Lecture Notes in Computer Science 13373

More information about this series at https://link.springer.com/bookseries/558

Pier Luigi Mazzeo · Emanuele Frontoni ·
Stan Sclaroff · Cosimo Distante (Eds.)

Image Analysis and Processing

ICIAP 2022 Workshops

ICIAP International Workshops
Lecce, Italy, May 23–27, 2022
Revised Selected Papers, Part I

 Springer

Editors
Pier Luigi Mazzeo 🆔
National Research Council
Lecce, Italy

Emanuele Frontoni 🆔
Università Politecnica delle Marche
Ancona, Italy

Stan Sclaroff 🆔
Boston University
Boston, MA, USA

Cosimo Distante 🆔
National Research Council
Lecce, Italy

ISSN 0302-9743   ISSN 1611-3349 (electronic)
Lecture Notes in Computer Science
ISBN 978-3-031-13320-6   ISBN 978-3-031-13321-3 (eBook)
https://doi.org/10.1007/978-3-031-13321-3

Preface

This volume contains 49 of the papers accepted for presentation at the workshops hosted by the 21st International Conference on Image Analysis and Processing (ICIAP 2022), held in Lecce, Italy, during May 23–27, 2022. ICIAP is organized every two years by CVPL, the group of Italian researchers affiliated with the International Association for Pattern Recognition (IAPR). The aim of the conference is to bring together researchers working on image processing, computer vision, and pattern recognition from around the world. Topics traditionally covered are related to computer vision, pattern recognition, and image processing, addressing both theoretical and applicative aspects.

In total, 16 different workshops were selected to complement ICIAP 2022 in Lecce.

All the 16 workshops have received a total of 157 submissions, and after a peer-review selection process, carried out by the individual workshop organizers, ultimately led to the selection of 96 papers, with an overall acceptance rate of 61%.

This volume contains 49 papers (out of 96) from the following workshops:

- Artificial Intelligence and Radiomics in Computer-Aided Diagnosis (AIRCAD)
- GoodBrother workshop on visual intelligence for active and assisted living
- Deep-Learning and High Performance Computing to Boost Biomedical Applications (DeepHealth)
- Intelligent Systems in Human and Artificial Perception (ISHAPE)
- Fine Art Pattern Extraction and Recognition (FAPER)
- PArts can woRth like The whole (PART)

The papers accepted for the other workshops are included in the companion volume (LNCS 13374).

AIRCAD, organized by Albert Comelli (Ri.MED Foundation, Italy), Cecilia Di Ruberto (Università di Cagliari, Italy), Andrea Loddo (Università di Cagliari, Italy), Lorenzo Putzu (Università di Cagliari, Italy), and Alessandro Stefano (IBFM-CNR, Italy), provided an overview of recent advances in the field of biomedical image processing in medical imaging using machine learning, deep learning, artificial intelligence, and radiomics features.

The GoodBrother workshop on visual intelligence for active and assisted living, organized by Sara Colantonio (ISTI-CNR, Italy), Francisco Florez-Revuelta (University of Alicante, Spain), Martin Kampel (Vienna University of Technology, Austria), and Peter Pocta (University of Zilina, Slovacchia), provided a forum for contributions presenting and discussing image- and video-based AAL applications, projects, and research as well as initiatives proposing ethical and privacy-aware solutions.

Deep-Learning and High Performance Computing to Boost Biomedical Applications (DeepHealth), organized by Federico Bolelli (Università degli Studi di Modena e Reggio Emilia, Italy), Jon Ander Gómez Adrián (Universitat Politècnica de València, Spain), and Stefano Allegretti (Università degli Studi di Modena e Reggio Emilia, Italy), aimed at exploiting heterogeneous HPC and big data architectures, assembled with state-of-the-art techniques in deep learning and computer vision.

The Workshop on Intelligent Systems in Human and Artificial Perception (ISHAPE), organized by Maria Di Summa, Nicola Mosca, and Vito Renò (STIIMA-CNR, Italy), aimed to collect cutting-edge contributions in the field of signal and image processing (e.g., computer vision systems, new algorithms, or machine/deep learning applications) as well as smart data fruition (virtual and augmented reality), ranging from new methodologies to innovative approaches in different domains.

The Workshop on Fine Art Pattern Extraction and Recognition (FAPER), organized by Gennaro Vessio and Giovanna Castellano (Università di Bari, Italy) along with Fabio Bellavia (Università di Palermo, Italy), provided an international forum for those wishing to present advancements in the state of the art, innovative research, ongoing projects, and academic and industrial reports on the application of visual pattern extraction and recognition for a better understanding and fruition of fine arts.

Finally, the PArts can woRth like The whole (PART) workshop, organized by Virginio Cantoni and Piercarlo Dondi (Università di Pavia, Italy) together with Fabio Narducci and Carmen Bisogni (Università di Salerno, Italy), aimed to collect contributions relating to problems that can be solved by segmenting and analyzing parts of an object.

We warmly thank all the workshop organizers who made such an interesting program possible and we hope that ICIAP 2022 has given us a chance to design a future where technologies allow people to live comfortably, healthily, and in peace.

May 2022   Pier Luigi Mazzeo
Emanuele Frontoni

Organization

General Chairs

Cosimo Distante — National Research Council, Italy
Stan Sclaroff — Boston University, USA

Technical Program Chairs

Giovanni Maria Farinella — University of Catania, Italy
Marco Leo — National Research Council, Italy
Federico Tombari — Google and TUM, Germany

Area Chairs

Lamberto Ballan — University of Padua, Italy
Francois Bremond — Inria, France
Simone Calderara — University of Modena and Reggio Emilia, Italy
Modesto Castrillon Santana — University of Las Palmas de Gran Canaria, Spain
Marco Cristani — University of Verona, Italy
Luigi Di Stefano — University of Bologna, Italy
Sergio Escalera — University of Barcelona, Spain
Luiz Marcos Garcia Goncalves — UFRN, Brazil
Javier Ortega Garcia — Universidad Autonoma de Madrid, Spain
Costantino Grana — University of Modena and Reggio Emilia, Italy
Tal Hassner — Facebook AML and Open University of Israel, Israel
Gian Luca Marcialis — University of Cagliari, Italy
Christian Micheloni — University of Udine, Italy
Fausto Milletarì — NVIDIA, USA
Vittorio Murino — Italian Institute of Technology, Italy
Vishal Patel — Johns Hopkins University, USA
Marcello Pelillo — Università Ca' Foscari Venice, Italy
Federico Pernici — University of Florence, Italy
Andrea Prati — University of Parma, Italy
Justus Piater — University of Innsbruck, Austria
Elisa Ricci — University of Trento, Italy
Alessia Saggese — University of Salerno, Italy
Roberto Scopigno — National Research Council, Italy

Filippo Stanco   University of Catania, Italy
Mario Vento   University of Salerno, Italy

Workshop Chairs

Emanuele Frontoni   Università Politecnica delle Marche, Italy
Pier Luigi Mazzeo   National Research Council, Italy

Publication Chair

Pierluigi Carcagni   National Research Council, Italy

Publicity Chairs

Marco Del Coco   National Research Council, Italy
Antonino Furnari   University of Catania, Italy

Finance and Registration Chairs

Maria Grazia Distante   National Research Council, Italy
Paolo Spagnolo   National Research Council, Italy

Web Chair

Arturo Argentieri   National Research Council, Italy

Tutorial Chairs

Alessio Del Bue   Italian Institute of Technology, Italy
Lorenzo Seidenari   University of Florence, Italy

Special Session Chairs

Marco La Cascia   University of Palermo, Italy
Nichi Martinel   University of Udine, Italy

Industrial Chairs

Ettore Stella   National Research Council, Italy
Giuseppe Celeste   National Research Council, Italy
Fabio Galasso   Sapienza University of Rome, Italy

North Africa Liaison Chair

Dorra Sellami   University of Sfax, Tunisia

Oceania Liaison Chair

Wei Qi Yan   Auckland University of Technology, New Zealand

North America Liaison Chair

Larry S. Davis   University of Maryland, USA

Asia Liaison Chair

Wei Shi Zheng   Sun Yat-sen University, China

Latin America Liaison Chair

Luiz Marcos Garcia Goncalves   UFRN, Brazil

Invited Speakers

Larry S. Davis   University of Maryland and Amazon, USA
Roberto Cipolla   University of Cambridge, UK
Dima Aldamen   University of Bristol, UK
Laura Leal-Taixe   Technische Universität München, Germany

Steering Committee

Virginio Cantoni   University of Pavia, Italy
Luigi Pietro Cordella   University of Napoli Federico II, Italy
Rita Cucchiara   University of Modena and Reggio Emilia, Italy
Alberto Del Bimbo   University of Firenze, Italy
Marco Ferretti   University of Pavia, Italy
Fabio Roli   University of Cagliari, Italy
Gabriella Sanniti di Baja   National Research Council, Italy

Endorsing Institutions

International Association for Pattern Recognition (IAPR)
Italian Association for Computer Vision, Pattern Recognition and Machine Learning
  (CVPL)
Springer

Institutional Patronage

Institute of Applied Sciences and Intelligent Systems (ISASI)
National Research Council of Italy (CNR)
Provincia di Lecce
Regione Puglia

Contents – Part I

Artificial Intelligence and Radiomics in Computer-Aided Diagnosis - AIRCAD

**Deep-Learning and High Performance Computing to Boost
Biomedical Applications - DeepHealth**

Contents – Part II

Artificial Intelligence for Preterm Infants' HealthCare - AI-Care

**Towards a Complete Analysis of People: From Face and Body to
Clothes - T-CAP**

Workshop on Small-Drone Surveillance, Detection and Counteraction Techniques - WOSDETC

Medical Imaging Analysis for Covid-19 - MIACOVID 2022

**Novel Benchmarks and Approaches for Real-World Continual
Learning - CL4REAL**

GoodBrother Workshop on Visual Intelligence for Active and Assisted Living

Case Study of a Low-Cost IoT Device with a Thermal Vision to Monitor Human Stool Behavior in the Home

Alicia Montoro-Lendínez$^{(\boxtimes)}$ ⓘ, David Díaz-Jiménez ⓘ,
José Luis López- Ruiz ⓘ, Javier Medina-Quero ⓘ,
and Macarena Espinilla-Estévez ⓘ

Department of Computer Science, University of Jaén, 23071 Jaén, Spain
{aml00074,ddj00003}@red.ujaen.es, {llopez,jmquero,mestevez}@ujaen.es

Abstract. Among the instruments for early detection are those for analysing gases in people's faeces, as it has been found that the presence of the intensity of certain compounds is related to the presence of cancer, diabetes or Alzheimer. The availability of sensor devices in recent years, together with the Internet of Things (IoT) paradigm, has made it possible to create low-cost systems that allow initial solutions to be tested for various real applications. Therefore, the aim of this contribution is to present the use case of a stool gas monitoring system in order to be the beginning of a solution for the early detection of this type of diseases. The proposed prototype integrates a thermal camera and MOX sensors to collect temperature and gas measurements immediately after a person has made deposition in their home. The measurements are monitored through an IoT platform and stored on a cloud server.

Keywords: Stool monitoring system · Volatile organic compounds (VOCs) · MOX sensors · Thermal camera · Internet of Things (IoT)

1 Introduction

Cancer remains the leading cause of death worldwide, with an estimated 10 million deaths in 2020. By shedding some light on cancer, it has been shown that early detection and early treatment reduces cancer mortality. To this end, population screening is carried out to identify potential cancer patients. These population screenings are carried out taking into account variables such as age and risk factors such as unhealthy eating habits, smoking, sedentary lifestyles and obesity [28].

In particular, for colorectal cancer (CRC), the third most common cancer in the world, its most frequent early detection tests are currently associated with many disadvantages, as they are painful, invasive, costly for the health system and sometimes even require patient conditioning and sedation [26,29]. Fecal

University of Jaen.

occult blood test (FOBT), colonoscopies, sigmoidoscopy, faecal immunochemical test (FIT), stool DNA tests and computed tomography colonography (CT colonography) [3] are some of the current early detection tests for CRC. Among them, FOBT is the test for excellence due to its low cost compared to the others. However, it is not enough because it requires a good infrastructure, a high amount of material and human resources such as administrative staff, nurses, specialists related to the digestive system and preventive medicine among others which end up raising the cost for the health system [21].

To overcome these limitations, on the one hand, the scientific studies on how the canine sense of smell is able to detect volatile organic compounds (VOCs) have been considered. These changes in VOCs detected in gases from the digestive system make it possible to identify patients with cancer in early stages [18,22], as well as other diseases such as diabetes or Alzheimer's disease [4,5]. Moreover, the nowadays and increasingly prevalent Internet of Things (IoT) paradigm, which has demonstrated its extraordinary usefulness in the healthcare sector [2,15,23].

On the other hand, the Active and Assisted Living (AAL) paradigm will be taken into account, which proposes technologies to improve the quality of life, people's well-being and health. Among its challenges are robust, accurate and non-intrusive data acquisition, which will also be found in this work [7,8].

Sampling of stool temperature is highly relevant and, moreover, at a general level for disease diagnosis or monitoring of diseases [11,17]. Therefore, this work focuses on the use of the thermal camera, which is integrated in an IoT system to monitor patients' bowel movements at home with the aim of being a first prototype to detect any anomaly with the advantages of small size, low cost, non-invasive and low energy consumption. The IoT system consisting of development boards, sensors and actuators is placed on the toilet seat to collect gas and thermal images. Subsequently, this data will be collected wirelessly to a central node, which is responsible, on one side hand, for storing the data (in a cloud server) for persistence and, on the other side, for allowing the visualisation of the data from an IoT platform.

This work will have the following structure. Section 2 reviews the works that deal with thermal cameras and gas sensors and low-cost monitoring systems that include these devices, both thermal cameras and gas sensors, for the prevention or diagnosis of diseases in the context of AAL. Section 3 reviews the architecture of the system where all its components will be described and presents the information processing proposed for the collection of sensor data, the persistence in the cloud server and the visualisation of the data in the IoT platform. A use case for the IoT system is presented in Sect. 4. Afterwards, Sect. 5 presents the limitations of the study and future work. And finally, Sect. 6 exposes the conclusions.

2   Related Works

In this section we review the literature on thermal cameras, gas sensors and smart gas and temperature monitoring systems related to the diagnosis of diseases. To do so, we will first review those works related to thermal camera or gas sensor type devices and, subsequently, systems which use sensors of this nature in the context of AAL.

2.1   Gas and Temperature Monitoring Devices

Regarding the devices responsible for monitoring gases, there are works that provide keys to detect VOCs such as the one presented by Malagú et al. [14]. In this work, several MOX (Metal Oxide Semiconductor) type sensors are used, which are also low cost compared to other technologies developed on the market to detect gases [9].

Alternatively, Movilla-Quesada et al. and Hofstetter et al. [10,16] in their works expose the use of MQ family sensors for gas collection in projects ranging from monitoring the concentration of ammonia in the environment and its possible adverse effects on poultry to monitoring greenhouse gas emissions in asphalt mixtures in recycled materials.

In terms of temperature monitoring, thermal cameras are an ideal choice, as well as being a good low-cost option, as their price is decreasing more and more in comparison to other technologies on the market. Other advantages of thermal cameras are their ease of use, the production of high resolution images in real time, making them a very useful device for a variety of applications, and, in addition, they are able to detect anomalies that are usually invisible to the human eye [20].

From the literature it was found that MOX-type sensors are the most suitable and cost-effective sensors for detecting VOCs. Likewise, thermal cameras are also an excellent low-cost option for monitoring temperatures and with adequate image resolution, while maintaining the anonymity of the user.

2.2   IoT System in the Context of Monitoring Diseases in AAL

Firstly, the literature reviews work with thermal cameras, such as Acharya et al. [1], which presents the use of these cameras for breast cancer detection using machine learning techniques. Likewise, Chekmenev et al. [6] present the use of thermal cameras but this time for the analysis of arterial pulse in a novel way. Another possibility is the combination of thermal and depth sensors as presented by Pramerdorfer et al. [19], which allows for person recognition and pose classification.Other authors have presented the use of the thermal camera in systems for the detection of accidents due to falls or unusual inactivity, which is an important tool for the independent living of people, especially the elderly [12,24,27].

Regarding of gas sensors, Liu et al. [13] present a system for diagnosing diabetes, whereby the breath of participants is analysed and the result is whether or not they suffer from this disease. Likewise, the analysis of VOCs for the early detection of cancer is addressed by Thriumani et al. [25], who present the use of an E-Nose, usually composed of an array of sensors, and machine learning classifiers to analyse samples of breast or lung cancer cells and healthy cells and identify them.

Therefore, the literature review demonstrates how gas and temperature sampling is very relevant. Therefore, our work aims to integrate both devices in a novel low-cost system which can be used at home without the need for medical staff or expensive installations.

3   Approach to Monitor Human Stool Behavior at Home

This section reviews the system architecture that will be composed of the different development boards, sensors and actuators in charge of collecting the key stool data from the toilet lid via the gas sensor and the thermal camera.

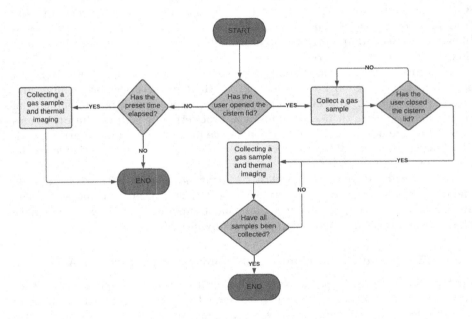

Fig. 1. Flowchart.

First of all, the flowchart (as shown in Fig. 1) which the system will realise is as follows:

– When the toilet lid is opened, the ESP32 (master) sends a signal to the ESP8266 (slave) for connection to the Wi-Fi network, the MQTT server and the Thinger platform. And it starts collecting and sending data from the gas sensor only.
– When the lid is closed, data collection and sending from the thermal camera starts and data collection and sending from the gas sensor continues.
– After a set time the ESP32 sends the signal to enter Deep Sleep mode to the ESP8266 and stops collecting and sending data from the gas sensor and thermal camera.

In addition, another operating mode has been implemented for when the lid is not open and where the person to be monitored is not involved. The purpose of this operating mode is usually to monitor the values under "normal" or "abnormal" conditions, e.g. the use of toilet cleaning agents could cause data errors. For this purpose, it is started after a preset time and as long as the ESP8266 development board is in idle mode. From this point on, thermal images of the values captured by the gas sensor are captured.

The components that make up the complete system are reviewed below. The development boards to be used are:

Lolin32 Lite (ESP32) development board

This board will be the master of the NodeMcu V3. Its main function is to execute a signal that stops the Deep Sleep mode of the NodeMcu V3. In this way, power consumption is significantly reduced. It will also be responsible for activating the alarm signal from the passive buzzer and collecting and transmitting data from the thermal camera and accelerometer.

NodeMcu V3 (ESP8266) development board

This is the slave board and the need to use this board in the IoT system is due to the power supply of the gas sensor. The supply voltage of the gas sensor is 5V and this board has a pin with this voltage output. Like the previous one, it incorporates Wi-Fi, which allows the collection and transmission of data from the gas sensor.

Raspberry Pi 3 Model B+ development board

It is the development board in charge of managing the data flow between the ESP32 and ESP8266 development boards, its main advantage is its high computational capacity with respect to its small size.

In addition, the following sensors will be included:

MQ2 gas sensor.

This MOX-type sensor detects the concentration of various gases present in the environment. In particular, it can measure liquefied petroleum gas (LPG), smoke, alcohol, propane, hydrogen, methane and carbon monoxide. This makes it ideal for collecting gas samples in depositions. However, one disadvantage is its 150 mAh power consumption, although this may seem low, it is a variable to be taken into consideration as it is a battery powered system.

Accelerometer sensor MMA8451

Because it can detect movement, tilt and orientation it is used within this IoT system to determine when the person being monitored is using the toilet, and therefore determine the start and end of the action. Also, the collection of samples is increased and after a set time, the alarm signal (passive buzzer) is activated.

Adafruit AMG8833 sensor IR thermal camera

It is structured in an 8×8 matrix of infrared thermal sensors. Its function is to obtain an image when the deposition has been performed. Its main advantage is that this type of thermal camera offers anonymity.

And finally, an actuator has been needed:

Passive buzzer.

The function of this actuator is to transform the electrical signals into very useful sound waves to warn the monitored person that the data collection has been completed and can flush the toilet.

This whole set will form the IoT system that will allow data to be collected and transmitted wirelessly to the central sink node. Regarding the protocol used for transmission between ESP8266, ESP32 and Raspberry Pi will be Message Queuing Telemetry Transport (MQTT) as this protocol is based on the publication and subscription being ideal for low-resource devices, as in the case of this project. Then, from this central node, the data will be stored in the cloud server for its persistence. Meanwhile, the information will be sent to the IoT platform for visualisation.

3.1   Database. MongoDB

In the database created in MongoDB, the data collected from the MQ2 sensor (in parts per million (ppm)), the thermal camera data, the data related to the lid opening and the raw data from the gas sensor (MQ2) will be stored. For this purpose, it was necessary to have four unrelated entities. For the transmission of the data, each data collection has been structured in its own way although they will have in common the fields, identifier (id), the name of the sensor, the measurement and the date of collection. An example of this is shown in the Table 1. The JSON format has also been used for sending, as this format allows the data to be easily understood, has a light data transmission and a high processing speed.

Table 1. Data collection for the entity THERMAL DATA

Thermal data	Description	Variable type
id	Unique identifier	ObjectId
img id	Image sequence number	Integer
control data	Indicates whether the data is a control sample	Boolean
Date	Date and time in international format	ISODate
Sensor	Sensor identifier	String
Thermal array	List of temperature values collected by the sensor	Array

3.2   IoT Platform. Thinger.io

For the visualisation of the data in real time, the choice was made for an IoT platform due to its ease of use was Thinger.io. The dashboard generated (as shown in Fig. 2) in Thinger.io consists of three line graphs. The first line graph, located at the top left, represents the historical maximum and minimum temperatures collected by the thermal cameras, the second line graph, located below the temperature graph, presents the historical values collected by the MQ2 sensor and, finally, the third line graph, located at the top right, represents whether the toilet is being used or not. In addition, the two meters included, one of them represents the last raw value obtained by the MQ2 sensor and the other one shows the value but in ppm.

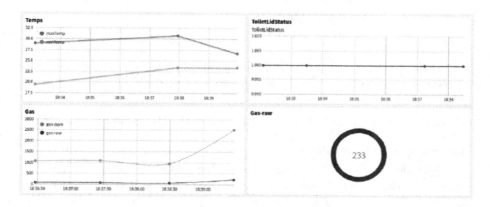

Fig. 2. Full dashboard

4   Case Study

This section presents the case study carried out to evaluate that the prototype of the low-cost IoT system for monitoring faecal gas is performing its function correctly. To do so, first, a user has to lift the toilet lid, make a bowel movement, close the toilet lid and when the alarm is triggered flush the toilet.

Table 2 presents the raw data for the gas sensor MQ2 when it is in active and idle state. From the data it can be seen that when the gas sensor is in the idle state the value obtained by the sensor fluctuates between the range of 160–190, while if the gas sensor is in the active state the value obtained by the sensor fluctuates between the range of 280–370. Therefore, it can be concluded that the gas collection when deposition is performed is correct.

Furthermore, Table 3 shows the data in ppm values for the MQ2 gas sensor when it is in an active state and when it is at rest. It can be seen that the ppm value is lower in the idle state and higher in the active state, as was the case with the raw data collected. For example, the resting value for alcohol is around 4.5 ppm while the active value is around 8.1 ppm. Similarly for propane, its resting state value is about 2.9 ppm while its active state value is about 4.66 ppm.

Table 2. Raw data obtained in active and resting state by the MQ2 sensor.

Gas Sensor MQ2 (raw values-voltage(V)*)	
Rest state	Active state
163-0.53V	338-1.09V
187-0.6V	362-1.17V
191-0.62V	287-0.93V
175-0.56V	324-1.05V
189-0.61V	345-1.11V
178-0.57V	359-1.16V
186-0.6V	295-0.95V
182-0.59V	333-1.07V
179-0.58V	356-1.15V
185-0.6V	358-1.15V

*ESP8266 development boards will return a value (raw value) ranging from 0 to 1023 which is equivalent to a voltage range between 0 and 3.3V (voltage).

Table 3. Data obtained in active and resting state by the MQ2 sensor in ppm values.

Gas Sensor MQ2 (ppm values)									
Alcohol Rest	Alcohol Active	CO Rest	CO Active	H_2 Rest	H_2 Active	LPG Rest	LPG Active	Propane Rest	Propane Active
4.5	9.8	15.5	38.5	4.4	8.3	2.2	4.2	2.9	5.4
4.6	8.6	16.3	33.1	4.5	7.5	2.2	3.8	3.0	4.9
4.3	8.1	15.0	30.9	4.3	7.1	2.1	3.6	2.8	4.7
4.5	7.5	15.5	28.4	4.4	6.7	2.2	3.4	2.9	4.4
4.9	6.5	17.4	23.8	4.8	5.9	2.4	3.0	3.1	3.9

Similarly, for temperature data collected by the thermal camera. On the one hand, in Fig. 3 it is observed that in the temperature map at certain points the temperature increases (maximum temperature of 29°C) due to the presence of the gases produced after the participant performs the deposition.

On the other hand, in Fig. 4 it can be seen that in the temperature map the temperature decreases in general (maximum temperature of 26.5°C) due to the elimination of these gases when flushing the tank.

Therefore, it can be concluded from this evaluation case that the low-cost IoT system is able to correctly monitor the gas in the faeces through the gas sensor and the thermal camera. Limitations of the study and future work.

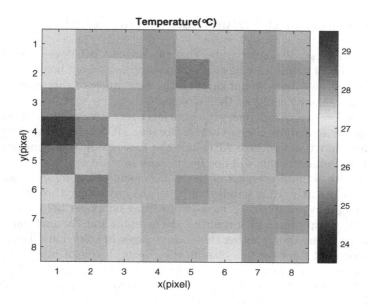

Fig. 3. After deposition

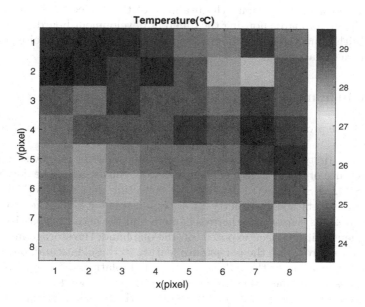

Fig. 4. After flushing the tank

5   Limitations of the Study and Future Work

Although the case study demonstrates that the low-cost IoT device with thermal vision is capable of monitoring human bowel movements from home, some of the limitations that have been found through the case study of this system and its possible improvements could be the following.

The incorporation of different gas sensors to cover a wider range of gases and also to improve sensitivity and accuracy. Because MOX sensors can be affected by humidity and temperature. Although the case study was conducted in a controlled environment, this will not be the case in reality.

Furthermore, an improvement of the management of incoming messages will be realised. Currently, it is handled in a single processing thread and if the sample throughput per second is increased, it may no longer behave correctly.

In addition, a protocol for acquiring gas samples and thermal images from different users to monitor whether there are changes in behaviour. The data can then be processed for real-time classification using artificial intelligence techniques. In this way, characteristics such as the type of deposition could be studied and inclusion criteria for the experimental control group could be generated in conjunction with the medical oncology team.

Although this work presents a prototype that is still in the design phase, it would be interesting to evaluate the usability of the device in the future. And replacing the breadboards housing the different development boards, sensors and actuators with a printed circuit board would reduce the size and noise generated by the swarm of cables.

6   Conclusions

In this work, we present the evaluation of a case study to monitor stool behaviour in the home.

To do this, first, the flowchart that the system performs is shown. Then, the IoT architecture of the system has been reviewed, consisting of the development boards, ESP32, ESP8266, (responsible for collecting data and both housed in the lid of the toilet) and Raspberry Pi 3, responsible for being the central sink node, the MQ2 gas sensor, the thermal camera and the actuator, passive buzzer.

Subsequently, it has been exposed, on the one hand, the storage in the MongoDB database, providing the persistence feature to these data and, on the other hand, the visualisation of these data from the IoT platform, Thinger.io.

Next, a case study has been presented where the low-cost device is evaluated. This evaluation presents the data collected by both the gas sensor and the thermal camera and shows how there is clearly a difference between the data when gases are presents and when they are not, which would allow for easy and quick monitoring of stool from home.

Finally, the limitations which have been found through the case study of the prototype and the future lines which can be carried out, especially in order to make improvements to it, have been exposed.

Acknowledgements. This result has been partially supported through the research projects REMIND project Marie Sklodowska-Curie EU Framework for Research and Innovation Horizon 516 2020, under grant agreement no. 734355, the Spanish Government by the project $RTI2018 - 098979 - A - I00MCIN/ AEI/10.13039/ 501100011033/$, FEDER "Una manera de hacer Europa" and the University of Jaén under Action 1 with code EI_TIC1_2021.

References

1. Acharya, U.R., Ng, E.Y.K., Tan, J.H., Sree, S.V.: Thermography based breast cancer detection using texture features and support vector machine. J. Med. Syst. **36**(3), 1503–1510 (2012)
2. Albín-Rodríguez, A.P., Ricoy-Cano, A.J., de-la Fuente-Robles, Y.M., Espinilla-Estévez, M.: Fuzzy protoform for hyperactive behaviour detection based on commercial devices. Int. J. Environ. Res. Public Health **17**(18), 6752 (2020). https:// doi.org/10.3390/IJERPH17186752
3. Bénard, F., Barkun, A.N., Martel, M., von Renteln, D.: Systematic review of colorectal cancer screening guidelines for average-risk adults: summarizing the current global recommendations. World J. Gastroenterol. **24**(1), 124 (2018). https://doi. org/10.3748/wjg.v24.i1.124
4. Boots, A.W., van Berkel, J.J.B.N., Dallinga, J.W., Smolinska, A., Wouters, E.F., van Schooten, F.J.: The versatile use of exhaled volatile organic compounds in human health and disease. J. Breath Res. **6**(2), 027108 (2012). https://doi.org/10. 1088/1752-7155/6/2/027108
5. Buszewski, B., Kesy, M., Ligor, T., Amann, A.: Human exhaled air analytics: biomarkers of diseases. Biomed. Chromatography **21**(6), 553–566 (2007). https:// doi.org/10.1002/BMC.835
6. Chekmenev, S.Y., Farag, A.A., Essock, E.A.: Thermal imaging of the superficial temporal artery: An arterial pulse recovery model. In: 2007 IEEE Conference on Computer Vision and Pattern Recognition, pp. 1–6. IEEE (2007)
7. Climent-Pérez, P., Florez-Revuelta, F.: Protection of visual privacy in videos acquired with RGB cameras for active and assisted living applications. Multimed. Tools Appl. **80**(15), 23649–23664 (2021)
8. Colantonio, S., Coppini, G., Giorgi, D., Morales, M.A., Pascali, M.A.: Computer vision for ambient assisted living: Monitoring systems for personalized healthcare and wellness that are robust in the real world and accepted by users, carers, and society. In: Computer Vision for Assistive Healthcare, pp. 147–182. Elsevier (2018)
9. Gomes, J., Rodrigues, J.J., Rabêlo, R.A., Kumar, N., Kozlov, S.: Iot-enabled gas sensors: technologies, applications, and opportunities. J. Sens. Actuator Netw. **8**(4), 57 (2019)
10. Hofstetter, D., Fabian, E., Lorenzoni, A.G.: Ammonia generation system for poultry health research using arduino. Sensors **21**(19), 6664 (2021). https://doi.org/ 10.3390/s21196664
11. Kaczmarek, M., Nowakowski, A.: Active IR-Thermal Imaging in Medicine. J. Nondestr. Eval. **35**(1), 1–16 (2016). https://doi.org/10.1007/s10921-016-0335-y
12. Kido, S., Miyasaka, T., Tanaka, T., Shimizu, T., Saga, T.: Fall detection in toilet rooms using thermal imaging sensors. In: 2009 IEEE/SICE International Symposium on System Integration (SII), pp. 83–88. IEEE (2009)
13. Liu, A., Tian, Y.: Design and implementation of oral odor detection system for diabetic patients. Chem. Eng. Trans. **68**, 385–390 (2018). https://doi.org/10.3303/ CET1868065

14. Malagù, C., Fabbri, B., Gherardi, S., Giberti, A., Guidi, V., Landini, N., Zonta, G.: Chemoresistive gas sensors for the detection of colorectal cancer biomarkers. Sensors **14**(10), 18982–18992 (2014). https://doi.org/10.3390/S141018982
15. Medina Quero, J., Fernandez Olmo, M.R., Pelaez Aguilera, M.D., Espinilla Estevez, M.: Real-time monitoring in home-based cardiac rehabilitation using wrist-worn heart rate devices. Sensors **17**(12), 2892 (2017). https://doi.org/10.3390/s17122892
16. Movilla-Quesada, D., Lagos-Varas, M., Raposeiras, A.C., Muñoz-Cáceres, O., Andrés-Valeri, V.C., Aguilar-Vidal, C.: Analysis of greenhouse gas emissions and the environmental impact of the production of asphalt mixes modified with recycled materials. Sustainability **13**(14), 8081 (2021). https://doi.org/10.3390/SU13148081
17. Ott, S.J., Musfeldt, M., Timmis, K.N., Hampe, J., Wenderoth, D.F., Schreiber, S.: In vitro alterations of intestinal bacterial microbiota in fecal samples during storage. Diagn. Microbiol. Infect. Dis. **50**(4), 237–245 (2004)
18. Politi, L., et al.: Discriminant profiles of volatile compounds in the alveolar air of patients with squamous cell lung cancer, lung adenocarcinoma or colon cancer. Molecules **26**(3), 550 (2021). https://doi.org/10.3390/MOLECULES26030550
19. Pramerdorfer, C., Strohmayer, J., Kampel, M.: Sdt: a synthetic multi-modal dataset for person detection and pose classification. In: 2020 IEEE International Conference on Image Processing (ICIP), pp. 1611–1615. IEEE (2020)
20. Rai, M., Maity, T., Yadav, R.: Thermal imaging system and its real time applications: a survey. J. Eng. Technol. **6**(2), 290–303 (2017)
21. van Rossum, L.G., et al.: Colorectal cancer screening comparing no screening, immunochemical and guaiac fecal occult blood tests: A cost-effectiveness analysis. Int. J. Cancer **128**(8), 1908–1917 (2011). https://doi.org/10.1002/ijc.25530
22. Schoon, G.A.A., De Jonge, D., Hilverink, P.: How dogs learn to detect colon cancer-optimizing the use of training aids. J. Veterinary Behav. **35**, 38–44 (2020). https://doi.org/10.1016/J.JVEB.2019.10.006
23. Sengan, S., Khalaf, O.I., Priyadarsini, S., Sharma, D.K., Amarendra, K., Hamad, A.A.: Smart healthcare security device on medical iot using raspberry pi. Int. J. Reliable Quality E-Healthcare (IJRQEH) **11**(3), 1–11 (2022). https://doi.org/10.4018/ijrqeh.289177
24. Sixsmith, A., Johnson, N.: A smart sensor to detect the falls of the elderly. IEEE Pervasive Comput. **3**(2), 42–47 (2004)
25. Thriumani, R., et al.: A preliminary study on in-vitro lung cancer detection using e-nose technology. In: 2014 IEEE International Conference on Control System, Computing and Engineering (ICCSCE 2014), pp. 601–605. IEEE (2014). https://doi.org/10.1109/ICCSCE.2014.7072789
26. Winawer, S., Zauber, A., HO MN, E.: Prevention of colorectal cancer by colonoscopic polypectomy. New England J. Med. **329**(27), 329 (1977). https://doi.org/10.1056/NEJM199312303292701
27. Wong, W.K., Lim, H.L., Loo, C.K., Lim, W.S.: Home alone faint detection surveillance system using thermal camera. In: 2010 Second International Conference on Computer Research and Development, pp. 747–751. IEEE (2010)
28. World Health Organization: Cancer. https://www.who.int/news-room/fact-sheets/detail/cancer (2022). Accessed Mar 09 2022
29. Zavoral, M., Suchanek, S., Zavada, F., Dusek, L., Muzik, J., Seifert, B., Fric, P.: Colorectal cancer screening in Europe. World J. Gastroenterol: WJG **15**(47), 5907 (2009). https://doi.org/10.3748/WJG.15.5907

Adults' Pain Recognition via Facial Expressions Using CNN-Based AU Detection

Noelia Vallez[1(✉)], Jesus Ruiz-Santaquiteria[1], Oscar Deniz[1], Jeff Hughes[2,3], Scott Robertson[3], Kreshnik Hoti[4], and Gloria Bueno[1]

[1] University of Castilla-La Mancha, ETSI Industrial, VISILAB, Ciudad Real, Spain
{Noelia.Vallez,Jesus.RAlegre,Oscar.Deniz,Gloria.Bueno}@uclm.es
[2] Curtin Medical School, Curtin University, Bentley, WA, Australia
j.d.hughes@curtin.edu.au
[3] Pain Check Ltd, Suite 401, 35 Lime Street, Sydney, NSW 2001, Australia
{jeff.hughes,scott.robertson}@painchek.com
[4] Division of Pharmacy, Faculty of Medicine, University of Prishtina,
Prishtina, Kosovo
kreshnik.hoti@uni-pr.edu
https://www.painchek.com/

Abstract. The identification of pain expression by facial analysis is a difficult problem with few effective solutions. Most of the existing facial expression recognition methods are based on the detection of different Action Units (AU) to identify simple expressions such as anger, joy or neutral. In this study, we propose using CNNs pre-trained on previously developed models for pain detection, such as the models included in PainChek, a point-of-care mobile application that uses automated facial assessment and analysis in the assessment of procedural pain in infants, to combine nine AUs identified in video images from the MORPH database without specific pain and from a proprietary database with joint pain. This work also analyses the variability of the AU detection method applied to images of individuals of different age, race and gender. For the database without specific pain, the mean amount of AUs considered as "not present" was 92.38% and 7.62% for "present", obtaining the worst results for the identification of AU6 and AU12 with 83.67% of "present" and 81.20% of "not present". For the joint pain database with ground truth labelled by AU and intensity, the mean accuracy for the 9 AUs was 84.98% with a sensitivity of up to 92% percent for AU25 and AU43.

Keywords: Pain facial expression · CNN · Action unit recognition

1 Introduction

The identification and management of pain is problematic, which is exacerbated by the lack of a simple, accurate, and reliable technique for assessing such pain [9]. This is true for both children and adults. Automated facial expression

P. L. Mazzeo et al. (Eds.): ICIAP 2022 Workshops, LNCS 13373, pp. 15–27, 2022.
https://doi.org/10.1007/978-3-031-13321-3_2

analysis is one of the few tools available for assessing emotions, including pain, in real time. In this respect, FACS (Facial Action Coding System) is the most used scheme to describe facial behaviors [15]. The FACS system [4,13] describes facial micro-gestures (i.e., mouth position, raise of the eyebrow, lid, etc.). These micro-gestures are called action units (AUs) and their relation to emotions and pain has been well studied and characterized in the literature [16,23]. In general, different AUs are triggered by different emotions and feeling states.

The definition of action units has allowed researchers to focus on expression recognition. Cakir and Arica [2] investigated the effective landmark patches for each AU on different size patches. Tian et al. [18] employed geometric parameters and Gabor wavelet features to feed a three-layer neural network, and the best recognition accuracy reached was 92.7% for AU9.

A different strategy was conducted by [8], were 90 models for 10 types of multiple AU views were trained. The architecture used 90 Bidirectional Long Short-Term Memory Recurrent Neural Networks (BLSTM-RNN) [7] to get temporal information, sent from a Convolutional Neural Network (CNN) [6]. However, the results showed an accuracy of 73.5%.

Figure 1 depicts the AUs used in this study to identify pain [15]. AUs are classified into two types based on their location on the face: upper and lower.

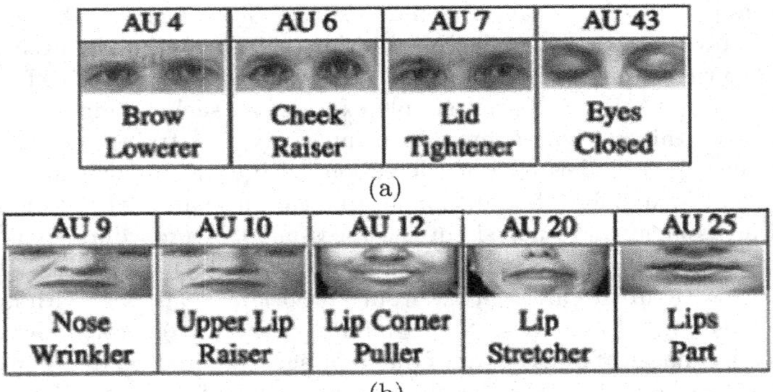

(a)

(b)

Fig. 1. Facial expressions used in this study: a) AUs of the upper face; b) AUs of the bottom face.

In this study we propose the use of these nine AUs to identify pain [10,11]. To accomplish this, we begin with the CNN model developed previously in *PainCheck Infant*, a mobile care application that utilizes automated facial analysis and evaluation to detect infant pain [9]. This technique has been expanded to include the analysis of adult pain. Thus, the purpose of this work is twofold: on the one hand, to evaluate the tool's inference ability to identify the AUs related to pain in a database that lacks labelled pain expressions (the MORPH database [14]) and, on the other hand, the ability to identify pain using a proprietary database of individuals experiencing joint pain.

Additionally, we will examine the effect of several factors on the detection of the considered AUs, such as the individuals' age and race. This will be discussed in greater detail in the following section, along with the database that was used. Then, in the Methodology section, we will examine the AUs' identification process, beginning with the detection of the face and concluding with AU classification. Finally, we will present the results of these analyses and the conclusions obtained from the research.

2 Materials

Two datasets have been used, the MORPH-4 (Morph version 4) dataset and a private one. The MORPH dataset is the largest longitudinal facial recognition database in the world [14]. This face dataset is composed of photos taken from 22038 individuals and composed of 132004 images along with the following metadata for age, gender, race, height, weight, and eye coordinates.

Figure 2 shows the race distribution of the 7 races present in the entire dataset [12]. As well as the distribution of age between 40 and over 80. Regarding the gender distribution, the database was divided into 66% men and 34% women.

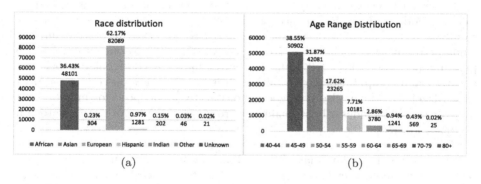

Fig. 2. a) Distribution of race in the dataset; b) Distribution of age in the dataset.

The private dataset consists of 101 video sequences, each one-minute long, with adults between ages 25 and 75 (each video corresponds to a different person). These individuals were suffering from joint pain and images were captured during a rehabilitation session. Two teams of FAC-coders extracted and labelled all frames containing pain to indicate active AU and grade pain intensity in five values (from A to E). Intensities C, D, and E, i.e., C+, were considered in this study. The study utilized 80842 images with the following number of images labelled as C+: AU4 = 8026, AU6 = 7999, AU7 = 7843, AU9 = 1867, AU10 = 4350, AU12 = 10889, AU20 = 1144, AU25 = 9319, and AU43 = 15414.

3   Methodology

3.1   Face Detection

Since the AU recognition process entails a first step where the face needs to be detected in the image, its results may be highly affected by the performance of the face detector. Despite the achievements in recent years with the introduction of deep learning, effective detection of small, blurred and partially occluded faces in the wild remains a challenging task. Furthermore, the trade-off between computational cost and accuracy is also an open research problem in this context.

The extraction of Eigenfaces was one of the first developed methods that extracted face descriptors for face recognition tasks [20]. It allowed the recognition of faces significantly faster by doing a Principal Component Analysis (PCA) and obtaining the so-called Eigenvectors. It also provided the ability to learn and recognize new faces in an unsupervised manner. Along with this method, further feature analysis on efficient descriptors was done [17], such as Linear Discriminant Analysis (LDA) [5], 2-D PCA [24] and Haar-like features [21,22]. The use of Histograms of Oriented Gradients descriptors was also proposed for feature extraction [3], which removed redundancy in the data, avoiding overfitting and providing robustness to facial detection.

Other machine learning approaches have been used to improve feature extraction methods such as RefineFace [25]. The method achieves state-of-the-art results and runs at 37.3 frames per second (fps) for VGA-resolution images. Another recent approach uses a triple loss function [26] to optimize a feature pyramid network (FPN) [19]. The method achieves a good balance between accuracy and computational cost, although it heavily relies on certain parameters. BlazeFace [1] can also be a good choice in terms of speed for mobile GPU inference, as it includes a lightweight feature extraction network capable to run at a speed of $200-1000+$ fps.

These techniques, along with facial feature recognition ones, can detect feature points (i.e., facial landmarks), bounding boxes, and surrounding facial components (i.e., mouth, eyebrow, etc.), to detect facial expressions. These facial expressions, uniquely identified by means of Facial Action Units (AUs), are defined in the Facial Action Coding System (FACS), which declares 48 different facial expressions [4,13].

Even with the achievements obtained with deep learning, long-hair, wrong-framed, or tiny faces remain as challenging cases. However, the self-learning mode is less sensitive to illuminance and registration error. Enormous amounts of labelled training data are crucial to train a deep-learning network. Nonetheless it is very challenging to label AUs because it is very time-consuming and there is no guarantee of an ideal result. Thus, challenges such as computational inexpensive detection methods as well as appropriate hardware are open lines for future development.

In our study all faces in the dataset were detected, cropped, and aligned. This tiling process starts by detecting the face using a CNN object detector. In this case, a MobileNetv2+SSD architecture is used. Then, a set of 68 landmarks are extracted to mark the position of the eyes, the mouth, the nose, and the face contour. The whole face is also marked with a bounding box. An example of the process is shown in Fig. 3.

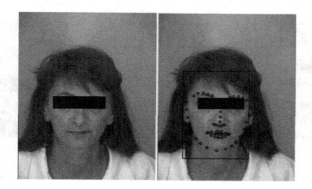

Fig. 3. Left: Example of an image before being landmarked. Right: Example of the same image after being landmarked in eyes, nose, eyebrows, and face contour.

Using these 68 points and the bounding-box of the face given by the CNN, all faces are centered and aligned. The resulting face is also divided into top and bottom sections to use only the sections related to each AU. The resulting tiles are then scaled to 50×50 pixels, as shown in Fig. 4.

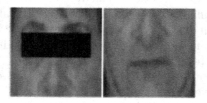

Fig. 4. Example of top and bottom images, scaled to 50×50 resolution.

To prove that the tiling process is deterministic, it was repeated three times, using the entire MORPH-4 dataset. In every run the result was exactly the same. In total, 131390 images were processed correctly but the method did not detect the face in 655 images. Therefore, an analysis was performed to find the reason why the method failed on those pictures.

3.2   Analysis of Non-detected Faces

The tiling failed in images with beards and/or long hair, as well as in images with low contrast or misaligned faces. These images were consequently removed from the dataset. Figure 5 illustrates deleted images in which the hair and beard are the cause of failures; as well as instances where images are not properly framed or have extremely low contrast.

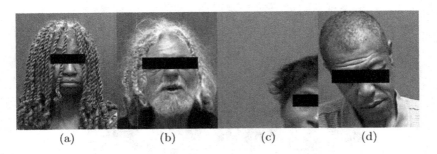

(a)   (b)   (c)   (d)

Fig. 5. Example of deleted images: a) hair covers the eyes; b) long hair and beard; c) and d) incorrect framing.

Additionally, some statistics were obtained to detect any sign of bias on tiling according to gender, race, or age.

Race and Age Distribution

Regarding the race distribution, although it appears in Fig. 6a (race distribution after tiling) and Fig. 6b (race distribution of deleted images) that the deleted images have a similar distribution to the remaining images, a goodness of fit test revealed the opposite. They do not share a common distribution, and thus they are significantly different. A goodness of fit test was also run on the deleted African and European individuals. A significant difference between Africans and Europeans' images was found (with respect to the total distribution of individuals). Others were not tested due to sample size issues.

For the age distribution, the deleted images are not distributed evenly. A goodness of fit test revealed a significant difference. As shown in Fig. 7a, the image quantity decreases as an individual's age increases. However, Fig. 7b revealed a slightly skewed distribution to the left. The distributions of individuals by age group, as well as the distributions of individuals after tiling and deleting individuals, are quite similar across different age ranges. The distribution of deleted individuals, on the other hand, is quite different.

Additionally, goodness of fit tests on deleted images were performed. These tests are designed to determine whether there are statistically significant

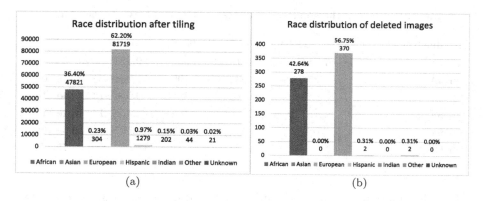

Fig. 6. Distribution of race among the images which: a) passed the tiling process and b) did not pass the tiling process.

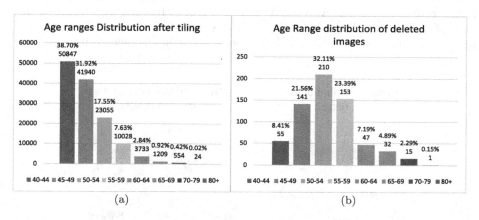

Fig. 7. Age distribution of images that a) passed tiling and b) did not.

differences between the various categories (except for 80+, which is not large enough). Table 1 shows the results of those test, where:

– H0: Age Ranges are equally distributed (p-value > 0.05)
– H1: Age Ranges are differently distributed (p-value < 0.05)

Gender Distribution
In terms of gender distribution, the deleted images do not follow the same pattern as the remaining images, as illustrated in Fig. 8. This was confirmed by performing a goodness of fit test, which revealed a significant difference.

Table 1. P-values of the goodness of fit tests performed between each range

p-value	40–44	45–49	50–54	55–59	60–64	65–69	70–79
40–44		7.28e−07	4.08e−19	1.41e−20	0.008	0.423	0.008
45–49			5.95e−05	1.23e−05	0.106	1.23e−05	9.77e−09
50–54				0.663	1.38e−06	9.55e−13	1.44e−16
55–59					3.48e−07	1.45e−13	1.52e−17
60–64						0.005	1.26e−05
65–69							0.075

The distribution of individuals after tiling and deletion across different age ranges indicates that the number of individuals is balanced between genders. Nonetheless, the number of deleted images indicates that males are deleted at a higher rate than females. As a result, a goodness of fit test was performed on the deleted individuals. The results established a statistically significant difference between the number of male and female individuals in the deleted images.

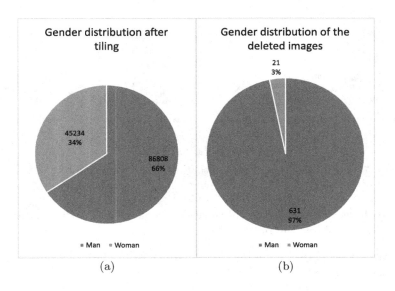

Fig. 8. Gender distribution in images that passed (a) and failed (b) tiling.

To obtain the AU predictions of this dataset, the previous model trained with the private dataset was used. The CNN architecture is composed by 3 blocks of 2D convolution + max pooling layers and a final fully connected network with 3 hidden layers, which generates the AU predictions. Several dropout operations are also included to mitigate overfitting during training. A different model was trained for each AU.

4   Results

4.1   Benchmark Results

The results in Table 2 show the rate of "not present" and "present" predictions that each AU obtained. An AU is present when the person in the frame is making the facial muscle movement described by it. Although we do not have the ground truth of this data, it is interesting to analyse the behaviour of the models. When classified by race, age range and gender, the results are quite different. Nevertheless, all results exhibit lower rates in AU12 and AU6 compared to the other ones.

Table 2. Not present and present rates (%) among all the AU.

Action unit	Not present rate	Present rate
AU4	97.70	2.30
AU6	83.67	16.33
AU7	90.48	9.52
AU9	98.94	1.06
AU10	91.15	8.85
AU12	81.20	18.80
AU20	96.93	3.06
AU25	98.00	2.00
AU43	93.37	6.63

Predictions by Race, Age and Gender

Table 3 shows the "not present" rate classified by AU and race among the total number of predicted images. It presents a high variability, which goes from a 66.27% rate to a 100% rate.

Table 3. Not present rate (%) among the different AUs and races.

Race	au4	au6	au7	au9	au10	au12	au20	au25	au43
African	97.33	78.22	97.23	98.46	77.91	66.27	93.21	97.55	98.18
Asian	98.68	66.78	83.88	99.01	96.38	84.87	99.67	99.67	94.08
European	97.94	86.98	86.51	99.22	98.83	89.80	99.08	98.29	90.49
Hispanic	96.72	80.22	92.42	99.30	94.06	87.80	97.34	96.33	96.95
Indian	98.02	84.65	92.57	99.01	91.58	89.60	99.01	98.51	96.04
Other	95.45	70.45	95.45	97.73	100.00	79.55	100.00	100.00	100.00
Unknown	85.71	66.67	90.48	95.24	90.48	76.19	100.00	100.00	95.24

Table 4 presents the "not present" rate classified by AU and age range over the total number of predicted images. Table 5 presents the "not present" rate classified by AU and gender.

Table 4. Not present rate (%) among the different AUs and age ranges.

Age range	au4	au6	au7	au9	au10	au12	au20	au25	au43
40-44	98.02	83.12	91.85	99.45	92.19	84.86	97.67	98.35	94.76
45-49	97.37	84.23	90.27	99.02	90.97	82.08	96.99	98.07	93.30
50-54	97.47	83.47	89.59	98.46	89.81	77.57	96.30	97.91	92.86
55-59	97.54	83.55	88.22	98.07	89.19	73.51	95.08	97.18	90.94
60-64	98.39	85.51	87.92	97.27	90.57	73.35	95.50	96.06	89.55
65-69	98.76	84.70	86.19	97.60	94.87	75.60	95.37	96.36	85.19
70-69	99.28	86.28	84.66	96.03	96.93	70.22	97.11	96.57	79.78
80+	100.00	83.33	70.83	100.00	95.83	66.67	100.00	100.00	83.33

Table 5. Not present rate (%) among the different AUs and both genders.

Gender	au4	au6	au7	au9	au10	au12	au20	au25	au43
Man	97.06	83.20	92.17	98.55	87.69	78.67	95.81	97.24	93.09
Woman	98.93	84.55	87.25	99.68	97.76	86.02	99.06	99.46	93.91

4.2 Classification Results

Each of the nine AU models was trained using a 5-fold cross-validation procedure (5fcv). Thus, the initial set of 101 videos was divided into five groups, four of which contained 20 videos and one of which contained 21, and a model was trained using four of the groups and tested using the remaining group. The test group is then switched by one of the training groups, and the process is repeated until all five groups are tested. This resulted in a total of 45 models.

The initial set was randomly partitioned into five groups while ensuring that the test set always contained a sufficient number of images labelled as C+. Moreover, we divide the data at the video level rather than the image level to avoid overfitting caused by having similar images in both the training and test sets. The total number of C+ images varies between 38 and 2820, depending on the group and AU. It is worth noting that AU43 has the highest number of images labelled as C+, while AU20 has the smallest.

The average and best values for the 5fcv are shown in Table 6. Additionally, we provide sensitivity and specificity values due to the unbalanced nature of our dataset, which contains more negative than positive samples. Except for the AU20, the majority of AU models perform well (mean accuracy of 84.98%, a sensitivity of 80.85% and specificity of 95.10%). This result is explained by the small number of images containing the AU20 'present' (1144, being it the smallest number among all AUs). Apart from AU20, AU9 has fewer images with the AU present than the others, which has an effect on the model's sensitivity. Therefore, adding more samples to these AUs will improve their models performance.

Table 6. 5fcv results. ACC = Accuracy, Sens = Sensitivity, and Spec = Specificity.

AU	Mean ACC	Best ACC	Best sens	Best spec
AU4	83.41	93.79	90.28	95.95
AU6	84.22	93.53	93.22	93.73
AU7	75.37	86.27	85.92	90.80
AU9	88.29	97.29	66.33	97.78
AU10	82.26	95.10	76.53	96.64
AU12	84.39	94.91	95.31	96.58
AU20	90.60	97.84	29.44	99.90
AU25	93.41	95.28	97.11	96.35
AU43	82.90	88.83	93.49	88.14
Mean	**84.98**	**93.65**	**80.85**	**95.10**

5   Conclusions

We present a method for detecting adult pain via facial expressions using CNN-based AU detection. For image pre-processing, a MobileNetv2+SSD architecture is used, and a CNN is used for AU predictions. The MORPH-4 dataset was used to demonstrate the tiling process's consistency and robustness. Also, dataset inference reveals a high proportion of 'non-present' AUs, which is consistent with a non-pain database. However, once all images are labelled, research on this topic may be conducted in the future.

To avoid overfitting, AU models were trained using 5fcv and the dataset was partitioned at the video level. They perform well on average, with a mean accuracy of 84.98%, a sensitivity of 80.85% and specificity of 95.10%. As a result, the proposed approach is well-suited for detecting the presence or absence of the studied AUs. From all the AUs, AU20 had the lowest sensitivity due to the low number of images with AU20 present. Gathering more videos with AU20 present is necessary to improve the model's results.

References

1. Bazarevsky, V., Kartynnik, Y., Vakunov, A., Raveendran, K., Grundmann, M.: BlazeFace: sub-millisecond neural face detection on mobile GPUs. arXiv preprint arXiv:1907.05047 (2019)

2. Cakir, D., Arica, N.: Size variant landmark patches for facial action unit detection. In: 2016 IEEE 7th Annual Information Technology, Electronics and Mobile Communication Conference (IEMCON), pp. 1–4 (2016)
3. Déniz, O., Bueno, G., Salido, J., De la Torre, F.: Face recognition using histograms of oriented gradients. Pattern Recogn. Lett. **32**(12), 1598–1603 (2011)
4. Ekman, P., Friesen, W.: Facial Action Coding System: A Technique for the Measurement of Facial movement. Consulting Psychologists Press, Palo Alto, CA (1978)
5. Etemad, K., Chellappa, R.: Discriminant analysis for recognition of human face images. Josa a **14**(8), 1724–1733 (1997)
6. Fukushima, K.: Neocognitron: a self-organizing neural network model for a mechanism of pattern recognition unaffected by shift in position. Biol. Cybern. **36**(4), 193–202 (2004)
7. Graves, A., Fernández, S., Schmidhuber, J.: Bidirectional lstm networks for improved phoneme classification and recognition. In: Proceedings of the 15th International Conference on Artificial Neural Networks: Formal Models and Their Applications - Volume Part II, pp. 799–804 (2005)
8. He, J., Dongliang, L., Yang, B., Cao, S., Sun, B., Yu, L.: Multi view facial action unit detection based on cnn and blstm-rnn. In: 2017 12th IEEE International Conference on Automatic Face & Gesture Recognition (FG 2017), pp. 848–853 (05 2017)
9. Hoti, K., Chivers, P., Hughes, J.: Assessing procedural pain in infants: a feasibility study evaluating a point-of-care mobile solution based on automated facial analysis. Lancet Digital Health **3**(10), e623–e634 (2021)
10. Kunz, M., Prkachin, K., Solomon, P.E., Lautenbacher, S.: Faces of clinical pain: inter-individual facial activity patterns in shoulder pain patients. Eur. J. Pain **25**(3), 529–540 (2021)
11. Lucey, P., Cohn, J.F., Prkachin, K.M., Solomon, P.E., Matthews, I.: Painful data: the UNBC-McMaster shoulder pain expression archive database. In: 2011 IEEE International Conference on Automatic Face & Gesture Recognition (FG), pp. 57–64. IEEE (2011)
12. U.S. Office of Management and Budget's: 1997 Standards for Maintaining, Collecting, and Presenting Federal Data on Race and Ethnicity. https://www.govinfo.gov/content/pkg/FR-1997-10-30/pdf/97-28653.pdf
13. Paul, E., Wallace, V.F.: Facial action coding system: The manual on CD ROM. A human face (2002)
14. Ricanek, K., Tesafaye, T.: Morph: a longitudinal image database of normal adult age-progression. In: 7th International Conference on Automatic Face and Gesture Recognition (FGR06), pp. 341–345. IEEE (2006)
15. Ruicong, Z., Mengyi, L., Dezheng, Z.: A comprehensive survey on automatic facial action unit analysis. Visual Comput. **36**(5), 1067–1093 (2020)
16. Schiavenato, M.: Facial expression and pain assessment in the pediatric patient: The primal face of pain. J. Specialists Pediatric Nursing **13**(2), 89–97 (05 2008)
17. Sun, C., Shrivastava, A., Singh, S., Gupta, A.: Revisiting unreasonable effectiveness of data in deep learning era. CoRR **abs/1707.02968** (2017)
18. Tian, Y.l., Kanade, T., Cohn, J.F.: Evaluation of gabor-wavelet-based facial action unit recognition in image sequences of increasing complexity. In: Proceedings of Fifth IEEE International Conference on Automatic Face Gesture Recognition, pp. 229–234. IEEE (2002)

19. Tsung-Yi, L., Piotr, D., Ross, B.G., Kaiming, H., Bharath, H., Belongie, B.: Feature pyramid networks for object detection. In: 2017 IEEE Conference on Computer Vision and Pattern Recognition (CVPR), pp. 936–944, December 2016
20. Turk, M., Pentland, A.: Eigenfaces for recognition. J. Cognitive Neurosci. 3(1), 71–86 (1991)
21. Viola, P., Jones, M.: Rapid object detection using a boosted cascade of simple features. In: Proceedings of the 2001 IEEE Computer Society Conference on Computer Vision and Pattern Recognition. CVPR 2001, vol. 1. IEEE (2001)
22. Viola, P., Jones, M.: Robust real-time face detection. Int. J. Comput. Vis. 57, 137–154 (05 2004)
23. Wilike, Diana, J.: Facial expressions of pain in lung cancer. Analgesia 1(2), 91–99 (1995)
24. Yang, J., Zhang, D., Frangi, A., Yang, J.y.: Two-dimensional pca: a new approach to appearance-based face representation and recognition. IEEE Trans. Pattern Anal. Mach. Intell. 26(1), 131–137 (2004)
25. Zhang, S., Chi, C., Lei, Z., Li, S.Z.: Refineface: refinement neural network for high performance face detection. IEEE Trans. Pattern Anal. Mach. Intell. 43(11), 4008–4020 (2021)
26. Zhenyu, F., et al.: Triple loss for hard face detection. Neurocomputing 398, 20–30 (2020)

In-bed Posture and Night Wandering Monitoring Using Force-Sensing Resistors

Xavier del Toro García[✉][iD], Jesús Fernández-Bermejo[iD],
Henry Llumiguano[iD], Javier Dorado[iD], Cristina Bolaños[iD],
and Juan C. López[iD]

Department of Technology and Information Systems, University of Castilla-La
Mancha, Ciudad Real, Spain
{xavier.deltoro,jesus.fruiz,henry.llumiguano,javier.dorado,
cristina.bolanos,juancarlos.lopez}@uclm.es

Abstract. Overnight postural changes and surveillance are two important issues to provide assistance to older individuals particularly when there is reduced mobility and cognitive decline. This paper presents a preliminary analysis of a cost-effective monitoring system based on force sensing resistors, to provide assistance to caregivers and facilitate the prevention of falls and pressure ulcers. A prototype of the proposed solution is presented, and the preliminary tests and measurements obtained using a real setup in a nursing home are analysed. The solution based on force-sensing resistors seeks simplicity, reduced costs, unobtrusiveness and privacy preservation. The prototype consists of 3 force-sensing resistor strips installed under the mattress and microcontroller board with wireless connectivity, to record measurements, transfer data, perform local analysis and generate warning messages. The positioning of the sensors has been analysed during the test to achieve a successful identification of the most relevant in-bed postures. The proposed solution can also be employed to monitor daily activities and assess sleep quality in combination with other sensors such as inertial measuring units in wearable devices or cameras.

Keywords: Assisted living · Activity recognition · Fall prevention ·
In-bed posture · Pressure ulcer prevention

1 Introduction

The demographic changes and increase of life expectancy is bringing new challenges in terms of ensuring the quality of life to older individuals and meeting the

---

This research was funded by H2020 European Union program under grant agreement No. 857159 (SHAPES project), by the Spanish MCIN/ AEI /10.13039/501100011033 grant TALENT-BELIEF (PID2020-116417RB-C44) and by GoodBrother COST action 19121. We would like to acknowledge the support received by the staff team at the nursing home of El Salvador in Pedroche (Spain).

P. L. Mazzeo et al. (Eds.): ICIAP 2022 Workshops, LNCS 13373, pp. 28–37, 2022.
https://doi.org/10.1007/978-3-031-13321-3_3

required economical and social efforts related to their increasing care needs. This challenges are being addressed by promoting Active and Healthy Aging (AHA) [1,2], while providing aids to extend independent living and support care givers to reduce the burden of their daily tasks, related the intensive care required in many cases. It is in this field that many digital solutions are being developed to provide the necessary technological leverage.

Poor quality of sleep affects a large portion of the elderly population, diminishing their health condition and quality of life [3]. Disorientation and wandering is also associated with dementia and Alzheimer, which has an increasing prevalence in elderly population. Wandering during nights and getting off the bed causes a high risk of falls and all the derived negative consequences, requiring night surveillance and the use of barriers in some cases to prevent them. In this context, the development of digital solutions that can monitor the sleep quality and detect situations in which the person is trying to get off the bed can be very beneficial and support the task of the care giver.

Reduced mobility also has high prevalence among elderly population. This condition requires adequate care to avoid pressure ulcers in the skin, also known as bed sores, particularly in those areas of body where and the pressure exerted by the bones and the conditions of humidity can cause them (e.g. hips, elbows, heels, back of the head, shoulder blades, etc.). This risk is particularly high in people with circulation problems, diabetes or poor nutrition. The appearance of pressure ulcers are also related to the quality of care that a person receives. In this context, there is a considerable number of previous works in the literature dedicated to the prevention of pressure ulcers, in which monitoring and pose estimation systems are proposed. A recent literature review has examined the most relevant works in this field of research [4], in which state-of-the-art sensors and classification techniques are identified. The type of sensor used in this type of applications includes: pressure sensors and mats [5,6], cameras [7], depth sensors [8], wearable devices with Inertial Measurement Units (IMUs) [9], and moisture and temperature sensors. Sometimes a combination of several types of sensors is used [10]. The majority of solutions rely on the use of an array of pressure sensors or a complete pressure mat. In the later case, there is a public dataset available [11] for training and testing of classification methods. It should be noted that when working with pressure data with high resolution, image processing techniques can be applied to the so-called pressure images. In general most of the aforementioned solution are used in conjunction with a classification algorithm to estimate in-bed postures. Some of the surveyed systems also provide alerts to the caregivers, so that appropriate postural changes are done during the time in bed. Similar solutions have also been presented recently in other fields with high relevance, such as the use of piezoelectric and PIR sensors to monitor sleep and pneumonia progression in COVID-19 patients [12].

In this paper, a prototype system based on the use of force-sensing resistor sensors is tested to detect the presence of a person on the bed and the event of getting off the bed, preventing possible falls. Furthermore, the proposed prototype is designed to detect the in-bed posture and postural changes required for people with reduced mobility and risk of pressure ulcers. The prototype has been deployed in the real environment of a nursing home for a preliminary assessment using an articulated bed. The system has been designed seeking simplicity, reduced cost, unobtrusiveness and the maximum preservation of privacy.

The paper is structured as follows: the next section describe the prototype, the sensor characteristics and positioning, as well as the microcontroller-based data logging and communication system and the instrumentation setup based on a multi-channel oscilloscope. Then, the experimental results are described in the following section, and the measurements of a sequence of in-bed movements are shown. Finally, the conclusion and further work are presented.

2 Prototype Description

The implemented prototype for in-bed posture and night wandering monitoring is shown in Fig. 1.

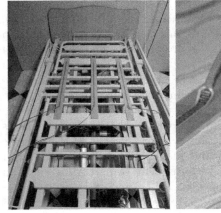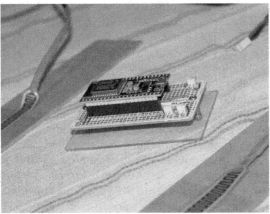

Fig. 1. Image of the implemented prototype being deployed in an articulated bed of a nursing home: Force-sensing resistor strips (left) and MCU board (right).

It consists of a set of 3 force-sensing resistor strips attached to Medium-density fibreboard (MDF) support. The sensor are connected to a Microcontroller Unit (MCU) board through 3 separate analog inputs by means of a resistive divisor. The total material cost of the prototype is below 100 Euro and it can be installed in less than 10 min.

2.1 Force-Sensing Resistors

The force-sensing resistors (FSR) are used as pressure sensors to detect the presence of a person and the posture on the bed. They are based on the polymer thick film (PTF) technology. The resistance of an FSR changes depending on the force exerted on the sensor. When no pressure is being applied, the resistance of the FSR is larger than $1\,M\Omega$. The higher is the pressure exerted, the lower the resistance between of the FSR. The main characteristics of the FSR strips employed are shown in Table 1 gives a summary of all heading levels.

Table 1. FSR strip characteristics.

Characteristic	Value
Model	SF15-600
Shape	Rectangular strip
Length	600 mm
Width	15 mm
Thickness	>0.35 mm
Weight	5 g
Measuring range	0 to 10 Kg
Force resolution	Continuous
Response time	10 ms
Temperature operation	−20 to 60 °C
Cost	<20 Euro

2.2 Sensor Positioning

The sensor strips have been positioned around the center of gravity of the body, that is the area around the hips and the waist, to receive the maximum pressure when a person is lying in the bed. The precise positioning is depicted in Fig. 2. It should be noted that the FSR can be easily integrated below the mattress due to their low thickness and it is only important to ensure that the mattress is well positioned on top of the bed frame and its weight is well distributed. This simplified sensor arrangement takes advantage of the fact that most postures of interest are mainly characterized by the weight distribution on the direction of the width of the mattress.

2.3 MCU and Connectivity

The FSR sensors are connected to a MCU Board, with and ESP32 MCU that incorporates wireless connectivity through both Bluetooth and WiFi. This MCU will be responsible for logging data, transferring data to a database and performing some local processing. The connection with the sensors is done through a voltage divider and an analog input as shown in Fig. 3.

According to the connection the voltage measured by the MCU will increase as the force applied to the sensor increases.

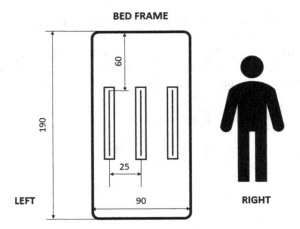

Fig. 2. FSR strip position with respect to the bed frame (all the measures are in cm).

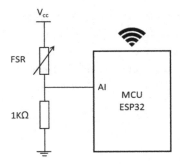

Fig. 3. Schematic of the FSR sensor connection with the MCU using a voltage divider. This connection is done for each FSR strip using a different analog input (AI).

2.4   Instrumentation for Preliminary Measurements

In order to record and analyse the preliminary measurements a high-precision and high-bandwidth oscilloscope with multiple channels has been employed. The model used is the Agilent InifiniiVision MSO7304A, with a 350 MHz bandwidth, shown in Fig. 4. 3 out of the 4 available channels have been employed to record the measurements during the preliminary tests performed on the test setup. In this way the 3 signals coming from the sensors installed in the bed frame can be simultaneously acquired. The recordings have been done using a sampling frequency of 40 kSa/s, which is more than sufficient to capture the signal dynamics observed and the response time of the sensors (10 ms).

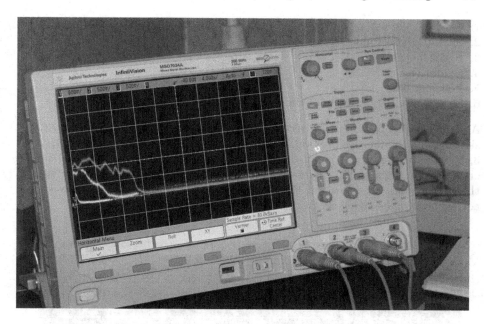

Fig. 4. 4-channel oscilloscope connected to the FSR strips during the preliminary measurements. The traces shown are the measured values during one of the tests performed.

3 Results

The validation of the proposed prototype was carried out using an articulated single bed (90 × 190 mm) in the nursing home of El Salvador in the village of Pedroche (Spain). This type of bed is generally used in the nursing homes and particularly with older persons having reduced mobility. The mattress type was also the one which is generally used in this cases, which has viscoelastic layer on top for a better adaptability to the body shape and to ensure a better distribution of pressure. Once the sensor were arranged as depicted in Figs. 1 and 2, different test were perform to register the measurements obtained from the 3 sensors. Measurements where both recorded using the MCU board (see Fig. 1) and the high-precision oscilloscope (see Fig. 4) for comparison and validation of the MCU board performance. During the tests 6 different positions were recorded for 11 different members of the research team (the left and right definition shown in Fig. 2 was considered), namely:

1. Off bed.
2. Sitting of the right edge of the bed.
3. Right foetus.
4. Center supine.
5. Left foetus.
6. Sitting of the right edge of the bed.

A sequence of positions was performed by each participant in the tests. Considering the numbering previously defined, the sequence followed was: 1, 2, 4, 3, 5, 6, 1. In this way a small dataset was recorded for future development of classification algorithms, currently in progress. The results obtained for two of the participants are shown in Figs. 5 and 6. The blue, green and yellow traces correspond to the right, central and left sensors respectively.

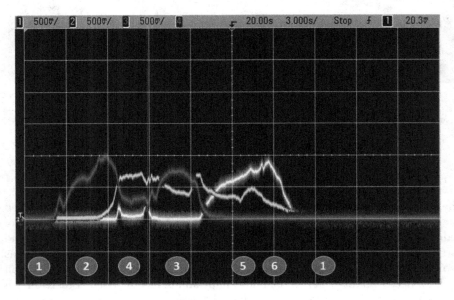

Fig. 5. Sensor measurements obtained by one of the participants (height = 165 cm and weight = 55 Kg).

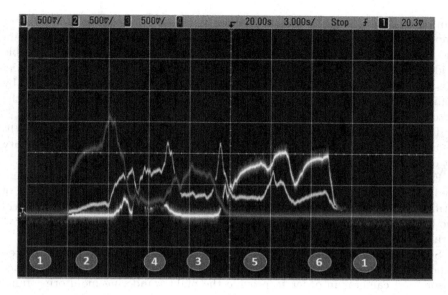

Fig. 6. Sensor measurements obtained by one of the participants (height = 190 cm and weight = 87 Kg).

The two cases depicted show the two extreme cases within the participants in terms of height and weight. It can be seen that in both cases it is possible to visually identify the sequence of movements performed by the participants. If we consider position 4, lying in the center of the bed in supinated position, we can see that for both, the amplitude of the central sensor (in green) is 0.7 V, which corresponds to 21% of the full measurement scale (i.e. 3.3 V). In this position, the difference in weight is compensated by the difference in height and similar pressure forces are measured. On the other hand, if we look at position 2 (sitting on the right edge of the bed) in the blue trace corresponding to the right sensor, the differences is in weight are apparent: 18% of the full scale in the case of Fig. 5 vs 30% of the full scale in Fig. 6, showing the correlation between weight and pressure while sitting on the edge of the bed.

It can be concluded that position 1, 2 and 6 can be clearly identified, which can be used to detect when the person has just or is about to stand up preventing risky situations a potential falls.

The signal-to-noise ratio in the measured signal is very low and further filtering techniques can applied if necessary to obtain smoother transitions to provide cleaner signals to the classification methods to be developed.

4   Conclusions and Further Work

A simple and cost-effective solution to monitor posture and presence in the bed has been presented in this paper. It has been shown that it is an unobstrusive solution that can be easily installed in conventional beds and beds adapted to people with reduced mobility, while privacy is kept in the context of the bedroom. The preliminary analysis of the recorded signals has shown that it is feasible to identify the basic positions tested during the assessment of the prototype. This solution has the potential to prevent the appearance of pressure ulcer by monitoring postural changes, and reduce the risk of fall by detecting when the person has left the bed or is sitting in the edge.

The analysis of the recorded signals is an ongoing task, and analytical methods to achieve dimensionality reduction, such us processing the center of gravity out of the 3 measurements are being investigated.

Further work will involve the development of classification techniques to identify in-bed postures, which is currently in progress. Moreover, the generation of notifications to caregivers when the person is about to get up from the bed will also be pursued. Future piloting of this solution is also considered in the context of the collaborating nursing home.

Sensor fusion will also be explored in the future, in the context of assisted homes for the elderly people, in combination with other sensors such as presence sensors and cameras in order to provide the night wandering monitoring functionality. The proposed solution can assist to this end by anticipating when the person is about to stand up from the bed.

References

1. Active and Healthy Living in the Digital World, European Commission. https://futurium.ec.europa.eu/en/active-and-healthy-living-digital-world. Accessed 6 Mar 2022
2. The European Innovation Partnership on Active and Healthy Ageing (EIP on AHA), European Commission. https://digital-strategy.ec.europa.eu/en/policies/eip-aha. Accessed 6 Mar 2022
3. Sun, X.H., Ma, T., Yao, S., et al.: Associations of sleep quality and sleep duration with frailty and pre-frailty in an elderly population Rugao longevity and ageing study. BMC Geriatr. **20**, 9 (2020). https://doi.org/10.1186/s12877-019-1407-5
4. Silva, A., Metrôlho, J., Ribeiro, F., Fidalgo, F., Santos, O., Dionisio, R.: A review of intelligent sensor-based systems for pressure ulcer prevention. Computers **11**(1), 6 (2022). https://doi.org/10.3390/computers11010006
5. Wai, A.P., et al.: Lying posture classification for pressure ulcer prevention. J. Healthcare Eng. **1**, 217–238 (2010). https://doi.org/10.1260/2040-2295.1.2.217
6. Caggiari, S., Worsley, P., Payan, Y., Bucki, M., Bader, D.: Biomechanical monitoring and machine learning for the detection of lying postures. Clin. Biomech. **80**, 105181 (2020). https://doi.org/10.1016/j.clinbiomech.2020.105181
7. Liu, S., Ostadabbas, S.: A vision-based system for in-bed posture tracking. In: 2017 IEEE International Conference on Computer Vision Workshops (ICCVW), pp. 1373–1382 (2017). https://doi.org/10.1109/ICCVW.2017.163
8. Chang, M.-C., et al.: In-bed patient motion and pose analysis using depth videos for pressure ulcer prevention. In: 2017 IEEE International Conference on Image Processing (ICIP), pp. 4118–4122 (2017). https://doi.org/10.1109/ICIP.2017.8297057

9. Monroy, E.B., Rodríguez, A.P., Estevez, M.E., Quero, J.M.: Fuzzy monitoring of in-bed postural changes for the prevention of pressure ulcers using inertial sensors attached to clothing. J. Biomed. Inf. **107**, 103476 (2020). https://doi.org/10.1016/j.jbi.2020.103476

10. Qidwai, U., Al-Sulaiti, S., Ahmed, G., Hegazy, A., Ilyas, S.K.: Intelligent integrated instrumentation platform for monitoring long-term bedridden patients. In: 2016 IEEE EMBS Conference on Biomedical Engineering and Sciences (IECBES), pp. 561–564 (2016). https://doi.org/10.1109/IECBES.2016.7843512

11. Pouyan, M.B., Birjandtalab, J., Heydarzadeh, M., Nourani, M., Ostadabbas, S.: A pressure map dataset for posture and subject analytics. In: 2017 IEEE EMBS International Conference on Biomedical & Health Informatics (BHI), pp. 65–68 (2017). https://doi.org/10.1109/BHI.2017.7897206

12. Dimitrievski, A., et al.: Towards detecting pneumonia progression in COVID-19 patients by monitoring sleep disturbance using data streams of non-invasive sensor networks. Sensors **21**, 3030 (2021). https://doi.org/10.3390/s21093030

Classifying Sport-Related Human Activity from Thermal Vision Sensors Using CNN and LSTM

Aurora Polo-Rodriguez$^{(\boxtimes)}$, Alicia Montoro-Lendinez, Macarena Espinilla, and Javier Medina-Quero

Department of Computer Science, University of Jaén, Jaén, Spain
{apolo,amlendin,mestevez,jmquero}@ujaen.es

Abstract. In this work, we describe a classification of five sport-related human activities which are sensed by a thermal vision sensor. First, we have collected several sport sessions of an inhabitant while developing: push-ups, sit-ups, jumping jacks, squats and planks. Second, we develop an ad-hoc augmentation of data to increase the sturdiness of the data collection and reduce overfitting. Third, a Deep Learning model has been evaluated to compute a sequence of images from the user in order to estimate the activity. A CNN extracts relevant features from spatial domain and LSTM network models the sequence of images to compute the final classification. The results show an encouraging performance and quick learning capabilities.

Keywords: Sport-related human activity · CNN and LSTM · Thermal sensor

1 Introduction

Monitoring of human activities by sensor devices is a a prolific and expanding field of research. [18]. Internet of Things (IoT) [1] has been extended the applications of Human Activity Recognition (HAR) by the deployment of multi-modal sensors [22]. At the beginning, binary sensors were proposed as low-cost devices to sense HAR in a low invasive way [13]. While in the 2010s wearable devices provided human perspective tracking, enabling support for health monitoring [15] and gesture recognition [16]. In addition, vision sensors have been proposed as multimodal devices together with audio sensors [17] to analyze the pattern recognition of inhabitants [26]. Based on the intrinsic privacy concerns of visible spectrum devices [19], thermal vision sensors have been proposed because they offer a high degree of privacy [19].

On the other hand, new trends on Deep Learning have developed the current state-of-the-art in HAR [21]. On wearable devices, Deep Learning has provided encouraging results in monitoring physical activity and human activities in several benchmarks [25]. In addition, conventional devices such as binary sensors,

P. L. Mazzeo et al. (Eds.): ICIAP 2022 Workshops, LNCS 13373, pp. 38–48, 2022.
https://doi.org/10.1007/978-3-031-13321-3_4

have enabled a very high performance in the fusion of fuzzy logic and Deep Learning models [13]. In the end, DL models have found an encouraging source in vision sensors, where data collection, preprocessing methods, feature extraction, and training process are exhaustively achieved by various convolutional neural network (CCN) [3] approaches.

In this work, we present a case study where thermal vision sensors and sequence Deep Learning models are integrated to classify sport-related human activity:

- Integration of a thermal device: FLIR Lepton camera connected on a Raspberry Pi that configures an IoT thermal vision sensor with data collection, distribution and computational capabilities.
- A Deep Learning model based on Convolutional Neural Networks (CNNs) and short-term memory (LSTM) is proposed to extract spatio-temporal features.
- A real-life case study is collected, evaluated and analyzed. A classification of five sport-related human activities (push-ups, sit-ups, jumping jacks, squats and planks) developed by 3 sessions are sensed by a thermal vision sensor.

The remainder of the paper is organised as follows: In Sect. 2, we review related works and methodologies; in Sect. 3, we describe the devices, architecture, and methodology of the approach; in Sect. 4, we present the results of a case study; in Sect. 5, we detail our conclusions and ongoing works.

2   Related Works

The use of sensors in different applications, such as, health and activity recognition are rapidly increasing worldwide since the last few years [4]. In fact, the emergence of thermal vision sensors has been a crucial change in activity recognition due to is an excellent approach to preserve privacy and non-invasiveness [7]. However, most of the scientific literature makes use of visible spectrum sensors, as extensive progress has been made in multimedia data analysis using Deep Learning [9]. Despite the high performance obtained through the use of visible spectrum sensors, indoor privacy is a recurring concern for users [5]. Whenever vision sensors are used, it is crucial that the user feels safe and comfortable with the environment, so that they can go about their daily activities without discomfort [10]. For this reason, in this work an IoT device based on thermal vision sensor has been proposed. In addition, the thermal vision sensor is robust to light and shadow problems which are presented in visible spectrum cameras [8]. The performance of these sensors has been highlighted in recent works for properly sensing data on pose classification [5,6], activity classification, fall detection and presence detection.

Going deeper in monitoring sport-related activities, which is the field on which this work focuses, several recent studies highlight. In [20], sequences of images were associated with a specific sport, such as hockey, through videos recorded with visible spectrum cameras using 3D CNNs. On the other hand, we found another specific systems [24] for real-time sports analysis based on motion and vision sensor integration such as tennis. However, few studies have classified general-purpose activities. We highlight the work for general-purpose recognition of sport activities [14], which identifies human behaviours by silhouette detection, body parts model and multidimensional cues from full-body silhouettes and an entropy Markov model. Last, we note that there is a lack of scientific proposals in which thermal vision sensors have been integrated for recognition of sport-related activities, highlighting in this topic the proposal in [6], an IoT-based privacy-preserving yoga posture recognition system employing a deep convolutional neural network and a low-resolution infrared sensor-based wireless sensor network.

Considering the challenge of sports classification and the recent success of CNNs in solving vision problems, the use of these deep learning models is the method that tends to work best [12]. In fact, the authors of [20] implement a 3D CNN based multi-label deep HAR system for multi-label class-imbalanced action recognition in hockey videos, as mentioned above. Due to their effectiveness in broad practical applications, LSTM networks have received extensive coverage in scientific journals and recent papers, as reported by the authors in [24], where they propose a long short term memory (LSTM)-based framework to integrate movement and vision data for training and classification. This work combines the use of 3D CNN with LSTM network model to increase accuracy by extracting only the important spatio-temporal features for each image sequence.

3   Materials and Methods

To introduce this section, we first describe the IoT device to collect data using a thermal device. Second, we detail the representation of sequence of data collected, pre-processing with data augmentation. Third, a deep learning model with CNN+LSTM is proposed.

3.1   IoT Thermal Vision Sensor

The collection of images from the thermal domain has been carried out through an IoT device consisting of a thermal vision sensor connected to a low-cost IoT board (Raspberry Pi 4). The thermal vision sensor is **FLIR Lepton 3.5, integrated with the PureThermal 2 Smart IO Module**. This device is notable for its high image resolution (160×120 pixels) despite its minimal size (much smaller than a coin), shown in Fig. 1. In addition, the images it captures are accurate and correctly calibrated as it is a high quality Long Wavelength Infra-Red camera. It is available for around €350.

The script developed in Python and executed through the Raspberry Pi makes a direct connection with the thermal vision sensor, requesting the capture of frames every 2 s. This allows for greater data collection and more naturalistic conditions.

Fig. 1. PureThermal 2 Smart I/O Module + FLIR Lepton 3.5

3.2   Data Collection and Augmentation

In this section we describe the definition of sequence from thermal vision streams.

Following a formal definition, a sensor s collects real-time data in the form of a pair $\overline{s_i} = \{s_i, t_i\}$, where s_i represents a given measurement and t_i the timestamp. In the case of a vision sensor, s_i is composed of a matrix of values of dimension WxH, where $s_i[x][y], x \in [0, W], y \in [0, H]$ represents the heat spot collected by the thermal sensor at position (x, y).

Thus, the data stream of the sensor source s is defined by $\overline{S_s} = \{\overline{s_0}, \ldots, \overline{s_i}\}$ and a given value at a timestamp t_i by $S_s(t_i) = s_i$. From the data stream $\overline{S_s}$, we define the size of a temporal sequence T which segments the stream to obtain a sequence of previous values $S^*(t^*)$ for each time point t^*:

$$S^*(t^*) = \{S_s(t^* - T) \to S_s(t^*T - 1) \to \ldots \to S_s(t^*)\}$$

This $S^*(t^*)$ represents the sequence of images which is computed by the DL model proposed here. In Fig. 2, we present an example of sequence of frames for $t^* = 5, T = 5, W = 160, H = 120$ in real conditions.

CNN learning needs a large amount of data [23], so we extend the number of learning cases from a limited set [2] and therefore, improving performance and reducing over-fitting [11].

We have developed an application to augment and enlarge (AAE) image data from the original dataset, collected by ACL through translation, rotation and scale transformations:

– *Translation.* The original image is relocated within a maximal window size $[t_x, t_y]^+$ using a random process which generates a random translation transformation $[t_x, t_y], t_x \in [0, t_x^+], t_y \in [0, t_y^+]$.

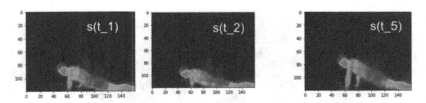

Fig. 2. Example of sequence of frames for $t^* = 5, T = 5, W = 160, H = 120$ in real conditions

- *Flipping* The image is flipped horizontally in a random process that applies the transformation to a percentage of F cases.
- *Rotation.* A random rotation is defined by a maximal rotation angle α in a random scale $s \in [1 - s^+, 1 + s^+]$.
- *Scale.* A scale factor s^+, which generate a random scale $s \in [1 - s^+, 1 + s^+]$.
- *Pixel alteration.* Each pixel $s_i[x][y]$ is modified by a threshold defined by δ using a normal distribution $N(\mu = s_i[x][y], \delta$.

In Fig. 3, we show an example of data augmentation with $[t_x, t_y]^+ = [-15, 15], F = 0.5, \alpha = 5°, [1 - s^+, 1 + s^+] = [0.8, 1.2], \delta = 0.05$.

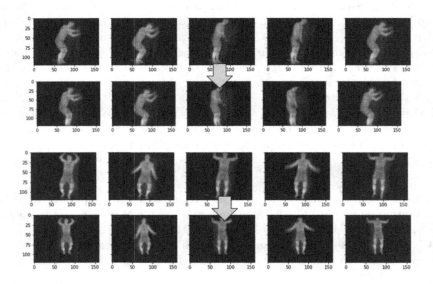

Fig. 3. Example data augmentation in two sequence of frames in real conditions.

3.3   DL Model for Learning from Image Sequences

Our proposed DL model to compute the sequence of frames collected by the thermal sensor is detailed in this section. Furthermore, as described in the "Related work" section, a suitable configuration for the extraction of spatial temporal features is the combination of CNN and LSTM.

First, CNNs are included to develop an automatic feature extraction for spatial information in the thermal frame values $s_i[x][y]$. A CNN with 7 layers of 2D convolutions is included. Each 2D convolution layer is defined by Conv2D(K,S,ST), where K defines the number of kernels, S the size of the convolution and ST the stride, whose stride $= 2$ value reduces the size from the input matrix to half size in the output matrix. Rectified linear unit activation function (ReLU) is also included in the inner layers to overcome the vanishing gradient problem and improve learning performance. In Fig. 4, we describe the CNN model proposed in this work.

Next, a LSTM network models the temporal sequence of spatial features extracted by the CNN for each frame. A 2 layers LSTM is integrated together with two dense multilayer perceptron-based layers which configure the final output of the neural network. In Fig. 4, we describe the temporal modelling of the DL model and the integrated CNN+LSTM model. Cross-entropy was defined as loss function that optimizes the Neural Network weights using the adam method optimization, which is a stochastic gradient descent for training deep learning models.

4   Case Study

In this section, we present the results obtained from a case study developed in real time in a real environment. The case study includes 3 scenes of a participant while performing sport-related human activities. Specifically, the participant performs push-ups, sit-ups, jumping jacks, squats and planks in one minute in sessions of 5–6 minutes duration. The developed dataset contains a total of 2089 images (without data augmentation).

The thermal sensor collected the image sequence at 2 FPS. Next, an external observer labelled the start and the end of each exercise. For learning purposes, a leave-session-out cross-validation is applied, where one of them is used for testing and other for learning the model.

First, we define $T = 5$ (2.5 s) as the number of frames which determines the input sequence for the model. The time-step between sampling data is defined to 1 s (exiting partial overlapping of data between consecutive sequences).

We have highlighted fast data collection, so data augmentation method is included (as described in Sect. 3.2). i) Translation is set to $[t_x, t_y]^+ = [-15, 15]$, ii) flipping percentage is set to $F = 0.5$, iii) maximal rotation is set to $\alpha = 5°$, iv) scale of image is set between $[1 - s^+, 1 + s^+] = [0.8, 1.2]$ and v) pixel modification is configure as standard deviation to $\delta = 0.05$.

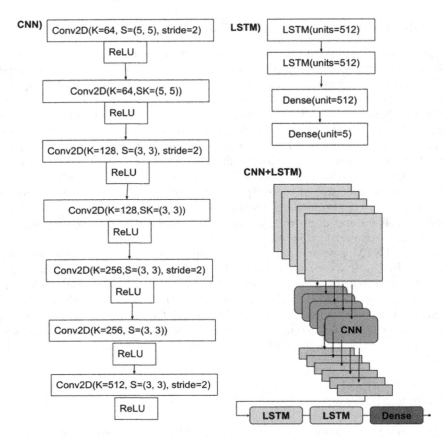

Fig. 4. Left) CNN model defined by Conv2D and ReLU layers. Top) LSTM and dense layers for final output configuration. Down) Representation of CNN+LSTM model.

4.1   Results

In this section, we describe the results thrown by the evaluation of the DL model proposed and data collected by the thermal sensor. The DL model has been configured with a batch size of 64 and a short learning of 10 epochs. The learning time in a iCore 17 16 GB RAM was 25 min. In Fig. 5, we show the confusion matrix and in Table 1 we describe accuracy, f1-score, precision and recall for each testing session.

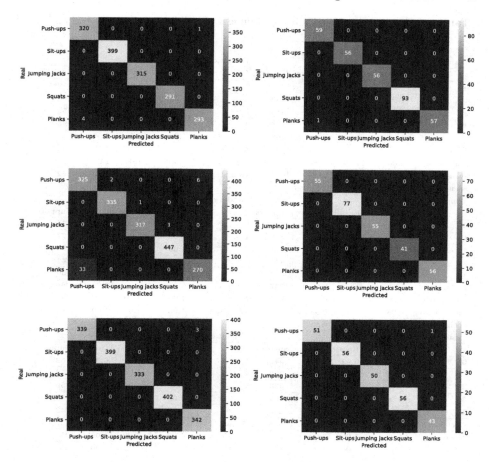

Fig. 5. Confusion matrices in training (**left**) and evaluation (**right**) for each scene shown in order: **Top)** Scene 1, **Middle)** Scene 2, **Bottom)** Scene 3.

As we observe from the data, the results are encouraging for learning in a straightforward way with a excellent accuracy. We note the training metrics are worse than testing metrics due to the impact of data augmentation in generating hard learning samples for learning purposes. However, it develops a sturdy model for evaluation purposes.

The data and source code developed in this work are available on GitHub: `://.com/AuroraPR/Sport-Related-Thermal`

Table 1. Classification metrics from training and validation of scenes 1, 2 and 3

Scene 1									
Training					Validation				
	Precision	Recall	f1-score	Support		Precision	Recall	f1-score	Support
0	0.99	1.00	0.99	321	0	0.98	1.00	0.99	59
1	1.00	1.00	1.00	399	1	1.00	1.00	1.00	56
2	1.00	1.00	1.00	315	2	1.00	1.00	1.00	56
3	1.00	1.00	1.00	291	3	1.00	1.00	1.00	93
4	1.00	0.99	0.99	297	4	1.00	0.98	0.99	58
Accuracy			1.00	1623	Accuracy			1.00	322
Macro avg	1.00	1.00	1.00	1623	Macro avg	1.00	1.00	1.00	322
Weighted avg	1.00	1.00	1.00	1623	Weighted avg	1.00	1.00	1.00	322
Scene 2									
Training					Validation				
	Precision	Recall	f1-score	Support		Precision	Recall	f1-score	Support
0	0.91	0.98	0.94	333	0	1.00	1.00	1.00	55
1	0.99	1.00	1.00	336	1	1.00	1.00	1.00	77
2	1.00	1.00	1.00	318	2	1.00	1.00	1.00	55
3	1.00	1.00	1.00	447	3	1.00	1.00	1.00	41
4	0.98	0.89	0.93	303	4	1.00	1.00	1.00	56
Accuracy			0.98	1737	Accuracy			1.00	284
Macro avg	0.97	0.97	0.97	1737	Macro avg	1.00	1.00	1.00	284
Weighted avg	0.98	0.98	0.98	1737	Weighted avg	1.00	1.00	1.00	284
Scene 3									
Training					Validation				
	Precision	Recall	f1-score	Support		Precision	Recall	f1-score	Support
0	1.00	0.99	1.00	342	0	1.00	0.98	0.99	52
1	1.00	1.00	1.00	399	1	1.00	1.00	1.00	56
2	1.00	1.00	1.00	333	2	1.00	1.00	1.00	50
3	1.00	1.00	1.00	402	3	1.00	1.00	1.00	56
4	0.99	1.00	1.00	342	4	0.98	1.00	0.99	43
Accuracy			1.00	1818	Accuracy			1.00	257
Macro avg	1.00	1.00	1.00	1818	Macro avg	1.00	1.00	1.00	257
Weighted avg	1.00	1.00	1.00	1818	Weighted avg	1.00	1.00	1.00	257

5   Conclusions and Ongoing Works

In this work, we have presented a Deep Learning model for processing thermal sequences of images to classify sport-related human activities. A configuration of CNN for extracting spatial features is integrated in a LSTM network which process the temporal dimension of the sequence to achieve excellent results.

A case study was collected with 3 sessions of 5 exercises: push-ups, sit-ups, jumping jacks, squats and planks. The data was augmented to extend the dataset, reduce overfitting and generate a robust model to noise and uncertainty in evaluation stage.

The encouraging performance of CNN+LSTM to classify human activities encourages the creation of a larger dataset. In this initial work, a single inhabitant and location is collected, but in future works we will focus on a multi domain and participant collection, where transfer learning, clustering and methods for pre-processing data will show new challenges to face.

References

1. Al-Sarawi, S., Anbar, M., Alieyan, K., Alzubaidi, M.: Internet of things (iot) communication protocols. In: 2017 8th International conference on information technology (ICIT), pp. 685–690. IEEE (2017)
2. Cireşan, D.C., Meier, U., Masci, J., Gambardella, L.M., Schmidhuber, J.: High-performance neural networks for visual object classification. arXiv preprint arXiv:1102.0183 (2011)
3. Dang, L.M., Min, K., Wang, H., Piran, M.J., Lee, C.H., Moon, H.: Sensor-based and vision-based human activity recognition: a comprehensive survey. Pattern Recogn. **108**, 107561 (2020)
4. De-La-Hoz-Franco, E., Ariza-Colpas, P., Quero, J.M., Espinilla, M.: Sensor-based datasets for human activity recognition-a systematic review of literature. IEEE Access **6**, 59192–59210 (2018)
5. Gochoo, M., Tan, T.H., Batjargal, T., Seredin, O., Huang, S.C.: Device-free non-privacy invasive indoor human posture recognition using low-resolution infrared sensor-based wireless sensor networks and dcnn. In: 2018 IEEE International Conference on Systems, Man, and Cybernetics (SMC), pp. 2311–2316. IEEE (2018)
6. Gochoo, M., et al.: Novel IoT-based privacy-preserving yoga posture recognition system using low-resolution infrared sensors and deep learning. IEEE Internet Things J. **6**(4), 7192–7200 (2019)
7. Griffiths, E., Assana, S., Whitehouse, K.: Privacy-preserving image processing with binocular thermal cameras. Proc. ACM Interact. Mob. Wearable Ubiq. Technol. **1**(4), 1–25 (2018)
8. Han, J., Bhanu, B.: Human activity recognition in thermal infrared imagery. In: 2005 IEEE Computer Society Conference on Computer Vision and Pattern Recognition (CVPR 2005)-Workshops, p. 17. IEEE (2005)
9. Hiriyannaiah, S., Akanksh, B.S., Koushik, A.S., Siddesh, G.M., Srinivasa, K.G.: Deep learning for multimedia data in IoT. In: Tanwar, S., Tyagi, S., Kumar, N. (eds.) Multimedia Big Data Computing for IoT Applications. ISRL, vol. 163, pp. 101–129. Springer, Singapore (2020). https://doi.org/10.1007/978-981-13-8759-3_4
10. Kong, X., Meng, Z., Meng, L., Tomiyama, H.: A privacy protected fall detection IoT system for elderly persons using depth camera. In: 2018 International Conference on Advanced Mechatronic Systems (ICAMechS), pp. 31–35. IEEE (2018)
11. Krizhevsky, A., Sutskever, I., Hinton, G.E.: Imagenet classification with deep convolutional neural networks. Adv. Neural Inf. Process. Syst. **25**, 1–9 (2012)
12. Martínez-González, A., Villamizar, M., Canévet, O., Odobez, J.M.: Efficient convolutional neural networks for depth-based multi-person pose estimation. IEEE Trans. Circ. Syst. Video Technol. **30**(11), 4207–4221 (2019)
13. Medina-Quero, J., Zhang, S., Nugent, C., Espinilla, M.: Ensemble classifier of long short-term memory with fuzzy temporal windows on binary sensors for activity recognition. Expert Syst. Appl. **114**, 441–453 (2018)
14. Nadeem, A., Jalal, A., Kim, K.: Automatic human posture estimation for sport activity recognition with robust body parts detection and entropy markov model. Multimedia Tools Appl. **80**(14), 21465–21498 (2021). https://doi.org/10.1007/s11042-021-10687-5
15. Nasiri, S., Khosravani, M.R.: Progress and challenges in fabrication of wearable sensors for health monitoring. Sens. Actuators A: Phys. **312**, 112105 (2020)
16. Ordóñez, F.J., Roggen, D.: Deep convolutional and LSTM recurrent neural networks for multimodal wearable activity recognition. Sensors **16**(1), 115 (2016)

17. Polo-Rodriguez, A., Vilchez Chiachio, J.M., Paggetti, C., Medina-Quero, J.: Ambient sound recognition of daily events by means of convolutional neural networks and fuzzy temporal restrictions. Appl. Sci. **11**(15), 6978 (2021)
18. Ramasamy Ramamurthy, S., Roy, N.: Recent trends in machine learning for human activity recognition-a survey. Wiley Interdisc. Rev. Data Min. Knowl. Disc. **8**(4), e1254 (2018)
19. Sixsmith, A., Johnson, N.: A smart sensor to detect the falls of the elderly. IEEE Perv. Comput. **3**(2), 42–47 (2004)
20. Sozykin, K., Protasov, S., Khan, A., Hussain, R., Lee, J.: Multi-label class-imbalanced action recognition in hockey videos via 3d convolutional neural networks. In: 2018 19th IEEE/ACIS International Conference on Software Engineering, Artificial Intelligence, Networking and Parallel/Distributed Computing (SNPD), pp. 146–151. IEEE (2018)
21. Wang, J., Chen, Y., Hao, S., Peng, X., Hu, L.: Deep learning for sensor-based activity recognition: a survey. Pattern Recogn. Lett. **119**, 3–11 (2019)
22. Yadav, S.K., Tiwari, K., Pandey, H.M., Akbar, S.A.: A review of multimodal human activity recognition with special emphasis on classification, applications, challenges and future directions. Knowl.-Based Syst. **223**, 106970 (2021)
23. Yamashita, T., Watasue, T., Yamauchi, Y., Fujiyoshi, H.: Improving quality of training samples through exhaustless generation and effective selection for deep convolutional neural networks. In: VISAPP, no. 2, pp. 228–235 (2015)
24. Zhang, C., Yang, F., Li, G., Zhai, Q., Jiang, Y., Xuan, D.: Mv-sports: a motion and vision sensor integration-based sports analysis system. In: IEEE INFOCOM 2018-IEEE Conference on Computer Communications, pp. 1070–1078. IEEE (2018)
25. Zhang, S., et al.: Deep learning in human activity recognition with wearable sensors: a review on advances. Sensors **22**(4), 1476 (2022)
26. Zhang, S., Wei, Z., Nie, J., Huang, L., Wang, S., Li, Z.: A review on human activity recognition using vision-based method. J. Healthcare Eng. **2017** (2017)

MIRATAR: A Virtual Caregiver for Active and Healthy Ageing

Maria J. Santofimia[1]([📧]) [iD], Felix J. Villanueva[1] [iD], Javier Dorado[1] [iD],
Ana Rubio[1] [iD], Jesus Fernández-Bermejo[1] [iD], Henry Llumiguano[1] [iD],
Xavier del Toro[1] [iD], Nirmalie Wiratunga[2] [iD], and Juan C. Lopez[1] [iD]

[1] Department of Technology and Information Systems,
University of Castilla-La Mancha, Ciudad Real, Spain
{mariajose.santofimia,felix.villanueva,javier.dorado,ana.rubio,
jesus.fruiz,henry.llumiguano,xavier.deltoro,juancarlos.lopez}@uclm.es
[2] School of Computing, Robert Gordon University, Aberdeen, UK
n.wiratunga@rgu.ac.uk

Abstract. Despite the technology advances in the field of virtual assistant and activity monitoring devices, older adults are still reluctant to embrace this technology, specially when it comes to employ it to manage health-related issues. This paper presents a work in progress for a virtual caregiver, based on the Internet of Thing paradigm, that employs different technological solutions for information gathering and intervention delivery. The ultimate goal of this virtual caregiver is to support people empowerment to actively contribute to frailty and multimorbidity management and risk mitigation. To this end, user acceptance and willingness to use the propose solution has to be ensured. This work in progress starts with the hypothesis that by embedding the proposed technology in a smart mirror device will improve user acceptance and willingness to use. This paper presents the vision and overall architecture and future work will address the evaluation of user acceptance and the use intention.

Keywords: Active and healthy ageing · Frailty and multimorbidity · Smart mirror

1 Introduction

The work in [7] defines care as *"the provision for the health, welfare and social well-being and needs of societies"*. Care is therefore what eventually holds society together, and without which life could not be sustained [11]. According to

This research was funded by H2020 European Union program under grant agreement No. 857159 (SHAPES project), by the Spanish MCIN/ AEI /10.13039/501100011033 grant TALENT-BELIEF (PID2020-116417RB-C44) and by GoodBrother COST action 19121.

P. L. Mazzeo et al. (Eds.): ICIAP 2022 Workshops, LNCS 13373, pp. 49–58, 2022.
https://doi.org/10.1007/978-3-031-13321-3_5

the Report on care work and care jobs for the future of decent work of the International Labour Organisation [4], there are 381 million workers in the global care workforce, most of them women working informally, representing 11.5% of the total global employment. Despite its relevance, this work is characterised for being unpaid or low-paid. This contrasts with the fact that, care works are, according to the UN Human Development Report [21], what drives market economies.

Spain is one of the few EU State Member countries that have decided to leverage the care economy in its recovery plan to face the COVID-19 crisis. The Spain's Recovery, Transformation and Resilience Plan proposes [12], specific measures to modernise and strengthen social services, such as developing "*new networks of tele-assistance, modernise dependency care systems and develop new residential infrastructure that facilitates the autonomy of elderly people and dependents, and the reorientation of the long-term caregiving system towards less institutionalised, more customer-centric model which is better connected with the primary healthcare network*".

The digital transformation of the care economy demands a step-change from a disease to a person-centred care model, in which the focus is moved from hospital care to home and community care [19]. This paradigm shift is particularly important for frailty and multimorbidity patients because they require regular care and supervision that, when not appropriately delivered, lead to acute episodes and hospital readmissions. According to the WHO [20] "*at least 80% of all heart disease, stroke and diabetes and 40% of cancer could be prevented*" by tackling the most common risk factors underlying the most prevalent chronic conditions, such as unhealthy diets, physical inactivity, hypertension or obesity.

Frailty and multimorbidity (understood as the condition of suffering from two or more chronic conditions) are the most relevant challenges faced by healthcare systems. Whereas improvements in acute care are close to its maximum, people die due to a range of other conditions like frailty and chronic diseases that could be avoided through better prevention policies and more effective care [13]. Multimorbidity is indeed very prevalent, reaching up to 90% of people over 65 [13]. This is, at the same time, very challenging because different professionals are involved in the treatment, medication is complex and involves polypharmacy with high risks of drugs interfering one to each other, or poor medication adherence. On the other hand, frailty, defined as "*a medical syndrome with multiple causes and contributors that is characterised by diminished strength, endurance, and reduced physiologic function that increases an individual's vulnerability for developing increased dependency and/or death*" [18], presents a community-dwelling older adult's prevalence of 12%, although in people aged 90+ it may be higher than 35%. Frailty is gaining attention as an important predictor of health outcomes in older adults. More specifically, this factor has been associated with death, institutionalisation, falls, reduced mobility, hospitalisation, and increased dependence in basic and instrumental activities of daily living [2]. More importantly, frailty, is potentially reversible with appropriate healthcare and lifestyle interventions, such as exercise [10], diet [16], polypharmacy control, or therapies against isolation. For all these reasons, frailty is actually considered the cornerstone of Geriatric Medicine and Healthcare for older adults [1].

The use of innovative technologies, such as wearable devices or virtual assistants, can play an important role in supporting the management of the aforementioned risk conditions. There are, however, limitations in the state of the art of such technologies that call for further research so that they can be successfully employed by older adults already dealing with multi morbidity and frailty. In this sense, off-the-shelf devices and Apps can be found for physical activity and weight management such as those of Fitbit [22], Apple Watch [3], Google Fit [17] or Xiaomi MiFit [8]. They all offer a range of functionalities for user engagement, monitoring, reminders for promoting a healthier lifestyle, etc. Most of these commercial solutions offer open APIs, so that third party applications can access the data they collect. So, efforts can be focused on what to do with the data rather than how to collect them. However, a recent study [15] concluded that there is little evidence that wearable devices, by themselves, could improve health outcomes in chronic patients, although they could improve motivation and physical activity. Most studies to date focus on healthy individuals rather than on those already suffering from a chronic condition or multimorbidity. On the other hand, the role that virtual assistants can play in improving motivation, engagement, and leading sustainable behaviour change may be essential for individual empowerment. From a technological point of view, voice assistants like "Hey, Siri", "Ok, Google" or "Alexa" are fully operational and have revolutionised the way we manage the interaction with our nearby devices and daily routines. However, little is known about both the willingness to use these assistants for health-related purposes and the aspects that contribute to their acceptance for these other purposes.

This paper presents a work in progress intended to provide a virtual caregiver to supports people empowerment to actively contribute to frailty and multimorbidity management and risk mitigation. To this end, the main risk factors negatively contributing to older aldult's health will be monitored, so that future risks can be predicted in advance, and appropriate interventions can be undertaken to prevent or mitigate them. The virtual caregiver proposed here, known as MIRATAR, runs on an innovative platform: a smart mirror. Mirrors, and more specifically their reflection, help us build our sense of self. For this reason, MIRATAR plans to exploit the human fascination for mirrors and the role they can play in enabling self-awareness. User acceptance and willingness to use is expected to be improved thanks to use of such a platform. Moreover, the smart mirror platform will run software solutions that will provide the virtual caregiver with the skills and required information to guide individuals towards an improved self-awareness and self-management of health.

This paper focuses in presenting the most relevant aspects of the virtual caregiver and it is organised as follow. First, Sect. 2 presents the vision for the MIRATAR virtual caregiver. Section 3 describes the most relevant technical details of the implemented virtual assistant. Finally, Sect. 4 presents the main conclusions drawn from this work in progress as well as the future works still needed to effectively achieved a comprehensive platform for frailty and multi-morbidity management and risk mitigation.

2   MIRATAR Concept and Vision

MIRATAR concept understands that a technological platform for integrated care, centred on frailty and multimorbidity management and risk mitigation has to address multiple dimensions and different roles, with different requirements. Figure 1 summarizes the MIRATAR vision.

Individuals or older adults will be willing to use the platform because it helps them to develop a greater sense of autonomous self-governance, and control over themselves and their condition. This will in turn drive change in behaviours towards healthier lifestyles, helps them in the management of chronic conditions and, ultimately, it gives them the assurance that any risk will be early iden-tified and therefore addressed and treated timeously. Although the platform is particularly aimed at providing care for patients with chronic diseases and multi-morbidities, its use should not be limited to those suffering from disease. Instead, it should be an active and positive support for all individuals to achieve and sus-tain healthier lifestyles. Because individuals, especially those already retired from work, develop their lives around the home environment, MIRATAR have focused on providing solutions for the home context. More importantly, the home context should be the place where integrated care, required by chronic patients, should be carried out, in a self-managed manner or assisted by caregivers. This will not only contribute to the sustainability of the healthcare system, but more impor-tantly to the quality of care received. In case it turns out that a person cannot be cared for at home anymore, the platform will be equipped with the possibility to warn about the risk that this moment might be near and provide information, to enable the users to instigate an informed discussion with their caregivers, physi-cians and close-ones early on. Due to the option to include data/information collected through the monitoring of health and lifestyle parameters, hospital admission might be reduced, and hospital discharges might be accelerated. This will not only help save cost but also enable better resource planning that can help save lives. Caregivers, healthcare professionals, and service providers will also be users of the MIRATAR platform. Caregivers and professionals will benefit from using the platform because of the relevant information it provides about the individual health and lifestyle. Medication intake, vital signs, physical activity performance are some of the aspects that both health and care professionals and caregivers will be interested in. The platform does also provide a place where to exchange information and knowledge with other professionals as well as to learn new evidence-based health and care pathways. Service providers will interact with MIRATAR in a double way, as service provider and data consumer. The platform should therefore implement the appropriate governance mechanisms to ensure that individuals, those who own the data, control, and manage who has access to their data. This will be accomplished by an approach based on

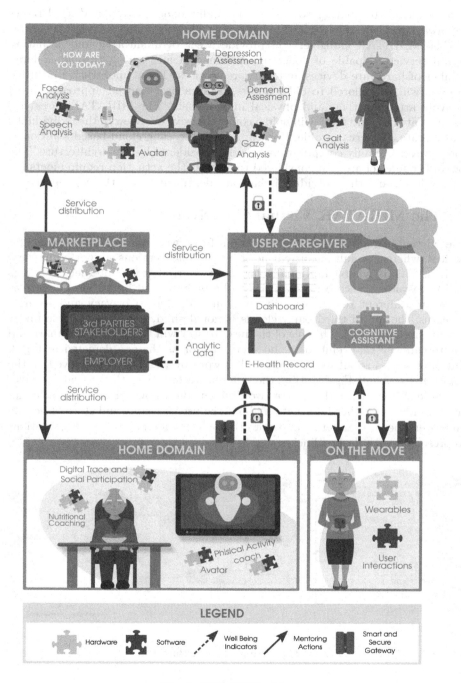

Fig. 1. MIRATAR vision

smart contract technology to ensure that individuals' privacy and legal rights are always in place.

The MIRATAR caregiver will provide a set of monitoring and actuation digital services capable of collecting information and acting through a large number of hardware devices and software services. These unobtrusive intuitive services will be tailored to older adults, using a user-centred approach aimed to avoid attention theft and physical impediments. The MIRATAR caregiver, installed at the cloud level, will hold a comprehensive overview of the individual's health state, patterns, profile, historic record, etc. The cloud-based solution is not however the only computational model considered by the architecture. The fog and edge level are also considered to address the actuation requirements (at the fog level) and the individual behaviour identification (at the edge level).

3   The MIRATAR Virtual Caregiver

The virtual caregiver needs information from wearable and environmental devices, whereas simultaneously it needs to run interventions supported in these devices. This is what traditionally has been referred to an Internet of Things (IoT) ecosystem. Such ecosystem has to be orchestrated by an interlocutor as there are different technologies involved in and, due to privacy and security concerns, the use of third party-clouds is not desired, nor even possible under certain circumstances. The role of the interlocutor will be played by a smart and secure gateway that, embed in the smart mirror as the one depicted in Fig 3, will have access to all technologies either wore by the user or deployed at the home environment. Fig 2 outline the different technologies the virtual caregiver will be equipped with. There are two different data flows. There are technologies intended to gather information about the user life style and state of health. Moreover, there are other technologies that are intended to deliver interventions (represented with dashed lines).

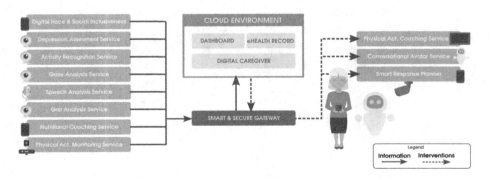

Fig. 2. The virtual avatar architecture

Based on the idea that the current healthcare approach, more disease oriented, has to evolve to a health promotion and disease prevention approach, this work spins around the idea that individuals should be responsible for their own health. To this end, individuals are encouraged to actively participate, assisted by innovative ICT technologies, in improving their health, well-being and quality of life. Key to achieving this will be promoting the development of greater personal autonomy in those individuals to take personal responsibility and accountability, by empowering their appreciation of their critical as well as experiential interests as part of their self-governance.

Verbal communication is gaining credit as an intuitive way of interacting with technology so, this approach stands out as a potential approach to successfully contribute to health self-management and self-governance. For this reason, the virtual caregiver has to be enhanced with conversational capabilities. This results in an innovative and multimodal assistant that will not only work on the smart mirror device but also in devices like phones, tablets, or desktop environments. This novel approach to delivering interventions intends to overcome the lack of engagement of traditional virtual assistants.

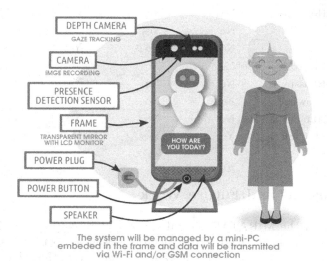

Fig. 3. The virtual avatar running in the smart mirror platform

The implementation of the virtual caregiver is supported in an open source toolkit known as Rhasspy[1]. There are different reasons supporting this option, in comparison to other solutions of the state of the art, which are compared and listed in Table 1 [6]. The same privacy and security concerns mentioned earlier when justifying the need for a smart and secure gateway is stated here to support the choice of open source solutions, running offline, over those commercial options requiring the use of an external cloud.

---

[1] https://rhasspy.readthedocs.io/en/latest/.

The proposed virtual caregiver assistant based on Rhasspy converts voice commands or requests into events, afterwards catered by the different services running on the smart mirror. It is therefore necessary to translate voice command into texts to which end the Deep Speech engine [5] has been employed. A dataset was collected, in Spanish language, employed to train the model. To this end, Fsticuffs [14] has been employed to train the intent recognition system. Further details of the voice assistant implementation and workflow are described in [9].

Table 1. Voice assistant comparisons

Assistant	Cloud-based	Works online	Open source
Google	Yes	Yes	No
Azurev	Yes	Yes	No
IBM	Yes	Yes	No
AWS	Yes	Yes	No
Houndify	Yes	Yes	No
Wit.ia	No	Yes	No
Vosk	No	No	Yes
Picovoice	No	No	Yes
Rhasspy	No	No	Yes
Snowboy	No	No	Yes
Almond & Ada	No	No	Yes
MyCroft	Yes	Yes	Yes

4   Conclusions and Future Work

The adoption of the MIRATAR virtual caregiver will empower individuals to take an active role in managing their health as well as to take responsibility in adopting healthier lifestyles in a sustainable manner so that changes can be adopted into the daily life of the individual. Nonetheless, these changes in habits and lifestyles will not necessarily offer immediate results, but rather these will be experienced in the long term and as a result of having lived a healthier, more self-directed life. This will eventually have an impact on the way individuals, health and care professionals and service providers interact. Also, adopting personalized and new health and care pathways will have an impact on the delivered quality of care. Overall, health systems will be less overwhelmed for different reasons. The knowledge and understanding of how frailty and multimorbidity interact will improve due to the data collected thanks to the proposed solutions. Moreover, machine learning and big data analytic will lead to relevant insights about how diseases behave, interact, or evolve. This will enable a better care and therefore, preventive measures that avoid, delay or minimize the associated risks.

MIRATAR will also impact the quality of services provided to society, in general, but more specifically to those that live in rural areas, hit by the depopulation phenomena. People living in these areas have to travel to access health services. For this reason, the innovative services proposed in this project, spinning around the smart mirror platform, are intended to provide at-home universal access to care.

Finally, future works are addressed to collect quantitative impact on health and well being that the proposed solution can have in older adults. To this end, a pilot study is expected to be conducted under the SHAPES project to evaluate such impact as a result of having used the proposed technology over a period of time.

References

1. Abizanda, P., Rodríguez-Mañas, L.: Function but not multimorbidity at the cornerstone of geriatric medicine. J. Am. Geriatr. Soc. **65**(10), 2333–2334 (2017)
2. Abizanda, P., Romero, L., Sanchez-Jurado, P.M., Martinez-Reig, M., Alfonso-Silguero, S.A., Rodriguez-Manas, L.: Age, frailty, disability, institutionalization, multimorbidity or comorbidity. which are the main targets in older adults? J. Nutr. Health Aging **18**(6), 622–627 (2014). https://doi.org/10.1007/s12603-014-0033-3
3. Abt, G., Bray, J., Benson, A.C.: Measuring moderate-intensity exercise with the apple watch: validation study. JMIR Cardio **2**(1), e8574 (2018)
4. Addati, L., Cattaneo, U., Esquivel, V., Valarino, I.: Care work and care jobs for the future of decent work. Op. cit (2018)
5. Amodei, D., et al.: Deep speech 2 : End-to-end speech recognition in english and mandarin. In: Balcan, M.F., Weinberger, K.Q. (eds.) Proceedings of The 33rd International Conference on Machine Learning. Proceedings of Machine Learning Research, 20–22 June 2016, vol. 48, pp. 173–182. PMLR, New York. https://proceedings.mlr.press/v48/amodei16.html
6. Astilleros, M.E.: Pasarela inteligente para el control remoto y la supervisión en entornos de envejecimiento activo y saludable. Ph.D. thesis, Escuela Superior de Informática. Universidad de Castilla-La Mancha (2021)
7. Barry, U., Jennings, C.: Gender equality: economic value of care from the perspective of the applicable EU funds: an exploration of an EU strategy towards valuing the care economy (2021)
8. de la Casa Pérez, A., et al.: Is the xiaomi mi band 4 an accuracy tool for measuring health-related parameters in adults and older people? an original validation study. Int. J. Environ. Res. Public Health **19**(3), 1593 (2022)
9. Chaparro, J.D., et al.: The shapes smart mirror approach for independent living, healthy and active ageing. Sensors **21**(23) (2021). https://doi.org/10.3390/s21237938, https://www.mdpi.com/1424-8220/21/23/7938
10. Clegg, A.P., Barber, S.E., Young, J.B., Forster, A., Iliffe, S.J.: Do home-based exercise interventions improve outcomes for frail older people? findings from a systematic review. Rev. Clin. Gerontol. **22**(1), 68–78 (2012)
11. Dowling, E.: The care crisis: what caused it and how can we end it? Verso Books (2021)

12. de España, G.: Plan de recuperación, transformación y resiliencia. componente 22. Report (2021). https://www.lamoncloa.gob.es/temas/fondos-recuperacion/Documents/05052021-Componente22.pdf
13. Forjaz, M.J., et al.: Application of the ja-chrodis integrated multimorbidity care model (imcm) to a case study of diabetes and mental health. Int. J. Environ. Res. Public Health 16(24), 5151 (2019)
14. Hansen, M., Vervloesem, K., Bachmann, M.: Rhasspy natural language understanding (2021). https://github.com/rhasspy/rhasspy-nlu. Accessed 2022
15. Jo, A., Coronel, B.D., Coakes, C.E., Mainous, A.G., III.: Is there a benefit to patients using wearable devices such as fitbit or health apps on mobiles? a systematic review. Am. J. Med. 132(12), 1394–1400 (2019)
16. Kojima, G., Avgerinou, C., Iliffe, S., Walters, K.: Adherence to mediterranean diet reduces incident frailty risk: systematic review and meta-analysis. J. Am. Geriatr. Soc. 66(4), 783–788 (2018)
17. Menaspà, P.: Effortless activity tracking with google fit. Brit. J. Sports Med. 49(24), 1598–1598 (2015)
18. Morley, J.E., et al.: Frailty consensus: a call to action. J. Am. Med. Direct. Assoc. 14(6), 392–397 (2013)
19. Organization, W.H., et al.: Interim report: placing people and communities at the centre of health services: Who global strategy on integrated people-centred health services 2016–2026: executive summary. World Health Organization, Technical report (2015)
20. Organization, W.H., et al.: Action plan for the prevention and control of noncommunicable diseases in the who European region. Technical report, World Health Organization. Regional Office for Europe (2016)
21. Qadir, U.: Un development programme (UNDP): human development report 2015-work for human development. Pak. Dev. Rev. 54(3), 277–278 (2015)
22. Ringeval, M., Wagner, G., Denford, J., Paré, G., Kitsiou, S., et al.: Fitbit-based interventions for healthy lifestyle outcomes: systematic review and meta-analysis. J. Med. Internet Res. 22(10), e23954 (2020)

From Garment to Skin: The visuAAL Skin Segmentation Dataset

Kooshan Hashemifard[✉][iD] and Francisco Florez-Revuelta[iD]

Department of Computing Technology,University of Alicante,
San Vicente Del Raspeig, 03690 Alicante, Spain
{k.hashemifard,francisco.florez}@ua.es

Abstract. Human skin detection has been remarkably incorporated in different computer vision and biometric systems. It has been receiving increasing attention in face analysis, human tracking and recognition, and medical image analysis. For many human-related recognition tasks, using skin detection cue could be a proper choice. Despite the vast area of usage and applications for skin detection, not many large or reliable skin detection datasets are available, and many of the existing ones, are originally created for other tasks such as hand tracking or face analysis. In this paper, we propose a methodology for extracting skin pixels from garment segmentation and recognition datasets. This is achieved by using deep learning methods to generate automatic skin label masks from them by exploiting human body and hair segmentation and provided garment masks. Following this approach, a large human skin segmentation dataset is introduced. A validation set is also manually segmented in order to evaluate the accuracy of the output skin masks. Finally, usual methods for skin detection and segmentation are evaluated on this new dataset.

Keywords: Skin segmentation · Dataset

1 Introduction

Padilla et al. [22] proposed a privacy-by-context approach to provide privacy in video data, particularly in active and assisted living applications. The context is given by a number of variables: (i) the observer; (ii) the identity of the person (to retrieve the privacy profile); (iii) the closeness between the person and observer (e.g., relative, doctor or acquaintance); (iv) appearance (dressed?); (v) location (e.g., kitchen); and (vi) ongoing activity or detected event (e.g., cooking, watching TV, fall). The automated recognition of these variables is a requirement to be able to provide privacy appropriately. Among these, appearance recognition, i.e.

This work is part of the visuAAL project on Privacy-Aware and Acceptable Video-Based Technologies and Services for Active and Assisted Living (https://www.visuaal-itn.eu/). This project has received funding from the European Union's Horizon 2020 research and innovation programme under the Marie Skłodowska-Curie grant agreement No 861091.

P. L. Mazzeo et al. (Eds.): ICIAP 2022 Workshops, LNCS 13373, pp. 59–70, 2022.
https://doi.org/10.1007/978-3-031-13321-3_6

determining the degree of nudity of a person, is one of them. Nudity estimation requires skin segmentation.

Skin classification is the act of separating skin pixels (or regions) in an image from non-skin ones which could be background pixels or body pixels covered by clothes [19]. Skin detection has been used in human biometric applications such as face analysis [21] and medical image analysis [3], as a preprocessing or validation step or to find the location of human beings and their body parts [29]. Skin segmentation is also an important task in other applications including content retrieval, robotics, sign language recognition, and human computer interaction [19]. For many human-related recognition and prediction tasks, using skin detection cue could be beneficial, since it can be insensitive to variables such as pose, rotation or facial expression.

Deep learning has been applied for semantic segmentation, which can also be exploited for skin segmentation. However, in order to perform adequately, deep learning methods usually rely on large datasets. The lack of large skin segmentation datasets is still a serious issue. Most of the datasets for this task are either small, noisy or suffering from low quality images, some are borrowed from other tasks such as hand tracking, face detection and face recognition and others are unavailable for public use. In addition to the dataset size, a dataset should cover a variety of poses and nonlinear illuminations, aging, makeups, complex backgrounds, different skin characteristics and colors, and also camera variations. All these problems have led many methods to not be experimented based on standard datasets. Therefore, many papers are validated based on random collection of personal or online public images [19]. However, the fact that developing a large-scale manually segmented dataset can be costly and time consuming cannot be ignored. The manual annotation process for segmentation is very demanding and labor-intensive [9]. As an example, annotating a single image in the Cityscapes dataset costs more than 1.5 h [4] and it will not be much less for a skin dataset due to variations of clothing or hair styles.

Therefore, the main aim of this work is to propose a methodology to create larger skin segmentation datasets, by exploiting available garment datasets in conjunction with deep learning methods for human body and hair segmentation in order to automatically generate ground truth skin labels for images. This tackles some of the problems mentioned above in order to build large human skin datasets. Following this approach, a new skin segmentation dataset (the visuAAL Skin Segmentation dataset) is introduced. A study on different preprocessing and postprocessing steps is done to evaluate the results, lower the segmentation noise and achieve the most precise masks possible. These evaluations are carried out employing a portion of randomly selected and manually segmented images from the dataset. Finally, usual and state-of-the-art algorithms for semantic segmentation and skin detection are evaluated on this dataset.

The remaining of this paper is organized as follows. Section 2 presents a brief review of existing human skin datasets. Section 3 proposes a methodology for generating skin annotations automatically. In Sect. 4 the details of the dataset, evaluation metrics and quality assessment are discussed, and Sect. 5 is dedicated

Table 1. Comparison between skin datasets.

Dataset	Year	Number of images	Annotation quality
Compaq	2002	13,640	Imprecise
TDSD	2004	554	Imprecise
ECU	2005	6,000	Precise
Schmugge	2007	845	Imprecise
MCG	2011	1,000	Imprecise
HGR	2012	1,558	Precise
Pratheepan	2012	78	Precise
SFA	2013	1,118	Precise

to baseline specification and measuring the performance of existing methods on the new dataset. Finally, Sect. 6 presents some conclusions and future work.

2   Skin Detection and Segmentation Datasets

While in skin detection it is very common for researchers to collect images and use their own datasets, there also exist popular human skin datasets. Though these datasets may not follow the same protocols (i.e., some considered eyebrows and lips as skin and some excluded them) or could be noisy, they still provide an opportunity to evaluate and compare the methods. Also, as mentioned before, some of them are not directly skin datasets but originally developed for face recognition and hand tracking tasks. Table 1 presents a summary of the main details of this datasets. Next, some of the main available datasets are described.

Compaq Dataset [14]. Compaq is one of the largest datasets including 13,640 images divided into two groups of skin and non-skin. Skin ground truths are semi-manually labeled. This dataset roughly contains 1 billion pixels in total, including more than 80 million skin pixels. Compaq has been widely used by the research community. However, low quality images and noisy labels are considerable issues.

ECU Dataset [24] . ECU consists of 4,000 high quality color images with high accuracy ground truth which are segmented manually for face detection and skin segmentation. Different skin types, backgrounds, and illuminations make this dataset more diverse. It contains 4.9 million skin pixels and 13.7 million non-skin pixels.

SFA Dataset [2]. This dataset is collected based on FERET [23] and AR [20] face images datasets. It includes 1,118 images. Though the ground truth is precise (lips, eyebrows and eyes are excluded), it mostly consists of face images only.

Fig. 1. Samples from the FashionPedia dataset.

Schmugge Dataset [27]. Schmugge et al. collected a general and diverse dataset consisting of 845 images with nearly 5 million skin pixels and 13.7 million non-skin pixels. The ground truths are generated in a semi-supervised way and are noisy.

HGR Dataset [15]. This dataset was collected by Kawulok et al. for hand gesture recognition and includes 1,558 images with different sizes, backgrounds and conditions.

MCG Dataset [12]. MCG-skin includes 1,000 images randomly collected from the web and social media. Images cover a variety of different backgrounds, skin colors and races, and illumination conditions with diverse quality and resolution. In this dataset, eyes, lips and eyebrows are labeled as skin.

TDSD Dataset [36]. It consists of 554 images randomly picked from the web with over 24 million skin pixels and 75 million non-skin pixels. Skin ground truths are labeled manually using Photoshop.

Pratheepan Dataset [31]. The images in this dataset are randomly collected from the web. The images were captured with a range of cameras using different color enhancement techniques and under different illuminations. Though the dataset is diverse in terms of background and lighting and the ground truths are very precise, it only consists of 78 images and is mostly used as a benchmark dataset for evaluation purposes.

3   Approach

As mentioned in Sect. 1, due to the difficulties of creating large skin segmentation datasets and overwhelming annotation process, a common alternative approach is to adapt datasets from homogeneous tasks. In this paper, we propose a methodology to take advantage of available fashion and garment datasets by

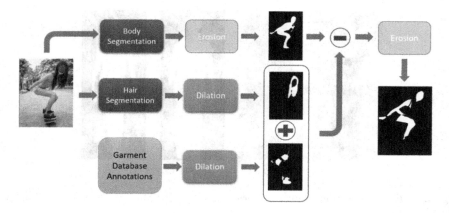

Fig. 2. Pipeline to obtain skin masks from garment masks.

using their provided clothing annotations, for instance, the masks provided by the FashionPedia [13] dataset are shown in Fig. 1. The approach proposed in this work is to obtain the skin areas as the inverse of those masks, as they provide a close result for skin segmentation. However, hair areas also need to be removed from the human body area. This approach is shown in Fig. 2.

There are several accurate methods for human body segmentation. Some of them have been tested in this work, namely DensePose [8], Mask R-CNN [11] and MediaPipe framework [18]. DensePose empirically works better than the other ones in abnormal or twisted body poses or camera rotations, since DensePose is specifically developed for human body segmentation and it is the one used in this paper. Mask R-CNN is a general segmentation method for predicting multiple object classes simultaneously. Furthermore, as shown in Fig. 3, extra margins add unwanted background that cannot get modified or erased easily from the output. In contrast, DensePose boundaries are much more precise. MediaPipe, even though it has a dedicated body segmentation model and performs acceptable in normal situation, its performance drops drastically with complex backgrounds or unusual body poses.

Although DensePose usually excludes most parts of the hair area from the body mask, a method is required to remove all remaining hair areas, for instance, hair covering torso areas. For this purpose, a PSPNet model [34] is trained on the Figaro dataset [30], a hair segmentation dataset with 1,000 images and manual precise ground truth. Using a pyramid pooling module, PSPNet can take object relationships into account, which leads to increase in accuracy for irregular hair styles and colors.

The three obtained masks (body area, clothing, and hair) are processed using mathematical morphology operators in order to remove noise and improve the results. An study to select these operators is presented in Sect. 4.2.

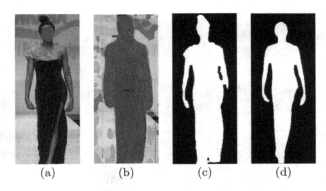

(a)   (b)   (c)   (d)

Fig. 3. Body segmentation results. (a) Original image, (b) Mask R-CNN, (c) MediaPipe and (d) DensePose.

4 Case Example: The visuAAL Skin Segmentation Dataset

In order to show the effectiveness of our methodology regarding the creation of datasets for skin segmentation, it is tested on a garment dataset. Next, fashion and garment datasets suitable for our work are explained. Then, a study is carried out on the quality of the results by defining proper evaluation metrics. Furthermore, error sources and ways to address them are discussed.

4.1 Fashion and Garment Datasets

There are several available fashion datasets with cloth labels, bounding box, pose and attributes from which few provide segmentation masks for each cloth parts too. A complete list of datasets is shown in [13]. Only FashionPedia [13], Deep-Fashion2 [7], Runway2Realway [32], and Modanet [35] have main garment and accessories segmentation at the pixel level. FashionPedia is the newest, consisting of 48,825 of everyday and celebrity event high quality images from different genders and skin colors, with exhaustive cloth segmentation and fine-grained attributes. It has the largest set of labeled cloth categories, and then fewer unlabeled cloth parts which could be mistakenly assigned as skin. To form the complete garment mask, all garment masks for a given image can be extracted and accumulated together. Therefore, We choose to validate our methodology using the FashionPedia dataset.

4.2 Dataset Quality Assessment

Putting aside the garment ground truth masks provided in FashionPedia, which can be assumed reliable, body segmentation and hair segmentation could impact the accuracy of the obtained skin masks. In order to measure the quality and

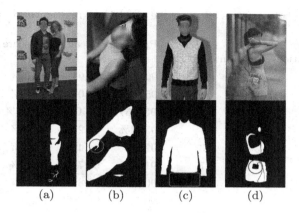

(a)   (b)   (c)   (d)

Fig. 4. Different error sources of the dataset. (a) Wrong detected body, (b) noisy body boundaries, (c) missed annotation in FashionPedia, (d) object covering body mask.

performance of the proposed methodology, 100 images were randomly selected and manually segmented using the CVAT open source image annotation tool [28].

The evaluation is carried out by comparing these manual ground truths with the masks generated by our algorithm. In semantic segmentation and skin detection, evaluation metrics quantify the difference between ground truth and output segmentation and the performance is usually evaluated using statistical measures including: Precision (P), Recall (R), F1-score (F1), Correct Detection Rate (CDR), a.k.a Accuracy, Intersection over Union (IoU), a.k.a Jaccard Index, and Dice Similarity Coefficient (DSC).

Given that in most images, the background is larger than the area covered by the person, causing class imbalance between skin and non-skin pixels, TN and CDR are not suitable metrics for skin segmentation evaluation. On the other hand, Precision and Recall and their integration (F1-score) are designed to deal with skewed datasets. IoU and DSC (which are highly correlated) have been proven to be more useful for segmenting small objects in an image and could be proper choices [6].

Figure 4 shows common error sources when generating the skin masks. First, DensePose might detect wrong body areas when several persons are in the image (since FashionPedia only provides garment mask for the main person in it). To address this issue, we compare the body area obtained with DensePose and the garment mask obtained from FashionPedia. If both overlap, the body and the garment masks belong to the same person. Otherwise the image is removed from the dataset.

The second issue is related to the accuracy of the body and hair segmentation. Though DensePose is much more accurate comparing to other methods, there are still cases in which body masks include some background pixels around body boundaries. This issue can also happen in hair removal as the segmentation model may fail to detect all the hair pixels. To address and reduce these errors, image processing operations and morphology filters are exploited. A study has

Table 2. Morphology filters effect on the visuAAL Skin Segmentation Dataset.

Body erosion	Garment dilation	Hair dilation	Skin erosion	Precision	Recall	F1-score	CDR
7	7	7	7	96.05%	85.94%	90.71%	98.58%
7	5	5	5	95.72%	88.07%	91.74%	98.72%
5	**1**	**3**	**1**	**93.45%**	**93.05%**	**93.25%**	**98.92%**
5	1	1	7	93.11%	93.27%	93.19%	98.90%
3	1	3	3	92.28%	94.49%	93.37%	98.92%
3	1	1	7	91.94%	94.72%	93.31%	98.91%
1	1	1	1	90.44%	95.8%	93.04%	98.85%
0	1	3	0	90.78%	95.56%	93.11%	98.86%

been done over 100 manually segmented images using grid search, to find appropriate filter sizes (between 0 and 9). The best results are presented in Table 2. We have employed the one in bold, as it gets good results in terms of F1-score and CDR, and precision and recall are balanced. For the body mask obtained with DensePose, erosion filters showed the best effect on the extra unwanted margins. For garment and hair masks, dilation filters are used to fill the small holes and cover errors in the boundaries between skin and cloth parts. Though these filtering may cause losing some amount of the actual skin pixels, they exclude the non-skin parts from skin masks which is much more important for the purpose of this dataset.

The third issue is due to wrong mask labels provided in the FashionPedia dataset. Although it includes very accurate garment annotations, there are images in which one part of clothing, for instance pants, are skipped or missed. In these cases, since there are no correct garment labels to get subtracted from body mask, those body parts would be assigned to skin class in the output. Although these cases are rare, they cannot be detected in an automatic labeling.

The last case are small clothing parts which classes are not included in the FashionPedia dataset such as necklaces and wristbands, and external objects which may exist in the body boundaries such as cups or phones. Since these parts are blocking the garment, they are not included in the garment annotations. Then, the pixels belonging to them will be added to the skin masks. These cases are also rare and the objects are mostly small. Therefore, they are ignored in this work, considering them as some amount of noise of our dataset.

4.3 The visuAAL Skin Segmentation Dataset

Applying the proposed methodology to the FashionPedia dataset, allows the creation of a new large-scale skin segmentation dataset, named the visuAAL Skin Segmentation Dataset. It contains 46,775 high quality images divided into a training set with 45,623 images, and a validation set with 1,152 images, from which 100 images have been annotated manually. The dataset is diverse, covering different

Fig. 5. Samples from the visuAAL Skin segmentation dataset.

Table 3. Traditional skin detection methods evaluation on the visuAAL Skin Segmentation Dataset.

Method	Precision	Recall	F1-score	CDR	DSC
Histogram	42.11%	74.14%	53.72%	89.72%	53.71%
Watershed	28.78%	82.90%	42.73%	82.12%	42.72%
Adaptive threshold	38.72%	60.93%	47.35%	89.10%	47.35%

indoor and outdoor backgrounds, skin tones and body poses. From the Fashion-Pedia dataset, non-skin and garment-only images and images containing multiple persons have been removed. Comparing to Table 1, it includes many more images than previous datasets for skin segmentation, and the annotations can be assumed relatively precise. Some samples of the visuAAL Skin Segmentation dataset with the corresponding skin masks are presented in Fig. 5. The dataset is available at https://github.com/visuAAL-ITN/SkinSegmentationDataset.

5 Baseline

Several existing methods for skin detection and semantic segmentation are tested on this new dataset to evaluate their performance. Some well-known traditional skin detection along with more recent deep learning segmentation architectures have been implemented. The experimented traditional methods are inspired by Adaptive Threshold [25], Histogram-based [33] and Watershed [16] methods. The poor performance of these methods showed in Table 3, can implies that they are highly biased on the reported datasets.

There are many works using semantic segmentation based methods as a backbone of their approach. Due to the lack of standard evaluation of these methods, we evaluated the most successful semantic segmentation architectures on our dataset, so that they can be used as a baseline to improve. These architectures include standard FCN [17], SegNet [1], UNet [26], HLNet [5] and DSNet [10]. Table 4 shows the results with these deep models.

Table 4. Semantic segmentation methods evaluation on the visuAAL skin segmentation dataset.

Method	Precision	Recall	F1-score	CDR	DSC
FCN	70.34%	84.88%	76.80%	97.11%	74.40%
SegNet	80.71%	80.12%	80.29%	97.75%	78.82%
UNet	82.66%	85.34%	83.83%	98.01%	82.38%
HLNet	76.50%	79.86%	78.01%	97.43%	76.08%
DSNet	85.80%	85.08%	85.40%	98.35%	84.14%

It is worth mentioning that in the skin segmentation task, Precision means the ratio of actual skin pixels to all predicted skin pixels by the model, and Recall is the percentage of detected skin pixels from all the skin pixels appearing in the image. Therefore, depending on the task, the metric priority can be different.

6   Conclusion

This paper presents a methodology for creating large-scale skin segmentation datasets from garment datasets by exploiting state-of-the-art deep learning and semantic segmentation methods. Unlike previous adapted datasets, which are mostly based on face or hand datasets, this dataset is based on the whole human body. This methodology has been validated by creating a new dataset, the visuAAL Skin Segmentation Dataset, which includes more images and in more diverse conditions than previous datasets. The efficiency of the obtained masks is validated by using a small sample of images manually annotated. In the near future, the dataset will also provide the skin areas related to each specific body part. Adding these annotations to the original garment datasets can make them more diverse and useful for different applications in human related segmentation tasks, and appearance and nudity detection. In future works, we aim at addressing the four issues presented in Sect. 4.2. To create a more precise version of the dataset, computer vision techniques will be used to remove non-skin areas, such as eyes, eye brows and lips. Additionally, object detection and segmentation methods can be exploited in the body boundaries in order to detect wrong or missing labels in the garment dataset. Finally, this methodology has been applied to the FashionPedia dataset. There are other bigger datasets with garment annotations at the pixel level. However, each of them have specific issues that need to be solved before applying the methodology, e.g. masks are not accurate or unlabeled clothes/accessories.

References

1. Badrinarayanan, V., Kendall, A., Cipolla, R.: Segnet: a deep convolutional encoder-decoder architecture for image segmentation. IEEE Trans. Pattern Anal. Mach. Intell. **39**(12), 2481–2495 (2017)

2. Casati, J.P.B., Moraes, D.R., Rodrigues, E.L.L.: SFA: a human skin image database based on feret and AR facial images. In: IX workshop de Visao Computational, Rio de Janeiro (2013)
3. Codella, N.C., et al.: Deep learning ensembles for melanoma recognition in dermoscopy images. IBM J. Res. Dev. **61**(4/5), 5–1 (2017)
4. Cordts, M., et al.: The cityscapes dataset for semantic urban scene understanding. In: Proceedings of the IEEE Conference on Computer Vision and Pattern Recognition, pp. 3213–3223 (2016)
5. Feng, X., Gao, X., Luo, L.: Hlnet: a unified framework for real-time segmentation and facial skin tones evaluation. Symmetry **12**(11), 1812 (2020)
6. Furtado, P.: Testing segmentation popular loss and variations in three multiclass medical imaging problems. J. Imaging **7**(2), 16 (2021)
7. Ge, Y., Zhang, R., Wang, X., Tang, X., Luo, P.: Deepfashion2: a versatile benchmark for detection, pose estimation, segmentation and re-identification of clothing images. In: Proceedings of the IEEE/CVF Conference on Computer Vision and Pattern Recognition, pp. 5337–5345 (2019)
8. Güler, R.A., Neverova, N., Kokkinos, I.: Densepose: dense human pose estimation in the wild. In: Proceedings of the IEEE Conference on Computer Vision and Pattern Recognition, pp. 7297–7306 (2018)
9. Hao, S., Zhou, Y., Guo, Y.: A brief survey on semantic segmentation with deep learning. Neurocomputing **406**, 302–321 (2020)
10. Hasan, M.K., Dahal, L., Samarakoon, P.N., Tushar, F.I., Martí, R.: Dsnet: automatic dermoscopic skin lesion segmentation. Comput. Biol. Med. **120**, 103738 (2020)
11. He, K., Gkioxari, G., Dollár, P., Girshick, R.: Mask r-cnn. In: Proceedings of the IEEE International Conference on Computer Vision, pp. 2961–2969 (2017)
12. Huang, L., Xia, T., Zhang, Y., Lin, S.: Human skin detection in images by MSER analysis. In: 2011 18th IEEE International Conference on Image Processing, pp. 1257–1260. IEEE (2011)
13. Jia, M., et al.: Fashionpedia: ontology, segmentation, and an attribute localization dataset. In: Vedaldi, A., Bischof, H., Brox, T., Frahm, J.-M. (eds.) ECCV 2020. LNCS, vol. 12346, pp. 316–332. Springer, Cham (2020). https://doi.org/10.1007/978-3-030-58452-8_19
14. Jones, M.J., Rehg, J.M.: Statistical color models with application to skin detection. Int. J. Comput. Vision **46**(1), 81–96 (2002)
15. Kawulok, M., Kawulok, J., Nalepa, J., Smolka, B.: Self-adaptive algorithm for segmenting skin regions. EURASIP J. Adv. Signal Process. **2014**(1), 1–22 (2014). https://doi.org/10.1186/1687-6180-2014-170
16. Khaled, S.M., et al.: Combinatorial color space models for skin detection in subcontinental human images. In: Badioze Zaman, H., Robinson, P., Petrou, M., Olivier, P., Schröder, H., Shih, T.K. (eds.) IVIC 2009. LNCS, vol. 5857, pp. 532–542. Springer, Heidelberg (2009). https://doi.org/10.1007/978-3-642-05036-7_50
17. Long, J., Shelhamer, E., Darrell, T.: Fully convolutional networks for semantic segmentation. In: Proceedings of the IEEE Conference on Computer Vision and Pattern Recognition, pp. 3431–3440 (2015)
18. Lugaresi, C., et al.: Mediapipe: a framework for building perception pipelines. arXiv preprint arXiv:1906.08172 (2019)
19. Mahmoodi, M.R., Sayedi, S.M.: A comprehensive survey on human skin detection. Int. J. Image Graph. Signal Process. **8**(5), 1 (2016)
20. Martinez, A., Benavente, R.: The AR face database, CVC. Copyright of Informatica (03505596) (1998)

21. Naji, S., Jalab, H.A., Kareem, S.A.: A survey on skin detection in colored images. Artif. Intell. Rev. **52**(2), 1041–1087 (2018). https://doi.org/10.1007/s10462-018-9664-9

22. Padilla-López, J.R., Chaaraoui, A.A., Gu, F., Flórez-Revuelta, F.: Visual privacy by context: Proposal and evaluation of a level-based visualisation scheme. Sensors **15**(6), 12959–12982 (2015)

23. Phillips, P.J., Moon, H., Rizvi, S.A., Rauss, P.J.: The feret evaluation methodology for face-recognition algorithms. IEEE Trans. Pattern Anal. Mach. Intell. **22**(10), 1090–1104 (2000)

24. Phung, S.L., Bouzerdoum, A., Chai, D.: Skin segmentation using color pixel classification: analysis and comparison. IEEE Trans. Pattern Anal. Mach. Intell. **27**(1), 148–154 (2005)

25. Rahmat, R.F., Chairunnisa, T., Gunawan, D., Sitompul, O.S.: Skin color segmentation using multi-color space threshold. In: 2016 3rd International Conference on Computer and Information Sciences (ICCOINS), pp. 391–396. IEEE (2016)

26. Ronneberger, O., Fischer, P., Brox, T.: U-net: convolutional networks for biomedical image segmentation. In: Navab, N., Hornegger, J., Wells, W.M., Frangi, A.F. (eds.) MICCAI 2015. LNCS, vol. 9351, pp. 234–241. Springer, Cham (2015). https://doi.org/10.1007/978-3-319-24574-4_28

27. Schmugge, S.J., Jayaram, S., Shin, M.C., Tsap, L.V.: Objective evaluation of approaches of skin detection using roc analysis. Comput. Vision Image Underst. **108**(1–2), 41–51 (2007)

28. Sekachev, B., et al.: opencv/cvat: v1.1.0 (2020). https://doi.org/10.5281/zenodo.4009388

29. Shaik, K.B., Ganesan, P., Kalist, V., Sathish, B., Jenitha, J.M.M.: Comparative study of skin color detection and segmentation in HSV and YCBCR color space. Procedia Comput. Sci. **57**, 41–48 (2015)

30. Svanera, M., Muhammad, U.R., Leonardi, R., Benini, S.: Figaro, hair detection and segmentation in the wild. In: 2016 IEEE International Conference on Image Processing (ICIP), pp. 933–937. IEEE (2016)

31. Tan, W.R., Chan, C.S., Yogarajah, P., Condell, J.: A fusion approach for efficient human skin detection. IEEE Trans. Ind. Inf. **8**(1), 138–147 (2011)

32. Vittayakorn, S., Yamaguchi, K., Berg, A.C., Berg, T.L.: Runway to realway: visual analysis of fashion. In: 2015 IEEE Winter Conference on Applications of Computer Vision, pp. 951–958. IEEE (2015)

33. Zarit, B.D., Super, B.J., Quek, F.K.: Comparison of five color models in skin pixel classification. In: Proceedings International Workshop on Recognition, Analysis, and Tracking of Faces and Gestures in Real-Time Systems. In Conjunction with ICCV 1999 (Cat. No. PR00378), pp. 58–63. IEEE (1999)

34. Zhao, H., Shi, J., Qi, X., Wang, X., Jia, J.: Pyramid scene parsing network. In: Proceedings of the IEEE Conference on Computer Vision and Pattern Recognition, pp. 2881–2890 (2017)

35. Zheng, S., Yang, F., Kiapour, M.H., Piramuthu, R.: Modanet: a large-scale street fashion dataset with polygon annotations. In: Proceedings of the 26th ACM International Conference on Multimedia, pp. 1670–1678 (2018)

36. Zhu, Q., Wu, C.T., Cheng, K.T., Wu, Y.L.: An adaptive skin model and its application to objectionable image filtering. In: Proceedings of the 12th annual ACM International Conference on Multimedia, pp. 56–63 (2004)

A Mobile Food Recognition System for Dietary Assessment

Şeymanur Aktı[1]([✉]), Marwa Qaraqe[2], and Hazım Kemal Ekenel[1]

[1] Istanbul Technical University, Istanbul, Turkey
{akti15,ekenel}@itu.edu.tr
[2] Hamad bin Khalifa University, Ar-Rayyan, Qatar
mqaraqe@hbku.edu.qa

Abstract. Food recognition is an important task for a variety of applications, including managing health conditions and assisting visually impaired people. Several food recognition studies have focused on generic types of food or specific cuisines, however, food recognition with respect to Middle Eastern cuisines has remained unexplored. Therefore, in this paper we focus on developing a mobile friendly, Middle Eastern cuisine focused food recognition application for assisted living purposes. In order to enable a low-latency, high-accuracy food classification system, we opted to utilize the Mobilenet-v2 deep learning model. As some of the foods are more popular than the others, the number of samples per class in the used Middle Eastern food dataset is relatively imbalanced. To compensate for this problem, data augmentation methods are applied on the underrepresented classes. Experimental results show that using Mobilenet-v2 architecture for this task is beneficial in terms of both accuracy and the memory usage. With the model achieving 94% accuracy on 23 food classes, the developed mobile application has potential to serve the visually impaired in automatic food recognition via images.

Keywords: Food recognition · Assistive technology · Computer vision

1 Introduction

The World Health Organization (WHO) estimates that at least 2.2 billion people are classified to be near or distance vision impaired [1]. The blind and visually impaired face challenges that are often overlooked to sighted people. Research in assistive technology has gained tremendous attention in the past decades to enable people that are visually impaired or blind to perform tasks comparable to sighted people, such as using a phone or computer (via screen reader). However, there still exists many challenges to visually impaired and blind. Among them is the simple task of identifying objects in their presence, which often requires visually impaired people to invoke other senses, such as touch, smell, and taste, to identify such objects.

© The Author(s), under exclusive license to Springer Nature Switzerland AG 2022
P. L. Mazzeo et al. (Eds.): ICIAP 2022 Workshops, LNCS 13373, pp. 71–81, 2022.
https://doi.org/10.1007/978-3-031-13321-3_7

With the abundance of food in today's society as well as the availability of international food locally, it becomes necessary to develop intelligent technology that can aid in the identification of food. Such systems are known as food recognition systems and can identify the type of food using images. Food recognition can be embedded in mobile systems for a diverse set of applications ranging from food tracking for diet management to an assistive technology application to aid visually impaired users identify foods via an image. Such a system will enable people with visual impairment to independently identify various food in real-time, which becomes particularly important i) if they are traveling to foreign countries and would like to identify various meals they will consume, ii) scan menus with images to identify foods in various food delivery applications or in menus at restaurants, and finally iii) to assist in food tracking for various reasons and objectives.

There has been work done in the literature that focuses on the development of food recognition systems through images. However, the majority of the work conducted on food recognition focuses on western style foods or popular international foods, such as sushi, ramen, etc. Middle Eastern cuisine has always been underrepresented in such food recognition applications, and limited work has investigated within this scope. Among the first to propose a food recognition system catering to foods communally consumed in the Middle East is [27]. In this paper, the authors implement a machine learning approach to develop the food recognition algorithm on a novel dataset collected by the authors. Their model is based on a feature extraction and classification stage and explore the capabilities of both early and late fusion techniques. In the early fusion technique, the authors combine the extracted features using different combination techniques. Ultimately, an accuracy of 80% was achieved on the developed dataset.

In this work, we also focus on Middle Eastern cuisine, and aim at enhancing the results of the food recognition model presented in [27]. The proposed approach led to a 10% absolute increase in the accuracy while also being more computationally efficient compared to the previous work.

2   Related Work

As nutrition is one of the most important factors for human development and health, it has become a subject for computer vision and deep learning fields. Researchers have been interested in food-related problems, such as estimating taste appreciation [36], generating pizza recipes [26], comprehension of cooking recipes [32], recipe generation from food images [28], and food portion estimation [10]. There has also been many systems developed for food image classification utilizing mobile devices [34], wearable sensors [18], and egocentric cameras [15].

There has been some work done for recognition of food images using computer vision methods and hand-crafted features such as SIFT (Scale-invariant Feature Transform) [19] features and color histograms [6], bag-of-words [3,35], pair-wise feature distribution of local features [33], bag-of-features with SIFT, color histogram and Gabor texture feature descriptors [16].

Given the advancement in intelligent algorithms, there has been a shift from the manual extraction of features from images to the automatic learning of such features by deep neural networks. As such, deep learning methods have proven their success on image classification tasks in many domains, including food recognition. In specific, [11] fine-tuned Inception-v3 architecture [31] on food images. The authors in [8] employed a deep residual network [13] for training large food datasets, whereas [25] and [4] used ensembled deep learning models for food recognition. Instead of using the deep convolutional networks for both extracting features and classifying them, [21] used convolutional networks only for feature extraction and used supervised machine learning methods for the classification of the features. A novel network developed specifically for food recognition is proposed in [20] where they exploit the vertical food traits which is common in the available food datasets. Similarly, [22] introduced the NutriNet as a novel deep convolutional network architecture for food recognition from images. Considering that the new food images could be included in the learning instead of using static datasets, [12] proposed an online continual learning method for food recognition. In order to develop more suitable food recognition models for mobile environments, [34] and [14] employed knowledge distillation methods resulting in more compact models without losing the performance. The work in [2] introduced a new data augmentation methodology for food datasets and exploited active learning for food classification to have a deeper insight regarding useful samples in the data. Finally, [24] tackled the multi-label food classification problem using a novel transfer learning framework.

The available datasets which are also used by some of the works above mostly focus on more generic type of foods [17,23] or specific cuisines such as fast-food image dataset [6], Japanese cuisine [16], Chinese cuisine [7], western cuisine [5] and more. Different from these datasets, in our study, we worked on Middle Eastern cuisine and improved the work presented in [27].

3 Method

For the identification of food items via images in real-time, an image classifier, thus, a deep learning model is trained for the classification of 23 classes of food images representing diverse Middle Eastern foods. The employed deep learning model architecture is chosen as a small and portable model providing a low process time for real-time inference. This section discusses the dataset and preprocessing measures taken, as well as the model development for the automatic food recognition task.

3.1 Dataset and Analysis

The dataset used was collected by [27] through crawling images from Google and Instagram that represent real-world Middle Eastern cuisine dishes with 27 classes [27]. Sample images from the dataset are shown in Fig. 1. After examining the dataset, it was found that this dataset has two main challenges, namely, i) low

Fig. 1. Sample images from the Middle Eastern cuisine dataset

inter-class difference between similar dishes and ii) class imbalance. To account for these limitations, two pre-processing steps are applied on the dataset prior to training, as discussed below.

Class Consolidation. Visual similarity between some of the classes in the food dataset was really high, and many of these classes have similar calorie values and ingredients used. Therefore, a subset of these classes are combined and assigned to a single class. The consolidated classes are listed below and examples from the combined classes can be seen in Fig. 2.

- Baklava & Kinafah: Baklava and kinafah are similar kind of dishes which are made of pistachio and syrup with similar calorie content. There exists a high visual similarity between these two classes as the color scales are the same most of the time. Thus, these two classes are combined in order to decrease the number of mispredictions among them.
- Khubz & Pita: These two classes are forms of bread. The bread type consumed widely in Middle Eastern countries is named as pita; however there are small variations of pita bread, such as khubz. As such, these classes were also consolidated.
- Salad: There are different types of salads in Middle Eastern cuisine such as tabouleh and fattoush. These salad types differ according to the way they are

cut and the dressing, but their ingredients are fairly similar and they have similar calorie content and have high visual similarities. Thus, salad, tabouleh and fattoush classes are combined into a single class.

Fig. 2. Samples from the combined classes

Data Augmentation. Another limitation with the dataset at hand was the imbalanced number of samples between classes. The distribution of the number of samples per class is given in Fig. 3. In order to overcome the class imbalance problem, some data augmentation techniques are applied on the underrepresented classes to reach a balanced dataset. Data augmentation is only applied on the classes which have less than 100 samples. The applied augmentation methods include horizontal flip, random crop, Gaussian noise, affine transforms, and contrast change, and are designed to generate images from different angles and in different lighting conditions, simulating real images that can be taken using a mobile phone.

These augmentation steps are applied in sequence to the images where their parameters are selected randomly for each run. Thus, various augmentations are obtained as it can be observed in Fig. 4. The dataset sizes before and after applying the data augmentation methods are presented in Table 1.

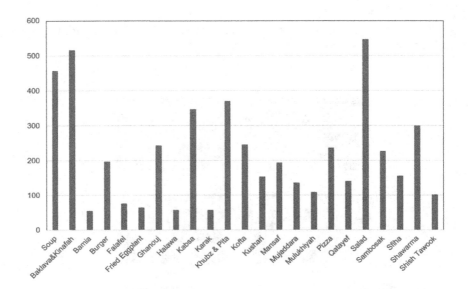

Fig. 3. Number of samples in each class before applying data augmentation.

Fig. 4. Augmented image samples. Original images are at the top and corresponding augmentations are given at the bottom

Table 1. Dataset size before and after data augmentation.

	Train set	Test set	Total
Without augmentation	4368	489	4857
With augmentation	5234	489	5723

3.2 Learning Model

The deep learning architecture for image classification model is chosen as Mobilenet-v2 [29]. This model is found to be suitable for our problem where the main aim is twofold, i) predicting the type of the food from the food images with high accuracy, and ii) the model should be lightweight and allow for low-latency predictions on a smartphone. Mobilenet-v2 is a relatively shallow architecture and is more convenient to adapt into the applications that might be used on mobile devices. Nevertheless, it maintains a promising performance for the image classification task, which makes it a good choice for a high-accuracy, low-latency food recognition solution.

A pre-trained model on ImageNet [9] is fine-tuned on the food recognition dataset. During fine-tuning, the last fully-connected layer of the model is replaced with a new fully-connected layer with the output size of 23, as the total number of classes in the dataset is 23. There are 20 blocks in the Mobilenet-v2 architecture and during training the weights for the first ten blocks are frozen and only the last ten blocks are fine-tuned on the food dataset. The learning rate for the last layer's parameters is 1e-03 and the learning rate for other layers' parameters is set to 1e-04. The cross-entropy loss and Adam optimizer are used with batch size of 128. The model is implemented with PyTorch and trained on Nvidia TitanX.

4 Experiments and Results

4.1 Experimental Setup

For the experimental analysis, the dataset is split into training and test sets. The training set includes 90% of the original samples. The remaining 10% is used in the test set. After augmentation, there were a total of 5234 samples in the training set and 489 samples in the test set, as given in Table 1. For the validation, 10-fold cross-validation is used.

4.2 Results

The classification results of the deep learning models are presented in Table 2 in terms of top-1 and top-5 accuracies. The Mobilenet-v2 model trained on the pre-processed dataset gives a satisfying top-1 accuracy where 94% of the test images are predicted correctly. Additionally, the model achieves a nearly perfect top-5 accuracy, showing that the correct label is found within the high confidence predictions almost all the time.

In order to assess the benefit of using Mobilenet-v2 for this task, we compared its performance with other larger networks such as ResNet-50 [13] and VGG-16 [30]. The results are listed in Table 2. Mobilenet-v2 performs comparable to ResNet-50 and significantly outperforms VGG-16. Moreover, the fine-tuned ResNet-50 model is ten times larger than the Mobilenet-v2 model in terms of the size, which makes the Mobilenet-v2 more efficient considering both the performance and compatibility with mobile devices. As we mentioned before, the food classification module is planned to be employed in the mobile devices, thus using a more compact model is an essential factor for an effective solution.

Table 2. Results of the food image classification models

	Top-1 accuracy	Top-5 accuracy
VGG-16	86.7%	97.5%
ResNet-50	94.0%	99.3%
Mobilenet-v2	**94.0%**	**99.5%**

In order to evaluate the effect of the adopted data pre-processing on the performance, several experiments have been conducted. The results of these experiments are presented in Table 3, where there are three studied scenarios; namely, (1) the Mobilenet-v2 architecture is trained without combining the classes that have high visual similarities, (2) Mobilenet-v2 architecture is trained using only the original data, without any data augmentation, (3) Mobilenet-v2 architecture trained on the pre-processed dataset as proposed in Sect. 3.1. The comparison between scenario (1) and scenario (3) indicates that the low inter-class difference between the food image classes drastically affects the performance as the top-1 accuracy increases by 4% as we combine the classes having high visual similarities. This is expected since most of the mispredicted validation samples in the initial training of the model on the original data were belonging to these classes.

The effect of data augmentation, although not significant, is still seen. Since the data augmentation is applied only the classes that have less than 100 samples in it, the amount of the augmented samples are relatively small and this can explain the limited contribution. Still, applying data augmentation compensates the negative effect of the class imbalance problem to some degree.

Table 3. Results of the experiments before and after the data pre-processing.

	Top-1 accuracy
Mobilenet-v2 (w/o combined classes, w/ augmentation)	90.0%
Mobilenet-v2 (w/ combined classes, w/o augmentation)	93.5%
Mobilenet-v2 (w/ augmentation and combined classes)	94.0%

As a qualitative analysis, some misclassified samples are given in Fig. 5. It can be observed that the mispredictions are mostly reasonable where the misclassified class samples and the ground truth class samples have similar visual patterns, such as kabsa and mansa or kofta and falafel classes. In addition, some of the images may contain overlapping dishes, such as the mansaf with khubz on top of it, thus causing misclassifications.

Fig. 5. Sample mispredictions

5   Conclusion

Food classification from images is seen as an important task for health and dietary assessment applications and assisting visually impaired people. The previous studies on food recognition mostly focus on generic types of food or specific cuisines whereas the application for Middle Eastern food recognition remained unexplored. Thus, in this paper, we have improved upon the study of [27] on Middle Eastern cuisine food recognition task and conducted several experiments on the proposed dataset. Due to the high inter-class similarity between certain classes, we consolidated some classes that have similar characteristics. Also, some data augmentation methods were applied on the underrepresented classes in the dataset to avoid the performance drop caused by class imbalance. During the experimentation, we proved that these two pre-processing steps have improved the performance of the model. We showed that using Mobilenet-v2 architecture for this task is beneficial in terms of both accuracy and the memory usage. The experimental results also show that the Mobilenet-v2 architecture performs as good as, or even better than ResNet-50 and VGG-16 which are more complex architectures. The processed dataset and the experimental results are expected to set a baseline for food recognition on Middle Eastern cuisine task.

References

1. Vision impairment and blindness (2021). https://www.who.int/news-room/fact-sheets/detail/blindness-and-visual-impairment

2. Aguilar, E., Nagarajan, B., Khantun, R., Bolaños, M., Radeva, P.: Uncertainty-aware data augmentation for food recognition. In: International Conference on Pattern Recognition (ICPR) (2021)
3. Anthimopoulos, M.M., Gianola, L., Scarnato, L., Diem, P., Mougiakakou, S.G.: A food recognition system for diabetic patients based on an optimized bag-of-features model. IEEE J. Biomed. Health Inf. **18**(4), 1261–1271 (2014)
4. Arslan, B., Memis, S., Battinisonmez, E., Batur, O.Z.: Fine-grained food classification methods on the UEC Food-100 database. IEEE Trans. Artif. Intell. **3**, 238–243 (2021)
5. Bossard, L., Guillaumin, M., Van Gool, L.: Food-101 – mining discriminative components with random forests. In: Fleet, D., Pajdla, T., Schiele, B., Tuytelaars, T. (eds.) ECCV 2014. LNCS, vol. 8694, pp. 446–461. Springer, Cham (2014). https://doi.org/10.1007/978-3-319-10599-4_29
6. Chen, M., Dhingra, K., Wu, W., Yang, L., Sukthankar, R., Yang, J.: PFID: Pittsburgh fast-food image dataset. In: International Conference on Image Processing (ICIP) (2009)
7. Chen, X., Zhu, Y., Zhou, H., Diao, L., Wang, D.: Chinesefoodnet: a large-scale image dataset for chinese food recognition. arXiv preprint arXiv:1705.02743 (2017)
8. Ciocca, G., Napoletano, P., Schettini, R.: Learning CNN-based features for retrieval of food images. In: International Conference on Image Analysis and Processing (2017)
9. Deng, J., Dong, W., Socher, R., Li, L.J., Li, K., Fei-Fei, L.: Imagenet: a large-scale hierarchical image database. In: Computer Vision and Pattern Recognition (2009)
10. Fang, S., et al.: Single-view food portion estimation: learning image-to-energy mappings using generative adversarial networks. In: International Conference on Image Processing (ICIP) (2018)
11. Hassannejad, H., Matrella, G., Ciampolini, P., De Munari, I., Mordonini, M., Cagnoni, S.: Food image recognition using very deep convolutional networks. In: International Workshop on Multimedia Assisted Dietary Management (2016)
12. He, J., Zhu, F.: Online continual learning for visual food classification. In: Intl. Conference on Computer Vision (ICCV) Workshops (2021)
13. He, K., Zhang, X., Ren, S., Sun, J.: Deep residual learning for image recognition. In: Computer Vision and Pattern Recognition (2016)
14. Heng, Z., Yap, K.H., Kot, A.C.: A compact joint distillation network for visual food recognition. In: International Conference on Acoustics, Speech and Signal Processing (ICASSP) (2021)
15. Jia, W., Li, Y., et al.: Automatic food detection in egocentric images using artificial intelligence technology. Public Health Nutr. **22**(7), 1168–1179 (2019)
16. Joutou, T., Yanai, K.: A food image recognition system with multiple kernel learning. In: International Conference on Image Processing (ICIP) (2009)
17. Kaur, P., Sikka, K., Wang, W., Belongie, S., Divakaran, A.: Foodx-251: a dataset for fine-grained food classification. arXiv preprint arXiv:1907.06167 (2019)
18. Liu, J., et al.: An intelligent food-intake monitoring system using wearable sensors. In: International Conference on Wearable and Implantable Body Sensor Networks (2012)
19. Lowe, D.G.: Distinctive image features from scale-invariant keypoints. Int. J. Comput. Vision **60**(2), 91–110 (2004)
20. Martinel, N., Foresti, G.L., Micheloni, C.: Wide-slice residual networks for food recognition. In: Winter Conference on Applications of Computer Vision (WACV) (2018)

21. McAllister, P., Zheng, H., Bond, R., Moorhead, A.: Combining deep residual neural network features with supervised machine learning algorithms to classify diverse food image datasets. Comput. Biol. Med. **95**, 217–233 (2018)
22. Mezgec, S., Koroušić Seljak, B.: NutriNet: a deep learning food and drink image recognition system for dietary assessment. Nutrients **9**(7), 657 (2017)
23. Min, W., et al.: ISIA food-500: a dataset for large-scale food recognition via stacked global-local attention network. In: ACM International Conference on Multimedia (2020)
24. Nagarajan, B., Aguilar, E., Radeva, P.: S2ML-TL framework for multi-label food recognition. In: International Conference on Pattern Recognition (2021)
25. Pandey, P., Deepthi, A., Mandal, B., Puhan, N.B.: FoodNet: recognizing foods using ensemble of deep networks. IEEE Signal Process. Lett. **24**(12), 1758–1762 (2017)
26. Papadopoulos, D.P., Tamaazousti, Y., Ofli, F., Weber, I., Torralba, A.: How to make a pizza: learning a compositional layer-based GAN model. In: Computer Vision and Pattern Recognition (2019)
27. Qaraqe, M., Usman, M., Ahmad, K., Sohail, A., Boyaci, A.: Automatic food recognition system for middle-eastern cuisines. IET Image Process. **14**(11), 2469–2479 (2020)
28. Salvador, A., Drozdzal, M., Giró-i Nieto, X., Romero, A.: Inverse cooking: recipe generation from food images. In: Computer Vision and Pattern Recognition (2019)
29. Sandler, M., Howard, A., Zhu, M., Zhmoginov, A., Chen, L.C.: Mobilenetv 2: inverted residuals and linear bottlenecks. In: Computer Vision and Pattern Recognition (2018)
30. Simonyan, K., Zisserman, A.: Very deep convolutional networks for large-scale image recognition. arXiv preprint arXiv:1409.1556 (2014)
31. Szegedy, C., Vanhoucke, V., Ioffe, S., Shlens, J., Wojna, Z.: Rethinking the inception architecture for computer vision. In: Computer Vision and Pattern Recognition (2016)
32. Yagcioglu, S., Erdem, A., Erdem, E., Ikizler-Cinbis, N.: RecipeQA: a challenge dataset for multimodal comprehension of cooking recipes. In: Empirical Methods in Natural Language Processing (2018)
33. Yang, S., Chen, M., Pomerleau, D., Sukthankar, R.: Food recognition using statistics of pairwise local features. In: Computer Society Conference on Computer Vision and Pattern Recognition (2010)
34. Zhao, H., Yap, K.H., Kot, A.C., Duan, L.: Jdnet: a joint-learning distilled network for mobile visual food recognition. IEEE J. Sel. Topics Signal Process. **14**(4), 665–675 (2020)
35. Zong, Z., Nguyen, D.T., Ogunbona, P., Li, W.: On the combination of local texture and global structure for food classification. In: International Symposium on Multimedia, pp. 204–211. IEEE (2010)
36. Zülfikar, İ.E., Dibeklioğlu, H., Ekenel, H.K.: A preliminary study on visual estimation of taste appreciation. In: International Conference on Multimedia & Expo Workshops (ICMEW) (2016)

Smart Diet Management Through Food Image and Cooking Recipe Analysis

Yinchao He[1]([✉]), Zeynep Hakguder[2], and Xu Shi[3]

[1] University of California-San Diego, La Jolla, CA 92093, USA
yih039@ucsd.edu
[2] Prorize LLC, Marietta, GA 30062, USA
[3] University of Nebraska-Lincoln, Lincoln, NE 68508, USA

Abstract. Food monitoring has become an indispensable practice for personal health management in increasingly growing populations. To facilitate this process, advanced image processing and AI technology have empowered automated recognition of food items and nutrients using food images taken by smart mobile devices. However, precision is often compromised for convenience, which is also applicable in food logging. In this study, we have explored new solutions that can help improve food recognition accuracy with a particular focus on domestic cooking, by leveraging advanced machine learning and natural language processing techniques, in conjunction with comprehensive food nutrient profiles in the knowledge base, as well as contextual ingredient information parsed from publicly available recipes. The optimized models were proved to be effective and have been integrated into an Android app named "FoodInsight".

Keywords: Image recognition · Recipe analysis · Transfer deep learning · Natural language processing · Recipe recommendation · Food intake monitoring

1 Introduction

High obesity rates and the associated risk of other serious health conditions such as diabetes, metabolic syndrome and cancer can be controlled by effective food monitoring and diet management.

Recent work on food image recognition mainly use deep neural networks for classification [10,15]. From a diet monitoring perspective, two major challenges are present. First, machine learning algorithms are limited by the quality of the datasets they are trained on. The training dataset should contain a large number of images closely related to food. Although there are some big food datasets available such as Food101 [1], UEC-FOOD100 [13], UEC-FOOD256 [11] containing dish images from American or a specific international cuisine, those pure food images are taken in a well-controlled manner, specific to a cuisine and

This research is supported by the NIH funded IDeA-CTR center at University of Nebraska Medical Center.

with items easier to separate. Next, food portion estimation from images is the second major challenge in automating diet monitoring from images. There are several approaches to tackle this problem by using predefined 3D food models [4], or predicted depth maps of eating scenes [14], or energy distribution maps [15]. Note that current solutions either estimate the content of the dish image as a whole or work with simplified geometrical models that need to be expanded to be of practical use in diet monitoring.

2 Objectives

To address aforementioned challenges, we aimed to explore in this study new computational solutions that can help improve food recognition accuracy in domestic cooking by leveraging advanced machine learning techniques, comprehensive nutrient profiles of food items in the knowledge base, and contextual, qualitative and quantitative information of ingredients parsed from known recipes.

Particularly, the core part of our approach is image classification, which represents a fundamental problem in computer vision. Given a high dimensional image, the aim of image classification is to assign the most likely label. The features that are used to predict the image class can either be engineered as it is done in traditional computer vision approaches or these can be learned by an algorithm as is the case in Convolutional neural networks (CNNs). In this study, we want to assign labels to food images via a reliable classification model.

Our second aim is to collectively classify multiple food images together given the cases that raw ingredients to prepare a meal appear in the same image. This is a structured prediction problem where there are dependencies within the labels. In our study, the classification of images of ingredients will be reevaluate based on the probability if those ingredients are present in the same recipe together. The aim is to take advantage of ingredients that the model has confidence in predicting and from co-occurrence information of ingredients in known recipes to ameliorate predictions for which the classifier is not highly confident. Hence, we want to find the set of labels that maximizes the conditional probability using an approach based on conditional random field (CRF) and techniques in natural language processing (NLP).

3 Related Work

Convolutional neural networks (CNNs) were used in classification of Food-101, UEC-FOOD100 and UEC-FOOD256 datasets [2,6,19,23,24]. These models were all trained and evaluated on images that are not in mobile setting. Images taken from mobile devices are harder to classify with models trained on these existing images. However, classification performance can be improved using contextual information such as user preference from past data.

Another source of contextual information is food item co-occurrence. These ideas are implemented in "Context based food image analysis" [8], where the co-occurrence information is modeled by a fully connected undirected graph.

Their dataset consists of images collected in natural eating conditions and has 56 categories and achieved 44% accuracy. Their food item co-occurrence model is updated as new images are taken by the user. Myers et al. predict both the food items in a given meal and their nutritional content in and out of the restaurant setting [14]. Their image model is a multi-label CNN classifier. In the restaurant setting, predicted food items are used to look up restaurant menus to retrieve the nutrition content. Out of the restaurants, estimating the nutrient content is hard due to hardness of volume estimation. Authors crowd sourced manual segmentation of images and compiled a segmented dataset of 201 food items to be used for volume estimation in conjunction with depth values calculated by another CNN.

Their segmentation system wasn't successful on real food data but they were able to get close to actual depth values with their depth prediction architecture. In addition to the classification based systems listed so far, object detection architectures have also been used for diet monitoring. Sun et al. use the YOLO [17] architecture to detect what food items are in the image and their position. Then, they look up a nutrition database to obtain and serve the per serving nutrient content in their mobile application [20]. Their dataset is restricted to mostly Japanese dishes.

4   Methodology

Image classification was done in two stages. This allowed supplementing the information in images of ingredients with information obtained from recipes. First, a deep learning model was used to obtain probabilities for each of the different food classes. Then, these probabilities were combined with co-occurrence probabilities of ingredients in recipes in a conditional random field.

Once the ingredients in the recipe are identified, either from pictures of raw ingredients or of whole prepared plates, a database of recipes can be searched to find most similar recipes which can be used to recommend ingredients.

4.1   Ingredient Image Classification Model

Ingredient Image Dataset. In order to train a ingredient recognition mode, we first collected images of ingredients that are commonly used in domestic cooking, which resulted a dataset containing 86,265 images on 130 classes of ingredients including vegetables, fruits, meat, cheese, egg, and etc. Each class has at least 240 and on average 663 images. The correlated images are collected from Google Images using ImageAssistant Batch Image Downloader that is a free image extractor developed by Mr.Pullywood. Each image in the dataset is at least 100×100 pixels. This dataset was divided into 80% *training*, 10% *testing* and 10% *validation* sets.

Ingredient Classification Model via Transfer Learning. Next, we transfer learned a classifier from InceptionV3 CNN architecture [21]. We started training the neural network with weights set to ImageNet [3] weights. We replaced the last classification layer of InceptionV3 with 130 nodes each corresponding to one of the ingredient classes.

We used a learning rate of $\alpha = 0.01$ with RMSProp optimization algorithm and set the number of training epochs to 1000. We used early stopping as regularization with a tolerance parameter set to $t = 10$. Tolerance parameter determines how many epochs the network continues training without any improvement on validation accuracy.

InceptionV3 is a convolutional neural network architecture with high classification performance and its training is less costly compared to other high performance convolutional neural networks. This architecture incurs less computational cost without a sacrifice on the classification accuracy by factorizing convolutions. They used a series of 3×3 convolutional filters instead of larger filter sizes and asymmetrically factorized of $n \times n$ filters into $1 \times n$ and $n \times 1$ filters.

Further, we have explored four other deep learning architectures on our dataset: ResNet50 [7], EfficientNet [22], DenseNet [9], and VGG16 [18] as a comparison.

4.2 Recipe Processing Using NLP

Recipe Dataset. Over 100 GB of recipe data is crawled using Python3 and Beautiful Soup from Allrecipes.com, which includes a total of 10,421 recipes of appetizers, desserts, main dishes, and soups from 21 types of cuisine from American, Argentinian, Australian and NewZealand, Brazilian, Canadian, Chilean, Chineses, Colombian, French, German, Greek, Indian, Israeli, Italian, Korean, Mexican, Peruvian, Spanish, Swiss, Thai, and UK. For each recipe, it consists of five components including recipe ID, recipe name, ingredients, serving information, and nutrients.

Ingredient Name Recognition via CRF. The first NLP task is to identify parts of a recipe ingredient item, where an item is composed of quantity, unit, ingredient name, and comments. An example ingredient item looks like below with the words bolded to differentiate from entity categories.

We first used a linear chain conditional random field to address the task of assigning a label from { "quantity", "unit", "name", "comment"}. We used 17 unigram templates and 1 bigram template to generate features on our data following [5]. The feature functions are defined using properties of the input. We used five properties, which are capitalization (C), if the input word is parenthesized or not (P), cap (CAP) on the limit of the ingredient list item (one of $\{4, 8, 12, 16, 20, 20+\}$), position (POS) of the word on the ingredient list item, and the word (W) itself.

We give an example input ingredient item from our dataset with its associated properties and BIO tag in Table 1. In our application, we want to find spans of text that are of interest and label those spans. BIO tagging [16] is a standard approach that transforms the span labeling problem to a word labeling problem.

Its labels capture both the position information of the word in an entity and the type of the entity.

Table 1. An example input with properties

Input	POS	CAP	C	P	BIO tag
1	1	8	0	0	B-QTY
Cup	2	8	1	0	B-UNIT
Mozzarella	3	8	1	0	B-NAME
,	4	8	0	0	OTHER
shredded	5	8	0	0	B-COMMENT

We trained our CRF model on New York Times cooking dataset released in 2015[1] using 20,000 ingredient items and tested on 2,000 ingredient items.

Ingredient Name Clustering. Next, We used string matching to group similar ingredients together after performing named entity recognition on our recipes collected from "AllRecipes.com". We started by removing plurality suffixes. Then, we divided the multi word ingredient names into their word constituents. We assumed the first and last words in an ingredient name would be most informative about the ingredient such as in "vine tomato" or "fig jam". We started our groups with single word ingredient names in our dataset and considered each single word ingredient name as the keyword of a group of ingredients. For ingredients with multiple names, if any word in the ingredient name agreed with the keyword of a cluster we placed the ingredient under that cluster. While doing that we prioritized the first and the last word in the ingredient name following our assumption.

4.3   Additional Validation

As an independent validation, we downloaded the Food.com dataset which contains both images and recipes (raw and processed) [12]. In total, the dataset contains more than 180,000 recipes and 13,627 ingredients. We removed rare ingredients which were listed in fewer than 100 recipes. We also removed entries that are not ingredients, e.g. tomato soup, aluminum foil. The resulting set had 10 distinct ingredients. Further, we mapped each ingredient to a super-ingredient, e.g. shredded beef was mapped to beef. These images from this dataset will be subject to the food recognition system and the identified recipe will be compared to the prediction results to examine if the prediction is desired at the recipe level or nutrient level.

---

[1] Available at https://github.com/nytimes/ingredient-phrase-tagger/blob/master/nyt-ingredients-snapshot-2015.csv.

5   Results

InceptionV3 Outperforms Other Architectures for Food Classification. We stopped training of InceptionV3 model when it stopped improving after achieving 85.84% validation accuracy with % testing accuracy. Several classes were classified with perfect score of 100%; e.g. ginger, lobster, crawfish, spaghetti squash; Monterey-Jack cheese was the class with lowest accuracy of 25%. We further investigated the breakdown of misclassified classes. The lowest performed class Monterey-Jack was classified solely as dairy products: butter, gouda, Swiss, pepper Jack and Colby Jack. Second worst class is chuck roast beef classified as other cuts of steak: T-bone, ribeye, tenderloin, eye of round steak and as pork loin chop.

While misclassifications listed above do not cause big problems for nutrient estimation, there are other classes that are mixed based on their similar visual characteristics, however nutritionally they are different. 13% of the parsley was classified as endive and 13% as kale. There are other cases for this type of misclassification in the validation dataset such as bananas classified as yellow squash, apple as shallot, white onion as melon, cucumber as zucchini. There is room for improvement in cases like these.

To compare with other deep learning architectures, we make sure all networks were transfer learned from weights learned on ImageNet dataset.

In Fig. 1, we show training loss plots which is negative log-likelihood, also corresponding to categorical cross-entropy in multi-class classification, given by

$$J(\theta) = -\frac{1}{m} \sum_i^m \sum_j^n \mathbb{I}_{y_i=j} \log p(y_i = j \mid \mathbf{x}; \theta) \tag{1}$$

where θ are network weights, $n = 130$ is the number of classes. m is the training set size for training loss and validation set size for validation loss in Eq. 1. In practice, this loss is calculated as average over batches. InceptionV3 and VGG16 weights adapted well to our dataset, while EfficientNet, ResNet50 and DenseNet losses didn't improve. In our experiments, the feature extraction phase was successful. During the fine-tuning phase, we didn't observe any improvement in loss.

Figure 2 shows validation accuracies over epochs. All network architectures except EfficientNet improve over time. However, DenseNet, ResNet50, and VGG16 plateau at significantly worse accuracies than InceptionV3. Hence, as our final model we use InceptionV3 architecture with weights frozen at the highest accuracy value.

We show a comparison of true and predicted classes in Fig. 3. Rows show true, columns show predicted classes. The counts row-wise normalised. As can be seen from the diagonal, model produces high class conditional accuracies.

Co-occurrence Information from Recipe Improves Ingredient Recognition. Ingredient information from recipes can be used to strengthen the predictions of the Inception model in cases where the ingredients can be visually confused but their use cases are different.

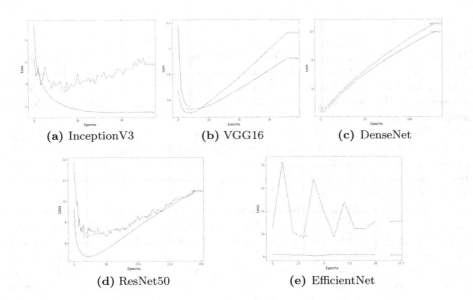

Fig. 1. Losses for different network architectures. Training loss is plotted in blue, validation loss is in orange. The lowest value of validation loss is marked on the plot. (Color figure online)

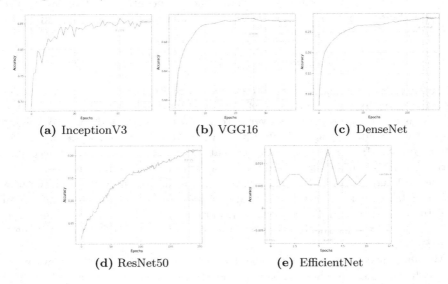

Fig. 2. Validation accuracies for different network architectures. The highest value of validation accuracy is marked on the plot.

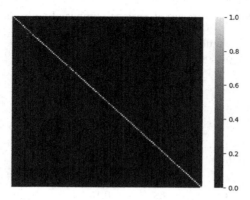

Fig. 3. Confusion matrix for InceptionV3. Rows are true, columns are predicted classes.

Recipe Parsing via CRF. We trained our linear chain CRF with the feature functions explained in Methods section to parse the ingredient entries into "ingredient name", "unit", "quantity" and "comment". We evaluated 2,000 ingredient items on a item and word level. Out of 2,000 items, our model predicted all of the words in 1,492 items correctly. These 2,000 items contain 11,450 words. Out of these 11,450, our model predicted 10,402 correctly. Our item level accuracy is 74.64% and word level accuracy is 90.85%.

We tested how the model would be affected when we incorporated ingredient co-occurrence information from recipes. Using the parser outputs for ingredient names, we calculated the co-occurrence frequencies of ingredient pairs and used these in our CRF model. We calculated the accuracy of the overall model by using n nodes, $n \in \{2, 3, \ldots, 9\}$. Our model performance declined as we increased the number of nodes in the model as shown in Table 2. Reported values are on 1,000 collages each containing n images sampled according to the co-occurrence frequencies. For each collage, we calculate the performance of the model on the collage and use these to calculate mean accuracy and standard deviation. We suspect the declining performance of our model is due to the way we process our recipes to group ingredients with same name but different representations together.

This grouping is done by a clustering process by string matching. We evaluated a few of the resulting ingredient name clusters qualitatively. This process reduced the 7,900 unique ingredient names in our dataset to 798 ingredient name clusters. We show a few representative clusters below:

– Banana: banana, banana ketchup, banana leaves, banana liqueur, banana pepper, banana pepper rings, banana peppers, banana quick bread muffin mix such the pillsbury brand, banana squash, banana blossoms, fluid banana liqueur, deveined yellow banana peppers, sweet banana peppers, bananas, ripe bananas, very ripe bananas, firm bananas

Table 2. Model accuracies at various number of nodes in the CRF

Number of nodes	Accuracy mean	Accuracy standard deviation
2	0.79	0.29
3	0.74	0.23
4	0.76	0.20
5	0.75	0.18
6	0.71	0.17
7	0.70	0.17
8	0.68	0.15
9	0.66	0.14

– Zucchini: baby zucchini, zucchini, zucchini long, extra zucchini, flowers pumpkin zucchini blossoms, flowers zucchini blossoms, spiralized zucchini, zucchini blossoms, zucchini matchsticks, zucchini squash, zucchinis
– Broccoli: California vegetables broccoli, broccoli florets, broccoli, broccoli carrots, broccoli crown, broccoli florets, broccoli flowerets, broccoli rabe, broccoli slaw, broccoli stalks, Chinese broccoli, dry rice chicken sauce mix broccoli, gailan broccoli, head romanesco broccoli, stalks gai lan broccoli, frozen broccoli

We can see that the clustering is successful overall, however some clusters may contain ingredient names that don't belong in the clusters as well, e.g. "sweet banana peppers" in "banana" cluster, "dry rice chicken sauce mix broccoli" in "broccoli" cluster.

Finding Similar Recipes Based on Food Images. First, we evaluated our similarity metrics defined using the weight of the cluster and rareness metric. We show top two similar recipe ingredients to a given random query ingredient set chosen from the recipes in our dataset for weight only ranking and weight and rareness based ranking in Table 3.

Results of the independent test should be included here. The known recipe and predicted ones can be evaluated by another coherence score calculation.

Table 3. Top 2 recipes with ingredients most similar to a given ingredient query set

Query	2 most similar according to weight
pepper, onion, oil, chicken, salt, soy sauce, clove	– chicken leg quarters, olive oil, black pepper, oregano, basil, garlic powder, salt
	– chicken wings, water, coriander, vegetable oil, cumin, black pepper, hot chile powder, salt
	– olive oil, oregano, garlic, lemon zest, lemon, black pepper, sea salt
	– chicken broth, chicken thighs, olive oil, lemon juice, oregano, garlic, black pepper, rosemary, cayenne pepper, salt
	– chicken tenderloins, green bell pepper, red bell pepper, onion, vegetable oil, paprika, chili powder, basil, garlic powder
pepper, chicken, carrot, onion, salt, rice, oil	– chicken broth, chicken breasts, rice, olive oil, oregano, garlic, black pepper, onion, salt
	– chicken broth, arborio rice, olive oil, white wine, garlic, onion flakes, black pepper, salt, parmesan cheese
	– chicken soup, chicken broth, chicken breasts, tomato sauce, canola oil, cumin, white pepper, chili powder, cayenne pepper, garlic powder, onion powder, salt
	– chicken broth, chicken thighs, onion, vegetable oil, white sugar, black pepper, salt

6 Conclusion

In this study, we have developed optimized models to recognize food images based on Inception V3 and conditional random field. In order to determine an optimal model for food image recognition, we compared Inception V3, VGC16, DenseNet, ResNet50, and EfficientNet through training loss, validation loss, and validation accuracy. Eventually, Inception V3 is seen as the best model because its weights adapted well to the dataset and it had the highest accuracy with 85.84% validation accuracy and 87.63% testing accuracy.

We also created a set of labels that maximizes the conditional probability using conditional random field and natural language processing, which ameliorated image prediction results through co-occurrence ingredients information in known recipes. The word level accuracy of recipe parsing via CRF with 90.85% is higher than the item level accuracy with 74.64%.

It is an ongoing effort to build a predictive model to estimate the weights of ingredients from the image. If food volume could be estimated through images, it will help achieve more accurate nutrient estimation. Then, food intake monitoring will be more meaningful and precise.

Acknowledgment. The project described is supported by the National Institute of General Medical Sciences, 1U54GM115458, which funds the Great Plains IDeA-CTR Network. The content is solely the responsibility of the authors and does not necessarily represent the official views of the NIH.

References

1. Bossard, L., Guillaumin, M., Van Gool, L.: Food-101 – mining discriminative components with random forests. In: Fleet, D., Pajdla, T., Schiele, B., Tuytelaars, T. (eds.) ECCV 2014. LNCS, vol. 8694, pp. 446–461. Springer, Cham (2014). https://doi.org/10.1007/978-3-319-10599-4_29
2. Ciocca, G., Napoletano, P., Schettini, R.: Food recognition: a new dataset, experiments, and results. IEEE J. Biomed. Health Inform. **21**(3), 588–598 (2016)
3. Deng, J., Dong, W., Socher, R., Li, L.J., Li, K., Fei-Fei, L.: Imagenet: a large-scale hierarchical image database. In: 2009 IEEE Conference on Computer Vision and Pattern Recognition, pp. 248–255. IEEE (2009)
4. Fang, S., Liu, C., Zhu, F., Delp, E.J., Boushey, C.J.: Single-view food portion estimation based on geometric models. In: 2015 IEEE International Symposium on Multimedia (ISM), pp. 385–390. IEEE (2015)
5. Greene, E.: Extracting structured data from recipes using conditional random fields, April 2015. https://open.blogs.nytimes.com/2015/04/09/extracting-structured-data-from-recipes-using-conditional-random-fields/
6. Hassannejad, H., Matrella, G., Ciampolini, P., De Munari, I., Mordonini, M., Cagnoni, S.: Food image recognition using very deep convolutional networks. In: Proceedings of the 2nd International Workshop on Multimedia Assisted Dietary Management, pp. 41–49 (2016)
7. He, K., Zhang, X., Ren, S., Sun, J.: Deep residual learning for image recognition. In: Proceedings of the IEEE Conference on Computer Vision and Pattern Recognition, pp. 770–778 (2016)
8. He, Y., Xu, C., Khanna, N., Boushey, C.J., Delp, E.J.: Context based food image analysis. In: 2013 IEEE International Conference on Image Processing, pp. 2748–2752. IEEE (2013)
9. Huang, G., Liu, Z., Van Der Maaten, L., Weinberger, K.Q.: Densely connected convolutional networks. In: Proceedings of the IEEE Conference on Computer Vision and Pattern Recognition, pp. 4700–4708 (2017)
10. Kagaya, H., Aizawa, K., Ogawa, M.: Food detection and recognition using convolutional neural network. In: Proceedings of the 22nd ACM International Conference on Multimedia, pp. 1085–1088 (2014)
11. Kawano, Y., Yanai, K.: Automatic expansion of a food image dataset leveraging existing categories with domain adaptation. In: Agapito, L., Bronstein, M.M., Rother, C. (eds.) ECCV 2014. LNCS, vol. 8927, pp. 3–17. Springer, Cham (2015). https://doi.org/10.1007/978-3-319-16199-0_1
12. Majumder, B.P., Li, S., Ni, J., McAuley, J.: Generating personalized recipes from historical user preferences. arXiv preprint arXiv:1909.00105 (2019)
13. Matsuda, Y., Hoashi, H., Yanai, K.: Recognition of multiple-food images by detecting candidate regions. In: 2012 IEEE International Conference on Multimedia and Expo, pp. 25–30. IEEE (2012)
14. Meyers, A., et al.: Im2calories: towards an automated mobile vision food diary. In: Proceedings of the IEEE International Conference on Computer Vision, pp. 1233–1241 (2015)

15. Pandey, P., Deepthi, A., Mandal, B., Puhan, N.B.: Foodnet: recognizing foods using ensemble of deep networks. IEEE Signal Process. Lett. **24**(12), 1758–1762 (2017)
16. Ramshaw, L., Marcus, M.: Text chunking using transformation-based learning (1999)
17. Redmon, J., Divvala, S., Girshick, R., Farhadi, A.: You only look once: unified, real-time object detection. In: Proceedings of the IEEE Conference on Computer Vision and Pattern Recognition, pp. 779–788 (2016)
18. Simonyan, K., Zisserman, A.: Very deep convolutional networks for large-scale image recognition. arXiv preprint arXiv:1409.1556 (2014)
19. Singla, A., Yuan, L., Ebrahimi, T.: Food/non-food image classification and food categorization using pre-trained googlenet model. In: Proceedings of the 2nd International Workshop on Multimedia Assisted Dietary Management, pp. 3–11 (2016)
20. Sun, J., Radecka, K., Zilic, Z.: Foodtracker: a real-time food detection mobile application by deep convolutional neural networks. arXiv preprint arXiv:1909.05994 (2019)
21. Szegedy, C., Vanhoucke, V., Ioffe, S., Shlens, J., Wojna, Z.: Rethinking the inception architecture for computer vision. In: Proceedings of the IEEE Conference on Computer Vision and Pattern Recognition, pp. 2818–2826 (2016)
22. Tan, M., Le, Q.: Efficientnet: rethinking model scaling for convolutional neural networks. In: International Conference on Machine Learning, pp. 6105–6114. PMLR (2019)
23. Tanno, R., Okamoto, K., Yanai, K.: Deepfoodcam: A dcnn-based real-time mobile food recognition system. In: Proceedings of the 2nd International Workshop on Multimedia Assisted Dietary Management, pp. 89–89 (2016)
24. Yanai, K., Kawano, Y.: Food image recognition using deep convolutional network with pre-training and fine-tuning. In: 2015 IEEE International Conference on Multimedia & Expo Workshops (ICMEW), pp. 1–6. IEEE (2015)

An Approach for Improving the Older people's Perception of Video-Based Applications in AAL Systems – Initial Study

Ivo Iliev[1]([✉]) and Galidiya Petrova[2]

[1] Department of Electronics, Faculty of Electronic Engineering and Technologies, Technical University of Sofia, 8 Kliment Ohridski Blvd., 1000 Sofia, Bulgaria
izi@tu-sofia.bg
[2] Department of Electronics, Faculty of Electronics and Automation, Technical University of Sofia – Plovdiv Branch, Sofia, Bulgaria

Abstract. It is an indisputable fact that the inclusion of video surveillance tools in the Active and Assistive Living (AAL) system contributes to a significant increase in reliability, especially in the detection of critical life-threatening conditions. Therefore, the efforts of researchers are focused on the development and implementation of innovative technological solutions and algorithms for image processing, which allow to overcome a number of privacy issues. Despite these efforts, the widespread use of video-based applications in AAL systems is still limited due to the older people's fears of being watched.

This study presents a new approach, consisting in the change of the synergy between the two main elements of AAL systems - the person in need of care and the video-based technological solution that detects/confirms the need for help. The essence of this approach is to provide a choice to the assisted person to activate/deactivate the video surveillance system depending on the personal assessment of his/her condition. This does not exclude the possibility that in the absence of a deactivation command, in a certain period after the announcement of the forthcoming activation, video monitoring to be turned on autonomously.

Initial studies were conducted with five people (75–84 years old) residents of an elderly hostel. When only accelerometer sensors were used to detect falls, the number of false alarms was quite high. After installing video cameras in the rooms of three of the participants, the number of confirmed alarms based on video analysis decreased to almost zero. For one of these three people, who had several incidents of falling out of bed in the previous period, 3 falls were registered with a camera in 24 days and were alerted on time.

Keywords: AAL · Assistance of elderly · Fall detection · Perception of video monitoring

1 Introduction

Over the last two decades, the interest of researchers and businesses has focused on the development of a variety of assistive devices and systems, and technologies for smart

P. L. Mazzeo et al. (Eds.): ICIAP 2022 Workshops, LNCS 13373, pp. 94–101, 2022.
https://doi.org/10.1007/978-3-031-13321-3_9

homes that will allow people to live independently until old age. The three generations of technology designed for supporting the independent living of adults are described in [1]. Specific features of the first generation include wearable devices for responding to an emergency situation that requires the user to initiate an alarm. Typically, the adult presses the button or pendant to raise the alarm in the event of an emergency, such as fall. The obvious benefits relate to the security and safety of the older people which reduce the stress levels for them and their relatives and caregivers. However, a specific weakness of this technology is demonstrated when the user has not capacity either physically or mentally to trigger the alarm or not wearing the device. A typical scenario is night going to the bathroom/toilet where the risk of falling is significant and in this high-risk situation the alarm will not be activated because the older person is not wearing the device. The second generation of AAL technologies overcomes some of the limitations of the first generation, by means of utilization of different sensors in order to detect potential emergency situations and call for assistance without relying to the older adult to trigger the alarm. Despite the obvious potential benefits, some users find these technologies intrusive and annoying, especially in the case of false alarms. The third generation of AAL technologies includes the integration of wearable devices and environmental sensors in the everyday environment not only for monitoring and assistance, but also for prevention. These systems integrate intelligent computer systems and assistive devices into everyday context, trying to be unobtrusive and easier to accept for older people.

A systematic literature review on AAL technologies, products and services regarding the interaction with users and involvement of end-users in the processes of development and evaluation of AAL is presented in [2]. The presented results show the need to improve the integration and interoperability of existing technologies and to promote user-oriented (user-centric) developments with a strong involvement of end-users in terms of usability and accessibility.

A systematic analysis of end-users' expectations from the services in an AAL system for older people monitoring and preventing dangerous situations, thus helping their independent living, is described in [3]. The study examines the usefulness and accessibility of specific services provided that could support independent living and improve the quality of life of older people in four identified categories, which include monitoring of physiological data, daily activities, environmental data and social interaction, in order to indicate a clear level of priority in each category of services from the point of view of end-users. Among the examined 45 parameters, events and situations considered as important to be detected and/or monitored, the highest priority levels were given to detection of fall and fear of falling in person activities monitoring, and monitoring of physiological parameters as heart rate, body temperature, blood glucose levels, blood oxygen levels and vital signs at night. Fear of falling is a major health problem among the elderly, present in older people who have fallen, but also in older people who have never had a fall [4].

Despite the high appreciation of the usefulness of these technologies and services, the older people have some concerns [3]. On the one hand, there are the concerns about privacy and intrusion into their personal space, especially with continuous video surveillance. On the other hand, the use of many different devices and technologies creates a feeling of insecurity in the end-users that they are unfamiliar and not be able to manage with them, and in the same time a fear of not being controlled by these devices. The older people have a feeling of losing control on these situations. In addition, they have concerns about possible additional costs they had to pay. In fact, keeping the costs of the devices and services low is a key requirement for older adults. The only way to make the monitoring devices and systems acceptable for the older people is to maintain reasonable compromise between usefulness and privacy and security issues, thus improving their perception.

In an extensive literature study on fall detection systems in old age [5], it is generally agreed that the use of different sensors that complement each other in different situations provides a more robust approach to falling detection. Thus high accuracy will be achieved while minimizing false alarms. For detection of falls as wearable devices the most popular and used are accelerometers, while for visual detection the Kinect (RGB-D depth cameras) and web cameras are most popular. The low-resolution IR thermal array sensors are a good choice to be used in the areas like dressing rooms, bathrooms and toilets.

Extensive literature studies have recently been published in the framework of COST Action CA19121 on audio and video-based solutions in AAL [6] and related ethical, social and privacy issues [7]. Despite the different application scenarios and diverse goals, the general requirements in the design of AAL solutions are to provide support in everyday life in an unobtrusive, convenient and user-acceptable way.

Trying to propose a solution for real life situations overcoming the above mention concerns of older people we employ a user-centered approach where the assisted person is a final element in the decision-making system for control and activating video surveillance.

In Sect. 2 the devices used and the algorithm for processing the data from the accelerometer to detect a fall are described. The proposed approach to improving the perception of the elderly by changing the role of the assisted person from a passive object of observation to an active subject controlling the video surveillance process and the initial results of our study are presented in Sect. 3. Section 4 continues with a discussion of how this approach can be further developed in specific scenarios. Finally, conclusions are drawn and future work is outlined.

2   Method and Devices for Falls Detection

To test the reliability and assess the personal perception of video-based fall detection solutions, two test systems were developed. In the first one, the detection is performed by analyzing the signals from a 3D accelerometer. In the second, images from a video camera are captured and processed. According to the plan of experimental studies, the results of two scenarios for tracking and detecting falls were considered.

Scenario 1: The assisted person wears the accelerometer sensor continuously and upon detection of a potential fall, the camera is activated, confirming or rejecting the occurrence of such an event.

Scenario 2: For overnight monitoring the video camera is turning on at regular intervals or when accelerometer alerts and the obtained frames are analyzed to detect potential falls.

A system configuration based on a 3D accelerometer built into a wristwatch was used. The smartwatch EZ *eZ430-Chronos* (Texas Instruments) was chosen because of the built-in accelerometer, the availability of a wireless interface for data transmission and especially because of the inclusion an USB emulator that connects the watch to a PC for real-time in-system programming and debugging (Fig. 1).

Fig. 1. Smartwatch EZ *eZ430-Chronos* with accessories for programming and debugging.

The data from the three axes of the accelerometer transmitted via the wireless interface to a laptop were processed in MATLAB with a fall detection algorithm including the following consecutive steps (Fig. 2):

- Summing of the samples on the three axes;
- Calculation of the first derivative of the summed signals to express rapid changes in acceleration;
- Raising to second power of the first derivative to express high-amplitude components;
- Application of threshold criteria to identify a sharp changes in the acceleration corresponding to potential fall.

With the developed system we had conducted preliminary laboratory tests with volunteers [8], both to assess the reliability of detecting falls and the ability to distinguish falls from daily/night activities such as: free movement indoors; movements during sleep, reading, watching TV, cooking. The obtained results had demonstrated a high degree of reliability and specificity.

An 1.0 Mega pixel IP camera HS-691B-M186I H.264 was chosen for the video monitoring. The camera is equipped with 9 Φ5 LED lights (IR distance: 10 m) for night-vision and a number of wired and wireless interfaces that allow connection to network architectures. In our configuration the images were transmitted wirelessly and processed by the same laptop to which the smartwatch with the accelerometer was also connected.

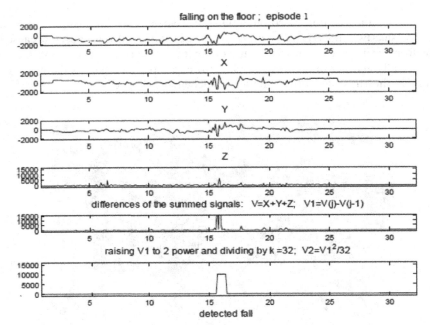

Fig. 2. Visualization of consecutive steps in the fall detection algorithm with an example of correct detection of a fall on the floor.

In order to be able to remotely control the video monitoring, an option has been added in which the camera can be turned on and off by the assisted person, via a smartwatch command or by pressing an additional emergency button.

3 Results

A series of tests were conducted with residents at hostel for adult to assess the reliability and personal perception of the solutions developed to detect falls. The tests complied with all rules for such non-medical study, including: detailed preliminary information and instructions to the participants; written consent for participation; supervision and permanent control by the management and staff of the institution.

Five people (75–84 years old) were involved in the studies. In accordance with Scenario1, they were given smartwatches and after a comprehensive explanation and consent on their part, an initial stage for collecting data from the accelerometer sensors was started. The recapitulation after seven days showed long periods with no connection of the assisted person with the system, as well as quite falsely detected falls. Some of these events were due to the removal of the smartwatch, but there were falsely detected falls for some trivial reasons, such as: hands shaking after washing, movements to repel insects, use of saltern, etc. Similar results were expected and they confirmed the difference between controlled laboratory tests and in-situ application. To a large extent, these problems can be overcome by including additional sensors located at different points on the body, but this would cause a significant discomfort and would not be acceptable by the participants.

To overcome these problems we considered to implement video cameras and verify the events detected by the accelerometers. Despite all detailed and comprehensive explanations about processes of images capturing, processing and storage, data encryption, authorized access, etc., the installation of cameras in the rooms of the participants was perceived completely negative. These terms and their meanings were completely incomprehensible and unacceptable from the participants.

The situation took a serious positive turn when the approach for video monitoring was changed. In case when potentially life-threatening condition (fall) is detected by accelerometer, the system announces, by audio or light timer during the night, that the video camera will be activated after 30 s (this interval is adjustable). If the assisted person is in good condition, not requiring video monitoring, he/she can cancel the camera activation in the specified period, otherwise the camera turns on. Three of adults agreed to install cameras in their rooms, having opportunity to control them remotely. In this way the highest priority in the decision-making process for activation/deactivation of the camera was given to the assisted people.

The experimental testing period of the system was one month. In daily monitoring (Scenario 1) the number of false alarms was reduced to almost zero due to a personal decision on the lack of need for video monitoring (cameras deactivation), despite incorrectly detected falls by the accelerometers.

One of these three people, with limited movement abilities, had several incidents of falling out of bed at night in a previous period. The staff had not helped him until the morning. When the cameras were turned on in half-hour image recording mode (Scenario 2), 3 falls were registered and alarmed for this person within 24 days. Two of the falls were detected only by the camera (Scenario 2). This allowed for timely assistance on the 5-th and 17-th minutes after the events. One of the falls was detected by the accelerometer and confirmed by a camera (Scenario 1).

4   Discussion

A core element in the proposed approach is the change in the synergy between the two main elements of AAL systems – the person in need of help and the technological solution detecting and confirming the need of help. This decision was in result of the hypothesis that if the assisted person was given the opportunity to make the final decision on turning the video cameras on or off, this would lead to easier perception of video surveillance. Three of the participants in this initial study agreed to install cameras in their rooms. The results of a one-month follow-up to detect falls and potentially life-threatening conditions confirmed the undeniable advantage of combining a traditionally used method such as accelerometry with video monitoring. The number of falsely detected events was reduced approximately to zero. During the test period there were three incidents (falls), which were correctly detected and alerted, so that timely assistance was provided to the person who fell into a helpless state.

Personally controlled video monitoring can be introduced for frailty people and people with cardiovascular diseases prone to heart attack, stroke, unstable blood pressure and other potentially life-threatening conditions.

The planned future research is aimed at expanding the possibilities for interactive communication between the assistive system and the assisted person. The inclusion of an audio communication system would allow remote control of cameras by voice commands, as well as automatic recognition of characteristic sounds (moaning, groaning, shouting for help) in cases of potentially life-threatening conditions confirmed by video monitoring. Video surveillance can be combined with other existing solutions for fall detection, such as smart floor coverings, audio systems with multiple microphones, infrared motion sensors.

5 Conclusion

The integration of video cameras is undoubtedly a major factor in increasing the reliability, especially in the recognition of life-threatening conditions by AAL systems. A significant part of the efforts of researchers and engineers are aimed at overcoming the main problem of video-based systems - the privacy. Despite the latest technological solutions, protocols and algorithms for transfer, image processing, standards for storage and access to personal data, potential users remain highly suspicious and almost always refuse video monitoring as an opportunity to receive an adequate care on-time. To overcome these obstacles, future technological implementations should provide an opportunity for easy personal control of the video monitoring process by users when they are able to do so. When users are unable to control the process, video-based systems must be automatically activated to explicitly confirm or denied a potential critical situation.

Acknowledgement. This research has been carried out in the frame of COST Action CA19121 NETWORK ON PRIVACY-AWARE AUDIO- AND VIDEO-BASED APPLICATIONS FOR ACTIVE AND ASSISTED LIVING (GoodBrother). This work was supported by the European Regional Development Fund within the Operational Programme "Science and Education for Smart Growth 2014 - 2020" under the Project CoE "National center of mechatronics and clean technologies" BG05M2OP001–1.001–0008.

References

1. Blackman, S., Matlo, C., Bobrovitskiy, C., Waldoch, A., Fang, M.L., Jackson, P., Mihailidis, A., Nygård, L., Astell, A., Sixsmith, A.: Ambient assisted living technologies for aging well: a scoping review. J. Intelligent Syst. https://doi.org/10.1515/jisys-2014-0136
2. Queirós, A., Silva, A., Alvarelhro, J., Pacheco Rocha, N., Teixeira, A.: Usability, accessibility and ambient-assisted living: A systematic literature review. Universal Access in the Information Society 14 27–66 (2015). https://doi.org/10.1007/s10209-013-0328-x
3. Cesta, A., Cortellessa, G., Fracasso, F.: Andrea orlandini a and marcello turno, user needs and preferences on AAL systems that support older adults and their carers. J. Ambient Intelligence Smart Environ. 10, 49–70 (2018). https://doi.org/10.3233/AIS-170471
4. Scheffer, A.C., Schuurmans, M.J., van Dijk, N., van der Hooft, T., de Rooij, S.E.: Fear of falling: Measurement strategy, prevalence, risk factors and consequences among older persons. Age Ageing 37, 19–24 (2008). https://doi.org/10.1093/ageing/afm169

5. Wang, X., Ellul, J., Azzopardi , G.: Elderly fall detection systems: a literature survey. Frontiers in Robotics and AI (2020). https://doi.org/10.3389/frobt.2020.00071
6. https://goodbrother.eu/wp-content/uploads/2022/03/GoodBrother-State-of-the-Art-of-Audio-and-Video-Based-Solutions-for-AAL.pdf
7. https://goodbrother.eu/wp-content/uploads/2022/03/GoodBrother-State-of-the-art-on-ethical-legal-and-social-issues-linked-to-audio-and-video-based-AAL-solutions.pdf
8. Iliev I., Tabakov S., Dotsinsky I.: Automatic fall detection of elderly living alone at home environment. Global J. Medical Res. 11(4), 48-54 (2011)

Parts Can Worth Like the Whole - PART 2022

Spectral Analysis of Masked Signals in the Context of Image Inpainting

Sylvie Le Hégarat-Mascle and Emanuel Aldea[(✉)]

SATIE Laboratory, Paris-Saclay University, Gif-sur-Yvette, France
{sylvie.le-hegarat,emanuel.aldea}@u-psud.fr

Abstract. This paper proposes a computationally efficient algorithm for evaluating a sum of squared differences in the image domain in the presence of arbitrary mask configurations. Among the many potential applications of this algorithm, we consider for illustration an image inpainting task. The results show that on a diverse sample of hundreds of simulated holes in the tested images, the proposed technique is more effective than the baseline normalized cross-correlation, even when the masks are properly dealt with by the baseline.

Keywords: Spectral analysis · Fourier domain · Image inpainting

1 Introduction

In image processing, a lot of tasks have been performed in the Fourier domain, given the capability of the Discrete Fourier Transform (DFT) to provide a discriminative spectral representation of a uniformly spaced discrete signal. Computationally wise, the DFT has been appealing as well due to the Fast Fourier Transform algorithm which allowed for addressing a wide range of applications in a practical manner. Specifically, image registration is a particularly suited task, since Fourier domain representations allow for recovering the translation offset, as well as for inferring the relative rotation and scale up to some extent [10,15–17]. The classification task may also be addressed with great success, as the spectra of images with rich content featuring real-world environments often contain diverse frequencies that may be exploited for robust discrimination [2,9,21].

One important but often irrelevant drawback of Fourier domain analysis is the requirement for the uniform sampling of the signal domain (in our case, the image domain). Although this does not raise particular concerns for most applications due to the widespread use of standard image sensors which sample uniformly the surrounding environment, in some cases either the support for the signal of interest might not satisfy the above constraint, or it is otherwise detrimental to process the entire domain indiscriminately. The most common situations are when 1) only some categories of objects in a scene should be considered for Fourier analysis and/or some categories of objects should be entirely ignored, 2) some context-specific masks underline the sub-part of interest in the

P. L. Mazzeo et al. (Eds.): ICIAP 2022 Workshops, LNCS 13373, pp. 105–114, 2022.
https://doi.org/10.1007/978-3-031-13321-3_10

field of view of the sensor, and 3) a part of multiple disjoint parts of the object of interest are visible. In all these circumstances, the absent area or the area containing irrelevant data would in fact contribute as well to the spectrum of the signal, and thus bias its representation and directly impact the subsequent analysis.

The community proposed various strategies for accounting for masked areas in a manner consistent with the Fourier transform, however these algorithms usually fail to preserve faithfully the spectrum of the regions of interest [8,13,20]. In contrast, Padfield [14] introduced an algorithm which directly and explicitly integrates the masking into the FFT algorithm steps. A normalized crossed-correlation (NCC) is computed in the Fourier domain, which is thereafter used for solving image registration. We propose to generalize this idea by extending the initial approach and demonstrate that 1) it may be used to compute other similarity criteria related to norms and 2) it may be applied to other tasks beyond registration.

2   Use of the Masked Fourier Transform

To measure the consistency between two areas of two different images, several criteria have been proposed, among them the NCC and the sum of squared differences (SSD). Both are computed on image subparts defined as spatial domains. To be able to compute a map giving the value of the considered consistency measure in one pass (in contrast with using a sliding window), we aim at formulating the consistency measure based on the Fast Fourier Transforms (FFT). Besides, we assume that the considered measure has to be evaluated on a domain which is not necessarily rectangular.

Let us consider f_1 and f_2 as the two considered images, with f_2 being the moving image. Let us denote by D_1 the f_1 2D domain and by $D_2(u,v)$ the f_2 translated/shifted by the 2D vector of coordinates (u,v). Then, $D_{u,v} = D_1 \cap D_2(u,v)$ denote the intersection (or overlap) between the two domains, so that the sums involved in the consistency measures are computed on $D_{u,v}$.

In [14], Padfield expressed the sums $\sum_{(x,y)\in D_{u,v}} 1$, $\sum_{(x,y)\in D_{u,v}} f_1(x,y)$ and $\sum_{(x,y)\in D_{u,v}} f_1(x,y)^2$ (and the corresponding expressions for f_2) after introducing the masks m_1 and m_2 corresponding to the indicator functions of the D_1 and D_2 domains, and their Fourier transforms $M_i = \mathcal{F}(m_i), i \in \{1,2\}$:

$$|D_{u,v}| = \sum_{(x,y)\in D_{u,v}} 1 = \mathcal{F}^{-1}(M_1 \cdot M_2^*)(u,v), \tag{1}$$

$$\overline{f_1} = \frac{1}{|D_{u,v}|} \sum_{(x,y)\in D_{u,v}} f_1(x,y) = \frac{\mathcal{F}^{-1}(F_1 \cdot M_2^*)(u,v)}{\mathcal{F}^{-1}(M_1 \cdot M_2^*)(u,v)}, \tag{2}$$

$$\sum_{(x,y)\in D_{u,v}} f_1(x,y)^2 = \mathcal{F}^{-1}(\mathcal{F}(f_1 \cdot f_1) \cdot M_2^*)(u,v), \tag{3}$$

with $F_i = \mathcal{F}(f_i), i \in \{1, 2\}$, and all the multiplications in these equations being elementwise (Hadamard product), and M_2^* denotes the complex conjuguate of the Fourier transform of M_2 (that is also the Fourier transform of the transposed of m_2).

2.1   Average of Squared Differences with masks

In this work, we derive the formulation of the Average of Squared Differences either centered or not centered, using the Fourier transform, i.e. without resorting to a sliding window. Indeed, conversely to the NCC measure, the SSD has been very popular due to its convenient summation properties, which are valuable for considering multichannel images such as color ones. Note that in the standard case, this measure is not normalized since the support has a set size and the normalization would be useless. In our case however, we will explicitly focus on the normalized (i.e., averaged with respect to the number of valid pixels) version since the masks will modify the support size.

Using the previous notations, we express the sum of the squared differences as follows:

$$SSD(u, v) = \sum_{(x,y) \in D_{u,v}} \left((f_1(x, y) - \overline{f_1}) - (f_2(x - u, y - v) - \overline{f_{2,u,v}}) \right)^2 \quad (4)$$

$$= \sum_{(x,y) \in D_{u,v}} f_1(x, y)^2 + \sum_{(x,y) \in D_{u,v}} f_2(x - u, y - v)^2 \quad (5)$$

$$-2 \sum_{(x,y) \in D_{u,v}} f_1(x, y) f_2(x - u, y - v) - |D_{u,v}| \left(\overline{f_1} - \overline{f_{2,u,v}} \right)^2$$

$$= \left[\mathcal{F}^{-1}(\mathcal{F}(f_1 \cdot f_1) \cdot M_2^*) + \mathcal{F}^{-1}(M_1 \cdot \mathcal{F}(f_2' \cdot f_2')) \right. \quad (6)$$

$$\left. - 2\mathcal{F}^{-1}(F_1 \cdot F_2^*) - \left(\mathcal{F}^{-1}(F_1 \cdot M_2^*) - \mathcal{F}^{-1}(F_2 \cdot M_2^*) \right)^2 \right] (u, v),$$

with f_2' being the f_2 image flipped (central symmetry).

The previous equation stands for the SSD with centered differences. In some cases, it might be advisable to consider the uncentered differences, and this version of the SSD is even simpler to express:

$$SSD(f_1, f_2) = \mathcal{F}^{-1}(\mathcal{F}(f_1 \cdot f_1) \cdot M_2^*) + \mathcal{F}^{-1}(M_1 \cdot \mathcal{F}(f_2' \cdot f_2')) - 2\mathcal{F}^{-1}(F_1 \cdot F_2^*). \quad (7)$$

Note that the computation of the uncentered SSD involves two less inverse Fourier transforms than that of the centered SSD. Then, the map of the average of squared differences (ASD) is provided by dividing pixel per pixel SSD map values (Eqs. (6) or (7)) by $\mathcal{F}^{-1}(M_1 \cdot M_2^*)$ map values:

$$ASD(f_1, f_2) = \frac{SSD(f_1, f_2)}{\mathcal{F}^{-1}(M_1 \cdot M_2^*)}. \quad (8)$$

2.2   Normalized Cross Correlation with Masks

In [14], following this reformulation of the intermediate terms which accounts for the impact of the masks m_1 and m_2 on the Fourier transform, the final evaluation of the NCC becomes:

$$NCC(f_1, f_2) = \frac{\mathcal{F}^{-1}(F_1 \cdot F_2^*) - \frac{\mathcal{F}^{-1}(F_1 \cdot M_2^*) \cdot \mathcal{F}^{-1}(M_1 \cdot F_2^*)}{\mathcal{F}^{-1}(M_1 \cdot M_2^*)}}{\sqrt{\mathcal{F}^{-1}(\mathcal{F}(f_1 \cdot f_1) \cdot M_2^*) - \frac{(\mathcal{F}^{-1}(F_1 \cdot M_2^*))^2}{\mathcal{F}^{-1}(M_1 \cdot M_2^*)}} \sqrt{\mathcal{F}^{-1}(M_1 \cdot \mathcal{F}(f_2' \cdot f_2')) - \frac{(\mathcal{F}^{-1}(M_1 \cdot F_2^*))^2}{\mathcal{F}^{-1}(M_1 \cdot M_2^*)}}}$$

$$(9)$$

3   Inpainting with the Masked Fourier Transform

Inpainting is a radical form of image restoration in which pixels inside a missing region of the image are filled with information provided by the surrounding areas, and potentially by the entire domain. The concept of self-similarity is central to this task, since the main underlying assumption is that repeating patterns from other parts of the image will be relevant for the missing area, and will thus be imported there as well. In the spatial domain, the inpainting task has been traditionally addressed, as an ill-posed problem, by total variation regularization, by dictionary based approaches [5,6], by diffusion with partial differential equations [11,22] or by some hybrid strategy [1,3]. Compared to these commonly encountered approaches, methods which use explicitly the Fourier transform of the deteriorated input image are less common. Some works focus on some specific cases of inpainting which are particularly suited for spectral analysis (e.g. removal of text overlay [18]). In [23], the FFT is used as an accelerating step for patch matching in exemplar based image inpainting, while in [12] the inpainting task is performed in the Fourier space of the image representation (i.e. some coefficients are assumed to be missing). In [19], the image is decomposed in decomposed in texture and non-texture components, then texture inpainting and denoising is performed in a subsequent step. In [7], the authors employ an alternative to the FFT, namely nonharmonic analysis, in order to minimize the impact of the side lobes appearing on truncated data. None of these works try to cope explicitly with the impact of the mask on the extracted frequencies, nor they propose a fully spectral, computationally efficient approach.

In this work, we propose to take advantage of the fact that we are able to compute a consistency criterion only considering the available pixels (i.e., fully disregarding the missing ones) thanks to the use of Fourier transform based expressions introduced in Sect. 2. Based on these latter, we are then able to propose an efficient strategy for solving the inpainting problem in which the mask represents the area to be filled. The proposed algorithm searches, for each area including missing pixels, another area which presents similar structures and colors than the ones near the missing pixels. This search can be performed globally or locally depending on the assumptions. We then expect such an approach to be all the more performing that the image presents repetitive structures or textures.

The global outline is given by Algorithm 1. In the considered algorithm, as well as in the conducted experiments in Sect. 4, we consider RGB images.

Algorithm 1. Inpainting by research of similar areas; input: RGB image I, search area side length l, boolean b_u indicating if ASD is centered; output: RGB image $\tilde{I}$. FFT stands for the Fast Fourier Transform and IFFT for the Inverse Fast Fourier Transform.

1: $L \leftarrow$ list of I areas with missing pixels
2: Initialize $\tilde{I}$ to I
3: **for** each element A_j of L **do**
4:    $(x, y) \leftarrow A_j$ center coordinates
5:    $d \leftarrow A_j$ min square bounding box side length
6:    $f_1 \leftarrow$ rectangular tile centered on (x, y) and having side length equal to l
7:    Cut a box of side length d at the center of f_1
8:    $n \leftarrow \lceil log_2(d) \rceil$
9:    $f_2 \leftarrow$ rectangular tile centered on (x, y) and having side length equal to 2^n
10:    $m_1 \leftarrow$ binary mask of f_1 valid pixels
11:    $M_1 \leftarrow$ FFT(m_1)
12:    $m_2 \leftarrow$ binary mask of f_2 valid pixels
13:    $M_2 \leftarrow$ FFT(m_2)
14:    $\check{M}_{12} \leftarrow$ IFFT$(M_1 \cdot M_2^*)$
15:    Initialize map S to 0 in every pixel
16:    **for** each channel k of f_1 **do**
17:       **for** $i \in 1, 2$ **do**
18:          $f_{i,k} \leftarrow$ channel k of f_i
19:          $F_i \leftarrow$ FFT$(f_{i,k})$
20:          $f_{i,k}^2 \leftarrow f_{i,k} \cdot f_{i,k}$
21:          $G_i \leftarrow$ FFT$(f_{i,k}^2)$
22:       **end for**
23:       $\check{F}_{12} \leftarrow$ IFFT$(F_1 \cdot F_2^*)$
24:       $\check{H}_{12} \leftarrow$ IFFT$(G_1 \cdot M_2^*)$
25:       $\check{H}_{21} \leftarrow$ IFFT$(M_1 \cdot G_2^*)$
26:       **if** b_u **then**
27:          $\check{J}_{12} \leftarrow$ IFFT$(F_1 \cdot M_2^*)$
28:          $\check{J}_{21} \leftarrow$ IFFT$(M_1 \cdot F_2^*)$
29:       **end if**
30:       $S \leftarrow S + \check{H}_{12} + \check{H}_{21} - 2\check{F}_{12} + b_u \left(\frac{\check{J}_{12} - \check{J}_{21}}{\check{M}_{12}} \right)$
31:    **end for**
32:    $S \leftarrow \frac{S}{\check{M}_{12}}$
33:    $(\hat{u}, \hat{v}) \leftarrow argmin_{(u,v)} S(u, v)$
34:    Fill the missing values in $\tilde{I}$ by pasting the values of I around $(x + \hat{u}, y + \hat{v})$
35: **end for**

However, it is straightforward to apply the proposed approach in another color space, or even to multispectral (or hyperspectral) images. The size l of the search area is an input parameter left to the user. Note that using a global search, the Fourier transforms associated to the search area (the whole image in this case) can be computed once at the beginning of the algorithm. However, in this case, we lose the support of a locality constraint. Note also that, to benefit from fast Fourier transform algorithms, l has to be a power of 2. In the extraction of f_1

and f_2 the original image can be padded with 0 (masked pixels) if necessary. Finally, since the patch that is researched in the image (around the area to fill) is extracted from the image itself, it is necessary to mask the pixels of the patch (to avoid to reselect the original patch location), which is simply done by "cutting" a box of patch size in original image (and filling it with black pixels).

4   Experimental Results

We performed experiments related to the inpainting task on images selected from the publicly available DAFNE challenge dataset [4]. As previously stated, the proposed algorithm is generally applicable to grayscale or color images, but the samples which are present in DAFNE offer a good diversity in terms of appearance and style of the content, with a good balance between repeating patterns and more singular structures. The hole creation process is performed by randomly and uniformly removing disk patches of content from the selected images.

Evaluation Metrics. Two widely used metrics are considered for the numerical evaluation. First, the Root Mean Squared Error (RMSE) is considered, then we also compute a metric which is more specific for benchmarking image reconstruction tasks, namely the peak signal-to-noise ration (PSNR). Although PSNR is partly related to the RMSE, it highlights better the method performance independently of the numerical range of the studied signal values.

Algorithm Variants. Based on the general idea for inpainting with the masked Fourier transform, we consider three variants depending on the similarity measure which is employed in searching for the most visually close data: (1) the normalized cross correlation (NCC, cf. Eq. (9)) computed on the intensity image, (2) a weighted sum of the three intensity-based criteria that may be potentially used: NCC, centered ASD (cf. Eq. (6) and Eq. (8)) and uncentered ASD (cf. Eq. (7) and Eq. (8)) called uASD, (3) the uASD computed on the three color channels (benefiting from good summation property), called 3D uASD.

Tables 1 and 2 show the obtained results in terms of evaluation metric statistics computed on 100 holes per fresco. We clearly see that the NCC is not sufficient to find a good image patch to fill a given hole, mainly since it is "only" based on intensity relative variations. Adding the two criteria based on squared differences significantly improves the results (between 2 and 8 dB depending on the considered fresco) while significantly reducing the standard deviation. Finally, the benefit of color information is also visible, varying however with the content of the fresco: the Lanzani fresco presents rather homogeneous colors (cf. Fig. 1, second line) whereas the Dellafrancesca fresco has a variety of colors (cf. Fig. 1, third line) allowing for a more significant improvement of performance.

Finally, let us have a qualitative look at the obtained results. Figure 1 shows the whole frescoes with simulated holes and the inpainting results from 3D uASD, while Fig. 2 shows some selected subareas. Indeed, Fig. 1 allows us to check quickly that holes have been filled with consistent values since at first

Table 1. RMSE statistics obtained on three frescoes for three algorithms based on different consistency measures; statistics (mean, median and standard deviation after ± symbol) are derived from 100 simulated holes. Best results are highlighted in green. (Best viewed onto the electronic version)

Algorithm	Tiepolo		Lanzani		DellaFrancesca	
	Mean	Median	Mean	Median	Mean	Median
NCC	35.64	31.76	36.32	33.92	35.85	30.01
	±27.67		±17.15		±21.73	
NCC+ASD +uASD	25.86	20.56	29.09	28.14	29.74	27.28
	±19.20		±11.52		±14.41	
3D uASD	24.74	20.13	28.69	26.99	27.40	25.28
	±19.02		±12.03		±13.81	

Table 2. PSNR statistics obtained on three frescoes for three algorithms based on different consistency measures; statistics (mean, median and standard deviation after ± symbol) are derived from 100 simulated holes. Best results are highlighted in green. (Best viewed onto the electronic version)

Algorithm	Tiepolo		Lanzani		**DellaFrancesca**	
	Mean	Median	Mean	Median	Mean	Median
NCC	47.61	41.66	41.58	40.35	42.76	42.79
	±21.87		±11.92		±13.14	
NCC+ASD +uASD	52.85	50.36	45.41	44.08	45.79	44.70
	±19.79		±10.66		±12.16	
3D ASD	54.0	50.78	45.88	44.91	47.66	46.23
	±19.92		±11.01		±12.56	

glance it is difficult to see the location of the simulated holes (without the help of the left image) whereas Fig. 2 allows us to evaluate the visual quality of the local reconstruction (fresco subareas of size 128 × 128 pixels), as well as to point out some remaining imperfections. Specifically, in Fig. 2, for each line considering details from a different fresco, left side shows a subarea that is rather well reconstructed (it is difficult to guess where the holes were even focusing on this subarea), while the right side shows a subarea with at least one partially flawed reconstruction: one hole filled with an incorrect shade of white (first line), a discontinuity in the leg of the soldier (second line) and appearing inconsistencies in the drapery of tunics (third line). However, all these imperfections are explainable and we hope to reduce them by searching in future works a patch candidate for the filling not only in translation but also in rotation.

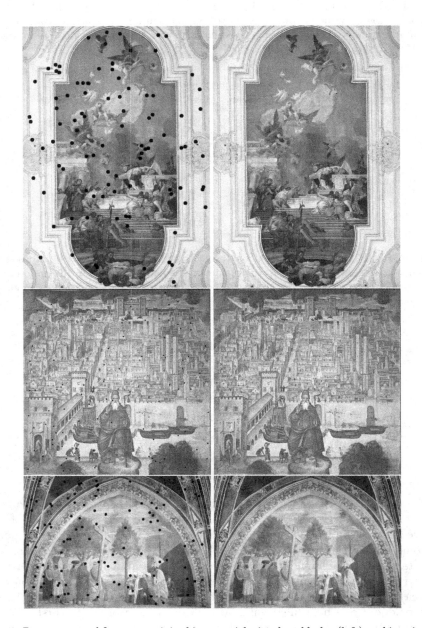

Fig. 1. Reconstructed frescoes: original image with simulated holes (left) and inpainting result (right); first line: Tiepolo fresco ("The Institution of the Rosary"), second line: Lanzani fresco ("Sant Antonio protegge Pavia"), and third line: Della Francesca fresco ("Exaltation of the Cross").

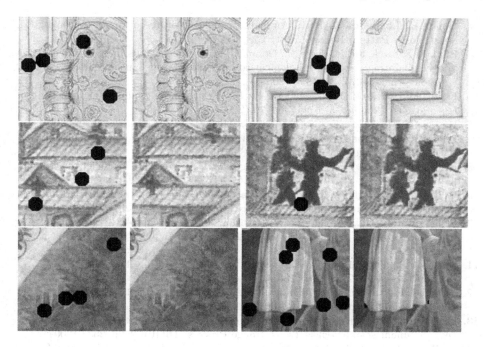

Fig. 2. Details of the reconstructed frescoes: simulated holes (left) and inpainting result (right); first line: Tiepolo fresco, second line: Lanzani fresco, and third line: Della Francesca fresco.

5   Conclusion

In this work, we extended the strategy initially proposed by [14] beyond NCC, to more consistency measures between masked image subparts. We have also addressed with success a novel task, namely inpainting, which has not been considered until now with these techniques, despite its suitability with the method assumptions. For future work, we intend to fully exploit the other properties of the Fourier transform (e.g. following Fourier-Mellin approach) which would allow us to perform more complex rotation and scaling invariant queries, and to characterize more in detail the computational advantage of the proposed algorithm.

References

1. Bugeau, A., Bertalmío, M., Caselles, V., Sapiro, G.: A comprehensive framework for image inpainting. IEEE Trans. Image Process. **19**(10), 2634–2645 (2010)
2. Chan, C.h., Pang, G.K.: Fabric defect detection by fourier analysis. IEEE Trans. Ind. Appl. **36**(5), 1267–1276 (2000)
3. Criminisi, A., Pérez, P., Toyama, K.: Region filling and object removal by exemplar-based image inpainting. IEEE Trans. Image Process. **13**(9), 1200–1212 (2004)

 4. Dondi, P., Lombardi, L., Setti, A.: Dafne: a dataset of fresco fragments for digital anastlylosis. Pattern Recogn. Lett. **138**, 631–637 (2020)
 5. Elad, M., Starck, J.L., Querre, P., Donoho, D.L.: Simultaneous cartoon and texture image inpainting using morphological component analysis (mca). Appl. Comput. Harmon. Anal. **19**(3), 340–358 (2005)
 6. Fadili, M.J., Starck, J.L., Murtagh, F.: Inpainting and zooming using sparse representations. Comput. J. **52**(1), 64–79 (2009)
 7. Hasegawa, M., Kako, T., Hirobayashi, S., Misawa, T., Yoshizawa, T., Inazumi, Y.: Image inpainting on the basis of spectral structure from 2-d nonharmonic analysis. IEEE Trans. Image Process. **22**(8), 3008–3017 (2013)
 8. Kaneko, S., Satoh, Y., Igarashi, S.: Using selective correlation coefficient for robust image registration. Pattern Recogn. **36**(5), 1165–1173 (2003)
 9. Kliangsuwan, T., Heednacram, A.: Fft features and hierarchical classification algorithms for cloud images. Eng. Appl. Artif. Intell. **76**, 40–54 (2018)
10. Konstantinidis, D., Stathaki, T., Argyriou, V.: Phase amplified correlation for improved sub-pixel motion estimation. IEEE Trans. Image Process. **28**(6), 3089–3101 (2019)
11. Masnou, S.: Disocclusion: a variational approach using level lines. IEEE Trans. Image Process. **11**(2), 68–76 (2002)
12. Mousavi, P., Tavakoli, A.: A new algorithm for image inpainting in fourier transform domain. Comput. Appl. Math. **38**(1), 1–9 (2019)
13. Orchard, J.: Efficient least squares multimodal registration with a globally exhaustive alignment search. IEEE Trans. Image Process. **16**(10), 2526–2534 (2007)
14. Padfield, D.: Masked object registration in the fourier domain. IEEE Trans. Image Process. **21**(5), 2706–2718 (2011)
15. Pan, W., Qin, K., Chen, Y.: An adaptable-multilayer fractional fourier transform approach for image registration. IEEE Trans. Pattern Anal. Mach. Intell. **31**(3), 400–414 (2008)
16. Reddy, B.S., Chatterji, B.N.: An fft-based technique for translation, rotation, and scale-invariant image registration. IEEE Trans. Image Process. **5**(8), 1266–1271 (1996)
17. Sheng, Y., Arsenault, H.H.: Experiments on pattern recognition using invariant fourier-mellin descriptors. JOSA A **3**(6), 771–776 (1986)
18. Sridevi, G., Srinivas Kumar, S.: Image inpainting based on fractional-order nonlinear diffusion for image reconstruction. Circuits Systems Signal Process. **38**(8), 3802–3817 (2019)
19. Thai, D.H., Gottschlich, C.: Simultaneous inpainting and denoising by directional global three-part decomposition: connecting variational and fourier domain-based image processing. Royal Society Open Science **5**(7), 171176 (2018)
20. Thevenaz, P., Ruttimann, U.E., Unser, M.: A pyramid approach to subpixel registration based on intensity. IEEE Trans. Image Process. **7**(1), 27–41 (1998)
21. Tsai, D.M., Wu, S.C., Li, W.C.: Defect detection of solar cells in electroluminescence images using fourier image reconstruction. Sol. Energy Mater. Sol. Cells **99**, 250–262 (2012)
22. Tschumperlé, D., Deriche, R.: Vector-valued image regularization with pdes: A common framework for different applications. IEEE Trans. Pattern Anal. Mach. Intell. **27**(4), 506–517 (2005)
23. Wang, H., Jiang, L., Liang, R., Li, X.X.: Exemplar-based image inpainting using structure consistent patch matching. Neurocomputing **269**, 90–96 (2017)

Bringing Attention to Image Anomaly Detection

Axel de Nardin$^{(\boxtimes)}$, Pankaj Mishra , Claudio Piciarelli ,
and Gian Luca Foresti

University of Udine, Italy, via delle Scienze 206, 33100 Udine, Italy
{denardin.axel,mishra.pankaj}@spes.uniud.it
{claudio.piciarelli,gianluca.foresti}@uniud.it

Abstract. Detecting anomalies in images is a task with several relevant real-world applications, e.g. industrial inspection. Building on the
existing RIAD (Reconstruction by Inpainting for visual Anomaly Detection) framework, we introduce an attention-based component to improve
the model performance. Furthermore we propose a different approach to
image masking which leverages the selection of multiple random patches
at a single scale in the original images. Through the provided experimental results we show how the novelties introduced by this work consistently
improve the performance of the baseline approach over the various classes
of the heterogeneous MVTec benchmark dataset across all the metrics
considered.

Keywords: Deep anomaly localization · Patch-based anomaly
localization · Attention-based anomaly localization · Self-supervised
learning

1 Introduction

Anomaly detection is referred to as the process of identifying novel samples that
exhibit significantly different traits compared to an accepted and predefined
model of normality. In real-life scenarios, like Visual Inspection Systems (VIS),
the novel sample can show a previously unseen and considerable difference from
the reference data, and labeling of novel examples is not possible. Systems that
can perform such a task in an autonomous way are in high demand, ranging from
banking [33], medical imaging [19], defect segmentation [23,27], inspection [27],
quality control [24], video surveillance [28], etc.

While this kind of task could be easy for a human being, the same does not
hold for an autonomous system trained over a small set of data. A significantly
pressing reason that makes this task challenging is the fact that, while it is
a classification problem, the traditional methods are intrinsically flawed by the
way they process the data. In fact, most often the industrial-grade data available
in real-life are highly imbalanced [21], or labeled data exist only for the normal
class.

P. L. Mazzeo et al. (Eds.): ICIAP 2022 Workshops, LNCS 13373, pp. 115–126, 2022.
https://doi.org/10.1007/978-3-031-13321-3_11

For this reason, most of the recent attempts to tackle this class of problems employ deep neural networks (DNN) with specific training setups to solve the anomaly detection task [1,4,5,10,17,20,22]. In particular, there are two major approaches that gained much popularity in dealing with this kind of problem, the Autoencoders [18] and Generative Adversarial Networks [16].

In this paper we are presenting an attention-based approach built upon the RIAD Framework [34] which leverages a patchwise inpainting process in order to detect and localize anomalies in images. In particular, while keeping the patch-wise structure of said approach, we modify the original reconstruction module of the framework by introducing an Attention U-Net model in place of the original U-Net. Furthermore, we propose a new approach for the masking process of the images which works on a higher number of overlapping patches at a single scale of the image instead of using a multiple scale approach. Finally we also propose a new evaluation setup which uses both an L2 and a multi scale GMS loss, instead of relying just on the latter, to generate the anomaly maps. We show how the combination of the two ideas significantly increases the overall performance of the model on the adopted dataset for the metrics considered.

The rest of the paper is organized as follows: in (Sect. 2) we provide a summary of the related works currently available in the literature, in (Sect. 3) we give an overview of the proposed framework by describing in detail the masking process and the attention-based reconstruction approach that characterize it. Finally in Sects. 4 and 5 we provide, respectively, a comparison of our model with its baseline counterpart as well as with other common approaches for anomaly localization, and the final remarks together with an overview of possible future works in this area.

2   Related Work

From the recent excerpts of the literature, the surveys published by Kiran et al. [14] and Pang Guansong et al. [26], excellently tried to discuss the Deep Anomaly Detection (DAD) methods based on learning (training approaches) and conceptual paradigms. Based on the adopted learning strategy, a DAD can be classified as a *Supervised, Semi-supervised or Unsupervised* method.

Supervised methods use properly labeled dataset and some generic techniques such as under-sampling the dominant class or oversampling the smaller class either by data duplication or by synthetic generation of new data to counter the pervasive highly-imbalanced datasets in real-life scenarios [7]. Although the supervised methods have improved their performance over time [29], they are not as popular as the semi-supervised or unsupervised ones, owing to the lack of labels in the training data and in particular for the anomalous instances. Semi-supervised learning exploits the availability of normal data in many practical applications like medical [13] and industrial fields [32]. A common approach is represented by the use of autoencoders which are trained only on the normal data in a semi-supervised way [21,22]. The idea is that the autoencoder, trained in such a fashion, will produce low reconstruction errors for the normal instances, while it will produce high reconstructions errors for the anomalies. Unsupervised methods rely only on the intrinsic features of the data, without any external information, such as instances labels, being provided. A popular unsupervised learning approach to anomaly detection is represented by Generative Adversarial Networks(GAN) [11]. Such generative networks are based on the two competing networks: a generator, which generates new unseen data resembling the training datasets, and a discriminator, which tries to discriminate between the original dataset and the generated dataset. For anomaly detection, these GAN networks are trained on the normal class (because of the easy availability and abundance of normal class data) much like autoencoders. At the time of testing, the generator is inverted, which provides the comparison between the latent space representation of the normal and the anomalous data [2,12].

We can also find in literature a new class of methods based on adopting different learning and scoring strategies of the networks [4,15,23,30]. They are based on a) Reconstruction-based approach, b) Latent space learning-based approach, c) Generative network-based approach. However, there is no strict division between each of the approaches, as many of these approaches overlap with one or more methods used. While all such methods are conceptually well categorized and discussed in detail by Pang et al. [26], the underlying assumption of these approaches is that the extracted deep features preserve the discriminative information while reducing the dimension of the input, which helps to separate anomalies from the normal instances. Moreover, recent approaches took the challenge of high-imbalanced classification task to a new-level by being able to perform anomaly localization (image-segmentation approach) from a single instance. The adaptability and capacity of such models can be well appreciated from the fact that they even don't need a pixel-precise ground truth to do the anomaly localization [5,17].

3   Methods

The approach we propose in the present paper is based on the framework presented in [34]. As in the original work, we try to address the problems of anomaly detection and localization via an inpainting approach that aims to reconstruct the missing parts of an image. The idea is to generate a set of random masks for each image before feeding it to the model, which then tries to reconstruct only the masked out regions hopefully ignoring the anomalies potentially contained in them, thus increasing the difference between the original images and the reconstructed ones specifically in those anomalous regions. The two main novelties we present in this work are, respectively, the introduction of a attention mechanism in our reconstruction process through the adoption of an Attention U-Net [25] instead of the original standard U-Net, and the adoption of a new masking process which will now be described in detail.

3.1   Masked Regions Generator

The masking approach we are proposing in the present works differs from the one used in the original work [34] in the fact that, instead of masking out non overlapping patches at multiple scales of the original image it focuses on patches of a single size. Our approach works by selecting N random, potentially over-lapping, masks consisting in a set of kXk regions which in total make up for the P percent of the total area of the input image, by setting the corresponding pixels to a value of 0. The masked instances are then fed to the model which tries to reconstruct the missing parts. Finally, the average of each reconstructed region of the input image is taken to determine the output of the model. The main intuition behind this approach is that, by reconstructing each patch of the original instance starting from different starting visible regions the robustness of the reconstructed image should improve, making it harder for it to contain the reconstruction of any eventual anomaly present in the corresponding input.

3.2   Model

The model we adopted for the Reconstruction module our framework is repre-sented by the popular Attention U-Net. This deep learning model was initially introduced [25] as a way to address the problem of Multi-class image segmenta-tion in biomedical images. The Attention U-Net differs from its original coun-terpart for the introduction of attention gates (Fig. 1) in the upsampling part of the network, which takes as their inputs a set of input features, represented by the output of the previous layer of the model (called the "gating signal") and the feature map obtained from the skip connection, which also defines the size of the output of the gate. This way a set of attention coefficients are learned in order to identify salient regions in the feature maps, relatively to the considered task.

4   Experiments

4.1   Datasets

The dataset we choose for the training and testing processes of the presented model is represented by the MVTec Anomaly Detection dataset [3]. This dataset, thanks to its heterogeneity, has become one of the most common benchmarks for works that try to address the problem of anomaly detection and localiza-tion in images. MVTec consists of 3629 training images and 1725 test images distributed over 15 classes, 10 of which represent different products while the remaining ones cover 5 different types of textures. The classes have been chosen in order to provide heterogeneous characteristics both regarding the appearance of the elements they represent and the type of anomalies by which they can be affected. The way in which the images have been collected is also heterogeneous as for some of the classes all the instances tend to be roughly aligned while for some other a random rotation is introduced. Moreover, three of the classes

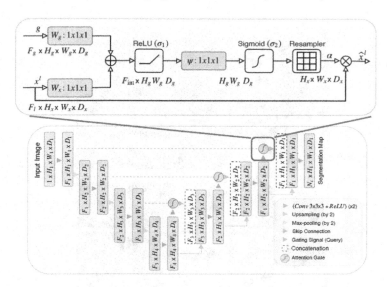

Fig. 1. Scheme representing the function of the attention gates for the Attention U-Net model [25]. The input features (x^l) are scaled with the attention coefficients (α) computed in the AG. These coefficients are obtained trough the use of additive attention computed between the input feature and the gating signal (g) which is collected from a coarser scale and provides the needed contextual information.

are characterized by the presence of grayscale images only, as this is a common occurrence in real-world industrial settings. As previously mentioned, the testing set also presents a high degree of heterogeneity. For each category an average of 5 different types of anomalies is provided for a total of 73 anomaly types across the dataset. Furthermore, MVTec does not only provide the labels for defective images at an instance level but also provides pixel-perfect Anomaly Maps which allow us to assess the quality of our model also on the anomaly localization task. A set of samples for the MVTec dataset is provided in Fig. 2.

4.2   Training Setup

The training of the model was performed using only the normal instances of the dataset, through a self-supervised approach. The maximum number of epochs allowed was set to 300, which proved to be enough for each model to converge, with an early stop in case the performance on the validation set wouldn't improve over the last 20 epochs. The total loss used to evaluate this performance was calculated as the sum between the Mean squared Error (MSE) loss, the Gradient Magnitude Similarity (GMS) loss, and the negative of the Structured Similarity Index (SSIM) between the original and the reconstructed images. The combination of these losses allows focusing both on the overall structure and the smaller

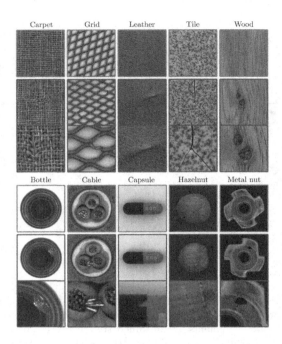

Carpet   Grid   Leather   Tile   Wood

Bottle   Cable   Capsule   Hazelnut   Metal nut

Fig. 2. Samples for 5 texture classes and 5 product classes of the MVTec dataset. For each category are shown a normal instance (top row), an anomalous one (middle row), and a close up of the anomalous region (bottom row)

details of the images. A formal description of the loss functions is given hereafter:

$$L_2(X, \hat{X}) = \sum_{i=0}^{h-1} \sum_{j=0}^{w-1} (X_{ij} - \hat{X}_{ij})^2 \tag{1}$$

$$L_{SSIM}(X, \hat{X}) = -\frac{(2\mu_X \mu_{\hat{X}} + c_1)(2\sigma_{X\hat{X}} + c_2)}{(\mu_X^2 + \mu_{\hat{X}}^2 + c_1)(\sigma_X^2 + \sigma_{\hat{X}}^2 + c_2)} \tag{2}$$

$$L_{GMS}(X, \hat{X}) = \frac{2g(X)g(\hat{X}) + C}{g(X)^2 + g(\hat{X})^2 + C} \tag{3}$$

$$L(X, \hat{X}) = \alpha * L_1(X, \hat{X}) + \beta * L_{SSIM}(X, \hat{X}) + \gamma * L_{GMS}(X, \hat{X}) \tag{4}$$

where:

- **X:** Is the original image
- $\hat{X}$: Is the reconstructed image
- **h, w:** Are the height and width of the image in pixel
- μ_x: Is average value of image x
- σ_x^2: Is variance of image x
- σ_{xy}: Is the covariance of x and y

- $c_1 \& c_2$: Are two variables used to stabilize the division with weak denominator
- $\mathbf{g(X)}$ is the gradient magnitude map for image $\mathbf{X}$ calculated as: $g(X) = \sqrt{(G * h_x)^2 + (G * h_y)^2}$ with h_x and h_y being 3×3 filters along the x and y dimensions respectively and $*$ being the convolution operation.
- $\boldsymbol{\alpha, \beta, \gamma}$: are the weights of every single loss in the total loss function, for this work we kept them all equal.

As we can notice the SSIM is negated in the total loss function, the reason behind this is that it represents a similarity measure defined in the interval $[-1, 1]$ where a value of 1 indicates that the compared images are completely identical, therefore by keeping the obtained values as they are we would have a maximization problem instead of a minimization one.

Finally, in Table 1 we provide the hyper-parameters employed for the model during the training process. The reported values have been selected empirically by trying to provide a good compromise between the quality of the predictions and the complexity of the model.

Table 1. Model hyperparameters

LR	Weight decay	Batch	Img size	# of masks	Patch sizes	Masked region (%)
1e^−4	1e^−4	16	128 × 128	20	16 × 16	33

4.3 Anomaly Localization Process

Another area in which we departed from the original RIAD framework is the one regarding how anomalous regions of the images are detected. Instead of relying on just the anomaly maps obtained by calculating the gradient magnitudes similarity between the input and the reconstructed images, we combined these with the anomaly maps resulting from the normalized, pixelwise, MSE between the two images by summing the values of each of their pixels. The idea behind this choice is that by taking in consideration different similarity measures between the original and the reconstructed images the reliability of the model in localizing the anomalies should improve.

4.4 Metrics

For the evaluation process of the performance of the model on the selected dataset, we opted to use two metrics. The first one is the Area Under the ROC Curve (AUROC), which plots the False Positive Rates obtained by the model versus its True positive Rates and then calculates the area under the resulting curve. This measure is a common metric for the addressed problems in recent works. Instead of considering the whole curve, we decided to set an upper limit for the FPR to 0.3 as proposed in [3]. This is because results with a high FPR tend to lead to meaningless detection and segmentation results, especially in real-world scenarios where they would lead to the rejection of many products not presenting any real defects. The second metric we adopted is the Area Under the Precision-Recall Curve, which has been chosen because it is particularly well suited for those problems where we are more interested in one specific class of the instances as it happens in the context of anomaly detection. Furthermore, another important property of this metric is that it is not affected by data imbalances in the test set.

4.5 Results

Hereafter we present the results achieved by our model on the MVTec dataset for the 2 different metrics considered, and show how they compare to the baseline on which our work is based, namely RIAD [34], as well as to other widely used approaches, represented by the ones reported in the most recent MVTec paper [3] from which we selected, for a fair comparison only those who didn't rely on additional data for pre-training. We additionally include, for the results regarding the ROCAUC score, a comparison with VT-ADL [23] which is of particular interest as it represents an alternative way of introducing the attention mechanism for the task of anomaly localization in images. In Table 2 and Table 3 are reported the aforementioned comparative results, for the ROCAUC and PRAUC metrics respectively. While the scores for the VT-ADL and baseline RIAD approaches have been calculated by us, which is of particular relevance especially for the latter as it allowed us to really analyze and understand the power represented by the introduction of the attention mechanism, for all the other models they have been gathered from the original paper.

Table 2. Normalized area under the ROC curve up to an average false positive rate per-pixel of 30% for each dataset category. The values in bold represent the best scores overall.

Class	f-anoGan [31]	l2-AE [6]	SSIM-AE [6]	Texture inspection [8]	Variation model [9]	VT-ADL [23]	RIAD [34]	Ours
Carpet	0.251	0.287	0.365	**0.874**	0.162	0.549	0.803	**0.906**
Grid	0.550	0.741	0.820	0.878	0.488	0.569	**0.966**	0.932
Leather	0.574	0.491	0.356	0.975	0.381	0.817	**0.983**	**0.983**
Tile	0.180	0.174	0.156	0.314	0.304	0.589	0.599	**0.719**
Wood	0.392	0.417	0.404	0.723	0.408	0.682	0.745	**0.768**
Bottle	0.422	0.528	0.624	0.454	0.667	0.687	0.893	**0.926**
Cable	0.453	0.510	0.302	0.512	0.423	0.751	0.665	**0.854**
Capsule	0.362	0.732	0.799	0.698	0.843	0.615	**0.965**	0.951
Hazelnut	0.825	0.879	0.847	0.955	0.802	0.926	0.944	**0.954**
Metal nut	0.435	0.572	0.539	0.135	0.462	0.711	0.706	**0.913**
Pill	0.504	0.690	0.698	0.440	0.666	0.748	**0.919**	0.903
Screw	0.814	0.867	0.885	0.877	0.697	0.771	0.881	**0.945**
Toothbrush	0.749	0.837	0.846	0.712	0.775	0.878	**0.974**	0.969
Transistor	0.372	0.657	0.562	0.363	0.601	0.689	0.731	**0.886**
Zipper	0.201	0.474	0.564	0.928	0.209	0.683	**0.951**	0.939
Mean	0.472	0.590	0.584	0.656	0.526	0.683	0.848	**0.893**

Table 3. Normalized area under the Precision Recall Curve for each dataset category. The values in bold represent the best scores overall.

Class	f-anoGan	l2-AE	SSIM-AE	Variation model	Texture inspection	RIAD	Ours
Carpet	0.025	0.042	0.035	0.017	**0.568**	0.223	0.292
Grid	0.050	0.252	0.081	0.096	0.179	**0.278**	0.208
Leather	0.156	0.089	0.037	0.072	**0.603**	0.600	0.555
Tile	0.093	0.093	0.077	**0.218**	0.187	0.157	0.198
Wood	0.159	0.196	0.086	0.213	**0.529**	0.322	0.290
Bottle	0.160	0.308	0.309	0.536	0.285	0.560	**0.571**
Cable	0.098	0.108	0.052	0.084	0.102	0.122	**0.369**
Capsule	0.033	0.276	0.128	0.226	0.071	0.184	**0.317**
Hazelnut	0.526	0.590	0.312	0.485	**0.689**	0.444	0.580
Metal nut	0.273	0.416	0.359	0.384	0.153	0.257	**0.712**
Pill	0.121	0.255	0.233	0.274	0.207	**0.567**	0.487
Screw	0.062	0.147	0.050	0.138	0.052	**0.163**	0.138
Toothbrush	0.133	0.367	0.183	0.416	0.140	0.456	**0.492**
Transistor	0.130	0.381	0.191	0.309	0.108	0.244	**0.525**
Zipper	0.027	0.095	0.088	0.038	**0.611**	0.605	0.312
Mean	0.136	0.241	0.148	0.234	0.299	0.339	**0.403**

As we can see for the ROCAUC metric the proposed model vastly outperforms all the other ones, achieving margins going from 4.5% to 42.1% on the mean value for the baseline RIAD and f-anogan models respectively, with a significant improvement (21%) also over VT-ADL, the only other approach using an attention-based mechanism. While the margin from the former is not as large as the one from other models it is definitely noteworthy and representative of the power of the attention mechanism. This aspect is also accentuated by the fact that our model achieved the best performance on most of the classes (10 out of 15) across all models. Regarding the PRAUC scores on the other hand we can see that, while the results achieved by our approach aren't as markedly better than the ones reported for the other approaches on the individual classes, where it obtains the top score in 6 out of 15 of them, it still proves to be the best performing model overall, again with a significant margin over the competition. Is it interesting to observe in particular how the improvement over the baseline RIAD model is even more significant for the PRAUC metric (6.4%), which can be considered a stricter evaluation metric, than it is for the formerly analyzed ROCAUC one (4.5%). Finally it's important to mention that the computational complexity of the proposed model is comparable to the original RIAD one as both the new mask generation process and the introduction of the attention gates introduce very little overhead.

5   Conclusions and Future Works

In the presented work we investigated the potential of the attention mechanism, and of an efficient masking process, in the context of Anomaly Localization, specifically through the introduction of an Attention U-Net as the reconstruction module for the already effective RIAD Framework, which used a traditional U-Net for this task. In particular we have shown how the proposed approach is able to outperform other more traditional models on the popular benchmark MVTec for the metrics considered, furthermore it provides a significant improvement in performance over its baseline counterpart which doesn't leverage the power of the Attention mechanism, showing the effectiveness of the latter. Even though the results obtained with this work clearly show the potential of attention-based approaches for anomaly detection, we think that further investigation in this area could lead to even more interesting outcomes. In future works we would like to build an entire framework which fully leverages the attention component as opposed to simply introducing it in a preexisting one. Furthermore, we believe that a higher degree of heterogeneity in the datasets considered for the benchmarking process would definitely provide a more complete picture of the capabilities of this approach in different real world scenarios.

Acknowledgement. This work was partially supported by the ONRG project N62909-20-1-2075 Target Re-Association for Autonomous Agents (TRAAA).

References

1. Abati, D., Porrello, A., Calderara, S., Cucchiara, R.: Latent space autoregression for novelty detection. In: Proceedings of the IEEE Conference on Computer Vision and Pattern Recognition, pp. 481–490 (2019)
2. Akcay, S., Atapour-Abarghouei, A., Breckon, T.P.: GANomaly: semi-supervised anomaly detection via adversarial training. In: Jawahar, C.V., Li, H., Mori, G., Schindler, K. (eds.) ACCV 2018. LNCS, vol. 11363, pp. 622–637. Springer, Cham (2019). https://doi.org/10.1007/978-3-030-20893-6_39
3. Bergmann, P., Batzner, K., Fauser, M., Sattlegger, D., Steger, C.: The MVTEC anomaly detection dataset: a comprehensive real-world dataset for unsupervised anomaly detection. Int. J. Comput. Vis. **129**(4), 1038–1059 (2021)
4. Bergmann, P., Fauser, M., Sattlegger, D., Steger, C.: Mvtec ad-a comprehensive real-world dataset for unsupervised anomaly detection. In: Proceedings of the IEEE Conference on Computer Vision and Pattern Recognition, pp. 9592–9600 (2019)
5. Bergmann, P., Fauser, M., Sattlegger, D., Steger, C.: Uninformed students: student-teacher anomaly detection with discriminative latent embeddings. In: Proceedings of the IEEE/CVF Conference on Computer Vision and Pattern Recognition, pp. 4183–4192 (2020)
6. Bergmann, P., Löwe, S., Fauser, M., Sattlegger, D., Steger, C.: Improving unsupervised defect segmentation by applying structural similarity to autoencoders. In: International Joint Conference on Computer Vision, Imaging and Computer Graphics Theory and Applications (2019)
7. Buda, M., Maki, A., Mazurowski, M.A.: A systematic study of the class imbalance problem in convolutional neural networks. Neural Netw. **106**, 249–259 (2018)
8. Böttger, T., Ulrich, M.: Real-time texture error detection on textured surfaces with compressed sensing. Pattern Recogni. Image Anal. **26**, 88–94 (2016)
9. Steger, C., Ulrich, M., Wiedemann, C.: Machine Vision Algorithms and Applications. Wiley (2018)

10. Cohen, N., Hoshen, Y.: Sub-image anomaly detection with deep pyramid correspondences. arXiv preprint arXiv:2005.02357 (2020)
11. Creswell, A., White, T., Dumoulin, V., Arulkumaran, K., Sengupta, B., Bharath, A.A.: Generative adversarial networks: an overview. IEEE Signal Process. Mag. **35**(1), 53–65 (2018)
12. Deecke, L., Vandermeulen, R., Ruff, L., Mandt, S., Kloft, M.: Image anomaly detection with generative adversarial networks. In: Berlingerio, M., Bonchi, F., Gärtner, T., Hurley, N., Ifrim, G. (eds.) ECML PKDD 2018. LNCS (LNAI), vol. 11051, pp. 3–17. Springer, Cham (2019). https://doi.org/10.1007/978-3-030-10925-7_1
13. Faust, K., et al.: Visualizing histopathologic deep learning classification and anomaly detection using nonlinear feature space dimensionality reduction. BMC Bioinform. **19**(1), 1–15 (2018)
14. Kiran, B.R., Thomas, D.M., Parakkal, R.: An overview of deep learning based methods for unsupervised and semi-supervised anomaly detection in videos. J. Imaging **4**(2), 36 (2018)
15. Klushyn, A., Chen, N., Kurle, R., Cseke, B., van der Smagt, P.: Learning hierarchical priors in vaes. In: Wallach, H., Larochelle, H., Beygelzimer, A., d'Alché-Buc, F., Fox, E., Garnett, R. (eds.) Advances in Neural Information Processing Systems, vol. 32, pp. 2866–2875. Curran Associates, Inc. (2019)
16. Lee, C.K., Cheon, Y.J., Hwang, W.Y.: Studies on the GAN-based anomaly detection methods for the time series data. IEEE Access **9**, 73201–73215 (2021)
17. Li, C.L., Sohn, K., Yoon, J., Pfister, T.: Cutpaste: self-supervised learning for anomaly detection and localization. In: Proceedings of the IEEE/CVF Conference on Computer Vision and Pattern Recognition, pp. 9664–9674 (2021)
18. Liu, B., Wang, D., Lin, K., Tan, P.N., Zhou, J.: Unsupervised anomaly detection by robust collaborative autoencoders (2021)
19. Ma, X., et al.: Understanding adversarial attacks on deep learning based medical image analysis systems. Pattern Recogn. **110**, 107332 (2021)
20. Mishra, N., Rohaninejad, M., Chen, X., Abbeel, P.: A simple neural attentive meta-learner. arXiv preprint arXiv:1707.03141 (2017)
21. Mishra, P., Piciarelli, C., Foresti, G.L.: A neural network for image anomaly detection with deep pyramidal representations and dynamic routing. Int. J. Neural Syst. **30**(10), 2050060–2050060 (2020)
22. Mishra, P., Piciarelli, C., Foresti, G.L.: Image anomaly detection by aggregating deep pyramidal representations. In: Del Bimbo, A., Cucchiara, R., Sclaroff, S., Farinella, G.M., Mei, T., Bertini, M., Escalante, H.J., Vezzani, R. (eds.) ICPR 2021. LNCS, vol. 12664, pp. 705–718. Springer, Cham (2021). https://doi.org/10.1007/978-3-030-68799-1_51
23. Mishra, P., Verk, R., Fornasier, D., Piciarelli, C., Foresti, G.L.: VT-ADL: a vision transformer network for image anomaly detection and localization. In: 30th IEEE/IES International Symposium on Industrial Electronics (ISIE), June 2021
24. Napoletano, P., Piccoli, F., Schettini, R.: Anomaly detection in nanofibrous materials by CNN-based self-similarity. Sensors **18**(1), 209 (2018)
25. Oktay, O., et al.: Attention u-net: Learning where to look for the pancreas. ArXiv abs/1804.03999 (2018)
26. Pang, G., Shen, C., Cao, L., Hengel, A.V.D.: Deep learning for anomaly detection: a review. ACM Comput. Surv. **54**(2), 1–38 (2021)
27. Piciarelli, C., Avola, D., Pannone, D., Foresti, G.L.: A vision-based system for internal pipeline inspection. IEEE Trans. Ind. Inform. **15**(6), 3289–3299 (2018). early access

28. Piciarelli, C., Micheloni, C., Foresti, G.L.: Trajectory-based anomalous event detection. IEEE Trans. Circ. Syst. Video Technol. **18**(11), 1544–1554 (2008)
29. Piciarelli, C., Mishra, P., Foresti, G.L.: Supervised anomaly detection with highly imbalanced datasets using capsule networks. Int. J. Pattern Recogn. Artif. Intell. **35**(8), 2152010 (2021)
30. Reiss, T., Cohen, N., Bergman, L., Hoshen, Y.: Panda: adapting pretrained features for anomaly detection and segmentation. In: Proceedings of the IEEE/CVF Conference on Computer Vision and Pattern Recognition, pp. 2806–2814 (2021)
31. Schlegl, T., Seeböck, P., Waldstein, S.M., Langs, G., Schmidt-Erfurth, U.: f-anogan: Fast unsupervised anomaly detection with generative adversarial networks. Med. Image Anal. **54**, 30–44 (2019)
32. Wang, J., Ma, Y., Zhang, L., Gao, R.X., Wu, D.: Deep learning for smart manufacturing: methods and applications. J. Manufact. Syst. **48**, 144–156 (2018)
33. Yu, P., Yan, X.: Stock price prediction based on deep neural networks. Neural Comput. Appl.**32**(6), 1609–1628 (2020)
34. Zavrtanik, V., Kristan, M., Skočaj, D.: Reconstruction by inpainting for visual anomaly detection. Pattern Recogn. **112**, 107706 (2021)

Workshop on Fine Art Pattern Extraction and Recognition - FAPER

Recognizing the Emotions Evoked by Artworks Through Visual Features and Knowledge Graph-Embeddings

Sinem Aslan[1] , Giovanna Castellano[2] , Vincenzo Digeno[2],
Giuseppe Migailo[2], Raffaele Scaringi[2], and Gennaro Vessio[2(✉)]

[1] Department of Environmental Science, Informatics and Statistics,
Ca' Foscari University of Venice, Venice, Italy
[2] Department of Computer Science, University of Bari Aldo Moro, Bari, Italy
`gennaro.vessio@uniba.it`

Abstract. Recognizing the emotion an image evokes in the observer has long attracted the interest of the community for its many potential applications. However, it is a challenging task mainly due to the inherent complexity and subjectivity of human feelings. Such a difficulty is exacerbated in the domain of visual arts, mainly because of their abstract nature. In this work, we propose a new version of the artistic knowledge graph we were working on, namely *ArtGraph*, obtained by integrating the emotion labels provided by the *ArtEmis* dataset. The proposed graph enables emotion-based information retrieval and knowledge discovery even without training a learning model. In addition, we propose an artwork emotion classification system that jointly exploits visual features and knowledge graph-embeddings. Experimental evaluation revealed that while improvements in emotion classification depend mainly on the use of visual features, the prediction of style, genre and emotion can benefit from the simultaneous exploitation of visual and contextual features and can assist each other in a synergistic way.

Keywords: Visual arts · Digital humanities · Computer vision · Deep learning · Knowledge graphs · Emotion classification

1 Introduction

With the increasing availability of digital collections of images and the growth of computational methods capable of processing them automatically, attention has been devoted to automatic methods that infer the emotions an image evokes in the observer [21,23]. This interest is motivated by the numerous applications this technology would bring, from semantic image retrieval to aesthetic evaluation and opinion mining. However, while fascinating, image emotion classification presents great challenges, mainly due to the inherent complexity and subjectivity of human feelings. A single image, in fact, can evoke multifaceted and subtle reactions; moreover, these can strongly depend on the observer's cultural background, if not on personal or situational factors [19,25].

P. L. Mazzeo et al. (Eds.): ICIAP 2022 Workshops, LNCS 13373, pp. 129–140, 2022.
https://doi.org/10.1007/978-3-031-13321-3_12

The difficulties raised by visual sentiment analysis are exacerbated in the domain of visual arts. Artworks, in fact, are abstract forms of art that often do not make it easy to grasp the real intentions of the artist and may not have an easily identifiable subject. Furthermore, the uncertainty associated with individual subjectivity is influenced by familiarity with the style or genre of the artwork or by the historical context [1,8]. In other words, *artwork emotion classification* poses new and intriguing challenges, which open up even wider applications as digitized art collections are a source of historically relevant information.

With the rise of deep learning, recent studies on artwork emotion classification are based on computer vision methods that primarily focus only on visual features of the artworks (e.g., [16,26]). However, as already noted in some recent works [3,24], other media, such as text, can be considered effective for expressing and categorizing emotions and, combined with visual stimuli, can lead to even more powerful systems. With a similar intent, we are currently working on *ArtGraph*, an artist knowledge graph (KG), which collects not only digital images of artworks but also other social, historical, more generally "contextual" features—expressed as text or metadata—which allow us to frame artworks in a more complex framework [6]. In the present study, we integrate into *ArtGraph* the emotional labels of artworks provided by the recently published *ArtEmis* dataset [1]. Our aim is to investigate whether context features can help provide better accuracy in emotion classification beyond pure visual features, and whether information about emotions is beneficial for the more classic task of recognizing the style or genre of an artwork and vice versa. The final goal of this line of research is the development of an automatic method capable of showing a high-level understanding of visual arts. In this context, affective capabilities cannot be neglected in the construction of a system called to perceive art.

In summary, the contributions of this paper are the following:

- We propose an artistic KG, built on our previous one, which integrates visual, contextual and emotional information about artworks.
- We propose a new method, extending our previous work, which jointly exploits these information in a multi-modal multi-task way to carry out the task of emotion (and of style and genre) classification.
- We report the results of some experiments aimed at studying if and to what extent the joint exploitation of visual, contextual and emotional information is beneficial to the system.

The rest of this paper is structured as follows. Section 2 reviews related work. Section 3 describes the combination of *ArtGraph* and *ArtEmis*. Section 4 presents the proposed method for artwork emotion classification. Section 5 reports the experimental setting and the results obtained. Finally, Sect. 6 concludes the paper and describes future developments of our research.

2   Related Work

Before the advent of modern convolutional neural network architectures, early works on artwork emotion classification used only low-level features to associate artworks with human-annotated labels. For example, Machajdik et al. [17] evaluated a number of low-level features, including color, texture, composition and content, for classifying abstract paintings in terms of emotion categories. Similarly, Sartori [22] adopted color and texture features to classify abstract paintings into positive and negative emotion classes. To improve the correlation between low-level features and high-level emotions, Zhao et al. [27] proposed to extract features based on various artistic aspects, such as balance, emphasis, harmony, movement, rhythm, and so on.

However, these features alone cannot detect more complex aspects that occur in an artwork. To overcome this limitation, deep learning-based methods have begun to spread in visual sentiment analysis in recent years, as they provide an end-to-end feature learning alternative to manual feature design [16,20,28]. In [8], Cetinic et al. focused on three different levels of image perception: the aesthetic evaluation of the image; the sentiment evoked by the image; and its memorability. The authors used several CNN models trained to predict the aesthetic, sentiment and memorability scores of natural images and explored these features in artistic images. Based on the correlation between predicted scores and human judgments, they studied how predicted aesthetics, sentiment, and memorability scores relate to different art styles and genres.

More recently, in addition to studying image captioning models, Achlioptas et al. [1] tackled the problem of predicting the expected emotional distribution of the emotional reaction to an artwork. To do this, they developed a ResNet32, pre-trained on ImageNet, minimizing the KL divergence between its output and the *ArtEmis* empirical user distribution. Furthermore, they tried to solve the same task using sequence models based on textual descriptions of the artworks. The main finding was that fine-grained emotion prediction in *ArtEmis* is a difficult task and is simplified when considering a positive vs. negative binary classification. In [24], Tashu et al. proposed a multi-modal approach to artwork emotion recognition, based on co-attention, that aims to use the information coming from the digitized painting, the title and emotion category through a weighted fusion. They showed how multi-modality improves uni-modal models. Similarly, in [3], Bose et al. tried to predict the emotions evoked in viewers by artworks using both textual and visual modalities. The experiments were conducted on the *ArtEmis* dataset. These recent studies suggest that artwork emotion classification can benefit from multiple inputs, not just visual ones.

In the more general domain of computational analysis of visual arts, the recent trend is indeed that of exploiting different input modalities together. Specifically, we are following a stream of papers encoding several information available about artworks in knowledge graphs, which can enhance deep learning models in tasks such as artwork attribute prediction and information retrieval (e.g., [10,12]). The problem of predicting artwork attributes using only visual features is a very challenging one, and researchers felt the need to use contextual information, along with visual features, to boost performance. In this work, we integrate the emotional data provided by *ArtEmis* into our artistic KG [6].

3   Materials

In this section, we describe the original *ArtEmis* dataset and the results of integrating the information it provides into *ArtGraph*.

3.1   ArtEmis

ArtEmis [1] is a large-scale dataset that associates human emotions with artworks and contains explanations in natural language of the rationale behind each triggered emotion. The dataset was built on top of *WikiArt* and contains 80,031 unique artworks, from 1,119 artists, which cover 27 styles and 45 genres. The authors collected emotions by asking at least 5 annotators to express their dominant emotional reaction. Specifically, after observing an artwork, annotators were asked to indicate their dominant reaction by selecting among *anger, disgust, fear, sadness, amusement, awe, contentment, excitement* and *something-else*. Hence, this is the categorical emotional model proposed by Mikels et al. [18] enlarged with a *something-else* ninth category. In total, 454,684 emotional responses were collected. Annotators were also asked to provide a detailed explanation for their choice, but these data have not been used in our study.

3.2   *ArtGraph*

A knowledge graph is a graph of data intended to accumulate and convey knowledge of the real world: nodes represent entities of interest; edges represent relations between entities [15]. For this reason, KGs are increasingly used for many applications such as recommendations and question answering. A KG can be particularly useful in the artistic domain as information is typically unstructured: a single artwork, in fact, is characterized by multiple attributes, and artworks and artists can be linked by multiple relationships. *ArtGraph*, first introduced in [6], is a KG in the art domain capable of representing and describing many concepts related to artworks and artists. We built the graph based on the 300 most popular artists in *WikiArt*, and since this encyclopedia does not provided rich information about artists, we also exploited DBpedia to retrieve artist metadata. More details are available in [6]. *ArtGraph* is a work in progress and, compared to the original version presented in [6], the currently released version now includes more nodes and edges [5].

3.3   Combining *ArtEmis* and *ArtGraph*

We integrated the emotion labels provided by *ArtEmis* into *ArtGraph* by adding to each artwork a relationship with an "emotion" node, corresponding to the most recurrent dominant reaction among those annotated by the evaluators. Table 1 presents the contextual comparison between the version of *ArtGraph* publicly available in [5] and the extension developed in the present work, which includes the emotion attributes of *ArtEmis*. For this study, we considered only

Table 1. Comparison between *ArtGraph* and the version involving emotion nodes attached to artworks.

KG	# nodes	# edges	# artists	# artworks
ArtGraph	135,038	875,416	2501	116,475
ArtGraph + *ArtEmis*	83,834	625,938	2501	65,252

the artworks in common between the two datasets, enriching them with the information about emotions. The version of the graph that includes emotions will be made available in a future release. It is worth noting that integrating emotion information into *ArtGraph* is already beneficial to end-users as it allows for information retrieval and knowledge discovery on the graph, even without training a learning model. The user, in fact, can browse the graph, for example to search for artworks or artists through a dominant emotion.

4 Methods

To perform the task of artwork emotion classification, we propose a modification of the method we have already experimented with in [6] that exploits both visual and knowledge graph-embeddings. In particular, we propose a "context-aware" *multi-modal multi-task* classification model that aims to simultaneously classify the style and genre of a given artwork and, furthermore, its aroused emotion. The scheme of the proposed model is shown in Fig. 1.

First, three-channel artwork images are resized to 224×224 pixels and propagated through a ResNet50 [14] pre-trained on ImageNet and fine-tuned to our image dataset. We take the global averaged pooled features which result in a *visual embedding* $\mathbf{h}_v \in \mathbb{R}^{2048}$. In parallel, we obtain a knowledge graph embedding $\mathbf{h}_g \in \mathbb{R}^{128}$ for the artwork node in *ArtGraph* using the well-known TransE node embedding algorithm [2]. Unlike node2vec [13], where each node is mapped into a multidimensional space regardless of type and attributes, TransE works better on heterogeneous graphs like *ArtGraph*. An embedding algorithm should be able to capture the various types of edges, as different edges indicate different relations. In particular, in TransE, a relationship is a triple (h, l, t), where h is the head entity, l is the relation and t is the tail entity. Similar to node2vec, entities are embedded in an entity space; however, the main innovation of TransE is that each relation l is also embedded into a vector l.

Visual and contextual embeddings are combined by concatenation, $(\mathbf{h}_v, \mathbf{h}_g)$, and fed to a fully-connected head, one for each task (style, genre and emotion classification), with as many output units as there are classes to predict. At training time, the overall network is asked to minimize the following loss:

$$\mathcal{L} = \sum_{i=1}^{T} \sum_{j=1}^{C} \ell\left(\mathbf{z}_{ij}, class_{ij}\right),$$

where T is the number of tasks, i.e. three, C is the number of classes for each task, while ℓ is the classic cross-entropy loss function between the predicted

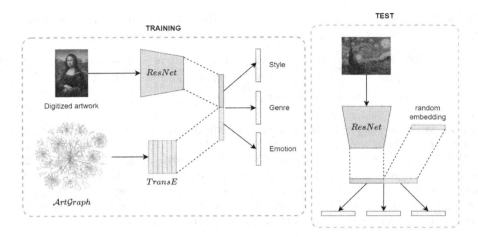

Fig. 1. Overview of the proposed classification method. The model works differently during training and testing. During training, both visual and graph embeddings are used for a given artwork to learn features to predict style, genre and emotion. At testing time, only visual features are used, but made "context-aware" during training.

output $\mathbf{z}_{ij}$ and the corresponding ground truth $class_{ij}$. This multi-task strategy allows the network to learn features that can be useful between tasks. Also, as the error is backpropagated to ResNet, the model learns a refinement of the visual embeddings that become more sensitive to contextual features [12].

At testing time, we assume that the context of the artwork just observed is not known, so the visual features are concatenated to randomly generated graph embeddings to still provide a prediction. Surprisingly, these "fake" features do not harm performance and allow the use of the model on artworks of which we only have information about pixels. This can be explained considering that the model tends to exclude the random embeddings and only use the visual embeddings that have been refined by the contextual information during training. Such a strategy is necessary, since extracting embeddings from a test graph implies that we inject knowledge about unobserved artworks into the model, leading to overly optimistic performance.

5   Experiments

In this Section, we describe the experimental setup and report and discuss the results obtained.

5.1   Setup

We implemented the proposed method in PyTorch and performed experiments on a system with i7-10700K CPU, NVIDIA RTX 3080 GPU, and 62.7 GB RAM. As baseline for comparing our method, we also experimented with:

- ResNet50 [14]: the backbone that we already used for visual feature extraction, fine-tuned to classify the emotion aroused by an artwork. This baseline was used to test whether any improvement was achieved using also contextual features versus using visual features alone.
- ContextNet [12]: the state-of-the-art method that learns to project visual features into the feature space of node2vec embeddings and does not concatenate them. We replicated the method on our KG and make it work with emotions.

It is worth noting that, for both ContextNet and our proposed method, we experimented with both node2vec and TransE to investigate whether and to what extent the choice of node embedding impacts performance. We have not compared our method with some recent work using graph neural networks (e.g., [10]), as they assume knowledge of graph topology at testing time. Instead, our goal was to test the effectiveness of the proposed method when a single novel artwork is "seen".

The overall data were split into 80% for training, 10% for validation and 10% for testing. For all three models, we used Adam as optimization algorithm, with a learning rate of 10^{-4}. The batch size was set to 64. All models were trained for 50 epochs, with an early stopping strategy on the validation set. As for the embeddings, for both node2vec and TransE we set their size to 128.

5.2   Results

Table 2 and 3 show the results obtained by the experimented methods in terms of classification accuracy when using a single- or multi-task learning strategy, i.e. optimizing the individual tasks separately or jointly. It is worth noting that, for the prediction of emotions, we performed both a multi-class classification, in which all labels were considered, and a simpler binary classification, in which emotions were grouped into positive or negative (the *something-else* label was considered positive). Additionally, for the multi-task experiment, we also measured accuracy for style and genre classification when optimized together, but without considering emotions.

First, we can see that using context features generally improves performance over using visual features alone. This confirms that attribute prediction methods benefit from the joint exploitation of visual and context features, as already noted in recent literature (e.g., [10,11]). Style and genre classification accuracy is improved by a large margin using context features, while emotion classification is only slightly improved. This indicates that the classification of style and genre benefits greatly from the knowledge encoded in the graph, while the classification of emotions is predominantly dominated by the visual features. Such a finding can corroborate the hypothesis that prior knowledge is less important than visual stimuli for the emotion the artwork evokes.

A second observation is that the proposed method is generally preferable to the state-of-the-art method, ContextNet, albeit with a slight margin. As also noted in our previous work [6], this indicates that we do a little better using the context features. For both ContextNet and the proposed method, however, there

Table 2. Single-task classification accuracy. The best results between this and the following table for each classification task are in bold.

Method	Style	Genre	Emotion (Multi-class)	Emotion (Binary)
ResNet50	41.40%	53.48%	43.78%	80.35%
ContextNet (node2vec)	60.57%	70.82%	43.97%	81.10%
ContextNet (TransE)	62.07%	69.57%	44.59%	81.20%
Proposed (node2vec)	61.59%	71.23%	43.53%	81.05%
Proposed (TransE)	**62.92%**	71.66%	43.35%	**81.57%**

Table 3. Multi-task classification accuracy. The tasks were jointly optimized with or without considering emotions. The best results between this and the preceding table for each classification task are in bold.

Method	No emotion		Emotion (Multi-class)			Emotion (Binary)		
	Style	Genre	Style	Genre	Emotion	Style	Genre	Emotion
ResNet50	42.09%	54.08%	41.91%	55.18%	40.78%	42.99%	55.85%	80.45%
ContextNet (node2vec)	61.06%	70.79%	60.49%	70.50%	44.89%	61.40%	71.01%	81.54%
ContextNet (TransE)	61.65%	71.98%	60.69%	70.95%	44.88%	60.91%	71.66%	81.25%
Proposed (node2vec)	61.62%	71.09%	62.35%	**72.26%**	44.88%	62.08%	70.98%	79.42%
Proposed (TransE)	61.80%	70.67%	61.45%	71.81%	**45.39%**	62.30%	71.44%	78.60%

Table 4. Comparison between the top-1 and top-2 accuracy of the proposed method with TransE for the multi-class emotion classification in the case of single- and multi-task learning.

Strategy	Top-1	Top-2
Single-task	43.35%	61.32%
Multi-task	45.39%	**63.27%**

is no predominant embedding technique between node2vec and TransE, even though 3 out of 4 best results were obtained using TransE. This was expected as TransE takes advantage of the heterogeneity of *ArtGraph*.

Regarding the comparison between single- and multi-task learning, we can observe that single-task learning is beneficial for style and binary emotion classification, while multi-task learning is beneficial for genre and multi-class emotion classification. This suggests that the prediction of genre and one of the multiple emotions improves if supported by features learned also for style; instead, predicting style and whether emotions are positive or negative does not benefit from such support. Finally, there is no agreement between the methods on whether or not emotions are useful in the multi-task strategy, even though the best results for the genre and multi-class emotion classification were obtained by predicting the three labels at the same time.

 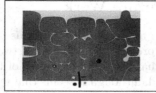 

Claude Monet
Predicted: *contentment*
Real: *contentment*

Victor Pasmore
Predicted: *something-else*
Real: *amusement*

Lev Lagorio
Predicted: *awe*
Real: *contentment*

Fig. 2. Examples of artworks and emotions predicted by the system. The emotion does not always correspond to the most common dominant reaction among the human evaluators, but it nevertheless corresponds to one of the other annotated ones.

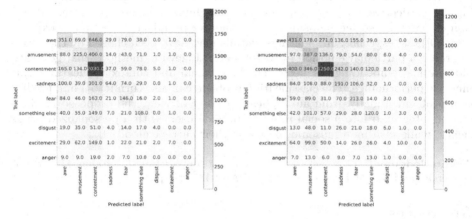

Fig. 3. Confusion matrices of the multi-class emotion classification with the original unbalanced training data (left) and when training data are more balanced (right).

Figure 2 shows examples of artworks and emotions predicted by the proposed method with TransE, which returned the best results for the multi-class emotion classification, showing competitive performance on style and genre. As we can see, the method is accurate in predicting the most recurring dominant emotion for some artworks, and when it fails, it still predicts one of the least recurring emotions as assessed by the annotators. This was expected as emotion labels are inherently subjective. This finding was also confirmed by computing the top-2 accuracy, as shown in Table 4.

Finally, as reported in [1], the emotion labels are highly unbalanced. In Fig. 3, we show the confusion matrices obtained by the method when trained on the original data, or when the majority classes, i.e. *contentment* and *awe*, are under-sampled. As we can see, performance improves slightly when these classes are under-sampled; however, in both cases the model makes confusion in predicting similar emotions, such as *contentment* and *awe* themselves, and in recognizing very rare classes such as *anger*.

6   Conclusion and Future Work

Classifying the emotion that an artwork could arouse in someone is a complex task. In this paper, we have proposed a model for artwork emotion classification that jointly exploits contextual and visual features of the artworks. The results obtained are encouraging and, although it seems that emotion categories depend mainly on visual features, there is an "entanglement" between style, genre and emotion that can be exploited for different applications in the automatic art analysis domain. On the other hand, affective capacities cannot be neglected in the construction of an automatic method which is asked to exhibit a high-level understanding of visual arts [7].

Many questions remain open. Using an unsupervised or semi-supervised learning approach can help better recognize emotion categories without relying on subjective and inherently conflicting human labels. Adopting attention or patch-based mechanisms may be another promising direction to explore (e.g., [9]), as, especially in paintings, details may have been chosen by the artist to arouse a particular emotion in the observer. Likewise, methods that generate more robust embeddings or better combine visual and contextual features can increase performance. The classification problem can also turn into a link prediction problem. Finally, from an application point of view, the proposed method can be integrated into a social robot to provide users with a personalized experience, while visiting a museum, based on their current mood [4].

Acknowledgment. G. V. acknowledges funding support from the Italian Ministry of University and Research through the PON AIM 1852414 project.

References

1. Achlioptas, P., Ovsjanikov, M., Haydarov, K., Elhoseiny, M., Guibas, L.J.: ArtEmis: affective language for visual art. In: Proceedings of the IEEE/CVF Conference on Computer Vision and Pattern Recognition, pp. 11569–11579 (2021)
2. Bordes, A., Usunier, N., Garcia-Duran, A., Weston, J., Yakhnenko, O.: Translating embeddings for modeling multi-relational data. In: Advances in Neural Information Processing Systems 26 (2013)
3. Bose, D., Somandepalli, K., Kundu, S., Lahiri, R., Gratch, J., Narayanan, S.: Understanding of emotion perception from art. arXiv preprint arXiv:2110.06486 (2021)
4. Castellano, G., De Carolis, B., Macchiarulo, N., Vessio, G.: Pepper4Museum: towards a human-like museum guide. In: AVI^{2}CH@ AVI (2020)
5. Castellano, G., Digeno, V., Sansaro, G., Vessio, G.: Leveraging knowledge graphs and deep learning for automatic art analysis. Knowl.-Based Syst. **248**, 108859 (2022). https://doi.org/10.1016/j.knosys.2022.108859. ISSN: 0950-7051
6. Castellano, G., Sansaro, G., Vessio, G.: Integrating contextual knowledge to visual features for fine art classification. In: Proceedings of the Workshop on Deep Learning for Knowledge Graphs (DL4KG 2021) (2021)
7. Castellano, G., Vessio, G.: Deep learning approaches to pattern extraction and recognition in paintings and drawings: an overview. Neural Comput. Appl. **33**(19), 12263–12282 (2021)

8. Cetinic, E., Lipic, T., Grgic, S.: A deep learning perspective on beauty, sentiment, and remembrance of art. IEEE Access **7**, 73694–73710 (2019)
9. David, L., Pedrini, H., Dias, Z., Rocha, A.: Connoisseur: provenance analysis in paintings. In: 2021 IEEE Symposium Series on Computational Intelligence (SSCI), pp. 1–8. IEEE (2021)
10. El Vaigh, C.B., Garcia, N., Renoust, B., Chu, C., Nakashima, Y., Nagahara, H.: GCNBoost: artwork classification by label propagation through a knowledge graph. In: Proceedings of the 2021 International Conference on Multimedia Retrieval, pp. 92–100 (2021)
11. Eyharabide, V., Bekkouch, I.E.I., Constantin, N.D.: Knowledge graph embedding-based domain adaptation for musical instrument recognition. Computers **10**(8), 94 (2021)
12. Garcia, N., Renoust, B., Nakashima, Y.: ContextNet: representation and exploration for painting classification and retrieval in context. Int. J. Multimedia Inf. Retrieval **9**(1), 17–30 (2019). https://doi.org/10.1007/s13735-019-00189-4
13. Grover, A., Leskovec, J.: node2vec: Scalable feature learning for networks. In: Proceedings of the 22nd ACM SIGKDD International Conference on Knowledge Discovery and Data Mining, pp. 855–864 (2016)
14. He, K., Zhang, X., Ren, S., Sun, J.: Deep residual learning for image recognition. In: Proceedings of the IEEE Conference on Computer Vision and Pattern Recognition, pp. 770–778 (2016)
15. Hogan, A., et al.: Knowledge graphs. Synth. Lect. Data Semant. Knowl. **12**(2), 1–257 (2021)
16. Li, L., Zhu, X., Hao, Y., Wang, S., Gao, X., Huang, Q.: A hierarchical CNN-RNN approach for visual emotion classification. ACM Trans. Multimedia Comput. Commun. Appl. (TOMM) **15**(3s), 1–17 (2019)
17. Machajdik, J., Hanbury, A.: Affective image classification using features inspired by psychology and art theory. In: Proceedings of the 18th ACM International Conference on Multimedia, pp. 83–92 (2010)
18. Mikels, J.A., Fredrickson, B.L., Larkin, G.R., Lindberg, C.M., Maglio, S.J., Reuter-Lorenz, P.A.: Emotional category data on images from the international affective picture system. Behav. Res. Methods **37**(4), 626–630 (2005). https://doi.org/10.3758/BF03192732
19. Pelowski, M., Specker, E., Gerger, G., Leder, H., Weingarden, L.S.: Do you feel like I do? A study of spontaneous and deliberate emotion sharing and understanding between artists and perceivers of installation art. Psychol. Aesthet. Creat. Arts **14**(3), 276 (2020)
20. Rao, T., Li, X., Xu, M.: Learning multi-level deep representations for image emotion classification. Neural Process. Lett. **51**(3), 2043–2061 (2020)
21. Rao, T., Li, X., Zhang, H., Xu, M.: Multi-level region-based convolutional neural network for image emotion classification. Neurocomputing **333**, 429–439 (2019)
22. Sartori, A.: Affective analysis of abstract paintings using statistical analysis and art theory. In: Proceedings of the 16th International Conference on Multimodal Interaction,. pp. 384–388 (2014)
23. Song, K., Yao, T., Ling, Q., Mei, T.: Boosting image sentiment analysis with visual attention. Neurocomputing **312**, 218–228 (2018)
24. Tashu, T.M., Hajiyeva, S., Horvath, T.: Multimodal emotion recognition from art using sequential co-attention. J. Imaging **7**(8), 157 (2021)
25. Tinio, P.P., Smith, J.K., Smith, L.F.: The walls do speak: psychological aesthetics and the museum experience. In: The Cambridge Handbook of the Psychology of Aesthetics and the Arts, pp. 195–218. Cambridge University Press (2015)

26. Yang, J., She, D., Lai, Y.K., Yang, M.H.: Retrieving and classifying affective images via deep metric learning. In: Proceedings of the AAAI Conference on Artificial Intelligence (2018)
27. Zhao, S., Gao, Y., Jiang, X., Yao, H., Chua, T.S., Sun, X.: Exploring principles-of-art features for image emotion recognition. In: Proceedings of the 22nd ACM International Conference on Multimedia, pp. 47–56 (2014)
28. Zhao, S., Zhao, X., Ding, G., Keutzer, K.: EmotionGAN: unsupervised domain adaptation for learning discrete probability distributions of image emotions. In: Proceedings of the 26th ACM International Conference on Multimedia, pp. 1319–1327 (2018)

Classification of Pottery Fragments Described by Concentration of Chemical Elements

Anna Maria Zanaboni[1]([✉])[iD], Dario Malchiodi[1,2][iD], Letizia Bonizzoni[3][iD], and Giulia Ruschioni[3][iD]

[1] Dipartimento di Informatica and DSRC, Università degli Studi di Milano, Milan, Italy
{annamaria.zanaboni,dario.malchiodi}@unimi.it
[2] CINI National Lab. on Artificial Intelligence and Intelligent Systems (AIIS), Roma, Italy
[3] Dipartimento di Fisica, Università degli Studi di Milano, Milan, Italy
letizia.bonizzoni@unimi.it, giulia.ruschioni@studenti.unimi.it

Abstract. In order to distinguish between archaeological pottery produced in the Etruscan city of Tarquinia and pottery produced in other coeval sites, we tested several supervised learning algorithms for classification. Pottery sherds were analised by X-ray fluorescence analysis and described in the dataset by the relative concentration of nine chemical elements. The dataset was unbalanced with about one fourth of negative samples, and contained repeated measures for each fragment; the number of repeated measures for each fragment ranged between two and seven. We carried out two types of experiments which differ in the way the repeated measures are exploited. The best performing models showed good performance, in terms of accuracy, sensibility and specificity.

Keywords: Machine learning · Classification · Ancient pottery

1 Introduction and Previous Work

Pottery sherds are the most abundant materials in archaeological excavations and are widely used to help in gathering knowledge of local furnace presence and commercial trades. The knowledge of the elemental chemical composition can be exploited to find out different geographical proveniences allowing to confirm the existence of fabric groups and supporting the hypothesis of a common origin for some fragments [4,11]. Clays can have a different composition within the same quarry and, on the other hand, be quite similar in different sites; for this reason, it is generally necessary to pay particular attention to minor and trace elements [6]. The classical approach in archeometric data analysis is to use unsupervised methods such as principal component analysis (PCA), hierarchical cluster analysis (HCA) and K-means clustering [8]. In particular, X-ray fluorescence (XRF) analysis coupled with unsupervised methods for data analysis has

P. L. Mazzeo et al. (Eds.): ICIAP 2022 Workshops, LNCS 13373, pp. 141–151, 2022.
https://doi.org/10.1007/978-3-031-13321-3_13

proved to be a useful tool to check for the presence of the same raw materials [10,12,14].

In [2] a wide set of supervised and unsupervised learning algorithms are considered for archaeometric data analysis. In [5] a robust methodology for classification of archaeological ceramic data described by elemental concentration is proposed, and experiments are carried out using k-nearest neighbors, learning vector quantization (LVQ) and decision trees. Machine learning algorithms for ancient pottery classification are also applied in [9,15].

We paid particular attention to the supervised classification methods: the aim of the present work was to verify the capability of supervised learning algorithms for the classification of ceramic samples described by chemical element concentrations.

The second section of the present paper is devoted to the description of data and how they were collected, followed by the statistical analysis of the dataset in the third section; in the fourth section we describe the learning scheme we used for the experiments, while results are illustrated in the fifth section. A brief discussion and some directions for future work can be found in the last section.

2   Data Collection

We considered 27 fragments of Etruscan *depurata* and *bucchero*[1] pottery, from the archaeological excavation at *Pian della Civita* in Tarquinia (Italy), dating from the VIII to the IV century B.C., classified as local production. For the class of non-local production we considered six fragments of black varnish fine pottery coming from the Greek colony of Velia, dating the same period, and three samples of non-local origin, even if no hypothesis on their provenance were made. The archaeological classification of the selected fragments has already been verified through chemical methods [3,7]. Due to the intrinsically inhomogeneous nature of ancient ceramics, more than one measure was considered for each fragment (from 2 to 7 depending on the dimension and conservation state of the fragment). Element concentrations were obtained through non-destructive quantitative XRF (X-Ray Fluorescence) analysis exploiting a portable spectrometer and making chemical analyses possible even when sample taking from the sherds is forbidden.

We considered nine elements, namely potassium (K), calcium (Ca), titanium (Ti), chromium (Cr), manganese (Mn), iron (Fe), zinc (Zn), rubidium (Rb), strontium (Sr), for which weight concentration was performed using a computational method (Lithos 3000 software) based on the fundamental parameters [3]. The chosen elements are those for which signals in the spectra allowed to perform reliable quantitative calculation. It is worth noting that XRF does not detect low atomic number (Z) elements; in particular, the spectrometer used for this work does not detect elements with Z below 18 (argon), most of all if they are present in low concentration.

---

[1] *Depurata* pottery and *Bucchero* are classes of Etruscan ceramics, characterized by a bulk without microscopically visible inclusions.

Quantitative analysis has been performed using a computational method based on the fundamental parameters, and considering the intensity ratio of the scattered peaks (namely, Compton and Rayleigh signals) to get information on effective absorption coefficient of low elements' matrix [3]. The concentrations obtained have been normalized to 100% to eliminate the differences among samples due to different silicate presence or firing temperatures, which could induce a different weight loss also in samples with similar raw materials. This procedure is particularly advisable whenever samples contain indefinite amounts of extraneous material [1] such as temper in archaeological ceramics.

3   Statistical Analysis

Our dataset consisted of 112 samples: 81 (72.3%) labelled as local production (the Tarquinia group) and 31 (27.7%) labelled as non-local production (the non-Tarquinia group). Different samples in the dataset could correspond to different measures for the same fragment: in the dataset we had 27 (75%) different fragments belonging to the Tarquinia group and 9 (25%) fragments belonging to the non-Tarquinia group.

Samples were described by the relative concentration of the nine elements K, Ca, Ti, Cr, Mn, Fe, Zn, Rb, Sr, as already mentioned in Sect. 2. We compared the two groups according to the Student's t test (for normal variables) or the Mann-Whitney U test (for non-normal variables), and normality was tested by the Shapiro-Wilk test ; in particular, Ca, Ti and Cr had a normal distribution both in the local and non local production groups. Figure 1 shows the boxplots of the chemical elements describing our data. Elements K, Ca and Fe have higher and widespread concentrations, while the other elements have a smaller concentration with a smaller range. As Table 1 shows, all the elements, except Sr, are statistically different in the two groups. In particular, objects coming from Tarquinia have a higher concentration of Ca than the samples from the other group, and this reflects the well known characteristic of Tarquinia raw material, rich in illitic-kaolinitic clays (all containing Ca), mostly if compared to surroundings Etruscan sites.

4   Learning Scheme

We learned from data the following models for classification, considering the implementations of the corresponding supervised learning algorithms provided by scikit-learn [13]: logistic regression (LR), linear discriminant analysis (LDA), support vector machines (SVM, focusing on their linear version as well as on the nonlinear implementations relying on polynomial and RBF kernels), binary decision trees (DT), random forests (RF), naive Bayes (NB) and k-nearest neighbors (KNN). For each of them, in order to find the best performing model

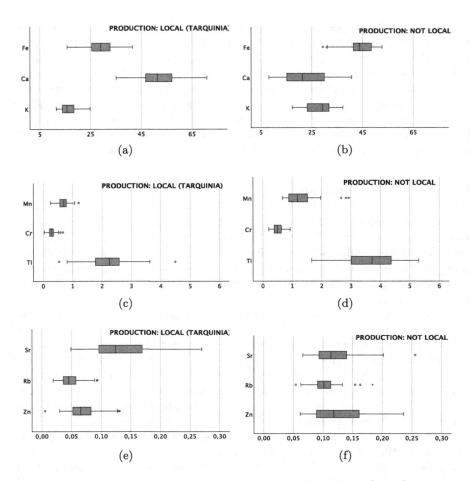

Fig. 1. Boxplots of chemical elements in the two groups: first column (a, c, e): Tarquinia local production pottery, second column (b, d, f) non local production pottery

and assess its generalization ability, we applied a nested k-fold cross-validation scheme (4 external and 3 internal folds), stratified over the two classes of local and non local production. In the inner cross-validation a grid search was devoted to the tuning of model hyper-parameters, while the outer cross-validation was used to assess generalization ability. The metric used for model selection was accuracy. The hyperparameters we considered for model selection and the corresponding grid values are listed in Table 2. In particular, for linear discriminant analysis we tried different solvers; for k-nearest neighbors we decided to consider at most eight neighbours, given the small number of negative examples in the dataset. We did not perform any model selection for Naive Bayes classification, using the default implementation in scikit-learn.

Table 1. Central position and dispersion values of elements in the two groups (T = Tarquinia, NT = non-Tarquinia, σ and IQR denote the standard deviation and interquartile range, respectively)

Element	Mean or median		p-value	σ or IQR	
	T	NT		T	NT
K	15.70	29.28	<0.001	4.72	5.59
Ca	52.13	22.69	<0.001	8.33	9.03
Ti	2.25	3.65	<0.001	0.68	0.96
Cr	0.29	0.53	<0.001	0.11	0.20
Mn	0.71	1.18	<0.001	0.23	0.69
Fe	29.08	43.73	<0.001	7.42	7.89
Zn	0.07	0.12	<0.001	0.03	0.07
Rb	0.05	0.10	<0.001	0.02	0.02
Sr	0.12	0.11	0.2	0.07	0.05

Performance for models comparison was evaluated by accuracy and, since the dataset was unbalanced, also specificity, sensibility and F1 score were considered.

Our data were already normalized between 0 and 1 and, as described in Sect. 4, the available descriptors had a different behaviour in the two groups; however we also considered the application of other scalers and some dimensionality reduction techniques, since pilot experiments showed that some combinations performed better than using just the raw data. So the learning pipeline started with two preprocessing steps, respectively related to scaling and dimensionality reduction. Both steps were included in the model selection phase; also in this case we relied on the implementations provided by scikit-learn, considering:

- for scaling: no processing, mean- and median-based standardization, normalization in the [0, 1] range, and quantile-based transformation onto the uniform distribution;
- for dimensionality reduction: no processing, PCA and truncated SVD (considering all possible values for the selected components, starting from 2).

Table 2. Model hyperparameters and grid values. For the sake of brevity, the column **Hyperparameters** shows the names used by scikit-learn.

Model	Hyperparameters	Grid values
LDA	solver	$\{svd, lsqr, eigen\}$
SVM	C	$logspace(-4, 3, 10)$ [a]
	kernel	$\{linear, polynomial, gaussian\}$ [b]
DT	criterion	$\{Gini\ index, entropy\}$
	max_features	$\{n, \sqrt{n}\}$ [c]
	max_depth	$range(2, 10) \cup \{\infty\}$
	min_samples_split	$range(2, 6)$
	min_samples_leaf	$range(2, 6)$
	ccp_alpha	$\{0, 0.5, 1, 1.5\}$
Same hyperparameters of DT +		
RF	n_estimators	$\{3, 5, 7, 9\}$
KNN	n_neighbors	$range(1, 8)$
	p	$range(2, 4)$
LR	penalty	$\{L1\ regularization, L2\ regularization\}$
	C	$logspace(-4, 3, 10)$

[a]in the table, $range(a, b)$ denotes the set of all integers from a (included) to b (excluded), while $logspace(a, b, n)$ denotes the set of n values evenly spaced between 10^a and 10^b on a logarithmic scale.
[b]the degree p of the polynomial kernel was selected in $\{2, 3, 5, 9\}$, while the parameter γ of the RBF kernel was selected in $logspace(-4, 3, 10)$, also allowing the predefined settings *auto* and *scale* of scikit-learn.
[c]n denotes the total number of features.

5   Experiments and Results

Since our dataset contained repeated measures for the same fragment, in some cases data points were not independent. For this reason we run two different types of experiments. In the first set we used the complete dataset as if all data were independent; this simple way of using data is affected by a bias and the learning process can easily lead to overfitting. In the other set of experiments we used data taking into account that some data points were not independent. As expected, in the latter set of experiments all the learning algorithms were less performing, but more reliable.

Type 1 Experiments. In these experiments stratification and subdivision in folds were run over the entire dataset, so that all the different measures of the same fragments contributed individually to the process.

For each learning algorithm, the hyperparameter configuration of the best performing model is shown in Table 3, while the performance of models on the test set is shown in Table 4.

Eight of the nine selected models showed an accuracy higher than 0.95, while the accuracy of support vector machines with a polynomial kernel was 0.93. All models performed well on the positive class (sensibility higher than 0.97). The same eight models with higher accuracy performed well on the negative class (specificity higher than 0.8), while specificity was acceptable (higher than 0.7) in the case of support vector machines with a polynomial kernel. Accuracy results were very good, but, due to the presence of repeated measures, we cannot exclude that some overfitting took place. Moreover, some measures of one fragment could fall in the training set while other measures of the same fragment could fall in the test set, so, in some sense, test set and training set where not "perfectly" disjoint.

Table 3. Characterisation of the best performing models found for each considered learning algorithm in type 1 experiments

Model	Best parameters
LR	StandardScaler + PCA($n = 2$)
	$C = 0.13$, max_iter: 5000, penalty: l2, solver: liblinear
DT	MinMaxScaler + PCA($n = 2$)
	ccp_alpha: 0, criterion: gini, max_depth: None, max_features: None
	max_leaf_nodes: 2, min_samples_leaf: 2, min_samples_split: 2
RF	MinMaxScaler + PCA($n = 2$), n_estimators: 3, ccp_alpha: 0
	criterion: gini, max_depth: None, max_features: None
	max_leaf_nodes: 2, min_samples_leaf: 2, min_samples_split: 2
SVM-rbf	RobustScaler + PCA($n = 2$, $C = 0.77$, gamma: scale
SVM-lin	MinMaxScaler + PCA($n = 2$), $C = 4.64$
NB	MinMaxScaler + PCA($n = 2$)
LDA	MinMaxScaler + TruncatedSVD($n = 3$), solver: svd
KNN	MinMaxScaler + TruncatedSVD($n = 2$), n_neighbors: 1, p: 2
SVM-poly	MinMaxScaler + TruncatedSVD($n = 3$), $C = 27.83$ degree: 2

Type 2 Experiments. In these experiments stratification and k-folds determination was done on the set of fragments rather than on measures. In particular, in the stratification process each fragment was considered just one time, and the fold containing the fragment contained all its available measures. This procedure introduces a little impurity in the learning mechanism, since now folds may have slightly different sizes, due to the fact that not all the fragments are represented by the same number of measures in the dataset.

However, we think that this experimental setting is still more worth than type 1 setting, because stratification is done over fragments and not over measures[2].

Table 4. Performances of the best performing model found for each considered learning algorithm in type 1 experiments, sorted by non-increasing accuracy

Model	Accuracy	Sensibility	Specificity	F1 score
LR	0.991 ± 0.015	0.988 ± 0.021	1.000 ± 0.000	0.994 ± 0.011
DT	0.982 ± 0.031	1.000 ± 0.000	0.929 ± 0.124	0.989 ± 0.020
RF	0.982 ± 0.031	1.000 ± 0.000	0.929 ± 0.124	0.989 ± 0.020
SVM-rbf	0.973 ± 0.030	0.988 ± 0.021	0.938 ± 0.108	0.982 ± 0.020
SVM-lin	0.964 ± 0.025	0.988 ± 0.021	0.906 ± 0.104	0.976 ± 0.017
NB	0.964 ± 0.025	1.000 ± 0.000	0.866 ± 0.101	0.976 ± 0.016
LDA	0.955 ± 0.030	1.000 ± 0.000	0.835 ± 0.112	0.971 ± 0.019
KNN	0.955 ± 0.059	0.988 ± 0.021	0.875 ± 0.217	0.971 ± 0.037
SVM-poly	0.929 ± 0.067	1.000 ± 0.000	0.741 ± 0.234	0.955 ± 0.041

For each learning algorithm the hyperparameter configuration of the best performing model is shown in Table 5, while model performance on the test set is shown in Table 6. Accuracy was higher than 0.93 for all the selected models, sensibility maintained high values (over 0.9), and specificity improved with respect to type 1 experiments, maintaining values over 0.7. In general, this set of experiments highly non linear models perform better. It can be noted that, even for best models, specificity showed lower values and higher dispersion than sensibility. The min-max scaler was the best choice for the majority of models and the choice of two principal components was in most cases the preferable way of transforming or selecting features.

---

[2] We also considered a variation of this experiment in which stratification was followed by a subsampling of the available measures, so as to ensure that each fold had approximately the same length. However, given the significantly high variance of the number of measures for the various fragments, we would have obtained folds with a very small number of negative cases, with a detrimental effect on the robustness of the estimate for model generalization ability.

Table 5. Characterisation of the best performing model found for each considered learning algorithm in type 2 experiments

Model	Best parameters
SVM-rbf	MinMaxScaler + TruncatedSVD($n = 2$), $C = 4.64$, gamma: 27.83
NB	MinMaxScaler + TruncatedSVD($n = 5$)
KNN	MinMaxScaler +TruncatedSVD($n = 2$), n_neighbors: 2, p: 2
DT	MinMaxScaler + PCA($n = 2$) ccp_alpha: 0, criterion: gini, max_depth: None, max_features: None max_leaf_nodes: 2, min_samples_leaf: 2, min_samples_split: 2
RF	MinMaxScaler + PCA($n = 2$), n_estimators: 3, ccp_alpha: 0 criterion: gini, max_depth: None, max_features: None max_leaf_nodes: 2, min_samples_leaf: 2, min_samples_split: 2
LR	MinMaxScaler + PCA($n = 2$) $C = 4.64$, max_iter: 5000, penalty: l1, solver: liblinear
SVM-poly	MinMaxScaler + TruncatedSVD($n = 2$), $C = 0.77$, degree: 3
SVM-lin	QuantileTransformer(n_quantiles=20) + PCA($n = 7$), $C = 0.77$
LDA	QuantileTransformer(n_quantiles=20) + TruncatedSVD($n = 6$), solver: svd

Table 6. Performances of the best performing model found for each considered learning algorithm in type 2 experiments

Model	Accuracy	Sensibility	Specificity	F1 score
SVM-rbf	0.985 ± 0.015	1.000 ± 0.000	0.951 ± 0.053	0.989 ± 0.012
NB	0.981 ± 0.020	0.986 ± 0.024	0.982 ± 0.031	0.986 ± 0.014
KNN	0.981 ± 0.020	0.986 ± 0.024	0.982 ± 0.031	0.986 ± 0.014
DT	0.977 ± 0.039	1.000 ± 0.000	0.875 ± 0.217	0.987 ± 0.023
RF	0.977 ± 0.039	1.000 ± 0.000	0.875 ± 0.217	0.987 ± 0.023
LR	0.977 ± 0.039	1.000 ± 0.000	0.875 ± 0.217	0.987 ± 0.023
SVM-poly	0.958 ± 0.056	0.986 ± 0.024	0.857 ± 0.208	0.973 ± 0.033
SVM-lin	0.943 ± 0.038	0.947 ± 0.064	0.906 ± 0.162	0.957 ± 0.032
LDA	0.932 ± 0.101	1.000 ± 0.000	0.732 ± 0.424	0.959 ± 0.057

6 Conclusions and Future Work

We applied several supervised learning algorithms to the problem of distinguishing pottery fragments produced locally in the site of Tarquinia from pottery fragments produced elsewhere. The pottery fragments were analyzed by chemical techniques and were described in the data set by the relative concentration of nine chemical elements. A simple statistical analysis of elemental concentration showed that the two classes were quite well distinct, so we could conclude that the selected nine chemical elements constitute a good set of features for representing this kind of data. As a consequence, most of the produced models showed a good performance, both in terms of accuracy and sensitivity. Specificity was less satisfactory, and this is due to the fact that the class of non local production contained fragments coming from different sites and was less characterized than the Tarquinia class.

Since the available dataset contained repeated measures for the same fragment, we defined two different experiment settings, in order to take into account (for stratification) distinct fragments rather than distinct measures; in fact the presence of distinct measures for the same fragment violates the data points independence requirement.

We are however aware of some limitations of the work, especially due to the fact that, in the available dataset, fragments produced outside Tarquinia consisted of elements coming from various sites, therefore it is somehow misleading to speak of the non-Tarquinia class; the corresponding examples rather represent an external environment to the class we were interested in. In other words, our classification problem was less similar to the problem of, say, distinguishing between red and blue, but it was more similar to the problem of recognizing if the color is, for example, red. For this reason, the next step will be to investigate the performance of one-class classification models, aiming at just recognizing one class rather than distinguishing between two classes. It is worth noting that this aspect is typical of the archaeological findings and reflects a real archaeological question. For this reason, the present work is of great interest for that field of application despite its limitations.

We also intend to compare classifications obtained with supervised learning to clustering results, since the final target of the project is to build a robust decision support system for the classification of objects whose labels are actually unknown.

Acknowledgements. Part of this work was done while D. Malchiodi was visiting scientist at Inria Sophia-Antipolis/I3S CNRS Université Côte d'Azur (France).

References

1. Aruga, R.: Closure of analytical chemical data and multivariate classification. Talanta **47**(4), 1053–1061 (1998). https://doi.org/10.1016/S0039-9140(98)00126-X
2. Baxter, M.J.: A review of supervised and unsupervised pattern recognition in archaeometry. Archaeometry **48**(4), 671–694 (2006). https://doi.org/10.1111/j.1475-4754.2006.00280.x
3. Bonizzoni, L., Galli, A., Milazzo, M.: XRF analysis without sampling of Etruscan depurata pottery for provenance classification. X-Ray Spectrom. **39**(5), 346–352 (2010). https://doi.org/10.1002/xrs.1263
4. Bruno, P., Caselli, M., Curri, M., Genga, A., Striccoli, R., Traini, A.: Chemical characterisation of ancient pottery from south of Italy by inductively coupled plasma atomic emission spectroscopy (ICP-AES): statistical multivariate analysis of data. Analytica chimica acta **410**(1–2), 193–202 (2000). https://doi.org/10.1016/S0003-2670(00)00734-0

5. Charalambous, E., Dikomitou-Eliadou, M., Milis, G.M., Mitsis, G., Eliades, D.G.: An experimental design for the classification of archaeological ceramic data from Cyprus, and the tracing of inter-class relationships. J. Arch. Sci. Rep. **7**, 465–471 (2016). https://doi.org/10.1016/j.jasrep.2015.08.010

6. Ciliberto, E., Spoto, G. (eds.): Modern Analytical Methods in Art and Archaeology, Chemical Analysis, vol. 155. Wiley, Hoboken (2000)

7. Fermo, P., Cariati, F., Ballabio, D., Consonni, V., Bagnasco Gianni, G.: Classification of ancient Etruscan ceramics using statistical multivariate analysis of data. Appl. Phys. A **79**(2), 299–307 (2004). https://doi.org/10.1007/s00339-004-2520-6

8. Fermo, P., Delnevo, E., Lasagni, M., Polla, S., de Vos, M.: Application of chemical and chemometric analytical techniques to the study of ancient ceramics from Dougga (Tunisia). Microchem. J. **88**(2), 150–159 (2008). https://doi.org/10.1016/j.microc.2007.11.012

9. Hazenfratz, R., Munita, C.S., Neves, E.G.: Neural Networks (SOM) applied to INAA data of chemical elements in archaeological ceramics from central amazon. STAR Sci. Technol. Archaeol. Res. **3**(2), 334–340 (2017). https://doi.org/10.1080/20548923.2018.1470218

10. Idjouadiene, L., Mostefaoui, T.A., Djermoune, H., Bonizzoni, L.: Application of X-ray fluorescence spectroscopy to provenance studies of Algerian archaeological pottery. X-Ray Spectrom. **48**(5), 505–512 (2019). https://doi.org/10.1002/xrs.3020

11. Jones, R.E.: Greek and Cypriot Pottery: A Review of Scientific Studies, vol. 1. British School at Athens (1986)

12. Padilla, R., Van Espen, P., Torres, P.G.: The suitability of XRF analysis for compositional classification of archaeological ceramic fabric: a comparison with a previous NAA study. Analytica Chimica Acta **558**(1–2), 283–289 (2006)

13. Pedregosa, F., et al.: Scikit-learn: machine learning in python. J. Mach. Learn. Res. **12**, 2825–2830 (2011). https://jmlr.csail.mit.edu/papers/v12/pedregosa11a.html

14. Romano, F., Pappalardo, G., Pappalardo, L., Garraffo, S., Gigli, R., Pautasso, A.: Quantitative non-destructive determination of trace elements in archaeological pottery using a portable beam stability-controlled XRF spectrometer. X-Ray Spectrom. Int. J. **35**(1), 1–7 (2006). https://doi.org/10.1002/xrs.880

15. Sun, H., Liu, M., Li, L., Yan, L., Zhou, Y., Feng, X.: A new classification method of ancient Chinese ceramics based on machine learning and component analysis. Ceram. Int. **46**(6), 8104–8110 (2020). https://doi.org/10.1016/j.ceramint.2019.12.037

Blind Deblurring of Hyperspectral Document Images

Marina Ljubenović[1]([✉]) [iD], Paolo Guzzonato[1,2] [iD], Giulia Franceschin[1] [iD],
and Arianna Traviglia[1] [iD]

[1] Center for Cultural Heritage Technology, Istituto Italiano di Tecnologia,
Venice, Italy
{marina.ljubenovic,paolo.guzzonato,giulia.franceschin,
arianna.taviglia}@iit.it
[2] Ca'Foscari University of Venice, Venice, Italy

Abstract. Most computer vision and machine learning-based approaches for historical document analysis are tailored to grayscale or RGB images and thus, mostly exploit their spatial information. Multispectral (MS) and hyperspectral (HS) images contain, next to the spatial information, a much richer spectral information than RGB images (usually spreading beyond the visible spectral range) that can facilitate more effective feature extraction, more accurate classification and recognition, and thus, improved analysis. Although utilization of a rich spectral information can improve historical document analysis tremendously, there are still some potential limitations of HS imagery such as camera induced noise and blur that require a carefully designed preprocessing step. Here, we propose a novel blind HS image deblurring method tailored to document images. We exploit a low-rank property of HS images (i.e., by projecting a HS image to a lower dimensional subspace) and utilize a text tailor image prior to performing a PSF estimation and deblurring of subspace components. The preliminary results show that the proposed approach gives good results over all spectral bands, removing successfully image artefacts introduced by blur and noise and significantly increasing the number of bands that can be used in further analysis.

Keywords: Document images · Hyperspectral image processing · Deblurring

1 Introduction

Automatic historical document analysis includes machine learning, computer vision, and pattern recognition based approaches for converting document images into a form that is easier for further manipulation (e.g., storage, systematic evaluation, information retrieval, and forensic analysis). Some of the common

This project has received funding from the European Union's Horizon 2020 research and innovation programme under grant agreement No. 101026453.

tasks in historical document analysis include layout analysis [1], optical character recognition [6,11], automatic transcription and translation [3], and information retrieval [7]. Most computer vision and machine learning-based approaches are tailored to grayscale or RGB images and thus, mostly exploit their spatial information (i.e., locations of the pixels in the spatial domain). Multispectral (MS) and hyperspectral (HS) images contain, next to the spatial information, much richer spectral information than RGB images (usually going beyond the visible spectral range). This information can further improve image analysis by facilitating more effective feature extraction and more accurate classification and recognition.

HS images are usually represented in a form of a 3-dimensional (3D) data cube, where 2D spectral bands corresponding to different wavelengths are stacked together along the spectral axis. These images are most commonly used in remote sensing applications [5]. In recent years, closed range HS images gain popularity in other computer vision applications in agriculture [20], chemistry [10], and cultural heritage [21]. HS imagery has been applied to tackle different problems in historical document analysis such as material identification and inks characterization [25], and removal of ageing-related artefacts (e.g., foxing and ink bleeding) [9]. It is shown in the literature that some materials used for the preparation of ancient documents (i.e., inks, supports, and bindings) have a unique fingerprint in the hyperspectral domain [4]. This fact can be utilized for material identification and digital source separation (e.g., separation of foxing artefacts or stains from inks) and ameliorate further image processing and analysis. Although utilization of rich spectral information can improve historical document analysis tremendously, there are still some potential limitations of HS imagery, such as camera induced noise and blur, that require a carefully designed preprocessing step.

Over years, many HS image restoration approaches were proposed, mostly tailored to MS and HS remote sensing images [19,28], where the low spatial resolution represents a major limitation for further data processing and analysis (e.g., satellite images usually have a spatial resolution of more than 10×10 m per pixel). For document image processing, where HS images are taken in the close range, image degradation induced by a camera, light conditions, and acquisition settings can corrupt all or only some spectral bands, making them unusable. These image degradation are often unavoidable and thus, prior denoising and deblurring represent a necessary preprocessing step for HS document image analysis.

To remove noise from HS images, the majority of state-of-the-art methods exploit characteristics of the HS data in the spectral domain such as a low-rank representation [28]. The low-rank assumption is widely utilized for other tasks such as spectral unmixing [27], classification [13], and super-resolution [12]. These tasks are commonly coupled with HS image deblurring where the point-spread function (PSF) of the imaging system is considered to be known and constant over bands. Additionally, remote sensing methods are designed for natural images, thus utilizing priors adjusted to these types of images. It is shown in the literature that images containing text follow different statistics compared to natural images (e.g., often contain only two colours and sharp transitions) and thus, require carefully designed or learned image priors [15, 24]. To learn an image prior, methods based on Gaussian mixture models [17] and specially designed dictionaries [16] have been proposed. These methods, tailored to RGB document images, do not exploit the high correlation between spectral bands: they can be applied to each band separately, leading to a higher sensitivity to the presence of noise and a time-consuming restoration process. Methods based on neural networks are also exploited in the past for text deblurring [8]. These methods, although providing good results on noiseless RGB images, are sensitive to even a small amount of noise (commonly present in bands of HS images corresponding to blue and near-infrared spectral regions).

Other remote sensing approaches, focused solely on deblurring, exploit different dimensionality reduction methods (e.g., *principal component analysis* [14] or *singular value decomposition* (SVD) [18]) to tackle blur present in HS images. Dimensionality reduction (i.e., projection of higher dimensional data to a lower-dimensional subspace) is a powerful tool as it allows for better differentiation between different spectral features. Additionally, by projecting data to a lower-dimensional subspace, useful information is usually preserved and noise reduced. Dimensionality reduction approaches are successfully used for the identification of endmembers (i.e., pure materials) in HS remote sensing data [23]. In document images, the number of endmembers is often limited (e.g., a document usually contains three materials: ink, support, and binding). Also, document HS images are particularly sensitive to poor light settings during acquisition which can introduce additional artefacts (e.g., shades).

Here, we propose a novel blind HS image deblurring method tailored to document images. We exploit a low-rank property of HS images and utilize a text tailor image prior to performing a PSF estimation and deblurring of subspace components. Specially designed samples containing lab-created and commercial inks on a printing paper are used to evaluate the performance of the proposed approach.

2   Proposed Method

Assuming additive noise, hyperspectral image deblurring is modelled as

$$\mathbf{Y} = \mathbf{HX} + \mathbf{N}, \tag{1}$$

where $\mathbf{Y} \in \mathbb{R}^{b \times n}$ and $\mathbf{X} \in \mathbb{R}^{b \times n}$ represent an observed and an underlying hyperspectral images, respectively, with the rows containing b spectral bands. Every band is a vectorized image containing n pixels. $\mathbf{H}$ and $\mathbf{N} \in \mathbb{R}^{b \times n}$ represent a blurring matrix and a Gaussian independent and identically distributed (i.i.d.) noise, respectively. Blurring matrix has the block-circulant-circulant-block (BCCB) form, where each block depict the cyclic convolution associated with a camera point spread function (PSF).

The spectral vectors $\mathbf{x}_i$, for $i = 1, ..., n$, live in a lower-dimensional subspace $\mathcal{S}_k$, where the number of dimensions $k \ll b$ [28] and thus, the underlying image $\mathbf{X}$ can be represented as

$$\mathbf{X} = \mathbf{EZ}, \tag{2}$$

where $\mathbf{E} = [\mathbf{e}_1, ..., \mathbf{e}_k] \in \mathbb{R}^{b \times k}$ stands for the subspace bases and $\mathbf{Z} \in \mathbb{R}^{k \times n}$ holds the representation coefficients of $\mathbf{X}$ in $\mathcal{S}_k$.

In the proposed method, we start by projecting the observed HS image to a lower dimension subspace by applying a state-of-the-art dimensionality reduction method (HySime) [22]. Then, we perform blind deblurring on each subspace component separately by using a text tailored image prior.

To estimate each sharp subspace component and blurring operator corresponding to that component, we solve the following optimization problem

$$\hat{\mathbf{z}}_i, \hat{\mathbf{h}}_i \in \underset{\mathbf{z}_i, \mathbf{h}_i}{\operatorname{argmin}} \frac{1}{2} ||\mathbf{y}_i - \mathbf{H}_i \mathbf{E} \mathbf{z}_i||_2^2 + \lambda \Phi(\mathbf{z}_i) + \gamma ||\mathbf{h}_i||_2^2, \tag{3}$$

where Φ represents a prior knowledge imposed to the underlying sharp image and λ and γ are regularization parameters that control a trade off between the data fidelity term and priors, respectively.

Following the formulation from [24], the image prior imposed on subspace components is formulated as a sum of two so-called l_0-norms on image intensities and gradients with the following form

$$\Phi(\mathbf{z}_i) = \alpha ||\mathbf{z}_i||_0 + ||\nabla \mathbf{z}_i||_0, \tag{4}$$

with α controlling the contribution of each component.

To solve the optimization problem from (3), we first fix the image $\mathbf{z}_i$ and estimate the blurring operator (by solving the least square minimisation). When blurring operator estimate is obtained, we apply a half-quadratic splitting optimization approach to obtain the sharp image (for more details about the optimization procedure, take a look at [26] and references therein).

3   Experiments

To test the proposed HS image deblurring method, we created several samples by using lab-created and commercial inks and a printing paper.

Lab-created inks. Five iron gall inks were prepared with simplified recipes based on the Madrid ink of Díaz Hidalgo *et al.* [2]. Inks have different gall:FeSO4 weight ratio, namely 1:1 for the first ink (Fig. 1(a), ink 01), 3:2 for the second ink (02), and 2:1 for the others (03, 04, and 05). For inks 01 to 03 iron sulfate was added to a solution obtained macerating galls powder in water for a week. For the ink 04 iron sulfate was grounded with the galls and macerated in water for a week. Ink 05 is akin to ink 03, but with the process shortened to one day. All the inks were filtered and contain the same amount of Arabic gum and water.

Galls (Q. infectoria), iron(II) sulfate heptahydrate, and Arabic gum powder (A. senegal) were purchased from Kremer.

Commercial inks. Commercial iron based inks (H_A, S_A, S_X) and copper based ink (S_V) were used as references. The commercial inks are: 1) Jacques Herbin Encre Authentique (H_A), 2) Roher & Klinger Schreibtinte Eisen-Gall-Tinte Scabiosa (S_A), 3) Roher & Klinger Schreibtinte Eisen-Gall-Tinte Salix (S_X), 4) Roher & Klinger Verdigris (S_V).

Samples of ink on (80 g/m^2) printing paper were written using steel and glass nibs. Inks spots were made with 10 μl spread and unspread drops.

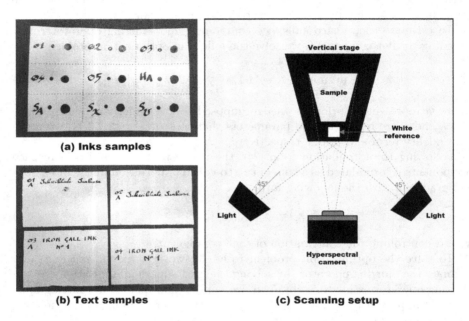

(a) Inks samples

(b) Text samples   (c) Scanning setup

Fig. 1. (a) Samples of different commercial and lab-created inks; (b) samples of text written with these inks; and (c) an illustration of the acquisition setup with a HS camera and two led lamps. (Color figure online)

The HS images are obtained by a hyperspectral camera based on time-domain Fourier Transform detection (NIREOS HERA Iperspettrale VIS-NIR). The camera has a spectral range from 400 to 1000 nm nm and the spatial resolutions 1280 × 1024 pixels. The camera was placed around 1.5 m from the sample that was mounted on a vertical stage. Two led lamps with a blue filter (5600 k) were set on each side of the camera, illuminating a sample at an angle of 45° (Fig. 1(c)).

4   Results and Discussion

We compared the proposed method with two state-of-the-art approaches for HS image deblurring: 1) The method that exploits the PCA dimensionality reduction approach and performs *total variation* (TV)-based deblurring only on the first few subspace components (PCA+TV) [14]; 2) The method based on the HySime approach followed by deblurring of subspace components tailored to remote sensing HS images (RS HS deblurring) [18]. For a fair comparison, we selected only methods tailored to HS images and not the ones developed for RGB or grayscale images as the latest may be sensitive to even a small amount of noise, often present in some HS bands.

The first step of the proposed method is dimensionality reduction: a HySime approach is applied to the observed HS image [22] to obtain subspace components. Figure 2 shows the first 10 subspace components of a sample containing nine different inks (five lab-created and four commercial). The useful information is visible in the first five subspace components, while the next five components contain mostly noise. The copper-based commercial ink (S_V) shows different behaviour in the subspace domain when compared with iron gall inks (lab-created and commercial).

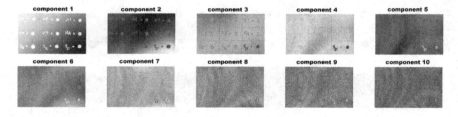

Fig. 2. Example of subspace components of a sample containing nine different inks.

The results obtained on the separate bands of HS document images are presented in Fig. 3. All three tested deblurring methods perform reasonably well on bands corresponding to medium frequencies (e.g., from 653 to 427 nm). PCA+TV introduces new artefacts on noisy bands (e.g., the band corresponding to 890 nm) and oversmooth small details in the image. Similarly, the method tailored to remote sensing images (RS HS deblurring) fails to fully remove noise from bands corresponding to the near-infrared (NIR) region ($\geq$793 nm). The proposed method performs optimally over the full spectral range and provides the sharpest resulting image.

Finally, we show the results in the form of an RGB composition (Fig. 4). As previously, we compared the results obtained by three HS image deblurring approaches. The three approaches give comparable results when tested on the images corrupted by a moderate blur (first and second rows), except the visible boundary artefacts visible when applying the PCA+TV approach. When an HS image is blurrier (third and fourth rows), the proposed method outperforms other tested approaches.

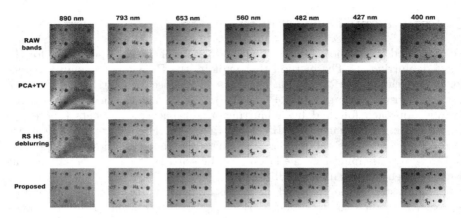

Fig. 3. Comparison of the results obtained by three approaches: the PCA and TV-based method (PCA+TV) [14], the deblurring method tailored to remote sensing images (RS HS deblurring) [18], and the proposed method.

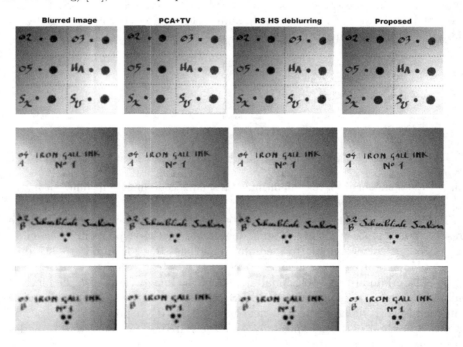

Fig. 4. RGB composition obtained on three different samples (blurred images presented in the first column); Methods: the PCA and TV-based method (PCA+TV) [14], the deblurring method tailored to remote sensing images (RS HS deblurring) [18], and the proposed method.

5   Conclusion

In this paper, we present a novel blind deblurring method tailored to hyperspectral images that contain text. The proposed method is based on the well-known low-rank characteristic of HS data and exploits a text-specific prior knowledge imposed on an underlying sharp HS image. The image prior is motivated by observing specific properties of text images. The behaviour of different lab-created and commercial inks in the visible and near-infrared spectral ranges was investigated to improve the restoration process. The preliminary results show that the proposed approach gives good results over all spectral bands, removing successfully image artefacts introduced by blur and noise and significantly increasing the number of bands that can be used in further analysis.

The proposed approach represents a (crucial) preprocessing step for historical document analysis where the important information may be hidden in the spectral ranges beyond visible light. Additionally, the proposed approach gives a new insight into the characterisation and identification of ancient inks. The future work will be focused on a more detailed examination of the behaviour of ancient materials in NIR and short-wave infrared wavelength ranges, together with the utilization of these ranges in the process of HS image restoration.

References

1. Cattoni, R., Coianiz, T., Messelodi, S., Modena, C.M.: Geometric layout analysis techniques for document image understanding: a review. ITC-irst Tech. Rep. **9703**(09), 1–68 (1998)
2. Díaz Hidalgo, R.J., et al.: New insights into iron-gall inks through the use of historically accurate reconstructions. Herit. Sci. **6**(1), 1–15 (2018)
3. Fischer, A., et al.: Automatic transcription of handwritten medieval documents. In: 2009 15th International Conference on Virtual Systems and Multimedia, pp. 137–142 (2009). https://doi.org/10.1109/VSMM.2009.26
4. George, S., Hardeberg, J.: Ink classification and visualisation of historical manuscripts: application of hyperspectral imaging. In: International Conference on Document Analysis and Recognition (ICDAR), pp. 1131–1135 (2015). https://doi.org/10.1109/ICDAR.2015.7333937
5. Govender, M., Chetty, K., Bulcock, H.: A review of hyperspectral remote sensing and its application in vegetation and water resource studies. Water SA **33**(2), 145–151 (2007). https://doi.org/10.4314/wsa.v33i2.49049
6. Govindan, V., Shivaprasad, A.: Character recognition–a review. Pattern Recognit. **23**(7), 671–683 (1990). https://doi.org/10.1016/0031-3203(90)90091-X
7. Hedjam, R., Cheriet, M.: Historical document image restoration using multispectral imaging system. Pattern Recognit. **46**(8), 2297–2312 (2013). https://doi.org/10.1016/j.patcog.2012.12.015
8. Hradiš, M., Kotera, J., Zemčík, P., Šroubek, F.: Convolutional neural networks for direct text deblurring. In: Proceedings of the British Machine Vision Conference, pp. 6.1–6.13. BMVA Press (2015). https://doi.org/10.5244/C.29.6
9. Joo Kim, S., Deng, F., Brown, M.S.: Visual enhancement of old documents with hyperspectral imaging. Pattern Recognit. **44**(7), 1461–1469 (2011). https://doi.org/10.1016/j.patcog.2010.12.019

10. Kamruzzaman, M., ElMasry, G., Sun, D.W., Allen, P.: Non-destructive prediction and visualization of chemical composition in lamb meat using NIR hyperspectral imaging and multivariate regression. Innov. Food Sci. Emerg. Technol. **16**, 218–226 (2012)

11. Narang, S.R., Jindal, M.K., Kumar, M.: Ancient text recognition: a review. Artif. Intell. Rev. **53**(8), 5517–5558 (2020). https://doi.org/10.1007/s10462-020-09827-4

12. Lanaras, C., Bioucas-Dias, J., Baltsavias, E., Schindler, K.: Super-resolution of multispectral multiresolution images from a single sensor. In: 2017 IEEE Conference on Computer Vision and Pattern Recognition Workshops (CVPRW), pp. 1505–1513 (2017). https://doi.org/10.1109/CVPRW.2017.194

13. Li, F., Ng, M.K., Plemmons, R.J.: Coupled segmentation and denoising/deblurring models for hyperspectral material identification. Numer. Linear Algebra Appl. **19**(1), 153–173 (2012). https://doi.org/10.1002/nla.750

14. Liao, W., et al.: Hyperspectral image deblurring with PCA and total variation. In: 2013 5th Workshop on Hyperspectral Image and Signal Processing: Evolution in Remote Sensing (WHISPERS), p. 4. IEEE (2013)

15. Ljubenović, M., Figueiredo, M.A.T.: Plug-and-play approach to class-adapted blind image deblurring. Int. J. Doc. Anal. Recognit. **22**(2), 79–97 (2019). https://doi.org/10.1007/s10032-019-00318-z

16. Ljubenovic, M., Zhuang, L., Figueiredo, M.A.: Class-adapted blind deblurring of document images. In: 2017 14th IAPR International Conference on Document Analysis and Recognition (ICDAR), vol. 01, pp. 721–726 (2017). https://doi.org/10.1109/ICDAR.2017.123

17. Ljubenović, M., Figueiredo, M.A.T.: Blind image deblurring using class-adapted image priors. In: 2017 IEEE International Conference on Image Processing (ICIP), pp. 490–494 (2017). https://doi.org/10.1109/ICIP.2017.8296329

18. Ljubenović, M., Traviglia, A.: Improved detection of buried archaeological sites by fast hyperspectral image deblurring and denoising. In: Liang, H., Groves, R. (eds.) Optics for Arts, Architecture, and Archaeology VIII, vol. 11784, pp. 128–137. International Society for Optics and Photonics, SPIE (2021). https://doi.org/10.1117/12.2593713

19. Loncan, L., et al.: Hyperspectral pansharpening: a review. IEEE Trans. Geosci. Remote Sens. Mag. **3**(3), 27–46 (2015). https://doi.org/10.1109/MGRS.2015.2440094

20. Mahesh, S., Jayas, D., Paliwal, J., White, N.: Hyperspectral imaging to classify and monitor quality of agricultural materials. J. Stored Prod. Res. **61**, 17–26 (2015). https://doi.org/10.1016/j.jspr.2015.01.006

21. Picollo, M., Cucci, C., Casini, A., Stefani, L.: Hyper-spectral imaging technique in the cultural heritage field: new possible scenarios. Sensors **20**, 2843 (2020). https://doi.org/10.3390/s20102843

22. Nascimento, J.M.P., Bioucas-Dias, J.M.: Hyperspectral signal subspace estimation. In: IEEE International Geoscience and Remote Sensing Symposium, pp. 3225–3228 (2007). https://doi.org/10.1109/IGARSS.2007.4423531

23. Nascimento, J., Dias, J.: Vertex component analysis: a fast algorithm to unmix hyperspectral data. IEEE Trans. Geosci. Remote Sens. **43**(4), 898–910 (2005). https://doi.org/10.1109/TGRS.2005.844293

24. Pan, J., Hu, Z., Su, Z., Yang, M.H.: Deblurring text images via l0-regularized intensity and gradient prior. In: 2014 IEEE Conference on Computer Vision and Pattern Recognition, pp. 2901–2908 (2014). https://doi.org/10.1109/CVPR.2014.371

25. Shiradkar, R., Shen, L., Landon, G., Heng Ong, S., Tan, P.: A new perspective on material classification and ink identification. In: Proceedings of the IEEE Conference on Computer Vision and Pattern Recognition, pp. 2267–2274 (2014)
26. Xu, L., Lu, C., Xu, Y., Jia, J.: Image smoothing via l0 gradient minimization. ACM Trans. Graph. **30**(6), 1–12 (2011). https://doi.org/10.1145/2070781.2024208
27. Zhao, X., Wang, F., Huang, T., Ng, M.K., Plemmons, R.J.: Deblurring and sparse unmixing for hyperspectral images. IEEE Trans. Geosci. Remote Sens. **51**(7), 4045–4058 (2013). https://doi.org/10.1109/TGRS.2012.2227764
28. Zhuang, L., Bioucas-Dias, J.M.: Fast hyperspectral image denoising and inpainting based on low-rank and sparse representations. IEEE J. Sel. Top. Appl. Earth Obs. Remote Sens. **11**(3), 730–742 (2018). https://doi.org/10.1109/JSTARS.2018.2796570

MyBottega: An Environment for the Innovative Production and Distribution of Digital Art

Nicola Noviello and Remo Pareschi(✉)

Stake Lab, University of Molise, Campobasso, Italy
`remo.pareschi@unimol.it`

Abstract. Recent years have seen a number of innovations that have set the stage for a radical expansion of digital art, from the point of view of both the production and the distribution of works. On the one hand, in fact, the advent of generative capabilities in Artificial Intelligence based on Deep Learning methodologies, such as in particular Generative Adversarial Networks (GANs), make radically innovative tools available to support artistic production; on the other hand, the processes of authentication of works of art made possible by blockchain technologies, such as Non-Fungible Tokens (NFTs), have seen the emergence on a large scale of digital art markets on the Web. These new modes of production and distribution need to be tightly integrated to fully express their potential for adoption. Drawing inspiration from the Italian Renaissance workshop (the "bottega"), which was a hugely successful environment for the production and distribution of art, we designed and implemented the MyBottega software architecture, in order to bring these innovations to the stakeholders (artists, curators, exhibitors, etc.) of today's digital art.

Keywords: Digital Art · GAN · NFT · Blockchain · Microservices

1 Introduction

The Italian Renaissance workshop, known as the "bottega", provided a highly successful environment for the apprenticeship of artistic skills and, consequently, the creation of works that have indelibly marked the history of art by geniuses such as Leonardo da Vinci, Raffaello Sanzio, Michelangelo Buonarroti, and other great artists. Its functioning relied upon teamwork, but also on a physical infrastructure including laboratories where the artists had tools and materials at their disposal to put their skills to use, as well as reception spaces for customers and visitors who could thus appreciate the shop products and negotiate and conclude orders. Five hundred years and more since then, the evolution of digital technologies, far from announcing a replacement of human creativity with the mechanization of artistic production, is defining the conditions for a rebirth of the Renaissance workshop in the virtual world of the Internet and the Web. And just as chisels, marbles, and blends of colors were made available to artists at the time, now they are offered algorithms that generate shapes and images. as well as digital markets for exhibiting and exchanging digital art. For this to be fully realized, it is a question of

P. L. Mazzeo et al. (Eds.): ICIAP 2022 Workshops, LNCS 13373, pp. 162–173, 2022.
https://doi.org/10.1007/978-3-031-13321-3_15

organizing these technological components in an architecture that gives new meaning and coherence to the artistic activity, both in the production and in the distribution of works, just like the production spaces and exhibition rooms in the Renaissance workshop did with respect to the previous epoch. While the technology has gone at a galloping pace in the development of the individual components that fit into this view, their organization is still missing. The MyBottega framework that we present here aims to make a contribution to remedying this lack.

1.1 Structure of the Paper

The rest of the article is structured as follows: Sect. 2 illustrates the trends of Web 3.0 and generative AI, driven respectively by blockchain technology and generative adversarial networks, and their convergence towards a new scenario for the world of art; Sect. 3 illustrates the differences and complementarities of MyBottega with respect to platforms and projects in related technological areas; Sect. 4 illustrates the principles underlying its design; Sect. 5 describes the MyBottega architecture as consequently designed and built; Sect. 6 concludes the article.

2 Web 3.0 and Generative AI: Two Converging Evolutions

The technological background that lays the foundations and motivations of MyBottega is twofold: on the one hand, the transition from the Web 2.0 of content transfer to the Web 3.0 of value transfer; on the other hand, the evolution in Artificial Intelligence of generative capabilities, thus overcoming, through technologies such as generative adversarial networks (GANs), the boundaries of analysis and classification within which AI was until recently confined. These two trends integrate and intertwine, with the effect of revolutionizing the methods of both distribution and production of works of art.

2.1 Non-fungible Tokens and the New Course in Art Distribution

Let's start with the transition to Web 3.0. Compared to the dawn of the Web, the Web 1.0 in which users still had neither faces nor profiles nor autonomy in the production of content, the Web 2.0 of social media, which began to materialize in the early 2000s, has thrust users into the limelight. However, it has also exploited and expropriated them by concentrating content management into a few hubs, namely social media sites like Meta (previously Facebook), Instagram, and YouTube that thus own all that is created online - from personal data to images, from behaviors to musical preferences. This is a high price to pay, as it involves the alienation of user personal content, which is extracted, processed, sold, and reinserted into algorithms that constantly propose and convey new content with the aim of generating additional revenue. This expropriation, disguised with concepts like "improving the user experience" or "free", has been characterized by some scholars as a novel form of exploitation, referred to as "surveillance capitalism" [1]. Tied as they are to the biggest hubs, even power users like professional online content creators have no choice but to play the game.

But since the advent of blockchain technology, starting with the Bitcoin in 2009 [2], the situation is reversing through the transition to Web 3.0, thus made possible by being based on the transfer of value. Blockchain technology is a digital ledger of transactions on ownership records. The management mechanism of a blockchain is totally decentralized, by taking place in peer-to-peer mode. In Web 2.0 users entrust and open their content to an elite of Internet oligopolists; in Web 3.0 they will have effective ownership of content. An important step forward in this direction, which right now is reshaping the art market, is given by the Non-Fungible Tokens (NFTs). NFTs are available on some of the major blockchains, including Ethereum [3], the second in size after that of Bitcoin as well as the one that led blockchain technology beyond the limited scope of cryptocurrencies. Anything whose property is transferable can be tokenized through the blockchain as an NFT so as to make its ownership programmable, verifiable, transferable, divisible, theft-proof, and cryptographically protected. A token is non-fungible in that it is unique and not replaceable with another token, while fungibility characterizes things like money. Thus, any digital content, such as text, music, images, and videos can be turned into an NFT and hence made a unique digital object, non-reproducible and usable only under the conditions to which it was bound at the time of its creation. This way, as much as files can be distributed on the Web, their origin and ownership are tracked forever on the blockchain.

Thus, by certifying ownership of ideas in the various ways in which these can be realized (graphic, textual, musical, etc.), NFTs provide content producers with the ability to sell directly to their audience without anyone else getting profit and without limiting dissemination. In Web 2.0, content that goes viral brings profits to the platform it spreads through. The verifiable ownership of NFTs reverses the course, redirecting the revenue stream to the owner of the work, according to what is established in a specific Smart Contract, i.e. a program that executes contractual conditions associated with the NFT. In this way, ideas can be turned into assets, thus making them proprietary and negotiable. Of course, NFTs don't work miracles, and a mediocre idea won't get bright because it is tokenized. As a matter of fact, there is plenty of tokenized junk currently floating on the Web. On the other hand, NFTs do make brilliant ideas tokenizable, hence protecting them from the rapacity of Web 2.0 predators.

2.2 Generative Artificial Intelligence to Boost Art Production

Let's turn now to content generators based on AI methodologies and in particular the aforementioned GANs, which are growing and maturing rapidly and can be applied to numerous domains. We are here specifically interested in their applicability to artistic contexts, in a range that includes changing the features of a face, applying the style of a famous artist on an image, generating photorealistic images of people who never existed, improving the resolution of a low-quality photo or video, creating images from text (text-to-image). GANs exploit Deep Learning techniques (such as Convolutional Neural Networks and Transformers) to solve generative modeling problems through the use of two sub-models: a Generator that is trained to output new instances from an input dataset and a Discriminator that classifies the generated items either as "real" (that is, belonging to the original domain) or "fake" (output by the Generator). The two models are trained together until the Discriminator is fooled 50% of the time, which means that the Generator is producing plausible instances [4].

The reverberations of this approach to art began to manifest in 2019 when the auction price of $ 432,500 was hit for a portrait of a fictional 19th-century aristocrat, Edmond de Belamy[1], to whose creation GAN technology contributed. From then on, works that made use of GANs and other digital generation tools became more and more widespread. We can ask ourselves if the direction in which we are moving is not in effect a prelude to the decline of human superiority in the field of artistic creation similar to what happened for strategy games such as chess. Here the event that changed history dates back to 1997, when an artificial player, the IBM Deep Blue program, won a match against Garry Kasparov, considered the greatest human player of all time. Since then, human skills have inexorably lost ground to artificial ones in both chess and other even more complex games such as Shogi and Go. We dare to say that for art this will not be the case. Our prediction is based on a simple observation: in the case of chess and other strategy games, right from the start, and therefore centuries before computers were invented and AI was talked about, it was man, albeit unwittingly, who went after and imitated the machine. Chess can in fact be tackled effectively through simple algorithms such as alpha-beta search, which is the basis of the now archaic and widely outclassed Deep Blue program that defeated Garry Kasparov at the time [5]. Today's chess programs use much more sophisticated methodologies, yet it was enough to equip an elementary algorithm with sufficient computational capacity to beat the greatest human player of all time. While human champions of chess and other strategy games can be said to use alternative tools, such as intuition and strategic finesse, to purely computational ones, they nevertheless compete in games in which algorithmic exploration of alternate moves works very effectively. It is therefore no surprise that machines overcame human players already 25 years ago and that every year the distance widens.

But in the case of art, the human component has always been predominant, and one aspect, in particular, appears beyond the reach of the machine: that is, the fragility, precariousness, and psychological and emotional complexity that characterize human existence. Paradoxical as it may sound, this weakness, if we can call it so, far away from the world of the artificial as can be, is at the root of the inspiration of great works of art in the past and there is no doubt that it will continue to be so in the future. On the other hand, according to a saying attributed to the famous inventor Thomas Edison, genius is 10% inspiration and 90% transpiration. In the field of art, this aphoristic remark translates into the fact that genius is not only in the spark that ignites the initial conception, but also in the process that from this embryonic element, in a demanding and exhausting cycle of reinterpretations and refinements, finally leads to light the work of art in its completeness - therefore, in effect, a progressive process of approximating the finished work by "trial and error" that has been proposed as a model of artistic production by Ernst Gombrich [6], one of the greatest theorists and art historians of the twentieth century, and indeed has striking similarities with the refinement progress of the generative capacities of GANs. This makes the production of works of art a matter as much of creativity and project management and, in fact, the great names in the history of the various artistic disciplines

---

[1] https://www.christies.com/en/lot/lot-6166184; Belamy in turn corresponds to a French rendition of the surname (Goodfellow) of the inventor of GANs.

undoubtedly belong to those who have been able to put together two apparently antinomic qualities: extreme creativity and the iron ability to manage a project in all its phases. Such individuals know both where to start and when to stop, and are not satisfied until the path has been covered in its entirety. For this purpose, in the field of the figurative arts, they have used the past tools for the construction and manipulation of physical works. Nowadays, similarly gifted individuals and teams can resort to tools suiting digital works, spearheaded by GANs, that can partly automate the cycles of revisiting and refinement that lead the work to its final form.

Of course, it should not be surprising if these new tools made available for artistic production will initially give ample space also to trivial outputs in which the paths opened by technology are not explored beyond the level of a glorified Photoshop. But this is not to be considered different from what was true for all the previous phases of the evolution of the artistic disciplines, namely that technical mastery is no guarantee for masterwork. There have been accomplished painting technicians, yet totally lacking creativity and originality, who had to be content with making a living as humble imitators or at best as skilled counterfeiters of the true masters. If therefore the forceful breakthrough of technology into artistic production has made it easy to imitate works of art, it has not, however, lowered the threshold that marks the passage from the banal work to the interesting one or even the masterpiece. We, therefore, expect that, after a period of adjustment necessary for learning and experimentation, those who can exploit these new means in an unprecedented and original way will emerge unequivocally.

3 Technological Background

While the inspiration for MyBottega is the Renaissance workshop, it is also important to place its contribution in the context of other developments associated with Machine Learning (ML) and NFTs. In this regard, the first question to ask is how MyBottega stands with respect to existing projects for the exploration and use of ML libraries and algorithms. Here the platforms to compare against are the so-called notebooks that have evolved from the open-source Jupyter Notebooks project[2], including the popular Google Colab[3], as well as Kaggle[4] (another Google project), Amazon Sagemaker Studio Lab[5], and IBM DataPlatform Notebooks[6]. The answer is simple and straightforward: these platforms offer excellent environments for programmers and data scientists, but are far removed from the world of art production. MyBottega, on the other hand, is conceived with the artist as the end user and gives space to roles played by other crucial stakeholders in the art ecosystem, such as gallery owners and curators. Therefore, it does not merely support a set of technologies, in that it also makes manageable, from start to finish, a process characterized by clearly defined organizational roles and business outcomes.

The relationship between MyBottega and NFT marketplaces is instead one of total complementarity. MyBottega, in fact, does not provide for the exchange of NFTs, while

---

[2] https://jupyter.org/
[3] https://colab.research.google.com/
[4] https://www.kaggle.com/
[5] https://aws.amazon.con/amazon/sagemaker
[6] https://dataplatform.cloud.ibm.com/

it does provide for NFT placement of finished works on existing markets. To this end, it connects to such marketplaces through the available APIs. Currently, only the two mega-hubs Opensea[7] and Rarible[8] are connected to, but more will be added. In this way, users will be able to choose marketplaces based not just on popularity but also on other relevant criteria such as security and protection against hacker attacks. The same applies to minting, namely the procedure for creating NFTs, pioneered by Ethereum and now supported by several other blockchains. MyBottega aims to interface with as many NFT-minting blockchains as possible, so as to let users choose based on criteria including diffusion of the type of minted NFT, blockchain robustness (determined by multiple factors, as shown in [7]), minting fees, and environmental sustainability of the minting procedure, i.e. the amount of electricity needed for its execution. The latter aspect has recently become very critical, given the negative impact of energy-wasteful operations, which could be penalized by supervisory and regulatory authorities in the future [8]. However, it is expected to be considerably mitigated once all major NFT-minting blockchains have replaced the wasteful Proof-of-Work consensus protocol with much more power-saving ones, such as Proof-of-Stake[9].

4 MyBottega: Design Principles

Basically, MyBottega takes its steps from the idea of supporting a supply chain in which artists produce digital works of art and galleries sell them on digital markets. To this aim, it makes use of an advanced client-server architecture that provides for distributed clients, such that it is possible to allocate distribution and production costs in relation to corresponding stakeholder roles. In fact, the gallery can delegate to the artist, or to the creative team, the installation of the microservices containing the GAN models and other applications on its own machine, while still being able to control the licenses through the JSON Web Token (JWT) Machine 2 Machine (M2M) technology that enables secure transmission of information between parties as a JSON object. It follows an assignment of roles in which the artist is placed at the production backend and the gallery operator at the marketing and distribution frontend while retaining a direct link between the two parties, just as the exhibition halls were directly linked to the production labs in the physical context of the Renaissance workshop.

Therefore, the following core functionalities of MyBottega concern two types of users, namely Admin users (galleries and curators) and end-users (artists and creators):

- **Authentication/Authorization**, which contains the user authentication functions, with the management of both the tokens to authenticate users in the main platform and the M2M tokens in case of user access to the distributed system. The function stores

---

[7] https://opensea.io/

[8] https://rarible.com/

[9] This essentially concerns Ethereum, where the majority of NFT minting still takes place, and which still uses pure Proof-of-Work. In fact, the other blockchains where NFT minting takes place either use other protocols or are layers on top of Ethereum. However, Ethereum. announced it will switch to Proof-of-Stake in the course of 2022 https://ethereum.org/en/developers/docs/consensus-mechanisms/pos/.

the data that is strictly necessary for authentication such as username and password, and also offers a registration service. In addition, user permissions are also managed, by issuing authorization tokens that enable users to access given features.

- **Profiling**, deals with the management of the data that characterize a user's profile, allowing it to be viewed and modified. It manages access to user data and those of other parties in a variety of ways according to the user's role.
- **Subscriptions**, which manage user terms of access, determining whether a particular user can use ML features like GANs through the main platform or whether she must use the generative components through the dedicated client. No particular logic is defined in the application of either function since this is a choice determined by the business/marketing aspects of the provided service. The choice will thus be left to the Admin user. A new user will default to a dedicated client and, if set by the Admin, will also be enabled on the main platform.
- **Galleries and Images**, which manages the creation, modification, and removal of the multimedia components that will be published on the merchant platform (currently only OpenSea and Rarible) for each individual user. Although the publication on the platform is done under the name of the service provider (the art gallery), individual users will be able to create their own galleries and images independently. There is no publication control function as this is a business model decision, but the concept of approval is made available in the data model. The data structure associated with this component also contains all the details about the revenue model.
- **Revenue history**, which, through integration with the NFT sales system, makes it possible to collect image sales information, acquire it via a webhook and upload it to a reporting program.

Thus, the core functionalities provide corresponding endpoints for the platform, where Admin users have access rights to all of them, while end users are limited to the endpoints for Profiles, Galleries and Images, and publication services on the NFT sales system and revenue reporting.

These core services are complemented by a set of GAN features in the form of microservices. As is known, the architectural approach based on microservices offers a series of advantages, compared to the traditional monolithic approach, for flexibility in both implementation and user interaction [9]. These characteristics are well suited to a business context in which a service provider (the gallery) aiming to promote digital artwork also provides tools to the creators of works of art so as to feed its merchant offer. We have therefore deployed our microservices through the well-known and renowned Docker technology[10], which offers reproducibility in diverse contexts, great portability, easy implementation on existing software, superior lightness compared to virtual machines and simplicity of use. Specifically, it makes possible for each microservice to be written in any programming language and to run different versions of microservices on the same machine without problems of conflicts or complicated configurations of virtual environments.

Each ML/GAN component (or microservice) is therefore implemented as an independent platform with its own software stack, which can be activated at the time of

---

[10] https://www.docker.com/

execution by inserting an M2M Token in the configuration. The token will be analyzed by the microservice, which will internally verify its authenticity and validate its authorization for use by synchronously calling the core platform, and will also authenticate the user by analyzing the JWT payload [10], since the JSON Web Tokens can be used versatilely in both authentication and authorization processes [11], offering the latter only the services for which it is authorized to operate. This means that the same ML/GAN microservice can be used by either a creative user or an Admin (as an extension of the functionality of the core platform) without any modification.

The design principles illustrated here, and represented in Fig. 1, are therefore functional to an architecture that combines construction solidity and organizational fluidity, so that every instance of MyBottega leads to the emergence of a micro-ecosystem, propelled by the gallery owner and at the same time capable of aggregating and promoting artists with the utmost openness and dynamism - just as the Renaissance workshops acted as attractors and promoters of creatives.

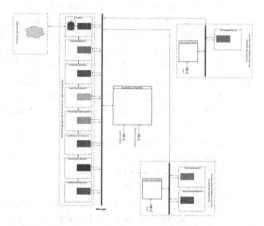

Fig. 1. A MyBottega ecosystem for digital creativity

The supported GAN components are listed and described in Table 1. Of course this is not a closed list, but is open to adding new components as technology evolves.

Table 1. Supported GAN components

Text-to-Image	Generation of images starting from a text entered by the user. For this service, the choice fell on an adversarial integration of the two transformer models VQGAN and CLIP, documented respectively in [12] and [13], on the WikiArt training dataset [14]
Faces-to-Image	Generation of faces from textual descriptions entered by the user. StyleGAN [15] was used for this component, an "alias-free" model developed by NVIDIA, used in combination with the CLIP transformer [13] as in the text-to-image component
Image-to-Image	Generation of images starting from an image and a text entered by the user. The component uses a conditional generative contradictory network (cGAN) [16] named pix2pix as described in [17]
Pre-trained Style Transfer	Generation of new images from input images coupled with style images where a new image is a restyled version of the input image according to the style image. It is very efficient, as it does not need training. A pre-built model developed by Google, called arbitrary-image-stylization [18], was used for this component, implemented on the basis of the approach described in [19]
Trainable Style Transfer	Like Pre-trained Style Transfer, except that it needs training. It is less efficient but more flexible. In this case, a GAN was built from scratch based on a standard implementation of DCGAN [20]
Pixel Art Generator	Generation of pixel art images whose style is parameterized with respect to a text entered by the user. The component uses Perception Engines [21] in combination with the generative transformer CLIP described in [13]
Image Enhancement	Quality improvement of a photographic image entered by the user. The component uses the GFP-GAN model, specialized in faces, called Towards Real-World Blind Face Restoration with Generative Facial Prior [22]

5   The MyBottega Architecture

Based on the design principles illustrated in the previous section, we can now proceed to illustrate the software architecture of MyBottega. Consistently with these principles, the architecture is based on two communicating structures, one occupied by the core functionalities and the other one by the GAN microservices.

The structure of the core functionalities is given in Fig. 2 and consists of 4 layers:

- **Client**, that provides the possibility of integrating any type of front-end/client as all core functions are accessible through REST APIs. In this way, web clients, mobile or desktop, independently developed according to their own front-end design choices, are able to interact in ways intended for administrative users and end-users. To obviate the need to distribute the workload for the generation of images through the use of GAN models, microservices called ClientML have been introduced, deployable on the main server or on a third machine, or on a machine available to the user and capable to perform the complex operations of ML models through an easy-to-use API layer.

- **API Layer**, which is made available to the Core platform and is divided into two types of endpoints: those designed for ClientML, usable exclusively through the M2M tokens, and those designed for the Core functions, usable through standard JWT tokens. Endpoints allow controlling all the functions defined within the Business Logic.
- **Business Logic,** where the application logic that implements all the functions concerning the personal data of users and their galleries and images reside, as well as the publication on marketplaces (eg OpenSea).
- **Data Layer**, which maintains the information data of the applications through a relational database and the images of the users through an archive bucket component.

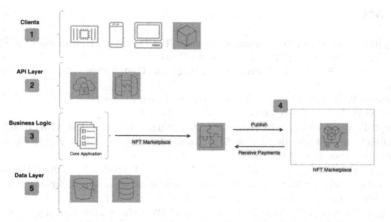

Fig. 2. Core Functionalities Structure in the MyBottega architecture

The GAN microservices structure follows a similar plan, however there are obvious differences in the functions absolved. In the first place, the Data Layer substantially works by proxy, in that data are not maintained in the structure itself but either are saved in the Data Layer of Core Functionalities or are saved in external storage. Second, the Client, API Layer and Business Logic components are dedicated to the synchronization of the ML modules with the user on one side and with the GAN models kept in the core on the other.

6   Conclusion

We illustrated the MyBottega software architecture for the development of ecosystems propitious and supportive to the production and distribution of digital art. In doing so we drew inspiration from a model that had a great success in the Renaissance, one of the highest and brightest points of human creativity. But, of course, our intent is rooted in the present, as given by the parallel and converging developments that have led to the digital protectability of works of art through the blockchain and to the generative applications of Artificial Intelligence; and looks towards a near future in which nothing stands in the way of the free circulation of creativity in a universe (or metaverse) of total digital fluidity.

The implementation of a working version of MyBottega has been carried out up to the level of technology readiness of a Proof-of-Concept and will be further developed so that it can soon be provided for experimentation. A presentation of the platform is available at https://presentation.mybottega.net.

Acknowledgments. We are grateful to Hervé Gallaire and to the anonymous reviewers for helpful comments on the previous version of the article.

References

1. Zuboff, S.: The Age of Surveillance Capitalism: The Fight for a Human Future at the New Frontier of Power. Public Affairs, New York (2018)
2. Nakamoto, S., Bitcoin, A.: A Peer-to-Peer Electronic Cash System. (2008). https://bitcoin.org/.
3. Ethereum White Paper. https://ethereum.org/. Accessed: 21 April 2022
4. Goodfellow, I.J., et al.: Commun. ACM **63**, 139–144 (2020)
5. Campbell, M., Hoane, A.J. Jr., Hsu, F.-H.: Deep Blue. Artif. Intell. **134**, 57-83 (2002)
6. Gombrich, E.: Art and Illusion. A Study in the Psychology of Pictorial Representation. Pantheon Books, New York (1960)
7. Garriga, M., Dalla Palma, S., Arias, M., De Renzis, A., Pareschi, R., Andrew Tamburri, D.: Blockchain and cryptocurrencies: A classification and comparison of architecture drivers. Concurrency Comput.: Practice Experience **33**(8), e5992 (2021)
8. Truby, J., Brown, R.D., Dahdal, A., Ibrahim, I.: Blockchain, climate damage, and death: policy interventions to reduce the carbon emissions, mortality, and net-zero implications of non-fungible tokens and Bitcoin. Energy Res. Social Sci. **88** 102499 (2022)
9. Newman, S.: Building Microservices: Designing Fine-Grained Systems. O' Really, Sebastopol, California (2015)
10. JSON Web Token (JWT). https://datatracker.ietf.org/doc/html/draft-ietf-oauth-json-web-token-32. Accessed: 21 April 2022
11. Web Authorization Protocol (Active WG). https://tools.ietf.org/wg/oauth/draft-ietf-oauth-jwt-bcp/. Accessed: 21 April 2022.
12. Patrick, E., Rombach, R., Ommer, B.: Taming Transformers for High-Resolution Image Synthesis. CVPR (2021)
13. Radford, A., Kim, J.W., Hallacy, C., Ramesh, A., Goh, G., Agarwal, S., Sastry, G., Askell, A., Mishkin, P., Clark, J., Krueger, G., Sutskever, I.: Learning Transferable Visual Models From Natural Language Supervision. ICML (2021)
14. https://github.com/cs-chan/ArtGAN/blob/master/WikiArt%20Dataset/README.md Accessed: 21 April 2022.
15. Karras, T., Aittala, M., Laine, S., Härkönen, E., Hellsten, J., Lehtinen, J., Aila, T.: Alias-Free Generative Adversarial Networks. CoRR abs/2106.12423 (2021)

16. Mirza, M., Osindero, S.: Conditional Generative Adversarial Nets. CoRR abs/1411.1784 (2014)
17. Isola, P., Zhu, J.-Y., Zhou, T., Efros, A.A.: Image-to-Image Translation with Conditional Adversarial Networks. CVPR (2017)
18. https://tfhub.dev/google/lite-model/magenta/arbitrary-image-stylization-v1-256/fp16/transf er/1 Accessed: 21 April 2022
19. Ghiasi, G., Lee, H., Kudlur, M., Dumoulin, V., Shlens, J.: Exploring the Structure of a Real-Time, Arbitrary Neural Artistic Stylization. BMVC (2017)
20. Radford, A., Metz, L., Chintala, S.: Unsupervised Representation Learning with Deep Convolutional Networks. ICLR (Poster) (2016)
21. dribnet/perception engines. https://github.com/dribnet/perceptionengines Accessed: 21 April 2022
22. Wang, X., Li, Y., Zhang, H., Shan, Y.: Towards Real-World Blind Face Restoration With Generative Facial Prior. CVPR (2021)

A Case Study for the Design and Implementation of Immersive Experiences in Support of Sicilian Cultural Heritage

Roberto Barbera[1], Francesca Condorelli[2], Giuseppe Di Gregorio[2],
Giuseppe Di Piazza[5], Mariella Farella[3,4,5], Giosué Lo Bosco[3,5],
Andrey Megvinov[5], Daniele Pirrone[5], Daniele Schicchi[3,5(✉)],
and Antonino Zora[5]

[1] Department of Physics and Astronomy, "E. Maiorana", University of Catania,
Piazza Universitá 2, 95131 Catania, Italy
`roberto.barbera@ct.infn.it`
[2] Department of Civil Engineering and Architecture, University of Catania,
Piazza Universitá 2, 95131 Catania, Italy
`condorelli@darc.unict.it`, `giuseppe.digregorio@unict.it`
[3] Department of Computer Science, University of Palermo, Via Archirafi 34,
90123 Palermo, Italy
`{mariella.farella,giosue.lobosco,daniele.schicchi}@unipa.it`
[4] National Research Council of Italy - Institute for Educational Technology,
Via Ugo La Malfa 153, 90146 Palermo, Italy
`mariella.farella@itd.cnr.it`
[5] Department of Sciences for Technological Innovation, Euro-Mediterranean Institute
of Science and Technology, Via Michele Miraglia, 20, 90133 Palermo, Italy
`{giuseppedipiazza,andreymegvinov,danielepirrone,antoninozora}@iemest.eu`

Abstract. Virtual Reality (VR) is a robust tool for sponsoring Cultural
Heritage sites. It enables immersive experiences in which the user can
enjoy the cultural assets virtually, behaving as he/she would do in the
real world. The covid-19 pandemic has shed light on the importance of
using VR in cultural heritage, showing advantages for the users that can
visit the site safely through specific devices. In this work, we present
the processes that lead to the creation of an immersive app that makes
explorable a famous cultural asset in Sicily, the church of SS. Crocifisso al
Calvario. The application creation process will be described in each of its
parts, beginning from the digital acquisition of the cultural asset to the
development of the user interface. The application is provided for three
different VR devices: smartphones equipped with cardboards, headsets,
and CAVE. The paper is supported by the 3DLab-Sicilia project, whose
main objective is to sponsor the creation, development, and validation of
a sustainable infrastructure that interconnects three main Sicilian centres
specialized in augmented and virtual reality.

Keywords: Virtual reality · Cultural heritage · CAVE · VR-headset ·
Virtual heritage

P. L. Mazzeo et al. (Eds.): ICIAP 2022 Workshops, LNCS 13373, pp. 174–185, 2022.
https://doi.org/10.1007/978-3-031-13321-3_16

1   Introduction

Virtual Reality (VR) [24], Augmented Reality (AR) [3], and Mixed Reality (MR) [11] are cutting edge technologies that promise to revolutionize the engagement of users during digital experiences. The functioning, related to their physical architecture, allows either projecting a user into a virtual world or including digital elements into the real world to interact with.

AR/VR and MR are commonly known as *immersive* technologies capable of enabling *immersivity*: the user's perception to being part of a non-physical world. Research on immersive technologies have drawn attention by showing fertile ground for supporting several application domains related to culture [14,23], medicine [1,2,16], education [12,13] and much more.

In detail, Virtual Reality simulates a realistic environment [25] by allowing the user to behave like he would do in the real world, for instance by moving around and exploring the digital environment. The interaction between the user and the environment is supported by programmable technologies capable of tracking the user's body to avoid the usage of classical input devices like mouse and keyboard configuring. VR is made accessible via several devices organized in categories based on the functions they offer and their price. The cheapest, as well as most commons, are mobile devices that, if combined with cardboard helmets (e.g. Google Cardboard), can offer a mid-quality immersive experience. VR headsets (e.g. Oculus Quest2) allow the user to enjoy a better experience providing functions such as head and eyes movement tracking, voice recording, and outputting sounds. Generally, VR headsets are equipped with specifically made physical controllers that improve the interactivity with the virtual world.

Mobile and wearable viewers are now within everyone's reach, a user ranging from the very young to evergreen IT shows particular attention in this direction. We are talking about a market that in the space of ten years has seen an evolution of hardware and software solutions that characterize it without comparison. Currently, VR technology has become potentially accessible to everyone, both from a business perspective, but also for the final consumer. In 2020, the economic impact of virtual reality and augmented reality reached a figure of around $ 29.5 billion. To understand the trend line, it is sufficient to consider that, at the end of 2017, the economic value of the software and hardware units sold was equal to 2.4 billion dollars, while at the end of 2016 there were 1.7 billion dollars. The scientific community is increasingly attentive to this sector, developing conferences, workshops, and dedicated events, with multidisciplinary involvement. Beyond the devices we have already described, the Cave Automatic Virtual Environment (CAVE) [17] is a technology created for providing immersive experiences to people without using headsets. It is a cube-shaped room whose walls act as displays for rear projections. In this environment, the user can feel a *sense of freedom* to move around and interact with the digital world since almost he/she wears glasses useful for tracking his/her movements inside the room.

In our previous work [5], we made it possible to visit Santa Maria La Vetere, a church built by the Normans around 1090 d.C. and located in Val di Catania, through cardboard, headsets, and CAVE. In [5], we also introduced a state of the art pipeline that describes the steps for the creation of general applications with the aim of virtual exploring cultural heritage sites. We benefit from the pipeline to implement a novel application that made accessible an antique church located in Catania. Thus, the aim of this paper is to present the processes that have led to the creation of the virtual experience alongside the achieved results that contribute to supporting the Sicilian cultural heritage. The application has been attained in the context of the 3dLab-Sicilia[1] project. 3DLab-Sicilia's main objective is to sponsor the creation, development, and validation of a sustainable infrastructure that interconnects three main Sicilian centres specialized in augmented and virtual reality. The project gives great importance to the cultural heritage, as well as to the tourism-related areas. Thus, we made explorable via VR devices an iconic Sicilian monument: the church of SS. Crocifisso al Calvario. This church is located in the municipality of Militello in Val di Catania. A brief demo of our work can be found here[2].

The paper is organized as follows: in Sect. 2 an overview of the state-of-the-art and current direction of this research topic is given; Sect. 3 describes the steps that lead to the development of the VR application (hereinafter pipeline) in the domain of cultural heritage; in Sects. 5 and 6 the procedures for the 3D scanning, the acquisition of the cultural asset, and the post-process of the point cloud to obtain the 3D model are reported; in Sect. 7 it is shown how the model is made accessible through virtual reality devices and CAVE. Finally, conclusions are given in Sect. 8.

2   Related Works

In the cultural heritage context, VR applications can be categorized on the basis of their purposes [7]. They have been successfully applied for supporting *education* by helping users to learn more about historical details of tangible and eventually non-tangible heritage assets. The embedding of virtual elements such as maps and virtual tour guides has been used as *exhibition* tool to enrich the visitor's experience. Moreover, VR has made nowadays possible the exploration of cultural heritage assets, giving also the opportunity to *explore* tangible assets in terms of viewing and manipulating operations. Finally, Virtual museums applications aim at proposing the experience of visiting physical museums virtually, including their tangible and intangible assets.

An example of an application created for the purpose of educating people about cultural heritage is shown in [20]. The application provides a gesture-based interface to allow the interaction of people by body movements with the virtual representation of tangible and intangible assets. Experiments show an increment of the user's engagement in the ancient Maya archaeology context. Authors of [18] tackle the problem of poor immersitivy in VR provided by mobile devices (e.g. smartphones). The problem of interacting with the virtual environment has been solved by presenting a system based on two smartphones in which one of them is used

---

[1] https://www.3dlab-sicilia.it.
[2] https://www.3dlab-sicilia.it/en/demo-della-chiesa-del-calvario/.

as the main display and the second one as a controller for implementing functions such as rotation and scale. In [4], HBIM and VR have been combined to virtually creating the Unesco World Heritage site of Lombardy known as *Santa Maria Delle Grazie*. Moreover, the paper presents a new methodology for creating intangible parts of monuments that have been lost through time.

To the best of our knowledge, there are a few similar works that have supported the cultural heritage of Sicily, an island that is well-known and rich in tangible and intangible cultural assets. A similar application is introduced in [9]. It is a virtual diving system that allows the user to explore *Cala Minnola*, an underwater archaeological site located near Levanzo (Aegadian Islands). In [6], the virtual reconstruction of the archaeological site of Ancient Noto has been made explorable. The application has been created in the context of the EFIAN project that aims at valorizing the ancient Noto by meeting the principles of the Italian Code for Cultural Heritage and Landscape. Finally, Selinunte temples, one of the foremost Greek colonies in Sicily, have been made virtually accessible through an approach based on high-resolution photo-realistic texture mapping onto 3D models [8].

3   The Pipeline

The virtual scenario that made the church of SS. Crocifisso al Calvario accessible has been implemented according to the pipeline shown in Fig. 1. This pipeline includes the sequence of steps that have led to the creation of the application deployed to cardboards, headsets, and CAVE. Firstly, the church of SS. Crocifisso al Calvario has been digitally acquired through 3D scanners. The output of the scanning process was a cloud of points that needed to be processed in order to obtain a 3D model in *obj* format. Such a model is then enriched with norms, meshes and textures through the use of specific techniques and computations. Once the object is created, it is imported into Unity3D, the software used in this work to implement the applications deployed on VR devices – i.e. smartphones in combination with cardboard, Oculus Quest 2 – and CAVE (Sect. 7).

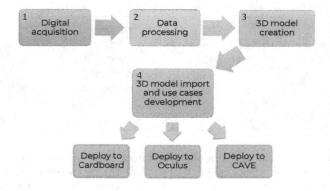

Fig. 1. The proposed Pipeline

4   The Sense of Detail

The attention to the product is differentiated by the user kind, ranging from the visual fascination for the youngest to the educational and cultural aspect for more mature ones. In the cultural heritage field, the recognition of details is essential, so that the virtualization realized with addictions of any kind must be credible. In the related immersive experience, correspondences take on undeniable importance. In this sense, geometric relationships, proportions, quality and detail are fundamental. Archaeological sites, religious and military architectures, present different criticalities amplified in the search for the quality of detail, where it is not always possible to foresee common pipelines. The case study of the church in question has focused on the need for different qualities in its parts. The portico in front of the entrance, a false construction of the seventeenth century, the work of the architect Francesco Battaglia is the element that embellishes the church (Fig. 2(a)), with a sferic vault (Fig. 2(b)). The beauty and harmony of the parts find balance in every aspect. Inside the church, there are various pictorial works along the walls of the nave (Fig. 2(c)), and along the intrados of the barrel vault (Fig. 2(d)). Near the transept, the architectural organization includes the two ends with the apse, the vault in the central area and the apse behind the altar. Already these elements make it clear how automatic decimation would not do justice to the entire system. Several works have been consulted in the literature for the semantic segmentation of point clouds [15,19]. This sector is still evolving to be applied to cultural heritage. During the acquisition phase with the 3D laser scanner, the resolution was calibrated according

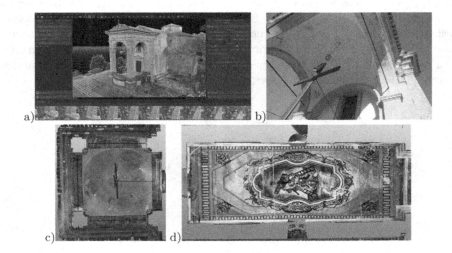

Fig. 2. a) The front porch, the work of the architect Francesco Battaglia, photogrammetric model developed with Zephyr; b) Detail of the seventeenth century portico, leaning against the pre-existing church; c) Bottom view of the vault of the portico, model from 3D laser scanner; d) Scan of the intrados of the barrel vault on the nave.

to the final quality of the detail, along the intrados of the nave vault the final acquisition was equal to about 1.6 mm, which combined with the photographic acquisition of HDR images brings colouration of the cloud points with a density comparable to a photographic image.

5   Digital Acquisition and Data Processing

The object of the survey described in this article is SS. Crocifisso al Calvario Church located in the municipality of Militello in Val di Catania. Different instruments were used for data acquisition: camera and drone for SFM reconstruction, laser scanner (Faro Focus 350S) for the points clouds. The data processing was carried out by the Scene software for the point clouds and the software Zephyr[3] for SFM reconstruction. In SS. Crocifisso al Calvario Church the survey by laser scanner of the outside has been organized by 16 station points, while for the inside part by 8 station points. A standard distance (about 5 m) between one station point and another one has been maintained for the survey of the outside (Fig. 3(a)), while it has been reduced near the apses and at the points of connection of inside and outside (Fig. 3(b)). Connection scans have been performed at the two access points so that there are many points in common to join the internal clouds with the external ones (Fig. 3(c,d)).

Fig. 3. a) Laser scanning 3D Survey of the outside: point of station; b) Laser scanning 3D Survey of the inside: point of station; c) Connection between the external and internal point cloud; d) Digital acquisition and data-processing of SS. Crocifisso al Calvario Church.

---

[3] https://www.3dflow.net/it/software-di-fotogrammetria-3df-zephyr/.

The scans (related to the outside, to the porch and the inside) were processed by the Scene software. A set of white reflective spheres (recognized by the program) was used as a target to improve the union and alignment of the scans. The scans were organized in different clusters in the program to simplify the automatic orientation procedures. The registration of all clusters ended with errors maintained below one centimetre.

The reconstruction of the SFM 3D model (Fig. 4) was made aligning about 500 photos (processing together photos taken by the camera with photos taken by the drone). The model created using the Scene software was then exported in .e57 format and imported into Zephyr. The two models were aligned, scaled and oriented by the control points procedure (choosing the homologous points in the different clouds). Point clouds of different origins (camera - drone and laser scanner) were then processed with the Zephyr software.

Fig. 4. Overall view of the SFM reconstruction - SS. Crocifisso al Calvario Church

To avoid overlapping of points (with different levels of detail), in the point cloud obtained by the photos of the drone and of the camera, the external context and only the roof of the church were maintained (deleting the external walls); while in the cloud obtained by the laser scanner, the external context was cut out (Fig. 5). A unique model was thus created by choosing the best parts of the different point clouds: the portico, the interiors (with a view of the vaults) and the external walls from the laser scanner survey; the external context and the roof starting from the camera and drone survey.

6   Point Cloud Processing

The point cloud is computed by Meshlab, a software that allows the processing of large 3D meshes, and also Blender, a software for 3D modelling used in the texturing phase of the model. To obtain the object model of the SS. Crocifisso al Calvario Church, the following steps were performed: a) Point cloud cleaning; b) Mesh reconstruction; c) Mesh simplification; d) Texturing.

To remove noise, markers and objects that can be hidden from the model (e.g. benches) the manual vertex selection and filter "Select outliers" of Meshlab

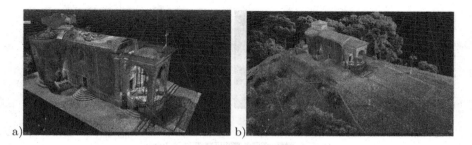

Fig. 5. View of the 3D reconstruction (photogrammetry and laser scanning) - SS. Crocifisso al Calvario Church

have been used. The selected points are deleted or moved to another layer. The outcome of this first stage is then transformed into a mesh. To do this, we leveraged the filter "Surface Reconstruction: Screened Poisson" by setting the *Reconstruction depth parameter* equal to 13 and leaving the value of the other parameters unchanged. A mesh with over 240.000.000 faces was obtained.

The resulting mesh needed to be simplified to have a smooth exploration experience. The simplification was done through the use of the filter "Simplification: Quadratic Edge Collapse Decimation" of Meshlab characterized by: *target number of faces* equal to 1.000.000, *quality threshold* equal to 1, *preserve normal*, *preserve topology*. The outcome is a simplified mesh composed of 1.000.000 faces.

During the texturing phase, UV mapping must be generated to project a 2D image onto the surface of a 3D model. This function splits the object making the application of 2D texture easier. The UV mapping is done through Blender exploiting the "Smart UV Project" function. It is applied to the simplified mesh to get a 3D model in .obj format in which the textures are projected. The file is imported into Meshlab alongside the processed point cloud to transfer the colours from the cloud to the texture. To carry on the process, the filters "Convert PerVertex UV into PerWedge UV" and the function "Transfer: Vertex attributes to texture" were applied subsequently selecting the *texture dimensions* to 16.384×16.384.

7   Use Case Development

The 3D representation of the SS. Crocifisso al Calvario church is passed as input to Unity 3D, which made the embedding of 3D models in VR applications easier through its tools, and a practical visual development environment. The application's goal is to allow the user to explore the cultural asset resembling the reality as much as possible. Thus, the user will be able to move around inside the SS. Crocifisso al Calvario church and admiring its details by getting close to the objects. The application is available for smartphones in combination with Cardboard, Oculus Quest 2 and CAVE (Fig. 6).

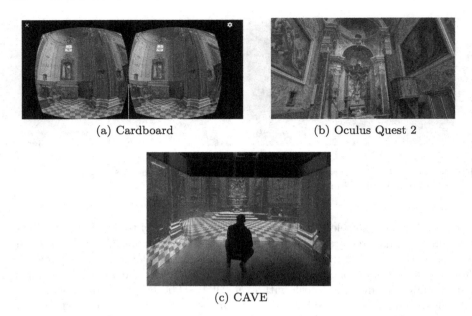

(a) Cardboard   (b) Oculus Quest 2

(c) CAVE

Fig. 6. Virtual exploration of the SS. Crocifisso al Calvario Church

The development of the applications for smartphones with Cardboard and Oculus Quest 2, was based on the use of plugins made available by Unity for the management of VR systems. The applications include the management system for lights and shadows, and they implement the way to allow the player's movements within the environment.

Unlike Oculus Quest 2, which allows the user's movements through physical controllers and the use of dedicated plugins (e.g. Oculus XR Plugin), the usage of smartphones combined with cardboards for the management of player's movements is provided by "trigger points". The trigger points are located in different places in the environment and they are used as means to teleport the user to a different area of the environment. Therefore, if the user looks at one of the trigger points (e.g., a point on the floor) for a certain time interval, the user's position will be set near that point.

The applications have been optimized to guarantee a user experience without breaks (e.g. lags in the navigation of the virtual environment). For this purpose, the lights have been pre-compiled and the shadows have been managed considering the computational resource of the subject device.

We have spent much time tackling the VR sickness or Cybersickness [10] problem, i.e., the feeling of lightheadedness, disorientation, or sickness caused by latency delay. Indeed, the delay can produce a dissonance between actions in the virtual environment and the body movements, generating a sense of disorientation. Such a problem is mainly related to the computational complexity of the system, thus we have down-scaled the texture resolution finding a good threshold between visual quality and computational effort. Choosing the correct resolution provides optimal navigation in the model, including a good level of detail.

A video recording of the exploration of the church wearing the Oculus Quest 2 can be found here[4]. For what concerns the CAVE, the development of the VR application has been focused on its physical structure. It is a 3-wall CAVE consisting of a front wall, a left side wall, and a right sidewall. The CAVE functioning is supported by two workstations that run the application and synchronize the imaging display among the walls. To enjoy the virtual tour by the CAVE, the user wears a tracking system composed of controllers and eyeglasses. The tracking data are sent to the workstations through the VRPN technology, and it is managed by Unity. In this way, the interaction between the user and the virtual environment can happen in real-time by mapping each user's action to a virtual environment update.

From the computational point of view, the CAVE uses high-performance hardware. With this device, it is possible to choose a higher texture resolution for the 3D models and real-time rendering of lights and shadows.

8   Conclusions

The SS. Crocifisso al Calvario church is a valuable cultural asset that we have made explorable by VR devices. The virtual tour has been developed according to a specific pipeline that has led to creating the 3D representation of the church, and the deployment of the app on smartphones equipped with cardboards, headsets, and CAVE.

VR devices have given different performances in terms of immersitivy and quality of the images. The oculus quest headset provides the best immersive effect, thanks to the architecture of the device that hides the real-world perception. The CAVE offers the best resolution despite the immersion effect being quite low. Finally, smartphones equipped with cardboards, though a low-cost solution for experiencing VR, is the worse in terms of both resolution and interactions capabilities. Following the presented approach we are working on the implementation of new apps related to new sites, making more evident the potentiality of VR devices and outlining the value of cultural assets in Sicily. Moreover, Virtual Assistants to embed in the virtual tour are being developed exploiting cutting edge methodologies known as Graph Neural Networks and Text Simplification [21, 22].

Acknowledgements. The following paper has been supported by the project "Creazione di una rete regionale per l'erogazione di servizi innovativi basati su tecnologie avanzate di visualizzazione" (3DLab-Sicilia), Grant No. 08CT4669990220, funded by Operational Program 2014–2020 of the European Regional Development Fund (ERDF) of the Sicilian Region. Daniele Schicchi acknowledges funding from the European Union PON project Ricerca e Innovazione 2014–2020, DM 1062/2021.

---

[4] https://www.3dlab-sicilia.it/en/demo-della-chiesa-del-calvario/.

References

1. Argo, A., et al.: Augmented reality gamification for human anatomy. In: Gentile, M., Allegra, M., Söbke, H. (eds.) GALA 2018. LNCS, vol. 11385, pp. 409–413. Springer, Cham (2019). https://doi.org/10.1007/978-3-030-11548-7_38
2. Arrigo, M., et al.: Heart mobile learning. In: 10th Annual International Conference on Education and New Learning Technologies, EDULEARN 2018, IATED Academy, pp. 10899–10905 (2018)
3. Azuma, R.T.: A survey of augmented reality. Presence Teleoperators Virtual Environ. **6**(4), 355–385 (1997)
4. Banfi, F., Bolognesi, C.M.: Virtual reality for cultural heritage: new levels of computer-generated simulation of a Unesco world heritage site. In: Bolognesi, C., Villa, D. (eds.) From Building Information Modelling to Mixed Reality. STCE, pp. 47–64. Springer, Cham (2021). https://doi.org/10.1007/978-3-030-49278-6_4
5. Barbera, R., et al.: A pipeline for the implementation of immersive experience in cultural heritage sites in Sicily. In: Proceedings of the 3rd International Conference on the Future of Heritage Science and Technologies (2022). In press
6. Barone, Z., Nuccio, G.: For a conscious fruition of the cultural heritage of ancient Noto (Sicily) - EFIAN project as opportunity for valorisation. Int. Arch. Photogramm. Remote Sens. Spat. Inf. Sci. **42** (2017)
7. Bekele, M.K., Pierdicca, R., Frontoni, E., Malinverni, E.S., Gain, J.: A survey of augmented, virtual, and mixed reality for cultural heritage. J. Comput. Cult. Herit. **11**(2), 1–36 (2018)
8. Beraldin, J.A., et al.: Virtual heritage: the cases of the Byzantine Cript of Santa Cristina and temple C of Selinunte. In: Proceedings of 10th International Conference on Virtual Systems and Multimedia (2004)
9. Bruno, F., et al.: Virtual reality technologies for the exploitation of underwater cultural heritage. In: Latest Developments in Reality-Based 3D Surveying and Modelling, pp.220–236 (2018)
10. Chang, E., Kim, H.T., Yoo, B.: Virtual reality sickness: a review of causes and measurements. Int. J. Hum. Comput. Int. **36**(17), 1658–1682 (2020)
11. Costanza, E., Kunz, A., Fjeld, M.: Mixed reality: a survey. In: Lalanne, D., Kohlas, J. (eds.) Human Machine Interaction. LNCS, vol. 5440, pp. 47–68. Springer, Heidelberg (2009). https://doi.org/10.1007/978-3-642-00437-7_3
12. Farella, M., Arrigo, M., Taibi, D., Todaro, G., Chiazzese, G., Fulantelli, G.: ARLectio: an augmented reality platform to support teachers in producing educational resources. CSEDU (2), 469–475 (2020)
13. Freina, L., Ott, M.: A literature review on immersive virtual reality in education: state of the art and perspectives. In: The International Scientific Conference eLearning and Software for Education. (2015)
14. Gaitatzes, A., Christopoulos, D., Roussou, M.: Reviving the past: cultural heritage meets virtual reality. In: Proceedings of the 2001 Conference on Virtual Reality, Archeology, and Cultural Heritage, pp. 103–110 (2001)
15. Griffiths, D., Boehm, J.: A review on deep learning techniques for 3D sensed data classification. Remote Sens. **11**(12), 1499 (2019)
16. John, B., Wickramasinghe, N.: A review of mixed reality in health care. In: Delivering Superior Health and Wellness Management with IoT and Analytics, pp. 375–382 (2020)

17. Manjrekar, S., Sandilya, S., Bhosale, D., Kanchi, S., Pitkar, A., Gondhalekar, M.: CAVE: an emerging immersive technology–a review. In: 2014 UKSim-AMSS 16th international conference on computer modelling and simulation, pp. 131–136. IEEE (2014)
18. Papaefthymiou, M., Plelis, K., Mavromatis, D., Papagiannakis, G.: Mobile virtual reality featuring a six degrees of freedom interaction paradigm in a virtual museum application. Institute of Computer Science (December) (2015)
19. Pierdicca, R., et al.: Point cloud semantic segmentation using a deep learning framework for cultural heritage. Remote Sens. **12**(6), 1005 (2020)
20. Richards-Rissetto, H., Robertsson, J., von Schwerin, J., Agugiaro, G., Remondino, F., Girardi, G.: Geospatial virtual heritage: a gesture-based 3D GIS to engage the public with ancient Maya archaeology. In: Archaeology in the Digital Era. Amsterdam University Press, pp. 118–130 (2014)
21. Schicchi, D., Pilato, G., Lo Bosco, G.: Attention-based model for evaluating the complexity of sentences in English language. In: Proceedings of 20th IEEE Mediterranean Electrotechnical Conference, MELECON 2020, pp. 221–225 (2020)
22. Schicchi, D., Pilato, G., Lo Bosco, G.: Deep neural attention-based model for the evaluation of Italian sentences complexity. In: Proceedings of 14th IEEE International Conference on Semantic Computing, ICSC 2020, pp. 253–256 (2020)
23. Tscheu, F., Buhalis, D.: Augmented reality at cultural heritage sites. In: Inversini, A., Schegg, R. (eds.) Information and Communication Technologies in Tourism 2016, pp. 607–619. Springer, Cham (2016). https://doi.org/10.1007/978-3-319-28231-2_44
24. Zhao, Q.: A survey on virtual reality. Sci. China Inf. Sci. **52**(3), 348–400 (2009)
25. Zheng, J., Chan, K., Gibson, I.: Virtual reality. IEEE Potentials **17**(2), 20–23 (1998)

Automatic Indexing of Virtual Camera Features from Japanese Anime

Gianluca Gualandris[1], Mattia Savardi[1] , Alberto Signoroni[2] ,
and Sergio Benini[1(✉)]

[1] Department of Information Engineering, University of Brescia, Brescia, Italy
g.gualandris002@studenti.unibs.it,
{mattia.savardi,sergio.benini}@unibs.it
[2] Department of Medical and Surgical Specialties, Radiological Sciences,
and Public Health, University of Brescia, Brescia, Italy
alberto.signoroni@unibs.it

Abstract. The position, orientation, and the distance of the camera in
relation to the subject(s) in a movie scene, namely *camera level, camera angle, and shot scale*, are essential features in the film-making process due to their influence on the viewer's perception of the scene. Since
animation techniques exploit drawings or computer graphics objects for
making films instead of camera shooting, the automatic understanding of
such "virtual camera" features appears harder if compared to live-action
movies. Exploiting a dataset of animated movies from popular directors
such as Hayao Miyazaki, Hideaki Anno and Mamoru Oshii, we finetune
pre-trained convolutional neural networks and use One Cycle Learning
Rate to reach convergence in a limited number of epochs. While some difficulties are revealed and discussed in classifying complex features, like
camera angle and camera level, showing F1 scores of respectively 61% and
68%, the classification of the shot scale reaches a score of about 80%, which
is comparable with state-of-the-art methods applied on live-action movies.
The developed models will be useful in conducting automated movie annotation for a wide range of applications, such as in stylistic analysis, video
recommendation, and studies in media psychology. The database and a
demo of the classifiers are available at https://cinescale.github.io/anime

Keywords: Camera angle · Camera level · Shot scale · Movies ·
Convolutional neural network · Anime

1 Introduction

The position of the camera, its orientation, and its distance in relation to the
subject(s) being framed, belong to the set of fundamental features to consider
during film production [2], along with others such as camera motion and editing,
just to name a few. Their importance is due to how such features greatly change
how a movie is experienced with or engaged by a spectator by altering his/her
perception, with the goal of obtaining a more powerful storytelling [9,30].

© The Author(s), under exclusive license to Springer Nature Switzerland AG 2022
P. L. Mazzeo et al. (Eds.): ICIAP 2022 Workshops, LNCS 13373, pp. 186–197, 2022.
https://doi.org/10.1007/978-3-031-13321-3_17

The orientation of the camera, namely *camera angle*, is often employed to show and establish a power dynamic between characters: using low or high angles while framing a character conveys a feeling of inferiority or, respectively, superiority, in the viewer [17, 24].

The distance of the camera from the main subject i.e., *shot scale*, influences the viewer's both lower and higher complexity responses: e.g., close-up shots increase viewers' character engagement responses, such as theory of mind, emotion recognition, and some empathy related processes in the viewers [4, 10]; conversely, longer shots allow the audience to better grasp a reference in space, time, or reality.

The height of the camera i.e., *camera level*, is also a tool for controlling storytelling: the camera positioned at eye/face level with the subject being shot represents a neutral setting for the scene, and it is widely used to show a natural conversation between the subjects (when eye contact is present it is often used to break through the fourth wall i.e., that imaginary wall that separates him from the audience). Ground level takes, instead, are often used to feature characters walking without revealing their face, thus forcing viewers' imagination to guess what it is happening at higher levels.

Such camera techniques have been studied so far mainly in the context of live-action cinema i.e., cinema made with live actors on real film sets. As opposed to live-action movies, animation techniques exploit hand drawings or computer graphics objects for making films instead of camera shooting: thus, a virtual camera system is used to display a view of such virtual world.

The automatic understanding of virtual camera features from animated movie frames appears harder if compared to live-action movies, as the animated movies domain brings with it further difficulties: a completely different use of geometries and colours, a substantial lack of visual depth, different anatomical proportions of bodies (e.g., anime-style eyes), greater freedom in the representation of objects and people, the use of styles of environments and characters ranging from realistic representation to extreme stylisation.

To the best of our knowledge, this is the first work that aims at investigating the problem of automatic indexing of virtual camera features directly from frames of animated movies. To accomplish this goal, three datasets (for shot scale, camera angle, and camera level, respectively) are built by manually annotating frames from fifteen Japanese animated films. Then, three Convolutional Neural Networks (CNNs) pretrained models learn from data using the One Cycle Learning Rate technique to obtain network convergence in a few tens of epochs, providing an advantage in terms of time consumed for training without a degradation of performance.

The rest of the paper is organized as follows. Section 2 presents previous work on the topic, while Sect. 3 describes the datasets used for training and testing, and the augmentation techniques used to compensate for the small amount of available data. Section 4 describes the CNN architectures and training practices used to build the models, while Sect. 5 presents the results and an overview of the classification problems encountered. Finally, conclusions are drawn in Sect. 6.

2 Related Work

No previous publication was found dealing with the automatic recognition of camera features such as camera level and camera angle, and only few regard shot scale. With respect to shot scale, many attempts rely on traditional machine learning approaches, defining sophisticated feature extraction pipelines: for example [7,31] use the relationship between the face-to-frame ratio (thus no scale can be recognized in case of scenes with no actors), while other studies on sport videos [12,13,33,35] evaluate the shot type based on dominant colour and camera movements. In [32] a new complete taxonomy for film semantics and shot type classification is proposed, also according to the distance between the camera and the subject. Similarly, [6] uses linear Support Vector Machines trained on homography parameters to classify frames into eight classes: Pan, Tilt, Zoom, Aerial, Bird eye, Crane, Dolly, and Establishing.

More recently, we are witnessing a simplification of the learning workflows by replacing sophisticated multistage pipelines with end-to-end deep learning models, which improve the overall results. After some attempts with traditional schemes on art movies [5], in [25] we first propose to measure shot scale with CNNs in live-action films. An improved version of this architecture is also used in [29], where shot scale turns to be useful for movie style classification. To enhance the recognition of shot scale, in [3] frames are preprocessed with Mask R-CNN and Yolact to obtain a semantic segmentation which improves on the existing studies. Other approaches on different video material deal with the classification of shots using CNNs in parliamentary debates [21], music concerts [20], and during sporting events [22].

Although a small but fairly active strand of research has been developed in recent years on the use of deep learning techniques applied to the field of animation movies, especially for cartoon character and emotion recognition [18, 34], as far as we know, no research has ever focused on extracting camera features from those.

3 Animated Movie Dataset

3.1 A Taxonomy for Virtual Camera Features

For the aim of this work, virtual camera features are classified into three categories: camera angle, camera level and shot scale. Camera angle accounts from five different classes: *Overhead, High, Neutral, Low, Dutch*, as shown in Fig. 1. It describes camera rotation along the lateral (High, Neutral, and Low) and longitudinal (Dutch) axes. In particular, an Overhead shot indicates a take looking down on a subject from an almost perpendicular angle. Camera level describes the height of the camera in the scene in relation to the subject(s) being framed on six different classes: *Aerial, Eye, Shoulder, Hip, Knee, Ground*, as shown in Fig. 2. In particular an Aerial level is used for shots taken from a considerable height, such as from a plane or a drone, and showing a large portion of the surroundings. Last, shot scale describes the distance from the camera to the

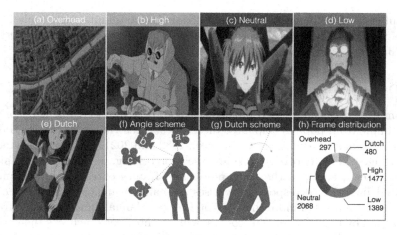

Fig. 1. Camera angle: examples of different classes, a reference scheme and data distribution. Shown frames belong to films a-b) 07, c-d) 02, e) 05 in Table 1.

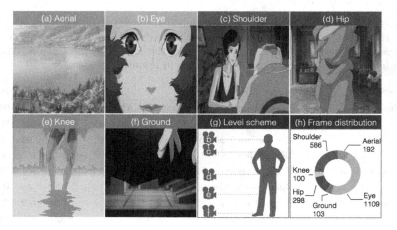

Fig. 2. Camera level: examples of different classes, a reference scheme and data distribution. Shown frames belong to films a) 13, b) 14, c) 07, d) 08, e) 05, f) 03 in Table 1.

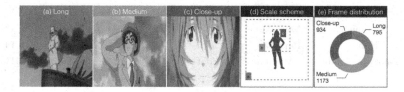

Fig. 3. Shot scale: examples of different classes, a reference scheme and data distribution. Shown frames belong to films a) 07, b) 10, c) 04 in Table 1.

main subject(s). Although the possible distances are infinite, shot scale is usually mapped into three categories: *Long shots*, *Medium shots*, and *Close-ups*, as in Fig. 3.

3.2 Dataset Annotation and Split

The complete list of films used in this work can be found in Table 1. It contains fifteen anime from popular Japanese directors such as Hayao Miyazaki, Hideaki Anno and Mamoru Oshii, directed between 1982 and 2021. We use twelve movies for training, while the other three are used for testing, as specified in Table 1. Table 2 instead, contains the total number of frames extracted and manually annotated into the corresponding classes for camera angle, camera level, and shot scale, for a total of more than 17,000 frames. Manual annotations on frames are provided by two independent coders, while a third person checks their coding and makes decisions in cases of disagreement. To the best of our knowledge this is the largest, and probably the unique database for automatic analysis of virtual camera features in animated movies.

Table 1. List of used films. For each film, a numerical index has been added for references in the text. The asterisk (*) indicates the movies in the test set. The Min column indicates the total duration of the films in minutes.

Director	Movie title	Year	Min	Ref
Hideaki Anno	Evangelion: 1.11 You Are (Not) Alone	2007	98	01
	Evangelion: 2.22 You Can (Not) Advance	2009	108	02
	Evangelion: 3.333 You Can (Not) Redo	2012	96	03
	*Evangelion: 3.0+1.01 Thrice Upon A Time	2021	155	04
Mamoru Oshii	Urusei Yatsura 2: Beautiful Dreamer	1984	101	05
	Ghost in the Shell	1995	83	06
Hayao Miyazaki	Porco Rosso	1992	102	07
	Spirited Away	2001	125	08
	Howl's moving castle	2004	119	09
	*The Wind Rises	2013	126	10
Isao Takahata	The Tale of the Princess Kaguya	2013	137	11
Hiroyuki Imaishi	Promare	2019	111	12
Makoto Shinkai	Your Name	2016	112	13
Satoshi Kon	Paprika	2006	90	14
Tomoharu Katsumata	*Arcadia of My Youth	1982	130	15

3.3 Data Augmentation

The initially extracted dataset is somehow unbalanced for classes which are rarely employed, such as Overhead and Dutch (for camera angle), Aerial, Hip, Knee and Ground (for camera level). To lessen the effect of this imbalance on training, more samples are artificially created through offline data augmentation. To compensate for low numerosity of Dutch shots, images belonging to Neutral camera angle are rotated by angles ranging from $\pm 10°$ to $\pm 30°$ to generate 217 artificial Dutch frames. The sample distributions for each class are illustrated in Figs. 1(h), 2(h), and 3(e), respectively.

Besides the artificial generation of new images, we implement on-the-fly augmentation by operating both geometric and chromatic transformations. With respect to geometric transformations, we apply a horizontal flip and a slight random rotation, avoiding transformations (such as the vertical flip) that would modify the semantics attached to the camera feature. Color augmentation techniques are also applied: b&w filters of varying intensity, swapping and pixel randomization of channels, and cutout regularization as described in [11].

4 Methods

4.1 Model Architecture

The architectures chosen for this work belong to the ResNet [15] and DenseNet [16] families: more specifically, the adopted variants are ResNet50 and DenseNet121. These architectures are chosen since they show superior performance on the ImageNet [23] challenge when compared to older models such as VGG16, while having comparatively fewer parameters. The framework and backend used for the implementation are Keras 2.3.0 [8] and Tensorflow 2.2.0 [1], respectively. To accept the images from the dataset, the input size is increased from 224×224 pixels to 256×256. The feature maps of the last convolutional layer are flattened and passed to two fully connected (FC) layers, with 256 and 128 hidden units, respectively, and with ReLU as activation function, to which *dropout regularization* and *batch normalization* strategies are applied to prevent overfitting, given the small number of samples. Last, the final layer is a FC with sigmoid activation function, with a number of neurons equal to the number of classes to be recognised for each classifier. Training is carried out on a workstation equipped with an GPU NVIDIA Titan Xp and takes about 1h for camera angle, 1.5h for camera level and 0.5h for shot scale.

Table 2. Number of frames annotated for each dataset. Images generated from augmentation procedures are not counted.

Camera-features	Training	Testing
Camera angle	5,494	2,948
Camera level	2,388	1,382
Shot scale	2,934	2,674

Table 3. Best results of tests performed with cross-validation.

Model	LR ranges [27]	Loss	F1-Score
ResNet50 (Angle)	$2 \cdot 10^2 - 2 \cdot 10^3$	0.9625 (±0.018)	0.577 (±0.015)
ResNet50 (Level)	0.023–0.0023	0.0485 (±0.049)	0.642 (±0.011)
ResNet50 (Scale)	0.005–0.0005	0.5583 (±0.009)	0.788 (±0.011)
DenseNet121 (Angle)	0.018–0.0018	1.019 (±0.012)	0.512 (±0.007)
DenseNet121 (Level)	0.025–0.0025	0.852 (±0.053)	0.602 (±0.012)
DenseNet121 (Scale)	0.02–0.002	0.518 (±0.021)	0.777 (±0.016)

4.2   Hyperparameters and Cross-validation

The training process makes use of Adam [19] as optimizer in all experiments. Instead of using traditional fixed or decaying learning rate, we adopt the methods for fast training of complex neural networks described in [28], which allow us to avoid the manual tuning of many hyperparameters such as momentum, learning rate, and weight decay. The chosen learning rate ranges from a minimum of 0.85 to a maximum of 0.95 [14,27]. The metric used for monitoring the performance of the networks is the F1-score, given the multi-label nature of the problem and the heavily imbalanced samples.

In order to evaluate the created model and the chosen hyperparameters, we adopt the k-fold cross-validation strategy ($k = 5$) with only the training dataset: this avoids the possibility that an incorrect static split of the dataset could generate a bias that would invalidate the analysis.

5   Results

In Table 3 we show the results obtained through the cross-validation training of ResNet and DenseNet based networks, for all the three types of camera-features. The obtained scores are calculated as the mean and variance of the loss and F1-Score calculated by averaging the performance on the validation datasets for each of the 5 folds of the cross-validation. From the results, it emerges that the best results for all camera features are obtained by the ResNet50 architecture.

As a consequence, we adopt the ResNet50 network for the next evaluation step, in which learning employs the whole training dataset, while the evaluation is performed on the test one. The obtained results are shown in the Table 4, where, due to the imbalance of samples, the weighted and unweighted measures differ greatly. While the performance obtained on shot scale (F1 = 0.80) is comparable to state-of-the-art similar systems on live-action movies [25], we lack proper state-of-the-art systems to compare the obtained F1-Scores of 0.61 for camera angle and 0.68 for camera level. However, considering the vastness and heterogeneity of the data domain, the limited availability and variety of usable data, and the unbalanced nature of some classes, the results on camera level and angle can be considered satisfactory.

Table 4. F1-Scores obtained from the trained neural networks. F1-Scores are calculated by considering total true positives, false negatives and false positives (F1-micro), or by the sum of the F1-Scores of each class, either weighted (F1-weighted) or arithmetic (F1-macro).

Model	F1-macro	F1-micro	F1-weighted
Camera angle	0.49	0.61	0.62
Camera level	0.59	0.68	0.69
Shot scale	0.80	0.80	0.80

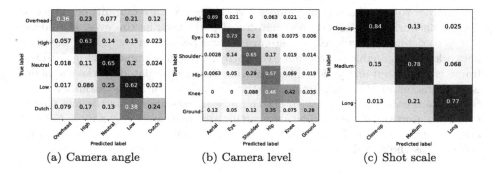

(a) Camera angle   (b) Camera level   (c) Shot scale

Fig. 4. Confusion matrices of the three models obtained on the test data.

5.1   Error Analysis

In Fig. 4 we show the confusion matrices obtained from evaluating the three models on the testing dataset. From inspecting the matrices, and by highlighting (using Grad-CAM [26]) the important regions for the prediction, we can make hypothesis about the main causes of wrongly predicted frames.

First, we notice that in most cases when the class has few images, the network is not able to generalise robust enough recognition patterns, and is inclined to choose other related classes. For example, this happens for the Overhead angle frames, which are often confused with High angle ones. Other rare classes, such as Dutch angle, together with Hip, Knee, and Ground level also suffer from this problem, as shown in Fig. 5(a), where a Dutch frame is wrongly classified as High. The only exception is constituted by the Aerial level images, which are clearly distinguishable from the other classes (i.e., they often depict wide open spaces and vast panoramas) so that the network is able to build a robust model even with relatively few images.

The confusion matrix in Fig. 4(b) shows that Knee and Ground levels are often misclassified as Hip, and similarly some Hip images are classified as Shoulder (as in Fig. 5(b)). The origin of this bias towards the recognition of higher levels is to be found in a specific joint use of camera level and camera angle (e.g., Hip level & Low angle camera: a tilted upward camera framing the subject's torso - a condition which makes the frame akin to a Shoulder level).

Another problem is the fact that the network is incapable of understanding the context of the various scenes. Many manual annotations rely on the knowledge of what is happening in the scene, whereas the network has to determine these responses solely on the basis of the visual stimuli. For example, in Close-up as in Fig. 5(c), it is difficult to discriminate whether the subject is standing (Neutral angle) or lying on the bed (Overhead angle) without context knowledge given by adjacent frames. Similarly, uncoherent results on sequential frames (e.g., the first frame in Fig. 5(g) is correctly classified as High angle, but the second in Fig. 5(h) is wrongly classified as Overhead) could be easily corrected by considering a moving processing window on frames.

Another source of errors in Camera level is the presence of multiple subjects. As the network relies on certain anatomical parts such as the eyes, shoulders, or hip to determine its level, if there are several persons in the frame, then the network is often unable to determine the correct camera reference: in Fig. 5(d) the frame is annotated as Eye level, but the classifier is stimulated by the shoulders of a character in the background, so the final classification is Shoulder level. Some less relevant problems with Dutch angle images arise from the fact that a consistent portion of the training set is artificially generated from simple Neutral angle images, as in Fig. 5(e), while in the test set many Dutch frames are visually complex, as the one shown in Fig. 5(f).

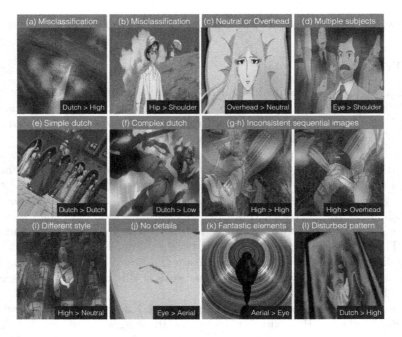

Fig. 5. Examples of some causes of misclassification. In the bottom right corner of the frame we show the predicted class and the correct one (Correct > Predicted). Frames are excerpted from the following movies in Table 1: a) 15, b) 10, c) 15, d) 10, e) 09, f) 04, g-h) 10, i-j-k) 04, l) 15.

There may be other reasons why models fail to classify images: for example, frames with different style from those with which it was trained on (Fig. 5(i)), or when the frame shows not enough details to be considered for classification, as in Fig. 5(j), or when it contains imaginary elements that have no equivalent in reality, as in Fig. 5(k). Finally, misclassification happens when the frame is disturbed by atypical patterns, such as when a glass is interposed between the figure and the camera, as in Fig. 5(l), or when using special lighting effects, color artifacts, or particle elements.

6   Conclusion

In this work, we have implemented three neural network models for the task of indexing virtual camera features such as camera angle, level, and shot scale in Japanese animated films. Starting from the definition of a strict taxonomy to distinguish between camera angle (Overhead, High, Neutral, Dutch, and Low), camera level (Aerial, Eye, Shoulder, Hip, Knee, and Ground), and shot scale (Long, Medium, and Close-up) we created a unique dataset of frame images extracted from fifteen Japanese animated films and manually classified them. We then designed a pre-trained CNN and suitably modified it to solve our classification problem using the transfer learning approach. For training, we relied on new techniques of learning able to guarantee the convergence of the network in a few epochs. Despite some critical aspects mainly due to the difficulty of the task on such a vast and heterogeneous domain, the little availability and variety of data which are currently available, and the resulting unbalance of some classes in the used dataset, the obtained performances are in line with those of similar systems operating on live-action movies [25]. From media psychology, it is well known that the choice of different camera features impact the viewer experience while watching a movie; thus, having an automated system capable of indexing different types of shots would provide noteworthy help to the theoretical study, especially in the field of animation movies that has only recently received attention from researchers in the deep learning field. Finally, beyond indexing for content retrieval, and stylistic analysis, gaining valuable insight into the nature of virtual camera techniques in anime, could be also useful for purposes such as movie recommendation and film therapy.

References

1. Abadi, M., et al.: TensorFlow: large-scale machine learning on heterogeneous systems (2015). https://www.tensorflow.org/
2. Arijon, D.: Grammar of the Film Language. Silman-James Press, Beverly Hills, CA (1976)
3. Bak, H.Y., Park, S.B.: Comparative study of movie shot classification based on semantic segmentation. Appl. Sci. **10**, 3390 (2020)
4. Benini, S., Savardi, M., Bálint, K., Kovács, A.B., Signoroni, A.: On the influence of shot scale on film mood and narrative engagement in film viewers. IEEE Trans. Affect. Comput. 1 (2019). https://doi.org/10.1109/TAFFC.2019.2939251

5. Benini, S., Svanera, M., Adami, N., Leonardi, R., Kovács, A.B.: Shot scale distribution in art films. Multimed. Tools Appl. **75**(23), 16499–16527 (2016). https://doi.org/10.1007/s11042-016-3339-9
6. Bhattacharya, S., Mehran, R., Sukthankar, R., Shah, M.: Classification of cinematographic shots using lie algebra and its application to complex event recognition. IEEE Trans. Multimed. **16**(3), 686–696 (2014). https://doi.org/10.1109/TMM.2014.2300833
7. Cherif, I., Solachidis, V., Pitas, I.: Shot type identification of movie content. In: 2007 9th International Symposium on Signal Processing and Its Applications, pp. 1–4 (2007)
8. Chollet, F., et al.: Keras (2015). https://keras.io
9. Cores Sarría, L.: The influence of camera angle in film narratives. Ph.D. thesis (2015). https://doi.org/10.13140/RG.2.2.23950.69444
10. Cutting, J.E., Armstrong, K.L.: Facial expression, size, and clutter: inferences from movie structure to emotion judgments and back. Atten. Percept. Psychophys. **78**(3), 891–901 (2015). https://doi.org/10.3758/s13414-015-1003-5
11. Devries, T., Taylor, G.W.: Improved regularization of convolutional neural networks with cutout. CoRR abs/1708.04552 (2017). http://arxiv.org/abs/1708.04552
12. Duan, L.Y., Xu, M., Tian, Q., Xu, C.S., Jin, J.: A unified framework for semantic shot classification in sports video. IEEE Trans. Multimedia **7**, 1066–1083 (2006). https://doi.org/10.1109/TMM.2005.858395
13. Ekin, A., Tekalp, A.M.: Robust dominant color region detection with applications to sports video analysis (2003)
14. Gugger, S.: The 1cycle policy. https://sgugger.github.io/the-1cycle-policy.html
15. He, K., Zhang, X., Ren, S., Sun, J.: Deep residual learning for image recognition. In: 2016 IEEE Conference on Computer Vision and Pattern Recognition (CVPR), pp. 770–778 (2016)
16. Huang, G., Liu, Z., van der Maaten, L., Weinberger, K.Q.: Densely connected convolutional networks (2018)
17. Huang, W., Olson, J.S., Olson, G.M.: Camera angle affects dominance in video-mediated communication. In: CHI 2002 Extended Abstracts on Human Factors in Computing Systems, pp. 716–717. Association for Computing Machinery, NY (2002). https://doi.org/10.1145/506443.506562
18. Jain, N., Gupta, V., Shubham, S., Madan, A., Chaudhary, A., Santosh, K.C.: Understanding cartoon emotion using integrated deep neural network on large dataset. Neural Comput. Appl. 1–21 (2021). https://doi.org/10.1007/s00521-021-06003-9
19. Kingma, D.P., Ba, J.: Adam: a method for stochastic optimization. In: Bengio, Y., LeCun, Y. (eds.) 3rd International Conference on Learning Representations, ICLR 2015, San Diego, CA, 7–9 May 2015, Conference Track Proceedings (2015). http://arxiv.org/abs/1412.6980
20. Lin, J.C., et al.: Coherent deep-net fusion to classify shots in concert videos. IEEE Trans. Multimed. **20**(11), 3123–3136 (2018). https://doi.org/10.1109/TMM.2018.2820904
21. Marín-Reyes, P.A., Lorenzo-Navarro, J., Santana, M.C., Sánchez-Nielsen, E.: Shot classification and keyframe detection for vision based speakers diarization in parliamentary debates. In: CAEPIA (2016)
22. Minhas, R.A., Javed, A., Irtaza, A., Mahmood, M.T., Joo, Y.B.: Shot classification of field sports videos using AlexNet convolutional neural network. Appl. Sci. **9**(3), 483 (2019). https://doi.org/10.3390/app9030483

23. Russakovsky, O., et al.: ImageNet large scale visual recognition challenge. Int. J. Comput. Vis. **115**(3), 211–252 (2015). https://doi.org/10.1007/s11263-015-0816-y
24. Sätteli, H.P.: The effect of different vertical camera-angles on faceperception (2010)
25. Savardi, M., Signoroni, A., Migliorati, P., Benini, S.: Shot scale analysis in movies by convolutional neural networks. In: 2018 25th IEEE International Conference on Image Processing (ICIP), pp. 2620–2624 (2018). https://doi.org/10.1109/ICIP.2018.8451474
26. Selvaraju, R.R., Das, A., Vedantam, R., Cogswell, M., Parikh, D., Batra, D.: Grad-CAM: why did you say that? Visual explanations from deep networks via gradient-based localization. CoRR abs/1610.02391 (2016). http://arxiv.org/abs/1610.02391
27. Smith, L.N.: Cyclical learning rates for training neural networks. In: 2017 IEEE Winter Conference on Applications of Computer Vision, WACV 2017, Santa Rosa, CA, 24–31 March 2017, pp. 464–472. IEEE Computer Society (2017). https://doi.org/10.1109/WACV.2017.58
28. Smith, L.N.: A disciplined approach to neural network hyper-parameters: Part 1 - learning rate, batch size, momentum, and weight decay. CoRR abs/1803.09820 (2018). http://arxiv.org/abs/1803.09820
29. Svanera, M., Savardi, M., Signoroni, A., Kovács, A.B., Benini, S.: Who is the film's director? Authorship recognition based on shot features. IEEE Multimed. **26**(4), 43–54 (2019). https://doi.org/10.1109/MMUL.2019.2940004
30. Tarvainen, J., Laaksonen, J., Takala, T.: Film mood and its quantitative determinants in different types of scenes. IEEE Trans. Affect. Comput. **11**(2), 313–326 (2020). https://doi.org/10.1109/TAFFC.2018.2791529
31. Tsingalis, I., Vretos, N., Nikolaidis, N., Pitas, I.: SVM-based shot type classification of movie content. In: Proceedings of 9th Mediterranean Electro Technical Conference. Istanbul, pp. 104–107 (2012)
32. Wang, H.L., Cheong, L.F.: Taxonomy of directing semantics for film shot classification. IEEE Trans. Circuits Syst. Video Technol. **19**(10), 1529–1542 (2009). https://doi.org/10.1109/TCSVT.2009.2022705
33. Xie, L., Chang, F., Divakaran, A., Sun, H.: Structure analysis of soccer video with hidden Markov models. In: 2002 IEEE International Conference on Acoustics, Speech, and Signal Processing (2001). https://doi.org/10.1109/ICASSP.2002.5745558
34. Zheng, Y., et al.: Cartoon face recognition: a benchmark dataset, pp. 2264–2272. Association for Computing Machinery, NY (2020). https://doi.org/10.1145/3394171.3413726
35. Zhou, Y.H., Cao, Y.D., Zhang, L.F., Zhang, H.X.: An SVM-based soccer video shot classification. In: 2005 International Conference on Machine Learning and Cybernetics, vol. 9, pp. 5398–5403 (2005). https://doi.org/10.1109/ICMLC.2005.1527898

Imageability-Based Multi-modal Analysis of Urban Environments for Architects and Artists

Theodora Pistola[1]([✉]), Nefeli Georgakopoulou[1], Alexander Shvets[2],
Konstantinos Chatzistavros[1], Vasileios-Rafail Xefteris[1], Alba Táboas García[2],
Ilias Koulalis[1], Sotiris Diplaris[1], Leo Wanner[2,3], Stefanos Vrochidis[1],
and Ioannis Kompatsiaris[1]

[1] Information Technologies Institute - CERTH, Thessaloniki, Greece
tpistola@iti.gr
[2] NLP Group, Pompeu Fabra University, Roc Boronat, 138 Barcelona, Spain
[3] Catalan Institute for Research and Advanced Studies (ICREA), Barcelona, Spain

Abstract. According to urban planner Kevin Lynch, imageability is the ability of a physical object to evoke a strong image in any viewer, making it memorable. The concept of imageability is important for architects and urban designers, so that their creations meet the needs of the citizens and improve the aesthetics of the place. Recently, computer vision and textual analysis techniques have been investigated for calculating the imageability of a place. In this paper, we propose a novel multi-modal system that utilises both visual and textual analysis methods to estimate the imageability score of a place. In addition, an image sentiment analysis deep learning model had been developed to provide supplementary information about the sentiment that is evoked to citizens by urban locations. Finally, a text generation algorithm is used to provide an explanation of the information extracted by the data analysis in a form of text to facilitate the works of architects and urban designers.

Keywords: Imageability · Urban design · Visual analysis · Text analysis

1 Introduction

1.1 The City Image and Imageability

The visual quality of a city or an art object is often associated with imageability according to Kevin Lynch or apparency according to Paul Stern respectively. Stern used this term in 1914 to describe the function of art as the creation of *images which by clarity and harmony of form fulfill the need of vividly comprehensible appearance* [2]. Imageability according to the urban planner Kevin Lynch [2] is *the quality of a physical object to evoke a strong image in any*

P. L. Mazzeo et al. (Eds.): ICIAP 2022 Workshops, LNCS 13373, pp. 198–209, 2022.
https://doi.org/10.1007/978-3-031-13321-3_18

observer, thus being memorable. As imageability first appeared in art and architecture, Paivio et al. [1] working in the field of Psycholinguistics proposed imageability as a measurement for quantizing the human perception of words and the ease with which they create a mental image. An attractive architectural and spatial environment can enlarge our sense of the present and heighten the intensity of human experience thus making it memorable. Nowadays, research in architecture can apply visual and textual assessment tools to articulate the relationship between physical forms, human behavior, sentiment and memory. The purpose of this work is to deploy a prototype that helps architects and artists to articulate proposals centered on improving the urban experience and consequently the imageability of selected urban spaces. Our approach is by engaging citizens in a design process centered in imageability and people's preferences which can provide a valuable consideration in conserving or changing certain areas in a city. Street view imagery (SVI) created opportunities for new approaches to urban and architectural design [25], enabling the assessment of images from the pedestrian perspective allowing to assess imageability remotely. Simultaneously advances in computer vision (CV) have created the means to process a great amount of images efficiently, and in natural language processing (NLP) methods have been proposed to estimate imageability through supervised machine learning, using word embeddings as explanatory variables [12]. In this work, we propose a multi-modal system that combines visual and textual analysis techniques, along with Lynch elements' information to calculate the imageability of urban spaces. Our goal is to determine the characteristics that contribute to a place's imageability to aid architects and urban planners create urban spaces with high imageability. Therefore every produced segment is categorized between the five lynch elements according to the one they most closely fit. For the presentation of the data analysis results to the architects and urban designers a text generation method is utilised. Our method has been applied to data collected from the city of L'Hospitalet de Llobregat.

1.2 Case Study

The case study concerns the design proposal of an outdoors space in a vibrant, modern city neighborhood (City de L'Hospitalet) aiming to attract citizens and users of public space through a participatory design process. L'Hospitalet de Llobregat is a city located in the metropolitan area of Barcelona. Being Catalonia's second city, with a population of more than 262.000 inhabitants, it faces major challenges regarding high urban density, high levels of multiculturalism and an industrial past, which has shaped the city. The past 20 years have brought intensive urban, economic and cultural programs creating today a dynamic metropolis that attracts artists, new companies and new population.

2   Related Work

In this section, we review related works that use visual and/or textual analysis techniques to compute the imageability of urban environments.

2.1   Related Visual Analysis Techniques

The authors of [18] present a crowdsourcing project aiming to investigate, at scale, which visual aspects of London neighborhoods make them appear beautiful, quiet, and/or happy by using modern image processing techniques. The researchers of [19] propose a novel approach for predicting the perceived safety of a scene from Google Street View Images, using the Place Pulse 1.0 dataset, by employing a new Convolutional Neural Network (CNN) architecture. In [20] the authors introduced the crowdsourced the Place Pulse 2.0 dataset, containing 110,988 images from 56 cities, and 1,170,000 pairwise comparisons provided by 81,630 online volunteers along six perceptual attributes: safe, lively, boring, wealthy, depressing, and beautiful. Using this dataset, they train a Siamese-like CNN that learns from a joint classification and ranking loss, to predict human judgements of pairwise image comparisons. The researchers of [21] created an annotated dataset from Street View Imagery (SVI) with four qualities, one of which is "imageability", using computer vision and machine learning techniques to acquire prediction scores for each one of the four qualities. Given the interdisciplinary character of this study, a better understanding may be provided-not only of how planning effects our experience of place, but also of how emotions, cognition, and actions impact community planning and development, as [32] indicate. Due to the low discussion on the effectiveness of integrating subjective measures with the SVI dataset, an effort towards measuring four important urban design theory perceptions via crowdsourcing, computer vision (CV), and machine learning (ML) took place, by collecting experts' ratings [22].

2.2   Related Textual Analysis Techniques

In [29], two social media-based indicators of imageability were proposed. The first one, the frequency of a place captured on Instagram, was linked to its perception as an architectural landmark and tourist attraction via keyword search and scene recognition algorithms while further validating results by a second step manual labelling. The second one, the frequency of a place mentioned on Twitter by name, was linked to its perceived niceness and relevance to everyday life. The approach is limited to a keyword search in messages lacking the deeper text analysis and therefore it does not reveal the elements that make the place more or less imageable. Working under the assumption that there is a relationship between the imageability of concepts, human perception, and the contents of Web-crawled images, the authors of [30] trained a regression model to assign imageability scores to individual classes of concepts having a large and balanced set of images. The classes were defined by merging three levels of hypernyms from WordNet [31], showing that the less variation in visual features the concept has across images the higher the imageability score is. This is inherent in concrete easy-to-grasp words like *car* in contrast to abstract words, which tend to be less imageable and have a much higher visual variety. The authors of [14] made a step further and assessed the imageability based on entire sentences that may contain many concepts at once. They added imageability feature vectors to the input of the neural LSTM-based text generation model with visual attention and showed promising results in generating imageability-aware image captions.

3   The Proposed Multi-modal System - Method

In this section, the contributing algorithms towards calculating imageability are presented. The process is based on data mining from the image's visual characteristics and corresponding comments while associating them with given weights towards the pipeline's objective. Hence the proposed system presented in Fig. 1 incorporates visual and textual analysis services, while also a module responsible for calculating realistic results that can be exploited by architects and designers in order to design engaging urban environments.

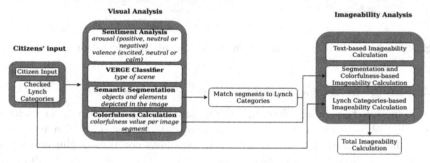

Fig. 1. The proposed multi-modal pipeline.

In order to fine-tune our system's algorithms, we asked for feedback related to imageability through questionnaires based on images from the city of L'Hospitalet de Llobregat. The questionaires ask for a score of how memorable the depicted place is, what objects or elements increase its memorability and if a specific scene (e.g., a park) can be detected in the image. Five people that come from artistic/design and technological background answered the questionaires and their answers were used as a guide to develop our multimodal system.

3.1   Visual Analysis Algorithms

3.1.1   Scene Recognition

Throughout this research we used publicly available DCNNs fine-tuned on the Places365 [9] dataset to extract place-related concepts. Specifically the utilized the VGG16-Places365 model with top-1 and top-5 accuracy 55.19% and 85.01% respectively. This research focuses on outdoor urban and architectural design, subsequently indoor information is irrelevant and the initial indoor classes of the pre-trained classifier are excluded. Doing so, from the initial 365 classes, finally 331 outdoor related classes are taken into consideration in the pipeline reducing the potential inserted noise towards estimating imageability, generating robust results.

building - 48.32%
Colorfulness: 52.04

road - 26.16%
Colorfulness: 6.32

sky - 13.87% -
Colorfulness: 4.89

car - 8.56% -
Colorfulness: 24.30

tree - 1.42% -
Colorfulness: 11.15

person - 0.86% -
Colorfulness: 8.20

sidewalk - 0.35% -
Colorfulness: 10.79

poster - 0.22% -
Colorfulness: 30.15

streetlight - 0.13% -
Colorfulness: 37.24

wall - 0.09% -
Colorfulness: 13.17

(a) Input image   (b) Image Semantic Segmentation result

Fig. 2. Example of image segmentation and colourfulness calculation per segment.

3.1.2   Image Semantic Segmentation

We also included an Image Semantic Segmentation algorithm in order to local-ize specific objects and elements in the analyzed images. The idea here is to extract the information about objects and elements composing the image and the amount of the image that each of them covers. To achieve this, we deployed the PixelLlib[1]0 framework with a DeepLabV3+ architecture [23] trained on the ADE20K dataset [24], which consists of 150 different classes of objects and ele-ments. Our algorithm provides the percentage that every localized class covers in the image while pixel-wise accuracy and mIOU are 82.52% and 45.65% respec-tively (Fig. 2).

3.1.3   Calculation of Colourfulness

Colour is one of the most important features in the images. Vivid colors make an image more memorable compared to less colorful images [26]. Based on this, we decided that it would be helpful to also include colour information to our imageability calculations. In [27] the authors propose an algorithm for the cal-culation of the overall colourfulness of an image, which, depending on its value, belongs to one of the following categories: 1) not colourful, 2) slightly colour-ful, 3) moderately colourful, 4) averagely colourful, 5) quite colourful, 6) highly colourful or 7) extremely colourful. The colourfulness calculation algorithm was defined after the authors conducted a psychophysical experiment using 20 non expert viewers, asking them to give a global colourfulness rating for a set of 84 images. The users had to choose among the above categories. Based on the above work, we developed an algorithm that computes the colourfulness value for every image segment extracted from the Image Semantic Segmentation algorithm.

---

[1] https://github.com/ayoolaolafenwa/PixelLib.

3.1.4 Image Sentiment Analysis

Image sentiment analysis facilitates designing multimodal systems by evaluating human emotional stimuli in order to shape architectural design rules. All sentiment extraction tasks, foster subjectivity risks that governs human emotions [3]. Utilizing Convolutional Neural Networks (CNNs) such as [5–8] are a potential effective way towards extracting a viewer's emotional stimulus and in this work the two dimensional representation system was followed, with three classes for valence(Positive, Neutral, Negative) and arousal(Excited, Neutral, Calm) as seen in Fig. 3a. Concerning the datasets content, 32.82% is derived from Unity virtual environments[2] of 3D spaces with multiple configurations depicting public spaces and urban cultural landmarks. In order to examine 3D space and its effect on human sentiment, a dataset was constructed, utilising GoogleForms[3]. Each image was followed by a question regarding the evaluation of three aforementioned valence and arousal classes. Doing so, two slightly unbalanced datasets were formed, as ground truth labels were retrieved based on the majority voting, while every image was annotated at least by 5 individuals, similarly to [4]. GoogleForms enabled to control the number and non-duplication of annotators' answers. Simultaneously the annotation process became less exhausting and error-prone, while the interface contained objectives details in Spanish, English and French.

For every of the aforementioned architectures the top Dense classification layers were discarded and replaced with new ones that fit the problem's needs. Hence, as seen in Fig. 3b, convolutional layers will work as feature extractors and the newly introduced top of every architecture will be capable of interpreting the found patterns. We employed 5-fold cross-validation, which means that each dataset is partitioned into k = 5 equally sized parts where 80% of the images are used for training and 20% for validation, while the produced models where tested on an independent test set. Furthermore, we applied a weighted optimization during the training phase to tackle the imbalanced data, where the significance

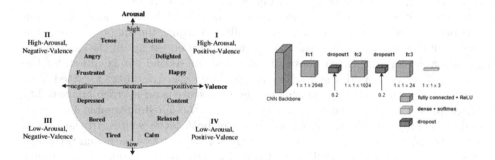

Fig. 3. a) Two dimensional valence - arousal representation. b) Newly inserted head on top of backbone CNN architectures.

[2] https://assetstore.unity.com/3d/environments.
[3] https://www.google.com/forms/about/.

of each sample is proportional to the number of samples in each class. That is, we give a minority class increased weight and a majority class reduced weight, while simultaneously image augmentation techniques were applied.

Throughout experiments every image was resized to $[224 \times 224 \times 3]$, batch size was set to 32, Adam optimizer was utilised with a 0.0001 learning rate for 20 epochs. Finally, the image sentiment analysis branch is based on two fine-tuned VGG-16 architectures, with a predictive ability of 61% and 60% valence and arousal respectively, estimating between three classes for each image.

3.1.5   Text-Based Imageability Assessment

Via text, citizens express their perception of urban space, taking forms: as it can be a short comment that shares an immediate experience or a long descriptive message pointing to social problems associated with public spaces arrangement. Multilingualism is another characteristic of texts, as people speak a variety of languages. These two peculiarities create a challenge in assessing imageability through text analysis[4]. Firstly, general-purpose concept extraction techniques applicable to texts of various nature (short spontaneous vs long thought-for messages) shall be used to detect concepts reflecting a mental image. Secondly, as shown in [10], there is no clear one-to-one correspondence between imageability ratings across languages due to variance in concepts dependent on cultural or socio-economic factors, therefore, every language shall be analysed using models incorporating these factors and result in different mappings to imageability ratings.

We opt for an open class pointer-generator-based concept extraction model that allows for transforming a sentence into a sequence of single- and multi-word concepts [11]. Similarly to [11], we trained this model on Wikipedia texts in several languages namely, English, Catalan, Spanish, and Greek). We use two dictionaries with imageability ratings to score concepts [12,13]. The first dictionary contains entries for 77 languages with 100K scores per language obtained automatically by transferring from one language to another with cross-lingual word embeddings trained on a crowdsourced dataset. We used the second small dictionary of 5.5K ratings of a higher quality to adjust the shape of the distribution of the first dictionary so that all the ratings ended up on the same scale. In case a concept appears in both dictionaries, the second one is chosen for the scoring. The text-based imageability is calculated over concepts extracted from a message by the pointer-generator model. One score is an average imageability of all concepts, another score - an average of the top-three imageable concepts , and the overall score is the harmonic mean of both latter scores. In the case of multi-word concepts, the rating of the headword is taken as a base, and ratings of the remaining words are used as modifiers similarly to the sentence imageability calculation in [14].

---

[4] In this work, we experimented with free-text comments that were apriori about spaces, as stated in Sect. 4. Therefore, we left other challenges such as the separation of texts about spaces and happenings in spaces for future research.

3.1.6   Imageability Computation

When the agreement of the place recognition between different subjects is high, this place has a high imageability score. Our novel multimodal imageability computation of the cities is based on the multimodal decision level fusion of image and textual information, along with users' annotation over the whole scene. Hence, computing imageability is divided into three different computations; segmentation-based, lynch-based, and text-based imageability respectively, while those three different scores are fused in a decision level manner.

For every segmentation-based imageability score, the segments are categorized into the five lynch elements. For example, the road and fence segment are assigned to the path and the edge element respectively. This categorization makes it easier to assess the agreement of different subjects in recognizing a place. Each lynch element is getting an imageability score based on the disagreement of the subjects in [16,17], since the imageability of cities is based on the ability of different subjects to recognize the same elements. The final segmentation-based imageability score is the weighted average score of each recognized element of each image, using as weights the segment percentage and the colourfulness. The lynch-based imageability is computed from the overall classification of the users over the different lynch elements. Again, the imageability score of each lynch element is computed based on the disagreement in [16,17]. The text-based imageability is computed as described in Sect. 3.1.5. The multimodal imageability computation is performed by averaging all of the sub-scores described above, having equal contribution towards the final multimodal imageability estimation.

3.1.7   Explanatory Text Generation

In order to provide interpretable system results to an end-user, an explanatory text generation module was designed taking as input numerical and categorical outcome values of pipelined components described in Sect. 3.1.1–3.1.6, aggregating the information, and verbalising it to form a natural text. Hence it works as an explainability feature of the proposed multi-model system. The backbone of the module was built within the graph-transduction framework FORGe [15], which is a multilayer grammar-based generator that features high portability to new languages and domains with little data requirements for the adaptation. The generator, following the precepts of the Meaning-Text Theory [28], is based on the notion of linguistic dependencies, such as semantic, syntactic, and morphologic relations between the components of the sentence. The other main component of the module is in charge of the projection of formal constructs, containing information from the output of visual and text analysis, onto the lexicalised semantic structures that the generator needs as input.

In the context of this paper, we developed the specific mapping between the extracted information in formal representation, creating 20 different predicate-argument templates associated with properties in the formal constructs. Regarding the grammar-based generator, we added 8 new rules and modified 33 existing

The place in the image forms a coherent scene, which has been classified as a campus. The image is fairly colourful. The overall imageability score, to which the colourfulness contributes in a positive way, is 5.8 out of 7. The most colourful element is the sky.
The image contains a hardly colourful sidewalk, which occupies 24% of the space. The image contains a quite colourful sky, which occupies 19% of the space. The image contains a slightly colourful building, which occupies 19% of the space. The image probably contains a quite colourful signboard, which occupies 4% of the space.
The visual analysis reveals that the image conveys a neutral emotion and a positive feeling. The analysis of the text indicates that the place is somewhat memorable (text-based imageability score of 6.5 out of 7). The most memorable element is "rotonda".

Fig. 4. The outcome of the text generation service.

ones to cover the required morpho-syntactic phenomena, including, for instance, the introduction of support verbs within subordinate clauses, the correct placement of adverbs, and the inflection of finite regular verbs. In addition to that, the lexicons were expanded with approximately 100 entries for each language (English, Spanish and Catalan) in order to comply with the provided inputs. In total, about 700 out of 2500 rules incorporated in FORGe are activated for a single output text. An example of generated text that corresponds to the image in Fig. 6a is shown in Fig. 4.[5]

4   Experiments and Results

4.1   Workshop

The "Instant Cities' workshop aimed to identify the citizens' perception of the city utilizing the categories as defined by Kevin Lynch's five elements: node, path, edge, district, and landmark. Following Lynch's categories, and the identified L'Hospitalet societal needs, an image dataset of everyday life around the city was compiled ready for use during the user workshop. The workshop involved 6 gender and age-balanced citizens and took place at the premises of the L'Hospitalet City Council on May 7th 2020. During the workshop the participants conducted virtual walks using a web based tool developed over Google Street View and Google Maps designed for data collection. During their navigation they were able to look around in any direction and bookmark elements of the city classifying them in Lynch's categories while also commenting on what influenced their decision. A dataset of 66 items was collected including text comments, images and Lynch classifications.

4.2   Results

In Fig. 6 the images with the maximum and minimum total imageability are presented, while image in Fig. 6 a) has 5.6379 and in b) 3.4773 respectively. In Fig. 6 all the segments included in the image (park, sidewalk, building) and the

---

[5] The concept "rotonda" is taken from user describing nearby roundabout which is not captured on the image.

classification of the image as node offer a high imageability score. In Fig. 6 b) the included car and motorbike segments highly influence the segmentation based imageability, but such segments do not offer to the total imageability of a city (Fig. 5).

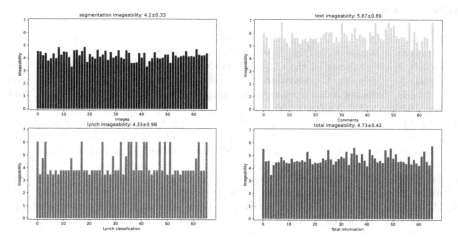

Fig. 5. Imageability results based on segmentation, text analysis, lynch classification, and the fused results. Along the x-axis are the ids of images, texts, and lynch classifications corresponding to the same input.

Fig. 6. a) Image with the maximum total imageability score. b) Image with the minimum total imageability score.

5 Conclusions

In this work, we presented a novel multi-modal system for the calculation of imageability of urban places, aiming to assist architects and urban designers to create places that meet the needs of citizens and improve the image of the location. The proposed system also extracts complementary sentiment information for every image of interest, while it provides all the information that derives from the data analysis in the form of text through a text generation technique.

Acknowledgments.. This work was supported by the EC-funded research and innovation programme H2020 Mindspaces: "Art-driven adaptive outdoors and indoors design" under the grant agreement No.825079.

References

1. Paivio, A., Yuille, J.C., Madigan, S.A.: Concreteness, imagery, and meaningfulness values for 925 nouns. J. Exp. Psychol. **76**, 1–25 (1968)
2. Lynch, K.: The Image of the City, vol. 11. MIT press, Cambridge (1960)
3. Ortis, A., Farinella, G., Battiato, S.: An overview on image sentiment analysis: methods. datasets and current challenges. ICETE, 290–300 (2019). https://doi.org/10.5220/0007909602900300
4. You, Q., Luo, J., Jin, H., Yang, J.: Robust image sentiment analysis using progressively trained and domain transferred deep networks. In: Proceedings of the Twenty-Ninth AAAI Conference on Artificial Intelligence, AAAI 2015, pp. 381–388. AAAI Press (2015)
5. Simonyan, K., Zisserman, A.: Very deep convolutional networks for large-scale image recognition. arXiv preprint arXiv:1409.1556 (2014)
6. He, K., Zhang, X., Ren, S., Sun, J.: Deep residual learning for image recognition. In: Proceedings of the IEEE Conference on Computer Vision and Pattern Recognition, pp. 770–778 (2016)
7. Huang, G., Liu, Z., Van Der Maaten, L., Weinberger, K.Q.: Densely connected convolutional networks. In: Proceedings of the IEEE Conference on Computer Vision and Pattern Recognition, pp. 4700–4708 (2017)
8. Chollet, F.: Xception: deep learning with depthwise separable convolutions. In: Proceedings of the IEEE Conference on Computer Vision and Pattern Recognition, pp. 1251–1258 (2017)
9. Zhou, B., Lapedriza, À., Khosla, A., Oliva, A., Torralba, A.: Places: a 10 million image database for scene recognition. IEEE Trans. Pattern Anal. Mach. Intell. **40**, 1452–1464 (2017). https://doi.org/10.1109/TPAMI.2017.2723009
10. Rofes, A., et al.: Imageability ratings across languages. Behav. Res. Methods **50**(3), 1187–1197 (2017). https://doi.org/10.3758/s13428-017-0936-0
11. Shvets, A., Wanner, L.: Concept extraction using pointer–generator networks and distant supervision for data augmentation. In: Keet, C.M., Dumontier, M. (eds.) EKAW 2020. LNCS (LNAI), vol. 12387, pp. 120–135. Springer, Cham (2020). https://doi.org/10.1007/978-3-030-61244-3_8
12. Ljubešić, N., Fišer, D., Peti-Stantić, A.: Predicting concreteness and imageability of words within and across languages via word embeddings. arXiv preprint arXiv:1807.02903 (2018)
13. Scott, G.G., Keitel, A., Becirspahic, M., Yao, B., Sereno, S.C.: The glasgow norms: ratings of 5,500 words on nine scales. Behav. Res. Methods **51**(3), 1258–1270 (2018). https://doi.org/10.3758/s13428-018-1099-3
14. Umemura, K., et al.: Tell as you imagine: sentence imageability-aware image captioning. In: Lokoč, J., et al. (eds.) MMM 2021. LNCS, vol. 12573, pp. 62–73. Springer, Cham (2021). https://doi.org/10.1007/978-3-030-67835-7_6
15. Mille, S., Carlini, R., Burga, A., Wanner, L.: FORGe at SemEval-2017 Task 9: deep sentence generation based on a sequence of graph transducers. In: Proceedings of the 11th International Workshop on Semantic Evaluation, Vancouver, pp. 920–923 (2017)

16. Meenar, M., Afzalan, N., Hajrasouliha, A.: Analyzing Lynch's city imageability in the digital age. J. Plan. Educ. Res., 0739456X19844573 (2019)
17. McCunn, L.J., Gifford, R.: Spatial navigation and place imageability in sense of place. Cities **74**, 208–218 (2018)
18. LNCS Homepage. www.springer.com/lncs. Accessed 21 Nov 2016
19. Quercia, D., O'Hare, N.K., Cramer, H.: Aesthetic capital: what makes London look beautiful, quiet, and happy?. In: Proceedings of the 17th ACM Conference on Computer Supported Cooperative Work & Social Computing, pp. 945–955 (2014)
20. Porzi, L., Rota Buló, S., Lepri, B., Ricci, E.: Predicting and understanding urban perception with convolutional neural networks. In: Proceedings of the 23rd ACM International Conference on Multimedia, pp. 139–148 (2015)
21. Dubey, A., Naik, N., Parikh, D., Raskar, R., Hidalgo, C.A.: Deep learning the city: quantifying urban perception at a global scale. In: Leibe, B., Matas, J., Sebe, N., Welling, M. (eds.) ECCV 2016. LNCS, vol. 9905, pp. 196–212. Springer, Cham (2016). https://doi.org/10.1007/978-3-319-46448-0_12
22. Qiu, W., Li, W., Liu, X., Huang, X.: Subjective street scene perceptions for Shanghai with large-scale application of computer vision and machine learning (No. 6166). EasyChair (2021)
23. Chen, L.C., Zhu, Y., Papandreou, G., Schroff, F., Adam, H.: Encoder-decoder with atrous separable convolution for semantic image segmentation. In: Proceedings of the European Conference on Computer Vision (ECCV), pp. 801–818 (2018)
24. Zhou, B., et al.: Semantic understanding of scenes through the ade20k dataset. Int. J. Comput. Vision **127**(3), 302–321 (2019)
25. Biljecki, F., Ito, K.: Street view imagery in urban analytics and GIS: a review. Landscape Urban Plan. **215**, 104217 (2021)
26. Isola, P., Xiao, J., Parikh, D., Torralba, A., Oliva, A.: What makes a photograph memorable? IEEE Trans. Pattern Anal. Mach. Intell. **36**(7), 1469–1482 (2013)
27. Hasler, D., Suesstrunk, S.E.: Measuring colorfulness in natural images. In: Human Vision and Electronic Imaging VIII, vol. 5007, pp. 87–95. International Society for Optics and Photonics (2003)
28. Mel'čuk, I.: Dependency Syntax. State University of New York Press, Albany (1988)
29. Huang, J., Obracht-Prondzynska, H., Kamrowska-Zaluska, D., Sun, Y., Li, L.: The image of the city on social media: a comparative study using "Big Data" and "Small Data" methods in the Tri-City Region in Poland. Landscape Urban Plan. **206**, 103977 (2021)
30. Kastner, M.A., et al.: Estimating the imageability of words by mining visual characteristics from crawled image data. Multimedia Tools Appl. **79**(3), 18167–18199 (2020). https://doi.org/10.1007/s11042-019-08571-4
31. Miller, G.A.: WordNet: a lexical database for English. Commun. ACM **38**(11), 39–41 (1995). https://doi.org/10.1145/219717.219748
32. Manzo, L.C., Perkins, D.D.: Finding common ground: the importance of place attachment to community participation and planning. J. Plan. Lit. **20**, 335–350 (2006)

Challenges in Image Matching for Cultural Heritage: An Overview and Perspective

F. Bellavia[1]($\boxtimes$)(iD), C. Colombo[2](iD), L. Morelli[3,4](iD), and F. Remondino[3](iD)

[1] University of Palermo, Palermo, Italy
`fabio.bellavia@unipa.it`
[2] University of Florence, Florence, Italy
`carlo.colombo@unifi.it`
[3] Bruno Kessler Foundation (FBK), Trento, Italy
`{lmorelli,remondino}@fbk.eu`
[4] University of Trento, Trento, Italy

Abstract. Image matching, as the task of finding correspondences in images, is the upstream component of vision and photogrammetric applications aiming at the reconstruction of 3D scenes, their understanding and comparison. Such applications are of special importance in the context of cultural heritage, as they can support archaeologists to digitally preserve, restore and analyze antiquities, but also to compare their changes over time. The success of deep learning, now firmly established, paired with the evolution of computer hardware, has led to many advances in image processing, including image matching. Despite this progress, image matching still offers challenges, in terms of the matching process itself but also on other practical and technical aspects. This paper gives an overview of the current status of the research in image matching with a particular focus on cultural heritage, presenting both strengths and weaknesses of the most recent approaches by means of visual comparisons on exemplar challenging image pairs. Besides assisting researchers and practitioners in the choice of the most suitable solution for a given task, this analysis also suggests lines of research worth to be investigated by the community in the near future.

Keywords: Image matching · Cultural heritage · SIFT · Deep learning · SfM

1 Overview

1.1 Introduction

Image matching [33] plays a key role in the design of reliable and effective vision and photogrammetric methods, which represent nowadays an essential resource in several fields of human knowledge and technology dealing with digital images. In particular, the preservation and valorization of cultural heritage can greatly

P. L. Mazzeo et al. (Eds.): ICIAP 2022 Workshops, LNCS 13373, pp. 210–222, 2022.
https://doi.org/10.1007/978-3-031-13321-3_19

benefit from images, which are often the unique source of data for retrieving valuable information [13,37]. The image matching task can be summarized as the detection of correct correspondences between two or more images of the same 3D scene, taken under different viewpoints, acquisition conditions or times. Image matching can be restricted to a sparse set of well characterized points extracted with traditional handcrafted methods or more recent learning-based approaches [25]. These sparse correspondences are normally used within the Structure-from-Motion (SfM) image orientation process, where they get refined by exploiting globally inherent geometric constraints in an optimization scheme known as bundle adjustment. The usual SfM output consists in the camera network configuration, i.e. the camera poses and calibration parameters, as well as a sparse 3D point cloud of the surveyed scene [31]. The recovered camera network configuration is then employed to obtain a finer and more complete 3D description of the scene by applying dense image matching methods, either pairwise or exploiting Multi View Stereo (MVS) [26,33]. Popular open source processing pipelines are COLMAP [29], OpenMVG+OpenMVS [23,24] and Meshroom [1], actively updated and extended by the research community. Several good commercial tools for professional use exist too.

1.2   Traditional Image Matching

Until recently, sparse image matching for SfM has been characterized by the following steps: (1) detecting keypoints, (2) localizing meaningful and salient regions of the image, (3) extracting these regions as patches, generally normalized in order to achieve invariance to image transformations, (4) computing the descriptor vectors associated to keypoints, whose distance is used to establish the candidate correspondences, (5) filtering the correspondences according to descriptor statistics, for instance using the best and second best overall distances, and (6) filtering the surviving matches by means of spatial global or local constraints, as those provided by epipolar geometry [14] exploited through RANdom SAmple Consensus (RANSAC) [12].

Scale Invariant Feature Transform (SIFT) [18] has dominated sparse image matching for nearly two decades. SIFT matching relies on blob-like keypoints, whose associated patches are normalized to become invariant to scale and rotation changes. For each patch, the SIFT descriptor is computed as the histogram of the gradient orientation, correspondences are then assigned according to the Euclidean distance between descriptors, and the Nearest Neighbor Ratio (NNR) strategy, often followed by RANSAC, is employed to rank them. SIFT provides a handcrafted, highly engineered and optimized matching approach, still valid today and able to obtain robust results. Indeed, all the previous mentioned SfM pipelines are based on SIFT (actually on RootSIFT [3], which introduces a slight variation in the descriptor computation). That said, further alternatives or extensions to the standard SIFT matching pipeline have been proposed with mixed fortunes during the years. The interested reader may refer to [2,15,19,33] for some recent and comprehensive reviews and comparisons.

1.3   Learning-Based Image Matching

As in other computer vision areas, the advent of deep learning has represented a breakthrough for image matching. Besides handcrafted approaches designed on the basis of human intuition and expertise, machine learning techniques have been employed with encouraging results mainly in the design of more robust and efficient keypoint descriptors, often referred to as data-driven descriptors [19]. A remarkable turning point was undoubtedly the L2-Net deep descriptor [35], which outperformed SIFT in many challenging scenarios. L2-Net is at the basis of the architecture for the HardNet descriptor [21], currently the state-of-the-art standalone descriptor according to several recent benchmarks [16], and employed successfully in many hybrid image matching pipelines [7].

Deep networks have progressively replaced the components of the image matching pipeline, moving from hybrid pipelines to full end-to-end deep architectures. For instance, besides descriptors, deep design has been successfully applied for the patch normalization, providing invariance to rotations and to more general affine transformations. OriNet and AffNet [22] are respectively two examples in this sense. As an additional step towards a full image matching deep architecture, end-to-end networks also integrated keypoint extraction (save for the last matching step). SuperPoint [10] can be considered a cornerstone in this evolution process, as it provides an effective way to train the whole network using synthetic images and homographic adaptations, thus without depending on handcrafted training data as with previous solutions [38]. Another successful strategy to overcome learning difficulties in end-to-end learning was demonstrated by DIScrete Keypoints (DISK) [36], that uses reinforcement learning. With the introduction of deep learning, alternatives to the detect-then-describe paradigm which binds the descriptor characterization to the keypoint definition, typical of the classic image matching pipelines, were also proposed. The detect-and-describe D2-Net [11] and the describe-to-detect D2D network [34], respectively treats as equal or gives more priority to the descriptor optimization than to the keypoint extractor. Another aspect that emerged is the gradual shift in the design of the network architecture and of the loss function towards solutions that strongly resemble their handcrafted counterparts, of which the respective deep equivalents appear as differentiable versions to be optimized on training data.

More recently, the final steps of the image matching pipeline have been absorbed into deep architectures too. This adaptation has started with the introduction of context normalization [39], which made it possible to effectively filter correspondences according to spatial constraints, and has gone further with the Order Aware Network (OANet) [40] up to the more recent SuperGlue [28]. This last state-of-the-art deep network is a full end-to-end deep architecture based on SuperPoint [10], able to associate and discard candidate matches on the basis of spatial information and descriptor statistics, relying for this last aspect on attentional graph neural networks. The Local Feature TRansformer (LoFTR) [32] futher added a coarse-to-fine schema to obtain semi-dense correspondences. Finally, it is worth mentioning the use of deep architectures such as in [17] for further refining the bundle adjustment 2D input and 3D output point localization, even if not directly involved in the matching process.

2   Analysis and Evaluation

2.1   Rationale

For the comparison of image matching pipelines in photogrammetry and computer vision applications, two criteria are generally and reasonably set out. On the one hand, there is the ability to establish matches in the case of severe image transformations, and on the other hand, the localization accuracy of the established matches. Often these two criteria tend towards opposite goals, as a better matching ability implies to include correspondences localized less accurately.

Several comparisons of image matching pipelines specifically designed for SfM have been proposed through the years. In this respect, the main problem researchers had to face was the unavailability of reliable Ground-Truth (GT) data. In order to circumvent this problem, [30] proposed to rank the matching methods according to specific statistics of the final SfM reconstructed 3D model, such as the number of register images, the mean reprojected error of the 3D points in the images, the track length and the point cloud size. As shown in [8], this solution does not correlate well with an accurate GT. A better approach is proposed in [16], which builds a pseudo GT by running a SfM pipeline on a rich set of images of the scene with a good coverage, and then verifies the matching pipelines indirectly according to the pose error obtained using a restricted and more challenging subset on the initial images. Another solution, explored by SimLocMatch[1], relies instead on synthetic rendered scenes as effective GT data. Finally, the approach employed in [8] makes use of accurate metric GT data provided by topological surveys in terms of ground control points. These points are used to establish check points upon which to measure pose errors very accurately, hence again providing an indirect evaluation of the image matching pipeline. Pseudo GTs generally offer a reasonable rough estimation, in particular in terms of matching ability, giving rise to an indirect evaluation that gets a method ranking very close to those obtained through a direct comparison on synthetic datasets. However, when it comes to analyze matching pipelines with high and similar levels of matching accuracy, the metric GT approach on real scenes leads to a better evaluation, even if the relative datasets are more difficult to obtain. It should also be taken into account that the level of scene complexity achieved by synthetic rendered images is inferior to that of real images and, as it was noted in [8], also the bundle adjustment setting, besides the image matching pipeline setup, may assume a critical role in the final pose estimation accuracy.

Among the most recent benchmark comparisons, the Image Matching Challenge (IMC)[2] has become an annual appointment to test the latest developments. Although currently only relying on pseudo GTs following [16], and not properly

---

[1] https://simlocmatch.com/ (currently offline).
[2] https://www.cs.ubc.ca/research/image-matching-challenge/current/.

focused on cultural heritage, it has represented a good starting point for any successive investigation aiming at a realistic snapshot of the current situation. In the lastest IMC (2021) the fully end-to-end networks SuperGlue, LoFTR and DISK, and the Hybrid Pipeline (HP [8]) based on HarrisZ$^+$ [7] obtained the best results, a ranking that was confirmed also by SimLocMatch. Some of these methods were included in other evaluations more focused on cultural heritage applications, where their superiority over other approaches was generally confirmed. In particular, [8] addressed the analysis of the metric accuracy of several matching methods on modern image datasets, while [20] employed the IMW benchmark configuration on historical images ranging from 1860 to today.

2.2   Results and Discussion

According to [8], in terms of SfM pose estimation accuracy, SIFT pipeline is still competitive and among the best with respect to the recent approaches when the camera network is robust and provides a good coverage of the scene, i.e. with "close" images having a high overlap and low relative distortions in terms of both viewpoint and illumination changes. However, when these assumptions are not satisfied, the ability to robustly match in the presence of strong image deformations, even if less accurately, becomes essential. In fact, this helps keeping image connections in the camera network and avoids failures in registering some images, which would affect the performance of the whole SfM pipeline. For this reason, the following discussion will not address the keypoint localization accuracy (and hence the camera pose accuracy), extensively covered by previous literature (see Sect. 2.1), but will focus instead on the ability of each pipeline to provide more or less precise correspondences in challenging scenarios that are likely to be found in cultural heritage: it is not-so-infrequent to have to register images acquired from different viewpoints (e.g. aerial and terrestrial images), by different cameras, with different illumination conditions and at different times (e.g. multitemporal images) with the aim to detect the occurred changes.

The chosen evaluation protocol that defines matches as correct is the one proposed in [6] and extended in [4] using hand-taken correspondences. These hand-taken matches are employed to obtain the epipolar geometry of the scene, so as to filter candidate matches on the basis of the epipolar error, and to compute a rough interpolated optical flow over the images to further refine filtered matches, since epipolar error only cannot be sufficient to disambiguate them. This protocol is reasonable for the qualitative evaluation through visual inspection presented hereafter, with a minimal probability of obtaining a wrong GT estimate. While providing a quantitative evaluation for challenging scenarios is in most cases unfeasible due to major difficulty to obtain an accurate metric GT, the proposed qualitative evaluation is sufficient to describe the potential and the limits of the compared methods. Besides, this setup does not employ synthetic images, and provides a direct evaluation on the true unconstrained matching ability of the evaluated methods.

The image matching pipelines included in this comparison are SIFT (used as reference), HP, DISK, SuperGlue and LoFTR. For SIFT, the VLFeat implementation is used[3], for HP and DISK the code available by the respective authors is employed, and for SuperGlue and LoFTR their respective Kornia implementations [27]. The matching ability on six different and challenging image pairs, with resolution from about 1024×768 to 1500×1000, of interest for cultural heritage is analyzed. As a good recommended practice [16], at the end of each matching pipeline DegenSAC [9] is executed to filter matches. Since the image pairs are quite challenging, the corresponding DegenSAC epipolar error threshold is set to 3 px, which is relatively high for precise photogrammetry applications, but can provide a better insight into the rough matching ability. Moreover, since this analysis concerns with a visual qualitative localization of the correspondences, error thresholds for evaluation are set to 40 px. Due to lack of space, only the most relevant matching results are shown. The reader is strongly invited to inspect the complete report, available as additional material together with the evaluation code and data[4].

Figure 1 shows the optical flow of the matches superimposed on one of the two images of the pair. The input images (shown alternated for the sake of clarity) represent the front side of the Temple of Neptune in Paestum (Italy), and were acquired by the same camera with fixed illumination conditions. The scene is approximately planar but presents a relatively high viewpoint distortion. SIFT was barely able to find a sufficient number of correspondences, while the other methods worked with no critical issues. Note that HP and SuperGlue found less correspondences but also less wrong matches (which can become an issue in photogrammetry applications as they can invalidate the bundle adjustment estimation) than DISK and LoFTR. Specifically, SuperGlue, HP, DISK and LoFTR found matches in increasing order. Wrong matches were relevant for LoFTR, and even more for DISK.

    (a) SIFT   (b) HP   (c) DISK   (d) SuperGlue   (e) LoFTR

Fig. 1. Matching results in terms of the optical flow for an image pair of the Temple of Neptune (Paestum, Italy), displayed alternating the two images. Correct and wrong matches are shown in green and red, respectively. (Color figure online)

Figure 2 still refers to the Temple of Neptune, but the image pair includes a terrestrial and an aerial image taken from an Unmanned Autonomous Vehicle

---

[3] https://www.vlfeat.org/.

[4] https://drive.google.com/drive/folders/1ws1SvRnym3FPh1J6K4lomTIqEsxR5k49.

(UAV), presenting large scale and illumination variations. Only DISK was able
to provide some correct matches, while the other methods failed (of these, only
LoFTR is reported in Fig. 2). Nevertheless, DISK was not able to correctly handle the scale variation but it was the only method able to correctly localize the
small image portion of corresponding regions at a similar scale.

Figure 3 includes an image pair from the Temple of Concordia (Agrigento,
Italy), taken with two different cameras within a time interval of about fifteen
years, before and after the restoration process to which the temple underwent.
Also in this case, the images present a relevant scale variation. SuperGlue and
LoFTR were the only methods able to detect correct matches, with SuperGlue
providing less wrong matches and a better distribution of the correct ones. In
general, it seems that the coarse-to-fine approach of LoFTR, once it has found
putative matching areas at the coarser scale, is quite indulgent in discarding
matches at the finer scale. Differently from the previous image pair, DISK was
not able to obtain correct matches, as well as SIFT and HP (not shown). Moreover, concerning HP, only an exiguous number of keypoints was detected in the
matching region of the second image, due to a relative low global contrast of this
area with respect to the whole image.

Figure 4 shows two images from the Temple of the Dioscuri (Agrigento, Italy),
taken in the same conditions and time interval of those reported for the Temple of

(a) DISK   (b) LoFTR

Fig. 2. Correct and wrong matching results on a challenging image pair of the Temple
of Neptune (Paestum, Italy), shown respectively in green and red. (Color figure online)

(a) DISK   (b) SuperGlue   (c) LoFTR

Fig. 3. Correct and wrong matching results on the image pair of the Temple of Concordia (Agrigento, Italy), shown respectively in green and red. (Color figure online)

Concordia. Only HP and SuperGlue were able to correctly find correspondences. DISK and LoFTR failed to provide matches, probably due to their inability to handle both the middle level image rotations and the repeating patterns that occur within the overlapped regions. Notice also that HP was able to find matches in the upper part, while SuperGlue was more effective in the in-between part. Moreover, DISK and LoFTR produced a large number of wrong matches. Conversely, SIFT (not shown), although unable to find correct correspondences, found a very low number of wrong matches.

Figure 5 reports the matching results on two aerial images taken from different UAV strips, presenting relevant perspective distortions and a significant relative rotation, a common situation in UAV or Autonomous Underwater Vehicle (AUV) surveys. Only HP was able to fully assign matches. The other methods failed: DISK, LoFTR and SuperGlue (the last one is not shown) due to their invariance to even moderate rotations, while SIFT since it is unable to tolerate the viewpoint distortion, although being invariant to rotations (as suggested by the presence of few correct matches). Note again that DISK, and to a minor extent LoFTR, provided more wrong matches than SuperGlue or SIFT.

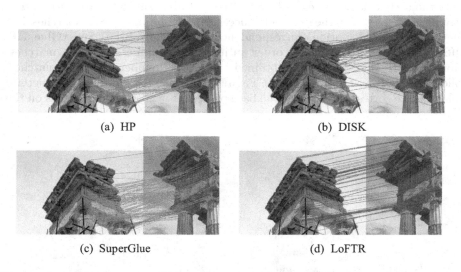

(a) HP   (b) DISK

(c) SuperGlue   (d) LoFTR

Fig. 4. Correct and wrong matching results on the image pair of the Temple of the Dioscuri (Agrigento, Italy), shown respectively in green and red. (Color figure online)

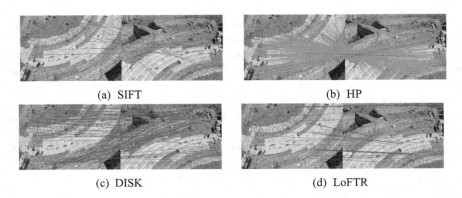

Fig. 5. Correct and wrong matching results on the image pair of the Ventimiglia Theatre (Ventimiglia, Italy), shown respectively in green and red. (Color figure online)

Finally, Fig. 6 presents the matching results on two views of an ancient vase from the archaeological area of Fiavé (Trento, Italy), subjected to a strong relative tilt change. All the methods succeeded in finding correct matches but they also produced spurious correspondences. Specifically, SIFT, SuperGlue, HP, DISK and LoFTR provided in order an increasing number of correct matches. Moreover, HP and SuperGlue obtained the lowest number of wrong matches, followed by DISK, LoFTR and SIFT. Note also that HP was the only method able to trace correspondences at the base plane, yet it missed the matches on the

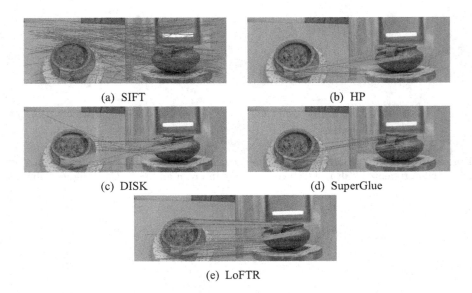

Fig. 6. Correct and wrong matching results on the image pair of an ancient vase (Fiavé, Italy), shown respectively in green and red. (Color figure online)

left upper part, that were detected instead by DISK and LoFTR. It is also worth mentioning that at the original input images resolution of 6048×4032 instead of the current processing resolution of 1500×1000, none of the methods was able to find correct matches, a fact that highlights the criticality of the detection scale.

3 Conclusions and Perspective

The presented investigation showed that recent learning-based image matching techniques provide an unquestionable advance with respect to traditional hand-crafted methods. However, there are still issues and not a clear winner, leaving large margins for improvement.

End-to-end LoFTR, DISK and SuperGlue are unable to handle average and high degrees of image rotation. This issue can be circumvented by rotating one of the input image (at least eight times for a tolerance to $45°$) but this would be computationally expensive, efficient solutions in this sense for handcrafted methods have been investigated [5]. Both DISK and LoFTR output a high number of matches, including wrong correspondences. In the case of failure, this can represent a critical issue that can mislead the next steps of the SfM pipeline, but also in case of success this can create problems due to computational requirements for data management. Furthermore, LoFTR outputs discrete keypoint locations for the first image and sub-pixel keypoint localizations for the second one, thus requiring some engineering in order to handle multiple images. On the other hand, the lower number of correspondences extracted by SuperGlue, inherited from Superpoint, can be limiting in some cases [25].

HP is rotation invariant, provides a reasonably high number of correct matches, outputs a low number of wrong correspondences in case of failure and is robust to viewpoint distortions similarly to end-to-end architectures. Nevertheless, it is less tolerant to strong scale variations, and can have issues related with the global image contrast. Being a modular pipeline, HP can be more easily adapted for specific tasks. For instance, removing OriNet from HP steps can improve the matching ability when there are no relevant rotations in the input images. Finally, the retraining of the standalone deep modules of HP requires less computational efforts than with a fully end-to-end network.

That said, SIFT still offers advantages in common-user non-challenging scenarios, which makes it still irreplaceable in commercial applications: SIFT is less computational expensive than its competitors with inferior hardware requirements, and provides state-of-the-art pose accuracy estimation in case of robust camera network input setups [25]. Moreover, it works without efforts with high resolution images (e.g. aerial image datasets), while its competitors cannot be launched using a high-end consumer-grade system configuration (with the exception of HP that runs much slower than SIFT with these images anyways). Multi-scale tiling can be devised in this case, which should also provide a solution in case of relevant scale changes, but again at the expense of increasing the computational cost, and probably decreasing the matching accuracy as the global overview of the scene is somewhat lost.

Although recent image matching approaches can be useful for research activities dealing with challenging SfM applications in cultural heritage, these methods are not yet fully ready and mature for common user applications. Effective solutions are still an open question, which offers new research opportunities and challenges to the scientific community, not only for the matching process itself but also in providing efficient and scalable solutions.

Acknowledgements. The authors would like to thank the Archaeological and Landscape Park of the Valley of the Temples of Agrigento (Italy), the Cultural Heritage Directorate of the Autonomous Province of Trento (Italy) and the Superintendence of the Imperia and Savona provinces (Italy) for providing some of the images used in this work.F. Bellavia is funded by the Italian Ministry of Education and Research (MIUR) under the program PON Ricerca e Innovazione 2014–2020, cofunded by the European Social Fund (ESF), CUP B74I18000220006, id. proposta AIM 1875400, linea di attività 2, Area Cultural Heritage.

References

1. AliceVision: Meshroom: A 3D reconstruction software (2018). https://github.com/alicevision/meshroom
2. Apollonio, F., Ballabeni, A., Gaiani, M., Remondino, F.: Evaluation of feature-based methods for automated network orientation. Int. Arch. Photogramm. Remote Sens. Spat. Inf. Sci. **XL–5**, 47–54 (2014)
3. Arandjelović, R., Zisserman, A.: Three things everyone should know to improve object retrieval. In: Proceedings of the IEEE Conference on Computer Vision and Pattern Recognition (CVPR) (2012)
4. Bellavia, F.: SIFT matching by context exposed. IEEE Trans. Pattern Anal. Mach. Intell. (2022). (early access)
5. Bellavia, F., Colombo, C.: Rethinking the sGLOH descriptor. IEEE Trans. Pattern Anal. Mach. Intell. **40**(4), 931–944 (2018)
6. Bellavia, F., Colombo, C.: Is there anything new to say about SIFT matching? Int. J. Comput. Vis. **128**(7), 1847–1866 (2020)
7. Bellavia, F., Mishkin, D.: HarrisZ$^+$: Harris corner selection for next-gen image matching pipelines. arXiv ePrint 2109.12925 (2021)
8. Bellavia, F., Morelli, L., Menna, F., Remondino, F.: Image orientation with a hybrid pipeline robust to rotations and wide-baselines. Int. Arch. Photogramm. Remote Sens. Spat. Inf. Sci. **XLVI–2/W1–2022**, 73–80 (2022)
9. Chum, O., Werner, T., Matas, J.: Two-view geometry estimation unaffected by a dominant plane. In: Proceedings of the IEEE Conference on Computer Vision and Pattern Recognition (CVPR) (2005)
10. DeTone, D., Malisiewicz, T., Rabinovich, A.: Superpoint: self-supervised interest point detection and description. In: Proceedings of the IEEE Conference on Computer Vision and Pattern Recognition (CVPR) (2018)
11. Dusmanu, M., et al.: D2-Net: a trainable CNN for joint detection and description of local features. In: Proceedings of the IEEE Conference on Computer Vision and Pattern Recognition (CVPR) (2019)
12. Fischler, M., Bolles, R.: Random sample consensus: a paradigm for model fitting with applications to image analysis and automated cartography. Commun. ACM **24**(6), 381–395 (1981)

13. Gruen, A., Remondino, F., Zhang, L.: Photogrammetric reconstruction of the Great Buddha of Bamiyan. Afg. Photogramm. Rec. **19**(107), 177–199 (2004)
14. Hartley, R.I., Zisserman, A.: Multiple View Geometry in Computer Vision. Cambridge University Press, Cambridge (2000)
15. Hartmann, W., Havlena, M., Schindler, K.: Recent developments in large-scale tie-point matching. ISPRS J. Photogramm. Remote Sens. **115**, 47–62 (2016)
16. Jin, Y., et al.: Image matching across wide baselines: from paper to practice. Int. J. Comput. Vis. **129**(2), 517–547 (2021)
17. Lindenberger, P., Sarlin, P., Larsson, V., Pollefeys, M.: Pixel-perfect structure-from-motion with featuremetric refinement. In: Proceedings of the IEEE International Conference on Computer Vision (ICCV) (2021)
18. Lowe, D.: Distinctive image features from scale-invariant keypoints. Int. J. Comput. Vis. **60**(2), 91–110 (2004)
19. Ma, J., Jiang, J., Fan, A., Jiang, J., Yan, J.: Image matching from handcrafted to deep features: a survey. Int. J. Comput. Vis. **129**(7), 23–79 (2021)
20. Maiwald, F., Lehmann, C., Lazariv, T.: Fully automated pose estimation of historical images in the context of 4d geographic information systems utilizing machine learning methods. ISPRS Int. J. Geoinf. **10**(11), 748 (2021)
21. Mishchuk, A., Mishkin, D., Radenovic, F., Matas, J.: Working hard to know your neighbor's margins: local descriptor learning loss. In: Proceedings of the Conference on Neural Information Processing Systems (NeurIPS) (2017)
22. Mishkin, D., Radenovic, F., Matas, J.: Repeatability is not enough: learning affine regions via discriminability. In: Proceedings of the European Conference on Computer Vision (ECCV) (2018)
23. Moulon, P., Monasse, P., Perrot, R., Marlet, R.: OpenMVG: Open multiple view geometry. In: Proceedings of International Workshop on Reproducible Research in Pattern Recognition (2016). https://github.com/openMVG/openMVG
24. OpenMVS: open Multi-View Stereo reconstruction library (2022). https://github.com/cdcseacave/openMVS
25. Remondino, F., Menna, F., Morelli, L.: Evaluating hand-crafted and learning-based features for photogrammetric applications. Int. Arch. Photogramm. Remote Sens. Spat. Inf. Sci. **XLIII–B2–2021**, 549–556 (2021)
26. Remondino, F., Spera, M., Nocerino, E., Menna, F., Nex, F.: State of the art in high density image matching. Photogramm. Rec. **29**(146), 144–166 (2014)
27. Riba, E., Mishkin, D., Ponsa, D., Rublee, E., Bradski, G.: Kornia: an open source differentiable computer vision library for PyTorch. In: Proceedings of IEEE/CVF Winter Conference on Applications of Computer Vision (WACV) (2020)
28. Sarlin, P.E., DeTone, D., Malisiewicz, T., Rabinovich, A.: SuperGlue: learning feature matching with graph neural networks. In: Proceedings of the 2019 IEEE Conference on Computer Vision and Pattern Recognition (CVPR) (2020)
29. Schönberger, J.L., Frahm, J.M.: Structure-from-Motion revisited. In: Proceedings of the IEEE Conference on Computer Vision and Pattern Recognition (CVPR) (2016), https://colmap.github.io/
30. Schönberger, J., Hardmeier, H., Sattler, T., Pollefeys, M.: Comparative evaluation of hand-crafted and learned local features. In: Proceedings of the IEEE Conference on Computer Vision and Pattern Recognition (CVPR) (2017)
31. Stathopoulou, E., Welponer, M., Remondino, F.: Open-source image-based 3D reconstruction pipeline: review, comparison and evaluation. Int. Arch. Photogramm. Remote Sens. Spat. Inf. Sci. **XLII-2/W17**, 331–338 (2019)

32. Sun, J., Shen, Z., Wang, Y., Bao, H., Zhou, X.: LoFTR: detector-free local feature matching with transformers. In: Proceedings of the IEEE Conference on Computer Vision and Pattern Recognition (CVPR) (2021)
33. Szeliski, R.: Computer Vision: Algorithms and Applications. Springer, Heidelberg (2022). https://doi.org/10.1007/978-1-84882-935-0
34. Tian, Y., Balntas, V., Ng, T., Laguna, A.B., Demiris, Y., Mikolajczyk, K.: D2D: keypoint extraction with describe to detect approach. In: Proceedings of the Asian Conference on Computer Vision (ACCV) (2020)
35. Tian, Y., Fan, B., Wu, F.: L2-Net: deep learning of discriminative patch descriptor in euclidean space. In: IEEE Conference on Computer Vision and Pattern Recognition (CVPR), pp. 6128–6136 (2017)
36. Tyszkiewicz, M.J., Fua, P., Trulls, E.: DISK: learning local features with policy gradient. In: Proceedings of the Conference on Neural Information Processing Systems (NeurIPS) (2020)
37. Vincent, M., Coughenour, C., Remondino, F., Gutierrez, M., Bendicho, V.L.M., Fritsch, D.: Rekrei: a public platform for digitally preserving lost heritage. In: Proceedings of the 44th CAA Conference (2016)
38. Yi, K.M., Trulls, E., Lepetit, V., Fua, P.: LIFT: Learned invariant feature transform. In: Proceedings of the European Conference on Computer Vision (ECCV) (2016)
39. Yi, K.M., Trulls, E., Ono, Y., Lepetit, V., Salzmann, M., Fua, P.: Learning to find good correspondences. In: Proceedings of the IEEE Conference on Computer Vision and Pattern Recognition (CVPR) (2018)
40. Zhang, J., et al.: Learning two-view correspondences and geometry using order-aware network. In: Proceedings of the IEEE International Conference on Computer Vision (ICCV). pp. 5844–5853 (2019)

Workshop on Intelligent Systems in Human and Artificial Perception - ISHAPE 2022

Virtual and Augmented Reality for Quality Control of Aircraft Interiors

Nicola Mosca$^{(\boxtimes)}$ ⬡, Gaetano Pernisco, Maria Di Summa, Vito Renò ⬡,
Massimiliano Nitti, and Ettore Stella

National Research Council of Italy - Institute of Intelligent Industrial Technologies
and Systems for Advanced Manufacturing (STIIMA), Bari, Italy
nicola.mosca@stiima.cnr.it

Abstract. Automation is a driving force in manufacturing, enabling to
ensure quality and scale during production and assembly. After a slow
start, civil aerospace industry efforts in automating production, assembly and testing, are gaining pace and novel technologies are being experimented for enabling automated assembly and inspection phases, which
are reliable and safe. In this context, a cluster of research projects were
devised for the improvement of assembly and inspection phases of aircraft
interiors, with a focus on cabin and cargo lining and hatrack elements of
single-aisle aircrafts. This paper is focused on the inspection phase which
follows the assembly, where a novel approach involving automated testing and human supervision aim to provide faster, safer and more flexible
inspection operations when compared with more traditional ways, using
virtual and augmented reality scenarios.

Keywords: Quality control · Report · Virtual reality · Mixed reality ·
Hololens

1 Introduction

Automated processes are key enablers of modern production chains. Industries
like the automotive ones, perhaps due to earlier exploitable economies of scale,
have achieved leaner and better processes faster than in other sectors, like the
aerospace industry. Moreover, even in the production chain, a few stages have
experienced successful automation efforts earlier than others. Assembly and testing, the latter in particular, have distinct aspects that tend to make them riskier
to tackle automatically: in most cases, some degrees of automation will most
likely provide a high return on investment, and yet the boundary conditions do
not enable to perform those process changes swiftly and without a systemic and
holistic view to the whole picture.

Supported from the European Union's Horizon 2020 research and innovation programme under grant agreement No 785410. The authors would like to acknowledge
industrial partner Protom Group S.p.A. for their support in the development of the
reporting interfaces.

P. L. Mazzeo et al. (Eds.): ICIAP 2022 Workshops, LNCS 13373, pp. 225–234, 2022.
https://doi.org/10.1007/978-3-031-13321-3_20

Cargo and cabin lining assembly and inspection, and, in general, aircraft manufacturing, is a case in point. As reported in a study by the U.S. Bureau of Labour Statistics in 1993 [8], total jet transport shipments averaged about 320 units per year between 1972 and 1991. Three decades later, the situation has not changed much, with productivity and production in the aerospace sector lagging behind automotive by orders of magnitude, with more recent statistics [1] putting global aircraft shipments in the order of about 2600 units in year 2019. This severely deter the willingness to automate tasks for productivity gains. And yet, while almost all the boundary conditions and ironies described in [8] persist, like combining the qualitative needs of a high-tech and complex manufacturing operation with the craftsmanship and low-volume numbers of a small handcraft boutique shop requiring highly qualified workers, the need to innovate and automate is stronger than ever.

Quality control performed by inspection officers is still performed most of the time with a low degree of automation. For instance, while inspecting cargo and cabin lining, workers are required to evaluate both geometric and appearance aspects of all visible panels. Manually performing geometric measurements between panels, like establishing that gap, step and parallelism, just to name a few, follow under acceptable ranges requires keeping attention over prolonged times. Cognitive fatigue is therefore a common issue as well as the human inability to perform quality control consistently for several hours: judging something differently at different times is bound to happen. Other factors must be considered as well, such as the ergonomic challenges present in certain environments, like in the cargo area, where inspection officers are most of the time required to work crouched, given the low ceiling. These reasons suggest just a few of the gains which could be obtained through more automation. But even so, some peculiar tasks, such as judging the appearance of panels, with all nuances attached to this assignment, suggests that the human element is still a fundamental part of the loop, even more so when it is possible to pair consistency, precision and accuracy of robotic inspections with the supervision of highly skilled inspection officers.

This paper reports on the automatic inspection of aircraft interiors panel assembly where robotic and human skills are used in conjunction. The work was performed as part of the VISTA project, acronym for "Vision-based Inspection Systems for automated Testing of Aircraft interiors", funded by the European Commission, with the objective of matching aerospace private sector needs with European research capabilities. The project required the development of an autonomous acquisition platform for scanning cargo and cabin environments, a methodology for automatically evaluating 3d and color information searching for geometric and surface defects. The methodology for the detection of geometrical defects has been presented in [10,12], while surface defects have been considered in [11]. At the end of automated processing, inspection officers can validate more effectively, efficiently and effectively reported measurements, through several means, including virtual and augmented reality renditions, which are the focus of this paper. Such solutions are devised for different scenarios and needs.

VR-like presentation can be useful for enabling validation of acquisitions and measurements taken by the autonomous robots in the factory when inspection officers cannot be present there, effectively enabling and making proficient smart working scenarios for quality control tasks. They are also useful for receiving additional feedback from co-workers in challenging situations, from the judgement point of view.

On the opposite, when the inspection officer can be physically present near the aircraft panels being inspected, an Hololens-based solution provides the worker with contextual information, enabling to localize problematic spots, overlaying measurements made by the automatic inspection.

The paper is organized in the following way. Related works are presented first. A brief description of geometrical and surface defects handled by the system is then presented. Afterwards, the architecture of the subsystem responsible for measurements reporting is explained, followed by results in both "on site" and "off site" scenarios. Last but not least, conclusions and future works are discussed.

2   Related Works

A recent literature review about the use of augmented reality in the manufacturing industry is presented in [4] and cover AR papers published from 2006 to early 2017. As reported in the review, most of the performed research work is connected to the automotive industry with 11 papers, opposed to just 3 papers dedicated to the aircraft/aerospace industry. Previous works in aerospace. The literature review provides an insight look to the industrial sector versus the application field of AR, showing that two of those works [5, 7] were related to maintenance and one to assembly operations [13]. However, no work in that period of time is about quality control, in the post-assembly phase.

Four use cases related to the use of Virtual and Augmented Reality for inspection and maintenance in the aerospace sector are reported in [6]. Among these, an AR solution for process guidance in inspecting and repairing of scarf profiles of fiber composite parts through milling is presented. An Hololens helmet is used for achieving the objective. Moreover, as in the work presented here, the correlation between physical and virtual world is performed with a marker and on the software side, Unity is used as well.

More recently, an AR-assisted system for the inspection of aviation connectors has been experimented [9]. In this case, inspectors are equipped with AR glasses while they scrutinize connectors for mismatched/missing pins. Images are wirelessly sent to a separate computer for processing using computer vision and deep learning techniques. The result is sent back as a list of misplaced-wire pins and missing-wire pins.

In summary, to the best of our knowledge, no semi-automated solution to quality control of aircraft interiors lining using VR-like and AR solutions has been presented so far.

3   A Brief Introduction to Geometrical and Surface Defects

VISTA project considered two categories of defects which can be present while inspecting aircraft interiors post-assembly: geometrical and surface defects.

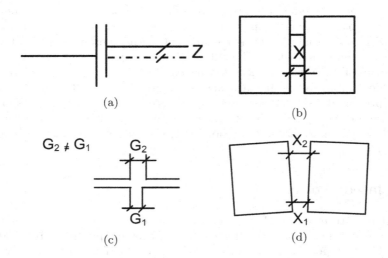

Fig. 1. Geometrical defects: a) step, b) gap, c) mismatch, d) parallelism

Geometrical defects are mostly related to the geometrical arrangements of panels, although they can be attributable to deformities on borders of a single panel as well. Specific examples of geometrical defects considered in the project are (see Fig. 1):

- step: it happens when two adjacent panels, which should be perceived as continuous, show a variation on the z-plane exceeding an allowable threshold limit;
- gap: it is the distance on a particular axis of interest (x, y or z) between adjacent panels closest ends, to be reported when outside a specific tolerance range;
- mismatch of tolerances: it is a defect which might be visible at the proximity of multiple panels (usually four) related to different gaps between any adjacent pairs;
- parallelism: it reports about the lack of parallelism of adjacent panels, by considering gap differences at the extreme ends of the shared edge.

On the other hand, surface defects are related to a single panel and are mostly related to roughness or unexpected color changes on its surface. Many types of surface defects exist, but most of them are related to panel anomalies already present before assembly.

For the sake of this work, only three types are relevant, post-assembly (see Fig. 2):

- scratches: a linear damage on the surface panel, usually caused by contact with a sharp object;
- bumps/dents: local concavity/convexity, usually rounded, which could be caused by inappropriate assembly or impact with a non-sharp object causing a local panel deformation;
- color/texture inhomogeneities: an expected change in color or texture on an otherwise uniform panel part

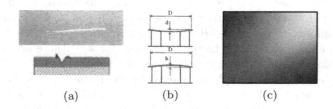

(a)   (b)   (c)

Fig. 2. Surface defects: a) scratches, b) bumps/dents, c) color/texture inhomogeneities

Most of these defects, either of the geometrical or surface types, must be corrected both for safety issues (for instance, a parallelism issue can be a signal of an inappropriately mounted panel), and for aesthetic/comfort considerations, with passengers appreciating well curated environments.

Moreover, it should be noted the importance of keeping a human inspector officer in the loop, considering the aesthetic/comfort considerations, which often involve more than just a few automated measurements for the sake of a correct judgement.

4 Reporting Sub-system

The solution is based on a client-server configuration where the main system, known in the project as the "supervisor", is responsible for handling interactions with all sub-systems, which are distributed among different physical devices. The supervisor, among other tasks, handles access to a centralized database containing the state of the automated inspection, including setup, configuration, acquired data and processed data. The latter ones are accessed through reporting clients, with the supervisor acting as the "middleman" for data access.

It is possible to access the processing results, and hence the reports, through different means, including but not limited to:

- Tablet app: reports are accessed through an Android or iOS application with a graphical 3d representation of the aircraft interiors obtained using Computer Aided Design (CAD) models or scanned data;

- Windows app: reports are accessed through Universal Windows Platform (UWP) on Windows 10+;
- Hololens app: reports are accessed through an UWP application specifically designed for Hololens 1, with the user able to overlay measurements of specific defects.

Moreover, it should be noted that the project focused on the development of a VR-like experience using a tablet or a desktop application, instead of a full-fledged VR environment using Oculus Quest 2 [3] or similar devices, since from the analysis the "immersion" factor for VR was perceived more akin to a "disconnection" from the physical environment, with limited, or any, additional benefits. On the other hand, providing contextual information in the real environment was perceived potentially more useful for the "on site" scenario, leading to the development of the Mixed Reality solution.

Although all solutions work basically in a similar way, there are some differences for exploiting the different medium and use cases.

For instance, the tablet application exploits the inspection environment (i.e. the acquisition was made in the cabin or the cargo) for the camera setup, so that the user is able to closely observe panels present in the cargo, present in the lower part of the aircrafts, or the cabin/passengers environment. Moreover, the application, exploiting the landscape mode, is able to present a list of defects on a left pane, and the 3d environment, with the selected defect properly highlighted, on the right pane. Users are able to select another defect and move into the virtual environment as well.

Selection of the inspection area (cargo or cabin) is handled differently in the augmented reality solution. As a matter of fact, the Hololens app requires to overlay synthetic information on the real scene, where cargo or cabin panels are physically installed. An image marker is used for this objective. This enables to "align" the physical and the virtual world and to initiate tracking, so that graphical information are always reported where needed, even after the user starts moving in the real environment. If a 3d scan of the environment is available, it can be composed on the Hololens view as well. A set of graphical panes can be used for changing color and transparency values for the synthetic data being shown, enabling users to fine-tune the experience based on preferences and needs.

In all reporting clients, the user can express a judgement on a specific defect, hence validating the results and potentially enhancing classification results in subsequent inspections. The system is designed to be multi-user, so that many opinions, whether needed and possible, can be collected.

From an engineering point of view, communication between server and clients is performed in a similar way, with a REST API using the JSON format for enabling the exchange of messages.

Considering the multi-platform support, all client solutions requiring the visualization of 3d environments, including the tablet and Hololens frontend, have been developed in Unity. From there, most variants of the same application can be obtained by tweaking a few parameters and "exporting" the project to different platforms.

The Hololens application, due to its nature, required the development of a more customized solution. In particular, the user interface had to be customized for handling the head-mounted display and the natural commands, like gestures and gaze. Moreover, it was important to "register" the virtual representation of the scene with the real one for achieving a flawless data overlay over panels, exploiting Hololens sensors for interpreting the scene and track the position of important objects.

Given the structured production environment for which the "on-site" system is devised, the usage of a solution based on an image marker was considered a feasible option. As a matter of fact, this is likely a good tradeoff for an Hololens based solution, considering the hardware limitation of the first iteration of the Mixed-Reality device. Thus, two different markers, one for the cargo and one for the cabin, at a known distance from the inspected panels, were used.

Once the marker is identified, the tracker can continue to work even moving away and with the image marker out of sight, thanks to Hololens inertial sensors, depth and color camera, all providing useful hints for an accurate tracking of user movements and place in the scene. A commercial off-the-shelf solution from the PTC company [2], namely Vuforia Engine, which can be integrated in Unity through a "package", was used for handling the AR scenario, while Vuforia Studio was exploited for creating the user interface based on the floating window. Three ways are available to list the defects: as text; on a 3d model; or over-imposed in augmented reality.

5   Results

The focus of this paper is about facilitating reporting of quality control issues for interior lining in single aisle aircrafts. In particular, for the sake of this project, lining and panels are inspected after mounting sidewalls and hatracks, but before installing airplane seats, as figures of VR-like and AR prototypes show.

Reporting is loosely coupled to the inspection phase: reporting enables to visualize inspection results and express a judgement on them, enabling inspector officers to decide what is correctly be considered a defect, triggering actions outside VISTA system boundaries, and what, instead is mis-classified, so that VISTA judgement can be fine-tuned for successive inspections.

A list of defects is available on the different versions of the reporting tool, and consists of the "list view" that is reported after the user has selected a processing timeline to inspect.

The user can then "engage" on a 3d view mode. This enables to split the screen in two parts, with the left side continuing to host the list of defects, while the rest of the screen is used for a VR representation of the environment (Fig. 3).

While the virtual reality application has been devised for analysing the measurements when the user/quality inspection officer is away from the production site, another possibility is available if the officer can work from the factory.

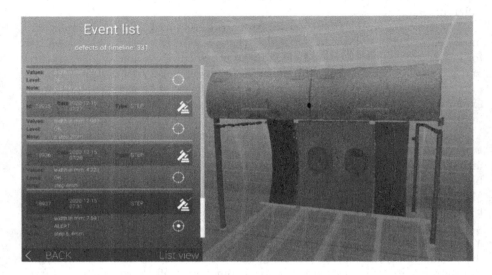

Fig. 3. Image from the tablet interface. The left pane reports a list of defects/measurements, with a 3d representation on the right.

Fig. 4. Floating window reporting the list of measurements in the event list in the Hololens application.

A particular version of the application is indeed capable of running on mixed-reality devices, such as the Microsoft Hololens, where, following an augmented reality approach, it is possible to walk freely in the area being inspected and "see" the position of the performed measurements and possible defects directly over imposed on the image of the environment.

While using the VISTA application on Hololens, the vision specs are capable of showing text, images and 3d models "co-existing" on the same scene. Since it is a stereoscopic device, virtual objects can be projected at a specified distance. The user is free to move in the environment, with some additional sensors (such as inertial sensors) taking care of tracking the user and update the position of the virtual objects from the new point of view. A floating window (see Fig. 4), which can be re-positioned in the environment at user's request, shows measurements data, while leaving most of the view "free" for showing virtual markers and objects overlaid on the real environment and panels.

6   Conclusions and Future Work

The paper has presented a novel way for enabling inspection officers to work better while evaluating geometrical and surface defects in aircraft interiors lining. The work was part of a larger effort aiming at enhancing productivity in aircraft lining assembly, using an autonomous platform for performing measurements in an accurate and consistent way. Moreover, 3d presentation interfaces, suited and customized for "on-site" and "off-site" scenarios enable inspection officers to improve results by validating them. Automation and apps also enable inspection officers to avoid working in non-ergonomic environments. The European project took place during pandemic times. The situation, although unfortunate, was able to highlight potential benefits provided by the new inspected modalities.

Naturally, there are some topics open to further investigation. First, it should be interesting to understand, experimentally, how much this change of inspection paradigm can really enhance working situations, both from a quality of life at work and productivity perspectives. Second, user interface, especially for the mixed reality solution, can be object of further investigation, to still improve user experience. Third, while the AR prototype was tested on a first-generation, it can be useful to explore the possible improvements using Hololens 2.

References

1. General aviation market data. http://www.fi-aeroweb.com/General-Aviation.html
2. Vuforia enterprise augmented reality (ar) software (2021). https://www.ptc.com/en/products/vuforia
3. Oculus quest 2: Our most advanced new all-in-one vr headset — oculus (2022). https://www.oculus.com/quest-2/?locale=en
4. Bottani, E., Vignali, G.: Augmented reality technology in the manufacturing industry: a review of the last decade. IISE Trans. **51**(3), 284–310 (2019). https://doi.org/10.1080/24725854.2018.1493244

5. De Crescenzio, F., Fantini, M., Persiani, F., Di Stefano, L., Azzari, P., Salti, S.: Augmented reality for aircraft maintenance training and operations support. IEEE Comput. Graph. Appl. **31**(1), 96–101 (2011). https://doi.org/10.1109/MCG. 2011.4

6. Eschen, H., Kötter, T., Rodeck, R., Harnisch, M., Schüppstuhl, T.: Augmented and virtual reality for inspection and maintenance processes in the aviation industry. Procedia Manuf. **19**, 156–163 (2018). https://doi.org/10.1016/j.promfg.2018. 01.022, https://www.sciencedirect.com/science/article/pii/S2351978918300222

7. Golański, P., Perz-Osowska, M., Szczekala, M.: A demonstration model of a mobile expert system with augmented reality user interface supporting m-28 aircraft maintenance. J. KONBiN **31**(1), 23–31 (2015). https://doi.org/10.2478/jok-2014-0020

8. Kronemer, A., Henneberger, J.E.: Productivity in aircraft manufacturing. Monthly Labor Rev. **116**(6), 24–33 (1993). http://www.jstor.org/stable/41844133

9. Li, S., Zheng, P., Zheng, L.: An AR-assisted deep learning-based approach for automatic inspection of aviation connectors. IEEE Trans. Ind. Inf. **17**(3), 1721–1731 (2021). https://doi.org/10.1109/TII.2020.3000870

10. Mosca, N., Patruno, C., Colella, R., Negri, S.P., Stella, E.: A ransac-based method for detecting post-assembly defects in aircraft interiors. In: 2020 IEEE 7th International Workshop on Metrology for AeroSpace (MetroAeroSpace), pp. 403–408 (2020). https://doi.org/10.1109/MetroAeroSpace48742.2020.9160295

11. Mosca, N., Patruno, C., Renò, V., Nitti, M., Stella, E.: Qualitative comparison of methodologies for detecting surface defects in aircraft interiors. In: 2021 IEEE 8th International Workshop on Metrology for AeroSpace (MetroAeroSpace), pp. 215–220 (2021). https://doi.org/10.1109/MetroAeroSpace51421.2021.9511778

12. Mosca, N., Renò, V., Nitti, M., Patruno, C., Stella, E.: Post assembly quality inspection using multimodal sensing in aircraft manufacturing. In: Stella, E. (ed.) Multimodal Sensing and Artificial Intelligence: Technologies and Applications II, vol. 11785, pp. 188–195. International Society for Optics and Photonics, SPIE (2021). https://doi.org/10.1117/12.2594104

13. Webel, S., Bockholt, U., Engelke, T., Gavish, N., Olbrich, M., Preusche, C.: An augmented reality training platform for assembly and maintenance skills. Rob. Auton. Syst. **61**(4), 398–403 (2013). https://doi.org/10.1016/j.robot.2012.09.013, https://www.sciencedirect.com/science/article/pii/S0921889012001674

Automatic Scoring of Synchronization from Fingers Motion Capture and Music Beats

Hamza Bayd$^{(\boxtimes)}$, Patrice Guyot, Benoit Bardy, and Pierre R. L. Slangen$^{(\boxtimes)}$

EuroMov Digital Health in Motion, Univ. Montpellier IMT Mines Ales, Ales, France
{hamza.bayd,patrice.guyot,pierre.slangen}@mines-ales.fr,
benoit.bardy@umontpellier.fr

Abstract. Thanks to various technological progresses such as musical rhythm estimation and motion capture systems, the evaluation of synchronization performances between motion and music beats is today possible. In this paper, we propose an innovative playful method to assess synchronization between hand motion and music. In this application, the hand gestures are tracked from live webcam motion capture based on MediaPipe open-source framework. Musical beats are estimated from the Librosa library. The synchronization between finger motion and beats is then computed from the dynamic time warping algorithm. A preliminary study was conducted with two different songs mixed with tempo beats at different intensities. The results are encouraging and show different levels of performance according to the tempo of the songs.

Keywords: Synchronization · Motion capture · Hand · Finger · Music beats · Dynamic time warping

1 Introduction

Synchronization between music and human movements is typically based on the perception of a common rhythm. Humans respond to rhythmic parameters of music by synchronizing movement pattern to the beat, that explain the close connection between the perceptual and audio-motor system. In general, synchronization between individuals are based on predictive abilities that are fed by visual and auditory perception [1]. During the last few years, significant progress has been made in challenging computer vision problems, including human pose estimation, in particular for neural network and motion capture (MoCap) technology. The task of human pose estimation from video, nowadays applied in various domains such as sign language recognition, is usually based on body landmarks or keypoints from each video frame. Moreover high level semantics from motion such as joint collection distance and temporal displacement of the body (visual information) can also be computed [3,4].

From the music side, beats are one of the most fundamental features linking to the accompanying movements. The ability to synchronize movements and music is primarily analyzed through the task of tapping. In more complex situations, such as walking, synchronization can be analyzed through the impact of the steps, and their correspondence with the strong beats of the music piece [2]. However, the way in which sound and visual information interact in the perception and production of synchronization, intentional or spontaneous, is still poorly understood [5]. In the present study, we propose a webcam beat-tracking software that measure and quantify in real time a synchronization score between natural movements of hands and the musical beats. The rest of this paper is structured as follows. Section 2 presents a short review of related works for musical rhythm, human pose estimation and synchronization. Sections 3 provides an overview of the developed system. In Sect. 4, we describe a preliminary experiment and discuss the results.

2   Related Works

2.1   Musical Rhythmic Features Extraction

Rhythm in music denotes the element of time. While a series of notes repeats in a regular cycle, they form a rhythmic pattern. Moreover to indicate the annotation timings for the respective notes, musical rhythm can also specify the duration and intensity. The best way to describe beat in real life is the moment when people taps feet or hand while listening to a song. The tempo in music is the number of beats per minute (bpm), and can change over the course of the music audio [8]. Some of the main characteristics that humans can understand and perceive when listening to music are tempo, rhythm, onset and tatum [7], as shown in Table 1.

Table 1. Characteristics of rhythm

Feature	Definition
Rhythm	The continuous repetition of a musical pattern with its variation as it moves over time
Tempo	The speed at which the music is played and is measured in beats per minute
Onsets	The time instant of the detectable start of a melodic note
Beat	The fundamental feature to the perception of timing in music usually grouped in bars
Downbeat	The first beat of a measure, the strongest in any meter
Tatum	Corresponds to the fastest perceived pulsation in the metrical structure

The music information retrieval is an interdisciplinary research field that enhances a wide range of applications such as beat tracking, structural analysis and music classification. It relies traditionally on features can be extracted in two domains, time domain or frequency domain, within different levels of abstraction. On one hand, low level features make sense for the machine as statistics features which are extracted directly from the audio such as amplitude envelope, energy, spectral centroid, spectrogram and MFCC (Mel Frequency Cepstral Coefficents) [6,14]. On the other hand, high-level features are related to the perception of rhythm.

Recent works on beat tracking are based on deep learning models to predict the beat position, using recurrent neural network and LSTM (Long Short Term Memory networks). These models directly process magnitude spectrograms at multiple levels and provide output feature recognizing beats and downbeats [10]. Furthermore, other researches relies on a temporal convolution network framework [9].

2.2   Human Movement and MoCap

Human movement can be mathematically described in terms of distance, displacement, speed and articulations. Table 2 shows detailed motion features. Skeleton-based action is defined as the problem of localizing human joints also known as 2D and 3D keypoints (hands, elbows, wrists, etc.) in images or videos. These features plays a critical role in various applications and has been widely used in multimedia applications such as human computer interaction [12]. For example, they make up the backbone for yoga, dance, and fitness applications [13]. A wide range of systems are available to collect continuous movement data. The most popular in the recent years is MoCap (motion capture), usually referring to motion representations in digital formats to allow quantitative analysis or real-time processing. Approaches can be split into two broad categories: marker-based approaches rely on infrared cameras and reflective markers (single or multiple instances), while marker-less approaches are only based on cameras (RGB-only images vs depth data RGB-D).

Table 2. Visual motion features

Feature	Definition
Body landmarks	The spatial location of human body articulation (keypoints) from visuals such as images and videos, each points described by three coordinates (x, y, z)
Articulation angles and orientation	Rotation between two adjacent body articulation with different orientation
Translation and rotation	translation and rotation related to the world coordinate axis (tx,ty,tz,rx,ry,rz)
Temporal displacement and acceleration	Predict spatiotemporal features and velocity from the previous frame to the current frame
Joint collection distances	Represent the changes over time of joint angles computed at each time frame and a fixed point of the skeleton

Human hand motion is highly articulate, but also highly constrained, which makes it difficult to model [17]. Vision-based hand pose estimation analysis has been an important research topic as this can play an essential role in enhancing the experience on a variety of technology disciplines and platforms in order to control devices or to interact with computer interfaces. This analysis process can be resumed in two steps: detection and tracking. The first major block will detect hand position that contains palm from frames of video. This can be achieved via an oriented hand bounding box by means of depth based methods [18], or alternatively by RGB based methods [16]. The second stage is the tracking pipeline that can track multiple hands in real-time by detecting the keypoints coordinates using regression model [19]. The hand can be also modelled in several aspects like shape, kinematical structure, dynamics, and semantics.

2.3   Audiomotor Synchronization

The human audio-motor systems are practically connected during musical performance. Moreover listening to music can easily encourage the motor system to act in the form of head nodding, foot tapping, and even dancing [24]. Further research on audio-motor systems is trying to test the ways in which audio-motor coordination is influenced by visual cues from a conductor's gestures [25]. Another popular tool for the systematic assessment of audio-motor system is the BAASTA (Battery for the Assessment of Auditory Sensorimotor and Timing Abilities) [26], that uses finger tapping with music and adaptive tapping to a sequence with a tempo change in order to evaluate the synchronization performance of the participants.

Musical cognition refers to the study of musical thinking field, that focuses to understand the mental processes and the way of human brain perception such as cortical activity during listening to the auditory rhythms through the methods of cognitive science, and neurological methods based on auditory motor synchronization [27]. Following this notion, recent research suggests that the processes of action-perception between neural and mechanical activities synchronize in different forms during musical activities, linking body movement and high level musical features [28].

3   Methodology

This section will present our approach to measure and quantify in real time the "synchronization score" between natural movements of hand (fingers) and the musical beats. Its workflow is presented in Fig. 1. Inspired by the success attained in hand tracking and music beat tracking methods, we propose to exploit these methods in order to evaluate the synchronization with temporal alignment using dynamic time warping (DTW) algorithms. This will be applied to measure similarity between two temporal sequences of motion and music beat while the participant is listening to the music using human computer interaction based on computer vision.

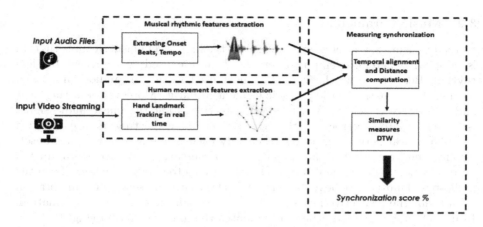

Fig. 1. Workflow method research

3.1 Motion Parameters

The presented process relies on MediaPipe [20], an open source framework to detect in real time the hand keypoints (x, y) captured by the camera [19]. The MediaPipe module predicts 21 hand landmarks based on three axes: x (horizontal), y (vertical) and z that represents the depth of landmark. Then the hand score, indicating the accuracy of hand presence in the input image is generated. Finally a simple classification occurs between left and right hand. In this study, the landmarks of index fingers are firstly determined. Figure 2 presents hand landmark in MediaPipe [20]. The left hand index finger is shown by coordinates [5,6,7,8] for example. These landmarks are then used to make condition of tapping based on position and the angle of articulation corresponding to image width and height.

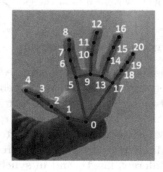

Fig. 2. The labeled keypoints generated by MediaPipe

3.2 Music Parameters

Instead of using low level acoustic features, the high level music features rhythm is adopted. Therefore tempo, onset and beat are used to represent musical rhythm. Beat in music theory is the most used feature in audio conditioned motion [15], that tracks the periodic element in music. Moreover detecting beat and tempo are closely related to onset detection. First the music audio signal is converted into spectrogram, then the coefficients of spectrogram are analyzed through neural network in order to classify each frame as onset or not onset. Finally, the beat location are founded by processing periodic patterns in the onset location. The public Librosa [21] is leveraged to extract the beats from the audio-based music. The beats features is a 1D vector, representing the annotation timings for the respective beats in which we consider it as rhythm information. Intuitively, the motion rhythm has to match the musical rhythm (Fig. 3).

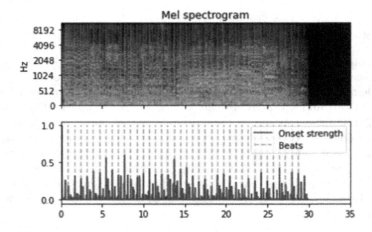

Fig. 3. Audio-based music waveform and the estimated beat positions

3.3 Similarity and Score of Synchronization

The aim of this paper is to develop more sophisticated methods for automated synchronization scoring between the hands movement and musical beat. As shown in the previous section we take temporal features with aggregation in real time from motion and music. Dynamic Time Warping is an algorithm that produces a better similarity measurement compared to others methods such as Hamming, Euclidean and Manhattan distance. The greatest advantage of DTW is to cope with signals of different length and in synchronization signals which move exactly at the same speed and time. Finally DTW can be used as a score component for synchronization between hand movement and musical beat [22]. The distance between two time series data n-dimensional space can be computed via the Euclidean distance $\mathbf{x} = [x_1, x_2, ..., x_n]$ and $\mathbf{y} = [y_1, y_2, ..., y_n]$

$$dist(\mathbf{x}, \mathbf{y}) = \|\mathbf{x} - \mathbf{y}\| = \sqrt{(x_1 - y_1)^2 + (x_2 - y_2)^2 + \cdots + (x_n - y_n)^2} \quad (1)$$

However, if the length of x is different from y, then the euclidean formula cannot be used to compute the similarity distance. Instead, a more flexible method must be developed to find the best mapping with the minimum distance from elements in x to those in y in order to compute the similarity synchronous.

Let x and y two vectors of lengths m and n:

$$D(i, j) = |x(i) - y(j)| + min \left\{ \begin{array}{c} D(i - 1, j) \\ D(i - 1, j - 1) \\ D(i, j - 1) \end{array} \right\} \quad (2)$$

DTW is used to align the signals and computes the euclidean distance at each frame across every other frames to reach the minimum path that will match the two signals.

4   Experiments

4.1   Set-up

The objective of this demo showcase is to present a real application based on our innovative and robust hand-music synchronisation system. The main objective is to study a playful configuration coupled with an innovative method using the webcam sensor, in order to improve the automatically generated synchronisation score between the music rhythm and the hand movements (see Fig. 4).

To test the synchronization, participants were asked to tap as regularly as possible with their two index fingers (Right and Left) in both directions and on the specific red button, in order to be synchronized to a rhythmic input music. We propose to the participants to test our demo in four difficulty levels to study the perception rhythm ability of each participant. The music was delivered over headphones at a comfortable sound volume level. The first "easy" level contains a clear beats pulse that were added in the background of the music, that can help the participants to match the beats rhythm easily. For the second level "moderate", the same musical audio is used but with low volume of the short pulses annotation... until level 4 "insane" that contains the audio music without beat pulses added to the original music. For this experiment two music clips of 35 s were selected, with different tempo and different style of music i.e. Ruby Baby *Act One* with 80 beats/minute including 39 beats, then Daft Punk *One More Time* but with 125 beats/minute and 65 of the placement beats.

Our algorithm was implemented in Python. All experiments are running on DELL with a Intel Core i5-8400H CPU 2.50 GHz × 8 processor and 16 GB of RAM, and the Ubuntu 20.04.2 operating system. The lived processed images video is refreshed at 25 frames per second, with 1280 × 720 resolution.

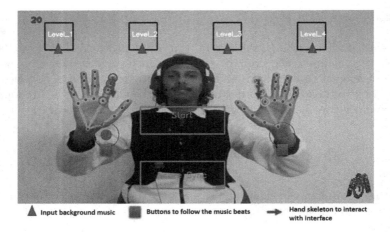

▲ Input background music   ■ Buttons to follow the music beats   ➡ Hand skeleton to interact with interface

Fig. 4. The screen contains four **black boxes** to choose the music. 4 options can be selected with audio music that has annotated timings for the respective **beats annotations** with lower pitched pulses in order to help the participant to match the beats rhythm on four difficulty levels. Then there are two **red buttons** in the center of the screen to follow the beats with the fingers, and it can be done by moving the index finger in both directions on the specific red button, in order to synchronize with the rhythms of the audio music in the background.

4.2 Results

The present study was carried out on 3 non-musicians students (2 males and 1 female, average age 21). This experiment was designed to investigate the level of synchronization at different intensity of beats annotation and to examine the impact of the tempo on the performance (slow-rhythm and fast-rhythm).

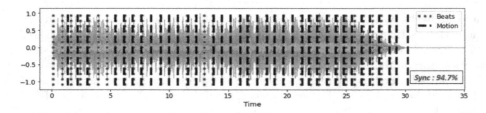

Fig. 5. Beat tracking for music waveform and motion beat, participant #2, lev moderate.

Figure 5 shows one of the 35 s music clip with aligned musical beats and motion beats for participant #2. Then the global synchronization score for every frame in the audio-video, the music beats marked by the green dashed line and the motion with the black dash-dotted line. It can be observed that the motion fingers tapping occur in very similar ways where the musical beats occur. The consecutive matched beats correspond to tapping index finger on left and right alternatively. For beat matching, the motion beats extracted from each frame and their corresponding input music beats are compared using euclidean distance and dynamic time warping. Then the score of synchronization is computed and displayed.

Table 3. Performance synchronization score (in percent)

Ruby Baby - *Act One* (80 bpm, 39 beats)			
Difficulty levels	Participant #1	Participant #2	Participant #3
Easy	93.2	**97.8**	95.4
Moderate	88.5	94.7	89.6
Hard	83.2	90.5	82.3
Insane	76.1	88.7	78.9
Daft Punk - *One more time* (123 bpm, 65 beats)			
Difficulty levels	Participant #1	Participant #2	Participant #3
Easy	**95.1**	86.8	88.7
Moderate	91.3	85.4	86.6
Hard	86.5	79.1	83.9
Insane	80.02	72.5	**70.4**

Results show fairly good performances of the participants. The best synchronization score (97.8%) is achieved for the song *Act One* at 80 bpm with an *easy* level of difficulty, and the smallest score (70.4%) for *One ore time* at 123 bpm with an *insane* level of difficulty. The average synchronization score is decreasing proportionally to the difficulty level. The overall average of synchronization score is higher (88.48%) for the first song at 80 bpm than for second one the (83.87%) at 123 bpm. This shows that the tempo impacts the ability of synchronization, in line with previous studies [29]. The overall best performance is achieved by participant #2 with 97.8% synchronization score. However the best performance with fast tempo is performed by participant #1 with 95.1% synchronization score.

Interviews were conducted with each participants after the experiments. The main feedback is that participants really appreciated the synchronization experience through this playful developed tools, and founded the application very easy to use. In addition, Participant 1's comments reveal that he is a fan of the *One more time* song. This could explain why he scores better on this song than on the first, unlike the other participants (Fig. 3).

5   Conclusion

In this paper, we propose an efficient and accurate playful method for the automatic notation of the synchronization of hand movements and musical rhythms, using the real-time webcam display and musical audio as input.

This also enables to test the level of synchronization for a musical piece by tapping fingers with the beat times position. Moreover, an experiment was conducted trough four difficulty, with beat pulses added to the music and different mixing levels. The results show that the synchronization score decreases proportionally as the level of difficulty increase.

Future work will consider increasing the number of participants in the experiment to achieve statistical processing of the data. We will also integrate novel multi-scale music features contribution, such as downbeat and tatum. In order to increase the robustness of our synchronization score method we will extract the peaks and calculate the phase difference between the musical beat and finger movements at each cycle.

Finally, motion capture will be generalized to the whole body using different features such as articulation, joint collection distance and temporal displacement of the body landmarks. This will produce accurate body movement descriptors leading to fine analysis of synchronization between the human body and fully-described music features of the listened song.

References

1. Bardy, B.G., et al.: Moving in unison after perceptual interruption. Sci. Rep. **10**(1), 1–13 (2020)
2. De Cock, V.C., et al.: Rhythmic abilities and musical training in Parkinson's disease: do they help? NPJ Parkinson's Dis. **4**, 1–8 (2018)
3. Kadir, M.E., et al.: Can a simple approach identify complex nurse care activity?. In: Adjunct Proceedings of the 2019 ACM International Joint Conference on Pervasive and Ubiquitous Computing and Proceedings of the 2019 ACM International Symposium on Wearable Computers (2019)
4. Sun, X., Li, C., Lin, S.: Explicit spatiotemporal joint relation learning for tracking human pose. In: Proceedings of the IEEE/CVF International Conference on Computer Vision Workshops (2019)
5. Ipser, A., et al.: Sight and sound persistently out of synch: stable individual differences in audiovisual synchronisation revealed by implicit measures of lip-voice integration. Sci. Rep. **7**(1), 1–12 (2017)
6. Ganesh, S.: Alexander Lerch. Tempo, Beat and Downbeat estimation for Electronic Dance Music (2018)
7. Fuentes, M.: Multi-scale computational rhythm analysis : a framework for sections, downbeats, beats, and microtiming (2019)
8. Sogorski, M., Geisel, T., Priesemann, V.: Correlated microtiming deviations in jazz and rock music (2018)
9. Davies,M.E., Böck, S.: Temporal convolutional networks for musical audio beat tracking. In: Proceedings of the 27th European Signal Processing Conference (EUSIPCO) (2019)

10. Böck, S., Krebs, F., Widmer, G.: Joint beat and downbeat tracking with recurrent neural networks. In: ISMIR (2016)
11. Sebastian, B., Davies, M.E.P., Knees, P.: Multi-task learning of tempo and beat: learning one to improve the other. In: ISMIR (2019)
12. Ren, Z,, et al.: Robust hand gesture recognition with kinect sensor. In: Proceedings of the 19th ACM International Conference on Multimedia (2011)
13. Zou, J., et al.: Intelligent fitness trainer system based on human pose estimation. In: Sun, S., Fu, M., Xu, L. (eds.) ICSINC 2018. LNEE, vol. 550, pp. 593–599. Springer, Singapore (2019). https://doi.org/10.1007/978-981-13-7123-3_69
14. Jensenius, A., Godøy, R., Wanderley, M.: Developing tools for studying musical gestures within the max/MSP/jitter environment. In: Proceedings of the International Computer Music Conference (2011)
15. Huang, R., et al.: Dance revolution: long-term dance generation with music via curriculum learning. arXiv preprint arXiv:2006.06119 (2020)
16. Sridhar, S., et al.: Real-time joint tracking of a hand manipulating an object from rgb-d input. In: Leibe, B., Matas, J., Sebe, N., Welling, M. (eds.) ECCV 2016. LNCS, vol. 9906, pp. 294–310. Springer, Cham (2016). https://doi.org/10.1007/978-3-319-46475-6_19
17. Wu, Y., Huang, T.S.: For vision-based human computer interaction. Studies (2001)
18. Gattupalli, S., et al.: Towards deep learning based hand keypoints detection for rapid sequential movements from RGB images. In: Proceedings of the 11th PErvasive Technologies Related to Assistive Environments Conference (2018)
19. Zhang, F., et al.: Mediapipe hands: on-device real-time hand tracking. arXiv preprint arXiv:2006.10214 (2020)
20. MediaPipe: Cross-platform ML solutions made simple. https://google.github.io/mediapipe/.2020
21. McFee, B., Raffel, C., Liang, D., Ellis, D.P., McVicar, M., Battenberg, E., et al.: librosa: audio and music signal analysis in python. In: Proceedings of the 14th Python in Science Conference (2015)
22. Cheong, J.H.: Four ways to quantify synchrony between time series data (2020). https://doi.org/10.17605/OSF.IO/BA3NY
23. Wu, Y., Huang, T.S.: For vision-based human computer interaction. Studies 5, 22 (2021)
24. Schalles, M.D., Pineda, J.A.: Musical sequence learning and EEG correlates of audiomotor processing. Behav. Neurol 2015, Article ID 638202, p. 11 (2015)
25. Colley, I.D., et al.: The influence of visual cues on temporal anticipation and movement synchronization with musical sequences. Acta Psychologica 191, 190–200 (2018)
26. Bella, S.D., et al.: BAASTA: Battery for the assessment of auditory sensorimotor and timing abilities. Behavior Research Methods 49(3), 1128–1145 (2017)
27. Damm, L., Varoqui, D., de Cock, V.C., Benoit, B.B., et al.: Why do we move to the beat? a multi-scale approach, from physical principles to brain dynamics. Neurosci. Biobehav. Rev. 112, 553–584 (2020)
28. https://mutor-2.github.io/MUTOR/units/12.html
29. Repp, B.H.: Sensorimotor synchronization: a review of the tapping literature. Psychon. Bull. Rev. 12, 969–992 (2005)

Performance of Recent Tiny/Small YOLO Versions in the Context of Top-View Fisheye Images

Benoît Faure[1], Nathan Odic[1], Olfa Haggui[2], and Baptiste Magnier[1(✉)]

[1] Euromov Digital Health in Motion, Univ. Montpellier,
IMT Mines Ales, Ales, France
{benoit.faure,nathan.odic}@mines-ales.org, baptiste.magnier@mines-ales.fr
[2] LIRMM, Univ. Montpellier, CNRS, Montpellier, France
olfa.haggui@lirmm.fr

Abstract. With the spreading of the computer vision field, human detection and tracking are problems more relevant than ever. However, due to the complexity of fisheye images, current lightweight detection models show difficulty when processing them. The aim of this article is to compare the performance on fisheye images of current real time detection solutions, specifically YOLOv3-tiny, YOLOv4-tiny and YOLOv5-small. Experiments carried out using a top-view fisheye camera, show faster performance but the very poor detection quality from YOLOv4-tiny. YOLOv5-small, while being slightly slower, gives a far better detection than both other solutions. The database created for this paper is available online. In conclusion, the current review shows YOLOv5-small is the best solution out of the 3 reviewed in a fast, real time, fisheye application.

Keywords: Human detection · YOLOv3 · v4 · v5 · Fisheye camera

1 Introduction and Motivations

Human detection is a challenging task owing to their variable appearance and wide range of poses [4], especially with fisheye camera. Indeed, a fisheye lens enables images to be acquired with a broad field of view [8,12,16]. However, pedestrians appear in different shapes, sizes and at various orientations. Unfortunately, most of the existing people-detection algorithms are designed for standard/perspective camera images where people appear upright. On the one hand, people-detection algorithms using classical feature extraction have been adapted to fisheye images [2,3,18]. On the other hand, the detection performances are improved with the great success of deep learning. For instance, the YOLO (You Only Look Once [14]) is a reliable detector based on Deep Convolutional Neural Network and remains commonly used for real-time object detection. Recently, different algorithms based on YOLO provide much faster and more accurate results than previous algorithms aimed at detecting people in fisheye images

P. L. Mazzeo et al. (Eds.): ICIAP 2022 Workshops, LNCS 13373, pp. 246–257, 2022.
https://doi.org/10.1007/978-3-031-13321-3_22

without any pre-processing [5,7]. Meanwhile, different YOLO versions exist, the last are: YOLOv3 [15], YOLOv4 [17], and YOLOv5 [10]. The small/tiny implementations of these versions are optimum regarding limited hardware resources. The aim of this article is to compare the person's detection performance of these versions on fisheye images. After discussing the differences between each algorithm, each YOLO version is trained on fisheye images, using fisheye datasets.

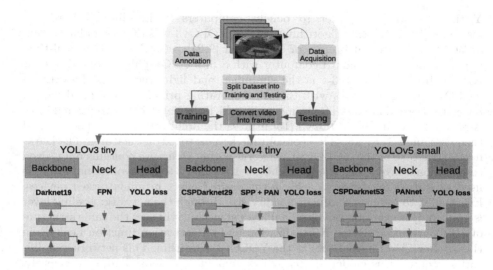

Fig. 1. Flow diagram of different YOLO architectures studied in this communication.

2   Detection Method

In this communication, human detection methods in top down fisheye cameras are evaluated. The detection model used in this paper is the state of the art method YOLO, the different versions of it we compared are shown in Fig. 1.

2.1   YOLO: An Architecture for Human Detection

This section details the developments of the YOLO architecture based on Deep Convolutional Neural Network detection model and its extensions: YOLOv3-tiny, YOLOv4-tiny and YOLOv5-small architectures. Originally, YOLO is a state of art Object Detector which can perform object detection in real-time with a good accuracy [14]. It treats the detection task as a regression downside and has been wide utilized in image process fields. There are various deep learning algorithms, but they are unable detecting an object in a single run. Meanwhile, YOLO makes the detection in a single forward propagation through a neural network, which makes it suitable for real-time applications. This property has made YOLO very popular amongst the other deep learning algorithms. Recently, several versions, e.g., YOLOv3 [15], also YOLOv4 [17], and lastly YOLOv5 [10], have additionally been developed to improve the classification performance on complicated datasets, and, to increase the quantity of data within the feature map. Usually, in the architecture of the YOLO algorithm, the head and neural network type are the same for all of the algorithms, whereas backbone, neck, and loss function are different, as detailed below.

YOLOv3-Tiny: In order to benefit computers having limited hardware resources, YOLOv3-tiny algorithm (denoted YOLOv3-t) is the preferable version of YOLOv3. Indeed, it is easy for YOLOv3-t [9,21] network to satisfy real-time requirements on a standard computer with a limited Graphics Processing Unit (GPU). In fact, YOLOv3-t is the simplified and light version of the original YOLOv3 [15]. It operates with the same operating principle as original model, but with a varied number of parameters in which the depth of convolutional layer is reduced. Originally, YOLOv3 [15] utilizes the architecture of darknet53, and then uses many 1×1 and 3×3 convolution kernels to extract features. The Darknet19 structure of the YOLOv3-t network, within structure contains only seven convolutional layers and small number of 1×1 and 3×3 convolutional layers is used as feature extractor to achieve the desired effect in miniaturized devices. Eventually, to reduce the dimensionality size through the network: pooling layer is applied. However, its convolutional layer structure still uses the same structure of 2D-Convolution, Batch Normalization and an activation function LeakyRelu (Leaky Rectified Linear Unit) as the YOLOv3 algorithm. This network simplification requires this model to occupy less amount of memory and, consequently, will improve the speed of the detection process.

YOLOv4-Tiny: As a modified version of YOLOv3, YOLOv4 [17] is used in this work with a derived version. Thus, YOLOv4-tiny (denoted YOLOv4-t) uses Cross Stage Partial Network (CSPNet) in Darknet, creating a new feature extractor backbone called CSPDarknet53. However, to help it achieve these fast speeds, YOLOv4-t [11] utilizes a couple of different changes from the original YOLOv4 network. Foremost, the number of convolutional layers in the CSP backbone are compressed with a total of 29 pre-trained convolutional layers. Additionally, the number of YOLO layers has been reduced to two instead of three and there are fewer anchor boxes for prediction. We can use YOLOv4-t for a faster training and a faster detection. Therefore, the neck is composed of a Spatial Pyramid Pooling (SPP) layer and PANet path aggregation. They are used for feature aggregation to improve the receptive field and short out important features from the backbone. In addition, the head is composed of YOLO layer. Fundamentally, the image is fed to CSPDarknet for feature extraction and then to path aggregation network PANet for fusion. At last, YOLOv4-t is the better option when compared with YOLOv4 as faster inference time is more important when working with a real-time object detection environment.

YOLOv5-Small: In this context, YOLOv5 is different from the previous releases. The v5 model has shown a substantial performance increase from its predecessors. In addition, YOLOv5 [10] comes with its various versions: YOLOv5-s, the small version, YOLOv5-m, the medium version, YOLOv5-l, the large version and YOLOv5-x, the extra-large version, each having its own unique characteristic. Since this study focuses on real-time detection, the speed is a factor of the utmost importance, hence the smallest version has been chosen as the representative of the YOLOv5 family for its performance analysis. The backbone is CSPDarknet53 and solves the repetitive gradient information in large backbones and integrates gradient change into feature map; that reduces the inference speed, increases accuracy, and reduces the model size by decreasing the parameters. Furthermore, it uses a path aggregation network (PANet) as neck to boost the information flow. PANet adopts a new feature pyramid network (FPN) that includes several bottom ups and top down layers. Consequently, this improves the propagation of low-level features in the model. The PANet improves the localization in lower layers, which enhances the localization accuracy of the object. In addition, the head in YOLOv5 is the same as YOLOv4 and YOLOv3, generating three different outputs of feature maps to achieve multi-scale prediction. Finally, it helps to enhance the prediction of small to large objects efficiently.

2.2 Dataset

Images in these datasets were resized to 640 × 640 pixels because YOLO requires square images whose height and width are multiples of 32. The image size of 640 × 640 was chosen based on preliminary tests with YOLOv5-s.

Public Datasets: Primarily, as a base for the algorithm, weights trained on the COCO dataset [13] were used. This dataset provides numerous images containing human examples. Even though the images presented are not fisheye and not necessarily top view, they gave a big data baseline for our model. The objective being, to start fisheye training with weights already able to recognize the general features of a human figure. A few benchmarks and datasets have been created in order to train and evaluate people detection algorithms for fisheye images. Such datasets are used to specialize our model on fisheye cameras. Fisheye images pose challenges not encountered in images taken with a standard lens. These include illumination variations across the image and big variations in the angle at which a person appears. Additionally, fisheye images distort figures in it. The distortion is much more prominent on the edge of the images, with big objects being affected the most. The distortion causes shrinking of the objects, this makes it harder for the YOLO algorithm to discern it.

The chosen dataset for specialization is the MIRROR Worlds dataset[1]. However, preliminary tests on these datasets gave poor detection results. That is because annotations of this dataset are imprecise, as shown in Fig. 2. These annotations were at times not bounding anything, or bounding completely different

---

[1] http://www2.icat.vt.edu/mirrorworlds/.

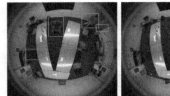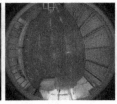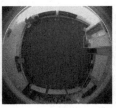

Fig. 2. Dataset MIRROR, originally not perfectly annotated.

Table 1. Experimental characteristics of the used datasets.

Database	MIRROR (new annotations)	Our dataset
Number of videos	19	31
Number of images for training	821	1492
Number of images for test	204	377 + 406
Moving camera	No	Yes

objects, objects that ended up being detected as human by the detection algorithm. We thus decided to relabel the MIRROR dataset using *roboflow*[2]. Subsequently, 1025 annotated images were obtained; the split for this dataset is 80% training and 20% test. Additionally, we decided to create a new dataset to further increase the variations in environments and situations the algorithm could find itself in.

Our Dataset: The images for the new dataset were collected in the CERIS laboratory of the IMT mines Alès. Videos were acquired with a fisheye camera (Basler ace acA2040-120uc) mounted on a pole and placed around 3m in height. Initially, images were pulled from videos from both inside and outside the laboratory's hangar. During each capture, the camera was static, 2–3 people moved around the camera taking different positions. Examples include sitting, lying down and crouching. Furthermore, the brightness level of the images is very low inside the hangar, outside, however the images are very clear. The split for this dataset is 80% train and 20% test; it is available online with tied annotations[3].

A second part of the dataset was made, the objective of which being to test the effectiveness of each algorithm (see Sect. 2.1) on images set in environments they were not familiar with. For this part of the dataset, images were pulled from videos taken outdoors and on the street outside. Consequently, these images are different from the one detailed previously. So far, 406 images were annotated, and between 0 and 3 discernible people appear in each image. Finally, the Table 1 represents the characteristics of the datasets we used with 406 annotated images of the different scene than others utilized only for the tests.

[2] https://roboflow.com/annotate.
[3] https://github.com/BenoitFaureIMT/CERIS_FishEye.

Data Annotation: Data labelling is an essential step in a supervised machine learning task requiring significant manual work. To annotate our new dataset, boxes containing people are manually annotated. In order to do so, the *Roboflow* Tool is used. From a technical aspect, the pixel representing the center of the BBox, as well as its height and width in pixels are defined. Consequently, each BBox is represented by five parameters:

- (x, y): pixel coordinates of the BBox center,
- w and h: width and height of the BBox respectively,
- class: ID of the object category.

The parameters x, y, w and h are essential for the evaluation presented in the next section, whereas the ID concerns mainly tracking processes.

3   Experiments and Evaluations

3.1   Evaluation Metrics

To analyze the progress of the network, we utilize the five following metrics: mean average precision 0.5 and 0.5:0.95, precision, recall and CIoU.

Mean Average Precision: After running the network on a certain number of images, of which the real BBox sizes and positions are known (i.e., called ground truth), the IoU (Intersection over Union) is computed between each detected BBox and all real BBoxes, the corresponding box with the highest IoU can be considered as the detected BBox: $IoU = \frac{Intersection\,area\,of\,both\,boxes}{Union\,area\,of\,both\,boxes}$. A threshold α is then set to compute the mean average precision mAP_α:

$$mAP_\alpha = \frac{Number\,of\,detections\,where\,the\,coressponding\,IoU \geq \alpha}{Number\,of\,detections\,from\,the\,neural\,network} \tag{1}$$

Moreover, it is possible to take the average of different values of α, to show the progress of the network over a range of metrics simultaneously. With this idea we declare $mAP_{0.5:0.95}$:

$$mAP_{0.5:0.95} = \frac{1}{10} \sum_{k=0}^{9} (mAP\,(0.5 + 0.05 * k)) \tag{2}$$

Precision: When a detected BBox obtains an IoU above 0, it is counted as a positive. However, the box of the detected object could be very inaccurate, for example by bounding only the top half, or by actually covering twice or thrice the area of the real box. To counter this problem, we set a threshold at 0.5, above which a detection is counted as a true positive, and below which, it is counted as a false positive: $precision = \frac{total\,amount\,of\,true\,positives}{number\,of\,true\,positives\,+\,number\,of\,false\,positives}$.

Recall: It represents the percentage of detections, which were not missed, a real BBox which was not detected represents a false negative and define the recall: $recall = \frac{total\,amount\,of\,true\,positives}{total\,amount\,of\,(true\,positives\,+\,false\,negatives)}$.

CIoU: Complete IoU bounding boss regression [22] allows for fast convergence towards the ground truth BBox. It is used in the training of YOLOv3-t, YOLOv4-t and YOLOv5-s. The metric combines the overlap between predicted and ground truth, as well as the center of the BBoxes and their aspect ratio.

3.2 Training of the Models

To train the different YOLO networks, we used the respective *PyTorch* implementations of each architecture. The definition for the architecture of YOLOv4-t was obtained from a github repository in [26], which based it on Ultralytics' yolov5 implementation. Finally, the definition for YOLOv3-t [24], YOLOv5-s [23] and the methods for training [25] the networks were obtained from the Ultralytics github repository, the company that developed the YOLOv5 architecture.

As mentioned in the Sect. 2.2, the training started using weights pre-trained on the COCO dataset [13]. Each YOLO version is then specialized on fisheye cameras, using first the MIRROR dataset (own annotated) before moving training onto our own dataset. We chose to train on the datasets in this order, as the context in which the network will be applied is expected to be closer to the environment we obtained images from. The settings for the training of each YOLO version are detailed in the Table 2.

Table 2. Training parameters for YOLOv3-t, YOLOv4-t and YOLOv5-s

Version	Training on MIRROR dataset			Training on our dataset			Hyper parameters
	Epochs	Batch size	Image size	Epochs	Batch size	Image size	
YOLOv3-t	100	64	640	50	64	640	Default
YOLOv4-t	100	64	640	50	64	640	Default
YOLOv5-s	100	64	640	50	64	640	Default

The batch size was maximized while considering the GPU's memory limitations could hold, this was done as to follow indications from Ultralytics on training the model. The image size was set to correspond to the size of COCO images and hyper-parameters were set to their default values. To quantify how close we are to overfitting the model, we observed the rate at which the CIoU increased. In an attempt to limit the risk of overfitting, epochs for both datasets were chosen as to stop training before this rate became negligible. The Fig. 3 represents the evolution of the CIoU during training on the MIRROR dataset (a) and our dataset (b). The graphs start very close to each other in (a) as they were all trained on the COCO dataset, however YOLOv5-s shows better performance in learning especially at the start of training where it begins converging much faster. In Fig. 3(b), the graphs start separate, this is due to the better score YOLOv5-s had at the end of training on the MIRROR dataset. The combination of these two graphs demonstrates a better learning performance of the YOLOv5-s model.

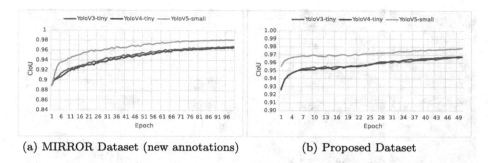

(a) MIRROR Dataset (new annotations)   (b) Proposed Dataset

Fig. 3. Evolution of CIoU during training of each YOLO model

Table 3. Performance of YOLOv3-t, YOLOv4-t and YOLOv5-s on the MIRROR dataset after being trained on it (computer equipped with GPU Tesla K80).

Version	Precision	Recall	$mAP_{0.5}$	$mAP_{0.5:0.95}$	Detection (ms)
YOLOv3-t	0.964	0.922	0.976	0.617	19.8
YOLOv4-t	0.947	0.952	0.975	0.587	14.7
YOLOv5-s	0.953	0.974	0.989	0.736	25.3

Table 4. Performance of YOLOv3-t, YOLOv4-t and YOLOv5-s on our dataset after being trained on both MIRROR and our new dataset (computer with GPU Tesla K80).

Version	Precision	Recall	$mAP_{0.5}$	$mAP_{0.5:0.95}$	Detection (ms)
YOLOv3-t	0.988	0.961	0.984	0.644	20.1
YOLOv4-t	0.976	0.936	0.976	0.626	15.2
YOLOv5-s	0.987	0.991	0.993	0.724	25.8

3.3 Performance of the Models on Images in a Familiar Context

The Table 3 gives the final metrics of the training and testing on the MIRROR dataset, while the Table 4 gives the final metrics of the testing on our dataset of models trained on both our dataset and the MIRROR dataset. The results are similar across all 3 versions for Precision, Recall and $mAP_{0.5}$, however YOLOv5-s has better results for $mAP_{0.5:0.95}$. In terms of the detection quality, YOLOv5-s performed best, with YOLOv3-t and YOLOv4-t as second and third place respectively. However, in detection speed the rankings are reversed, the increase in speed from YOLOv4-t comes from the small size of the neural network (weight file is 6.3Mo) relative to YOLOv3-t (17.4Mo) and YOLOv5-s (14.5Mo).

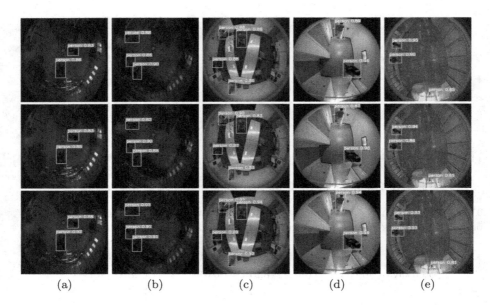

(a)   (b)   (c)   (d)   (e)

Fig. 4. People detection on top-view fisheye images. The used algorithms for the detection are in the first row: YOLOv3-t, second row: YOLOv4-t and third row: YOLOv5-s. Images in (a)–(b) correspond to our new image dataset whereas in (c)–(e), they are tied to MIRROR dataset with new annotations.

Table 5. YOLOv3-t, YOLOv4-t and YOLOv5-s performances in an unfamiliar context.

Version	Precision	Recall	$mAP_{0.5}$	$mAP_{0.5:0.95}$	Detection (ms)
YOLOv3-t	0.374	0.221	0.207	0.054	19.8
YOLOv4-t	0.191	0.109	0.089	0.021	14.4
YOLOv5-s	0.820	0.656	0.739	0.389	24.2
GPU	Tesla K80				

To finish testing, all 3 models were used to detect people in the same dataset they were trained on. A sample of the data obtained is shown in Fig. 4. All 3 algorithms perform well in both a dark (a)–(b) and light (c)–(e) contexts. The algorithms were also able to detect and bound small entities as shown in column (e) of Fig. 4.

3.4   Performance of the Models on Images in an Unfamiliar Context

Results shown previously (Sect. 3.3) give a very optimistic view of the algorithms performance. However, the high similarity between the BBoxes provided by each model, as well as the very high performance in low light contexts possibly indicates a partial memorization of the dataset. To investigate this, all 3 trained YOLO versions were tested on the second part of our dataset. As the images and contexts differ greatly in comparison to images our models were trained on, it would give a better indication of the models performance.

The Table 5 summarizes the results obtained in the test, the rankings are consistent with the results obtained previously; however the distance between each model is much bigger. On all precision metrics, YOLOv5-s performs much better than the other two metrics. The $mAP_{0.5}$ of the model is at 0.739, meaning that the algorithm is capable of bounding it's detection relatively well. Furthermore, the model displays a high precision (0.82), indicating the low number of false positives in an unfamiliar context. Finally, the recall is at 0.656, it indicates that the model missed around 35% of detection; this figure is high, but in the context of a tracking algorithm could be negligible if compensated properly.

The Fig. 5 shows a sample of the images obtained from the tests. While these images have been selected, they represent quite well the obtained images. In that respect, YOLOv5-s outperforms the other networks, but still has its limitations, as shown by the metrics discussed previously. Column (e) shows two false negatives, one (center) is due to the black clothes on a dark background, and another (bottom left) appears when the person walks into the very edge of the image. This same person was detected a few frames before in the column (d). This column also shows a false negative (center) and a false positive (top left) also appearing at the edge of the frame where cars can be seen distorted. Nevertheless, looking at columns (a), (b) and (c) where the images are very clear, YOLOv5-s was able to properly detect all people present in the picture.

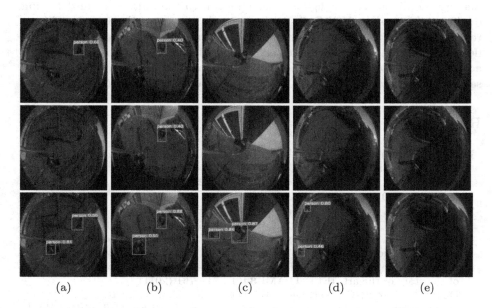

(a)   (b)   (c)   (d)   (e)

Fig. 5. People detection on top-view fisheye images on a new dataset without training on the same data. The used algorithms for the detection are in the first row: YOLOv3-t, second row: YOLOv4-t and third row: YOLOv5-s.

While it is true that YOLOv3-t and YOLOv4-t both have faster detection speeds than YOLOv5, the difference between each algorithm is about 5ms. The detection speeds of YOLOv5-small are fast enough to be used in real time cases (i.e., >10 fps), making detection speed a secondary factor in the comparison of each network. The difference is further dwarfed by the very high performance of YOLOv5-s on detection metrics in comparison to YOLOv3-t and YOLOv4-t. We expect YOLOv4-t's very poor performance to come from it's small size, because of it, it memorized the dataset rather than learn important features.

4   Conclusion

This paper presents a comparison in the performance of YOLOv3-tiny, YOLOv4-tiny and YOLOv5-small when applied to a problem involving fisheye images. During training, even though YOLOv5-s shows slightly better convergence, all 3 networks give similar detection scores. However, the same cannot be said about the networks' performance on datasets pulled from contexts they are unfamiliar with. In these cases, YOLOv5-s surpasses both YOLOv3-t and YOLOv4-t by a large margin, while giving itself acceptable detection performances. Moreover, while YOLOv5-s displays the slowest detection time, it is a small disadvantage as the detection speeds are still fast enough (25ms per frame) for real time applications. To further the argument in favor of YOLOv5-s, YOLOv4-t and YOLOv3-t have detection times of the same order of magnitude as YOLOv5-s, making the differences negligible in comparison to the differences in detection quality. Subsequently, YOLOv5-s is the best solution out of the 3 proposed for a real time, fisheye detection application. This solution was retained to act as the detection portion of a real time tracking algorithm [6,19,20], applied to videos acquired from a top-view fisheye camera, and mounted on an aerial drone or for security cameras. As a reminder, the dataset is available online (see Sect. 2.2).

References

1. Ahmed, I., Ahmad, M., Ahmad, A., Jeon, G.: Top view multiple people tracking by detection using deep SORT and YOLOv3 with transfer learning: within 5G infrastructure. Int. J. Mach. Learn. Cybern. **12**(11), 3053–3067 (2020). https://doi.org/10.1007/s13042-020-01220-5
2. Chiang, A.T., Wang, Y.: Human detection in fish-eye images using HOG-based detectors over rotated windows. In: IEEE ICMEW, pp. 1–6 (2014)
3. Demirkus, M., Wang, L., Eschey, M., Kaestle, H., Galasso, F.: People detection in fish-eye top-views. In: VISIGRAPP (5: VISAPP), pp. 141–148 (2017)
4. Dollar, P., Wojek, C., Schiele, B., Perona, P.: Pedestrian detection: an evaluation of the state of the art. IEEE TPAMI **34**(4), 743–761 (2011)
5. Duan, Z., Tezcan, O., Nakamura, H., Ishwar, P., Konrad, J.: RAPiD: rotation-aware people detection in overhead fisheye images. In: IEEE/CVF CVPR Workshops, pp. 636–637 (2020)
6. Haggui, O., Tchalim, M.A., Magnier, B.: A comparison of OpenCV algorithms for human tracking with a moving perspective camera. In: IEEE EUVIP (2021)

7. Haggui, O., Bayd, H., Magnier, B., Aberkane, A.: Human detection in moving fisheye camera using an improved YOLOv3 framework. In: IEEE MMSP (2021)
8. Hansen, P., Corke, P., Boles, W.: Wide-angle visual feature matching for outdoor localization. Int. J. Rob. Res. **29**(2–3), 267–297 (2010)
9. He, W., Huang, Z., Wei, Z., Li, C., Guo, B.: TF-YOLO: an improved incremental network for real-time object detection. Appl. Sci. **9**, 3225 (2019)
10. Iyer, R., Ringe, P.S., Iyer, R.V., Bhensdadiya, K.P.: Comparison of YOLOv3, YOLOv5s and MobileNet-SSD V2 for real-time mask detection. Int. Res. J. Eng. Technol. **8**(7), 1156–1160 (2021)
11. Jiang, Z., Zhao, L., Li, S., Jia, Y.: Real-time object detection method based on improved YOLOv4-tiny. arXiv preprint arXiv:2011.04244 (2020)
12. Kumler, J.J., Bauer, M.L.: Fish-eye lens designs and their relative performance. In: Current Developments in Lens Design and Optical Systems Engineering, vol. 4093, pp. 360–369. International Society for Optics and Photonics (2000)
13. Lin, T.-Y., et al.: Microsoft COCO: common objects in context. In: Fleet, D., Pajdla, T., Schiele, B., Tuytelaars, T. (eds.) ECCV 2014. LNCS, vol. 8693, pp. 740–755. Springer, Cham (2014). https://doi.org/10.1007/978-3-319-10602-1_48
14. Redmon, J., Divvala, S., Girshick, R., Farhadi, A.: You only look once: unified, real-time object detection. In: IEEE CVPR, pp. 779–788 (2016)
15. Redmon, J., Farhadi, A.: Yolov3: an incremental improvement. arXiv preprint arXiv:1804.02767 (2018)
16. Scaramuzza, D., Ikeuchi, K.: Omnidirectional Camera. Springer, Heidelberg (2014). https://doi.org/10.1007/978-0-387-31439-6
17. Shaniya, P., Jati, G., Alhamidi, M.R., Caesarendra, W., Jatmiko, W.: YOLOv4 RGBT human detection on unmanned aerial vehicle perspective. In: IEEE IWBIS, pp. 41–46 (2021)
18. Wang, T., Chang, C.W., Wu, Y.S.: Template-based people detection using a single downward-viewing fisheye camera. In: IEEE ISPACS, pp. 719–723 (2017)
19. Wojke, N., Bewley, A., Paulus, D.: Simple online and realtime tracking with a deep association metric. In: IEEE ICIP, pp. 3645–3649 (2017)
20. Talaoubrid, H., Vert, M., Hayat, K., Magnier, B.: Human tracking in top-view fisheye images: analysis of familiar similarity measures via hog and against various color spaces. J. Imaging **8**(4), 115 (2022)
21. Xiao, D., Shan, F., Li, Z., Le, B.T., Liu, X., Li, X.: A target detection model based on improved tiny-yolov3 under the environment of mining truck. IEEE Access **7**, 123757–123764 (2019)
22. Zheng, Z., Wang, P., Liu, W., Li, J., Ye, R., Ren, D.: Distance-IoU Loss: Faster and better learning for bounding box regression. In: AAAI (2020)
23. Ultralytics yolov5s [source code] (2021). https://github.com/ultralytics/yolov5/blob/master/models/yolov5s.yaml
24. Ultralytics yolov5-tiny [source code] (2021). https://github.com/ultralytics/yolov5/blob/master/models/hub/yolov3-tiny.yaml
25. Ultralytics train [source code] (2021). https://github.com/ultralytics/yolov5/blob/master/train.py
26. Yolov4-tiny [source code]. https://github.com/WongKinYiu/PyTorch_YOLOv4/blob/u5_preview/models/yolov4-tiny.yaml

Cloud-Based Visually Aided Mobile Manipulator Kinematic Parameters Calibration

Stefano Mutti[1,3]([✉])(iD), Vito Renò[2], Massimiliano Nitti[2], Giovanni Dimauro[3], and Nicola Pedrocchi[1]

[1] CNR-STIIMA, Via Alfonso Corti 12, 20133 Milan, Italy
[2] CNR-STIIMA, Via G. Amendola 122, 70126 Bari, Italy
[3] Department of Computer Science, University of Bari, Bari, Italy
stefano.mutti@stiima.cnr.it

Abstract. Mobile manipulators are often comprised of an extensive kinematic chain resulting from an industrial robot mounted on top of an autonomous mobile robot. In such a way, the system not only retains the parameters embedded in the two sub-systems, hence DH parameters for the industrial robot and odometry parameters for the mobile robot, but also includes the relative transformation between the two parts and an additional transformation for a camera mounted on the kinematic chain.In this complex setup, it is relatively simple to introduce kinematic inaccuracies, or in some cases, to operate the system in such a way that the kinematic parameters vary(e.g., rubber wheels on high payload).Estimating the values of such parameters might be too demanding for the on-board computing system.In this work, we propose a cloud-based visually aided parameter estimation method, which constantly receives data from the mobile manipulator and generates better estimates of the kinematic parameters through an UKF dual estimation.The overall system architecture is presented to the reader, together with the reasons for relying to a cloud based paradigm, for then giving a theoretical analysis and real world experiments and results.

1 Introduction

Industrial Mobile Manipulators (IMMs)[1] have seen a substantial industrial employment increase in the latest years, thanks to their extensive dexterity and applicability in many scenarios. This dexterity comes as a result of embedding an Industrial robots (IRs) systems, on top of an AMR, resulting in a complex kinematic chain that relies on the AMR positioning capability and the IR dexterity. Such a system often includes a camera mounted on the IR proximity, which might compensate for the overall system open loop uncertainty, but raises the

---

[1] For the nomenclature and acronym, refer to RiA R15.08 where Autonomous Mobile Robots (AMR), Industrial Mobile Manipulator (IMM), Autonomous Guided Vehicle (AGV) *etc.* are defined.

P. L. Mazzeo et al. (Eds.): ICIAP 2022 Workshops, LNCS 13373, pp. 258–268, 2022.
https://doi.org/10.1007/978-3-031-13321-3_23

overall kinematic complexity by adding a rigid transform to the chain. In such scenarios, an external pose has to be retrieved as part of the system's tasks, adopting the provided camera images, where the precision is affected by the kinematic parameters of the overall system, the hand - eye precision, and the transformations taking part in kinematic chain. This problem amplifies in complex IMMs, where often the relative transformation of the components are not accurately known and might vary during the tasks, as results of different robotic payloads or conditions. On the topic of robotic calibration, many recent works address the problem by taking advantage of visual systems. In [1], a closed-loop kinematic calibration method to improve absolute position accuracy with point and distance constraints is introduced, while in [2] an optical-tracking marker fixed to the system's camera is employed on the Da Vinci robotic surgery system. While some methods only apply to IRs, in [3] a 2D based positional features based method specifically tailored to IMM is introduced, and in [4] an improved method for hand-eye calibration in IMM systems is devised. Following the results in [5–7], it is clear that parameter estimation algorithms have become a computationally expensive task, especially for modern embedded devices that are at the core of IMMs control systems. Furthermore, when it comes to visually aided methods, the computational complexity and data volume are considerably increased, making on-board embedded systems not ideal for the task. To this aid, a considerable research effort lately focused on cloud/edge computing paradigms for robotic systems, moving classical control problems and optimization on the cloud side. In [8], an IR cloud control scheme is optimized on the wireless connection properties and cloud resources, while in [9] a service based cloud server acts as a motion planner and controller for an AMR. Many cloud based works deal with mobile robotics classical problems, such as mapping, localization and path planning, especially in presence of a multitude of mobile robots, refer to [10–12] for a complete overview. Generically, cloud computing frameworks in robotics might be employed when computing capability positive affects the tasks [13], and latency between the robotic systems and the cloud is manageable, low, or taken into account by the control criteria [14–16].

1.1   Contribution

The authors have already investigated the potential of employing a UKF locally on an on-board computing system [17], where the kinematic parameters of an autonomous mobile robot are estimated, improving its odometry and docking performance. Noticeably, the UFK based model estimation together with the system's covariance computation is quite computationally expensive to be execute on-board. The contribution of this work consists of devising a cloud based framework that performs the estimation, based on the visual and kinematic data sent by the robot. Section 2 introduces the problem and concepts, while Sect. 3 unveils the background fundamentals to the newly devised method introduced in Sect. 4, along with the system model and architecture. Finally, Sect. 5 gathers the experimental phase and draws the conclusions and possible future works.

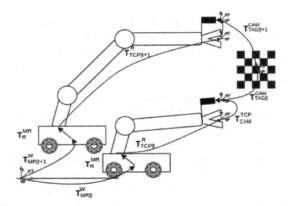

Fig. 1. Mobile manipulator system sketch including reference frames

2   Problem Formulation

Consider an IMM, on which a camera is fixed in the proximity of the Tool Center Point (ee) frame, and a visual tag, rigidly fixed in the environment, is used to retrieve the camera tag transformations during the system evolution, as shown in Fig. 1. General frames in such systems are W, the world fixed frame, M, the frame fixed to the mobile robot, R, the frame of the robot base, ee, the end-effector, C the camera frame, and T the frame bound to the external visual tag fixed to the world.

In such system, the forward kinematic (**FK**) computes the value of the W - ee transformation, as a function of its Denavit Hartenberg (DH) parameters DH_C, odometry parameters such as the radius r and generic model dependent distance l_{xy}, and the rigid transformations present in the kinematic chain.

Hence, provided an IMM, the transformation $trTeeW|t$ takes the following form:

$$^{ee}\mathbf{T}_W|t = \mathbf{FK}\left(\boldsymbol{\theta}_{ir}|t, \boldsymbol{\theta}_{imm}|t, r, l_{xy}, \boldsymbol{DH}\right) \tag{1}$$

The system chain groups also the $^C\mathbf{T}_{ee}$ transformation matrix (the hand-eye transformation), and the $^T\mathbf{T}_C$ which is evaluated at each position using visual pose estimation algorithms, depending on the visual tag nature. Finally, the parameters to be estimated are the DH parameters of the robotic arm, $^C\mathbf{T}_{ee}$, $^R\mathbf{T}_M|t$, and the kinematic parameters of the mobile robot that contribute to the odometry, hence r and l_{xy}. From the system description, a kinematic-based model, which characterizes the complete state of the system transformations at each iteration, has to be devised to consequently perform a dual UKF based estimation on both the system state and on the parameter's value. At each estimation step, the complete odometry of the IMM has to be computed from its initial state, a task that raises the computational demand of the system. Furthermore, introducing probabilistic pose composition allows the uncertainty propagation in the kinematic chain, unregarding its nature, providing the UKF with a reasonable estimation of the state covariance matrix. Combining the state dynamic computation with the pose estimation from the image and the covariance computation, increases the needed computation capability required to have a prompt result, hence a cloud based solution is the optimal condition to increase the system overall performance.

3   Background

3.1   Unscented Kalman Filter

Consider a discrete time nonlinear dynamical system:

$$\zeta^{t+1} = F(\zeta^t, u^t, v^t, e) \tag{2}$$
$$y^t = G(\zeta^t, w^t, b) \tag{3}$$

where t denotes the time index, ζ the state vector, u the system input, y the system output, and e and b are generic constant parameters. The model also includes the state and measurement noises v and w, which are zero-mean white noises with a known covariance matrix. The system dynamic model F and the output function G are known and include some unknown constant parameters that must be estimated. In order to estimate the constant parameters by mean of the Kalman filtering theory, the parameters have to be given a dummy dynamic, and to be included in the state vector:

$$x^{t+1} = \begin{bmatrix} \zeta^{t+1} \\ e^{t+1} \\ b^{t+1} \end{bmatrix} = \begin{bmatrix} F(\zeta^t, u^t, v^t) \\ e^t \\ b^t \end{bmatrix} \tag{4}$$

where x is the enlarged state, and the unknown parameters e and b have a fake dynamic because their value at instant $t+1$ is the same as at instant t. The original Kalman filter theory can be adopted in linear dynamical systems to estimate the state value optimally, but, with nonlinear state or output functions, variants of the original filter exist, such as the extended Kalman filter (EKF) or the Unscented Kalman filter (UKF). Considering the strong non-linearity of the system in study, and the additional complexity brought by the hand-eye problem, a UKF is employed due to its increased reliability in nonlinear system identification [18], and robustness to parameter initial value [19]. On the one hand, the inaccuracies of the EKF, coming from the error introduced by the linearization of the dynamic model, might harm the filtering capability and stability. On the other hand, the UKF keeps the original nonlinear dynamic model, using the unscented transform algorithm [20] to propagate the state uncertainty[2].

---

[2] The unscented transformation is a method to compute the evolution of a random variable through a nonlinear map.

3.2   Probabilistic Pose Composition

Following the definitions contained in [21], we exploit the Lie Groups and Algebra to associate uncertainty with rigid transformation and propagate this uncertainty in rigid chains. The goal consist of describing a transformation $^i\mathbf{T}_j$ by a mean value, denoted by an on-top bar, and its associated sigma co-variance matrix:

$$\{^i\mathbf{T}_j, \boldsymbol{\Sigma}_{i,j}\}, \tag{5}$$

Following the operators described in [21], we define a random variable in $SE(3)$ as:

$$\mathbf{T} = exp(\boldsymbol{\xi}^\wedge)\bar{\mathbf{T}} \tag{6}$$

where $\boldsymbol{\xi} \in R^6$ is the noise perturbation, defined as a zero-mean Gaussian $p(\boldsymbol{\xi}) = \mathcal{N}(0, \boldsymbol{\Sigma})$, where $\boldsymbol{\Sigma}$ is its 6×6 co-variance matrix.

To compose random poses on SE(3), the mean value operates under the standard group multiplication operation:

$$^i\mathbf{T}_k = {}^i\mathbf{T}_j{}^j\mathbf{T}_k \tag{7}$$

$$^i\mathbf{T}_k = {}^i\mathbf{T}_j{}^j\mathbf{T}_k \tag{8}$$

while using the probabilistic description introduced the covariance results in:

$$exp(\boldsymbol{\xi}_i^\wedge){}^i\mathbf{T}_k = exp(\boldsymbol{\xi}_i^\wedge){}^i\mathbf{T}_j exp(\boldsymbol{\xi}_j^\wedge){}^j\mathbf{T}_k$$
$$= exp(\boldsymbol{\xi}_i^\wedge)exp(Ad_i{}_{\bar{\mathbf{T}}_j}(\boldsymbol{\xi}_j^\wedge)){}^i\mathbf{T}_j{}^j\mathbf{T}_k$$
$$exp(\boldsymbol{\xi}_i^\wedge) = exp(\boldsymbol{\xi}_i)exp(Ad_i{}_{\bar{\mathbf{T}}_j}(\boldsymbol{\xi}_j^\wedge)^\wedge). \tag{9}$$

Such formulation computes the covariance matrix as $E[\xi\xi^T]$, approximated to the fourth-order, using the Baker-Campbell-Hausdorff formula.

Given this probabilistic interpretation of rigid transformations, we can now associate to every link of our kinematic chain a definition as in (5), using as mean value the nominal transformation of the link, and as $\boldsymbol{\Sigma}$ a matrix that describes the uncertainty of the nominal parameter. For further details regarding composition, inversion, and join of uncertain poses, refer [21].

4   System Architecture and Model Design

4.1   System Architecture

The overall system architecture is comprised by the local system, hence the robot and is controller, and a cloud computing server, as shown in Fig. 2. Generically, modern IMMs are controlled by embedded real-time devices that are tailored on the control, navigation, and localization algorithm needed by the system, making the offloading of services a reasonable choice, in order to not aggravate the control algorithms that need real time performances. The estimation service initialization requires the local robotic system to send the initial kinematic parameters to the cloud side, in order to set the dynamic model. Then, the local system gathers the real time data during its tasks, such as the tag pictures, joints position and wheels speed, and continuously send the data to the cloud platform during the estimation phase. Concurrently, the cloud side evolves the dynamic model using the received data and generates a new parameters estimate ad every iteration, returning the values to the local system. In order to do this, the cloud side is endowed with different specific devices. Namely, a graphical processing unit based image processing module which computes the tag position from the images, the IMM dynamic system module that simulates the system evolution at every iteration, and a kinematic covariance model, which computes the state covariance from the received IMM data.

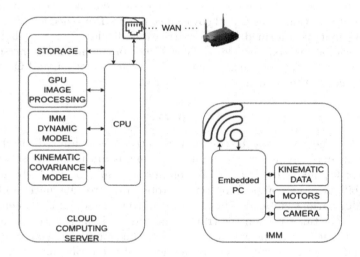

Fig. 2. Local and cloud system architecture

4.2 Model Design

In order to properly employ the method to retrieve the system parameters, a complete system model is needed, including the forward kinematic and all the elements that have to be estimated. Our discrete-time model state describes the transformation between the camera poses at successive steps, as $^{C|t}\mathbf{T}_{C|t+1}$, computed composing the kinematic transformations of the system, given the actual value of the parameters, and the system's inputs. Then, the model state is augmented to include the constant parameters that have to be estimated, such as $\boldsymbol{DH}$, r, l_{xy}, $^{R}\mathbf{T}_{M}$, and $^{C}\mathbf{T}_{ee}$, depending on the estimation aim. Hence, the state of the system is composed as follows:

$$x^{t+1} = \begin{bmatrix} ^{C|t}\mathbf{T}_{C|t+1} \\ \boldsymbol{DH}|t+1 \\ r|t+1 \\ l_{xy}|t+1 \\ ... \end{bmatrix} = \begin{bmatrix} F(...|t,...|t+1) \\ \boldsymbol{DH}|t \\ r|t \\ l_{xy}|t \\ ... \end{bmatrix} \tag{10}$$

where the value of the first element depends on the kinematic chain parameters and input at two consecutive instants $t, t+1$, while the output function, corresponds to the same $^{C|t}\mathbf{T}_{C|t+1}$ transform computed by the camera at two consecutive time instants $t, t+1$ corresponds to:

$$y^t = {}^{C|t}\mathbf{T}_{C|t+1} = {}^{C|t}\mathbf{T}_T{}^T\,\mathbf{T}_{C|t+1} \tag{11}$$

The transformations in the model are described by a 6-sized vector, using $x, y, z, \alpha, \beta, \gamma$ where $\alpha\beta\gamma$ are the Euler angles. Moreover, to finalize the system model, a proper value of the covariance matrices of the noises acting on the state $\mathbf{Q}$, on the output $\mathbf{R}$, and the initial covariance matrix $\mathbf{P}$ are needed. Specifically, the state $\mathbf{Q}$ matrix is formed by sub-matrices as displayed in 12, where $\mathbf{Q_1}$, a 6×6 dimensional matrix, provides the covariance of the minimal representation elements $(x, y, z, \alpha, \beta, \gamma)$ of the kinematic chain transformation, and $\mathbf{Q_2}$ contains the covariances of the elements to be estimated.

$$\mathbf{Q} = \begin{bmatrix} \mathbf{Q_1} & \mathbf{0} \\ \mathbf{0} & \mathbf{Q_2} \end{bmatrix} \tag{12}$$

While the measurement $\mathbf{R}$ covariance matrix has a limited effect on the identification performance when calibrated cameras are used, the state covariance matrix $\mathbf{Q_1}$ needs to be precisely computed to aid the UKF, by means of the probabilistic pose composition on the robot forward kinematic and on the rigid transformations embedded in the system. To this end, all the kinematically parameters that takes part in the transformation $^{C|t}\mathbf{T}_{C|t+1}$, need to be defined as in (5). In such way, the mean part yields the nominal initial value, while the diagonal covariance matrix yields the nominal value variance at the proper position, as highlighted in the following:

$$\left\{ \begin{bmatrix} & & & x \\ f(\alpha, \beta, \gamma) & & & y \\ & & & z \\ 0 & 0 & 0 & 1 \end{bmatrix}, \begin{bmatrix} \sigma_x^2 & & & & & \\ & \sigma_y^2 & & & & \\ & & \sigma_z^2 & & & \\ & & & \sigma_\alpha^2 & & \\ & & & & \sigma_\beta^2 & \\ & & & & & \sigma_\gamma^2 \end{bmatrix} \right\} \tag{13}$$

The complete chain covariance can be computed at every iteration time, as $\mathbf{Q_1}|t$, using (9).

4.3   Methodology

The overall method consists of a data acquisition phase on the local machine and an asynchronous concurrent data processing on the cloud side. To locally acquire the needed data, the IMMs is moved acting on all its inputs, in order to extensively cover the working space of the system. The data logged are the joint positions of the robotic arm, the wheels' speed, and the camera images, which are sent to the cloud side after every iteration. During the data acquisition, on the cloud side, the $\mathbf{Q_1}$ matrix is computed propagating the covariance matrix relative to all the links of the kinematic chain, using (9), where every link of the robot is according (6), with a diagonal Σ covariance matrix associated. Specifically, the diagonal values have been assigned a value equivalent to 1% of the related quantities in $\bar{\mathbf{T}}$. Other relevant values for the UKF covariance matrices have been set after an extensive design of the experimental phase, in which we have tried multiple values and compared the results. Their values are the following:

$$
\mathbf{Q_2} = \begin{bmatrix} 1e^{-5} & & \\ & \ddots & \\ & & 1e^{-5} \end{bmatrix} \quad \mathbf{R} = \begin{bmatrix} 5e^{-4} & & \\ & \ddots & \\ & & 5e^{-4} \end{bmatrix} \quad \mathbf{P} = \begin{bmatrix} 1e^{-3} & & \\ & \ddots & \\ & & 1e^{-3} \end{bmatrix} \tag{14}
$$

where $\mathbf{R}$ is a 6×6 matrix, and both $\mathbf{P}$ and $\mathbf{Q_2}$ dimension is system dependent.

In order to devise an improvement criterion, given the set of all the $^T\mathbf{T}_W$ transformations acquired, and using i as the iteration index, as their minimal representation version $[x\ y\ z\ \alpha\ \beta\ \gamma]$, we compute the iteration standard deviation SD_i of all the same components for all the data in the set.

Finally, at every cloud side estimation iteration, we compare the standard deviations for each element of the 6-dimension vector from $^T\mathbf{T}_W$, with the assumption that a lower SD_i for a given element results in a better system precision.

5   Experiment

In the following experiments, we used the ROS framework [22] for the robot control and communication, OpenCV libraries [23] for the visual tag position identification and filterpy for the UKF [24]. The UKF parameters are tuned according to [25]. The initial value for $^C\mathbf{T}_{ee}$ is computed according to [26]. As a cloud side, a computer using 12 core i7-8700 CPU and an Nvidia Quadro P2000 is employed. The cloud side - client connection has a round-trip time of 27 ms.

5.1   Mobile Manipulator Experiment

The setup consists of an UR10e robot fixed on an omnidirectional platform, using a DALSA Nano XL-M5100 25 MP camera fixed in proximity to the $\{ee\}$ to acquire the images. Every data package that is sent to the cloud side, at the end of every step, has a dimension of 27 MB, primarily due to the size of the camera image, where a higher resolution lead to a better tag pose estimation, and as a consequence a better parameter estimation too. The local system takes an average time of 2.9 s to transfer the data to the cloud side, where the actual bottleneck lies on the on-board WiFi board. During the experimental phase,

20 random configurations have been acquired and sent to the cloud side, repeating the experiments 10 times for statistical relevance. At every repetition, the initial values of the estimation parameters have been disturbed by a $U(-0.005, 0.005)$ uniformly distributed noise. The aim of the experiment is the estimation of r and l_{xy}, the DH parameters, and the fixed transformations between the mobile robot and the robotic arm base and the hand-eye matrix, respectively. The processing time on the cloud side relative to every iteration, which consists of retrieving the tag position from the image (510 ms), and evolving the dynamic system on step (120 ms), takes an average of 630 ms. In Fig. 3 is shown the trend of the SD_i for every element of the $^T\mathbf{T}_W$ transformation, evaluated on the complete data set. It is clearly noticeable the precision improvement for every element of the transformation, a the general consensus reached at the end of the estimation, even with different initial values.

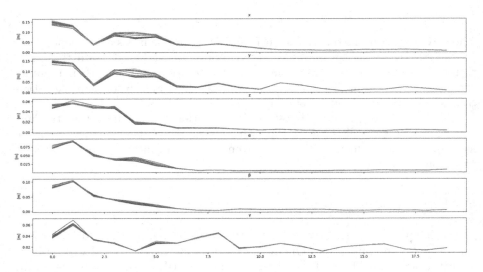

Fig. 3. Trend of the SD_i for every element of the $^T\mathbf{T}_W$, valued with the estimation data returned at every step. Relative improvements values are [x:13%, y:12%, z:5.3%, α:4.6%, β:6.5%, γ:2.1%]

6   Conclusion and Future Works

This paper has proposed a cloud based architecture for the kinematic parameter estimation of an IMM, using an UKF on the system model. The architecture exploits the computing power on the cloud side in order to provide the local system with a prompt estimation of the kinematic parameters. The choice of outsourcing the computing showed promising results and appears to be a valid alternative for systems with a limited computing power, as normally occurs for IMMs. Future works might investigate the automatic configuration generation for the IMM, in order to generate a better data rate to feed the cloud side and information richer data. As well as further investigating image compression techniques and package sending criteria with the aim of reducing the network-transferred packed size, while preserving the embedded information used by the estimation algorithm (e.g. SVD or deep autoencoders based image compression).

References

1. Wang, R., Wu, A., Chen, X., Wang, J.: A point and distance constraint based 6r robot calibration method through machine vision. Robot. Comput. Integr. Manuf. **65**, 101959 (2020)
2. Özgüner, O., et al.: Camera-robot calibration for the Da Vinci robotic surgery system. IEEE Trans. Autom. Sci. Eng. **17**(4), 2154–2161 (2020)
3. Shah, M., Bostelman, R., Legowik, S., Hong, T.: Calibration of mobile manipulators using 2D positional features. Measurement **124**, 322–328 (2018)
4. Zhou, Z., Li, L., Wang, R., Zhang, X.: Experimental eye-in-hand calibration for industrial mobile manipulators. In: 2020 IEEE International Conference on Mechatronics and Automation (ICMA), pp. 582–587. IEEE (2020)
5. Xuan, J.-Q., Xu, S.-H., et al.: Review on kinematics calibration technology of serial robots. Int. J. Precis. Eng. Manuf. **15**(8), 1759–1774 (2014)
6. Bostelman, R., Hong, T., Marvel, J.: Survey of research for performance measurement of mobile manipulators. J. Res. Nat. Inst. Stand. Technol. **121**, 342 (2016)
7. Yang, M., Yang, E., Zante, R.C., Post, M., Liu, X.: Collaborative mobile industrial manipulator: a review of system architecture and applications. In: 2019 25th International Conference on Automation and Computing (ICAC), pp. 1–6. IEEE (2019)
8. Huang, Z., Wang, Q.: Industrial robot control system optimized by wireless resources and cloud resources based on cloud edge multi-cluster containers. Int. J. Syst. Assur. Eng. Manage. 1–10 (2021). https://doi.org/10.1007/s13198-021-01254-0
9. Vick, A., Vonásek, V., Pěnička, R., Krüger, J.: Robot control as a service—towards cloud-based motion planning and control for industrial robots. In: 2015 10th International Workshop on Robot Motion and Control (RoMoCo), pp. 33–39. IEEE (2015)
10. Dey, S., Mukherjee, A.: Robotic SLAM: a review from fog computing and mobile edge computing perspective. In: Adjunct Proceedings of the 13th International Conference on Mobile and Ubiquitous Systems: Computing Networking and Services, pp. 153–158 (2016)
11. Tzafestas, S.G.: Mobile robot control and navigation: a global overview. J. Intell. Robot. Syst. **91**(1), 35–58 (2018). https://doi.org/10.1007/s10846-018-0805-9
12. Dyumin, A., Puzikov, L., Rovnyagin, M., Urvanov, G., Chugunkov, I.: Cloud computing architectures for mobile robotics. In: 2015 IEEE NW Russia Young Researchers in Electrical and Electronic Engineering Conference (EIConRusNW), pp. 65–70. IEEE (2015)
13. Saha, O., Dasgupta, P.: A comprehensive survey of recent trends in cloud robotics architectures and applications. Robotics **7**(3), 47 (2018)
14. Li, S., Zheng, Z., Chen, W., Zheng, Z., Wang, J.: Latency-aware task assignment and scheduling in collaborative cloud robotic systems. In: 2018 IEEE 11th International Conference on Cloud Computing (CLOUD), pp. 65–72. IEEE (2018)

15. Shukla, S., Hassan, M.F., Tran, D.C., Akbar, R., Paputungan, I.V., Khan, M.K.: Improving latency in Internet-of-Things and cloud computing for real-time data transmission: a systematic literature review (SLR). Clust. Comput. 1–24 (2021). https://doi.org/10.1007/s10586-021-03279-3

16. Cesen, F.E.R., Csikor, L., Recalde, C., Rothenberg, C.E., Pongrácz, G.: Towards low latency industrial robot control in programmable data planes. In: 2020 6th IEEE Conference on Network Softwarization (NetSoft), pp. 165–169. IEEE (2020)

17. Mutti, S., Pedrocchi, N.: Improved tracking and docking of industrial mobile robots through UKF vision-based kinematics calibration. IEEE Access 9, 127664–127671 (2021)

18. Wan, E.A., Van Der Merwe, R.: The unscented Kalman filter for nonlinear estimation. In: Proceedings of the IEEE 2000 Adaptive Systems for Signal Processing, Communications, and Control Symposium (Cat. No. 00EX373), pp. 153–158. IEEE (2000)

19. Fiorenzani, T., Manes, C., Oriolo, G., Peliti, P.: Comparative study of unscented Kalman filter and extended kalman filter for position/attitude estimation in unmanned aerial vehicles. In: Institute for Systems Analysis and Computer Science (IASI-CNR), Rome, Italy, Report, p. 08 (2008). http://www.iasi.cnr.it/new/publications.php/id_p/2/anno/0/id_autore/0/id_tipologia/6/rep/3459. http://www.iasi.cnr.it/ResearchReports/R08008

20. Julier, S., Uhlmann, J., Durrant-Whyte, H.F.: A new method for the nonlinear transformation of means and covariances in filters and estimators. IEEE Tranans. Autom. control 45(3), 477–482 (2000)

21. Barfoot, T.D., Furgale, P.T.: Associating uncertainty with three-dimensional poses for use in estimation problems. IEEE Trans. Robot. 30(3), 679–693 (2014)

22. Stanford Artificial Intelligence Laboratory et al.: Robotic operating system. www.ros.org

23. Bradski, G.: The OpenCV library. Dr. Dobb's J. Softw. Tools 25, 120–123 (2000)

24. Labbe, R.: filterpy. https://github.com/rlabbe/filterpy

25. Van Der Merwe, R.: Sigma-Point Kalman Filters for Probabilistic Inference in Dynamic State-Space Models. Oregon Health and Science University (2004)

26. Park, F.C., Martin, B.J.: Robot sensor calibration: solving AX = XB on the Euclidean group. IEEE Tranans. Robot. Autom. 10(5), 717–721 (1994)

Deep Learning Approaches for Image-Based Detection and Classification of Structural Defects in Bridges

Angelo Cardellicchio[1]([⊠])[iD], Sergio Ruggieri[2][iD], Andrea Nettis[2][iD],
Cosimo Patruno[1][iD], Giuseppina Uva[2][iD], and Vito Renò[1][iD]

[1] Institute of Intelligent Industrial Technologies and Systems for Advanced
Manufacturing (STIIMA) National Research Council of Italy, Bari, Italy
{angelo.cardellicchio,cosimo.patruno,vito.reno}@stiima.cnr.it
[2] Dipartimento di Ingegneria Civile, Ambientale, del Territorio, Edile e di Chimica
(DICATECH), Politecnico di Bari, Bari, Italy
{sergio.ruggieri,andrea.nettis,giuseppina.uva}@poliba.it

Abstract. The paper presents a study about the defect detection on structural elements of existing reinforced concrete bridges through a machine-learning approach. In detail, the proposed methodology aims to explore the possibility of automatically recognising deficiencies on bridges' elements, e.g., cracks, humidity, by employing a training of existing convolutional neural networks on a set of photos. The initial database, characterized by 2.436 images, has been firstly selected and after has been classified by domain experts according to the requirements of the new Italian guidelines on structural safety of existing bridges. The results show a good effectiveness and accuracy of the proposed methodology, opening new scenarios for the automatic defect detection on bridges, mainly aimed to support management companies surveyors in the phase of in-situ structural inspection.

Keywords: Damage detection · Bridge inspection · Machine learning

1 Introduction

Over the last years, the dramatic collapse of several existing Italian bridges, such as the Polcevera viaduct or the Massa Carrara and Torino - Savoia bridges, has led to public concerns from Italian institutions, and a deep focus by the scientific community on the monitoring and maintenance of such structures. As a response to this unfortunate series of events, the Italian government released new guidelines on structural safety of existing bridges [1] to perform an accurate risk evaluation and health assessment of these structures.

© The Author(s), under exclusive license to Springer Nature Switzerland AG 2022
P. L. Mazzeo et al. (Eds.): ICIAP 2022 Workshops, LNCS 13373, pp. 269–279, 2022.
https://doi.org/10.1007/978-3-031-13321-3_24

However, defining the risk class of an existing bridge is strongly dependent from the results of in-situ inspections, in which domain experts must accurately survey the bridge *element-by-element*. Hence, especially for complex structures, performing an accurate inspection of structural elements requires high effort. Specifically, a careful surveyor may employ one working day to assess structural elements belonging to about four to five bridge bays. Furthermore, even the most careful expert may be subject to drops in attention, which may mislead and undermine the results of the whole inspection. This implies that there is an urgent necessity to support surveyors performing in-situ inspection of existing bridges, to both optimise costs and avoid risks related to misjudgements due to the human factor.

To respond to these need, we propose a representation learning technique to train a reliable and automatic tool for detecting defects in existing bridges. Specifically, starting from a dataset previously labelled by domain experts, a series of convolutional neural networks (*CNNs*) have been trained and tested, with the aim to identify some specific defects and support the surveyors' work. Preliminary results show good potentials, and the tool has been designed to be scalable enough to be embedded in mobile devices, such as smartphones and tables, which may be carried along the surveyor during the inspection.

The paper is organised as follows. In Sect. 2, an overview of similar approaches already in literature is provided. In Sect. 3, an overview of the methodology is provided, along with the results achieved by this first round of experiments. Finally, in Sect. 4, a perspective of future works to enhance and expand the methodology is provided.

2 Related Works

Machine learning has found several applications in various fields of civil and structural engineering, such as earthquake engineering, structural properties identification and structural health monitoring [2,3]. As for deep learning, its application to image understanding has proven to be one of the most promising approach in structural health monitoring, and has been used to create tools and datasets to define simplified (yet effective) vulnerability index of existing buildings [4,5].

As for bridge damage detection, CNNs have been used to automatically detect damages performing pixel-based analysis to identify cracks and damages [9–11,13]. Another approach is the one proposed in [14], where authors describe a tool for defect detection and localization via neural networks named *DDLNet*, achieving detection and localization accuracy of 80.7% and 86% on a test dataset of 823 images, respectively. Furthermore, in [8] authors leveraged transfer learning to improve results achieved in terms of accuracy on small datasets.

Object detection techniques have also been used to automatically highlight defects and damages. As an example, in [6] a sliding window to perform damage detection on several regions of the original image has been employed. However, as this approach has proven itself to be relatively slow, more recent works have been focused on using either two-stage detectors, such as Faster R-CNN [12], or one-stage detectors, such as YOLO [16] and SSD [15].

Specifically, in [7] authors used Faster R-CNN to identify five types of damages, such as concrete cracks, steel and bolt corrosion, and delamination, showing a mean average precision of 87.8%. Another example is the work proposed by [17], where several base networks are tested in a SSD-based approach on a dataset consisting of 9.053 images and 15.435 instances of road damages and defects. Furthermore [17] focuses on the portability of this approach, developing a smartphone application which can be used to demonstrate achieved results.

3 Methodology

3.1 Building the Dataset

As for the reference dataset for bridge defects, it has been created using a two-steps procedure with data selection and enrichment. The first step, specifically data selection and labelling, began by collecting 2.685 images from real surveys on existing bridges in Southern Italy. These surveys have been performed by domain experts with a specific focus on structural elements of bridges, such as girders, deck, piles and pile caps, each one presenting different kinds of damages or defects. Afterwards, a labelling procedure has been performed on each image, identifying observed defects in accordance to [1].

Considering the extremely fine granularity on defect classes defined by [1], the first response to the initial labelling was the awareness of having an inadequate amount of data to perform multi-class classification on more than 50 classes that may show very slight differences when visually compared.

272   A. Cardellicchio et al.

(a) Crack.

(b) Corroded steel reinforcement.

(c) Deteriorated concrete.

(d) Honeycombs.

(e) Moisture spots.

(f) Pavement degradation.

Fig. 1. A series of sample frames from the dataset used for network training.

As a consequence, several defect typologies have been logically grouped under higher-level categories; as an example, the existing differentiation in cracks (i.e., vertical, horizontal and diagonal) has not been considered, and all cracks have been grouped into a single class. In this way the deep learning model can be trained focusing on macro categories, thus capturing the main differences in patterns among the different classes. Therefore, seven classes of defects have been defining after the first phase: (1) *corroded/oxidized steel reinforcement*, (2) *cracks*, (3) *deteriorated concrete*, (4) *honeycombs*, (5) *moisture spots*, (6) *pavement degradation* and (7) *shrinkage cracks*.

To improve the quantity of data used for processing, a data enrichment and augmentation procedure has been performed as the second step. To this end, we used the Get-VULMA tool, developed within the framework of the VULMA project [4], to gather several images belonging to each one of the aforementioned classes.

Thanks to the images gathered in the second step, we were also able to remove poor quality images from the overall dataset, leaving only high resolution and clearly focused patches for learning. However, we explicitly selected to not remove images that presented occlusions, as they may be representative of real-case scenarios, and can be used to improve machine learning performance.

The results of this two-steps procedure has led to the definition of the dataset used in the present work, made of 2.436 high quality images and organized as shown in Table 1. Samples of images belonging to the dataset are shown in Fig. 1.

Table 1. Number of images per each class in the reference dataset.

Class	# of images
Corroded steel reinforcements	404
Cracks	603
Deteriorated concrete	227
Honeycombs	252
Moisture spots	670
Pavement degradation	185
Shrinkage cracks	96

3.2 Damage Classification

Framing the Problem. Despite the two-steps procedure, we note that the dataset is somehow unbalanced, especially for pavement degradation and shrinkage. Furthermore, the number of images and defect instances is currently not adequate to train complex object detection model, such as YOLO in its latest revisions, which require more than 1500 images per class to be trained properly with transfer learning [18]. As a consequence, we decided to frame our problem as a *damage classification* task, where frames containing pre-selected defects are provided to neural network architectures and classified accordingly.

Furthermore, let us note that several of the classes may present high visual correlation, such as corroded steel reinforcements and deteriorated concrete; hence, we decided to frame the classification task as a *one-vs-all* problem, where the neural network is trained to determine whether a frame represents a single damage or not. To this end, the multi-class problem is effectively re-framed as a series of binary problems, where a cascade of parallel neural network can effectively determine the nature of the defect by adopting a hard consensus at decision level.

As a consequence, the analysis has been carried on the binary tasks enlisted in Table 2.

Table 2. Binary tasks defined for the one-vs-all problem.

Task name	Identifier	Description
CR	All types of cracks	States whether the damage is related to cracks
CO-SR	Corroded and oxidized steel reinforcement	States whether the damage is related to corroded steel reinforcement
DC	Deteriorated concrete	States whether the damage is related to deteriorated concrete
HC	Honeycombs	States whether the damage is related to honeycombs
MS	Moisture spots	States whether the damage is related to moisture
PD	Pavement degradation	States whether the damage is related to pavement degradation or none
S-CR	Shrinkage cracks	States whether the damage is related to shrinkage

Network Training. Several base CNNs architectures have been proposed in recent years, some of which are specifically intended to be extremely lightweight and, therefore, perfectly deployable on mobile devices. Hence, the selection of the architectures to use to evaluate the performance on the aforementioned binary problems has been driven by two factors.

1. The need to define a baseline for the problem starting from a series of well-assessed classic models.
2. The need to compare the baseline achieved by classic models with lightweight models, that is, model which can be easily deployed on constrained (and even low-power) devices, such as tables and smartphones.

As a consequence, we selected five different base network architectures, specifically InceptionV3 and ResNet50V2 as classic models, and DenseNet121, MobileNetV3 and NASNetMobile for lightweight models.

Due to the limited quantity of available data, the training has been performed for each model using both transfer learning and fine tuning on a workstation equipped with NVIDIA GeForce RTX 3070 GPU with 8 GBs of RAM. Each dataset has been split according to a classic 70/30% in training and validation samples. Furthermore, random data augmentation in form of horizontal and vertical flipping has been applied. Each image has first been scaled down to 224×224 pixels, and the preprocessing procedure shown in Table 3 has been performed.

Table 3. Preprocessing steps taken for each architecture.

Network architecture	Preprocessing steps
InceptionV3	Input RGB values scaled in the range $[-1, 1]$
ResNet50V2	Input RGB values scaled in the range $[-1, 1]$
NASNetMobile	Input RGB values scaled in the range $[-1, 1]$
DenseNet121	Input RGB values scaled in the range $[0, 1]$
MobileNetV3	Input RGB values scaled in the range $[-1, 1]$

Results in terms of accuracy after twenty epochs of transfer learning are shown in Table 4, while results in terms of accuracy after ten epochs of fine tuning are shown in Table 5.

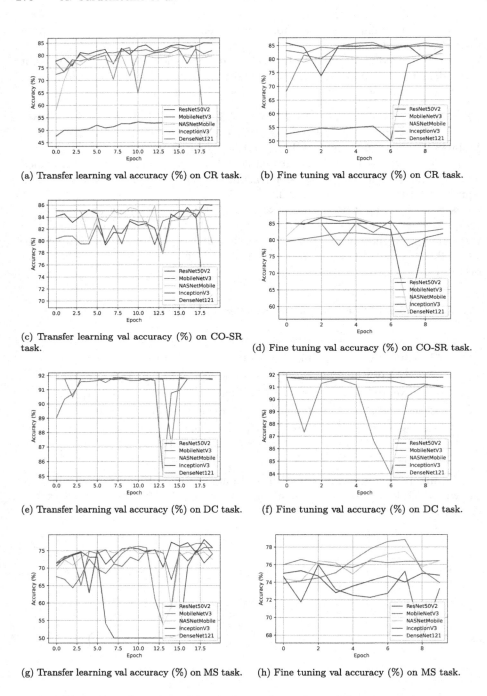

(a) Transfer learning val accuracy (%) on CR task.

(b) Fine tuning val accuracy (%) on CR task.

(c) Transfer learning val accuracy (%) on CO-SR task.

(d) Fine tuning val accuracy (%) on CO-SR task.

(e) Transfer learning val accuracy (%) on DC task.

(f) Fine tuning val accuracy (%) on DC task.

(g) Transfer learning val accuracy (%) on MS task.

(h) Fine tuning val accuracy (%) on MS task.

Fig. 2. Results achieved by the networks on four of the seven tasks.

Table 4. Transfer learning accuracy (in %) comparison for the *one-vs-all* problem formulation with the selected five neural network architectures.

Task	DenseNet121	InceptionV3	ResNet50V2	MobileNetV3	NASNetMobile
CR	53.33	50.89	**84.89**	81.78	79.63
CO-SR	85.03	85.04	**85.92**	70.96	79.63
DC	90.78	90.82	**91.78**	91.71	91.70
HC	90.37	**90.40**	89.03	90.14	90.30
MS	74.09	74.01	**75.90**	75.83	72.08
PD	**92.81**	89.89	89.88	92.41	90.01
S-CR	96.05	96.04	**96.47**	95.91	96.01

Table 5. Fine learning accuracy (in %) comparison for the *one-vs-all* problem formulation with the selected five neural network architectures.

Task	DenseNet121	InceptionV3	ResNet50V2	MobileNetV3	NASNetMobile
CR	**85.19**	79.70	83.33	84.30	81.93
CO-SR	81.92	85.03	81.85	83.26	**85.40**
DC	91.10	**91.78**	**91.78**	90.96	**91.78**
HC	90.37	90.37	**90.96**	89.56	90.44
MS	73.94	73.26	74.77	**76.43**	**76.43**
PD	89.89	**93.44**	89.88	92.25	89.88
S-CR	96.05	96.04	96.12	**96.13**	96.05

In Fig. 2 results in terms of validation accuracy over all the epochs of transfer learning and fine tuning are provided for four of the seven tasks, specifically CR, CO-SR, DC and MS. The rationale behind this choice will be further clarified in Sect. 3.3.

3.3   Discussion

With reference to Tables 4 and 5, it is immediate to notice that there are some differences looking at the percentages achieved before and after the fine tuning step (the best score is highlighted in bold for each task). In fact, before the fine tuning, ResNet50V2 architecture performs the best for identifying all the defects except HC and PD, whilst after the fine tuning step the results become generally higher as expected, but the best performing network is different for each considered task. For example, for CR detection, the fine tuning step suggests to employ DenseNet121 (32% accuracy gain w.r.t. the pure transfer learning approach) instead of ResNet50V2. Similar considerations can be made for the other tasks. This suggests to use an ensemble strategy to assign a label if the classification problem is solved with many binary classifiers as proposed in this work. To summarize, we highlight the following three main aspects:

1. Networks generally achieve a reasonably high level of accuracy, even before the fine tuning, with the exception of DenseNet121 on cracks and all the networks on moisture, which is the most challenging task currently in the dataset. This is mainly related to both the visual appearance of cracks and moisture spots, which appear sometimes extremely similar, and the co-existence of both corroded/oxidized steel reinforcement and deteriorated concrete within the same frame. However, it should be noted that DenseNet121 gains its accuracy after the fine tuning.
2. Accuracy tends to be extremely similar and almost saturated for different network on the same task, thus suggesting that for the higher-level classification presented in this work, maybe some specific custom models or architecture can be investigated too.
3. In some cases, results decrease after fine tuning. In the worst case, this may be due to overfitting and/or saturation effects. For this reason, in the future, we will increase the dataset examples to overcome these kind of issues that may arise with the current problem formulation on our dataset.

4   Conclusions and Future Works

In this paper, we presented the initial assessment for a methodology to identify structural damages in existing bridges by using transfer learning and fine tuning, along with a dataset composed by a mixture of images acquired both from real surveys and online web services.

Despite the fact that the dataset appears to be extremely challenging, some improvements can be made to the method itself. Specifically, future works will focus on the following aspects.

1. *Improving the quality of the dataset*, by achieving a proper number of images for each defect class, under varying conditions.
2. *Extensive use of data balancing techniques.*
3. *Use of improved architectures and techniques*, such as hyperparameters optimization, to improve accuracy results.
4. *Address of the multi-class problem*, fusing the cascade of single binary tasks.
5. *Address the problem of damage localisation*, exploiting architectures oriented to object detection such as YOLO and SSD.

References

1. Ministero delle Infrastrutture e dei Trasporti. Linee Guida per la Classificazione e Gestione del Rischio, la Valutazione della Sicurezza ed il Monitoraggio dei Ponti Esistenti (2020). (in Italian)
2. Xie, Y., Ebad Sichani, M., Padgett, J.E., DesRoches, R.: The promise of implementing machine learning in earthquake engineering: a state-of-the-art review. Earthq. Spectra **36**(4), 1769–1801 (2020). https://doi.org/10.1177/8755293020919419

3. Sun, H., Burton, H.V., Huang, H.: Machine learning applications for building structural design and performance assessment: state-of-the-art review. J. Build. Eng. **33**, 101816 (2020). https://doi.org/10.1016/j.jobe.2020.101816

4. Ruggieri, S., Cardellicchio, A., Leggieri, V., Uva, G.: Machine-learning based vulnerability analysis of existing buildings. Autom. Constr. **132**, 103936 (2021). https://doi.org/10.1016/j.autcon.2021.103936

5. Cardellicchio, A., Ruggieri, S., Leggieri, V., Uva, G.: View VULMA: data set for training a machine-learning tool for a fast vulnerability analysis of existing buildings. Data. **7**(1), 4 (2022). https://doi.org/10.3390/data7010004

6. Cha, Y.J., Choi, W., Büyüköztürk, O.: Deep learning-based crack damage detection using convolutional neural networks. Comput. Civ. Infrastruct. Eng. **32**, 361–378 (2017). https://doi.org/10.1111/mice.12263

7. Cha, Y.J., Choi, W., Suh, G., Mahmoudkhani, S., Büyüköztürk, O.: Autonomous structural visual inspection using region-based deep learning for detecting multiple damage types. Comput. Civ. Infrastruct. Eng. **33**, 731–47 (2018). https://doi.org/10.1111/mice.12334

8. Zhu, J., Zhang, C., Qi, H., Lu, Z.: Vision-based defects detection for bridges using transfer learning and convolutional neural networks. Struct. Infrastruct. Eng. **16**(7), 1037–1049 (2020). https://doi.org/10.1080/15732479.2019.1680709

9. Zhang, A., et al.: Automated pixel-level pavement crack detection on 3D asphalt surfaces using a deep-learning network. Comput. Aided Civ. Infrastruct. Eng. **32**(10), 805–819 (2017). https://doi.org/10.1111/mice.12297

10. Yang, X., Li, H., Yu, Y., Luo, X., Huang, T., Yang, X.: Automatic pixel-level crack detection and measurement using fully convolutional network. Comput. Aided Civ. Infrastruct. Eng. **33**(12), 1090–1109 (2018). https://doi.org/10.1111/mice.12412

11. Yang, L., Li, B., Li, W., Liu, Z., Yang, G., Xiao, J.: Deep concrete inspection using unmanned aerial vehicle towards CSSC database. In: Proceedings of the IEEE/RSJ International Conference on Intelligent Robots and Systems (pp. 24–28, September 2017

12. Ren, S., He, K., Girshick, R., Sun, J.: Faster R-CNN: towards real-time object detection with region proposal networks. Adv. Neural Inf. Process. Syst. **28**, 91–99 (2015)

13. Kim, I., Jeon, H., Baek, S., Hong, W., Jung, H.: Application of crack identification techniques for an aging concrete bridge inspection using an unmanned aerial vehicle. Sensors **18**(6), 1881 (2018). https://doi.org/10.3390/s18061881

14. Li, R., Yuan, Y., Zhang, W., Yuan, Y.: Unified vision-based methodology for simultaneous concrete defect detection and geolocalization. Comput. Aided Civ. Infrastruct. Eng. **33**(7), 527–544 (2018). https://doi.org/10.1111/mice.12351

15. Liu, W., et al.: SSD: single shot MultiBox detector. In: Leibe, B., Matas, J., Sebe, N., Welling, M. (eds.) ECCV 2016, Part I. LNCS, vol. 9905, pp. 21–37. Springer, Cham (2016). https://doi.org/10.1007/978-3-319-46448-0_2

16. Redmon, J., Divvala, S., Girshick, R., Farhadi, A.: You only look once: unified, real-time object detection. In: Proceedings of the IEEE Conference on Computer Vision and Pattern Recognition, pp. 779–788 (2016). https://doi.org/10.1109/CVPR.2016.91

17. Maeda, H., Sekimoto, Y., Seto, T., Kashiyama, T., Omata, H.: Road damage detection and classification using deep neural networks with smartphone images. Comput. Aided Civ. Infrastruct. Eng. **33**(12), 1127–1141 (2018). https://doi.org/10.1111/mice.12387

18. https://github.com/ultralytics/yolov5. Accessed 23 Mar 2022

MONstEr: A Deep Learning-Based System for the Automatic Generation of Gaming Assets

Michele Brocchini[1], Marco Mameli[1(✉)], Emanuele Balloni[1,2],
Laura Della Sciucca[1,3], Luca Rossi[1], Marina Paolanti[1,2], Emanuele Frontoni[1,2],
and Primo Zingaretti[1]

[1] VRAI Vision Robotics and Artificial Intelligence Lab, Dipartimento di Ingegneria
dell'Informazione (DII), Università Politecnica delle Marche, Via Brecce Bianche 12,
60131 Ancona, Italy
S1077335@studenti.univpm.it, {m.mameli,l.rossi}@pm.univpm.it,
p.zingaretti@univpm.it
[2] Department of Political Sciences, Communication and International Relations,
University of Macerata, 62100 Macerata, Italy
{emanuele.balloni,marina.paolanti,emanuele.frontoni}@unimc.it
[3] Department of Humanities, University of Macerata, 62100 Macerata, Italy
laura.dellasciucca@unimc.it

Abstract. In recent years, we have witnessed the spread of computer graphics techniques, used as a background map for movies and video games. Nevertheless, when creating 3D models with conventional computer graphics software, it is necessary for the user to manually change the placement and size. This requires expertise of computer graphics architecture and operations, which is time demanding. Applying Artificial Intelligence (AI) to games is currently an established research field. Starting from such premises, in this paper MONstEr (dEEp lEArNiNG GENErAtiON AssEt) a system for the automatic generation of virtual asset for videogames is presented. MONstEr exploits the principle of Deep Learning (DL) and in particular Generative models to automatically design new assets for videogames. The DL pipeline is the core of this system and it is based on a Deep Convolutional Generative Adversarial Network followed by Pixel2Mesh architecture for the 3D models generation. The approach was applied and tested on a newly collected dataset of images, "GameAssetDataset" which comprises characters representation extracted thanks a web crawler algorithm specifically developed for its acquisition. MONstEr expedites the implementation of solutions for new gamining environments, requiring only a small intervention in the 3D construction to insert the object in the game scene.

1 Introduction

A highly developed sector in the entertainment industry concerns games, especially those in digital form, used for recreational purposes but also for educational or rehabilitative purposes. The videogames industry has grown considerably in recent years and the gaming business occupies much of the leisure time of people. However, there are a number of elements, including the standardization of rules, the high cost of production and the economic crisis that many companies are still facing, which has led the gaming industry to no longer produce innovative elements, except in the graphic department. Mainly in the last years, there is a greater interest by this sector in research in the field of Artificial Intelligence (AI) on the different production mechanisms of videogames. The development process of a game in general can be revolutionized with the introduction of automatic systems that replace the manual method for the creation of any content that forms the game itself. The application of the algorithms, generally search-based or falling into the category of evolutionary computation, allows to create through a Procedural Content Generation (PCG) [1], any element of a game. The keystone of this methodology is the concept of randomness: through the use of a few parameters, the application of the PCG method should ensure a creation of a large number of possible contents of a game, all different from each other. In this way, more immersive games can be automatically create, which customize and modify the content according to the characteristics of each individual player, with costs less than the manual development process. According to [5,17], there are several motivations of using PCG method in videogames. Among these we mention: the reduction of costs and time promoting the artistic and technological progress of games of any platform, a reduction in the use of mass memory, the automatic creation of new rules, levels, stories and characters. For this purpose, given the increasing interest that AI approaches have had in recent times, the idea was to apply new methodologies to the problem of content generation. In this respect, a new methodology has been introduced called PCGML (Procedural Content Generation via Machine Learning) [16] which is the generation of game content from machine learning models trained on existing content. This approach is different from the traditional PCG since it does not imply a research in the content space, but the model directly creates the content. An interesting application of deep learning (DL) is the use of neural networks as generative models (Generative Adversarial Network, GAN) [4]: algorithms capable of replicating the distribution of input data in order to be able to then generate new values from that distribution. This model is able to learn the data distribution of a dataset and create synthetic data that have similar features to the real data and they have been applied in many application that concern image processing [10,14], dataset collection [23] and other related application [11,22].

In this context, our work aim to propose a system named MONstEr (dEEp lEArNiNG GENErAtiON AssEt) that automatically generates virtual assets for videogames. First of all, we have collected a novel available dataset of images of different representations of characters from different videogames using the web crawling algorithm [13]. Then the dataset has been used to implement a Deep Convolutional Generative Adversarial Network (DCGAN) [14], to generate novel graphical asset for videogames. Finally, a Pixel2Mesh [19] architecture is added in cascade to DCGAN with the aim to automatically generate without texture the three-dimensional character from the bi-dimensional image. To the best of our knowledge, this is the first work that propose a completely automated approach to realize 3D objects in a short time and without human intervention. MONstEr has the task to produce starting bases of 2D and 3D models for gaming assets.

The main contributions of our work can be summarized as follows:

- The collection of a novel available dataset that overcome the limit for which there are not pre-existing and accessible datasets, suitable for our aim, containing a large number of characters images;
- the creation of an architecture that implement a GAN based algorithm in combination with a Pixel2Mesh system by automatically generating novel 2D assets and from these 3D characters.

The remainder of the paper is organised as follows: Section 2 presents some interesting works of the literature that use GAN to generate objects in different sector. Section 3 presents how the dataset was collected, and what is the architecture of the neural network presented. Section 4 describes the results obtained and related comments are reported and in Sect. 5 we summarise the conclusions and identify possible the future developments aimed at improving the achieved results.

2   Related Works

This section aims at reviewing some interesting works that adopt GANs [4] to generate objects in different fields of applications, not only for game.

In fact GANs have been used for generating 3D objects also in other application domains. In [20], the authors propose an architecture named 3D Generative Adversarial Network (3D-GAN), that generates 3D objects by combining volumetric convolutional networks [12,21] and GAN. The authors highlight that the generative representation is useful for synthesizing high-quality realistic objects and discriminative representation is useful for recognizing 3D objects. In addition, both provide rich semantic information about 3D objects, and allow for similar performance to recent supervised methods and enhance other unsupervised methods. They also demonstrate that the network combined with a variational autoencoder (VAE) [8] makes it possible to directly reconstruct a 3D object from a 2D input image, solving a challenging problem for computer vision.

In order to solve this last mentioned problem, the work presented by [2] uses a GAN architecture to create three-dimensional objects departing from their bidimensional projection from different unknown views. They implement a novel GAN (PrGAN) that has in input binary images of the same 2D object and in output its 3D rendering. To demonstrate the efficiency of the approaches they make a comparison with traditional GAN trained on 3D objects, obtaining comparable results for several objects and in a totally unsupervised manner.

Considering the gaming sector, the work of [15] proposes architecture consisted of a GAN model based on a U-Net generator. The aim is to propose a solution for gaming teams of character designers and animators to reduce the cost of the resource creation pipeline. In particular, we intend to reduce time necessary to create a new character, starting from the rough sketch up to the final sprites, that are similar to those created by the artist team. To obtain a feedback about the results, the design team have evaluated 207 sprites generated.

Also for the gaming sector, the paper of [18] proposes a novel GAN architecture (Conditional Embedding Self-Attention Generative Adversarial Network, CESAGAN) and a new bootstrapping training procedure. The architecture proposed generates a large number of levels and diversified from each other. Levels are generated by sampling the generator network and all levels generated are tested for playability. The playable levels that are different from the levels used for the training set are added to the training set to train continuously the GAN.

Gonzalez et al. [3] present an approach that uses a Convolutional Variational Autoencoder (CVAE) architecture to modify Pokémon sprites based on a target Pokémon type. Moreover, they solve the problem of low training data, using a Transfer Learning approach. The authors use VAE [8] since it is useful to create variations of existing content, but in future they plan to use GAN. In fact, according to [9], generative VAEs can produce blurry images.

It is placed in a similar context the work of [7] that, unlike the previous one, uses a GAN architecture to generate game icons. In this way they solve the problem to create icons manually, operation that takes a significant amount of time. Moreover, to create an unlimited number of unique icons is a very big opportunity for the video game creators and then for the users. To verify the validity of the method and so the attractive appearance of the icons, they use three methods: Fretchet Inception Distance (FID) [6] metric, a study of 50 observers, and the visual evaluation of two experts.

3   Materials And Methods

In this section, we introduce MONstEr for automatic contents generation for video games as well as the novel dataset used for evaluation: "GameAsset-Dataset". MONstEr comprises three important stages that will be detailed in the following subsections:

1. Generation of GameAssetDataset;
2. 2D asset generation;
3. 3D asset generation.

Figure 1 schematically represents the workflow of MONstEr.

3.1   GameAssetDataset

In this work, it is constructed a new dataset of characters representations for overcoming the limitations of the ones publicly available. To collect the images, it is implemented a web crawler algorithm that is able to search images starting from chosen keywords. Since our aim was to generate new monsters, our web crawler retrieves raw information from the internet. The crawler scans

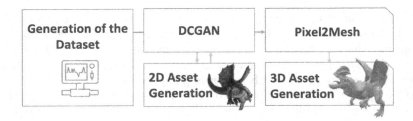

Fig. 1. MONstEr workflow. It comprises three important phases: dataset collection with a web crawler algorithm, 2D asset generation by training a DCGAN followed by a Pixel2mesh for the 3D asset generation.

well-known web applications and any websites that have been denoted as relevant by gaming experts. GameAssetDataset contains 2700 monsters images and some example are showed in Fig. 2.

Fig. 2. Monsters images of GameAssetDataset.

3.2 Deep Learning Pipeline

The DL pipeline is the key core of MONstEr. It is composed of two phases: 2D Asset generation and 3D Asset generation. This allows to automatic generate new 3D models for gaming environment.

2D Asset Generation. At the first stage, MONstEr uses a DCGAN network [14] that has a signal noise as input and an image in output. DCGANs are able to create photorealistic original images using a combination of two Deep Neural Networks (generator and discriminator) that compete with each other. When both networks are sufficiently trained to ensure that the images produced by the generator are considered satisfactory, we can use the network to create novel and realistic content.

The epoch number used for the first training phase was 750. It has been performed a pretraining using the CelebA dataset[1], which contains over 200000 images of celebrities.

3.3 3D Asset Generation

In the first step of the workflow production for the 3D models generation, we subdivided the dataset in 5 categories: 1) monsters with an excrescence on the back, 2) monsters without an excrescence on the back, 3) winged monsters, 4) big-legged monsters, 5) long-tailed monsters (as shown in Figs. 3 and 4). For each category we considered a 3D asset used as label for the pixel2mesh algorithm (Figs. 3 and 4).

(a)   (b)

(c)   (d)

(e)   (f)

Fig. 3. Dataset subdivision (1). (a) and (b): winged monsters. (c) and (d): long-tailed monsters. (e) and (f): monsters with an excrescence on the back.

---

[1] https://www.kaggle.com/jessicali9530/celeba-dataset.

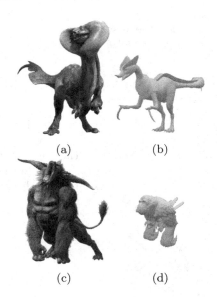

Fig. 4. Dataset subdivision (2). (a) and (b): monsters without an excrescence on the back. (c) and (d): big-legged monsters

We have chosen the Pixel2Mesh algorithm since it provides a high 3D shape estimation accuracy [19]. Pixel2Mesh can predict both the vertices and faces of a 3D model from a single image by deforming a mesh model, usually an ellipsoid. The target model must be homeomorphic from the mesh of the model, so using a mesh of the convex model as an ellipsoid can introduce many false faces on highly non-converted objects such as chairs and lamps.

4   Results and Discussions

During the experimental phase, to validate the efficiency of the proposed architecture in the generation of virtual asset, we train the two network for 500 epochs in the case of the DC-GAN and for 750 epochs for the Pixel2mesh. We used the 85% of the total amount of images for the training phase which took about 5 h. This phase was done by using a GPU RTX 2080TI with a memory of 11 GB, pytorch 1.8.2, a RAM of 128 GB and a CPU Intel Xeon E5 2.47 G.Hz. Subsequently, during the test phase, CPU was used to check the correct operation of the framework even without the use of a GPU. Analyzing the response times on the CPU, these are on average of about 40 s, while those of inference on the GPU are of 10 s. After training, the generation of 2D asset is satisfactory even if not completely precise, as showed in Fig. 5. Nonetheless, the results are appropriate for the generation of 3D assets. As Fig. 6 shows, during the generation of 3D objects there are generation errors that can be quickly corrected with a graphic.

Fig. 5. An example of monster generated.

Errors in generation are also due to an excessive generalization of the association classes of 3D objects to 2D images. In spite of this excessive generalization, the 3D generation allows to obtain good quality starting results for a graph. In Fig. 6a, it is possible to immediately notices a problem in the generation of the tail that presents a set of points that do not respect the shape of the rest of the structure. Another error is the absence of spines in the hind legs. In Fig. 6b, the generation respects the structure of the mesh better, but there are errors that can be corrected by a graph. In particular, the scales of the original element are not generated on the tail and the wings are not complete. An error is the incomplete generation of the eye bodies. In the case of the monster with a growth on its back, the errors are visible even without the need to visualize the single structure, in fact the area of the back in the generated mesh does not present the details present in the original mesh as well as in the area of the head. In Fig. 6d, the generation defects occur on the beak and in the area of the lower claws, in the first case with errors in the positioning of the vertices while in the second case with some absence of points and faces in the mesh that make it not complete. Finally, the generation of the winged monster in Fig. 6e presents the greatest criticality in the area of the head, which is not complete with vertices and faces, and in the generation of the wings where there are generations of additional vertices that lead to the presence of artefacts as visible in the right wing of the same. Concerning quantitative evaluation, Table 1 reports intersection-over-union (IoU) results for each single category of monster. IoU allows to obtain a quantitative value to evaluate the 3D reconstruction using a single input image.

Table 1. IoU of each category for 3D reconstruction

Category 1	Category 2	Category 3	Category 4	Category 5
0.34	0.43	0.40	0.47	0.38

From these analyses, and analysing the reference meshes, in addition to the problems of GAN generation, the errors in 3D generation are also due to the different complexity of the starting meshes, both the number of vertices and the structure itself. However, these results show the effectiveness and the suitability of the proposed approach for gaming content generation.

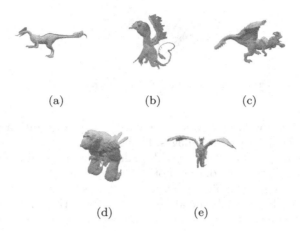

(a)   (b)   (c)

(d)   (e)

Fig. 6. Generated monsters from Pixel2mesh

5   Conclusions and Future Works

Methods based on AI aims to solve issues that involve high costs of production, time consuming and need many qualified person. In recent years, there is a great interest in research in the field of AI on the production mechanisms of videogames. The development process of a game in general can be changed by introducing automatic systems that replace the manual method for the creation of any content for the game. In this context, in this paper we have presented an architecture that we named MONstEr able to automatically generate novel graphical assets for videogames. We have implemented an approach based on a DCGAN in combination with a pixel2mesh algorithm to generate original 2D and from this 3D object. We have implemented a simple architecture that is able to solve time and cost problems related to the creation of novel assets for videogames. In addition, we have presented an automatic mechanism for the generation of original characters, by transforming two dimensional images into three-dimensional costumes that often went beyond the imagination of the designer. Moreover, since in literature there are not dataset necessary for the training of the MONstEr architecture, we have collected a novel dataset named "GameAssetDataset" obtained from different dataset, that will be made available for the scientific community. In future, we aim to optimize the results, by increasing the dataset and so the input data during the training phase, with the purpose to achieve higher generalization performance of the architecture. Moreover, we intend to integrate the architecture in an open source environment as blender.

References

1. Browne, C.B.: Automatic generation and evaluation of recombination games. Ph.D. thesis, Queensland University of Technology (2008)
2. Gadelha, M., Maji, S., Wang, R.: 3D shape induction from 2D views of multiple objects. In: 2017 International Conference on 3D Vision (3DV), pp. 402–411. IEEE (2017)
3. Gonzalez, A., Guzdial, M., Ramos, F.: Generating gameplay-relevant art assets with transfer learning. arXiv preprint arXiv:2010.01681 (2020)
4. Goodfellow, I., et al.: Generative adversarial nets. Adv. Neural Inf. Process. Syst. **27** (2014)
5. Hendrikx, M., Meijer, S., Van Der Velden, J., Iosup, A.: Procedural content generation for games: a survey. ACM Trans. Multi. Comput. Commun. Appl. (TOMM) **9**(1), 1–22 (2013)
6. Heusel, M., Ramsauer, H., Unterthiner, T., Nessler, B., Hochreiter, S.: Gans trained by a two time-scale update rule converge to a local nash equilibrium. Adv. Neural Inf. Process. Syst. **30** (2017)
7. Karp, R., Swiderska-Chadaj, Z.: Automatic generation of graphical game assets using GAN. In: 2021 7th International Conference on Computer Technology Applications, pp. 7–12 (2021)
8. Kingma, D.P., Welling, M.: Auto-encoding variational bayes. arXiv preprint arXiv:1312.6114 (2013)
9. Kingma, D.P., Welling, M.: An introduction to variational autoencoders. arXiv preprint arXiv:1906.02691 (2019)
10. Liu, Z., Luo, P., Wang, X., Tang, X.: Deep learning face attributes in the wild. In: Proceedings of the IEEE International Conference on Computer Vision, pp. 3730–3738 (2015)
11. Mathieu, M., Couprie, C., LeCun, Y.: Deep multi-scale video prediction beyond mean square error. arXiv preprint arXiv:1511.05440 (2015)
12. Maturana, D., Scherer, S.: Voxnet: a 3D convolutional neural network for real-time object recognition. In: 2015 IEEE/RSJ International Conference on Intelligent Robots and Systems (IROS), pp. 922–928. IEEE (2015)
13. Nigam, A.: Web crawling algorithms. Int. J. Comput. Sci. Artif. Intell. **4**(3), 63 (2014)
14. Radford, A., Metz, L., Chintala, S.: Unsupervised representation learning with deep convolutional generative adversarial networks. arXiv preprint arXiv:1511.06434 (2015)
15. Serpa, Y.R., Rodrigues, M.A.F.: Towards machine-learning assisted asset generation for games: a study on pixel art sprite sheets. In: 2019 18th Brazilian Symposium on Computer Games and Digital Entertainment (SBGames), pp. 182–191. IEEE (2019)
16. Summerville, A., et al.: Procedural content generation via machine learning (PCGML). IEEE Trans. Games **10**(3), 257–270 (2018)
17. Togelius, J., Yannakakis, G.N., Stanley, K.O., Browne, C.: Search-based procedural content generation: a taxonomy and survey. IEEE Trans. Comput. Intell. AI Games **3**(3), 172–186 (2011)
18. Torrado, R.R., Khalifa, A., Green, M.C., Justesen, N., Risi, S., Togelius, J.: Bootstrapping conditional GANS for video game level generation. In: 2020 IEEE Conference on Games (CoG), pp. 41–48. IEEE (2020)

19. Wang, N., Zhang, Y., Li, Z., Fu, Y., Liu, W., Jiang, Y.G.: Pixel2mesh: generating 3D mesh models from single RGB images. In: Proceedings of the European Conference on Computer Vision (ECCV), pp. 52–67 (2018)

20. Wu, J., Zhang, C., Xue, T., Freeman, W.T., Tenenbaum, J.B.: Learning a probabilistic latent space of object shapes via 3D generative-adversarial modeling. In: Proceedings of the 30th International Conference on Neural Information Processing Systems, pp. 82–90 (2016)

21. Wu, Z., et al.: 3D shapenets: a deep representation for volumetric shapes. In: Proceedings of the IEEE Conference on Computer Vision and Pattern Recognition, pp. 1912–1920 (2015)

22. Yang, L.C., Chou, S.Y., Yang, Y.H.: Midinet: a convolutional generative adversarial network for symbolic-domain music generation. arXiv preprint arXiv:1703.10847 (2017)

23. Yu, F., Seff, A., Zhang, Y., Song, S., Funkhouser, T., Xiao, J.: LSUN: construction of a large-scale image dataset using deep learning with humans in the loop. arXiv preprint arXiv:1506.03365 (2015)

Surface Oxide Detection and Characterization Using Sparse Unmixing on Hyperspectral Images

Tarek Zenati[1,2], Bruno Figliuzzi[1(✉)], and Shu Hui Ham[2]

[1] Center for Mathematical Morphology, Mines Paris, PSL Research University,
35, rue Saint Honoré, 77305 Fontainebleau, France
`bruno.figliuzzi@minesparis.psl.eu`
[2] ArcelorMittal R&D Maizières SA, Voie Romaine, 57280 Maizières-lès-Metz, France

Abstract. In this article, we present a novel methodology based on hyperspectral images to detect the presence of surface layers of selected oxides on steel sheets. Our approach consists in precomputing a dictionary of reflectance spectra in order to formulate the problem as a sparse regression problem. The methodology is validated through experiments conducted with reflectance spectra simulated for random geometrical settings incorporating several distinct oxides. These experiments demonstrate that the methodology is able to estimate the presence of selective oxides with high recall and precision metrics.

Keywords: Hyperspectral imaging · Sparse hyperspectral unmixing · Convex optimization

1 Introduction

During steel-sheets manufacturing, laboratory characterization of surface defects is an essential process for guaranteeing the quality of the production. To improve the mechanical performance of steel sheets, a number of alloying elements including manganese, aluminium or silicon are usually incorporated to the steel. It becomes therefore important to prevent the formation of selective oxides at the surface, which could significantly impact the wettability of the sheet surface [13]. The development of image processing techniques aimed at detecting the formation of oxides has therefore been an active topic of research over the past few years [9,20,21].

Hyperspectral camera technology is increasingly being used for laboratory control in the industry and is an interesting axis of development for steel surfaces characterization [12–14]. Spectral information can indeed be exploited to detect the formation of specific chemical species at the surface. However, due to the limited spatial resolution of hyperspectral sensors, the spectra measured at each pixel location are often highly mixed and potentially incorporate the contribution of several oxide species.

P. L. Mazzeo et al. (Eds.): ICIAP 2022 Workshops, LNCS 13373, pp. 291–302, 2022.
https://doi.org/10.1007/978-3-031-13321-3_26

Hyperspectral unmixing (HU) has been a challenging subject over the past few years for academical researchers and industrials. HU aims at detecting the present materials - also referred to as endmembers - in measurements images by identifying their spectral signatures. HU can be a difficult problem due to the complexity of the optical model describing the mixing process [3,7,11,15]. A classical assumption in HU is to consider that elementary spectra are combined linearly to form the observed spectrum. Under the linear model assumption, several algorithms have been developed over the years to perform unmixing, and efficient algorithms are now available to perform HU [1,6,10,18,22]. However, these algorithms are barely applicable in our case where the optical model describing the formation of the observed spectra is strongly nonlinear. An alternative approach is to try to build a dictionary containing an exhaustive list of the spectra of the elementary chemical species that can be present at the surface. The observed spectrum can then be recovered as a linear combination of a small number of spectra taken from the dictionary. HU is therefore conveniently formulated as a sparse regression problem whose objective is to jointly identify the materials within each pixel and to quantify their respective abundances [16]. Classically, a l^1 penalty is used to promote sparse solutions [2,5,23]. In our case, it is possible to determine in advance the oxides that can potentially form at the surface. The main difficulty is that the chemical species are usually structured into several layers with infinitely many possible thicknesses, therefore making the construction of the spectra dictionary a difficult task.

This article introduces a novel methodology for solving the HU problem for detecting the formation of chemical oxides on a surface and for estimating the thickness of the oxide layers. In particular, we demonstrate that by selecting reference thicknesses and by linearizing the optical model around these, it becomes possible to construct a dictionary containing a reasonnable number of elementary spectra. Our main contribution is therefore to formulate the problem of the oxide determination within the sparse HU framework.

The paper is organized as follows. Section 2 and 3 present the optical model developed to describe the spectra formation and the inversion algorithm. The proposed methodology is illustrated and discussed on a synthetic dataset in Sect. 4. Conclusions are finally drawn in the last section.

2   Optical Model

2.1   Optical Modelization for Oxides

We describe in this section the physical model used to compute the optical reflectance of a system composed of a stack of homogeneous layers in the xy plane. We denote by z the direction orthogonal to the layers. According to the superposition principle, the electric field E can be decomposed onto a field E_f propagating forward and a field E_b propagating backward [25]:

$$E = E_f e^{ik_z z} + E_b e^{-ik_z z}, \qquad (1)$$

where k_z is the $z-$component of the wave vector. Let us denote by z_k the location of the interface separating the layers k and $k+1$. Then, we have:

$$\begin{pmatrix} E_f(z_k^-) \\ E_b(z_k^-) \end{pmatrix} = \underbrace{\frac{1}{t_{k,k+1}} \begin{pmatrix} 1 & r_{k,k+1} \\ r_{k,k+1} & 1 \end{pmatrix}}_{T_{k,k+1}} \begin{pmatrix} E_f(z_k^+) \\ E_b(z_k^+) \end{pmatrix},$$ (2)

where $t_{k,k+1}$ and $r_{k,k+1}$ are the Fresnel coefficients for transmission and reflection, respectively. Similarly, the relationship between the electric fields entering and leaving the k-th layer is:

$$\begin{pmatrix} E_f(z_k^+) \\ E_b(z_k^+) \end{pmatrix} = \underbrace{\begin{pmatrix} e^{ik_z h_k} & 0 \\ 0 & e^{-ik_z h_k} \end{pmatrix}}_{T_{k+1}(h)} \begin{pmatrix} E_f(z_{k+1}^-) \\ E_b(z_{k+1}^-) \end{pmatrix},$$ (3)

In the presence of a single layer of oxide on a steel substrate, since there is no electric field propagating backward in the steel, the system is described by the equation:

$$\begin{pmatrix} E_i(0^+) \\ E_r(0^+) \end{pmatrix} = \underbrace{T_{1,2} T_2(h) T_{2,3}}_{T(h)} \begin{pmatrix} E_t(h^-) \\ 0 \end{pmatrix},$$ (4)

where E_i, E_r and E_t correspond to the incident, reflected and transmitted fields, respectively. Hence, the global transmission and reflection coefficients t and r for the system can easily be computed from the coefficients of $T(h)$ as a function of the layer thickness:

$$r = \frac{[T(h)]_{21}}{[T(h)]_{11}}, \qquad t = \frac{1}{[T(h)]_{11}}.$$ (5)

Finally, it is straightforward to compute the reflectance, which is simply defined as $R(h) = |r(h)|^2$.

Interestingly, it is possible to linearize the model around any reference thickness h. When $\Delta h \ll \lambda$, we find indeed that:

$$T(h + \Delta h) \simeq T(h) + \Delta h \, T_{1,2} \underbrace{\begin{pmatrix} ik_z e^{ik_z h} & 0 \\ 0 & -ik_z e^{-ik_z h} \end{pmatrix} T_{2,3}}_{\partial T/\partial h}$$ (6)

Therefore, at first order in $\Delta h/\lambda$, we get:

$$r(h + \Delta h) \simeq r(h) + \Delta h \underbrace{\frac{1}{r(h)} \left(\frac{1}{[T(h)]_{21}} \left[\frac{\partial T}{\partial h}(h) \right]_{21} - \frac{1}{[T(h)]_{11}} \left[\frac{\partial T}{\partial h}(h) \right]_{11} \right)}_{\partial r/\partial h}$$ (7)

Eq. (7) allows us to express the reflectance around any reference thickness h as the linear combination of only two terms: the reflectance at the reference thickness and its gradient with respect to the thickness. We display in Fig. 1 a comparison between the reflectance computed with the model for a single layer of a mixture of manganese and aluminium oxides (Mn-AlO) with thickness 400nm and the corresponding first order approximation around the reference thickness 300nm. We note that there is a good agreement between both computed reflectances.

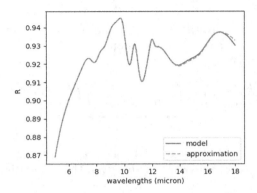

Fig. 1. Comparison between the optical model and its first order approximation for a layer of Mn-AlO (Color figure online)

3 Sparse Unmixing Approach

In this section, we assume that the measured reflectance spectra results from a linear combination of a small number of elementary spectra $S_i(h_i; \lambda)$ generated by a layer of thickness h_i of some oxide i:

$$S(\lambda) = \sum_{i=1}^{n} \beta_i S_i(h_i; \lambda). \tag{8}$$

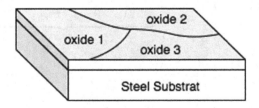

Fig. 2. Mixed oxide on a steel substrat

In this equation, the parameter λ corresponds to the wavelength, and the coefficients $\{\beta_i, i = 1, \ldots, n\}$ can be interpreted as the abundances or surface fractions of the different oxides present at the surface. This model can be interpretated as an approximation of the optical interactions occuring in the geometrical setting described in Fig. 2, where distinct layers of oxide are present in the region probed by the hyperspectral sensor.

One way of approaching the problem of determining the presence of an oxide, and its thickness if applicable, is to pre-calculate, for each oxide, the reflectance spectra corresponding to different reference thicknesses and to collect all pre-calculated spectra in a dictionary D. This dictionary takes the form of a matrix of size $L \times N$ whose columns correspond to the calculated spectra, L here designating the number of wavelengths. The problem of determining the elementary reflectance spectra is then reformulated as the search for a linear combination involving a small number of elementary spectra from the dictionary D that makes it possible to reconstruct the observed spectrum $S(\lambda)$ with good precision.

Let us consider an observed spectrum S. Our objective is to find a sparse vector β such that $S = D\beta$, and therefore express S as a linear combination of a small number of pre-calculated oxide spectra. From a mathematical perspective, this can be formulated as the following optimization problem:

$$\hat{\beta} = \underset{\beta \in \mathbb{R}}{\operatorname{argmin}} \|S - D\beta\|^2 + \gamma\|\beta\|_0. \tag{9}$$

In formulation (9), β corresponds to the coefficients of a vector selecting the elements of the dictionary D used for the reconstruction of the observed spectrum S. The quantity $\|\beta\|_0$ refers to the number of non-zero components of the vector β:

$$\|\beta\|_0 = \#\{i \in \{1, ..., N\}, \beta_i \neq 0\}. \tag{10}$$

Formulation (9) can be interpreted as the search for a compromise between a vector of coefficients β which allows on the one hand to properly reconstruct the measured reflectance through the minimization of the term $\|S - D\beta\|^2$, and on the other hand, is parsimonious through the minimization of the term $\|\beta\|_0$. The positive parameter γ allows to weight the parsimony influence and the quality of the reconstruction: a high value of γ thus favors parsimonious solutions to the detriment of the reconstruction accuracy.

A major problem related to formulation (9) is that the considered optimization problem is difficult to solve in practice. In particular, to obtain an exact solution, it is necessary to consider all possible combinations of parameters, which implies a combinatorial complexity. Different algorithms have nevertheless been developed in the literature in order to obtain approximate solutions to the problem, such as the *orthogonal matching pursuit* (OMP) [19].

An alternative to formulation (9) is to consider a penalty by the l^1 norm instead of the l^0 norm in the optimization problem. Penalization by the l^1 norm indeed leads to the obtaining of parsimonious solutions. The new formulation of the problem therefore takes the following form :

$$\hat{\beta} = \arg \min_{\beta \in \mathbb{R}^N} \|S - D\beta\|^2 + \gamma\|\beta\|_1, \tag{11}$$

where the norm l^1 of the vector β is given by $\|\beta\| = \sum_{i=1}^{N} |\beta_i|$.

The advantage of this second formulation, known under the name of *Least Absolute Shrinkage and Selection Operator* (LASSO [24]) is that the problem considered is convex and that there is therefore a great variety of solving algorithms [4,5,8].

3.1 Algorithm

The problem is approached by precomputing, for each possible oxide appearing at the substrat surface, the reflectance spectra corresponding to different reference thicknesses, before grouping the precomputed spectra in a dictionary D. Estimation and characterization of the oxides present on the observed surface are carried out in two steps:

1. Firstly, by solving problem (11), we seek to identify the oxides present on the studied surface, and obtain a first approximation of their respective thicknesses.
2. Secondly, the estimation can optionally be refined by using the spectrum gradient calculated around the estimated thickness to improve the thickness estimation.

Step 1. We first solve the optimization problem (11) for decreasing values of the parameter γ using a proximal gradient descent and by adding a constraint of positivity on the coefficients of the solution:

$$\forall i \in \{1, \ldots, N\}, \hat{\beta}(\gamma)_i \geq 0. \tag{12}$$

We start with a high value of γ which results in obtaining a highly parsimonious $\hat{\beta}(\gamma)$ solution, before gradually reducing the value of γ until the following criterion is satisfied:

$$\sum_{i=1}^{N} \hat{\beta}(\gamma)_i = 1 \tag{13}$$

The fact that the coordinate i of the solution $\hat{\beta}(\gamma)$ is non-zero indicates that it was necessary to select the oxide corresponding to the column i of the dictionary D to reconstruct the observed spectrum. As the reconstruction problem is penalized by the l^1 norm, only a small number of coefficients are non-zero, and only a small number of oxides are involved in the reconstruction of the spectrum. The criterion (13) is relatively easy to interpret: when it is satisfied, the quantity $D\hat{\beta}(\gamma)$ can be seen as a weighted average of different elements of the dictionary.

As a general rule, nothing prevents the vector $\hat{\beta}(\gamma)$ from selecting columns of D corresponding to the same oxide, but for different thicknesses. We therefore estimate the thickness of each oxide effectively selected by the vector $\hat{\beta}(\gamma)$ by calculating the average of the selected thicknesses, weighted by the value of the coefficients of $\hat{\beta}(\gamma)$. More precisely, for a given oxide $\mathcal{O}$, let us denote by $\hat{\beta}(\gamma, \mathcal{O})$ the vector such that:

$$\forall i \in \{1, N\}, \hat{\beta}(\gamma, \mathcal{O})_i = \begin{cases} \hat{\beta}(\gamma)_i \text{ if the i-th column refers to oxide } \mathcal{O} \\ 0 \text{ otherwise} \end{cases} \tag{14}$$

Finally, let $h \in \mathbb{R}^N$ and $\sigma \in \mathbb{R}^N$ be the vectors containing, for all $n \in \{1, \ldots, N\}$ the thicknesses of the pre-calculated spectra in the columns of D. For a given oxide $\mathcal{O}$, we estimate the thickness of the oxide layer to be:

$$h(\mathcal{O}) = \frac{h^T \hat{\beta}(\gamma, \mathcal{O})}{\|\hat{\beta}(\gamma, \mathcal{O})\|_1} = \frac{1}{\|\hat{\beta}(\gamma, \mathcal{O})\|_1} \sum_{i=1}^{N} h_i \hat{\beta}(\gamma, \mathcal{O})_i. \tag{15}$$

Step 2 (optional). During the first step of the algorithmic processing, we were able to estimate, by solving the optimization problem (11), which were the oxides present on a given surface. Let us suppose that K distinct oxides were identified. We denote by $\{h_k, k = 1, \ldots, K\}$ the layer thicknesses corresponding to these oxides. The estimation of the real thickness of the k-th oxide layer can be improved by using the gradient of the spectrum associated with the oxide, as computed at the thickness h_k estimated during the first step. We have indeed

$$S_k(h; \lambda) = S_k(h_k; \lambda) + (h - h_k) \frac{\partial S_k}{\partial h}(h_k; \lambda) + o(|h - h_k|). \tag{16}$$

As a consequence, we can try to find the observed spectrum in the form:

$$S(\lambda) = \sum_{k=1}^{K} \alpha_k \left(S_k + (\tilde{h}_k - h_k) \frac{\partial S_k}{\partial h} \right), \tag{17}$$

where $S_k := S_k(h_k; \lambda)$ et $\partial S_k / \partial h := \partial S_k / \partial h(h_k, \lambda)$ and $\tilde{h}_k$ is a new estimation of the thickness of the oxide layer. In this equation, the unknowns are the coefficients α_k, which correspond to the respective abundances of each of the spectra, as well as the thicknesses $\tilde{h}_k$ for each oxide. The determination of these coefficients can quite simply be carried out by considering the least squares regression problem:

$$\hat{\alpha}, \hat{h}_k = \text{argmin}_{\alpha \in \mathbb{R}^K, \tilde{h}_k \in \mathbb{R}^K} \sum_{k=1}^{K} \left\| \alpha_k \left(S_k + (\tilde{h}_k - h_k) \frac{\partial S_k}{\partial h} \right) - S \right\|_2^2. \tag{18}$$

4   Results and Discussion

We present and discuss in this section the numerical experiments conducted to evaluate the proposed algorithm. In these experiments, we use the optical properties of $K = 5$ distinct oxides, including aluminium oxide (Al_2O_3), silicon dioxide (SiO_2), manganese oxide (MnO) and mixtures of manganese and aluminium oxides (MnAlO, Mn+AlO) obtained from measurements conducted in [13]. All these oxides have a significant probability of formation on steel substrates. Based upon the optical properties of the oxides, we construct a dictionary D based upon

8 reference thicknesses ranging from 20 to 300 nm. For each pair of oxide and thickness, we compute the corresponding reflectance for 186 wavelengths ranging uniformly from 6.5 to 12.6 microns. We incorporate the reflectance of the substrate in the dictionary. The shape of the dictionary D is therefore 41×186.

4.1 Single Oxide Characterization

In a first experiment, we randomly select one of the oxides and a random thickness h between 10 nm and 350 nm according to a uniform law. Using the optical model described in Sect. 2, we compute the optical response of a layer of the selected oxide with thickness h. This procedure allows us to simulate the obtaining of experimental reflectances.

Next, using the dictionary D, we apply the algorithm described in Sect. 3 to estimate the proportion of each one of the considered oxides at the surface and their respective thicknesses. The algorithm outputs two $(K+1) \times 1$ vectors indicating the abundance and the thickness estimated for the substrate and for each oxide. These vectors are then compared to the actual geometrical settings. The results of the experiments are based upon the generation of $N = 1000$ random samples. In Fig. 3, we compare the reconstructed and the simulated reflectance spectra for two oxide layers, composed of a layer of SiO_2 (120 nm) and of a layer of AlO+Mn (183 nm). In the figure, the reconstructed reflectance is the reflectance computed from the optical model with the abundances and thicknesses estimated by the algorithm. We can note the good agreement between the reconstruction and the simulation for both layers, which is partly due to the fact that the generated spectra are noise free. For the first (resp. second) layer, the estimated thickness for the oxide is 121 nm (resp. 183 nm). In table 1, we present the confusion matrix associated to our experiment. The column (resp. row) entries correspond to the material associated with the highest estimated abundance (resp. to the actual material). Cell $C_{i,j}$ therefore indicate the number of layers containing the i-th oxide that were classified as containing the j-th oxide. Overall, we note that the algorithm is able to properly identify the main oxide in 97% of the cases. The principal source of error corresponds to oxide layers that have been wrongly classified as substrate. These layers are usually very thin layers, whose reflectance is extremely close to the one of the substrate.

Since multiple oxides can potentially be detected by the algorithm, the confusion matrix only provides an incomplete view of the detection result. In table 2, we present our results in terms of precision and recall. In the presented results, an oxide is considered to be detected by the algorithm if its associated abundance is strictly greater than 0. Overall, the precision and the recall reach high values around 0.95 and 0.99 for samples with a single oxide.

Finally, to quantify the error regarding the thickness estimation, we report in table 2 the Euclidean distance between the thickness estimation and the actual thickness, averaged over the samples for which the detected oxide with highest abundance is the one actually present at the surface. The results are reported for an algorithm run with and without the refinement step. With the refinement step, we note that the estimation error decreases significantly.

Table 1. Confusion matrix

	Substrate	Al2O3	SiO2	MnO	MnAlO	Mn+AlO
Substrate	189	0	0	0	0	0
Al2O3	17	138	0	0	0	0
SiO2	1	0	158	0	0	0
MnO	10	0	0	160	0	0
MnAlO	0	0	0	0	156	0
Mn+AlO	2	0	0	0	0	163

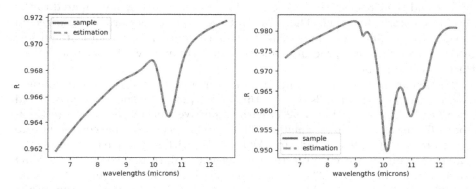

Fig. 3. Spectrum recovery in the presence of a single layer of oxide (left: SiO_2, 120 nm; right: AlO+Mn, 183 nm) (Color figure online)

Table 2. Detection and characterization performances

Performance indicator	Single oxide	Multiple oxides
Recall	0.993	0.772
Precision	0.948	0.892
Thickness error (nm)	0.37	9.2
without refinement (nm)	3.5	11.3

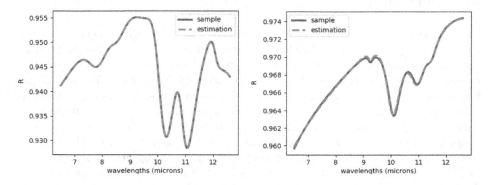

Fig. 4. Reflectance recovery in the presence of a multiple layers of oxides (left: mixture of SO_2 and MnAlO; right: mixture of MnO and Mn+AlO) (Color figure online)

4.2 Multiple Oxides Characterization

In a second experiment, we randomly select k oxides, with k selected randomly between 1 and 3, and k random thicknesses $\{h_1, \ldots, h_k\}$ between 10 nm and 350 nm according to a uniform law. Surface fractions $\{\beta_1, \ldots, \beta_k\}$ are drawn for the selected oxides according to a uniform Dirichlet distribution with dimension k. Based upon model (8), we can then compute the optical response of the corresponding geometry.

As previously, using the dictionary D, we rely on the algorithm described in Sect. 3 to estimate the proportion of each one of the considered oxides at the surface and their respective thicknesses. The estimation is then compared to the actual geometrical setting. The results of the experiments are summarized in table 2. We obtain a precision of 0.89 and a recall of 0.77 for the case of multiple oxides. The refinement procedure allows to slightly improve the accuracy of the thickness estimation.

We display in Fig. 4 the results of the estimation on two generated samples. The first sample corresponds to a mixture of SO_2 (23.7%, estimation: 23.8%) and MnAlO (76.3%, estimation: 76.2%) with respective thicknesses 206nm (estimation: 207 nm) and 79 nm (estimation: 79 nm). The second sample corresponds to a mixture of MnO (29.6%) and Mn+AlO (70.4%) with respective thicknesses 126 nm and 140 nm. However, our estimation yields a mixture of SO_2 (71.4%), MnO (23.3%) and Mn+AlO (5.3%) with respective thicknesses 63 nm and 233 nm and 680 nm. In this case, the proposed approach fails to properly estimate the correct proportion of oxides and even to identify the actual oxides present at the surface. However, as can be observed in Fig. 4, the spectrum is still reconstructed with high accuracy. This example illustrates one intrinsic difficulty related to our approach: when the elements of the dictionary D are strongly correlated, as it is the case for the reflectance spectra in D, different combinations of spectra can lead to the same reconstruction. In this case, the l^1 penalization does not guarantee the recovery of the observed reflectance spectrum with the correct volume fraction of oxides.

5 Conclusion

In this article, we presented a novel methodology based on hyperspectral images to detect the presence of surface layers of selected oxides on steel sheets. Numerical experiments demonstrated that the methodology is able to estimate the presence of selective oxides with high recall and precision metrics. The main limitation of the proposed approach is that the precomputed spectra are strongly correlated, so that very different combinations of oxides can potentially lead to similar reflectance spectra. This issue could potentially be dealt with by trying to incorporate spatial information by enforcing consistency between the estimation conducted at neighbor pixels. Total variation based algorithms have notably been proposed in the literature to that end [17]. Finally, an obvious perspective for this study will be to apply the proposed algorithm to real experimental data.

In this case, a major issue will be related to the presence of measurement noise in the observed spectra, which could complicate their analysis. This will be the subject of subsequent research.

References

1. Ambikapathi, A., Chan, T.H., Ma, W.K., Chi, C.Y.: Chance-constrained robust minimum-volume enclosing simplex algorithm for hyperspectral unmixing. IEEE Trans. Geosci. Remote Sens. **49**(11), 4194–4209 (2011)
2. Beck, A., Teboulle, M.: A fast iterative shrinkage-thresholding algorithm for linear inverse problems. SIAM J. Imaging Sci. **2**(1), 183–202 (2009)
3. Bioucas-Dias, J.M., Plaza, A., Dobigeon, N., Parente, M., Du, Q., Gader, P., Chanussot, J.: Hyperspectral unmixing overview: Geometrical, statistical, and sparse regression-based approaches. IEEE J. Sel. Top. Appl. Earth Observations Remote Sens. **5**(2), 354–379 (2012)
4. Boyd, S., Boyd, S.P., Vandenberghe, L.: Convex optimization. Cambridge University Press (2004)
5. Bubeck, S.: Convex optimization: algorithms and complexity (2014). arXiv preprint arXiv:1405.4980
6. Dobigeon, N., Moussaoui, S., Coulon, M., Tourneret, J.Y., Hero, A.O.: Joint Bayesian endmember extraction and linear unmixing for hyperspectral imagery. IEEE Trans. Signal Process. **57**(11), 4355–4368 (2009)
7. Dobigeon, N., Tourneret, J.Y., Richard, C., Bermudez, J.C.M., McLaughlin, S., Hero, A.O.: Nonlinear unmixing of hyperspectral images: models and algorithms. IEEE Signal Process. Mag. **31**(1), 82–94 (2013)
8. Efron, B., Hastie, T., Johnstone, I., Tibshirani, R., et al.: Least angle regression. Ann. Stat. **32**(2), 407–499 (2004)
9. Ferté, M.: Étude et analyse de couches minces par techniques multi-spectroscopiques pour une application sur une ligne de galvanisation. Ph.D. thesis, Université de Lorraine (2014)
10. Figliuzzi, B., Velasco-Forero, S., Bilodeau, M., Angulo, J.: A Bayesian approach to linear unmixing in the presence of highly mixed spectra. In: Blanc-Talon, J., Distante, C., Philips, W., Popescu, D., Scheunders, P. (eds.) ACIVS 2016. LNCS, vol. 10016, pp. 263–274. Springer, Cham (2016). https://doi.org/10.1007/978-3-319-48680-2_24
11. Halimi, A., Altmann, Y., Dobigeon, N., Tourneret, J.Y.: Nonlinear unmixing of hyperspectral images using a generalized bilinear model. IEEE Trans. Geosci. Remote Sens. **49**(11), 4153–4162 (2011)
12. Ham, S., Ferté, M., Fricout, G., Depalo, L., Carteret, C.: In-situ spectral emissivity measurement of alloy steels during annealing in controlled atmosphere. QIRT **2016**, 315–321 (2016)
13. Ham, S.H.: Propriétés physico-chimiques des oxydes de surface et analyse des données de l'imagerie hyperspectrale. Physicochemical properties of surface oxides and data analysis of hyperspectral imaging. Ph.D. thesis, Université de Lorraine (2018)
14. Ham, S.H., Ferie, M., Carteret, C., Fricout, G., Angulo, J., Capon, F.: Hyperspectral imaging as an analytical tool for thin single and multilayer oxides characterization: a laboratory study. In: 2016 8th Workshop on Hyperspectral Image and Signal Processing: Evolution in Remote Sensing (WHISPERS), pp. 1–5. IEEE (2016)

15. Heylen, R., Parente, M., Gader, P.: A review of nonlinear hyperspectral unmixing methods. IEEE J. Sel. Top. Appl. Earth Observations Remote Sens. **7**(6), 1844–1868 (2014)
16. Iordache, M.D., Bioucas-Dias, J.M., Plaza, A.: Sparse unmixing of hyperspectral data. IEEE Trans. Geosci. Remote Sens. **49**(6), 2014–2039 (2011)
17. Iordache, M.D., Bioucas-Dias, J.M., Plaza, A.: Total variation spatial regularization for sparse hyperspectral unmixing. IEEE Trans. Geosci. Remote Sens. **50**(11), 4484–4502 (2012)
18. Li, J., Bioucas-Dias, J.M.: Minimum volume simplex analysis: A fast algorithm to unmix hyperspectral data. In: IGARSS 2008–2008 IEEE International Geoscience and Remote Sensing Symposium. vol. 3, pp. III-250. IEEE (2008)
19. Mallat, S.G., Zhang, Z.: Matching pursuits with time-frequency dictionaries. IEEE Trans. Signal Process. **41**(12), 3397–3415 (1993)
20. Masci, J., Meier, U., Ciresan, D., Schmidhuber, J., Fricout, G.: Steel defect classification with max-pooling convolutional neural networks. In: The 2012 International Joint Conference on Neural Networks (IJCNN), pp. 1–6. IEEE (2012)
21. Masci, J., Meier, U., Fricout, G., Schmidhuber, J.: Multi-scale pyramidal pooling network for generic steel defect classification. In: The 2013 International Joint Conference on Neural Networks (IJCNN), pp. 1–8. IEEE (2013)
22. Nascimento, J.M., Dias, J.M.: Vertex component analysis: a fast algorithm to unmix hyperspectral data. IEEE Trans. Geosci. Remote Sens. **43**(4), 898–910 (2005)
23. Parikh, N., Boyd, S.: Proximal algorithms. Found. Trends Optim. **1**(3), 127–239 (2014)
24. Tibshirani, R.: Regression shrinkage and selection via the lasso. J. Roy. Stat. Soc.: Ser. B (Methodol.) **58**(1), 267–288 (1996)
25. Tolstoy, V.P., Chernyshova, I., Skryshevsky, V.A.: Handbook of Infrared Spectroscopy of Ultrathin Films. John Wiley & Sons, Hoboken, USA (2003)

FakeNED: A Deep Learning Based-System for Fake News Detection from Social Media

Laura Della Sciucca[1,2], Marco Mameli[1(✉)], Emanuele Balloni[1,3], Luca Rossi[1], Emanuele Frontoni[1,3], Primo Zingaretti[1], and Marina Paolanti[1,3]

[1] VRAI Vision Robotics and Artificial Intelligence Lab, Dipartimento di Ingegneria dell'Informazione (DII), Università Politecnica delle Marche, Via Brecce Bianche 12, 60131 Ancona, Italy
{laura.dellasciucca,emanuele.balloni,emanuele.frontoni, marina.paolanti}@unimc.it, {m.mameli,l.rossi}@pm.univpm.it, p.zingaretti@univpm.it
[2] Department of Humanities, University of Macerata, 62100 Macerata, Italy
[3] Department of Political Sciences, Communication and International Relations, University of Macerata, 62100 Macerata, Italy

Abstract. Social networks are increasingly present in our daily life. They allow us to remain in contact with friends regardless of distances, to share posts, images, videos, to be part of communities or come across articles and news. Everything develops so quickly that formality and content are no longer given too much importance. Therefore, it is through the development of these social networks that the need to distinguish fake news from real ones has developed. In this paper, we propose FakeNED a system for the detection of fake news on social networks. It comprises a multimodal Deep Learning (DL) approach of extracting features both from the text and from the images of the article. For the first extraction, we implemented a BERT-based (Bidirectional Encoder Representations from Transformers) method with an initial pre-trained phase followed by a fine-tuning final phase. For the latter, we used a VGG-16 to develop the image feature extraction. The extracted features were then given as input to a Fully Connected Layer in order to obtain the final output. We conduct our experiments on Fakeddit dataset through which we obtained a result which outperforms the state-of-art models. Moreover, FakeNED includes a service for allowing users to easily estimate the truth of social media content.

1 Introduction

Nowadays social networks have become an integral part of our daily life, it's so easy to access to them since our smartphones are always on our hands. This simplicity, together with the speed of access, determines the constant use of these platforms by their users; everyone can post a contribution, give feedback, share articles, and express its own opinion with minimum authentication. Furthermore, it's the fastest and cheapest way to access daily news. Unfortunately, these free

P. L. Mazzeo et al. (Eds.): ICIAP 2022 Workshops, LNCS 13373, pp. 303–313, 2022.
https://doi.org/10.1007/978-3-031-13321-3_27

sharing platforms have no control over the veracity of posts and it is often difficult even for the users themselves to check the reliability of a content.

These factors have therefore influenced the huge and uncontrolled development of fake news, false or misleading information presented with the aim of damaging the reputation of a person or entity or even manipulate people's thinking and decisions. In fact, the huge spread of false information brings negative impact to individual and society, for this reason it is increasingly urgent to find a solution to the automatic detection of fake news.

The aim of this paper is to propose FakeNED, a fake news detection system, taking into account information coming not only from the text of the post but also from eventual images attached on it, in order to obtain a larger number of features to analyze. The experiments have been assessed on Fakeddit [10], a multimodal dataset consisting of over 1 million samples from multiple categories of fake news. In addition to the novel deep learning (DL) approach, which combines two different kind of social media data (text and image), FakeNED includes a user friendly service that allow people to easily judge the truth of the content of the news shared on social network.

This paper is structured as follows: Sect. 2 gives an overview of the background knowledge of related studies; in Sect. 3 there is a detailed description of the methods and the entire workflow together with the required materials; Sect. 4 presents an explanation of the results obtained accompanied by conclusions in Sect. 5.

2   State of Art

Nowadays the detection of fake news is a problem on which several studies have focused [4,8,13,16]. Multiple fake news detection approaches have been defined during the years. In particular, as described in [17] it is possible to distinguish between two different methods:

– News content based learning which focuses its attention on the informative content presented in the news article and on the writing style and linguistic pattern in the content.
– Social context based learning focused on studying news propagation and the credibility of news creators and propagators.

Many works study the correlation between fake news detection and the writing style. The work of Jiang et al. [5] uses term frequency, term frequency-inverse, document frequency and embedding techniques to obtain text representation for machine learning and DL models. A similar approach is used by Nikam et al. [12] where Naive Bayes and passive aggressive machine learning algorithms are estimated with TF-IDF feature extraction method. The work of Verma et al. [18] proposes a two-phase benchmark model named WELFake based on word embedding (WE) over linguistic features for fake news detection using machine learning classification. For what concern the research of Devlin et al. [1] and of Kaliyar et al. [6], they base the study on BERT which alleviates the constraint of unidirectionality. Another bidirectional approach is applied by Ghinadya et al. [3] with Bidirectional LSTM (Bi-LSTM). The work of Zhi et al. [20] instead, divided the input of the model into two parts, one is the concatenation of news, market data and sources, the other one is comments.

On the other hand, other studies have focused more on the second approach which take into account even the social context; in the paper of Kaliyar et al. [7] input data is passed using a three-dimensional tensor vector. In this tensor, the engagement between news and user is concatenated with user-community information. Another important work with a similar approach is the one made by Ni et al. [11] which propose a novel neural network model, multi-view attention networks (MVAN), to detect fake news based on the source tweet and its propagation structure. MVAN consists of three components. The first is text semantic attention networks. Its role is to obtain the semantic representation of the source tweet text information. The second is propagation structure attention networks. It captures the hidden information in the propagation structure of a tweet. The last generates the final detection result by concatenating text semantic representation and propagation structure representation. Ramezani et al. [14] propose a work where input features were not only message context and user information but even the message post time.

None of the projects mentioned so far takes into consideration features which come from eventual images attached to the post. Qi et al. [17] proposed the Multi-domain Visual Neural Network (MVNN) model utilizing the visual information in frequency and pixel domains to evaluate whether the given image is a fake-news or real-news image. Li et al. [9] base their study not only on text content features, but even on propagation features, image features, and user features. Another multi-modal approach is the one followed by Zhang et al. [19], in fact they proposed BERT-Based Domain Adaptation Neural Network (BDANN) which comprises three main modules: a multi-modal feature extractor, a domain classifier and a fake news detector. Specifically, the multi-modal feature extractor employs the pretrained BERT model to extract text features and the pretrained VGG-19 model to extract image features. The extracted features are then concatenated and fed to the detector to distinguish fake news. Another multi-modal approach is the one proposed by Zhou et al. [21], they developed a Similarity-Aware FakE news detection method (SAFE) which investigates multi-modal (textual and visual) information of news articles.

In this light, FakeNED adopts a multimodal DL approach to estimate the truth of social media content considering the image, the accompanying text and the text embedded in the picture. It also include a user friendly service for allowing users to quickly evaluate if a shared news on social network is fake or real.

3   Materials and Methods

Within this section, the methodologies used for the development of FakeNED have been reported. Specifically, in the first subsection the entire multimodal

DL approach, which are the key core of FakeNED are described, the second subsection presents the description of the dataset used while the results will be commented in the next section. Besides the analysis and the detection, Fakeddit arranges a service that allows users to easily and effectively recognise the news found. (Section 4). Figure 1 schematically depicts the entire FakeNED workflow.

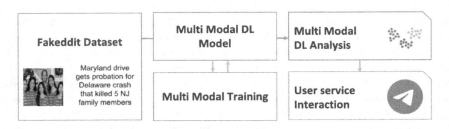

Fig. 1. FakeNED workflow. It comprises three important phases. The data collection and processing, the DL-based analysis and the design of a service for users.

3.1   FakeNED Multimodal Deep Learning Phase

The approach followed in this work is multi-modal (Fig. 2) which means that features extracted come not only from the news text but also from images attached to it. In particular, the multi-modal feature extractor employs the pre-trained BERT model to extract text features and the pretrained VGG-16 model to extract image features. The feature extraction is then followed by an agglomeration phase in which a single one-dimensional tensor is passed to fully connected layers for classification in order to produce the final output.

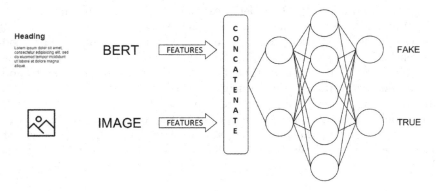

Fig. 2. Representation of the methodology used. The Image block is based on the VGG-16 network.

Firstly, BERT Bidirectional Encoder Representations from Transformers [?] is adopted since it can analyze the whole context of the word by viewing the other words nearby. Its implementation is composed of two steps: pre-training and fine-tuning. One of the fundamental parts of BERT is composed of the transformers which are in turn composed by:

- Encoder made up of 6 layers each, made up in turn of 2 substrates: a self-attention layer and a fully connected layer.
- Decoder: made up of 6 layers each, made up in turn of 2 substrates: also composed of 6 layers, each consisting of 3 substrates: the first two identical to the encoder while the third one is used for normalization of the output.
- Multi-head attention: this block constitutes the substantial difference with respect to the structures previously used. It allows the model to fetch information from different representations inserted in different positions.

There are two dimensions of BERT (base and large) and the one chosen for this work consists of 12 layers, 768 hidden layers and 12 self-attention, with a total number of parameters equal to 110M.

VGG16 [15] is the Convolutional Neural Network used in our work in order to classify images. During training, great importance must be given to the initialization of the weights, in fact, bad initialization can lead to instability and blocking of the training itself. In this regard, a fairly superficial configuration was used, so it can be subsequently trained with a random initialization, which has been carried out to the first four layers and to the last three layers completely connected to the network. On these levels the learning rate was not changed, this allows them to be able to change the weights during the same. Finally, to increase the training set, some images have been randomly cropped and rotated.

ViT. The Vision Transformer is it is based on the same idea and architecture as BERT for NLP [2]. It extracts patches from the input image and makes use of positional embedding. It also applies the attention mechanism to extract features from images. The feature that distinguishes the transformers from the classic convolutional networks is the need for a very high amount of data to be towed, in fact the architecture used here has been pretrained on ImageNet-21K which includes about 14M of images. The request for such a large amount of data allows the transformer to generalize the extraction of the features and therefore, precisely for the extraction tasks they do not need to be towed or fine-tuned but can be used directly for the extraction task and that is why tasks that are used within the workflow.

3.2 Fakeddit Dataset

DL is an efficient way to develop automatic fake news detection. Furthermore, since our approach was not only based on the analysis of the text, but also on the feature extraction from images attached on posts, another fundamental element to solve this issue is to use a good dataset. For this reason, we have decided to use Fakeddit. As described in paper [10], it is a dataset consisting of samples from multiple categories of fake news which comes from Reddit, one of the top 20 website in the world by traffic. In this social news and discussion website, users can post submissions about different areas of interest, called subreddits, which have their own theme. Specifically, Fakeddit includes over 1 million submissions belonging to 22 different subreddits guaranteeing a variation on the contents. In fact, collecting submissions from different subreddits give us the possibility to consider a very wide range from a thematic point of view, from political news to everyday posts. These submissions have been published by approximately 300,000 different users over a period of approximately 10 years. Furthermore, users have the possibility to vote positively, negatively or to comment on submissions.

We collected these submissions through API pushshift and various processing levels have been defined to ensure that the data was correct and pertinent to the topic covered in the subreddits.

Firstly, there are the Reddit moderators themselves who regulate the flow of posts within the various channels. We then continue with the analysis of the individual submissions, focusing above all on the number of positive and negative votes. In fact, a particular element is considered off topic if it receives a number of positive votes far lower than the number of negative votes. Specifically, the popularity of Reddit has allowed this level to be particularly efficient. Finally, 10 elements are randomly analyzed to verify the success of the previous processes.

The fact of having considered such a large number of users and the fact of having data relating to the last decade has allowed DL models to be able to elaborate a modern language and perspectives, fundamental for the correct execution of the task. At the end of this analysis, all numbers, punctuation marks and words that refer directly to a particular Reddit theme are removed.

Here are some examples taken from the dataset:

As showed in the Table 1 there are some examples in the dataset that do not have an image attached, these samples are discarded for the present work. After this pre-processing of the dataset we have obtained a dataset composed by 628262 rows, where: 57853 are dedicated to the test, 57906 are dedicated to the validation set and 512503 are used for the training set.

4   Results and Discussions

In this section, the results of our experiments are reported. The training and the test are carried out with NVIDIA RTX 2080Ti GPU that has 11GB of V-RAM. Specifically, the confusion matrix in Fig. 3 and the results related to the validation and testing phases were reported together with the related graphs.

The confusion matrix shows us the predictions on the columns and the real status on the rows. In this way, it is easy to compute:

Table 1. Example of a few lines from Fakeddit

User	Title	Code	Image presence	Image	Number of comments
Avrata27	This leaf in the shape of an upvote-downvote	1560608711.0	True	q3kyrhxe5j431.jpg	22
	This flower in my neighbor-hood	1557764025.0	False		17
massivecoiler	They phoned me with shocking news	1537557926.0	True	vd77x3li7nn11.jpg	15

- True Positives (TP): these are the cases in which the machine has correctly labeled the actually positive data ("news"). In the test they constitute 61% of cases.
- True Negatives (TN): are all those values that the machine identifies as false ("fake news") as they actually are. In the test they represent 27% of cases.
- False Positives (FP): cases in which the machine has identified the data as news but this is actually fake news. In the test they represent 0.069 % of cases.
- False Negatives (FN): cases where the news was predicted as fake news by the machine. In the test they represent 12 % of cases.

Continuing with the analysis of the results, we therefore analyzed the value of accuracy, defined by considering the number of positive predictions by the model with respect to the total. Specifically, the accuracy obtained in the test phase was equal to 87.79 %, while the value of F1 score was 91 %. These results indicate that FakeNED outperform the state-of-art models. In fact, by considering the performances of the SAFE model [21], it is possible to deduce that its results are lower than those obtained with FakeNED. SAFE reached an accuracy value of about 87.4 % with an F1 score of 89.6 %. In addition, even the values obtained with BDANN model [19] are lower than those obtained with FakeNED.

For what concern the difference between predicted values and actual ones, we have obtained a value of Test Loss equal to 0,5794.

In Figs. 4a and 4b validation accuracy and validation loss are reported. As expected, the first increases with increasing epochs, the latter decreases as the epochs increase.

Considering the multimodal approach chosen for this work, the results demonstrate the suitability and the effectiveness of the proposed method.

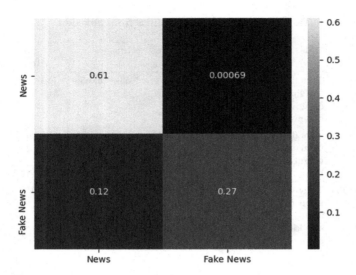

Fig. 3. Confusion matrix

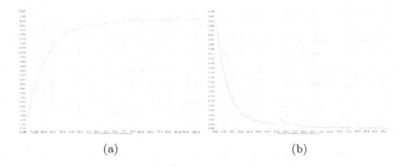

(a)   (b)

Fig. 4. Validation accuracy 4a and loss 4b

4.1   User Service Interaction

Thanks to the model obtained through training on Fakeddit, it was possible to create a service based on a bot and accessible at the following link `t.me/IsFakeNewsBot`. This bot, as showed in the Fig. 5 is based on the input of an image accompanied by a caption that can be shared via telegram. The image represents the visual content linked to the news and the caption will contain the title of the news. Once this data has been received, it will be separated, preprocessed to obtain model input and finally analysed by the model. The output of the model will be processed to obtain the string that will be shared to the user through a standard telegram response message.

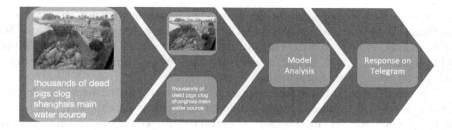

Fig. 5. The workflow of the execution of the bot that give access to the service.

The results inherent to a fake news and a real news are shown in Fig. 6

(a)   (b)

Fig. 6. Example of the result obtained by the user service interaction

5   Conclusions and Future Works

Starting from the problem of Fake News detection, we implemented DL approaches in order to solve problems related to the dissemination of news. In particular, through the use of BERT and Covolutional Neural Networks, as much information as possible was extracted and processed from the elements of the dataset, Fakeddit, entirely made up of Reddit posts composed of images and text.

All this was carried out with the aim of distinguishing, in the most correct way possible, fake news compared to actually true news. Our experimental analysis, built on top of the bidirectional transformers, shows that the approach used for the detection of fake news turns out to be more efficient than state-of-the-art techniques. In fact, as reported in Sect. 4, the accuracy produced in the test phase testifies how the model developed is effective and reliable for filtering news.

In a future work, a wider dataset and a greater diversification of the elements treated would allow the model to learn other fields of information than the one treated. Furthermore, another improvement could be obtained by analyzing the figure of the author who writes the article. In a future work, thanks to the functions associated with the various social accounts, it could be possible to implement an index, based on user behavior, which influences the model's decision on whether or not the news is true.

The service available for the users can be improved in the future by implementing a system to analyse the content of web pages. In this way, the information needed for the model can be extracted directly from the links. This improvement can be also add for the model, it would be useful to use more images as visual input linked to the news. Thus, the model will be modified considering the input linked to the news.

References

1. Devlin, J., Chang, M., Lee, K., Toutanova, K.: BERT: pre-training of deep bidirectional transformers for language understanding (2018). CoRR abs/1810.04805, http://arxiv.org/abs/1810.04805
2. Dosovitskiy, A., et al.: An image is worth 16x16 words: transformers for image recognition at scale (2020). arXiv preprint arXiv:2010.11929
3. Ghinadya, Suyanto, S.: Synonyms-based augmentation to improve fake news detection using bidirectional LSTM. In: 2020 8th International Conference on Information and Communication Technology (ICoICT), pp. 1–5 (2020). https://doi.org/10.1109/ICoICT49345.2020.9166230
4. Islam, M.R., Liu, S., Wang, X., Xu, G.: Deep learning for misinformation detection on online social networks: a survey and new perspectives. Soc. Netw. Anal. Min. **10**(1), 1–20 (2020). https://doi.org/10.1007/s13278-020-00696-x
5. Jiang, T., Li, J.P., Haq, A.U., Saboor, A., Ali, A.: A novel stacking approach for accurate detection of fake news. IEEE Access **9**, 22626–22639 (2021). https://doi.org/10.1109/ACCESS.2021.3056079
6. Kaliyar, R.K., Goswami, A., Narang, P.: FakeBERT: fake news detection in social media with a BERT-based deep learning approach. Multimedia Tools Appl. **80**(8), 11765–11788 (2021). https://doi.org/10.1007/s11042-020-10183-2
7. Kaliyar, R.K., et al.: Deepnet: An efficient neural network for fake news detection using news-user engagements. In: 2020 5th International Conference on Computing, Communication and Security (ICCCS), pp. 1–6 (2020). https://doi.org/10.1109/ICCCS49678.2020.9277353
8. Kesarwani, A., Chauhan, S.S., Nair, A.R.: Fake news detection on social media using k-nearest neighbor classifier. In: 2020 International Conference on Advances in Computing and Communication Engineering (ICACCE), pp. 1–4 (2020). https://doi.org/10.1109/ICACCE49060.2020.9154997
9. Li, D., Guo, H., Wang, Z., Zheng, Z.: Unsupervised fake news detection based on autoencoder. IEEE Access **9**, 29356–29365 (2021). https://doi.org/10.1109/ACCESS.2021.3058809
10. Nakamura, K., Levy, S., Wang, W.Y.: Fakeddit: a new multimodal benchmark dataset for fine-grained fake news detection (2020). arXiv preprint arXiv:1911.03854
11. Ni, S., Li, J., Kao, H.Y.: Mvan: multi-view attention networks for fake news detection on social media. IEEE Access **9**, 106907–106917 (2021). https://doi.org/10.1109/ACCESS.2021.3100245

12. Nikam, S.S., Dalvi, R.: Machine learning algorithm based model for classification of fake news on twitter. In: 2020 Fourth International Conference on I-SMAC (IoT in Social, Mobile, Analytics and Cloud) (I-SMAC), pp. 1–4 (2020). https://doi.org/10.1109/I-SMAC49090.2020.9243385

13. Prelog, L., Bakić-Tomić, L.: The perception of the fake news phenomenon on the internet by members of generation z. In: 2020 43rd International Convention on Information, Communication and Electronic Technology (MIPRO), pp. 452–455 (2020). https://doi.org/10.23919/MIPRO48935.2020.9245169

14. Ramezani, M., Rafiei, M., Omranpour, S., Rabiee, H.R.: News labeling as early as possible. In: Proceedings of the 2019 IEEE/ACM International Conference on Advances in Social Networks Analysis and Mining (Aug 2019). DOI: https://doi.org/10.1145/3341161.3342957

15. Simonyan, K., Zisserman, A.: Very deep convolutional networks for large-scale image recognition. arXiv 1409.1556 (09 2014)

16. Snell, N., Fleck, W., Traylor, T., Straub, J.: Manually classified real and fake news articles. In: 2019 International Conference on Computational Science and Computational Intelligence (CSCI), pp. 1405–1407 (2019). https://doi.org/10.1109/CSCI49370.2019.00262

17. Uppal, A., Sachdeva, V., Sharma, S.: Fake news detection using discourse segment structure analysis, pp. 751–756 (01 2020). https://doi.org/10.1109/Confluence47617.2020.9058106

18. Verma, P., Agrawal, P., Amorim, I., Prodan, R.: Welfake: Word embedding over linguistic features for fake news detection. In: IEEE Transactions on Computational Social Systems, PP. 1–13 (04 2021). https://doi.org/10.1109/TCSS.2021.3068519

19. Zhang, T., et al.: BDANN: BERT-based domain adaptation neural network for multi-modal fake news detection. In: 2020 International Joint Conference on Neural Networks (IJCNN), pp. 1–8 (2020). https://doi.org/10.1109/IJCNN48605.2020.9206973

20. Zhi, X., et al.: Financial fake news detection with multi fact CNN-LSTM model. In: 2021 IEEE 4th International Conference on Electronics Technology (ICET), pp. 1338–1341 (2021). https://doi.org/10.1109/ICET51757.2021.9450924

21. Zhou, X., Wu, J., Zafarani, R.: SAFE: similarity-aware multi-modal fake news detection (2020). CoRR abs/2003.04981, https://arxiv.org/abs/2003.04981

Artificial Intelligence and Radiomics in Computer-Aided Diagnosis - AIRCAD

Radiomics Analyses of Schwannomas in the Head and Neck: A Preliminary Analysis

Giuseppe Cutaia[1,2] , Rosalia Gargano[3], Roberto Cannella[1,2] , Nicoletta Feo[1],
Antonio Greco[1], Giuseppe Merennino[1], Nicola Nicastro[4], Albert Comelli[5(✉)] ,
Viviana Benfante[5,6] , Giuseppe Salvaggio[1] , and Antonio Lo Casto[1]

[1] Section of Radiology - Department of Biomedicine, Neuroscience and Advanced Diagnostics
(Bi.N.D.), University Hospital "Paolo Giaccone", Via del Vespro 129, 90127 Palermo, Italy
[2] Section of Gastroenterology & Hepatology, Department of Health Promotion, Mother and
Child Care, Internal Medicine and Medical Specialties, PROMISE, University of Palermo,
90127 Palermo, Italy
[3] Department of Biomedicine, Neurosciences and Advanced Diagnostic (Bi.N.D.),
Otorhinolaryngology Section, University of Palermo, Palermo, Italy
[4] Servizio Di Diagnostica Per Immagini, La Maddalena S.P.A, via San Lorenzo Colli 312/D,
90146 Palermo, Italy
[5] Ri.MED Foundation, Via Bandiera 11, 90133 Palermo, Italy
acomelli@fondazionerimed.com
[6] Department of Health Promotion, Mother and Child Care, Internal Medicine and Medical
Specialties, Molecular and Clinical Medicine, University of Palermo, 90127 Palermo, Italy

Abstract. The purpose of this preliminary study was to evaluate the differences
in Magnetic Resonance Imaging (MRI)-based radiomics analysis between cerebellopontine angle neurinomas and schwannomas originating from other locations
in the neck spaces. Twenty-six patients with available MRI exams and head and
neck schwannomas were included. Lesions were manually segmented on the precontrast and postcontrast T1 sequences. The radiomics features were extracted by
using PyRadiomics software, and a total of 120 radiomics features were obtained
from each segmented tumor volume. An operator-independent hybrid descriptive-
inferential method was adopted for the selection and reduction of the features,
while discriminant analysis was used to construct the predictive model. On precontrast T1 images, the original_glcm_InverseVariance demonstrated a good performance with an area under the receiver operating characteristic (AUROC) of
0.756 (95% C.I. 0.532–0.979; p = 0.026). On postcontrast T1 images, the orig-
inal_glcm_Idmn provided a good diagnostic performance with an AUROC of
0.779 (95% C.I. 0.572–0.987; p = 0.014). In conclusion, this preliminary analysis
showed statistically significant differences in radiomics features between cerebellopontine angle neurinomas and schwannomas of other locations in the neck
spaces.

Keywords: Magnetic resonance imaging · Head and neck cancer · Texture
analysis · Radiomics

© The Author(s), under exclusive license to Springer Nature Switzerland AG 2022
P. L. Mazzeo et al. (Eds.): ICIAP 2022 Workshops, LNCS 13373, pp. 317–325, 2022.
https://doi.org/10.1007/978-3-031-13321-3_28

1 Introduction

Schwannomas, also known as neurinomas, are rare tumors originating from the Schwann cells, which are frequently benign, with a low risk of malignant degeneration [1]. About 25–45% of schwannomas originate in the head and neck spaces, with the most common location being the carotid space [1]. Intracranial schwannomas originate from the cranial nerves, with the vestibulocochlear nerve being the most common involved nerve.

Magnetic resonance imaging (MRI) is the most accurate noninvasive imaging technique for the assessment of head and neck schwannomas [2]. Due to its high contrast resolution, MRI provides a high accuracy for the staging and preoperative differential diagnosis of head and neck schwannomas [2]. These lesions are characterized by the hyperintensity on T2 images, hypointensity on T1 sequences and enhancement after contrast agent administration. However, the characterization of schwannomas may be affected by the radiologists' experience and may vary according to the different origins from the and neck spaces.

Radiomics represent a new frontier of advances image analysis, allowing the extraction of a large number of quantitative features from radiological images that cannot be assesses by human eyes [3]. Radiomics has been largely applied in the oncologic patients, providing promising results for the differential diagnosis of focal lesions and correlation with histopathological characteristics of tumor aggressiveness, prediction treatment response after locoregional or systemic therapies, and prediction of prognosis in patients undergoing complete surgical resection [4–7]. In the head and neck region, radiomics has been applied for the characterization of salivary gland tumors and oral cavity cancers [8, 9]. Radiomics applications in benign lesions are scant, especially in the head and neck tumors [10–12].

The purpose of this preliminary study was to evaluate differences in MRI-based radiomics features between cerebellopontine angle neurinomas and schwannomas originating from other locations in the neck spaces.

2 Materials and Methods

This retrospective study was approved by the local IRB with a waiver for informed consent due to its retrospective design.

2.1 Population

Between January 2017 and September 2021, 856 consecutive patients were referred to our radiological Department to perform an MRI exam of the head and neck. The MRI exams were acquired for at least one of the following clinical indications: (a) diagnostic workup in a patient with a palpable neck mass; (b) study in patients with head and neck injuries; (c) follow-up in patients with known and untreated head and neck pathology; (d) follow-up in patients with a history of head and neck cancer undergoing radiotherapy and/or surgery. The following patients were excluded from the study: (a) patients with incomplete examinations; (b) patients with reported allergic reactions to the contrast agent; (c) patients treated with radiotherapy and/or surgery; (d) patients without lesions on MRI diagnosed as schwannomas. Our final population consisted of 26 patients (14 men and 12 women), age range 51 to 88 years (mean age: 67.5 ± 7.6 years).

2.2 MRI Technique

All patients underwent preoperative MRI examinations using the same clinical 1.5-T MRI system (Achieva, Philips, Amsterdam, Netherlands) with a dedicated head and neck coil. The standard MRI protocol includes axial and coronal T1 and T2 turbo spin-echo sequences, sagittal T1 sequence, 3D T2 sequence, and the following sequences after injection of contrast agent: 3D T1 ultrafast spoiled gradient echo sequence, axial and coronal spectral presaturation with inversion recovery (SPIR) and axial turbo spin-echo T1 sequences. The precontrast and postcontrast T1 sequences were acquired with the following scanning parameters: repletion time (TR), 500 ms; echo time (TE), 8 ms; flip angle, 69°, slice thickness of 3 mm. A weighted-based dose of 0.1 ml/Kg mmol/Kg of gatobenate dimeglumine or gadoteridol (Multihance or Prohance, Bracco Imaging Italia srl, Milan, Italy) were administered followed by 20-mL saline flush at the same injection rate, using an automatic injector (Medrad Spectris Solaris EP MR Injection System, Bayer Healthcare, Berlin, Germany).

2.3 Qualitative Imaging Analysis

A board-certified radiologist with thirty years of experience in the head and neck imaging assessed the lesions in an independent workstation using Horos software (https://www.horosproject.org/). The radiologist was blinded to the patients' clinical characteristics. The qualitative analysis of the tumors included the assessment of morphological and signal intensity characteristics.

2.4 Segmentation and Radiomics Features Extraction

Manual segmentation of schwannomas and neurinomas was performed by a radiologist with 5 years of experience on MRI, blinded to the patients' clinical information. Each MRI exam was imported into an open source DICOM viewer (Horos, https://www.horosproject.org/). The contours of the lesions were manually traced within the lesion margins including the whole tumor visible on consecutive slices on the precontrast and postcontrast T1 sequences in the axial plane, using a contouring tool (closed polygon). Example of lesion segmentation is provided in the Fig. 1.

The radiomics parameters were extracted by using PyRadiomics (3.0) software [13], which automatically obtained a total of 120 radiomics features from each segmented tumor volume, including first order texture features (which provide information related to the distribution of the gray level within the ROI, without considering the spatial relationships between the voxels), second order (which take into account the spatial relationships between the voxels), and third order features (evaluating the spatial relationship between three or more voxels). The texture parameters were obtained from the histogram analysis of the gray levels (e.g. mean, variance, asymmetry, kurtosis, and percentiles), the co-occurrence matrix was calculated in five measurements (e.g. contrast, correlation, sum of squares, inverse difference moment [IDM], sum average, sum variance, sum entropy, difference variance, difference entropy), while the run-length matrix was calculated in four directions (eg run length nonuniformity [RLN], gray-level nonuniformity normalized [GLNN], long run emphasis [LRE], short run emphasis [SRE]). The detailed description of the radiomics parameters is available in the online manual of PyRadiomics [13].

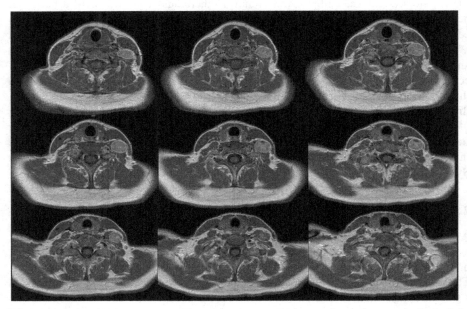

Fig. 1. Example of lesion segmentation on postcontrast T1 images in a schwannoma in the left paravertebral space of the neck.

2.5 Computational and Statistical Analyses

Computational analysis of radiomics features was conducted by a senior scientist in biomedical imaging (with 9 years of experience on image and data processing and analysis). The analyzed lesions were grouped into cerebellopontine angle neurinomas and schwannomas originating in other the neck spaces.

An operator-independent statistical hybrid method was adopted for the selection and reduction of features, while discriminant analysis was used to construct the predictive model. To identify the most discriminant features and reduce redundancy of radiomics features with high correlation, a new descriptive-inferential mixed sequential approach was used [14]. Particularly, for each feature, the point-biserial correlation coefficient between features and dichotomous variable was calculated assuming a value of 1 or 0 for the reference standard. Subsequently, the features were sorted in descending order based on the absolute value of the point-biserial correlation coefficient. Then, a cycle began to add one column at a time performing a logistic regression analysis. Next, the p-value of the current iteration was compared to the p-value of the previous iteration. The loop stopped when the p-value of the current iteration did not decrease from the previous iteration. In this way, the most discriminating features were identified [15].

The discriminant analysis was used to create a predictive model in our dataset. We trained the discriminant analysis with the most discriminant features to evaluated differences between cerebellopontine angle neurinomas and schwannomas in other neck spaces. The training activity had to be performed only one time and, once completed, the discriminant analysis was able to classify the newly encountered radiomics texture. To generate the formative input for the classifier, the results of the expert radiologist's assessment were used as gold standard. In our study, the k-fold (with k = 5 [16]) strategy was used to split data into training and validation sets. In this way, the studies were divided into k-folds. One of the folds was used as the validation set and the remaining folds were combined in the training set. This process was repeated k-times using each fold as the validation set and the other remaining sets as the training set. To ensure disjointed validation sets, the leave-one-out approach was not adopted. In this way, more robust results can be obtained in implementing the classification model [17]. Receiver operating characteristics (ROC) with 95% confidence intervals (95% CI) and areas under the ROC curve (AUROC) were calculated to evaluate the diagnostic performance of the most discriminating selected parameters on precontrast and postcontrast T1 images. Sensitivity, specificity, and accuracy were calculated. The system used to provide the proposed computational statistical analysis was implemented in the Matlab R2019a simulation environment (MathWorks, Natick, MA, USA), running on an Intel Core i7 3.5 GHz, 16 GB iMac computer 1600 DDR3 MHz memory and OS X El Capitan.

3   Results

3.1   Population

The final population included 26 patients. The characteristics of the study population are reported in Table 1. Twelve patients (46.2%, mean age of 61 ± 16 years) had cerebellopontine angle neurinomas (median diameter of 15 mm, interquartile range of 13–18 mm), while the other 14 patients (53.8%, mean age of 57 ± 18 years) had schwannomas of the head and neck (median diameter of 18 mm; interquartile range of 14–25 mm). In the neck, the lesions' location included the carotid space (n = 6), the prevertebral space (n = 3), the posterior cervical space (n = 2), the buccal space (n = 2), and the parapharyngeal space (n = 1). Imaging examples of lesions included in the study population are illustrated in Fig. 2 and Fig. 3.

Table 1. Characteristics of the study population.

Characteristics	Number (%)
Sex	14 (53.8%)
Males	12 (46.2%)
Females	
Age (years)	67.5 ± 7.6
Location	12 (46.2%)
Cerebellopontine angle	14 (53.8%)
Neck spaces	

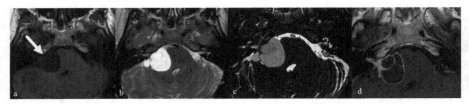

Fig. 2. MRI of a cystic neurinoma of the right cerebellopontine angle on T1 (a), T2 (b), FIESTA (c), and postcontrast T1 sequences (d).

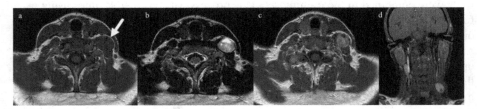

Fig. 3. MRI of a schwannoma of the left prevertebral space on T1 (a), T2 (b) postcontrast T1 sequences (c), and coronal image after contrast agent administration (d).

3.2 Performance of Radiomics

The most discriminative radiomics features with their diagnostic performance are presented in the Table 2.

On precontrast T1 images, the original_glcm_InverseVariance demonstrated a good performance in the differentiation between cerebellopontine angle neurinomas and schwannomas from other neck spaces, with an AUROC of 0.756 (95% C.I. 0.532–0.979; p = 0.026), sensitivity of 98.3%, specificity of 94.0%, and accuracy of 96.0% (Fig. 4).

On postcontrast T1 images, the original_glcm_Idmn provided a good diagnostic performance in the differentiation between cerebellopontine angle neurinomas and schwannomas from other neck spaces, with an AUROC of 0.779 (95% C.I. 0.572–0.987; p = 0.014), sensitivity of 55.6%, specificity of 84.7%, and accuracy of 71.6% (Fig. 5).

Table 2. Selected radiomics features and their performance for the differentiation between cerebellopontine angle neurinomas and schwannomas from other neck spaces.

Feature	Sensitivity	Specificity	Accuracy	AUC (95% CI)	p value
Original glcm InverseVariance	98.3%	94.0%	96.0%	0.756 (0.532–0.979)	0.026
Original glcm Idmn	55.6%	84.7%	71.6%	0.779 (0.571–0.987)	0.014

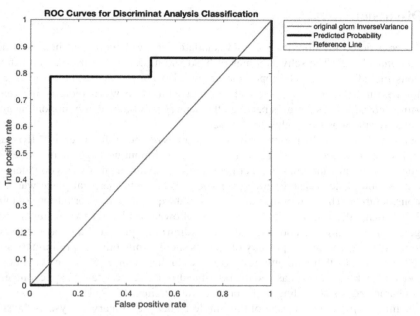

Fig. 4. Receiver operating characteristics curve of original_glcm_InverseVariance on precontrast T1 sequence.

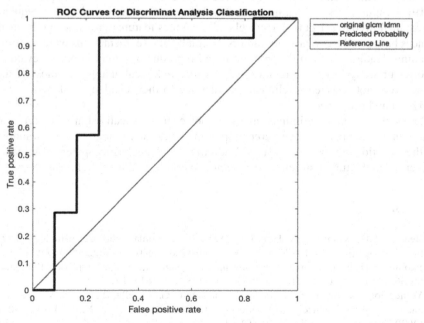

Fig. 5. Receiver operating characteristics curve of original_glcm_Idmn on postcontrast T1 sequence.

4 Discussion

MRI is considered the noninvasive gold standard for the diagnosis of head and neck schwannomas [1, 2]. The schwannomas of head and neck can be observed in different locations including the cerebellopontine angle (also known as vestibular or acoustic neurinomas) and other neck spaces [1, 2]. The aim of this study was to identify differences in texture and radiomics features between the neurinomas of the cerebellopontine angle and the schwannomas from other neck spaces.

Our population of 26 patients allowed to analyze the differences in MRI-based radiomics features between 12 patients with cerebellopontine angle neurinomas and 14 patients with schwannomas in other neck spaces. Texture analysis was conducted on precontrast and postcontrast T1 images. In both cases, only the axial plane was taken into consideration. The extraction and analysis of the quantitative information contained within the manually traced volume of interest allowed to identify two features (original_glcm_InverseVariance and original_glcm_Idmn) that provided a good accuracy to differentiate between the two primary of lesions site. Despite this is a preliminary study with a small sample, there are only few evidences in the literature regarding the imaging of head and neck schwannomas and the possible differences in imaging appearance and tumor characteristics according to the primary tumor site [10–12, 18].

The most important limitation of this single-center preliminary analysis is the small number of included lesions, due to the rarity of the disease in the general population. In addition, since radiomics features can vary greatly in relation to experimental extraction conditions, a study on the robustness of the extracted features should be performed as in [19]. Despite the small sample, our novel descriptive-inferential mixed sequential approach allowed to select two uncorrelated radiomics features showing significant differences between the two primary tumors. Secondly, the segmentations were performed by a single radiologist and the inter-observed reproducibility could not be evaluated. Finally, our study lacked correlation with histopathological analysis as most of these tumors were not resected in clinical practice due to their challenging location in the deep head and neck spaces.

In conclusion, this preliminary analysis showed a statistically significant difference in radiomics features between cerebellopontine angle neurinomas and schwannomas of other locations in the neck spaces. Radiomics analysis has the potential to capture differences in the tumor structure that cannot be established by radiologists' eyes.

References

1. Beaman, F.D., Kransdorf, M.J., Menke, D.M.: Schwannoma: radiologic-pathologic correlation. Radiographics **24**, 1477–1481 (2004). https://doi.org/10.1148/rg.245045001
2. Skolnik, A.D., et al.: Cranial nerve schwannomas: diagnostic imaging approach. Radiographics **36**, 1463–1477 (2016). https://doi.org/10.1148/rg.2016150199
3. Vernuccio, F., Cannella, R., Comelli, A., Salvaggio, G., Lagalla, R., Midiri, M.: Radiomics and artificial intelligence: new frontiers in medicine. Recent. Prog. Med. **111**(3), 130–135 (2020). Italian. https://doi.org/10.1701/3315.32853
4. Cutaia, G., et al.: Radiomics and prostate MRI: current role and future applications. J. Imaging. **7**, 34 (2021). https://doi.org/10.3390/jimaging7020034

5. Giambelluca, D., et al.: PI-RADS 3 lesions: role of prostate mri texture analysis in the identification of prostate cancer. Curr. Probl. Diagn. Radiol. (2019). https://doi.org/10.1067/j.cpr adiol.2019.10.009

6. Stefano, A., Gioè, M., Russo, G., Palmucci, S., Torrisi, S.E., Bignardi, S., Basile, A., Comelli, A., Benfante, V., Sambataro, G., Falsaperla, D., Torcitto, A.G., Attanasio, M., Yezzi, A., Vancheri, C.: Performance of radiomics features in the quantification of idiopathic pulmonary fibrosis from HRCT. Diagnostics **10**(5), 306 (2020) https://doi.org/10.3390/DIAGNOSTICS1 0050306

7. Cannella, R., la Grutta, L., Midiri, M., Bartolotta, T.V.: New advances in radiomics of gastrointestinal stromal tumors. World J. Gastroenterol. **26**, 4729–4738 (2020). https://doi.org/10.3748/WJG.V26.I32.4729

8. Vernuccio, F., Arnone, F., Cannella, R., Verro, B., Comelli, A., Agnello, F., Stefano, A., Gargano, R., Rodolico, V., Salvaggio, G., Lagalla, R., Midiri, M., Lo Casto, A.: Diagnostic performance of qualitative and radiomics approach to parotid gland tumors: which is the added benefit of texture analysis?. Br. J. Radiol. **94**(1128) (2021). https://doi.org/10.1259/bjr.20210340

9. Yu, B., et al.: Prediction of the degree of pathological differentiation in tongue squamous cell carcinoma based on radiomics analysis of magnetic resonance images. BMC Oral Health **21**, 1 (2021). https://doi.org/10.1186/s12903-021-01947-9

10. Langenhuizen, P.P.J.H., et al.: Radiomics-based prediction of long-term treatment response of vestibular schwannomas following stereotactic radiosurgery. Otol. Neurotol. **41**, e1321–e1327 (2020). https://doi.org/10.1097/MAO.0000000000002886

11. Chen, L., et al.: MRI-based radiomics for differentiating orbital cavernous hemangioma and orbital schwannoma. Front. Med. **8**, 2679 (2021). https://doi.org/10.3389/fmed.2021.795038

12. Zhang, M., et al.: Machine learning approach to differentiation of peripheral schwannomas and neurofibromas: a multi-center study. Neuro. Oncol. (2021). https://doi.org/10.1093/neu onc/noab211

13. Van Griethuysen, J.J.M., et al.: Computational radiomics system to decode the radiographic phenotype. Cancer Res. **77**, e104–e107 (2017). https://doi.org/10.1158/0008-5472.CAN-17-0339

14. Barone, S., et al.: Hybrid descriptive-inferential method for key feature selection in prostate cancer radiomics. Appl. Stoch. Model. Bus. Ind. **37**, 961–972 (2021). https://doi.org/10.1002/asmb.2642

15. Alongi, P., et al.: Radiomics analysis of 18F-Choline PET/CT in the prediction of disease outcome in high-risk prostate cancer: an explorative study on machine learning feature classification in 94 patients. Eur. Radiol. **31**(7), 4595–4605 (2021). https://doi.org/10.1007/s00 330-020-07617-8

16. Stefano, A., Comelli, A.: Customized efficient neural network for covid-19 infected region identification in ct images. J. Imaging. **7**, 131 (2021). https://doi.org/10.3390/jimaging7 080131

17. Russo, G., et al.: Feasibility on the use of radiomics features of 11[C]-MET PET/CT in central nervous system tumours: Preliminary results on potential grading discrimination using a machine learning model. Curr. Oncol. **28**, 5318–5331 (2021). https://doi.org/10.3390/cur roncol28060444

18. George-Jones, N.A., Chkheidze, R., Moore, S., Wang, J., Hunter, J.B.: MRI texture features are associated with vestibular schwannoma histology. Laryngoscope. **131**, E2000–E2006 (2021). https://doi.org/10.1002/lary.29309

19. Stefano, A., et al.: Robustness of pet radiomics features: impact of co-registration with mri. Appl. Sci. **11**, 10170 (2021). https://doi.org/10.3390/app112110170

A Shallow Learning Investigation for COVID-19 Classification

Luca Zedda, Andrea Loddo$^{(\boxtimes)}$, and Cecilia Di Ruberto

Department of Mathematics and Computer Science, University of Cagliari, Cagliari, Italy
l.zedda12@studenti.unica.it, {andrea.loddo,dirubert}@unica.it

Abstract. COVID-19, an infectious coronavirus disease, triggered a pandemic that resulted in countless deaths. Since its inception, clinical institutions have used computed tomography as a supplemental screening method to reverse transcription-polymerase chain reaction. Deep learning approaches have shown promising results in addressing the problem; however, less computationally expensive techniques, such as those based on handcrafted descriptors and shallow classifiers, may be equally capable of detecting COVID-19 based on medical images of patients. This work proposes an initial investigation of several handcrafted descriptors well known in the computer vision literature already been exploited for similar tasks. The goal is to discriminate tomographic images belonging to three classes, COVID-19, pneumonia, and normal conditions, and present in a large public dataset. The results show that kNN and ensembles trained with texture descriptors achieve outstanding accuracy in this task, reaching accuracy and F-measure of 93.05% and 89.63%, respectively. Although it did not exceed state of the art, it achieved satisfactory performance with only 36 features, enabling the potential to achieve remarkable improvements from a computational complexity perspective.

Keywords: Computer vision · Shallow learning · Image processing · COVID-19 detection · Texture features · CT scan images

1 Introduction

COVID-19 is a disease caused by the SARS-CoV-2 virus, declared a pandemic by the World Health Organisation on 11 March 2020. At the time of writing, COVID-19 has more than 458 million confirmed cases and has caused more than six million deaths [24]. The infection starts in the throat's mucous membranes and spreads to the lungs through the respiratory tract. COVID-19 is a highly contagious disease; therefore, rapid screening is essential for timely diagnosis and treatment. Diagnosis of COVID-19 infection by imaging-based methods has been reported to give accurate results, both for screening and quantifying the amount of damage [7]. At the same time, attempts are being made to develop rapid diagnostic techniques for detecting COVID-19 using chest X-ray (CXR)

© The Author(s), under exclusive license to Springer Nature Switzerland AG 2022
P. L. Mazzeo et al. (Eds.): ICIAP 2022 Workshops, LNCS 13373, pp. 326–337, 2022.
https://doi.org/10.1007/978-3-031-13321-3_29

and chest computed tomography (CT) images that radiologists frequently analyze. Like many other types, manual diagnosis of COVID-19 is time-consuming, prone to human error, and requires the help of a competent radiologist. The presence of an experienced radiologist is also necessary because abnormalities in the early stages of COVID-19 may resemble other lung diseases such as severe acute respiratory syndrome (SARS) or viral pneumonia (VP), which may delay the diagnosis and treatment of COVID.

In particular, CXR is the most easily accessible and fastest form of imaging with the fewest side effects on the human body. CXR imaging has traditionally been used for the detection of pneumonia and cancer. Although it can detect COVID-19 infection, it fails to provide fine-order details of infected lungs. CT is a more sophisticated technique for assessing is used to evaluate the level of infection. CXR imaging can be used to detect COVID-19; however, to assess the level of severity of infection, a CT scan is mandatory [1].

For these reasons, any automated solution designed to diagnose COVID-19 should also consider other respiratory disorders to develop a more comprehensive and robust diagnostic system [28].

In this manuscript, our focus is on computed tomography from a machine and deep learning point of view. CT is a widely explored medical imaging technique that allows non-invasive visualisation of the interior of an object [2,8,15,32,33] and is widely used in many applications, such as medical imaging for clinical purposes [14,18,23,30].

Two CT scans of COVID-19 and non-COVID-19 are shown in fig. 1.

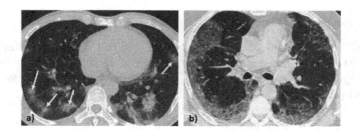

Fig. 1. (a) represents a CT of the lungs of a patient with COVID-19, in which there are traces of ground glass opacity indicated by red arrows. (b) shows a CT of the lungs of a non-COVID-19 patient with diffuse opacity in the outer parts of the lungs. These images are courtesy of [35]. (Color figure online)

The main target of this study is an early investigation regarding the extent to which two types of handcrafted (HC) features can be beneficial for the classification of the CTs of patients. We focus our work on invariant moments and texture features, which are widely employed in the context of MR and CT imaging [26], to train several shallow classifiers.

We performed a three-class classification on the public COVIDx CT-2A dataset, divided explicitly into COVID-19, pneumonia, and healthy cases; we investigated the robustness of the descriptors analyzed through five different machine learning classifiers; we aim to demonstrate how this task can be faced employing HC features, even with low-end devices, for a real-time diagnosis.

Moreover, several works in the context of COVID-19 diagnostics have considered small or private datasets or lacked rigorous experimental methods, potentially leading to overfitting and overestimation of performance [28,29]. For this reason, we carefully selected an extended dataset composed of multi-source CT images on which to conduct the experiments described. Roberts et al. [28] have recently shown that most of the datasets used in the literature for the diagnosis or prognosis of COVID-19 suffer from duplication and quality problems. It has already been provided with train, validation, and testing splits.

Our proposed approach achieves promising results on COVID-19 identification, although it is only a preliminary analysis that does not consider deep learning methods, for example.

The rest of the manuscript is organized as follows. section 2 illustrates the dataset, our approach, and the setup. In Sect. 3 the experimental results are given and discussed. Finally, in Sect. 4 we draw the findings and directions for future works.

2   Materials and Methods

A publicly available dataset has been used in this study, as detailed in Sect. 2.1, while the evaluation metrics are described in Sect. 2.4.

2.1   Dataset: COVIDx CT-2A

COVIDx CT-2A [9] is an open-access dataset. At the time of writing, it consisted of 194,922 CT images of 3745 patients from 15 different countries, aged 0–93 years (median age 51), belonging to a particular class clinically verified by experienced pathologists.

Specifically, the classes are COVID-19, indicating CT images of COVID-19 positive patients, pneumonia, and patients in a normal condition.

The countries involved are part of a multinational cohort that consists of patient cases collected by the following organizations and initiatives from around the world:

1. China National Center for Bioinformation (CNCB) [34] (China);
2. National Institutes of Health Intramural Targeted Anti-COVID-19 (ITAC) Program (hosted by TCIA [12], countries unknown);
3. Negin Radiology Medical Center [27] (Iran);
4. Union Hospital and Liyuan Hospital of the Huazhong University of Science and Technology [20] (China);
5. COVID-19 CT Lung and Infection Segmentation initiative annotated and verified by Nanjing Drum Tower Hospital [17] (Iran, Italy, Turkey, Ukraine, Belgium, some countries unknown);

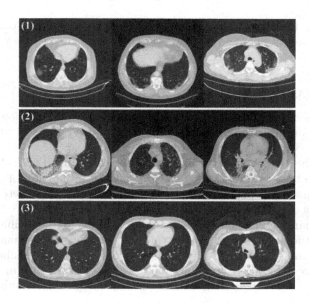

Fig. 2. Sample CT images from the COVIDx CT dataset. From top to bottom, the images in (**1**) represent coronavirus pneumonia due to SARS-CoV-2 infection (NCP), (**2**) are common pneumonia (CP), and (**3**) are healthy lungs. Images are courtesy of [10].

6. Lung Image Database Consortium (LIDC) and Image Database Resource Initiative (IDRI) [4] (countries unknown);
7. Radiopaedia collection [5] (Iran, Italy, Australia, Afghanistan, Scotland, Lebanon, England, Algeria, Peru, Azerbaijan, some countries unknown).

Figure 2 shows some sample images taken from the dataset.

2.2   Feature Extraction

We evaluated two different feature sets: invariant moments and texture features.

The invariant moments computed were the **Hu** [13] and **Zernike** moments. The former are invariant to changes in scale, translation, and rotation, while the latter are orthogonal and represent image properties without redundancy [22]. The order of the Zernike moments is 6, as higher orders would reduce the system's performance by adding features representing irrelevant details or noise [6].

As texture features, the rotationally invariant Gray Level Co-occurrence Matrix (GLCM), as proposed in [25], and the rotationally invariant **LBP** features [21] have been computed. In both cases, we focused on the finest textures, so we computed four GLCMs with $d = 1$ and $\theta = [0°, 45°, 90°, 135°]$ and the LBP map in the neighborhood identified by r and n equal to 1 and 8, respectively. From the GLCMs we extracted 26 features [11] and converted them to the rotationally invariant features Har_{ri} [25]). The LBP map is converted to a rotationally invariant one, and its histogram is used as the feature vector LBP_{ri} [21].

2.3 Shallow Classifiers

The classification algorithms considered in this study were as follows: **kNN** (k-Nearest Neighbors) (kNN), **Decision Tree** (DT), **Naive Bayes** (NB), **Ensemble** (Ens), and **Support Vector Machine** (SVM).

To ensure the heterogeneity of the training set, we trained each classifier with stratified 10-fold cross-validation to ensure that the proportion of positive and negative examples is respected in all folds. For each case, we selected the model with the largest area under the ROC curve (AUC).

The hyperparameters characterizing each classifier were not fine-tuned. Our goal for this study was not to obtain the best absolute performance but only to understand the extent to which the descriptors used were feasible for analysis. Furthermore, several authors have empirically observed that in many cases, the use of tuned parameters cannot significantly exceed the default values of a classifier [3, 31].

However, to make the results reproducible, we specify the values of the hyperparameters chosen. For the kNN classifier, the distance metric adopted was the euclidean, and the number of nearest neighbors is 3, with an inverse squared distance weighting function. For the Decision Tree classifier, the maximum number of splits to control the depth of the trees is 50. The distribution chosen to model the data is normal for the Naive Bayes classifier with a normal kernel. The ensemble classifier was Random Undersampling Boosting (RUSBoost), the students were decision trees. Finally, for the SVM classifier, we used a linear kernel.

2.4 Metrics

The performance measures used to quantify the performance are the accuracy (A), precision (P), specificity (SP), sensitivity (SE), F1-score (F1) as following defined:

$$accuracy = \frac{TP + TN}{TP + TF + FP + FN}, \tag{1}$$

$$precision = \frac{TP}{TP + FP}, \tag{2}$$

$$specificity = \frac{TN}{FP + TN}, \tag{3}$$

$$recall = \frac{TP}{TP + FN}, \tag{4}$$

$$F1 = \frac{2 * precision * recall}{precision + recall} = \frac{2 * TP}{2 * TP + FP + FN}. \tag{5}$$

Accuracy measures the number of correctly labeled items belonging to the positive class divided by the items correctly or incorrectly labeled as belonging to the same class. Specificity measures the proportion of correctly identified negatives (the true negative rate), while sensitivity measures the proportion of correctly identified positives (the true positive rate). The fourth measure is accuracy, defined as the ratio of correctly labeled instances to the entire pool of cases. The last is the F1 score, which conveys the balance between precision and recall.

2.5 Experimental Setup

The images were not preprocessed or augmented because this work is used as a basis for further investigation. We retained the dataset splits provided by the authors and did not use any randomization approach to make the studies repeatable.

In addition, COVIDx CT-2A has already been divided by the authors according to the following percentages: 70%, 20%, and 10% for training, validation, and testing, respectively. For the sake of reproducibility, we left this division unchanged.

Finally, all the experiments have been conducted on a single machine with the following configuration: Intel(R) Core(TM) i9-8950HK @ 2.90GHz CPU with 32 GB RAM and NVIDIA GTX1050 Ti 4GB GPU.

3 Experimental Results and Discussion

Three main results obtained from the experiments are reported. In particular, Fig. 3 and Fig. 4 show the general behavior of the four sets of descriptors with two different metrics, accuracy, and F-measure, respectively. We give a general indication of the descriptors' effectiveness for the task.

Next, we analyze the performance class by class, remembering that the problem is divided into three classes. Figure 5 show the performance of the accuracy and F-measure computed for the best combination of descriptor and classifier.

Figure 4 shows that the configuration based on the kNN classifier trained with LBP features can achieve the highest performance, with 93.05% accuracy and 89.63% F-measure. Overall, it seems clear that texture outperformed the moment features in this scenario, as both HAR and LBP achieved the highest performance with every classifier except SVM.

Although the DT and Ensemble strategies achieved interesting results, kNN seems the most suitable for this task, especially when trained with LBP descriptors, being the only one above 89% on both metrics.

In general, looking at accuracy, there are no distinct performance differences between the texture descriptors to justify one over the other. In the case of SVM, the accuracy achieved with HAR as a descriptor is even higher than LBP.

However, the scenario changes when looking at the results of multiclass classification performance evaluated using both metrics computed for all classes.

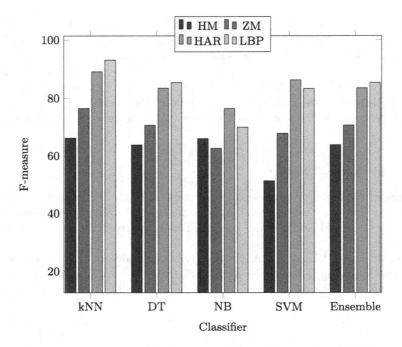

Fig. 3. Accuracy trends with the different classifiers adopted.

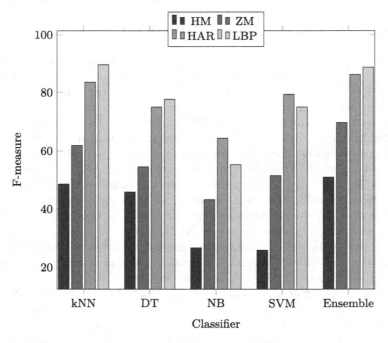

Fig. 4. F-measure trends with the different classifiers adopted.

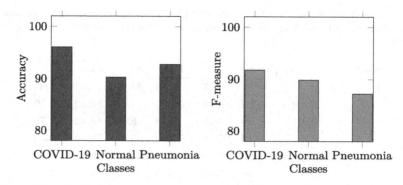

Fig. 5. Classwise F-measure computed from the best model: kNN with LBP features.

In particular, Fig. 4 shows that the F-measure values are generally lower than the accuracy. However, the texture descriptors helped keep the performance high, especially LBP, which reached 89.63% with the kNN classifier.

As a general rule, on the one hand, the results provided by the numerous experiments conducted seem to show that the kNN trained with LBP features can perform the multiclass classification task with performance that outperforms any other combination of descriptors and classifier analyzed. Moreover, as represented by Fig. 5, this solution seems to be the most robust, achieving the highest results in each comparative test.

A final statement concerns the number of features extracted from each descriptor. More specifically, 36 features were extracted from the LBP descriptor, while HAR, ZM, and HM had 26, 10, and 7, respectively. If we consider the number of discriminating features, the results obtained with LBP features can be considered satisfactory in a low-resource environment, even compared to the computational cost of using a CNN, and open the way for possible combinations of heterogeneous features.

The behavior expressed by texture features and LBP, in particular, is due to their high representation power in MR and CT imaging, even for fine-grained analysis [19]. However, the accuracy metric does not represent the detail of the multiclass problem addressed in this work. For this reason, we adopted the F-measure to have a more unambiguous indication of which features are best suited for the task. Figure 4 confirms that, in terms of F-measure, the kNN and ensemble classifiers benefit from texture features in general and LBP in particular, outperforming all the rest.

Furthermore, Table 1 shows the metrics computed with all the classifiers and descriptors. As can be seen, the LBP descriptors are the best and second-best performing, with kNN and ensemble, respectively. It is also notable the result obtained with the same classifiers trained with $HARri$ features, clearly being the second-best descriptor. It must be noted that with only 36 and 26 features, the mentioned classifiers can achieve more than 90% accuracy.

Table 1. Weighted average performance computed using the five different shallow classifiers trained with each of the four descriptors. The best results is in black bold, while red indicates the second-best.

Classifier	Descriptor	Size	A	P	SP	SE	F1
DT	HM	7	63.73	52.56	48.97	74.55	45.85
	HARri	26	83.43	76.06	74.44	86.52	75.10
	LBP	36	85.30	77.48	78.70	88.42	77.75
	ZM	10	70.61	56.50	56.09	78.54	54.54
Naive Bayes	HM	7	65.95	44.52	35.47	68.24	26.71
	HARri	26	76.38	65.39	65.13	81.27	64.37
	LBP	36	69.90	54.80	57.84	77.14	55.33
	ZM	10	62.54	51.44	46.03	73.85	43.26
SVM	HM	7	51.20	27.88	25.63	62.25	25.90
	HARri	26	86.23	79.41	79.80	88.85	79.38
	LBP	36	83.29	74.81	76.14	86.70	75.11
	ZM	10	67.76	53.95	54.33	76.76	51.50
Ensemble	HM	7	67.77	56.66	53.43	77.20	51.00
	HARri	26	90.75	86.15	86.37	92.52	86.25
	LBP	36	92.43	88.57	88.97	93.89	88.75
	ZM	10	81.30	71.10	70.83	86.58	69.77
kNN	HM	7	66.18	52.55	50.45	75.81	48.56
	HARri	26	89.07	83.50	83.66	91.17	83.56
	LBP	36	**93.05**	**89.66**	**89.63**	**94.33**	**89.63**
	ZM	10	76.45	63.87	63.39	82.97	61.89

Table 2. Comparison of this work with the state of the art on COVIDx CT-2A.

Method	Accuracy	N. features
COVID-Net CT-1 [10]	94.5%	>1,000
COVID-Net CT-2 L [10]	98.1%	>1,000
COVID-Net CT-2 S [10]	97.9%	>1,000
Bit-M [36]	99.2%	>1,000
Loddo [16]	98.87%	1,024
This work	93.05%	36

As presented in Table 2, these results cannot outperform the 98.87% accuracy obtained in a previous work that employed only CNNs for the same task [16], and others using deep learning strategies. However, a satisfactory accuracy has been obtained with an enormously smaller quantity of features (only 36 for LBP) compared to that works. It opens the field to further improvements, e.g., with features combination or by using this indicator to realize attention mechanisms to drive CNNs towards the right portions of the images needed to perform a correct diagnosis.

4   Conclusions

In this study, we have investigated the performance of some handcrafted features, invariant moments, and texture for a three-class classification of CT images. In particular, we have performed an early investigation of the feature feasibility for the classification task that involves COVID-19 and pneumonia classes.

This investigation can be considered a novel, rapid and lightweight approach for the diagnosis of COVID-19 to address the problem of faster diagnosis and patient prioritization. It can potentially also confirm the severity. The task is faced with five different shallow classification methods, each one trained with four different categories of handcrafted descriptors.

We worked on a dataset composed of 194,922 images, of which about 19,000 have been exploited in testing the mentioned descriptors. Among all the experiments, the kNN classifier trained with LBP features reached a weighted accuracy of 93.05% and an F-measure of 89.63%, being the best performer. In any case, the texture features generally demonstrated high representative power with both kNN and ensemble strategies.

These results show significant and promising results regarding the state of the art, even though we planned several further investigations. First of all, we aim to propose a system able to combine the potential of CNNs, expressed in [16], with the features presented in this work. To cite some examples, they can be combined, even with the ones extracted from CNNs, or their indicators can even be used to realize attention-based mechanisms to drive CNNs towards the right portions of the images to perform a correct diagnosis. Secondly, we plan to extend this work to generalize it to different diseases and conditions. Finally, we aim to further study these methods to test their robustness across multiple datasets and assess their feasibility in clinical practice.

References

1. Aggarwal, P., Mishra, N.K., Fatimah, B., Singh, P., Gupta, A., Joshi, S.D.: Covid-19 image classification using deep learning: advances, challenges and opportunities. Comput. Biol. Med. **144**, 105350 (2022)
2. Ahmad, M., Ai, D., Xie, G., Qadri, S.F., Song, H., Huang, Y., Wang, Y., Yang, J.: Deep belief network modeling for automatic liver segmentation. IEEE Access **7**, 20585–20595 (2019)
3. Arcuri, A., Fraser, G.: Parameter tuning or default values? an empirical investigation in search-based software engineering. Empir. Softw. Eng. **18**(3), 594–623 (2013)
4. Armato, S.G., III., et al.: The lung image database consortium (lidc) and image database resource initiative (idri): a completed reference database of lung nodules on ct scans. Med. Phys. **38**(2), 915–931 (2011)

5. Bell, D.J.: Covid-19 (2021). https://radiopaedia.org/articles/covid-19-4. Accessed 9 Aug 2021
6. Di Ruberto, C., Putzu, L., Rodriguez, G.: Fast and accurate computation of orthogonal moments for texture analysis. Pattern Recogn. **83**, 498–510 (2018)
7. Fang, Y., et al.: Sensitivity of chest CT for Covid-19: comparison to RT-PCR. Radiology **296**(2), E115–E117 (2020)
8. Furqan Qadri, S., et al.: Automatic deep feature learning via patch-based deep belief network for vertebrae segmentation in CT images. Appl. Sci. **9**(1), 69 (2019)
9. Gunraj, H.: Covid-net open source initiative - Covidx CT-2 dataset (2020). https://www.kaggle.com/hgunraj/covidxct, Accessed 30 June 2021
10. Gunraj, H., Sabri, A., Koff, D., Wong, A.: Covid-net ct-2: enhanced deep neural networks for detection of Covid-19 from chest CT images through bigger, more diverse learning (2021)
11. Haralick, R.M., Shanmugam, K., Dinstein, I.H.: Textural features for image classification. IEEE Trans. Syst. Man Cybern. SMC **3**(6), 610–621 (1973)
12. Harmon, S.A., et al.: Artificial intelligence for the detection of Covid-19 pneumonia on chest CT using multinational datasets. Nat. Commun. **11**(1), 1–7 (2020)
13. Hu, M.K.: Visual pattern recognition by moment invariants. IRE Trans. Inf. Theory **8**(2), 179–187 (1962)
14. Isaac, A., Nehemiah, H.K., Isaac, A., Kannan, A.: Computer-aided diagnosis system for diagnosis of pulmonary emphysema using bio-inspired algorithms. Comput. Biol. Med. **124**, 103940 (2020)
15. Liu, M., Dong, J., Dong, X., Yu, H., Qi, L.: Segmentation of lung nodule in CT images based on mask R-CNN. In: 9th International Conference on Awareness Science and Technology, iCAST 2018, Fukuoka, Japan, September 19–21, 2018, pp. 1–6. IEEE (2018)
16. Loddo, A., Pili, F., Di Ruberto, C.: Deep learning for Covid-19 diagnosis from CT images. Appl. Sci. **11**(17), 8227 (2021)
17. Ma, J., et al.: Towards efficient Covid-19 CT annotation: a benchmark for lung and infection segmentation. arXiv e-prints pp. arXiv-2004 (2020)
18. Ma, L., Liu, X., Gao, Y., Zhao, Y., Zhao, X., Zhou, C.: A new method of content based medical image retrieval and its applications to CT imaging sign retrieval. J. Biomed. Inf. **66**, 148–158 (2017)
19. Maheshwari, S., Sharma, R.R., Kumar, M.: LBP-based information assisted intelligent system for Covid-19 identification. Comput. Biol. Med. **134**, 104453 (2021)
20. Ning, W., et al.: Open resource of clinical data from patients with pneumonia for the prediction of Covid-19 outcomes via deep learning. Nat. Biomed. Eng. **4**(12), 1197–1207 (2020)
21. Ojala, T., Pietikäinen, M., Maempaa, T.: Multiresolution gray-scale and rotation invariant texture classification with local binary pattern. IEEE Trans. Pattern Anal. Mach. Intell. **24**(7), 971–987 (2002)
22. Oujaoura, M., Minaoui, B., Fakir, M.: Image annotation by moments. In: Moments and Moment Invariants - Theory and Applications, vol. 1, pp. 227–252 (2014)
23. Oulefki, A., Agaian, S., Trongtirakul, T., Laouar, A.K.: Automatic Covid-19 lung infected region segmentation and measurement using CT-scans images. Pattern Recogn. **114**, 107747 (2021)
24. University of Oxford: Coronavirus pandemic (Covid-19) - the data (2021). https://ourworldindata.org/coronavirus-data. Accessed 30 June 2021

25. Putzu, L., Di Ruberto, C.: Rotation invariant co-occurrence matrix features. In: Battiato, S., Gallo, G., Schettini, R., Stanco, F. (eds.) ICIAP 2017. LNCS, vol. 10484, pp. 391–401. Springer, Cham (2017). https://doi.org/10.1007/978-3-319-68560-1_35

26. Putzu, L., Loddo, A., Ruberto, C.D.: Invariant moments, textural and deep features for diagnostic MR and CT image retrieval. In: Tsapatsoulis, N., Panayides, A., Theocharides, T., Lanitis, A., Pattichis, C.S., Vento, M. (eds.) Computer Analysis of Images and Patterns - 19th International Conference, CAIP 2021, Virtual Event, September 28–30, 2021, Proceedings, Part I, vol. 13052, pp. 287–297 (2021)

27. Rahimzadeh, M., Attar, A., Sakhaei, S.M.: A fully automated deep learning-based network for detecting Covid-19 from a new and large lung CT scan dataset. Biomed. Signal Process. Control **68**, 102588 (2021)

28. Roberts, M., Driggs, D., Thorpe, M.E.A.: Common pitfalls and recommendations for using machine learning to detect and prognosticate for Covid-19 using chest radiographs and ct scans. Nat. Mach. Intell. **3**, 199–217 (2021)

29. Signoroni, A., et al.: Bs-net: learning Covid-19 pneumonia severity on a large chest x-ray dataset. Med. Image Anal. **71**, 102046 (2021)

30. Sivaranjini, S., Sujatha, C.: Deep learning based diagnosis of Parkinson's disease using convolutional neural network. Multimedia Tools Appl. **79**(21), 15467–15479 (2020)

31. Soda, P., et al.: Aiforcovid: Predicting the clinical outcomes in patients with COVID-19 applying AI to chest-x-rays: an Italian multicentre study. Med. Image Anal. **74**, 102216 (2021)

32. Tu, X., et al.: Automatic categorization and scoring of solid, part-solid and non-solid pulmonary nodules in CT images with convolutional neural network. Sci. Rep. **7**(1), 1–10 (2017)

33. Zhang, B., et al.: Ensemble learners of multiple deep CNNs for pulmonary nodules classification using CT images. IEEE Access **7**, 110358–110371 (2019)

34. Zhang, K., et al.: Clinically applicable AI system for accurate diagnosis, quantitative measurements, and prognosis of Covid-19 pneumonia using computed tomography. Cell **181**(6), 1423–1433 (2020)

35. Zhao, J., Zhang, Y., He, X., Xie, P.: Covid-CT-dataset: a CT scan dataset about Covid-19. arXiv preprint arXiv:2003.13865 (2020)

36. Zhao, W., Jiang, W., Qiu, X.: Deep learning for covid-19 detection based on CT images. Sci. Rep. **11**(1), 1–12 (2021)

Shape Prior Based Myocardial Segmentation with Anatomically Motivated Pose Model

Navdeep Dahiya[1]([✉]) [iD], Marina Piccinelli[2] [iD], Ernest Garcia[2] [iD],
and Anthony Yezzi[1] [iD]

[1] Georgia Institute of Technology, Atlanta, GA 30332, USA
ndahiya3@gatech.edu
[2] Emory University, Atlanta, GA 30322, USA

Abstract. We extend the shape-prior based geometric approach developed for myocardial segmentation in cardiac CT imagery by incorporating minimal user input in the form of anatomical constraints to guide the segmentation process resulting in significantly improved results. The shape-prior based geometric approach involves estimating coefficients of a low-dimensional principal component analysis based shape representation along with a set of rigid 3D pose parameters of three separate surfaces corresponding to left (LV)/right (RV) ventricles and Epicardium (Epi) by optimizing a novel Chan-Vese *like* image appearance model with gradient descent. We enhance this framework by allowing experienced clinical users to identify the centers of the three anatomies in apical slices and a common anatomical cardiac base slice. We integrate this minimal user input as anatomical constraints in the segmentation process by replacing the rigid 3D pose model with a novel blended model which incorporates rigidity only within 2D slices while incorporating nonrigid effects of shear and torsion along the third (axial) dimension. With this new formulation we achieved significantly improved segmentation results in terms of average symmetric surface-to-surface distances (mm): LV 1.05 $\pm$ 0.27; RV 1.7 $\pm$ 0.40; Epi 1.22 $\pm$ 0.56 compared to LV 2.3 $\pm$ 0.50; RV 1.13 $\pm$ 0.21; Epi 3.3 $\pm$ 0.50 with rigid 3D pose model.

Keywords: Cardiac segmentation · Principal component analysis · Shape priors · Anatomical modeling

1 Introduction

In 2015, the American Heart Association (AHA) reported [6] that heart disease is the No. 1 cause of death in the United States, killing nearly 787,000 people in 2011 alone. Among various types of heart diseases, coronary artery disease is the most common, killing nearly 380,000 people annually. Further, the direct and

This work was supported by the National Institutes of Health (NIH) grant number R01-HL-143350.

indirect costs of heart disease total more than \$320 billion. Consequently, early and cost-effective diagnosis of heart diseases is an important requirement for clinical practitioners worldwide. Coronary Computed Tomography Angiography (CCTA), a non-invasive imaging technique, is becoming increasingly popular for cardiac examination, mainly due to its superior spatial resolution compared to magnetic resonance imaging (MRI). This imaging modality is currently widely used for the diagnosis of Coronary Artery Disease (CAD). For the purposes of both routine cardiac diagnosis as well as multimodality image fusion [4,22], segmentation of important cardiac structures such as left (LV)/right (RV) ventricles, myocardium (Myo) and epicardium (Epi) is an important requirement.

Computer vision and image processing deal with the problem of automatically extracting useful information from digital imagery including different medical imaging modalities. There are a plethora of techniques available for various computer vision tasks. Medical imagery, in general, suffers from poor contrast, low signal to noise ratio (SNR), weak or missing edges or smearing of edges due to patient movement. To overcome the shortcomings of the image acquisition process and inherent complexity of the heart anatomy, many different classes of techniques have been proposed over the years to aid diagnosis and prognosis of cardiac diseases in various imaging modalities and data acquisition protocols.

Active Shape and Appearance Models [11–14] based techniques have been very influential in the field of medical image processing, and have been used for both LV and RV segmentation [1,2,19]. Atlas based segmentation is another class of techniques that have become increasingly popular in recent years and now being used for cardiac segmentation as well [23].

Active contour models have been widely used in medical image segmentation because of their flexibility and robustness. [17] proposed a model-based segmenter that incorporated shape information as a prior model to restrict the flow of the geodesic active contour [5,27]. In contrast to these edge-based active contour models which utilize image gradient to stop the evolving contours on the object boundaries, region-based models [7], which minimizes the Mumford-Shah [8,20] energy functional have shown to be more robust to noise and initial placement of contours. These methods are more global in nature and avoid taking image intensity derivatives. In recent years, Deep Learning [3,9,29] based methods have also become quite prominent and successful in variety of computer vision tasks including medical image segmentation.

2   Relationship to Previous Work

In [24] the authors developed a parametric model using pose and shape parameters for segmentation, where they describe the segmenting curve as a linear combination of eigenvectors that are obtained by performing PCA on the variations from the mean shape. [25] and [24] use the Chan-Vese image model which models the image as piece-wise constant function and the evolution of the segmenting curve depends upon the pixel intensities within entire regions. The statistics of entire regions (such as sample mean and variance) are used to direct the movement of the curve toward the boundaries of the image.

More formally, the Chan-Vese energy is defined as:

$$E_{cv} = \int_{R^u} (I - \mu)^2 d\mathbf{x} + \int_{R^v} (I - \nu)^2 d\mathbf{x} \tag{1}$$

where R^u and R^v are the regions inside and outside the segmenting curve. The optimal choice for the constants μ and ν are the region means.

In [15,16] we customized these frameworks for the task of 3D CCTA imagery by introducing several high level constraints and making use of PCA based shape priors for three anatomical regions, LV, RV, and Epi simultaneously. We estimate a set of pose and shape parameters for each segmenting curve via gradient descent procedure to minimize an energy functional designed specifically for the myocardial segmentation task.

In the training phase of this framework, shape prior models comprising of mean shapes and principal modes of shape variation are built for each of the three anatomical regions, LV, RV and Epi. A binary image alignment procedure is first applied to a set of training shapes (expert manual segmentations for LV/RV/Epi) to remove shape difference due to pose variations and then the aligned binary masks were converted to signed distance function (SDF) representations. After image alignment, mean shapes and n *Eigen Shapes* (principal modes of variation) are extracted using a PCA [24] procedure applied to the set of mean offset aligned SDFs corresponding to each of the training shapes.

Using the shape priors, pre-pose shape-prior model is synthesized by adding first k modes to the mean level set function Ψ_{mean} like so:

$$\Psi(w, \mathbf{x}) = \Psi_{mean}(\mathbf{x}) + \sum_{i=1}^{k} w_i u_i(\mathbf{x}) = \Psi_{mean}(\mathbf{x}) + w \cdot U_k(\mathbf{x})$$

where w_i are the weights associated with each of the k eigen-shapes. A set of L pose parameters $p = (p_1, \ldots, p_L)$ are added to define an invertible shape-independent domain transformation $g(p, \mathbf{x})$ (such as translation, rotation, or scaling) which maps any given spatial location $\mathbf{x}$ to $\hat{\mathbf{x}} = g(p, \mathbf{x})$ and whose inverse mapping in turn maps each such location $\hat{\mathbf{x}}$ back to its original location $\mathbf{x} = g^{-1}(p, \hat{\mathbf{x}})$ leading to the following shape prior model:

$$\hat{\Psi}(w, \hat{\mathbf{x}}) = \hat{\Psi}_{mean}(\hat{\mathbf{x}}) + \sum_{i=1}^{k} w_i \hat{u}_i(\hat{\mathbf{x}}) = \hat{\Psi}_{mean}(\hat{\mathbf{x}}) + w \cdot \hat{U}_k(\hat{\mathbf{x}})$$

The zero levelset of $\hat{\Psi}$ is used as a representation of the evolving shapes. By varying the weights w_i and pose parameters p the function $\hat{\Psi}$ is varied leading to indirectly deforming the shape boundaries. Since the ultimate goal is myocardial segmentation, we used the 3D shape prior models for LV, RV and Epi simultaneously which implicitly divides the image into 4 regions with myocardium being defined as the region bounded by LV, RV, and Epi and the Background (BG) as the region outside Epi shape. This formulation allowed us to impose high level constraints to customize the model for the task of myocardial segmentation.

In order to define the task of myocardial segmentation, we developed a Chan-Vese *like* model for the interior region of the Epicardium i.e. RV, LV and Myocardium with integral terms over LV, RV, Myo and background (BG). We defined the Myo domain to be everything inside epicardium but outside RV and LV and background to be everything outside epicardium. This basic definition of the energy functional directly led to a coupling between the different regions. To further customize the model for myocardial segmentation, we derived a mathematical formulation for enforcing a strict ordering of the image statistics of different regions in the appearance model which makes the segmentation even more robust to initial contour placement. Additionally, to deal with the very complex region surrounding the epicardium composed of different types of tissues exhibiting different intensity ranges, we modeled the background as a binary cluster, one cluster exhibiting very low and the other very high image intensities.

Instead of using the model separately for each region which doesn't allow the shapes to be constrained to not overlap with each other, we used all three priors simultaneously with high level constraints. Our model included a coupling energy functional with an overlap penalty between distinct regions which effectively couples the three priors. It was a purely regularization term which induced a repulsive force whenever regions overlap. The developed shape models were defined directly in 3D space instead of operating in a slice-by-slice manner.

The piecewise constant image appearance model was defined as follows:

$$
\begin{aligned}
E_{coupled} = w_{LV} \int_{LV} (I - \mu_{LV})^2 d\hat{\mathbf{x}} + w_{RV} \int_{RV} (I - \mu_{RV})^2 d\hat{\mathbf{x}} \\
+ w_{Myo} \int_{Myo} (I - \mu_{Myo})^2 d\hat{\mathbf{x}} \\
+ w_{BG} \int_{BG} \min \left((I - c_{lo})^2, (I - c_{hi})^2 \right) d\hat{\mathbf{x}}
\end{aligned}
\tag{2}
$$

with the following image intensity ordering constraint:

$$
c_{lo} \leq \mu_{Myo} \leq \mu_{RV} \leq \mu_{LV} \leq c_{hi}
\tag{3}
$$

In the above formulation c_{lo} and c_{hi} referred to dark and bright binary cluster centers for the complex background region and all integral terms have tunable penalty factors[1]. The coupling overlap penalty was defined as follows:

$$
E_{overlap} = \beta_{LR} \left(\int_{LV \cap RV} d\hat{\mathbf{x}} \right) + \beta_L \left(\int_{LV \cap BG} d\hat{\mathbf{x}} \right) + \beta_R \left(\int_{RV \cap BG} d\hat{\mathbf{x}} \right)
\tag{4}
$$

This overlap penalty energy term penalized the amount of intersection between LV and RV, LV and BG, and RV and BG with tunable penalty factors.

---

[1] These penalties are experimentally determined for each case. Typically, in some cases RV and Myo penalties need to be tuned to allow proper segmentation of RV in extreme poor contrast cases while LV (= 0.5) and BG (= 1.0) penalties remain fixed.

Finally, an optimal set of pose and shape parameters were obtained for each of the three shapes by minimizing the proposed energy functional w.r.t. the pose and shape parameters. This was achieved via a gradient descent based parameter optimization procedure. Due to the complexity of cardiac CT imagery, and complex non-convex energy functional, a direct application of gradient descent produced sub-optimal results. We devised and used a novel automated, shape-adaptive [28] way to choose the parameter weighting dynamically during the fitting process together with momentum based gradient descent resulting in a robust and reliable optimization process.

Using the above formulation for cardiac segmentation, we showed good segmentation results for LV, RV and Myocardium. However, the results were unsatisfactory particularly near the anatomical apex and base and the thin septum region. This is common concern in automatic cardiac segmentation where we see worse results in apical and basal slices even for manual expert segmentations [3].

In this work, we extend the shape prior based segmentation framework to incorporate minimal user input utilized maximally to guide the segmentation process achieving significantly improved results. We let the clinician identify the LV, RV and Epi apex centers and select a common base slice and use these inputs as anatomical constraints for the segmenting surfaces. We formulate a new blended pose model which incorporates the user inputs by replacing the rigid 3D pose model with a novel blended model which incorporates rigidity only within 2D slices while incorporating non-rigid effects of shear and torsion along the third (axial) dimension. This blended model accounts for shearing and torsion explicitly rather than relying on shape priors. We provide the details of blended pose formulation and experimental results in the following sections. We show results comparable to latest deep learning based methods and in a separate concurrent paper [30] show that our technique can be used with Deep Learning methods to further improve their results.

3   Approach: Blended Pose

Using shape prior-based models coupled with a customized piece-wise constant appearance model, we saw good segmentation results on our testing datasets. However, we identified clinically unacceptable results in several anatomical regions, particularly near the apical, basal and septum regions of the heart anatomy. One of the main causes of sub-par results was the presence of shearing and torsion in the heart anatomy. When there is a large amount of shear and torsion in the anatomy a large part of the PCA budget is spent in accounting for these pose variations. Since the base of the anatomy is much larger than the apex regions it leads to worse results near the apex and septum regions due to the larger portion of PCA budget being consumed by the base regions.

Figure 1 shows example RV shapes with varying amounts of torsion and shearing due to the motion of heart muscles required to pump blood. Figure 1b clearly shows a large amount of torsion where the small slices (apex) are twisted in relation to the larger slices at the RV anatomical base. Figure 1d clearly shows

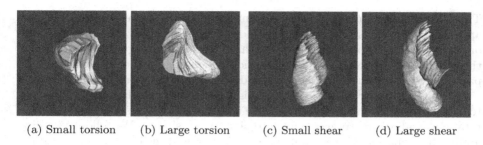

(a) Small torsion   (b) Large torsion   (c) Small shear   (d) Large shear

Fig. 1. Example of different amounts of torsion and shear in RV anatomy

a larger amount of shearing compared to the RV shape in Fig. 1c. In Fig. 1d, the smaller slices on the top (apex) of RV are leaning forward. The center of the apex doesn't line up with the center of the base (larger slices at the bottom). This causes a large portion of the PCA budget being spent in capturing these shear and torsion shape variations which further are dominated by the larger base regions while neglecting important shape variations near the smaller apex region. During the fitting process, the model tends to respond to these large shape variations near the RV base leading to worse results near clinically important apex and septum regions.

In order to overcome these shortcomings, we decided to leverage minimal user input to guide the segmentation process. It is common in clinical practice for user to select a few points (landmarks) of interest for various purposes. We worked with our clinical collaborators to identify minimal user input that we could exploit maximally to constraint the segmentation process. We decided to let clinical user to identify apex centers for LV, RV, Epi shapes and a common base slice for all three anatomies and incorporated these anatomical constraints in the shape prior model. We formulated a new blended pose model to not only incorporate these anatomical constraints but also explicitly include shear and torsion as a part of the pose model.

In order to incorporate the user provided anatomical constraints and also account for shear and torsion, we develop a blended pose model which incorporates rigidity only within 2D slices while incorporating non-rigid effects of shear and torsion along the third (axial) dimension. We select a center point in the apex slice of the three shapes and a common base slice for all three shapes. Then we use two sets of rigid 2D pose parameters, one each for apex and base slice for each shape separately i.e. two sets of poses for each of the three shapes. We fix the translation of the apex pose but allow the base pose to freely move in order to estimate a 2D translation. During fitting, we estimate the in-plane rotation and a uniform scale for the apex pose and in-plane rotation, a uniform scale and 2D translation for the base pose. We then take a convex combination of these two 2D poses for the remaining slices between the apex and base slices.

This is done using a normalized z coordinate which is 0 at the base and 1 at the apex slice. This leads to only the apex pose being applied to the apex slice and only the base pose to the base slice, with all remaining image slices in-between these two slices receiving a blended version depending on the z coordinate of a particular slice which allows shearing and torsion along the axial dimension.

Fixing the apex translation and allowing the base to translate freely allows us to account for shearing in the data. Since the two sets of poses have independent rotation, it allows us to account for torsion in the shapes. We follow a similar approach during the PCA training process. We discard the manual segmentation below the selected base slice of all the training datasets. This allows us to capture only meaningful shape variations, especially in RV.

More formally, we now linearly blend the separate apex and base pose parameters themselves as a function convex weights $w(z)$ and $1 - w(z)$ depending on $z \in [z_b, z_a]$ where z_b and z_a represent the z-coordinate for the base and apex slice respectively. As such our spatial mapping $\hat{\mathbf{x}} = g(\mathbf{p}, \mathbf{x})$ now takes the form

$$\hat{\mathbf{x}} = g\left(\mathbf{p}(\mathbf{x}, \mathbf{p}_a, \mathbf{p}_b), \mathbf{x}\right) = g\left(\underbrace{\ldots, p_k(z\,,\, p_{a,k}\,,\, p_{b,k}), \ldots}_{\text{each pose parameter}}, \mathbf{x}\right)$$

where the pose vector (now dependent upon the z-coordinate of $\mathbf{x}$) is given by

$$\mathbf{p}(\mathbf{x}, \mathbf{p}_a, \mathbf{p}_b) = \underbrace{w(z)}_{\in [0,1]} \mathbf{p}_a + (1 - w(z))\, \mathbf{p}_b$$

and where $\mathbf{p}_b = (p_{b,1}, \ldots, p_{b,L})$ and $\mathbf{p}_a = (p_{a,1}, \ldots, p_{a,L})$ represent the new double set of pose parameters corresponding to the base and apex poses respectively. In the above formulation, we may consider several choices for the blending factor $w(z)$ as well. An obvious choice for the blending factor would be

$$w(z) = \underbrace{\frac{z - z_b}{z_a - z_b}}_{0 \leq \bar{z} \leq 1}, \qquad 1 - w(z) = \underbrace{\frac{z_a - z}{z_a - z_b}}_{1 - \bar{z}}$$

where $\bar{z}$ represents a normalized z-coordinate which starts at 0 on the base slice z_b and reaches 1 on the apex slice z_a. In this case the blending factor matches the normalized coordinate itself and therefore changes linearly. However, we could allow a variable rate of change by making the blending factor depend upon a parameter γ. We considered other schemes including:

- **Quadratic Blending**: $\bar{w}_\gamma(\bar{z}) = \left[1 + \gamma\,(1 - \bar{z})\right]\bar{z}, \quad -1 \leq \gamma \leq 1$
- **Power Law 0 Blending**: $\bar{w}_\gamma(\bar{z}) = \bar{z}^\gamma, \quad 0 < \gamma < \infty$
- **Power Law 1 Blending**: $\bar{w}_\gamma(\bar{z}) = (1 - \bar{z})^\gamma, \quad 0 < \gamma < \infty$

During the training process, for each of the training datasets, we select an apex and same base slice for all three shapes before image alignment and PCA process. We manually select the base slice to be the slice just before the dramatic change in RV shape occurs for each dataset. The apex slices are selected separately for each shape as all three shapes have different anatomical apexes. We then use the blended pose formulation to align the training datasets to a common reference shape. In this training step shape variations due to shearing and torsion are removed leaving the PCA model to capture actual shape variations. This process of blended pose based alignment and PCA is run to obtain a set of mean shapes and principal components for each shape, RV, LV, and Epi.

We developed the mathematical formulation of this technique, including all the gradient expressions needed for implementing the gradient descent procedure, created the implementations and then trained and tested new models.

4   Experimental Results

4.1   Imaging Data

In collaboration with clinical researchers in Emory University, we acquired a database of ninety one clinical ECG-gated contrast-enhanced CCTA imaging datasets. The data base was created with images acquired at different clinical and research centers as a result of current and previous collaborations [21] involving the laboratory of Nuclear Cardiology at Emory University. To facilitate manual segmentation of cardiac CCTA images, datasets were re-oriented along the cardiac short-axis (SA) and resampled with an isotropic image spacing equal to the original in-plane image resolution creating a volume of $512 \times 512 \times 512$ voxels. An in-house developed software was used for the manual segmentation performed by members of the team expert in cardiac anatomy. Three borders were identified on the volumes: the left (LV) and right ventricle (RV) endocardia and the biventricular epicardium (EPI). Binary images were constructed from the profiles and three-dimensional (3D) surface models extracted with the Marching Cube algorithm [18].

We selected forty six short-axis images out of the total ninety one for the training phase of our algorithms to prepare PCA based shape prior models as described in the previous sections. To accelerate the testing process as well as reduce image processing times and computer memory requirements a scaled-down version of each image was created with a spacing 3 times the original one and a dimension of $170 \times 170 \times 170$ voxels. We prepared the shape prior models at original $512 \times 512 \times 512$ resolution and then downsampled the trained mean shape and principal components to the same resolution of $170 \times 170 \times 170$. We used twenty principal components during all our experiments.

4.2   Qualitative Results

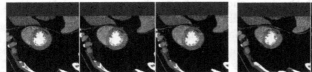
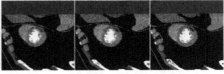

(a) Bad septum with rigid 3D pose   (b) Better septum with blended pose

Fig. 2. Illustration of better segmentation results in septum region with the new blended pose and anatomical constraints compared to rigid 3D pose.

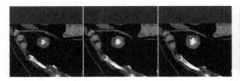
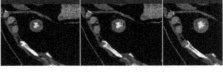

(a) Bad apex segmentation with 3D pose   (b) Better segmentation with blended pose

Fig. 3. Illustration of better segmentation results around apex with the new blended pose and anatomical constraints compared to rigid 3D pose

Figures 2 and 3 show results of applying the new blended pose model incorporating user provided anatomical constraints versus the original rigid 3D pose formulation [15, 16] to test cases. PCA models for the both the blended pose and rigid 3D pose are trained from same set of training images. In Fig. 2, rigid 3D pose fails to segment the septum region of the myocardium correctly whereas the blended pose does a much better job. Similarly, in Fig. 3, the new blended pose formulation segments the small apex region much better than rigid 3D pose. These better results are partly due to the torsion being separately accounted for in the pose model rather than relying on the shape model to capture it. The addition of the anatomical constraints helps to overcome the deficiencies caused by lack of contrast in many cases. Whenever the image contrast is poor, especially for the RV/Myocardium region, the rigid 3D pose approach fails to capture correct boundaries. In the case of blended pose formulation whenever there is a lack of image contrast the anatomical constraints can kick in and help drive the segmentation to the correct boundaries. The apex occupies less volume compared to the rest of the anatomy, however, it is still clinically very important to segment this area well. The blended pose model helps to do just that.

Table 1. DSC and surface-to-surface distances

DSC and Surface-to-Surface Distances

	DSC		ASSD [mm]	
	Blended Pose	Rigid 3D Pose	Blended Pose	Rigid 3D Pose
LV Endo	0.92 ± 0.03	0.91 ± 0.02	1.05 ± 0.27	1.7 ± 0.40
RV Endo	0.90 ± 0.04	0.85 ± 0.03	1.22 ± 0.56	2.3 ± 0.50
Heart Epi	0.95 ± 0.04	0.89 ± 0.02	1.13 ± 0.21	3.3 ± 0.50

4.3   Quantitative Results

To further test the benefits of the blended pose formulation, we compute several
quantitative measures on segmentations generated on the testing set of 45 CCTA
datasets. We compute dice coefficient (DSC) and average symmetric surface to
surface distance (ASSD). ASSD measures average distance between voxels of a
pair of surfaces. We also compute the physiologically relevant LV and RV chambers volume (Vol), and biventricular myocardial mass (Myo Mass) for automated
and manual segmentations. We use pearson correlation coefficient (R) between
manual and automated segmentations for the two techniques to assess and compare the performance in extracting LV, RV, and Myocardial Mass.

Table 1 shows the computed DSC and surface-to-surface distance metrics
using 45 test cases. All three anatomies have an average DSC score of more
than 0.90 which is generally clinically acceptable. Epicardium shows the highest
accuracy with an average DSC score of approximately 0.95 with low variation
across the testing datasets. RV is the hardest to segment and consequently has
the lowest average DSC scores (0.90 ± 0.04). Along similar lines, the average
surface to surface distance (ASSD) is close to 1 mm for both Epi and LV but
is larger (at 1.22 mm) for RV. In all computed metrics, the blended pose formulation achieves much better results compared to using rigid 3D pose without
any anatomical constraints. LV DSC scores are similar but the blended pose
formulation produces much better surface to surface distance metrics.

Table 2 shows the Pearson correlation coefficients (R) between the manual
and automatic segmentation metrics for the two techniques of blended pose vs
3D pose. We see excellent results for the LV endocardium detection (R = 0.99)
for both techniques but we see significant improvement in using the blended pose
formulation for RV endocardium (R = 0.97 blended vs R = 0.75 3D pose) and
myocardium mass (R = 0.90 blended vs R = 0.67 3D pose).

Table 2. Chamber volumes and myocardial mass

Clinical Parameters Correlation (R)		
	Blended Pose	Rigid 3D Pose
LV Vol [mL]	0.99	0.99
RV Vol [mL]	0.97	0.75
Myo Mass [g]	0.90	0.67

A recent publication [29], reported the results of evaluation of 10 different algorithms (including Deep Learning based methods) on a whole heart segmentation challenge (including LV and RV chambers) in both cardiac CT and MRI images. The best average DSC reported was 0.923 for LV and 0.909 for RV for the CT datasets whereas we achieved a very close DSC of 0.92 for LV and 0.90 for RV. These metrics are also very close to the inter-observer variability of manual segmentations of 0.937 ± 0.013 for LV and 0.90 ± 0.02 for RV in cardiac MRI images (CT results not available) as reported in [29].

5   Conclusion

In this paper, we presented a technique to incorporate user defined anatomical constraints in PCA based shape prior model optimized for a Chan-Vese *like* energy functional for myocardium segmentation in Cardiac CT imagery. We showed a blended pose formulation that not only incorporates minimal user defined anatomical constraints and explicitly accounts for torsion and shearing in the pose model. With this formulation we showed results that are significantly improved compared to a previous rigid 3D pose approach and are competitive with other recent approaches including deep learning based techniques.

References

1. van Assen, H.C., Danilouchkine, M.G., Dirksen, M.S., et al.: A 3-D active shape model driven by fuzzy inference: application to cardiac CT and MR. IEEE Trans. Inf. Technol. Biomed. **12**(5), 595–605 (2008)
2. van Assen, H.C., Danilouchkine, M.G., Frangi, F.F., et al.: A 3D-ASM for segmentation of sparse and arbitrarily oriented cardiac MRI data. Med. Image Anal. **10**(2), 286–303 (2006)
3. Bernard, O., Lalande, A., Zotti, C., et al.: Deep learning techniques for automatic MRI cardiac multi-structures segmentation and diagnosis: is the problem solved? IEEE Trans. Med. Imaging **37**(11), 2514–2525 (2018). https://doi.org/10.1109/TMI.2018.2837502
4. Blankstein, R., Di Carli, M.F.: Integration of coronary anatomy and myocardial perfusion imaging. Nat. Rev. Cardiol. **7**(4), 226–236 (2010). https://doi.org/10.1038/nrcardio.2010.15
5. Caselles, V., Kimmel, R., Sapiro, G.: Geodesic active contours. Int. J. Comput. Vis. **22**(61), 61–79 (1997)

6. CDC: Heart disease: Scope and impact (2015). http://www.theheartfoundation. org/heart-disease-facts/heart-disease-statistics/
7. Chan, T., Vese, L.: An active contour model without edges. In: International Conference on Scale-Space Theories in Computer Vision, pp. 141–151 (1999)
8. Chan, T., Vese, L.: A level set algorithm for minimizing the Mumford-shah functional in image processing. In: IEEE Workshop on Variational and Level Set Methods in Computer Vision, pp. 161–168 (2001)
9. Chen, C., Qin, C., Qiu, H., et al.: Deep learning for cardiac image segmentation: a review. Front. Cardiovasc. Med. **7** (2020). https://doi.org/10.3389/fcvm.2020. 00025
10. Chen, Y., Thiruvenkadam, S., Huang, F., et al.: On the incorporation of shape priors into geometric active contours. In: IEEE Workshop on Variational and Level Set Methods in Computer Vision, pp. 145–152 (2001)
11. Cootes, T., Edwards, G., Taylor, C.: Active appearance models. IEEE Trans. Pattern Recognit. Mach. Intell. **23**(6), 681–685 (2001)
12. Cootes, T., Taylor, C.: Smart snakes. In: Proceedings of British Machine Vision Conference, pp. 266–275 (1992)
13. Cootes, T.F., Edwards, G.J., Taylor, C.J.: Active appearance models. In: Burkhardt, H., Neumann, B. (eds.) ECCV 1998. LNCS, vol. 1407, pp. 484–498. Springer, Heidelberg (1998). https://doi.org/10.1007/BFb0054760
14. Cootes, T., Taylor, C., Cooper, C., et al.: Active shape models - their training and application. Comput. Vis. Image Underst. **61**(9), 38–59 (1995)
15. Dahiya, N., Yezzi, A., Piccinelli, M., et al.: Integrated 3D anatomical model for automatic myocardial segmentation in cardiac CT imagery. Comput. Methods Biomech. Biomed. Eng. Imaging Vis. **7**(5–6), 690–706 (2019). https://doi.org/10. 1080/21681163.2019.1583607
16. Dahiya, N., Yezzi, A., Piccinelli, M., Garcia, E.: Integrated 3D anatomical model for automatic myocardial segmentation in cardiac CT imagery. In: Tavares, J.M.R.S., Natal Jorge, R.M. (eds.) ECCOMAS 2017. LNCVB, vol. 27, pp. 1115–1124. Springer, Cham (2018). https://doi.org/10.1007/978-3-319-68195-5_123
17. Leventon, M., Grimson, E., Faugeras, O.: Statistical shape influence in geodesic active contours. In: Proceedings of the IEEE Conference on Computer Vision and Pattern Recognition, vol. 1, pp. 316–323 (2000)
18. Lorensen, W.E., Cline, H.E.: Marching cubes: a high resolution 3D surface construction algorithm. SIGGRAPH Comput. Graph. **21**(4), 163–169 (1987). https:// doi.org/10.1145/37402.37422
19. Mitchell, S.C., Lelieveldt, B., Van Der Geest, et al.: Multistage hybrid active appearance model matching: segmentation of left and right ventricles in cardiac MR images. IEEE Trans. Med. Imaging **20**(5), 415–423 (2001)
20. Mumford, D., Shah, J.: Optimal approximations by piecewise smooth functions and associated variational problems. Commun. Pure Appl. Math. **42**(6), 577–685 (1989)
21. Piccinelli, M., et al.: Diagnostic performance of the quantification of myocardium at risk from MPI SPECT/CTA 2G fusion for detecting obstructive coronary disease: a multicenter trial. J. Nucl. Cardiol. **25**(4), 1376–1386 (2017). https://doi.org/10. 1007/s12350-017-0819-x
22. Rizvi, A., Han, D., Danad, I., et al.: Diagnostic performance of hybrid cardiac imaging methods for assessment of obstructive coronary artery disease compared with stand-alone coronary computed tomography angiography: a meta-analysis. JACC Cardiovasc. Imaging **11**(4), 589–599 (2018)

23. Shahzad, R., Bos, D., Budde, R.P.J., et al.: Automatic segmentation and quantification of the cardiac structures from non-contrast-enhanced cardiac CT scans. Phys. Med. Biol. **62**(9), 3798 (2017)
24. Tsai, A., Yezzi, A., Wells, W., et al.: A shape-based approach to the segmentation of medical imagery using level sets. IEEE Trans. Med. Imaging **22**, 137–154 (2003)
25. Vikram, A., Ganapathy, B., Abufadel, A., et al.: A regions of confidence based approach to enhance segmentation with shape priors. In: Proceedings of the of SPIE-IS&T Electronic Imaging, SPIE, pp. 7533–12 (2010). https://doi.org/10.1117/12.850888
26. Weese, J., Kaus, M., Lorenz, C., Lobregt, S., Truyen, R., Pekar, V.: Shape constrained deformable models for 3D medical image segmentation. In: Insana, M.F., Leahy, R.M. (eds.) IPMI 2001. LNCS, vol. 2082, pp. 380–387. Springer, Heidelberg (2001). https://doi.org/10.1007/3-540-45729-1_38
27. Yezzi, A., Kichenassamy, S., Kumar, et al.: A geometric snake model for segmentation of medical imagery. IEEE Trans. Med. Imaging **16**, 199–209 (1997)
28. Yezzi, A., Dahiya, N.: Shape adaptive accelerated parameter optimization. In: 2018 IEEE Southwest Symposium on Image Analysis and Interpretation (SSIAI), pp. 1–4 (2018). https://doi.org/10.1109/SSIAI.2018.8470380
29. Zhuang, X., Li, L., Payer, C., et al.: Evaluation of algorithms for multi-modality whole heart segmentation: an open-access grand challenge. Med. Image Anal. **58**, 101537 (2019). https://doi.org/10.1016/j.media.2019.101537
30. Bignardi, S., Dahiya, N., Comelli, A., et al.: Combining convolutional neural networks and anatomical shape-based priors for cardiac segmentation. To appear. In: AIRCAD 2022 1st International Workshop on Artificial Intelligence and Radiomics in Computer-Aided Diagnosis

PET Images Atlas-Based Segmentation Performed in Native and in Template Space: A Radiomics Repeatability Study in Mouse Models

Paolo Giaccone[1,2], Viviana Benfante[1,3,4(✉)], Alessandro Stefano[4], Francesco Paolo Cammarata[4], Giorgio Russo[4], and Albert Comelli[1]

[1] Ri.MED Foundation, Via Bandiera 11, 90133 Palermo, Italy
[2] Unit of Computer Systems and Bioinformatics, Department of Engineering, Università Campus Bio-Medico di Roma, Via Alvaro del Portillo 21, 00128 Rome, Italy
[3] Department of Health Promotion, Mother and Child Care, Internal Medicine and Medical Specialties, Molecular and Clinical Medicine, University of Palermo, 90127 Palermo, Italy
viviana.benfante@unipa.it
[4] Institute of Molecular Bioimaging and Physiology, National Research Council (IBFM-CNR), 90015 Cefalù, Italy

Abstract. Image segmentation is a task of the utmost importance in computer vision, especially in the biomedical field where accurate delineation of an organ or lesion can make a difference in patient's survival. Although there are several approaches, the Atlas-based co-registration method is most appropriate for low-contrast functional images, where organ boundaries are not easily recognizable. This technique is strongly dependent on the template choice and can even lead to inaccurate results if unproperly tuned; however, two different pipelines were similarly adopted in literature either warping the Atlas to the target image or warping the target image to the Atlas. This, unless proved to be equivalent, may result ambiguous, hence in this study we investigated the two algorithms equivalence employing a preclinical dataset of mice undergoing micro-PET/CT scans after chelator injection. We focused on seven selected organs (namely heart, bladder, stomach, spleen, liver, kidneys and lungs), and for each of them we computed the percentage of PET radiomics features with significant variations between the two algorithms. Our results showed that the two approaches considerably differed. Specifically, a mean significant difference of about 40% was found in the radiomics features extracted following the two different pipelines, posing the need to distinguish between the two registration output spaces.

Keywords: Radiomics · Micro PET/CT · Atlas · Segmentation · Normalization · Mouse

1 Introduction

The ability to locate multiple targets in an image is the first step to understand what that image shows. This applies to both human beings and machines: segmentation is

P. L. Mazzeo et al. (Eds.): ICIAP 2022 Workshops, LNCS 13373, pp. 351–361, 2022.
https://doi.org/10.1007/978-3-031-13321-3_31

preliminary to semantic classification and interpretation of any image. In the biomedical field, medical physicians are involved in the manual delineation of organs or lesions in anatomical and functional scans of the human body for diagnostic purposes, in the fine-tuning of a localized treatment, as well as to evaluate the efficacy of a therapy in a follow-up screening [1]. Unfortunately, such gold-standard is tedious, time-consuming and, by consequence, error-prone. Hence, due to its relevance and prohibitive burden, automated segmentation algorithms have been a challenging task for decades, leading to the development of several tools to support the clinical practice [2]. The techniques that are widely used for medical image segmentation can be mainly divided into the following categories based on: thresholding, regions, edges, active contours, clustering and artificial intelligence [3–5]. All these approaches, either supervised or unsupervised, differently exploit the gray-level gradient of the scan, requiring the target to be clearly visible a priori; thus, they are dependent on the quality of tissue contrast, as well as susceptible to intensity artifacts, such as noise, bias or partial volume effect [6, 7]. An alternative solution, which turned the segmentation problem into a registration task, is the atlas-based strategy. The usage of a template image allowed researchers to define a common coordinate system that may be used to locate similar volumes of interest (VOIs) in multiple subjects for reproducibility reasons [8, 9]. Furthermore, this technique proved to be more appropriate for low-resolution scans [10] because the registration procedure is primarily guided by the high-contrast structures (e.g.: bones or lungs), while the multiple segmentation of less visible regions can be basically obtained through the alignment with the template parcellation.

The atlas-based segmentation performance depends on many aspects and is primarily influenced by the registration procedure, which must be suitable for the degree of variability in question; for instance, a rigid or affine deformation might account for brain images misalignment [11], while whole-body scans could require more sophisticated non-linear warping [8]. Besides, these models can even lead to inaccurate outcomes if unproperly tuned in terms of similarity metrics, interpolation and other settings [9]. In particular, a fundamental aspect which was rarely considered in literature is the registration output space: there was plenty of works that registered the Atlas to the target image and propagated the labels accordingly, thus segmenting in the subject-specific space [8, 12]; on the other hand, some authors reverted the process by warping the target image to the Atlas space, which is commonly referred to as *spatial normalization*, and applying the basic atlas parcellation to segment the regions of interest [13, 14]. Both these workflows were referred to as atlas-based segmentation but, unless proved to be equivalent, this may result ambiguous. To our knowledge, whether segmenting in native or in template space was never considered as a relevant aspect, hence we assessed its actual impact on the obtained outcomes. In this paper, we investigated these two registration alternatives, making use of a preclinical dataset of Balb/C nude strain mice [15], who underwent micro-Positron Emission Tomography/Computerized Tomography (PET/CT) scans after a [^{64}Cu]chelator injection (see Sect. 2.1 for the detailed description of the preclinical test), and employing a 3D whole-body mouse atlas for the segmentation of seven PET VOIs: heart, bladder, stomach, spleen, liver, kidneys and lungs.

To assess the equivalence of the two approaches, that is the possibility to change the moving with the target image, usual metrics, like accuracy or dice score, could not be adopted due to lack of any ground truth; besides, common anatomical measures were not suitable because the deformations between native and template spaces did not preserve the volume. Hence, we quantitatively evaluated the functional information provided by both VOIs groups in terms of radiomics features [16–18]. Radiomics already proved to have a significant predictive potential in medicine. In this study we used these features as a novel comparative method. Specifically, we employed a total of 108 features, concerning shape, histogram and texture, for each VOI in both pipelines to conduct a repeatability study, reporting the percentage of radiomics measures that exhibited a statistically significant difference ($p < 0.05$) between the two registration approaches [19].

2 Materials and Methods

2.1 Dataset

Nine 6-week-old female Balb/C nude strain mice were used (CAnN.Cg-Foxn1nu/Crl - Charles River/Envigo) weighing $18,0 \pm 0,7$ g. Animals were randomly housed in individually ventilated cages (IVC), using a stocking density of 3 mice per cage at a constant temperature (23–25 °C) with ad libitum access to food and water. All animals were scanned with an Albira Si micro-PET/CT for the assessment of the biodistribution of the [^{64}Cu]chelator at three time points after injection [15]. A sulfur-containing derivative of tetraazacyclododecane (cyclen) described in [20] was used as a bifunctional chelator of ^{64}Cu in these experiments. At the time of the examination the animals were anesthetized with isofluorane (4% for induction, 2% for maintenance) and the radio-pharmaceutical complex was injected intra venous in the tail with an activity of about 7 MBq in a maximum volume of 50 μl. The PET acquisition was performed in three pre-established times (1 h, 4 h and 24 h) and the main vital parameters were constantly monitored. Mice were divided into three groups of three subjects each: group 1 (micro-PET/CT acquisition after 1 h from administration of the radiolabeled chelator), group 2 (acquisition after 4 h) and group 3 (acquisition after 24 h). In addition to the functional examination, a morphological scan (CT) was concurrently performed which, being co-registered with PET images, allowed to associate the functional information with the organs to be studied.

2.2 PET/CT Image Acquisition and Segmentation

Micro-PET/CT dataset was acquired using a preclinical micro-PET/CT (Albira Si, Bruker), made available by the CAPiR (Center for Advanced Preclinical Research in vivo), University of Catania, Italy. The CT dataset was acquired using 600 views in a low-resolution configuration, an initial horizontal position of 37 mm, a FOV of 64 mm, an X-ray energy of 35 kV, a current of 200 μA, and the size of each CT-voxel was equal to $500 \times 500 \times 500$ μm^3. The Digital Image COmmunications in Medicine (DICOM) images were obtained using a 3D filtered back projection algorithm. The PET images were re-constructed using the 3D Maximum-Likelihood Expectation-Maximization algorithm with a total of 12 iterations. PET-voxel was equal to 500×500

$\times$ 500 μm^3. The extremely low resolution did not allow other techniques to be used but the atlas-based for organs segmentation, as displayed in Fig. 1.

All PET/CT scans were spatially pre-processed and segmented through co-registration with a standard template space as follows. First, a custom-made MAT-LAB® algorithm was implemented to rescale the CT images intensity range (from the Hounsfield scale to an 8-bit grayscale format), as well as to segment and remove every non-mouse-related structure from the CT scans, like the animal holder. After image cleaning, the CT scans were co-registered with the 3D whole-body Digimouse Atlas [21]; this template was assessed to be more appropriate for this study due to the similarity of the anatomical mouse model used, as well as the imaging modalities from which it was constructed (i.e.: PET, X-ray CT and cryosection images of normal nude mice). Despite the multimodal template, in our co-registration pipeline, only the CT part of the Atlas was used as its functional part relates to the [^{18}F]FDG uptake, and therefore the involvement of such information would have implied an a-priori biodistribution pattern which may have altered our results. The following two registration pipelines were adopted.

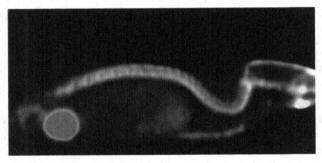

Fig. 1. PET/CT image of a mouse scanned 1 h after administration of the radioactive compound.

Warping Atlas to CT. A three-steps registration was performed to overlap the 3D whole-body Digimouse Atlas with CT scans. The registration procedure consisted of a semi-automated linear alignment, performed through ITK-Snap software, followed by an automated non-linear warping, accomplished with the Elastix toolkit, which was further enhanced by small local refinements achieved by the landmark registration tool of 3DSlicer. More in details, for each mouse, the atlas was first manually pre-aligned to match the subject-specific coordinate system, by means of a rigid roto-translation, so to ease the convergence of the subsequent automated algorithm. Then, the optimal affine transform, employing mutual information as the similarity metric, linear interpolation and a multi-resolution approach, was estimated, involving only half-resolution at the coarsest level and full resolution at the finest because of the poor raw data quality. After-wards, the non-linear intensity-based registration step was performed by a B-spline deformation model, whose metric, optimization routine and other parameter settings were chosen as in [22]. This procedure allowed to properly overlap the global mouse shape outline and it considerably improved the registration of the main anatomical structures with highest contrast, such as the spine, skull and limbs; nevertheless, the expected misalignments in low-contrast tissues of interest, such as the bladder, as well as some slight residual differences in the lungs contour, required some local refinements; thus, a thin-plate spline mapping through multiple landmarks definition, where the fiducial markers were manually positioned by visual inspection, was generated. Finally, all these estimated linear and non-linear transforms were exploited to propagate the binary masks of the atlas into each subject-specific space, but, due to resolution shrinkage, some tiny masks, like pancreas or adrenal glands, got fragmentary and were discarded from the selected set of VOIs.

Warping CT to Atlas. The second registration procedure was similar to the first one, except for the switch between the moving and the reference images. Each CT scan was first manually pre-aligned to the standard coordinate space by means of a rigid roto-translation. Next, the optimal affine transform was automatically estimated employing mutual information as the similarity metric, linear interpolation and a multi-resolution approach. Afterwards, the non-linear intensity-based deformation was performed, together with the landmark registration step. The thin-plate spline mapping was defined, as before, by manually locating the fiducials markers on the anatomical structures with highest contrast, such as the spine, skull, limbs, paws and lungs, as well as on the mouse shape outline. Finally, the estimated linear and non-linear transforms of the CT images were exploited to spatially normalize the respective PET scans which were then segmented by the basic Digimouse Atlas labels, focusing only to the previously selected set of VOIs.

2.3 Extraction of Radiomics Features

After atlas co-registration, organs of interest (i.e.: heart, bladder, stomach, spleen, liver, kidneys and lungs) were identified and exported as binary masks. Before proceeding to the feature extraction process, the PET DICOMs were modified to incorporate the standardized uptake value (SUV), as reported in [23]. The SUV is the most common semi-quantitative parameter used to estimate biodistribution in PET images. In this way the functional information was entered directly into DICOM so that the extracted features took them into account: the SUV normalizes the voxel activity considering acquisition time, administered activity, and mouse weight. In other words, PET images were converted to SUV images, thus taking into account factors that would otherwise be ignored during radiomics analysis. At this point, both PET and masks images were used to extract 108 radiomics features using an Image Biomarker Standardization Initiative (IBSI) [24] compliant analysis software, namely PyRadiomics [25], since one of the main points in radiomics studies is to increase the reproducibility of the extracted features [19]. Many feature classes were extracted, like shape descriptors, first-order statistics, and the following texture matrices: grey level co-occurrence matrix (GLCM), grey level run-length matrix (GLRLM), grey level dependence matrix (GLDM), grey level size-zone matrix (GLSZM) and neighbouring grey level dependence matrix (NGLDM).

2.4 Statistical Analysis

The performance results of the proposed approaches were obtained using the two-way analysis of variance (ANOVA), which allowed to determine whether there were any statistically significant differences between the means of two or more categorical groups in two independent variables, by comparing the within-groups and between-groups variability. In other words, the two-way ANOVA considered the mean of the variances of each group, as well as the variance of the means between groups, determining if one of these groups was statistically different from the others. In our case, for each radiomics feature of every VOI, the two independent variables referred to the mouse identity and the segmentation algorithm; as it is, despite genetically identical because belonging to the same strain, it was not possible to neglect the differences caused by the individual functional behaviour of the single mouse, whose identity thus was regarded as an independent variable. Furthermore, we separately considered the three different time points after the [^{64}Cu]chelator injection, because comparing these three physiological states, although reasonable in a biodistribution study, would have altered our algorithmic performance considerations.

Specifically, there were two null hypotheses, one per independent variable, but the most important one referred to the segmentation algorithms:

$$H_0 : \mu_{:,1}^{i,j} = \mu_{:,2}^{i,j} \tag{1}$$

with $i = 1,2\ldots108;\ j = 1,2\ldots7$, where $\mu_{:,1}$ and $\mu_{:,2}$ are the average, over the three mice of the same group, of the i-th feature extracted from the j-th VOI through the first and the second atlas-based segmentation approach respectively (see Sect. 2.2).

If, the two-way ANOVA returned a statistically significant result on the segmentation variable ($p < 0.05$), we rejected (1) and accepted the alternative hypothesis: the registration procedure had a significant impact on the feature value. Then, for every organ, we considered those features with p-value < 0.05 to compute the percentage of significantly different radiomics features between the two algorithms.

3 Results

Figure 2 shows the 3D segmented skeleton of the Digimouse atlas overlapped with a representative mouse, both before and after the two registration procedures; quantitatively, warping the atlas to the CT images allowed to reach registration accuracies ranging from 87.5% to 91%, with a mean performance of 89% ± 1%, in terms of intensity correlation; on the other hand, warping the CT images to the atlas led to correlation values in the range of 71.9%–79.4%, with a mean score of 76.2% ± 2%. Such discrepancies were primarily due to the non-linear registration step which, in the latter case, was prevalently handcrafted.

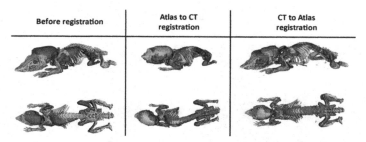

Fig. 2. Qualitative assessment of the two registration workflows, evaluated through the overlapping of standard (yellow) and real (red) segmented bone structures. (Color figure online)

After co-registrations, radiomics features of PET scans were extracted from seven different targets: heart, bladder, stomach, spleen, liver, kidneys, and lungs. As expected, the two-way ANOVA, conducted separately on the three different time points after the [^{64}Cu]chelator injection, highlighted very few significant differences in the feature values due to the mouse phenotypical variability which, however, had to be considered for statistical rigour. As shown in the right half of Figs. 3, 4 and 5, the mouse variable collected very low percentages of significantly different radiomics features in every VOI.

On the other hand, the statistical analysis revealed a substantial difference on the segmentation variable according to the proposed radiomics evaluation (about 40% over the entire dataset), which challenges the equivalence of the two atlas-based segmentation procedures. Specifically, the first mice group, whose PET scans were acquired 1 h after the radio-metal administration, showed a mean difference of 37% in radiomics features across the selected VOIs and, out of 108 considered features, the significant variations between the two algorithms amounted to:

- 22 features (equals to 20.37%) in the cardiac region
- 58 features (equals to 53.70%) in the bladder district
- 40 features (equals to 37.04%) in the stomach area
- 36 features (equals to 33.33%) in the spleen region
- 54 features (equals to 50.00%) in the liver area
- 38 features (equals to 35.19%) in the kidneys district
- 32 features (equals to 29.63%) in the lung region

These results are summarized in Figure 3.

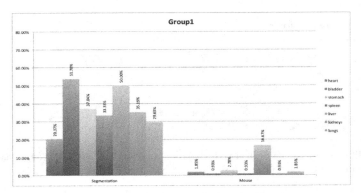

Fig. 3. Two-way ANOVA results on the first group of mice, showing the percentages of radiomics features with significant dependence on the segmentation (left) and the mouse variable (right) for each VOI

In the second group of mice, which were scanned after 4 h from the contrast agent administration, the analyses showed a mean difference of 46.82% in the radiomics features across the selected VOIs and, as shown in Fig. 4, the significant variations between the two algorithms consisted of:

- 74 features (equals to 68.52%) in the cardiac region
- 46 features (equals to 42.59%) in the bladder district
- 44 features (equals to 40.74%) in the stomach area
- 31 features (equals to 28.70%) in the spleen region
- 62 features (equals to 57.41%) in the liver area
- 51 features (equals to 47.22%) in the kidneys district
- 46 features (equals to 42.59%) in the lung region

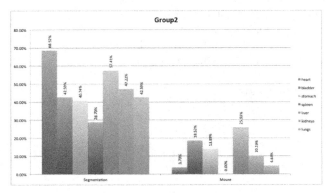

Fig. 4. Two-way ANOVA results on the second group of mice, showing the percentages of radiomics features with significant dependence on the segmentation (left) and the mouse variable (right) for each VOI

Finally, Fig. 5 shows that the third mice group, whose PET scans were acquired 24 h after the [^{64}Cu]chelator injection, exhibited again a mean difference of 37% in the radiomics features across the selected VOIs and, out of 108 features, the significant variations between the two algorithms amounted to:

- 29 features (equals to 26.85%) in the cardiac region
- 36 features (equals to 33.33%) in the bladder district
- 38 features (equals to 35.19%) in the stomach area
- 37 features (equals to 34.26%) in the spleen region
- 56 features (equals to 51.85%) in the liver area
- 37 features (equals to 34.26%) in the kidneys district
- 47 features (equals to 43.52%) in the lung region

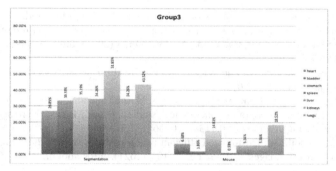

Fig. 5. Two-way ANOVA results on the third group of mice, showing the percentages of radiomics features with significant dependence on the segmentation (left) and the mouse variable (right) for each VOI

4   Conclusions

PET image segmentation is a crucial task in the biomedical field both for clinical [26] and preclinical studies [27]. The atlas-based techniques are a valid solution which proved to reach better performances in low-resolution images [10], but inaccurate results if unproperly tuned [8]. Hence, in this paper we focused on a detail which was rarely considered in literature: the segmentation output space. We investigated two alternative atlas co-registration pipelines by warping either the target image to the template, or the template to the target image. Both methods were similarly used in literature [8, 9, 14] but, unless proved to be equivalent, this may result ambiguous.

We employed a preclinical dataset of Balb/C nude strain mice undergoing micro-PET/CT scans at three different time points after [^{64}Cu]chelator injection; successively, we evaluated the two pipelines equivalence focusing on the functional uptake of seven selected organs (heart, bladder, stomach, spleen, liver, kidneys and lungs), computing the percentage of radiomics features with significant variations within each of the VOI.

Our results, despite potentially biased to some extent due to some non-linear registration differences, revealed substantial variation between the two approaches according to the proposed radiomics evaluation: more specifically, over the entire dataset, we found a mean significant difference of about 40% in the radiomics features across the selected VOIs, which challenges the equivalence of the two atlas-based segmentation procedures.

These outcomes will need future endeavours to be validated, both using different datasets and comparing the results with a reliable gold-standard, as well as employing an ensemble of atlases through the so-called multi-atlas segmentation technique, which can provide better capture of anatomical variability [28]. Moreover, future experiments will apply the proposed radiomics repeatability evaluation metrics to assess those available software packages that equivalently perform both segmentation pipelines as in [29].

References

1. Alongi, P., et al.: Radiomics analysis of 18F-Choline PET/CT in the prediction of disease outcome in high-risk prostate cancer: an explorative study on machine learning feature classification in 94 patients. Eur. Radiol. **31**(7), 4595–4605 (2021). https://doi.org/10.1007/s00 330-020-07617-8
2. Litjens, G., et al.: A survey on deep learning in medical image analysis (2017). https://doi. org/10.1016/j.media.2017.07.005
3. Comelli, A., Stefano, A., Benfante, V., Russo, G.: Normal and abnormal tissue classification in positron emission tomography oncological studies. Pattern Recognit. Image Anal. **28**, 106–113 (2018). https://doi.org/10.1134/S1054661818010054
4. Stefano, A., Comelli, A.: Customized efficient neural network for covid-19 infected region identification in CT images. J. Imaging. **7**, 131 (2021). https://doi.org/10.3390/jimaging7 080131
5. Comelli, A., et al.: Tissue classification to support local active delineation of brain tumors. In: Communications in Computer and Information Science, pp. 3–14. Springer, Cham (2020).https://doi.org/10.1007/978-3-030-39343-4_1
6. Soret, M., Bacharach, S.L., Buvat, I.I.: Partial-volume effect in PET tumor imaging. J. Nucl. Med. **48**, 932–945 (2007). https://doi.org/10.2967/jnumed.106.035774
7. Stefano, A., Gallivanone, F., Messa, C.L., Gilardi, M.C.L., Castiglioni, I.: Metabolic impact of Partial Volume Correction of [18F]FDG PET-CT oncological studies on the assessment of tumor response to treatment. Q. J. Nucl. Med. Mol. Imaging. **58**, 413–423 (2014)
8. Li, X., Yankeelov, T.E., Peterson, T.E., Gore, J.C., Dawant, B.M.: Automatic nonrigid registration of whole body CT mice images. Med. Phys. **35**, 1507–1520 (2008). https://doi.org/ 10.1118/1.2889758
9. Elfarnawany, M., Alam, S.R., Agrawal, S.K., Ladak, H.M.: Evaluation of non-rigid registration parameters for atlas-based segmentation of CT images of human cochlea. Med. Imaging 2017 Image Process. **10133**, 101330Z (2017). https://doi.org/10.1117/12.2254040
10. Payette, K., et al.: An automatic multi-tissue human fetal brain segmentation benchmark using the Fetal Tissue Annotation Dataset. Sci. Data. **8**, 1–14 (2021). https://doi.org/10.1038/s41 597-021-00946-3
11. Zaitsev, M., Akin, B., LeVan, P., Knowles, B.R.: Prospective motion correction in functional MRI. Neuroimage **154**, 33–42 (2017). https://doi.org/10.1016/j.neuroimage.2016.11.014
12. Liu, Q., et al.: Fully automatic multi-atlas segmentation of CTA for partial volume correction in cardiac SPECT/CT. Phys. Med. Biol. **62**, 3944–3957 (2017). https://doi.org/10.1088/1361-6560/aa6520

13. Gispert, J.D., et al.: Influence of the normalization template on the outcome of statistical parametric mapping of PET scans. Neuroimage **19**, 601–612 (2003). https://doi.org/10.1016/S1053-8119(03)00072-7
14. Rajagopalan, V., Pioro, E.P.: Disparate voxel based morphometry (VBM) results between SPM and FSL softwares in ALS patients with frontotemporal dementia: which VBM results to consider? BMC Neurol. **15** (2015). https://doi.org/10.1186/s12883-015-0274-8
15. Benfante, V., et al.: A new preclinical decision support system based on PET radiomics: a preliminary study on the evaluation of an innovative 64Cu-Labeled chelator in mouse models. J. Imaging. **8**, 92 (2022). https://doi.org/10.3390/jimaging8040092
16. Vernuccio, F., Cannella, R., Comelli, A., Salvaggio, G., Lagalla, R., Midiri, M.: Radiomics and artificial intelligence: new frontiers in medicine. Recent Prog. Med. **111**(3), 130–135 (2020 Mar). Italian. https://www.recentiprogressi.it/archivio/3315/articoli/32853/
17. Barone, S., et al.: Hybrid descriptive-inferential method for key feature selection in prostate cancer radiomics. Appl. Stoch. Model. Bus. Ind. **37**, 961–972 (2021). https://doi.org/10.1002/asmb.2642
18. Stefano, A., et al.: Performance of radiomics features in the quantification of idiopathic pulmonary fibrosis from HRCT. Diagnostics. **10**, 306 (2020). https://doi.org/10.3390/diagnostics10050306
19. Stefano, A., et al.: Robustness of pet radiomics features: impact of co-registration with MRI. Appl. Sci. **11**, 10170 (2021). https://doi.org/10.3390/app112110170
20. Tosato, M., et al.: Copper coordination chemistry of Sulfur Pendant Cyclen derivatives: an attempt to hinder the reductive-induced Demetalation in 64/67Cu radiopharmaceuticals. Inorg. Chem. **60**, 11530–11547 (2021). https://doi.org/10.1021/ACS.INORGCHEM.1C01550/SUPPL_FILE/IC1C01550_SI_001.PDF
21. Dogdas, B., Stout, D., Chatziioannou, A.F., Leahy, R.M.: Digimouse: a 3D whole body mouse atlas from CT and cryosection data. Phys. Med. Biol. **52**, 577–587 (2007). https://doi.org/10.1088/0031-9155/52/3/003
22. Baiker, M., Staring, M., Löwik, C.W.G.M., Reiber, J.H.C., Lelieveldt, B.P.F.: Automated registration of whole-body follow-up MicroCT data of mice. Med. Image Comput. Comput. Assist. Interv. **14**, 516–523 (2011).https://doi.org/10.1007/978-3-642-23629-7_63
23. Stefano, A., et al.: A graph-based method for PET image segmentation in radiotherapy planning: a pilot study. In: Petrosino, A. (ed.) Lecture Notes in Computer Science (including subseries Lecture Notes in Artificial Intelligence and Lecture Notes in Bioinformatics), pp. 711–720. Springer-Verlag Berlin (2013). https://doi.org/10.1007/978-3-642-41184-7_72
24. Fornacon-Wood, I., et al.: Reliability and prognostic value of radiomic features are highly dependent on choice of feature extraction platform. Eur. Radiol. **30**, 6241–6250 (2020). https://doi.org/10.1007/s00330-020-06957-9
25. Van Griethuysen, J.J.M., et al.: Computational radiomics system to decode the radiographic phenotype. Cancer Res. **77**, e104–e107 (2017). https://doi.org/10.1158/0008-5472.CAN-17-0339
26. Comelli, A., Stefano, A.: Active surface for fully 3D automatic segmentation. In: Del Bimbo, A., et al. (eds.) Lecture Notes in Computer Science (including subseries Lecture Notes in Artificial Intelligence and Lecture Notes in Bioinformatics), pp. 357–367. Springer International Publishing, Cham (2021). https://doi.org/10.1007/978-3-030-68763-2_27
27. Raccagni, I., et al.: [18F]FDG and [18F]FLT PET for the evaluation of response to neoadjuvant chemotherapy in a model of triple negative breast cancer. PLoS One **13** (2018). https://doi.org/10.1371/journal.pone.0197754
28. Heckemann, R.A., Hajnal, J.V., Aljabar, P., Rueckert, D., Hammers, A.: Automatic anatomical brain MRI segmentation combining label propagation and decision fusion. Neuroimage **33**, 115–126 (2006). https://doi.org/10.1016/j.neuroimage.2006.05.061
29. Esteban, O., et al.: fMRIPrep: a robust preprocessing pipeline for functional MRI. Nat. Methods. **16**, 111–116 (2019). https://doi.org/10.1038/s41592-018-0235-4

MRI-Based Radiomics Analysis for Identification of Features Correlated with the Expanded Disability Status Scale of Multiple Sclerosis Patients

Valentina Nepi[1,2], Giovanni Pasini[1,2], Fabiano Bini[2], Franco Marinozzi[2], Giorgio Russo[1], and Alessandro Stefano[1(✉)]

[1] Institute of Molecular Bioimaging and Physiology, National Research Council (IBFM-CNR), 90015 Cefalù, Italy
alessandro.stefano@ibfm.cnr.it

[2] Department of Mechanical and Aerospace Engineering, Sapienza University of Rome, Eudossiana 18, 00184 Rome, Italy

Abstract. Multiple Sclerosis (MS) is considered a neurodegenerative disease that can cause multiple injuries within the Central Nervous System (CNS). MS can be diagnosed and qualitatively investigated with nuclear Magnetic Resonance (MR). In this study, a radiomics analysis is carried out considering 30 patients who underwent through MR studies consisting of T_1-weighted (T_1W), T_2-weighted (T_2W), Fluid Attenuated Inversion Recovery (FLAIR), and post-contrast administration T_1W (T_1WKS) images. Since radiomics features can vary greatly in relation to experimental extraction conditions, a first analysis is conducted by calculating the average percentage variations among features as the intensity bin size varies. A second analysis relates to the implementation of the predictive model based on the clinical outcome, namely the Expanded Disability Status Scale (EDSS) of MS. To this aim, the extracted features are reduced, selected, and then used to build the predictive model based on a machine learning algorithm, namely the Linear Discriminant Analysis (LDA). The k-fold strategy is used to split data into training and validation sets. Performance metrics of each model associated with the four MR images (T_1W, T_2W, FLAIR, and T_1WKS) as the bin size varies resulted in optimal predictive values close to 80%.

Keyword: Radiomics · Multiple Sclerosis · Machine Learning · Image Analysis · MRI

1 Introduction

Multiple Sclerosis (MS) is one of the world's most common disorders that causes non-traumatic neurological disability among young adults, between 20 and 40 years old. MS is considered as a neurodegenerative disease because its lesions can occur anywhere in the Central Nervous System (CNS) changing its morphology and structures. MS lesions

P. L. Mazzeo et al. (Eds.): ICIAP 2022 Workshops, LNCS 13373, pp. 362–373, 2022.
https://doi.org/10.1007/978-3-031-13321-3_32

are typically regarded as White Matter Lesions (WML) because, during an MS attack, the T-lymphocytes cells of immune system mistakenly recognize the internal protective layer of axons (i.e., the *myelin*). In fact, once the axons layer is identified as "foreign", T-cells start to destroy it, triggering inflammatory processes, and generating pathological tissues, called *sclerosis lesions* or *plaques*.

The MS is typically diagnosed based on the presenting signs and symptoms of patients, in combination with clinical, laboratory, and radiologic evidence of lesions. In particular, the Magnetic Resonance Imaging (MRI) is currently considered the best paraclinical test for MS diagnosis since it can detect areas of MS lesions in the 95% of cases [1].

There are four typical MRI-scans (i.e., sequences) capable to detect MS plaques: the T_1-weighted (T_1W), the T_2-weighted (T_2W), the Fluid Attenuated Inversion Recovery (FLAIR), and the post-contrast administration T_1-weighted (T_1WKS) images. MS lesions usually appear hyperintense in the MRI sequences, except for T_1W images where lesions appear as hypointense areas, also known as "Black Holes" (BHs), since they are displayed darker than the surrounding normal-appearing tissue.

For the patient neurological assessment and the evaluation of MS disability degree it is important to assign an Expanded Disability Status Scale (EDSS) number [2]. EDSS ranges from 0 to 10 with a 0.5-unit increment starting from 1.

Radiomics is an emerging research field based on a deep analysis and mining of data features to convert biomedical images into high-dimensional and mineable data. These data, called "*radiomics features*", are quantitative metrics that can be extracted from MRI or Computer Tomography (CT), and Positron Emission Tomography (PET) scans. The most important and commonly used features can be grouped into three large classes:

1) Shape Features, or Morphological Features, that describe geometric characteristics of the Volume of Interest (VOI), such as Mesh or Voxel Volume.
2) 1st Order Statistical Features, describing grey levels distribution within the VOI, such as Entropy or Kurtosis.
3) Texture Features, used to obtain information about grey levels patterns within the VOI and are the most complex.

All the aforementioned features reveal quantitative, predictive, or prognostic associations between biomedical/radiological images and medical outcomes since they can capture tissue and lesion properties. This approach enables the evaluation of how features change over time and the creation of personalized support models for clinical decision, such as therapy response assessment or diagnosis [3–7].

Every radiomics workflow starts [8, 9] with image acquisition using the abovementioned diagnostic techniques. After image reconstruction, a VOI is selected using an appropriate segmentation method, e.g. those proposed in [10–12], that defines the target for feature extraction. The calculation of these features is performed through an image-processing software. Afterwards, a statistical model that allows the selection of features able to predict a clinical outcome is built. Finally, a classification model needs to be performed.

Among all the tools used for radiomics, one of the most popular is 3D Slicer [13], a free, open-source and multi-platform software package widely used for medical, biomedical, and related imaging researches. The tool has a Radiomics extension, PyRadiomics [14], that is an open-source Image Biomarkers Standardization Initiative (IBSI) [15] compliant python package for the extraction of radiomics features. However, feature selection and the subsequent machine learning algorithm cannot be carried out through those tools and are conducted outside 3D Slicer.

The aim of this work is to make a complete radiomics study, from PyRadiomics feature extraction to model validation, focusing the attention on mean percentage variations of features varying bin size parameter and on model performance in relation to four MRI sequences.

2 Materials and Methods

The analysis is made with a notebook whose specifications are:

1. MotherBoard ASUSTek COMPUTER INC. X550JX
2. CPU Intel Core i7-4720HQ @ 2.60 GHz, 2594 MHz
3. GPU NVIDIA GeForce GTX 950M
4. RAM DDR3 8,00 GB
5. Windows 10 Home v. 21H2 64-bit

2.1 Dataset

The studied dataset is composed of MRI-scans [16, 17] that are performed on 30 patients affected by MS. Each patient MR scan consists of a 2D T_1W, a 2D T_2W, a 3D FLAIR, and a 2D T_1WKS. With reference to the study [16], all the medical images are acquired by the same 3T Siemens Magnetom Trio MR system at the University Medical Center Ljubljana (UMCL) to ensure identical acquisition protocol. Moreover, all the images are already pre-processed [16, 18, 19], and T_1W and T_2W are resampled into FLAIR image space. In addition to these four scans, each patient WML segmentation, obtained in native FLAIR image space and based on multi-raters' consensus [16], is part of the provided dataset. All the MRI-scans packages and the consensus segmentations are available [16] in NIfTI [20] format. Finally, the dataset is supplemented by a.csv file in which are indicated all the characteristics of MS patients as age, sex, MS type [21], and EDSS [2].

Three patients have no indication about the EDSS, and they are therefore excluded from this study. The radiomics feature extraction is firstly conducted for 27 patients and this part of both the study and the results is identified with the "*global*" caption.

In addition, as the disease name suggests, the MS has multiple focus areas that are separated by their own definition in nature. Since only one lesion mask is available for lesions of each patient, an operation called "islands effect" is performed in 3D Slicer [13] on the provided consensus segmentation to have masks as many as diseased areas. The 3D Slicer tool removes all connected regions that have a voxel count less than a certain number chosen by operator, being the connected regions defined as a group of voxels which touch each other but are surrounded by zero valued voxels. The tool essentially creates a unique segment for each connected region of the loaded consensus mask. After its application, the features extraction is repeated. The outcomes of this step are marked in the results section as "*islands*".

2.2 Feature Extraction

The feature extraction is performed with 3D Slicer v4.11.20200930 and its extension of PyRadiomics v3.0.1. A total of 107 features is obtained.

As recommended by the IBSI standard [15], there are three parameters that must be considered in a radiomics study:

1. A *Spatial Resampling*, with the aim of modifying the (x,y,z) dimensions of voxels and make them isotropic.
2. An *Intensity Rescaling*, that is a normalization to exclude voxels that are defined "outliers".
3. An *Intensity Discretization,* that is conceptually equivalent to the creation of a histogram.

Since the available images in [17] are pre-processed [16], the provided T_1W and T_2W scans are already co-registered [18], normalized [19], and lastly resampled into FLAIR image space. In this way, among the three IBSI parameters above-mentioned, only the *Intensity Discretization* is varied in this study, choosing different Fixed Bin Size (FBS) values, to assess the average percentage variations among the extracted features (for more information see the next section). The used PyRadiomics configuration is summarized in Table 1.

Table 1. IBSI recommended configuration for feature extraction.

Pre-processing	PyRadiomics
Spatial resampling	None
Intensity rescaling	Default: relative $I \in (min, max)_{VOI}$
Intensity discretization	FBS (5, 25, and 32)

2.2.1 Intensity Discretization

The *Intensity Discretization* consists in grouping the original intensity values according to specific range intervals (bins). Let w_b the width for every intensity interval, i.e., w_b is the bin width, $X_{gl,min}$ and $X_{gl,k}$ the gray level intensities before and after discretization, respectively the minimum referred within VOI and the value of the k voxel, discretized intensities are computed as follows:

$$X_{d,k} = \left[\frac{X_{gl,k} - X_{gl,min}}{w_b} \right] + 1 \qquad (1)$$

Since the first part of this study focuses on calculation of how much different bin sizes can affect the extracted features, three different bin sizes are considered: 5, 25 and 32. These choices are justified because:

- 5 is the bin used in radiomics study for white matter hyperintensities [22].
- 25 is the default value preset in 3D Slicer PyRadiomics [14].
- 32 is in line with a radiomics study in which it's indicated as good compromise when T_1W and T_2-FLAIR sequences are investigated [23].

2.2.2 Mean Percentage Variations of Extracted Features

Let:

- i the index of every single extracted feature and $i = 1:107$.
- $x_i (w_{bk})$ the value for the i-th feature calculated for the w_{bk} bin size with $k = 1,2,3$.
- $b_1 = 25$, $b_2 = 32$ and $b_3 = 5$.

To detect how features change varying bin size, the percentage variation is calculated considering the w_{25} value as reference (i.e., the PyRadiomics default) and increasing (w_{32}) or decreasing (w_5) its value as presented in Sect. 2.2.1.

For the first comparison, from w_{25} to w_{32} (reported as $w_{25}\_w_{32}$), the absolute percentage variation is calculated as follows:

$$\Delta x_i \% (w_{25}\_w_{32}) = \left| \frac{x_i(w_{32}) - x_i(w_{25})}{x_i(w_{25})} \cdot 100 \right| \tag{2}$$

This formula is also valid for the second comparison, with w_5 replacing w_{32}.

The mean μ_i of the absolute percentage variation referred to all n_{global} (=27) analysed patients and to the i-th feature is:

$$\mu_i = \frac{\sum \Delta x_i \% (w_{25}\_w_{32})}{n_{global}} \tag{3}$$

2.2.3 Mean Percentage Variations of Extracted Features Within Same Class

Let the index of each feature class defined as $j = 1:7$, each one containing its own total number n_j of features, the i-th features can be regrouped as follows [14]:

- *Shape class* if $i = 1:14, j = 1$ and $= n_j 14$.
- *First-order* class if $i = 15:32, j = 2$ and $= n_j 18$.
- "*glcm*" the Gray Level Co-occurrence Matrix class if $i = 33:56, j = 3$ and $n_j=24$.
- "*gldm*" the Gray Level Dependence Matrix if $i = 57:70, j = 4$ and $= n_j 14$.
- "*glrlm*" the Gray Level Run Length Matrix class if $i = 71:86, j = 5$ and $n_j=16$.
- "*glszm*" the Gray Level Size Zone Matrix class if $i = 87:102, j = 6$ and $= n_j 16$.
- "*ngtdm*" the Neighborhood Gray Tone Difference Matrix class if $i = 103:107, j = 7$ and $n_j=5$.

Considering each j-th class, the mean μ_j and the standard deviation σ_j are calculated as follows:

$$\mu_j = \frac{\sum \mu_i}{n_j} \tag{4}$$

$$\sigma_j = \sqrt{\frac{\sum (\mu_i - \mu_j)^2}{n_j}} \tag{5}$$

2.3 Feature Selection

The feature selection algorithm used in this study is a hybrid method consisting of a point biserial correlation index in combination with a logistic regression model [24]. The aim of such algorithm is to sort features assigning them a score and to select the most discriminant features.

The hybrid algorithm works for binary classification. A dichotomous outcome is then chosen and two n_{pat} patient subsets are generated as follows:

$$clinical_{outcome}(EDSS) = \begin{cases} 0, EDSS < 4 & (n_{pat} = 8) \\ 1, EDSS \geq 4 & (n_{pat} = 19) \end{cases} \tag{6}$$

Since EDSS not only considers the disability severity referred to human functional systems [2] but also the patient ability to ambulate, the value of 4 is chosen as threshold. An EDSS ≥ 4 underlies the first walking disorder because the MS patient is fully ambulatory without aid for 500 m.

2.4 Predictive Model

In order to build predictive model and evaluate its performance, a Linear Discriminant Analysis (LDA) [25] is used. In particular, a K-fold Cross validation and K-fold Stratified Cross Validation is used to perform model validation. With k = 3, three models are generated. For each one the Receiver Operating Characteristic (ROC) curve and Area Under Curve (AUC) value are obtained. Finally, the averaged ROC curve of the generated ROC curves and its related AUC value are computed.

2.5 "Islands"

As anticipated in the Sect. 2.1, the "islands effect" of 3D Slicer [13] is performed on the provided consensus segmentation. To realize this study part, a 64 minimum voxel size is set. Through this operation, the initial dataset of n_{global} patients is incremented since the total number of generated islands is $n_{islands} = 1860$.

This procedure is repeated for all the four available sequences. An example of this application is displayed in Fig. 1. In this way, more data are available to support the development of a radiomics signature. All the steps analyzed for the initial n_{global} patients are implemented on the $n_{islands}$ samples: the feature extraction, the calculation of their mean percentage variation, the feature selection and the model evaluation are performed again on this "new increased" dataset. In addition, and with reference to the Sect. 2.3, the imbalance of the two n_{pat} subsets associated with the dichotomous clinical outcome is reduced as follows:

$$clinical_{outcome}(EDSS) = \begin{cases} 0, EDSS < 4(n_{pat} = 862) \\ 1, EDSS \geq 4(n_{pat} = 998) \end{cases} \tag{7}$$

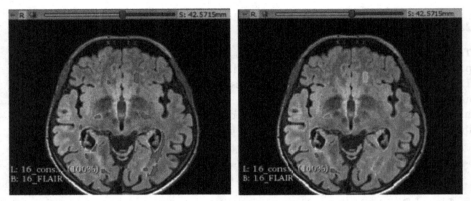

Fig. 1. The "islands effect" is applied on the 16th patient and FLAIR sequence. On the left the initial consensus mask, on the right the same mask edited by 3D Slicer "islands" tool.

3   Results and Discussion

Overall, this study can be considered split in two parts.

1) The first one is dedicated to investigate how much features change focusing the attention on the mean percentage variation of extracted features within same class as the FBS varies.
2) The other one is concentrated to the mean AUC of the predictive models.

All the phases of this radiomics study are reproduced with reference to three different w_{bk} bin size (as mentioned in Sect. 2.2.1, $b_1 = 25$, $b_2 = 32$, and $b_3 = 5$) and for the entire set of available MR sequences. Results are provided in separated tables (Table 2 and Table 3). The "*global*" and the "*islands*" refer to the n_{global} and $n_{islands}$ dataset respectively, while the columns indicate the bin change. Results are shown with reference to the single sequence and only the most and the least robust feature class are reported in the rows. Moreover, for each sequence, the best mean AUC of the predictive models (both "*global*" and "*islands*") is reported choosing the highest obtained value and clearly specifying with which w_{bk} is possible to achieve it.

3.1 Global Results

In the *global* study, varying the FBS, the mean percentage variation of shape feature class is approximately 0% for all the sequences. In particular, increasing the FBS from 25 to 32, the T_2W and T_1WKS analyses are significant since all feature classes experience a 0% variation (see Table 2). For FLAIR and T_1W studies, the least robust class is the glszm. Decreasing the w_{bk} from 25 to 5, the least robust class is the glcm in all the sequences.

Table 2. Mean percentage variations of feature classes obtained in the *global* study.

FLAIR	$w_{25}\_w_{32}$	$w_{25}\_w_5$
Most robust	0% ± 0% (shape_class)	0.86% ± 0.33% (shape_class)
Least robust	40.26% ± 37.12% (glszm_class)	2847.27% ± 10848.01% (glcm_class)
T_2W	$w_{25}\_w_{32}$	$w_{25}\_w_5$
Most robust	0% ± 0% (all_feature_classes)	0.37% ± 0.33% (shape_class)
Least robust	None	8934.00% ± 34111.93% (glcm_class)
T_1W	$w_{25}\_w_{32}$	$w_{25}\_w_5$
Most robust	0% ± 0% (shape_class)	0.37% ± 0.33% (shape_class)
Least robust	55.34% ± 62.74% (glszm_class)	3138.60% ± 12499.58% (glcm_class)
T_1WKS	$w_{25}\_w_{32}$	$w_{25}\_w_5$
Most robust	0% ± 0% (all_feature_classes)	0.37% ± 0.33% (shape_class)
Least robust	None	7827.34% ± 33507.04% (glcm_class)

3.2 Islands Results

The results obtained in the *islands* study about shape feature class are the opposite of the *global* one: increasing w_{bk}, a mean percentage variation almost equal to 0% is obtained, vice versa decreasing w_{bk} a 0% variation is obtained (see Table 3).

Table 3. Mean percentage variations of feature classes obtained in the *islands* study.

FLAIR	$w_{25}\_w_{32}$	$w_{25}\_w_5$
Most robust	0.25% ± 0.17% (shape_class)	0% ± 0% (shape_class)
Least robust	2521099.64% ± 5636426.94% (ngtdm_class)	14571.01% ± 39358.81% (glszm_class)
T_2W	$w_{25}\_w_{32}$	$w_{25}\_w_5$

(*continued*)

Table 3. (*continued*)

FLAIR	$w_{25}\_w_{32}$	$w_{25}\_w_5$
Most robust	0.25% ± 0.17% (shape_class)	0% ± 0% (shape_class)
Least robust	55.48% ± 49.38% (glszm_class)	3299.89% ± 12213.90% (glcm_class)
T_1W	$w_{25}\_w_{32}$	$w_{25}\_w_5$
Most robust	0.25% ± 0.17% (shape_class)	0% ± 0% (shape_class)
Least robust	96842.95% ± 216407.36% (ngtdm_class)	3400.13% ± 11308.51% (glcm_class)
T_1WKS	$w_{25}\_w_{32}$	$w_{25}\_w_5$
Most robust	0.25% ± 0.17% (shape_class)	0% ± 0% (shape_class)
Least robust	158444.79% ± 354156.82% (ngtdm_class)	3125.70% ± 9925.39% (glszm_class)

In particular, increasing w_{bk} the T_2W analysis is characterized by the glszm as least robust class, where in the other MRI sequences there is the ngtdm class. Decreasing the w_{bk} the least robust class, as in the global case, continues to be the glcm in T_2W and T_1W sequences. Instead, the least robust class for FLAIR and T_1WKS is the glszm.

3.3 Predictive Model

The performance metrics of the predictive models are evaluated considering the mean AUC of the averaged ROC curves. The best mean AUC values are listed in Table 4. Focusing the attention on the first column and the w_{bk} values, this last is in agreement with the bin size choice 5 and 32 recommended in the two above mentioned radiomics studies [22, 23] (see Sect. 2.2.1.).

Table 4. Highest mean AUC results of the predictive models obtained for each studied sequence.

Study modality	Mean_AUC
FLAIR_global_w_5	0.83
FLAIR_islands_w_5	0.85
T_2W_global_w_5	0.85
T_2W_islands_w_5	0.78
T_1W_global_w_{32}	0.86
T_1W_islands_w_{32}	0.75
T_1WKS_global_w_5	0.85
T_1WKS_islands_w_5	0.78

As an example, Fig. 2 shows the two best ROC curves referred to the predictive model obtained in *global* (on the left) and *islands* (on the right) study.

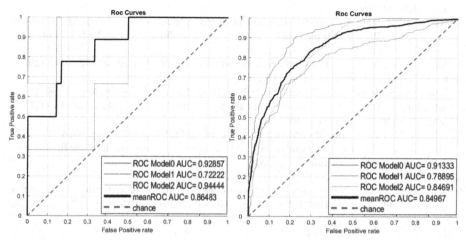

Fig. 2. The ROC Curves and the related AUC values. The light blue, pink and yellow curves refer to each generated model. The black curve is the mean ROC. The $T_1W\_global\_ w_{32}$ is on the left, the FLAIR_islands_ w_5 is on the right.

4 Conclusions

These results confirm that intensity discretization is an important parameter because increasing or decreasing the bin width has a significant influence over some radiomics feature values.

The shape features class always experiences a lower mean percentage variation confirming its role of the most robust class because it depends on the target geometry.

Furthermore, with an LDA model, it can be concluded that an optimal predictive value (~80%) is obtained in all the considered sequences. The higher value for the *global* and the *islands* studies is achieved for the bin width set on 32 and 5, respectively. This confirms the choice made in previous studies to use these values for radiomics MRI analysis [23] and, particularly, for white matter hyperintensity [22]. In another paper [26], 50 was used as a fixed number of bins indicating the potential of conventional MRI and quantitative MRI radiomics in MS-related biomarker development. An analysis based on this value will be subject of future research.

Our work tries to study how much the lack of a practical guideline might impact on the radiomics results, and therefore on their repeatability and reliability. The IBSI seeks to provide recommendations but not standardised protocols. Without the latter, the radiomics deeply depends on the parameters chosen by the operator, as affirmed in [27].

Future work will aim to apply the proposed methodology on a larger initial dataset and to carry out a more in-depth analysis of the texture features. Finally, deep learning methods will be also considered, e.g. [28, 29].

References

1. Grossman, R.I., McGowan, J.C.: Perspectives on multiple sclerosis. Am. J. Neuroradiol. **19**, 1251–1265 (1998)
2. Kurtzke, J.F.: Rating neurologic impairment in multiple sclerosis: An expanded disability status scale (EDSS). Neurology **33**, 1444–1452 (1983). https://doi.org/10.1212/wnl.33.11. 1444
3. Mayerhoefer, M.E., et al.: Introduction to radiomics. J. Nucl. Med. **61**, 488–495 (2020). https://doi.org/10.2967/JNUMED.118.222893
4. Vernuccio, F., Cannella, R., Comelli, A., Salvaggio, G., Lagalla, R., Midiri, M.: Radiomics and artificial intelligence: New frontiers in medicine. Recenti Prog. Med. **111**, 130–135 (2020). https://doi.org/10.1701/3315.32853
5. Alongi, P., et al.: Radiomics analysis of 18F-Choline PET/CT in the prediction of disease outcome in high-risk prostate cancer: An explorative study on machine learning feature classification in 94 patients. Eur. Radiol. **31**(7), 4595–4605 (2021). https://doi.org/10.1007/s00 330-020-07617-8
6. Stefano, A., et al.: Performance of radiomics features in the quantification of idiopathic pulmonary fibrosis from HRCT. Diagnostics. **10**, 306 (2020). https://doi.org/10.3390/diagno stics10050306
7. Lambin, P., et al.: Radiomics: Extracting more information from medical images using advanced feature analysis. Eur. J. Cancer. **48**, 441–446 (2012). https://doi.org/10.1016/j.ejca. 2011.11.036
8. Comelli, A., et al.: Radiomics: A new biomedical workflow to create a predictive model. In: Papież, B.W., Namburete, A.I.L., Yaqub, M., Noble, J.A. (eds.) MIUA 2020. CCIS, vol. 1248, pp. 280–293. Springer, Cham (2020). https://doi.org/10.1007/978-3-030-52791-4_22
9. van Timmeren, J.E., Cester, D., Tanadini-Lang, S., Alkadhi, H., Baessler, B.: Radiomics in medical imaging—"how-to" guide and critical reflection. Insights Imaging **11**(1), 1–16 (2020). https://doi.org/10.1186/s13244-020-00887-2
10. Stefano, A., et al.: A graph-based method for pet image segmentation in radiotherapy planning: A pilot study. In: Petrosino, A. (ed.) ICIAP 2013. LNCS, vol. 8157, pp. 711–720. Springer, Heidelberg (2013). https://doi.org/10.1007/978-3-642-41184-7_72
11. Comelli, A., et al.: Tissue classification to support local active delineation of brain tumors. In: Zheng, Y., Williams, B.M., Chen, K. (eds.) MIUA 2019. CCIS, vol. 1065, pp. 3–14. Springer, Cham (2020). https://doi.org/10.1007/978-3-030-39343-4_1
12. Agnello, L., Comelli, A., Ardizzone, E., Vitabile, S.: Unsupervised tissue classification of brain MR images for voxel-based morphometry analysis. Int. J. Imaging Syst. Technol. **26**, 136–150 (2016). https://doi.org/10.1002/ima.22168
13. Fedorov, A., et al.: 3D Slicer as an image computing platform for the quantitative imaging network. Magn. Reson. Imaging. **30**, 1323–1341 (2012). https://doi.org/10.1016/j.mri.2012. 05.001
14. Van Griethuysen, J.J.M., et al.: Computational radiomics system to decode the radiographic phenotype. Cancer Res. **77**, e104–e107 (2017). https://doi.org/10.1158/0008-5472.CAN-17-0339
15. Zwanenburg, A., et al.: The image biomarker standardization initiative: Standardized quantitative radiomics for high-throughput image-based phenotyping. Radiology **295**, 328–338 (2020). https://doi.org/10.1148/radiol.2020191145
16. Lesjak, Ž, et al.: A novel public MR image dataset of multiple sclerosis patients with lesion segmentations based on multi-rater consensus. Neuroinformatics **16**(1), 51–63 (2017). https:// doi.org/10.1007/s12021-017-9348-7
17. Quantim knowledge-base: https://www.quantim.eu/. Accessed 11 Apr 2022

18. Klein, S., Staring, M., Murphy, K., Viergever, M.A., Pluim, J.P.W.: Elastix: A toolbox for intensity-based medical image registration. IEEE Trans. Med. Imaging. **29**, 196–205 (2010). https://doi.org/10.1109/TMI.2009.2035616
19. Tustison, N.J., et al.: N4ITK: Improved N3 bias correction. IEEE Trans. Med. Imaging. **29**, 1310–1320 (2010). https://doi.org/10.1109/TMI.2010.2046908
20. NIfTI background: https://nifti.nimh.nih.gov/. Accessed 11 Apr 2022
21. Kim, W., Kim, H.J.: Multiple sclerosis. J. Korean Med. Assoc. **52**, 665–676 (2009). https://doi.org/10.5124/jkma.2009.52.7.665
22. Bretzner, M., et al.: MRI radiomic signature of white matter hyperintensities is associated with clinical phenotypes. Front. Neurosci. **15**, 850 (2021). https://doi.org/10.3389/fnins.2021.691244
23. Carré, A., et al.: Standardization of brain MR images across machines and protocols: Bridging the gap for MRI-based radiomics. Sci. Rep. **10**, 1–15 (2020). https://doi.org/10.1038/s41598-020-69298-z
24. Barone, S., et al.: Hybrid descriptive-inferential method for key feature selection in prostate cancer radiomics. Appl. Stoch. Model. Bus. Ind. **37**, 961–972 (2021). https://doi.org/10.1002/asmb.2642
25. Tharwat, A., Gaber, T., Ibrahim, A., Hassanien, A.E.: Linear discriminant analysis: A detailed tutorial. AI Commun. **30**, 169–190 (2017). https://doi.org/10.3233/AIC-170729
26. Lavrova, E., et al.: Exploratory radiomic analysis of conventional vs. quantitative brain MRI: Toward automatic diagnosis of early multiple sclerosis. Front. Neurosci. **15**, 1–14 (2021). https://doi.org/10.3389/fnins.2021.679941
27. Stefano, A., et al.: Robustness of pet radiomics features: Impact of co-registration with MRI. Appl. Sci. **11**, 10170 (2021). https://doi.org/10.3390/app112110170
28. Stefano, A., Comelli, A.: Customized efficient neural network for Covid-19 infected region identification in CT images. J. Imaging. **7**, 131 (2021). https://doi.org/10.3390/jimaging7080131
29. Salvaggio, G., et al.: Deep learning network for segmentation of the prostate gland with median lobe enlargement in T2-weighted MR images: Comparison with manual segmentation method. Curr. Probl. Diagn. Radiol.2021https://doi.org/10.1067/j.cpradiol.2021.06.006

matRadiomics: From Biomedical Image Visualization to Predictive Model Implementation

Giovanni Pasini[1,2], Fabiano Bini[2], Giorgio Russo[1], Franco Marinozzi[2], and Alessandro Stefano[1(✉)] (iD)

[1] Institute of Molecular Bioimaging and Physiology, National Research Council (IBFM-CNR), 90015 Cefalù, Italy
alessandro.stefano@ibfm.cnr.it

[2] Department of Mechanical and Aerospace Engineering, Sapienza University of Rome, Eudossiana 18, 00184 Rome, Italy

Abstract. The development of radiomics tools allows the extraction of quantitative features from medical images, thus enhancing the available information for clinicians. However, to date, these tools do not allow the user to complete the radiomics workflow by stopping at the feature extraction step. Therefore, a new software, namely *matRadiomics*, was developed as a user-friendly tool with the aim of allowing the user to carry out all the steps of a radiomics study. Using a single tool, i) biomedical images can be imported and inspected, ii) the target can be identified and segmented, iii) features can be extracted from the target, iv) reduced and selected, and v) used to build a predictive model using machine learning algorithms. As result, two different feature extractors can be chosen, a Matlab-based extractor, and the Pyradiomics extractor naturally integrated into matRadiomics. Extracted features can be selected using a hybrid descriptive-inferential method, while selected features can be used to train three different classifiers: Linear Discriminant Analysis, K-Nearest Neighbors, and Support Vector Machines. Models' validation is performed using K-Fold Cross Validation and K-Fold Stratified Cross Validation. Finally, the performance metrics of each model are shown in the graphical interface of matRadiomics. In conclusion, the result of this study was the development, implementation, and validation of an innovative and complete radiomics tool that accompanies the researcher throughout the whole radiomics workflow.

Keywords: Radiomics · Software package · Machine learning · Image analysis · PET · MRI · CT

1 Introduction

Radiomics is a rapidly evolving research field whose initial aim is the extraction of quantitative parameters, commonly called radiomics features, from medical images. Radiomics features can be extracted from Positron Emission Tomography (PET) [1],

Magnetic Resonance Imaging (MRI) [2], and Computed Tomography (CT) [3] images. Extracted features can be grouped into three large classes: Shape Features, or Morphological Features, 1st Order Statistical Features, and Texture Features. The goal of Shape Features is to describe geometric characteristics of the Volume of Interest (VOI), such as Mesh Total Volume and Total Surface, while 1st Order Statistical Features are used to describe grey levels distribution within the VOI, such as Kurtosis and Skewness. Texture Features, which are the most complex, can be used to obtain information about grey levels patterns within the VOI [4].

Moreover, radiomics data are mineable, thus they can be used to identify personalized predictive and/or prognostic models to support the medical decision process [5]. Radiomics features can be used to check the characteristics of a lesion and its evolution over time, potentially capturing the evolution of the disease, and improving the prediction of patient overall survival and/or outcome [6–8]. Radiomics could be further used to predict and monitor response to immunotherapy treatment when used in combination with Immuno-PET radiotracers [9, 10]. Therefore, radiomics should not be limited only to its initial aim of extracting features, but it is further extended to the construction of a predictive model, which is its final goal. Accordingly, radiomics is divided into a workflow that starts from target identification and ends with the construction of a predictive model. The steps are: i) target identification, ii) target segmentation, iii) feature extraction, iv) feature selection, and v) predictive model implementation [11, 12].

Among all the tools used for radiomics, LIFEx [12] and PyRadiomics [13] are the most popular. LIFEx is an image biomarker standardization initiative (IBSI) [14] compliant freeware that allows the user to fulfill the first three steps of the workflow from target identification to feature extraction. IBSI addresses the main issue in the feature extraction process: the reproducibility of the extracted features. For this reason, the IBSI was introduced for the standardization of radiomics features [15]. LIFEx can be used to interact with its User Interface (UI). On the other hand, PyRadiomics is an open-source IBSI compliant python package that can only be used to carry out feature extraction and does not have its own UI. Its advantage is that it can be integrated into other software solutions, such as 3D Slicer that works as PyRadiomics UI. The major issue with both tools is that the radiomics workflow stops at the feature extraction step.

Aim of this work was the development, implementation, and validation of an innovative tool designed to carry out all the steps of the radiomics workflow mentioned above. The tool, written in Matlab r2021a Update 5 [16] and Python 3.7.0 [17], was called matRadiomics. matRadiomics supports macOS and Windows operating systems, includes an innovative algorithm for feature selection, has a user-friendly interface, and integrates PyRadiomics, which makes it a software alternative for 3D Slicer, but with the advantage that the radiomics workflow can be completed within the same tool.

2 Materials and Methods

matRadiomics can be installed on desktop Personal Computers (PCs), Laptops, and Notebooks and runs under macOS and Windows operating systems.

The tool has been implemented into a Desktop PC whose specifications are:

1. MotherBoard ASUS PRIME X470-PRO

2. CPU AMD Ryzen 5 2600
3. GPU NVIDIA GeForce GTX 1060 6 GB
4. RAM DDR4 16 GB
5. Windows 10 Home 64-bit

and into a MacBook Pro (Retina, 13 in., Early 2015) whose specifications are:

1. CPU Intel Core I5 dual core @2.7 GHz
2. GPU Intel Iris Graphics 6100 1536 MB
3. RAM DDR3 8 GB
4. macOS Catalina

2.1 matRadiomics Architecture Design

The system architecture of the matRadiomics tool consists of four layers (Fig. 1):

- The first layer is the matRadiomics Graphical User Interface (GUI), which receives the user input.
- The second layer is the matRadiomics Model, which processes the user requests.
- The third layer is the Matlab layer which supports image/data handling and processing, feature selection, and calls python modules.
- The fourth layer is the Python layer, which is called by the Matlab layer in order to accomplish special operations.

More details are provided in the next section.

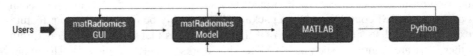

Fig. 1. The matRadiomics architecture

2.2 Software Design

matRadiomics tool has been developed in Matlab r2021a Update 5 [16], and ad-hoc utilities were implemented using Python 3.7.0 [17]. Three modules (namely, Dicom Module, Pyradiomics Module, and Classification Module) were written in Python, and they are initialized at matRadiomics startup. In fact, Matlab naturally integrates other programming languages such as Python, Java, and C/C++, whose modules and libraries can be called directly from the Matlab main code.

In total seven Python libraries were used: pydicom, pyradiomics, pandas, numpy, scikit-learn, openpyxel, and xldr.

matRadiomics user-friendly interface was designed using the AppDesigner [18] tool and was developed with the aim of simplifying the radiomics workflow. The use of

Matlab and its AppDesigner simplified the design of the graphical interface and the implementation of the whole radiomics workflow, while the use of Python allowed using proven libraries with extended documentation and solved some computational speed issues.

2.2.1 Reading Dicom Files

The Dicom Module has been implemented to read DICOM (Digital Imaging and Communications in Medicine) Files [19]. Using Pydicom library the full list of DICOM attributes and image voxel data are read [20]. Attributes and images are displayed in matRadiomics UI. Automatic rescaling of voxel intensities is performed while reading images. This procedure is also used to convert voxel intensities to activity for PET scans, and to Hounsfield Units for CT scans.

2.2.2 Viewing Imported Images

Functions for displaying all the images data were implemented. The user can scroll through them either by rotating the mouse wheel or by interacting with a slider. Moreover, the current slice number and some DICOM attributes are constantly updated.

2.2.3 Target Identification and Segmentation

This step represents the process of defining the 3D VOI in the image in such a way as to avoid distortions in feature extraction. This is an important issue in radiomics studies where target segmentation is manually obtained. Consequently, the use of an operator-independent segmentation system is highly recommended [21, 22]. For this reason, functions for drawing a starting region of interest (ROI) and for automatic segmentations were implemented. The area that contains the target can be identified by drawing a freehand contour that surrounds it. This ROI can also be moved within the image. Then, contour coordinates are then stored in memory. After that, segmentation can be performed using a thresholding algorithm. The percentage of threshold relative to the maximum voxel intensity within the ROI and the slices within which the thresholding algorithm must work can be manually adjusted. The segmentation process ends with the generation of a binary VOI that overlaps the images.

2.2.4 Feature Extraction

Two extractors have been implemented in matRadiomics, as reported in the two next sections.

matRadiomics Extractor

Functions for pre-processing and feature extraction were written. The segmented volume can be spatial resampled, re-segmented, and discretized. Functions for the extraction of Shape Features and 1st Order Statistical Features were implemented. Shape Features are based on the mesh representation of the segmented volume, which is displayed in matRadiomics UI when the extraction process is completed. Mesh representation is obtained using a Marching Cubes algorithm [23–25]. 1st Order Statistical Features can be extracted from the non-discretized segmented volume and from the discretized volume. For the extraction of Texture Features an existing IBSI compliant Matlab package, called Radiomics Toolbox [26, 27], has been integrated into matRadiomics. Results obtained using matRadiomics extractor were validated by making use of images, and segmentations provided by the IBSI [14] manual. The configuration in Table 1 was set in matRadiomics, and the results were compared to those reported in the IBSI manual.

Table 1. Reference manual configuration for extraction

Extractor	Spatial resampling	Re-segmentation	Discretization
matRadiomics	NO	[−500,400] HU	Bin width = 25

Pyradiomics Extractor
Pyradiomics integration was carried out using the Pyradiomics Module. Pre-processing and extraction options can be set by interacting with matRadiomics UI, then they are sent to the Pyradiomics Module which processes them. Once the extraction is complete, results are displayed in matRadiomics UI. Pyradiomics integration was validated by comparing the features extracted from 27 patients affected by Multiple Sclerosis (MRI images) [28], using PyRadiomics integrated in matRadiomics and PyRadiomics used externally.

The configuration used is reported in Table 2.

Table 2. Extraction configuration used in order to validate PyRadiomics integration

Extractor	Spatial resampling	Re-segmentation	Discretization
Pyradiomics	NO	NO	Bin width = 32

2.2.5 Feature Selection

The Feature Selection algorithm used in matRadiomics is the reproduction of the algorithm proposed in [29]. In this study, a hybrid method consisting of the Point Biserial Correlation in combination with logistic regression was proposed.

Briefly, this algorithm sorts features based on the absolute value of the point biserial correlation index, then the subset of the most important features is extracted by iteratively building a regression logistic model. In addition to the mentioned method, two other methods have been implemented: T-Test and Relieff. All the algorithms are meant to assign a score to the features [30–32].

matRadiomics Feature Selection Scheme can be seen in Fig. 2.

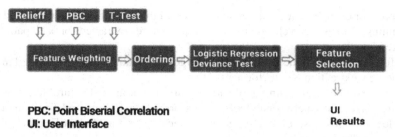

Fig. 2. Feature selection process implemented in the matRadiomics tool

The Classification Module was written to build predictive models. Python scikit-learn library was used to implement functions that allow model validation, model training, and model performance evaluation. K-fold Cross validation and K-fold Stratified Cross Validation can be selected to perform model validation. Linear Discriminant Analysis (LDA) [33], K-Nearest Neighbors (KNN) [34] and Support Vector Machines (SVM) [35] were implemented.

The aim of the Classification Module is to obtain performance metrics like accuracy, true positive rate, and false positive rate for each model produced by the K-fold cross-validation. Then these metrics are sent back to the matRadiomics model in order to build the Receiver operating characteristics (ROC) curves and display results.

The average ROC curve is computed as the global performance metric. It is calculated as an average of the ROC curves generated for each k group produced by the cross validation. Moreover, Area Under Curve (AUC) values are computed for each ROC and for the average ROC. Accuracy values, mean accuracy, and total confusion matrix are displayed in matRadiomics UI.

3 Results and Discussion

3.1 Walk-Through

- On the program start-up, the user is presented with matRadiomics UI. Five tabs are shown: Segmentation Tab, Feature Extraction Tab, Feature Selection Tab, Selected Features Tab, and Model Training Tab.
- Before importing files, the user needs to create a series that is the "Series folder" containing all the features extracted for the chosen study type.
- The user can import DICOM files.
- DICOM Attributes will be shown in the segmentation tab together with the images.
- The user can identify the target using the Draw ROI tool allowing to draw the ROI.
- The user can automatically segment the target using the Threshold Tool.
- In the feature Extracted Tab the user can set the extraction options and then click on the "Extract Features" button to start the feature extraction process.
- Extracted features are shown in a table in the same tab.
- The process can be repeated for different patients and the extracted features are shown one below the other in the same table in the Extracted Features Tab.

- Features for each patient are automatically saved in the "Series folder" created at the beginning. The user can choose to save all the features extracted for each patient in a single.xlsx file.
- The file containing all the features extracted for each patient can be imported in order to add new extraction results for new patients.
- Feature Extracted can be imported and they are shown in the Feature Selection Tab.
- The user can choose between Point Biserial Correlation, Relieff, and T-test algorithms to select the most discriminative features. Clicking on the "Select Features" button starts the selection process.
- Results are visible in the Selected Features Tab.
- Selected features can be saved in a .xlsx file and can be subsequently imported in order to build the predictive model.
- After importing the selected features, they are displayed in the Model Training Tab.
- Model Training options can be set, and results are displayed in the same Tab.

3.2 Functions

3.2.1 Reading DICOM and Displaying Images

The Segmentation Tab is shown in Fig. 3. The full list of DICOM attributes, the search bar, the current slice, the "Draw ROI" and "Threshold" buttons are shown.

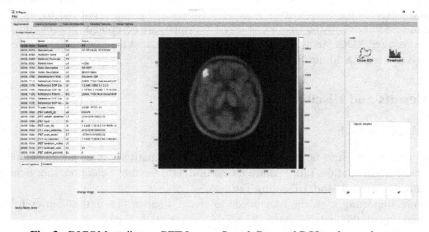

Fig. 3. DICOM attributes, PET Image, Search Bar, and ROI tools are shown.

3.2.2 Target Individuation and Segmentation

Figure 4 and Fig. 5 are examples of target identification and segmentation.

The target is surrounded by a blue closed line, while the segmentation is shown in transparent purple color overlapping the images.

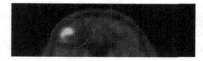

Fig. 4. ROI created with the Draw ROI tool (Color figure online)

Fig. 5. Segmentation created with the Threshold tool (Color figure online)

3.2.3 Feature Extraction

The Extracted Features Tab is shown in Fig. 6 with related features and 3D target volume.

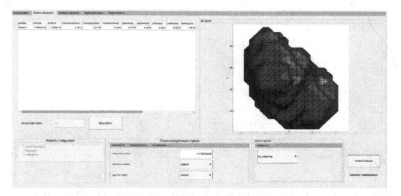

Fig. 6. Feature Extracted Tab, and extraction options are shown.

3.2.4 Feature Selection Results

Feature selection results are shown in Fig. 7. In red the features selected by the hybrid model.

3.2.5 Predictive Model

Performance metrics are shown in Fig. 8. Examples of ROC curves using LDA and accuracies are shown in the figure.

3.3 Validation

matRadiomics Extractor was validated by comparing results extracted with matRadiomics and those reported in the IBSI manual. Both Shape Features and 1st Order

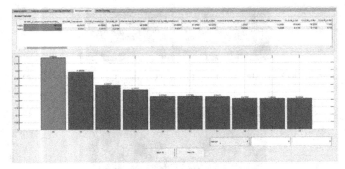

Fig. 7. In red the features selected using the hybrid method. Features are sorted by scores (Color figure online).

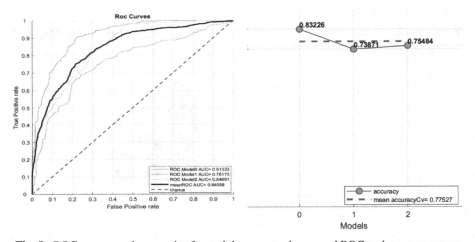

Fig. 8. ROC curves, and accuracies for each k group, and averaged ROC and mean accuracy.

Statistical Feature values fall within the ranges reported in the reference manual. We couldn't perform an accurate comparison of Texture Features because the configuration used in the manual could not be reproduced in matRadiomics. However, as reported in Sect. 2.2.4, these features were obtained using the IBSI compliant Matlab package, called Radiomics Toolbox [26, 27]. Results obtained using PyRadiomics integrated into matRadiomics, and PyRadiomics used externally were the same for all the 27 patients affected by Multiple Sclerosis [28].

4   Conclusions

The matRadiomics tool was developed with the purpose of completing the radiomics workflow and simplifying it in such a way that physicians, radiologists, or researchers can use it easily without any programming knowledge. The user can interact with matRadiomics UI in order to import images, identify the target, segment the target, extract features, select the most discriminative features and build the predictive model within the same application. Specifically, an innovative hybrid method based on the point bise-rial correlation in combination with logistic regression [29] was implemented to improve the quality of the predictive model obtained using three different machine learning algo-rithms, namely LDA, KNN, and SMV. Moreover, the aim of this work was to build a tool that could be used intensively to produce a large amount of data, useful for research purposes, and support the medical diagnosis. Although more tests need to be done to ensure results reliability, matRadiomics is a tool that simplifies radiomics and how it is performed. In particular, future analyses will be performed to compare our results with those of LIFEx.

References

1. Alongi, P., et al.: Choline PET/CT features to predict survival outcome in high risk prostate cancer restaging: A preliminary machine-learning radiomics study. Q. J. Nucl. Med. Mol. Imaging (2020). https://doi.org/10.23736/S1824-4785.20.03227-6
2. Cutaia, G., et al.: Radiomics and prostate MRI: current role and future applications. J. Imaging. **7**, 34 (2021). https://doi.org/10.3390/jimaging7020034
3. Stefano, A., et al.: Performance of radiomics features in the quantification of idiopathic pulmonary fibrosis from HRCT. Diagnostics **10**, 306 (2020). https://doi.org/10.3390/DIA GNOSTICS10050306
4. Mayerhoefer, M.E., et al.: Introduction to radiomics. J. Nucl. Med. **61**, 488–495 (2020). https://doi.org/10.2967/jnumed.118.222893
5. Cuocolo, R., et al.: Clinically significant prostate cancer detection on MRI: A radiomic shape features study. Eur. J. Radiol. **116**, 144–149 (2019). https://doi.org/10.1016/j.ejrad. 2019.05.006
6. Alongi, P., et al.: Radiomics analysis of 18F-Choline PET/CT in the prediction of disease outcome in high-risk prostate cancer: An explorative study on machine learning feature clas-sification in 94 patients. Eur. Radiol. **31**(7), 4595–4605 (2021). https://doi.org/10.1007/s00 330-020-07617-8
7. Vernuccio, F., Cannella, R., Comelli, A., Salvaggio, G., Lagalla, R., Midiri, M.: Radiomics and artificial intelligence: New frontiers in medicine. Recenti Prog. Med. **111**, 130–135 (2020). https://doi.org/10.1701/3315.32853
8. Comelli, A., et al.: Radiomics: A new biomedical workflow to create a predictive model. In: Papież, B.W., Namburete, A.I.L., Yaqub, M., Noble, J.A. (eds.) MIUA 2020. CCIS, vol. 1248, pp. 280–293. Springer, Cham (2020). https://doi.org/10.1007/978-3-030-52791-4_22
9. Liberini, V., et al.: The future of cancer diagnosis, treatment and surveillance: A systemic review on immunotherapy and immuno-PET radiotracers. Molecules **26**, 2201 (2021). https:// doi.org/10.3390/molecules26082201
10. Laudicella, R., et al.: [68Ga]DOTATOC PET/CT Radiomics to Predict the Response in GEP-NETs Undergoing [177Lu]DOTATOC PRRT: The "Theragnomics" Concept. Cancers. 14, 984 (2022). https://doi.org/10.3390/cancers14040984
11. van Timmeren, J.E., Cester, D., Tanadini-Lang, S., Alkadhi, H., Baessler, B.: Radiomics in medical imaging—"how-to" guide and critical reflection. Insights Imaging **11**(1), 1–16 (2020). https://doi.org/10.1186/s13244-020-00887-2
12. Nioche, C., et al.: Lifex: A freeware for radiomic feature calculation in multimodality imaging to accelerate advances in the characterization of tumor heterogeneity. Cancer Res. **78**, 4786–4789 (2018). https://doi.org/10.1158/0008-5472.CAN-18-0125

13. Van Griethuysen, J.J., et al.: Computational Radiomics System to Decode the Radiographic Phenotype. Cancer Res. **77**, 104–107 (2017). https://doi.org/10.1158/0008-5472.CAN-17-0339
14. Zwanenburg, A., et al.: The image biomarker standardization initiative: Standardized quantitative radiomics for high-throughput image-base phenotyping. Radiology **295**, 328–338 (2020). https://doi.org/10.1148/radiol.2020191145
15. Stefano, A., et al.: Robustness of pet radiomics features: Impact of co-registration with MRI. Appl. Sci. **11**, 10170 (2021). https://doi.org/10.3390/app112110170
16. MathWorks: MATLAB. https://it.mathworks.com/products/matlab.html. Accessed 11 Apr 2022
17. Python. https://www.python.org/. Accessed 11 Apr 2022
18. MathWorks: MATLAB App Designer. https://it.mathworks.com/products/matlab/app-designer.html. Accessed 11 Apr 2022
19. Pianykh, O.S.: Digital Imaging and Communications in Medicine (DICOM). Springer, Berlin (2012). https://doi.org/10.1007/978-3-642-10850-1
20. Pydicom. https://pydicom.github.io/. Accessed 11 Apr 2022
21. Comelli, A., Stefano, A., Benfante, V., Russo, G.: Normal and abnormal tissue classification in positron emission tomography oncological studies. Pattern Recognit. Image Anal. **28**, 106–113 (2018). https://doi.org/10.1134/S1054661818010054
22. Stefano, A., Comelli, A.: Customized efficient neural network for covid-19 infected region identification in CT images. J. Imaging. **7**, 131 (2021). https://doi.org/10.3390/jimaging7080131
23. Lorensen, W.E., Cline, H.E.: Marching cubes: A high resolution 3D surface construction algorithm. In: Proceedings of the 14th Annual Conference on Computer Graphics and Interactive Techniques, SIGGRAPH 1987, pp. 163–169. ACM (2016). https://doi.org/10.1145/37401.37422
24. Lewiner, T., Lopes, H., Vieira, A.W., Tavares, G.: Efficient implementation of marching cubes' cases with topological guarantees. J. Graph. Tools **8**, 1–15 (2012). https://doi.org/10.1080/10867651.2003.10487582
25. Hammer, P.: Marching cubes - file exchange - matlab central. https://it.mathworks.com/matlabcentral/fileexchange/32506-marching-cubes. Accessed 11 Apr 2022
26. Vallieres, M., et al.: Radiomics Toolbox. https://github.com/mvallieres/radiomics. Accessed 11 Apr 2022
27. Fornacon-Wood, I., et al.: Reliability and prognostic value of radiomic features are highly dependent on choice of feature extraction platform. Eur. Radiol. **30**(11), 6241–6250 (2020). https://doi.org/10.1007/s00330-020-06957-9
28. Lesjak, Ž, et al.: A novel public MR image dataset of multiple sclerosis patients with lesion segmentations based on multi-rater consensus. Neuroinformatics **16**(1), 51–63 (2017). https://doi.org/10.1007/s12021-017-9348-7
29. Barone, S., et al.: Hybrid descriptive-inferential method for key feature selection in prostate cancer radiomics. Appl. Stoch. Model. Bus. Ind. **37**, 961–972 (2021). https://doi.org/10.1002/asmb.2642
30. Zhao, Z., Morstatter, F., Sharma, S., Alelyani, S., Liu, H.: Advancing feature selection research. ASU Feature Selection Repository. https://jundongl.github.io/scikit-feature/OLD/home_old.html. Accessed 11 Apr 2022
31. Robnik-Šikonja, M., Kononenko, I.: Theoretical and empirical analysis of ReliefF and RReliefF. Mach. Learn. **53**, 23–69 (2003). https://doi.org/10.1023/A:1025667309714
32. Kenji, K., Larry, A.R.: A practical approach to feature selection. In: Proceedings of the Machine Learning Proceedings 1992, pp. 249–256. Morgan Kauffman, San Francisco (1992). https://doi.org/10.1016/B978-1-55860-247-2.50037-1

33. Comelli, A., et al.: Active contour algorithm with discriminant analysis for delineating tumors in positron emission tomography. Artif. Intell. Med. **94**, 67–78 (2019). https://doi.org/10.1016/j.artmed.2019.01.002
34. Comelli, A., et al.: K-nearest neighbor driving active contours to delineate biological tumor volumes. Eng. Appl. Artif. Intell. **81**, 133–144 (2019). https://doi.org/10.1016/j.engappai.2019.02.005
35. Comelli, A., et al.: A kernel support vector machine based technique for Crohn's disease classification in human patients. In: Barolli, L., Terzo, O. (eds.) CISIS 2017. AISC, vol. 611, pp. 262–273. Springer, Cham (2018). https://doi.org/10.1007/978-3-319-61566-0_25

Assessing High-Order Interdependencies Through Static O-Information Measures Computed on Resting State fMRI Intrinsic Component Networks

Simone Valenti[1,2], Laura Sparacino[1], Riccardo Pernice[1] (ID), Daniele Marinazzo[3], Hannes Almgren[4], Albert Comelli[2](✉) (ID), and Luca Faes[1] (ID)

[1] Department of Engineering, University of Palermo, Palermo, Italy
[2] Ri.MED Foundation, Via Bandiera 11, Palermo, Italy
acomelli@fondazionerimed.com
[3] Department of Data Analysis, Ghent University, Ghent, Belgium
[4] Department of Clinical Neurosciences, University of Calgary, Calgary, AB, Canada

Abstract. Resting state brain networks have reached a strong popularity in recent scientific endeavors due to their feasibility to characterize the metabolic mechanisms at the basis of neural control when the brain is not engaged in any task. The evaluation of these states, consisting in complex physiological processes employing a large amount of energy, is carried out from diagnostic images acquired through resting-state functional magnetic resonance (RS-fMRI) on different populations of subjects. In the present study, RS-fMRI signals from the WU-Minn HCP 1200 Subjects Data Release of the Human Connectome Project were studied with the aim of investigating the high order organizational structure of the brain function in resting conditions. Image data were post-processed through Independent Component Analysis to extract the so-called Intrinsic Component Networks, and a recently proposed framework for assessing high-order interactions in network data through the so-called O-Information measure was exploited. The framework allows an information-theoretic evaluation of pairwise and higher-order interactions, and was here extended to the analysis of vector variables, to allow investigating interactions among multiple Independent Component Networks (ICNs) each composed by several brain regions. Moreover, surrogate data analysis was used to validate statistically the detected pairwise and high-order networks. Our results indicate that RSNs are dominated by redundant interactions among ICN subnetworks, with levels of redundancy that increase monotonically with the order of the interactions analyzed. The ICNs mostly involved in the interactions of any order were the Default Mode and the Cognitive Control networks, suggesting a key role of these areas in mediating brain interactions during the resting state. Future works should assess the alterations of these patterns of functional brain connectivity during task-induced activity and in pathological states.

Keywords: Functional magnetic resonance imaging (fMRI) · O-Information (OI) · Complex networks · High-order interactions · Resting State Networks (RSN) · Independent Component Analysis (ICA)

© The Author(s), under exclusive license to Springer Nature Switzerland AG 2022
P. L. Mazzeo et al. (Eds.): ICIAP 2022 Workshops, LNCS 13373, pp. 386–397, 2022.
https://doi.org/10.1007/978-3-031-13321-3_34

1 Introduction

Since its discovery, functional magnetic resonance imaging (fMRI) has been fundamental in understanding the complex processes underlying the time-varying metabolic
activation of particular areas of the human brain, in different physio-pathological states
and experimental conditions, both in response to tasks and in resting conditions (the so-
called resting state fMRI, RS-fMRI) [1, 2]. This technique is widely applied especially
when it is not possible to directly interact with or let the patient perform the task, such
as with pediatric, sedated and/or neurologically compromised patients [3–5]. In fact,
recent studies have shown how the brain is essentially driven by intrinsic activity, not
related to mental task-, sensory- or motor-induced stimulation and consuming the most
of brain energy demand, and that external stimulus can only modulate but not determine
its trend. RS-fMRI functional brain connectivity patterns have been investigated also
in clinical settings to provide an assessment for diagnosis, prognosis, and treatment of
individual patients.

The functional behavior of multiple resting state networks (RSN) has been assessed in
the context of end-stage organ disease patients compared to healthy controls and surgical
neuro-oncology planning, using the tools of graph theory, seed-based analysis and basic
measures of functional connectivity such as Pearson correlation [5, 6] or other techniques
such as dynamic causal model for assessing effective connectivity [7, 8]. Specifically, the
Pearson correlation coefficient quantifies the strength of the linear pairwise interactions
between two variables or groups of variables, e.g. two subsets of voxels in the case of
fMRI data. The correlation coefficient has been often employed to assess the degree
of interdependency between different areas of the brain in the context of functional
connectivity [5, 6]. On the other hand, the directionality of pairwise interactions has been
assessed through effective connectivity approaches which investigate the direction of the
information flow exchanged between two different brain areas [7, 8]. In this context, RS-
fMRI has allowed to identify specific spontaneous activity patterns or modifications that
can be associated with the changing of neurologic deficits due to organ diseases or after
surgery. Such activity patterns are often described and graphically displayed by a circular
graph named "connectome", consisting of a set of nodes representing brain areas and
edges depicting their multiple interconnections [9, 10].

The analysis of the human connectome based on RS-fMRI measurements is a consolidated but also evolving research field, where several methodological issues still
need to be addressed. A main question is which type of measure to adopt to quantify
connectivity and how to assess the significance of the measured connections. Several
studies report the use of thresholding methods applied to bivariate correlation measures to select only the most relevant connections within these complex networks, but
in the literature an unequivocal way to set the optimal threshold has still not been identified [11, 12]. Moreover, it has been shown that the threshold selection may strongly
depend on the algorithms used to identify intrinsic component networks (ICN) and on
the size of the whole analyzed network. ICNs are groups of independent components
(IC), extracted from RS-fMRI images through independent component analysis (ICA)
[13], and are indicative of different areas of the brain which can be anatomically separated but are activated synchronously (i.e., they are temporally coherent), following the
same oscillation patterns in resting-state conditions. Another emerging issue is the need

to use connectivity measures which go beyond the framework of pairwise interactions. Approaches such as the Pearson correlation or dynamic causal modeling are, indeed, confined to a bivariate framework which does not take into account higher-order interactions, i.e. interactions involving more than two variables or groups of variables. It is indeed increasingly evident that complex brain networks such as those probed by RS-fMRI recordings display emergent behaviors which cannot be described solely in terms of the interaction between pairs of network nodes. To address such complex high-order interactions, new measures typically devised within the frame of information theory, are being defined and increasingly used in multivariate biomedical datasets [14–16].

In this work, starting from the consolidated concept of mutual information (MI), which quantifies the amount of information shared between groups of random variables, we have applied recently defined measures of static interdependence (i.e., interdependence between equal-time points in two time series) for assessing high-order redundant and synergistic contributions brought by adding a target ICN to a source system already composed of a given number of ICNs [14–16]. Specifically, in broad terms, while synergy arises from statistical interactions that can be found collectively in a network but not in parts of it considered separately, redundancy refers to group interactions that can be explained by the communication of sub-groups of scalar or vector variables. In this way, we are able to assess and describe brain interactions occurring at higher orders, i.e. between more than two brain areas, thus overcoming the limitations of the above-indicated approaches that instead operate mostly pairwise. Mostly redundant connectivity patterns were identified in our analyses and their statistical significance was assessed through surrogate data testing, without the need for applying arbitrary thresholding procedures.

2   Materials and Methods

2.1   Dataset

In this study, we used a subset of the public database WU-Minn HCP 1200 Subjects Data Release from Human Connectome Project (HCP), that includes high-resolution 3T MR scans from young healthy adult twins and non-twin siblings (ages 22–35) using four imaging modalities: structural images (T1w and T2w), RS-fMRI, task-fMRI (t-fMRI), and high angular resolution diffusion imaging (d-MRI). RS-fMRI scans were acquired in a darkened room for approximately 15 min, for a total of about 1200 frames per run.

Subjects were asked to stay with eyes open relaxingly fixating on a projected white crosshair on a dark background. Images were collected using the acquisition parameters indicated in Table 1. For further details we refer the reader to [17].

Table 1. RS-fMRI acquisition settings [17].

Parameter	Value
Sequence	Gradient-echo EPI
Repetition time (TR)	720 ms
Time to echo (TE)	33.1 ms
Flip angle	52°
FOV	208 × 180 mm (RO × PE)
Matrix	104 × 90 (RO × PE)
Slice thickness	2.0 mm; 72 slices; 2.0 mm isotropic voxels
Multiband factor	8
Echo spacing	0.58 ms
BW	2290 Hz/Px

2.2 Data Processing and Independent Component Analysis

The dataset was processed first with the minimal preprocessing pipelines for the Human Connectome Project [18], and then with a smoothing algorithm using a Gaussian kernel of 6 mm Full Width at Half Maximum (FWHM). After this preprocessing pipeline, RS-fMRI data were decomposed using the common technique of independent component analysis (ICA). Group ICA of fMRI Toolbox (GIFT, http://icatb.sourceforge.net) [13, 19, 20], performed using the Infomax algorithm [21], was used to compute $C = 100$ spatially independent components (ICs). After spatial reconstruction and visual inspection of the 100 components, $C' = 53$ components-of-interest, with anatomical distribution schematized in Table 2, were selected for this work.

Table 2. ICN decomposition of the RS-fMRI.

Name	ICs	Area/domain
ICN_AD (1)	66, 76	Auditory domain
ICN_CB (2)	48, 77, 26, 88	Cerebellum
ICN_CC (3)	71, 65, 42, 93, 53, 83, 75, 31, 90, 78, 81, 95, 73, 70, 54, 96, 27	Cognitive control
ICN_DM (4)	20, 35, 29, 52, 34, 24, 85	Default mode
ICN_SC (5)	30, 41, 99, 45, 50	Subcortical
ICN_SM (6)	2, 5, 8, 4, 23, 97, 74, 79, 69	Sensorimotor
ICN_VS (7)	6, 1, 25, 13, 14, 43, 19, 7, 98	Visual

2.3 Static O-Information

This section presents the framework to measure static interactions among Q stationary random variables $X = \{X_1, \ldots, X_Q\}$, grouped in M blocks $Y = \{Y_1, \ldots, Y_M\}$. The ith block has dimension M_i, so that $Q = \sum_{i=1}^{M} M_i$. The activity of the complex network formed by the M interacting systems can be described by the mutual information (MI) between blocks, here denoted as $I_{Y_i; Y_j}$ when computed for the two vector variables Y_i and Y_j. Higher-order interactions are assessed by means of the O-Information (OI), a novel measure which generalizes the MI to groups of variables [14–16]. The OI of N random vectors taken from the set $Y = \{Y_1, \ldots, Y_M\}$ is defined as:

$$\Omega_{Y^N} = \Omega_{Y_{-j}^N} + \Delta_{Y_{-j}^N; Y_j}, \tag{1}$$

where $Y^N = \{Y_{i_1}, \ldots, Y_{i_N}\}$, $i_1, \ldots, i_N \in \{1, \ldots, M\}, N \leq M$, is the analyzed group of random vectors, $Y_{-j}^N = Y^N \backslash Y_j$ is the subset of random vectors where Y_j is removed ($j \in \{i_1, \ldots, i_N\}$), and where the quantity

$$\Delta_{Y_{-j}^N; Y_j} = (2 - N) I_{Y_{-j}^N; Y_j} + \sum_{\substack{m \neq 1 \\ m \neq j}}^{N} I_{Y_{-mj}^N; Y_j} \tag{2}$$

is the variation of the OI obtained with the addition of Y_j to Y_{-j}^N, being $Y_{-mj}^N = Y^N \backslash \{Y_j, Y_m\}$. In this framework, if the sign of the OI increment is positive ($\Delta_{Y_{-j}^N; Y_j} > 0$) the information brought by Y_j to Y_{-j}^N is redundant, while a negative OI increment means that the influence of Y_{-j}^N on Y_j is dominated by synergy. In other words, if OI > 0 the system is redundancy-dominated, while OI < 0 means that the system is synergy-dominated; if OI $= 0$, synergy and redundancy are balanced in the analyzed network. Note that, since $\Omega_{Y^2} = 0$ for any pair of variables, when $N = 3$ random vectors are considered, i.e. $Y = \{Y_i, Y_k, Y_j\}$, the OI in (1) reduces to the OI increment:

$$\Delta_{Y_i, Y_k; Y_j} = -I(Y_j; Y_i, Y_k) + I(Y_j; Y_i) + I(Y_j; Y_k), \tag{3}$$

In this case, the OI increment in (3) coincides with the well-known interaction information, measuring the difference between synergy and redundancy when a target variable is added to a bivariate source vector process [22].

The calculation of the measures (1) and (2) requires an approach to compute the MI between vector random variables. In this work, assuming that the observed variables have a joint Gaussian distribution, we exploit the linear parametric representation to compute MI [23]. Specifically, we consider two generic zero-mean vector variables Z_1 and Z_2 containing respectively n and m random variables with a number t of observations, assuming that Z_1 and Z_2 take the role of Y_j and Y_{-mj}^N in (2). The two variables are related by the following linear regression model:

$$Z_1 = A Z_2 + U, \tag{4}$$

where variable Z_1 is predicted using an $n \times m$ coefficient matrix A which weights the regressors Z_2, and U is a vector of n zero-mean white noises (prediction errors). In this context, the MI between the two variables, which is defined as [24]:

$$I_{Z_1; Z_2} = H(Z_1) - H(Z_1 | Z_2), \tag{5}$$

can be estimated exploiting the relation between entropy and variance valid for Gaussian variables, i.e. expressing the entropy of the predicted variable as $H(Z_1) = \frac{1}{2}log\big((2\pi e)^n|\Sigma_{Z_1}|\big)$ and the conditional entropy of the predicted variables given the predictor as $H(Z_1|Z_2) = \frac{1}{2}log\big((2\pi e)^n|\Sigma_U|\big)$, where Σ_{Z_1} is the $n \times n$ covariance of the predicted variable and where Σ_U is the $n \times n$ covariance of the prediction errors [25].

2.4 Data Analysis and Statistical Analysis

Static interactions among $Q = 53$ stationary random variables of length $t = 1195$ observations, which are realizations of the 53 selected ICs, grouped in $M = 7$ blocks representing the 7 identified ICNs $Y_1, \ldots, Y_7$ (Table 2), were investigated. The functional connectivity between groups of ICNs, from order $N = 2$ to order $N = M = 7$, was assessed through exploitation of the MI and of the novel OI measure defined in Sect. 2.3. We performed ordinary least squares identification of the linear regression models defined as in (4) to assess the pairwise interaction ($N = 2$) between two ICNs through the MI measure, as well as to assess higher-order interactions through the OI measure computed for orders N from 3 to 7 considering all possible combinations of ICNs, herein referred to as "multiplets". Specifically, we analyzed the following number of multiplets: 35 of order $N = 3$; 35 of order $N = 4$; 21 of order $N = 5$; 7 of order $N = 6$; 1 of order $N = M = 7$.

Surrogate data analysis was carried out to evaluate the number of subjects whose MI and OI values were statistically significant. Specifically, 20 surrogates were generated according to a circular shift procedure which randomly shifts in time the ICs data for each given subject. For each ICN, the lag of the shifted samples (k) was chosen randomly between 10 and 1010 in order to ensure a larger variability of the shift, and this k was chosen the same for each IC belonging to the ICN. This choice was done to maintain within-network interdependencies (i.e., interactions among the scalar components of the vector variable Y_i), while destroying dependencies between different networks (i.e., interactions between any pair of variables taken from Y_i and Y_j, $i, j = 1, \ldots, 7$). The resulting surrogates are realizations of independent identically distributed random variables with the same marginal probability distribution as the original variables under analysis, but with destroyed correlation structure [26]. When the maximum value of the considered measure (MI or |OI|) among all the surrogates computed for a given subject was less than the same measure computed on the original time series for the same subject, we considered this measure as significant and added the subject to the total number of significant ones.

To investigate statistical differences between different multiplets within the same order, we carried out a Student t-test for paired data and corrected for multiple comparisons using the Bonferroni-Holm correction. Since the number of paired combinations was found to be extremely high, especially for low orders where the number of multiplets was higher, we focused the analysis only on a subset of multiplets. Specifically, triplets (multiplets of order $N = 3$) were chosen where the Default Mode (DM) was present, while higher-order multiplets (orders from the 4th to the 6th; the 7th order was not considered as constituted by a single multiplet) were selected as those combinations whose roots of 3th, 4th and 5th order contained the DM component [27, 28]. In this way, we identified 15, 19, 12 and 3 multiplets for orders 3th, 4th, 5th and 6th to analyze, respectively.

3 Results and Discussion

Figure 1(a) and 1(b) display two connectograms, whose edges map functional connections between different ICNs in terms of MI values (Fig. 1(a)) or number of subjects who showed statistically significant MI values (Fig. 1(b)). The application of surrogate data analysis led us to statistically validate our measures. With reference to Fig. 1(b), we found a significant percentage of MI values for pairs of ICNs in the interval [90–100] %. Despite results regarding significant subjects in OI measures are not shown here for brevity, significant percentages between 50% and 100% were reported for multiplets of order 3, while percentages between 95% and 100% were found for multiplets of order 4. Full significance (100%) was detected for multiplets of higher order.

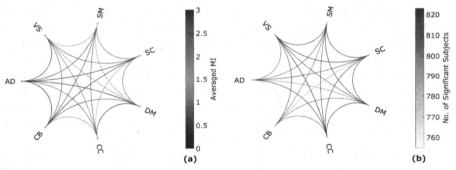

Fig. 1. Connectomic map. Edges represent functional connections between different ICNs in terms of MI values averaged on the whole set of subjects (*panel a)*) or number of significant subjects (*panel (b)*), while the 7 nodes represent the ICNs identified through ICA.

This finding shows that higher-order interdependencies, characterized by higher redundancies as shown in Fig. 2, are much more significant than lower order connectivity patterns. The reason for this increase may be related to the increasingly stronger connectivity which characterize the structure of higher order network interdependencies. Figure 1(a) depicts that links between DM and CC (i.e. Cognitive Control) networks, between CC and SM (i.e. Sensorimotor) networks and between CC and VS (i.e. Visual) networks are characterized by the highest MI values. With reference to Table 2 and Fig. 3, these networks, described by the index 3 for CC, 4 for DM, 6 for SM and 7 for VS, are mostly connected with redundant pathways.

The distribution of the O-Information index as a function of the order of the interaction is depicted in Fig. 2, where each grey dot represents the value of the interaction averaged on all the 823 subjects for each multiplet. Increasing the interaction order leads to find an increase in redundancy within the considered network. Indeed, the type of information brought by an ICN when it is added to a lower-order network seems to become more and more redundant with increasing numbers of analyzed ICNs, suggesting that high order group interactions can be better explained by the communication of sub-groups.

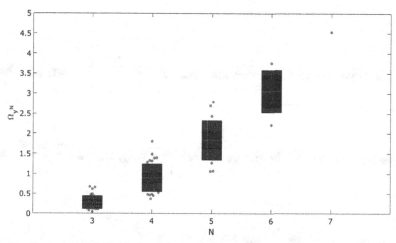

Fig. 2. Distributions and individual values (averaged over 823 subjects) of the O-Information computed for each multiplet as a function of the interaction order N. Each point represents a given multiplet intended as a combination of ICNs. Darker and light blue areas represent 1 standard deviation and 95% confidence interval, respectively, while red line is the mean value of the distribution.

Figure 3a), b), (c) and (d) show the distributions of the O-Information values of order 3, 4, 5 and 6, respectively, for all the multiplets specified in Sect. 2.4, and results of statistical analyses. The t-test revealed the presence of significant differences between the OI values of most pairs of multiplets, while only a few pairs of combinations were found to have mean OI values not significantly different between each other; these pairs are connected in the figure with red dashed lines. While it remains clear that increasing the order interaction leads to higher redundancy, the interpretation of the differences between OI values obtained from different combinations of ICNs is not straightforward. The addition of a given ICNs to pre-existing networks may cause diverse redundancy fluctuations in the same subjects. In other words, starting from a given combination of ICNs, an additional ICN inserted among those remaining generates a specific redundancy increment which is peculiar to that ICN and is different from the one that would be produced inserting another ICN. Such behavior suggests that high-order interactions between cerebral areas are very complex and strongly depend on the brain connections under analysis.

Specifically, our results show that higher redundant contributions were found for multiplets containing as "root" system the ICNs CC and DM, with addition of ICNs SC (Subcortical), SM (Sensorimotor) and VS (Visual) as also demonstrated in Fig. 1, where the highest values of MI were found between these networks. Then, the complex and high order communications between these subsets of ICNs seem to be responsible for most of the redundancy patterns found in our analyses. A main limitation of our analysis consists in the difficult interpretation of the results from a physiological point of view and the inability of generalization of the results, given the absence of a control condition to refer to.

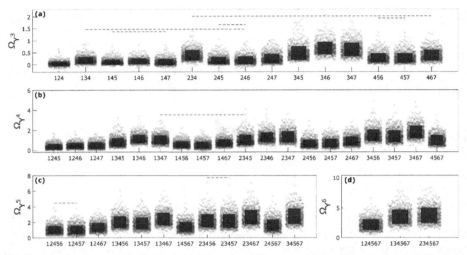

Fig. 3. Distributions and individual OI values for different multiplets of order 3 *(a)*, 4 *(b)*, 5 *(c)* and 6 *(d)*. Darker and light blue areas represent 1 standard deviation and 95% confidence interval, respectively, while red line is the mean value of the distribution. With reference to Table 2, each ICN is indicated by a number as follows: (1) AD; (2) CB; (3) CC; (4) DM; (5) SC; (6) SM; (7) VS. Pairwise t-tests showed statistical differences for most pairs of distributions, except for those highlighted by red dashed lines.

4   Conclusion

In this work we computed measures of high-order interaction between vector-valued variables for the evaluation of the information shared between several pairs of RSNs in the brain. With respect to the common methodologies found in the literature, mostly based on the use of Pearson correlation and on thresholding approaches for the selection of the most significant connectivity links [6, 11, 12], our tools allow to detect redundancy and synergy in complex systems starting from the well-known measure of mutual information [14–16]. In this context, O-Information measures provide additional information if compared to the Pearson correlation index and other pairwise functional connectivity measures. In our work, calculation of the O-Information has allowed us to investigate the complex higher-order structures consisting not only in just single pairs of voxel subsets, but instead multiplets of voxel subsets which share multivariate information. The assessment of the statistical significance of the interactions of any order was performed through surrogate data testing in place of selecting an adequate threshold, a procedure which strongly depends on the methodology used to extract ICNs and lacks standardization.

We found that RSNs are dominated by redundant interdependencies which tend to increase in strength as the order of the analyzed interaction grows. In particular, multiplets containing CC, DM, SM and VS networks show highest values of MI and mostly redundant trends over all the orders of OI measures. Physiological interpretations of the obtained findings are not straightforward, especially because the underlying mechanisms constitute the basis of the human brain activity, and such a clearer enlightenment could come from the comparisons between different experimental conditions (resting-state, task-induced states) and populations of subjects (healthy controls, diseased patients). Indeed, further utilizations of our proposed methodological approach should consider more heterogeneous datasets and different clinical settings. Moreover, future studies should focus on the proper selection of the most relevant networks in resting state, i.e., the ones which interact more between each other in redundant or synergistic ways. The proposed framework could also be applied to different fMRI data (e.g., task-induced states) or used to analyze multiplets where signals belonging to different organs are included, in order to assess for instance brain-heart interactions according and to investigate the role on brain activity of peripheral physiological oscillations on brain activity [29].

References

1. Glover, G.H.: Overview of functional magnetic resonance imaging. Neurosurg. Clin. N. Am. **22**, 133–139 (2011). https://doi.org/10.1016/j.nec.2010.11.001
2. Chow, M.S., Wu, S.L., Webb, S.E., Gluskin, K., Yew, D.: Functional magnetic resonance imaging and the brain: a brief review. World J. Radiol. **9**, 5 (2017). https://doi.org/10.4329/wjr.v9.i1.5
3. Duyn, J.: Spontaneous fMRI activity during resting wakefulness and sleep. Prog. Brain Res. **193**, 295–305 (2011). https://doi.org/10.1016/B978-0-444-53839-0.00019-3
4. Fox, M.D., Raichle, M.E.: Spontaneous fluctuations in brain activity observed with functional magnetic resonance imaging. Nat. Rev. Neurosci. **8**, 700–711 (2007). https://doi.org/10.1038/nrn2201
5. Agnello, L., Comelli, A., Ardizzone, E., Vitabile, S.: Unsupervised tissue classification of brain MR images for voxel-based morphometry analysis. Int. J. Imaging Syst. Technol. **26**, 136–150 (2016). https://doi.org/10.1002/ima.22168
6. Ran, Q., Jamoulle, T., Schaeverbeke, J., Meersmans, K., Vandenberghe, R., Dupont, P.: Reproducibility of graph measures at the subject level using resting-state fMRI. Brain Behav. **10**, 2336–2351 (2020). https://doi.org/10.1002/brb3.1705
7. Almgren, H., Van de Steen, F., Razi, A., Friston, K., Marinazzo, D.: The effect of global signal regression on DCM estimates of noise and effective connectivity from resting state fMRI. Neuroimage **208**, 116435 (2020). https://doi.org/10.1016/j.neuroimage.2019.116435
8. Almgren, H., Van de Steen, F., Kühn, S., Razi, A., Friston, K., Marinazzo, D.: Variability and reliability of effective connectivity within the core default mode network: a multi-site longitudinal spectral DCM study. Neuroimage **183**, 757–768 (2018). https://doi.org/10.1016/j.neuroimage.2018.08.053
9. Behzadi, Y., Restom, K., Liau, J., Liu, T.T.: A component based noise correction method (CompCor) for BOLD and perfusion based fMRI. Neuroimage **37**, 90–101 (2007). https://doi.org/10.1016/j.neuroimage.2007.04.042

10. Sparacia, G., et al.: Resting-state functional connectome in patients with brain tumors before and after surgical resection. World Neurosurg. **141**, e182–e194 (2020). https://doi.org/10.1016/j.wneu.2020.05.054

11. De Vico Fallani, F., Latora, V., Chavez, M.: A topological criterion for filtering information in complex brain networks. PLoS Comput. Biol. **13**, 1–18 (2017). https://doi.org/10.1371/journal.pcbi.1005305

12. Garrison, K.A., Scheinost, D., Finn, E.S., Shen, X., Todd, R., Program, N.: The (in)stability of functional brain network measures across thresholds. NeuroImage **118**, 651–661 (2016). https://doi.org/10.1016/j.neuroimage.2015.05.046

13. Calhoun, V.D., Adali, T., Pearlson, G.D., Pekar, J.J.: A method for making group inferences from functional MRI data using independent component analysis V.D. J. Neurotrauma **32**, 655–659 (2015). https://doi.org/10.1089/neu.2014.3723

14. Faes, L., et al.: A Framework for the time- and frequency-domain assessment of high-order interactions in brain and physiological networks. XX, pp. 1–11 (2022)

15. Stramaglia, S., Scagliarini, T., Daniels, B.C., Marinazzo, D.: Quantifying dynamical high-order interdependencies from the O-information: an application to neural spiking dynamics. Front. Physiol. **11**, 1–11 (2021). https://doi.org/10.3389/fphys.2020.595736

16. Rosas, F.E., Mediano, P.A.M., Gastpar, M., Jensen, H.J.: Quantifying high-order interdependencies via multivariate extensions of the mutual information. Phys. Rev. E. **100**, 32305 (2019). https://doi.org/10.1103/PhysRevE.100.032305

17. Elam, J.S., Van Essen, D.: WU-Minn HCP 1200 subjects data release reference manual. Encycl. Comput. Neurosci. **2017**, 35 (2013). https://doi.org/10.1007/978-1-4614-7320-6_5 92-1

18. Glasser, M.F., et al.: The minimal preprocessing pipelines for the human connectome project and for the WU-Minn HCP consortium. Neuroimage **80**, 105–12404 (2013). https://doi.org/10.1016/j.neuroimage.2013.04.127.The

19. Fu, Z., Du, Y., Calhoun, V.D.: The Dynamic Functional Network Connectivity Analysis Framework. Engineering **5**, 190–193 (2019). https://doi.org/10.1016/j.eng.2018.10.001

20. Sako, Ü., Pearlson, G.D., Kiehl, K.A., Wang, Y.M., Andrew, M., Calhoun, V.D.: A method for evaluating dynamic functional network connectivity and task-modulation. App. Schizophrenia **23**, 351–366 (2010). https://doi.org/10.1007/s10334-010-0197-8.A

21. Bell, A.J., Sejnowski, T.J.: An information-maximization approach to blind separation and blind deconvolution. Neural Comput. **7**, 1129–1159 (1995)

22. Faes, L., Marinazzo, D., Stramaglia, S.: Multiscale information decomposition: exact computation for multivariate Gaussian processes. Entropy **19**, 1–18 (2017). https://doi.org/10.3390/e19080408

23. Barrett, A.B., Barnett, L., Seth, A.K.: Multivariate granger causality and generalized variance. Phys. Rev. E - Stat. Nonlinear, Soft Matter Phys. **81**, (2010). https://doi.org/10.1103/PhysRevE.81.041907

24. over, T.M., Thomas, J.A.: Elements of Information Theory. John Wiley & Sons, New York (2012)

25. Pernice, R., et al.: Multivariate correlation measures reveal structure and strength of brain – body physiological networks at rest and during mental stress. Front Neurosci. **14** (2021). https://doi.org/10.3389/fnins.2020.602584

26. Paluš, M.: Detecting phase synchronization in noisy systems. Phys. Lett. Sect. A Gen. Solid State Phys. **235**, 341–351 (1997). https://doi.org/10.1016/S0375-9601(97)00635-X

27. Raichle, M.E.: The brain's default mode network. Annu. Rev. Neurosci. **38**, 433–447 (2015). https://doi.org/10.1146/annurev-neuro-071013-014030

28. Greicius, M.D., Krasnow, B., Reiss, A.L., Menon, V.: Functional connectivity in the resting brain: a network analysis of the default mode hypothesis. Proc. Natl. Acad. Sci. U. S. A. **100**, 253–258 (2003). https://doi.org/10.1073/pnas.0135058100
29. Wu, G.R., Marinazzo, D.: Sensitivity of the resting-state haemodynamic response function estimation to autonomic nervous system fluctuations. Philos. Trans. R. Soc. A Math. Phys. Eng. Sci. **374**, 20150190 (2016)

Place Cell's Computational Model

Camille Mazzara[1,2] (iD), Albert Comelli[2(✉)] (iD), and Michele Migliore[3] (iD)

[1] Department of Health Promotion, Mother and Child Care, Internal Medicine and Medical Specialties, Molecular and Clinical Medicine, University of Palermo, 90127 Palermo, Italy
[2] Ri.MED Foundation, Via Bandiera 11, 90133 Palermo, Italy
acomelli@fondazionerimed.com
[3] Institute of Biophysics, National Research Council, Palermo, Italy

Abstract. Hippocampal Place Cells play a pivotal role in spatial navigation. These cells have the particular characteristic of firing at a low rate during navigation throughout most of the environment, except when the animal is within a restricted spatial region called place field. The biophysical mechanisms underlying their formation or remapping following external sensory inputs are poorly understood. Recent experimental evidence clearly showed that, in the CA1 hippocampal region, the interaction between a properly timed association of inputs from the entorhinal cortex and the CA3 region can induce a novel place field formation. On CA1 pyramidal neurons, these different inputs are spatially segregated: the input from entorhinal cortex targets the most distal apical dendritic regions, while the CA3 input arrives onto proximal dendrites. The conditions under which this interaction can explain the formation of a place field in a CA1 pyramidal neuron are not fully understood. In this work, we present a series of simulations using a morphologically and biophysically detailed model of a CA1 pyramidal neuron. We tested the model by simulating a mouse random spatial navigation in a small room with objects. Following a reward signal activated during the navigation in the distal dendrites, as a forward traveling depolarization envelope, the neuron was able to selectively potentiate only the synapses coding for the object present in the visual field. Subsequent navigation through the same environment resulted in the neuron firing as expected for a place cell.

Keywords: Place Cells · Spatial navigation · Computational model

1 Introduction

Hippocampal place cells (PCs) have a principal role in representation of the spatial environment in the brain [1]. PCs act as a cognitive map, they are observed by monitoring extracellularly recorded action potentials from pyramidal cells in the Cornu Ammonis 1 (CA1) and Cornu Ammonis 3 (CA3) area of the hippocampus of liberally behaving rats [2, 3]. A PC becomes active when an animal enters a specific position in its environment, which is known as the place field, so reflects the presence and topography of various environmental cues.

The properties of hippocampal PCs in primates are comparable to those in rodents, with the exception that in primates the speed of the information has a better impact on

© The Author(s), under exclusive license to Springer Nature Switzerland AG 2022
P. L. Mazzeo et al. (Eds.): ICIAP 2022 Workshops, LNCS 13373, pp. 398–407, 2022.
https://doi.org/10.1007/978-3-031-13321-3_35

PC activity than on directional information [4, 5]. In the human hippocampus, there are also cells that respond only to specific spatial positions [6]. The activity of PCs strongly depends on the properties of the external environment. Only one set of active PCs describes a place [7, 8] and different combinations of PCs fire in distinct environments [9].Furthermore, if the characteristics of the environment (such as the shape, color, or the number of cue cards in the walls of the room explored by the animal) are changed, a new firing pattern is produced [10]. Also, an alteration of the relative position of cues produces geometric changes in place fields [11], and rotating the cue card causes an equal rotation of the PCs [10].

There are experiments suggesting that synaptic plasticity and extra-hippocampus inputs play a major role in PCs formation. It has been shown that the stability of the Place Field strongly correlates with the attention needed to perform a task: when a rat does not pay attention to the external environment in which it walks, the place fields become unstable after 3–6 h and these animals are unable to carry out spatial tasks. Conversely, when a rat pays attention to the surrounding space, for example, because a food reward, place fields are stable for days. Research on primates shows that this mechanism depends on the dopaminergic system.

In spite of the intense experimental effort, a detailed understanding of the cellular processes that may be involved, or need to interplay, in such a way to turn a CA1 pyramidal neuron into a PC, is still missing. A major obstacle in the experimental investigation of these mechanisms, may be that the process of turning a CA1 pyramidal cell into a place cell requires an exquisite interaction of independent and well timed inputs at the level of individual dendrites. Although dependent on the plastic properties of the system, the current computational models of PCs are implemented through simplified neural networks, with two or more layers, consisting of neuron-like elements [12, 13]. In our model the PC is a single CA1 neuron implemented with the system of nonlinear differential equations of A.L. Hodgkin and A.F. Huxley. The construction of our model and its functioning are based on the experimental studies discussed by Bittner et al. (2015) [14]. Two spatially segregated inputs, interacting with appropriate timing, lead to the formation of a dendritic Plateau Potential that causes a strong depolarization propagating along the whole neuron. The dendritic Plateau Potential induces a rapid and temporary change in synaptic weight and dendritic excitability. All these combined signals rapidly induce the new formation of place fields.

In the CA1 region of the hippocampus, the interaction between a properly timed association of inputs from the entorhinal cortex (EC) and the CA3 region can induce a novel place field formation [14]. On CA1 pyramidal neurons, these different inputs are spatially segregated: the input from EC targets the most distal apical dendritic regions, while the CA3 input arrives onto proximal dendrites. The conditions under which this interaction can explain the formation of a place field in a CA1 pyramidal neuron are not fully understood. In this work, we present a morphologically and biophysically detailed model of a CA1 pyramidal neuron that shows how a PC is formed. We have included the passive properties and currents of sodium, potassium and the current I_h (h-channel), typical of CA1 neurons.

The I_h current is a hyperpolarization-activated, non-specific, cation current with a reversal potential of -30 mV; it is expressed at increasing densities in the apical dendrites, where it has a key role in modulating the integration of synaptic signals.

2 Materials and Methods

The neuron morphology was modeled using the NEURON simulation environment (v7.5, Carnevale and Hines 2006). The channel kinetics were based on those used in a previously published paper on the binding properties of CA1 hippocampal pyramidal neurons [15, 16], and validated against a number of experimental findings on CA1 pyramidal neurons. In particular, there are non-specific I_h current [15, 16], Na$^+$ and K$_{DR}$ currents, two A-type potassium currents (K$_A$, for proximal and distal dendrites) and a M-type potassium current K$_M$. The K$_A$ and I_h peak conductance increased linearly with distance from the soma [17–20] and the K$_M$ was inserted in the soma and in the axon.

2.1 Synaptic Inputs and Plasticity

Excitatory synapses were implemented with an AMPA and a NMDA component, as in Gasparini et al. (2004) [20].

As in Bianchi, D. et al. 2014 [21], synaptic weights change in accordance with a Spike Time Dependent Plasticity (STDP) law. Consequently, the induction of LTP or LTD is driven by the correlation between the presynaptic and postsynaptic activation:

$$g_{peak}(t) = g_{peak}^0 + A(t) \tag{1}$$

$$A(t) = A(t-1) * \left(1 - d * \frac{e^{-\frac{((tpost-tpre)-M)^2}{2V^2}}}{V\sqrt{2\pi}} \right) \tag{2}$$

$$for \ (t_{post} - t_{pre}) > 0 \ and$$

$$A(t) = A(t-1) * \left(g_{peak}^{max} - g_{peak}^0 - A(t-1) \right) * p * e^{-\frac{(tpost-tpre)}{\tau}}$$
$$for \ (t_{post} - t_{pre}) > 0 \tag{3}$$

in which:

- A is always ≥ 0 and represents the improvement of synaptic weights;
- The constants $M = -24$, $V = 6.32$, and $\tau = 2$ and the parameters $d = 0.3$, and $p = 1$ have been chosen in such a way that they replicate the experimental results (Nishiyama et al. 2000);
- g_{peak}^0 indicates the initial peak conductance and g_{peak}^{max} its maximum value.

LTD (Long Term Depression) is generated when $(t_{post} - t_{pre}) < 0$, on the contrary, LTP (Long Term Potentiation) is produced when $(t_{post} - t_{pre}) > 0$.

$t_{pre} \neq 0$ when there is a synaptic activation, while $t_{post} \neq 0$ when there is a dendritic spike.

If the local synaptic signal is not high enough to generate a dendritic spike, the synaptic activity does not change as there is neither a t_{pre} nor a t_{post}. A dendritic spike can occur if the synapse is strong enough to generate it or if the signals around it are strong enough to cause a depolarization to propagate, which in addition to the depolarization of the synapse causes the dendritic spike.

The construction of the model and its functioning are based on the experimental studies discussed by Bittner and collaborators [14]. Our computational model of a PC is illustrated in Fig. 1 and represents a CA1 pyramidal neuron in which two spatially segregated inputs lead the neuron to fire only in particular positions (Place Fields). One of the two inputs comes from the axons of the third layer of the entorhinal cortex (EC3) that innervate the most distal apical tuft dendrite regions of the CA1 neuron, the second input, on the other hand, starts from the hippocampal CA3 region and forms synapses onto the proximal perisomatic dendrites. These different inputs positively modulate the firing of earlier established place fields and quickly produce new place field arrangement to provide feature selectivity in CA1 that is a function of both EC3 and CA3 input. Experimentally it has been seen that if the two afferent input streams interact with appropriate timing, they lead to the formation of a dendritic Plateau Potential that causes a strong depolarization that propagates throughout the neuron [14].

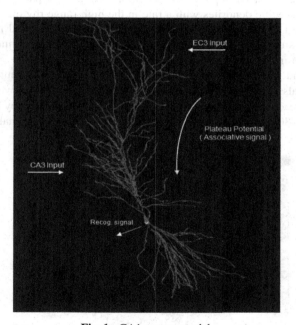

Fig. 1. CA1 neuron model.

On the basis of these experimental results, we simulated a propagating Plateau Potential by activating, at different times, 200 ms long current injection steps along the longitudinal axis of the neuron, in four different apical dendritic locations. In this way, the dendritic Plateau Potential induces a rapid and temporary change in the synaptic weight and dendritic excitability.

Our simulated pyramidal Ca1 cell is tuned to a certain object, which means that when the mouse sees one particular object (in our case a clue), some of its dendrites are activated at a frequency in the gamma rhythm range. As seen experimentally, neurons are selectively activated by impressively distinct pictures of given individuals, landmarks or objects and in some cases even by letter strings with their names [22–24]. In the same way, our simulated cell fires when the recognition of this specific object occurs. Specific features of visual input independently activate different dendrites, eliciting local dendritic action potentials that can generate somatic output [15, 25, 26]. It has been suggested by theoretical models that the recognition of an object is given by the preferential activation of 7 specific dendrites [15]. For this reason, in our model a clue is recognized by the union of seven dendrites that recognize seven different parts of the clue. A set of seven synapse pairs (one AMPA and one NMDA) positioned in different dendrites will activate at a higher rate (gamma) when the mouse sees a specific clue, while another set of seven synapse pairs will activate when it sees a different clue. By marking each coordinate with a blue dot it is noticed that the neuron spikes in a spatial area similar to the Place Field. All synapses have an activation rate in the theta rhythm (3 Hz). This rate changes if the mouse receives visual inputs. The vision of an object (or part of it) will activate the synapses of specific dendrites with a rate in the high range rhythm (80 Hz). These rates were chosen as suggested by both experimental and theoretical results. Lisman and collaborators demonstrate that working memory, which they define as the ability to actively retain information in the mind, is organized by oscillatory processes in the order of theta and gamma [27]. Computational modeling based on neuronal activation models in animals suggests that a presumed mechanism facilitating working memory is the periodic reactivation (or replay) of informations coordinated by theta (3–8 Hz) and gamma (30–80 Hz) neural oscillations [28]. Furthermore, neuronal activity in the

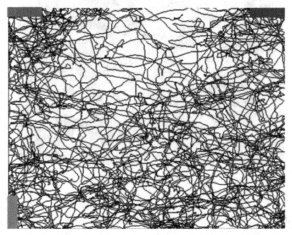

Fig. 2. The environment that the mouse explores during the test: a square arena with clues inside it. The black line represents the mouse's trajectory.

gamma range (30–100 Hz) is believed to play an important role in attention, memory tasks [29] and in other cognitive functions [30].

We simulated the environment in which the mouse navigates as a square arena having three visual inputs, i.e. three clues positioned in different portions of the space (Fig. 2).

In order to make the simulation faster, two programs have been created: one to write the trajectory that the mouse executes and another one to read the spatial coordinates of this trajectory. The trajectory (black line in Fig. 2) is random and built in a way that changes the mouse direction once the border of the arena has been reached. The field of view of the mouse is 90° and decreases with increasing distance. During the simulation, the mouse travels a random trajectory during which, depending on the direction and position of the head, one or more clues, or even parts of clues, can enter its field of vision. During navigation, the hippocampus plays a fundamental role, being an essential area for orienting oneself within the surrounding space. Based on different mathematical models, each part of an object is encoded in a single dendrite [15, 25, 26]. All synapses have an activation frequency of the order of the theta rhythm (3 Hz), this discharge frequency changes if the mouse receives visual inputs coming from the shaffer collaterals. Only visual inputs have been implemented in the model but olfactory, vestibular, etc. inputs can be added later.

3   Results

Figure 3A shows part of the trajectory of the mouse during space navigation. At a certain instant of time the four IClamps that simulate the presence of the Plateau Potential were activated. The blue circles identify the spatial coordinates in which the neuron spikes in the presence of the Plateau Potential.

In the presence of these signals (when the red bar enters the mouse's visual field), the synapses (with frequency equal to 80 Hz) produce a long-lasting increase in signal transmission and provoke dendritic spikes, causing the activation of the neuron.

Therefore, in Fig. 3B the increase in the synaptic weights of all the synapses of the model is evident during the activation period of the IClamps. The synaptic weights of the synapses that code for the red bar are represented in red; on the other hand, the synaptic weights of the synapses that code for the blue bar are represented in blue. As can be seen from the graph, the synapses that do not code for the object that the mouse is looking at (red bar) do not strengthen.

In the presence of the Plateau Potential, which in our model translates into the activation of the 4 different IClamps, a CA1 pyramidal neuron can self-tune into a place cell. In fact, in the figure we see the first spikes of the neuron (blue circles), a sign of the Place Field's initial formation. So, as the experimental data, also this model shows that, in the CA1 region of the hippocampus, an interaction between a distal input from the Entorhinal Cortex and a proximal input from the CA3 area of the hippocampus, induces the formation of new Place Fields [14].

A

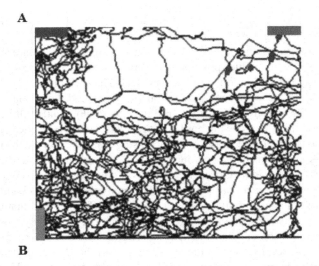

B

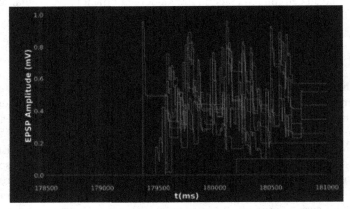

Fig. 3. Place field's initial formation. (Color figure online)

4   Discussion and Conclusions

Spatial navigation is the ability to plan and execute a path from one location to another. Depending on the task animals used different types of navigation strategies. There are a few other models of place cells. However, none of them uses a detailed morphological and biophysical implementation, which allow a direct comparison with experimental recordings. For example, Hartley et al.'s model [31] is implemented with artificial cells that respond to the presence of any wall at a given distance and direction; the cumulative suprathreshold activity of a population of these cells causes Place Cell-like firing. In this model, there is no learning. Burgess et al.'s [32] model extended the Hartley's model adding connections between cells with experience-dependent plasticity; this model produces Place Cells that encode position relative to specific objects, but place cells are still implemented with artificial point-neuron elements, which fire proportionally to the weighted cumulative input activity, and synaptic plasticity is modulated exclusively by the postsynaptic firing rate. In our model, a Place Cell more naturally emerges from synaptic weights evolving according to a physiologically plausible dynamics in which dendritic location, activation time, and postsynaptic activity all concur in transforming a pyramidal CA1 neuron into a Place Cell.

We have created the first computational model capable of simulating the creation of a PC on a single CA1 neuron having all its characteristic biophysical properties. Based on these experimental data, in this work, we simulated the spatial navigation of a mouse in a small arena. Each clue inside this arena is associated with a particular set of synapses: when a clue enters the mouse's field of view, the firing rate of some synapses changes. This activity associated appropriately with the distal input causes the activation of the cell. In this way, during the trajectory, the place cell fires only when the mouse is inside a restricted area of the environment.

The results suggested how, to what extent, and under what conditions of synaptic activity a CA1 pyramidal neuron can self-tune into a place cell. Place Cells are specific to the external environment: when the animal enters a new environment, a new Place Field is formed within a few minutes and remains stable for weeks to months. In the near future we will test this model under different conditions, such as longer simulations to test place field's stability, and changes caused by alteration of the relative position of the objects, as experimentally observed [11]. Furthermore, we will explore whether the rotation of the objects causes an equal rotation of the place cells, confirming the experimental observation that a mouse in behavioral tests does not get disoriented during the rotation [31–33], or if the neuron can represent different Place Cells when tuned to different objects.

This work presents a computational model that suggests the biophysical and neuro-physiological mechanisms underlying the formation of a Place Cell. A limitation of our current model is that the synaptic inputs need to be carefully preset, to represent input clues; we have found that a simple set of random synapses will not be able to generate the activity required to properly activate LTP and create a Place Cell. However, rather than a real limitation we consider this shortcoming as a model prediction, suggesting that the process of wiring a CA1 pyramidal neuron with preceding brain regions cannot be random but requires a substantial preprocessing; we plan to further investigate this issue in the near future, to be able to use the model for a better understanding of hippocampus-dependent cognitive functions and dysfunctions.

A possible future implication is to integrate the model into the full-scale hippocampal network that is being implemented within the Human Brain Project EU Flagship (https://www.humanbrainproject.eu/en/brain-simulation/hippocampus/) to generate population level activity at macroscopic level. What we expect to obtain are activity maps with place fields formation that can be directly compared with those seen experimentally. Through the development of artificial intelligence algorithms (Machine Learning and Deep Learning) the activation maps obtained experimentally could be first analyzed and then compared with *in silico* experiments able to reproduce both physiological and patho-logical conditions. The results can thus be used to make with the model experimentally testable predictions on how to implement innovative treatments of brain diseases.

References

1. Burgess, N., O'Keefe, J.: Neuronal computations underlying the firing of place cells and their role in navigation. Hippocampus **6**, 749–762 (1996). https://doi.org/10.1002/(sici)1098-106 3(1996)6:6%3c749::aid-hipo16%3e3.0.co;2-0

2. O'Keefe, J., Dostrovsky, J.: The hippocampus as a spatial map. Preliminary evidence from unit activity in the freely-moving rat. Brain Res. **34**, 171–175 (1971). https://doi.org/10.1016/0006-8993(71)90358-1

3. Fox, S.E., Ranck, J.B.: Localization and anatomical identification of theta and complex spike cells in dorsal hippocampal formation of rats. Exp Neurol. **49**, 299–313 (1975). https://doi.org/10.1016/0014-4886(75)90213-7

4. Hazama, Y., Tamura, R.: Effects of self-locomotion on the activity of place cells in the hippocampus of a freely behaving monkey. Neurosci Lett. **701**, 32–37 (2019). https://doi.org/10.1016/J.NEULET.2019.02.009

5. Hazama, Y., Tamura, R.: Data on the activity of place cells in the hippocampal CA1 subfield of a monkey performing a shuttling task. Data Brief. **26** (2019). https://doi.org/10.1016/J.DIB.2019.104467

6. Ekstrom, A.D., et al.: Cellular networks underlying human spatial navigation. Nature **425**, 184–187 (2003). https://doi.org/10.1038/NATURE01964

7. O'Keefe, J., Nadel, L.: The Hippocampus as a Cognitive Map. Clarendon Press, Oxford (1978)

8. Wilson, M.A., McNaughton, B.L.: Dynamics of the hippocampal ensemble code for space. Science **261**, 1055–1058 (1993). https://doi.org/10.1126/SCIENCE.8351520

9. Alme, C.B., Miao, C., Jezek, K., Treves, A., Moser, E.I., Moser, M.B.: Place cells in the hippocampus: eleven maps for eleven rooms. Proc. Natl. Acad. Sci. U S A. **111**, 18428–18435 (2014). https://doi.org/10.1073/PNAS.1421056111

10. Muller, R.U., Kubie, J.L.: The effects of changes in the environment on the spatial firing of hippocampal complex-spike cells. J. Neurosci. **7**, 1951–1968 (1987). https://doi.org/10.1523/JNEUROSCI.07-07-01951.1987

11. Fenton, A.A., Csizmadia, G., Muller, R.U.: Conjoint control of hippocampal place cell firing by two visual stimuli. I. The effects of moving the stimuli on firing field positions. J. Gen. Physiol. **116**, 191–209 (2000). https://doi.org/10.1085/JGP.116.2.191

12. Sharp, P.E.: Computer simulation of hippocampal place cells. Psychobiology **19**(2), 103–115 (2013). https://doi.org/10.3758/BF03327179

13. Zipser, D.: Biologically plausible models of place recognition and goal location. In: McClelland, J.L., Rumelhart, D.E., PDP Research Group (eds.) Parallel Distributed Processing: Explorations in the Microstructure of Cognition, vol. 2, pp. 432–470. MIT Press, Cambridge (1986)

14. Bittner, K.C., et al.: Conjunctive input processing drives feature selectivity in hippocampal CA1 neurons. Nat. Neurosci. **18**, 1133–1142 (2015). https://doi.org/10.1038/NN.4062

15. Migliore, M., Novara, G., Tegolo, D.: Single neuron binding properties and the magical number 7. Hippocampus **18**, 1122–1130 (2008). https://doi.org/10.1002/HIPO.20480

16. Migliore, M., Cannia, C., Canavier, C.C.: A modeling study suggesting a possible pharmacological target to mitigate the effects of ethanol on reward-related dopaminergic signaling. J. Neurophysiol. **99**, 2703–2707 (2008). https://doi.org/10.1152/JN.00024.2008

17. Hoffman, D.A., Magee, J.C., Colbert, C.M., Johnston, D.: K+ channel regulation of signal propagation in dendrites of hippocampal pyramidal neurons. Nature **387**, 869–875 (1997). https://doi.org/10.1038/43119

18. Magee, J.C.: Dendritic hyperpolarization-activated currents modify the integrative properties of hippocampal CA1 pyramidal neurons. J. Neurosci. **18**, 7613–7624 (1998). https://doi.org/10.1523/JNEUROSCI.18-19-07613.1998

19. Migliore, M.: On the integration of subthreshold inputs from Perforant Path and Schaffer Collaterals in hippocampal CA1 pyramidal neurons. J Comput. Neurosci. **14**, 185–192 (2003). https://doi.org/10.1023/A:1021906818333

20. Gasparini, S., Migliore, M., Magee, J.C.: On the initiation and propagation of dendritic spikes in CA1 pyramidal neurons. J. Neurosci. **24**, 11046–11056 (2004). https://doi.org/10.1523/JNEUROSCI.2520-04.2004

21. Bianchi, D., et al.: Effects of increasing CREB-dependent transcription on the storage and recall processes in a hippocampal CA1 microcircuit. Hippocampus **24**, 165–177 (2014). https://doi.org/10.1002/HIPO.22212

22. Quiroga, R.Q., Reddy, L., Kreiman, G., Koch, C., Fried, I.: Invariant visual representation by single neurons in the human brain. Nature **435**, 1102–1107 (2005). https://doi.org/10.1038/NATURE03687

23. Fried, I., MacDonald, K.A., Wilson, C.L.: Single neuron activity in human hippocampus and amygdala during recognition of faces and objects. Neuron **18**, 753–765 (1997). https://doi.org/10.1016/S0896-6273(00)80315-3

24. Kornblith, S., Quian Quiroga, R., Koch, C., Fried, I., Mormann, F.: Persistent single-neuron activity during working memory in the human medial temporal lobe. Curr. Biol. **27**, 1026–1032 (2017). https://doi.org/10.1016/J.CUB.2017.02.013

25. Migliore, M., de Blasi, I., Tegolo, D., Migliore, R.: A modeling study suggesting how a reduction in the context-dependent input on CA1 pyramidal neurons could generate schizophrenic behavior. Neural. Netw. **24**, 552–559 (2011). https://doi.org/10.1016/J.NEUNET.2011.01.001

26. Kastellakis, G., Silva, A.J., Poirazi, P.: Linking memories across time via neuronal and dendritic overlaps in model neurons with active dendrites. Cell Rep. **17**, 1491–1504 (2016). https://doi.org/10.1016/J.CELREP.2016.10.015

27. Lisman, J.: Working memory: the importance of theta and gamma oscillations. Curr Biol. **20** (2010). https://doi.org/10.1016/J.CUB.2010.04.011

28. Fuentemilla, L., Penny, W.D., Cashdollar, N., Bunzeck, N., Düzel, E.: Theta-coupled periodic replay in working memory. Curr. Biol. **20**, 606–612 (2010). https://doi.org/10.1016/J.CUB.2010.01.057

29. Jensen, O., Kaiser, J., Lachaux, J.P.: Human gamma-frequency oscillations associated with attention and memory. Trends Neurosci. **30**, 317–324 (2007). https://doi.org/10.1016/J.TINS.2007.05.001

30. Gray, C.M.: Synchronous oscillations in neuronal systems: mechanisms and functions. J. Comput. Neurosci. **1**, 11–38 (1994). https://doi.org/10.1007/BF00962716

31. Hartley, T., Burgess, N., Lever, C., Cacucci, F., O'Keefe, J.: Modeling place fields in terms of the cortical inputs to the hippocampus. Hippocampus **10**, 369–379 (2000). https://doi.org/10.1002/1098-1063(2000)10:4%3c369::aid-hipo3%3e3.0.co;2-0

32. Barry, C., Burgess, N.: Learning in a geometric model of place cell firing. Hippocampus **17**, 786–800 (2007). https://doi.org/10.1002/HIPO.20324

33. Yoder, R.M., Clark, B.J., Taube, J.S.: Origins of landmark encoding in the brain. Trends Neurosci. **34**, 561–571 (2011). https://doi.org/10.1016/J.TINS.2011.08.004

34. Knierim, J.J., Rao, G.: Distal landmarks and hippocampal place cells: effects of relative translation versus rotation. Hippocampus **13**, 604–617 (2003). https://doi.org/10.1002/HIPO.10092

35. Knierim, J.J., Kudrimoti, H.S., McNaughton, B.L.: Place cells, head direction cells, and the learning of landmark stability. J. Neurosci. **15**, 1648–1659 (1995). https://doi.org/10.1523/JNEUROSCI.15-03-01648.1995

Automatic Liver Segmentation in Pre-TIPS Cirrhotic Patients: A Preliminary Step for Radiomics Studies

Anna Maria Pavone[1,2], Viviana Benfante[1,3,4] (iD), Alessandro Stefano[4] (iD),
Giuseppe Mamone[5(✉)] (iD), Mariapina Milazzo[5] (iD), Ambra Di Pizza[5] (iD),
Rosalba Parenti[2] (iD), Luigi Maruzzelli[5] (iD), Roberto Miraglia[5] (iD), and Albert Comelli[1] (iD)

[1] Ri.MED Foundation, Via Bandiera 11, 90133 Palermo, Italy
[2] Section of Physiology, Department of Biomedical and Biotechnological Sciences, University of Catania, Via S. Sofia n. 97, Torre Biologica,, 95123 Catania, Italy
[3] Department of Health Promotion, Mother and Child Care, Internal Medicine and Medical Specialties, Molecular and Clinical Medicine, University of Palermo, 90127 Palermo, Italy
[4] Institute of Molecular Bioimaging and Physiology, National Research Council (IBFM-CNR), 90015 Cefalù, Italy
[5] Department of Diagnostic and Therapeutic Services, IRCCS-ISMETT (Mediterranean Institute for Transplantation and Advanced Specialized Therapies), Via Tricomi 5, 90127 Palermo, Italy
gmamone@ismett.edu

Abstract. The aim of this study is to present a deep learning (DL) algorithm for accurate liver delineation in high-resolution computed tomography (CT) images of pre-transjugular intrahepatic portosystemic shunt (TIPS) cirrhotic patients. In this way, we aim to improve the methodology performed by medical physicians in radiomics studies where the use of operator-independent segmentation methods is mandatory to correctly identify the target and to obtain accurate predictive models.

Two DL models were investigated: UNet, the most widely used DL network for biomedical image segmentation, and the innovative customized efficient neural network (C-ENet). 111 patients with liver contrast-enhanced CT examinations before TIPS procedure were considered. The performance of the two DL networks was evaluated in terms of the similarity of their segmentations to the gold standard.

The results show that C-ENet can be used to obtain accurate (dice similarity coefficient = 87.70%) segmentation of the liver region outperforming UNet (dice similarity coefficient = 85.33%). In conclusion, we demonstrated that DL can be efficiently applied to rapidly segment cirrhotic liver images, without any radiologist supervision, to produce user-independent results useful for subsequent radiomics studies.

Keywords: Segmentation · Deep learning · UNet · C-ENet · Liver · Cirrhosis · TIPS

© The Author(s), under exclusive license to Springer Nature Switzerland AG 2022
P. L. Mazzeo et al. (Eds.): ICIAP 2022 Workshops, LNCS 13373, pp. 408–418, 2022.
https://doi.org/10.1007/978-3-031-13321-3_36

1   Introduction

Liver cirrhosis is a progressive and chronic disease, characterized by the alteration of liver function that evolves into an irreversible condition, during its late stages. In recent years, the incidence of liver cirrhosis has increased worldwide [1, 2]. The most common risk factors for the development of liver cirrhosis are viral hepatitis infections, obesity, autoimmune disease, alcohol-dependent liver diseases, and non-alcoholic steatohepatitis [3]. The resulting chronic inflammation leads to an architecture replacement with fibrous partitions and regenerative nodules, altering liver parenchyma and vascular structure and causing chronic liver failure and hepatocellular carcinoma [4, 5]. Indeed, aberration of the hepatic structure induces an increase in resistance to portal blood, with a consequent rise in portal pressure [2]. Portal hypertension (PH) is a pathological condition associated with other complications, such as refractory ascites, hepatorenal syndrome, gastric and esophageal variceal bleedings, and hepatic encephalopathies [6]. Due to these severe manifestations, PH must be monitored and treated promptly.

Transjugular Intrahepatic Portosystemic Shunt (TIPS) is an accepted radiological treatment in the event of failure of standard treatments, especially for severe cirrhotic patients, such as nonsurgical candidates [7]. Indeed, TIPS is configured as an effective no-surgical technique in the case of refractory ascites, with a success of up to 85% [6]. This procedure involves the insertion of a stent through the hepatic parenchyma, to connect one portal vein branch to the adjacent hepatic vein [8].

However, TIPS rescue treatments lead to a high incidence of complications (20%-54% of cases), including hepatic encephalopathy (HE), probably due to the already liver impairment [6]. In this field, diagnostic imaging plays an essential role in improving clinical decision-making. Deep-learning (DL) methods allow for many purposes to be achieved automatically [9, 10]. According to an objective view, DL exploits algorithms to create synthetic images and to perform behavior identifications, image classifications, and segmentations [11, 12]. Moreover, convolution neural networks (CNN) are feed-forward neural networks applied primarily to medical imaging, such as computer tomography (CT) [13], magnetic resonance imaging (MRI) [14], or also Contrast-Enhanced Ultrasound (CEUS) images [15].

In pathological liver imaging, DL is considered a successful method for automatically detecting high-level features, improving liver tumor detection and segmentation studies [16] to analyze the morphology and to set liver tumor classification, including hepatocellular carcinoma (HCC). While liver volume per se is not critical for the TIPS procedure, it is useful for extracting radiomics features from the whole liver rather than from a single slice. Indeed, the features extracted from a single slice may reflect only a portion of the liver and not be representative of the entire hepatic disease; this is due to the heterogeneity of the disease distribution in the hepatic parenchyma. For example, Mitrea et al. performed HCC diagnostic studies, applying innovative CNN algorithms from CEUS images, which capture more detailed images than CT and MRI [17]. The implementation of pattern matching and DL (PM-DL) algorithms was instead carried out by Zheng et al. They performed identification analyses to investigate the differences between benign cirrhosis-associated nodules and malignant lesions of HCC [18]. In other studies, CNN algorithms were applied to classify four liver stages of disease, from healthy tissue to evolved HCC after cirrhosis [19]. Moreover, artificial intelligence is also used to improve segmentation techniques. This is the case of Alberto A. Perez, et al. that used CNN to detect a threshold in hepatomegaly disease by automating liver segmentation. To achieve this, they used DL CT imaging, making comparisons among several algorithms, including a modified 3D U-Net, and CycleGAN [19].

In this context, our aim was to apply CNN, including customized efficient neural network (C-ENet) [20], and UNet to improve accurate image segmentation, object detection, and to make accurate classifications for future radiomics studies [21]. These comparisons were applied to cirrhotic liver imaging in pre-TIPS patients.

2   Materials and Methods

2.1   Patients

Since its retrospective nature, this study was approved from institutional review board of our hospital, and written informed consent was waived. This is a tertiary hospital specialized in liver diseases and liver transplantation, with many years of experience performing TIPS procedures. From May 2015 to June 2019, a total of 130 consecutive patients underwent TIPS using controlled expansion stents were collected from our institutional electronic medical records. These patients were hospitalized due to variceal bleeding or refractory ascites. Nine patients with liver transplantation, one patient with complete portal vein thrombosis, and nine with problems during the manual segmentation phase were excluded. Finally, 111 patients were consecutively enrolled (80 males and 31 females; mean age 59; median age 59; range 25–79 years). In these patients, liver contrast-enhanced CT examinations were performed within 20 months before TIPS procedure (range 0–600 days).

2.2   TIPS Procedure

Previous studies have already described technical details of TIPS procedure [7]. In this study, all procedures were performed using the so called "controlled expansion stents", that are covered stents made of nitinol (Viatorr; Gore, Phoenix, AZ) which dilatation caliber may be customized in each patient, reducing the risk of HE and/or liver failure. The goal of the TIPS procedure is to reduce the portosystemic pressure gradient to less than 12 mmHg.

2.3   CT Examination

CT examinations were performed with a 64-detector VCT scanner (GE, Milwaukee, USA) and stored in our Picture Archiving and Communication System (PACS). CT scan parameters were: tube voltage 120 kV; tube current range 100–400 mA; gantry rotation time 0.5 s; matrix 512×512; detector collimation of 64×0.625 mm; slice thickness 2.5 mm; intervals 0 m; pitch 0.984: noise index 18; large body FOV; ASIR 30%. The examinations were acquired withhold breath and craniocaudal direction. Unenhanced scan was followed by contrast-enhanced imaging with a contrast agent (Iopromide, Bayer Healthcare, Germany) injected at 1.5 mL $\times$ Kg and a rate of 4.0 mL/s using an automatic power injector.

The CT scan protocol included a multiphasic dynamic study with arterial, portal venous and delayed phase, respectively acquired with a delay of 30 s, 65 s, and 180 s after bolus tracking.

2.4 Manual Segmentation

Two board-certified diagnostic radiologists with at least 16 years of experience in liver imaging reviewed the CT images. The radiologists were blinded to the patients' clinical characteristics.

The liver analysis has been performed drawing ROIs along the whole hepatic pro-file on all the CT axial images obtaining a whole liver volume.

The two radiologists manually drew the ROIs in consensus on both unenhanced and portal venous phase images in an independent workstation (ADW 4.7, GE, Mil-waukee, USA).

2.5 The Proposed Deep Learning Model

C-ENet is a custom neural network model which is based on ENet, which in turn is characterized by high precision and fast inference and whose architecture is well described in [22]. The customization of ENet to obtain C-ENet (which means custom-ENet) is due to the fact that the output of $128 \times 64 \times 64$ is replaced by an output of $256 \times 64 \times 64$. This causes on average an increase in the DSC distribution and a lower variability compared to the starting network [20]. In this study, this customized network is compared with the most promising technique in the biomedical field, namely UNet [23].

2.6 Loss Function

The biomedical image segmentation process can be characterized by a well-known issue: the target region may be smaller than the surrounding tissue. In this way, most of the voxels are tagged as a background. This process causes data imbalance in the DL method. This imbalance issue can be solved through particular loss functions, such as the Tversky loss function proposed in [24]. Through the following formulas, the dice similarity coefficient and a penalty approach are applied to optimize the segmentation:

$$T(\alpha\beta) = \frac{\sum_{i=1}^{N} p_{0i} g_{0i}}{\sum_{i=1}^{N} p_{0i} g_{0i} + \alpha \sum_{i=1}^{N} p_{0i} g_{1i} + \beta \sum_{i=1}^{N} p_{1i} g_{0i}} \quad (1)$$

where p_{0i} is the probability of voxel I is inside the target, and p_{1i} is the probability of voxel I is outside the target. The ground truth training label g_{0i} is 1 for target and 0 for background, and vice versa for the label g_{1i}. By adjusting the parameters, α and β, the trade-off can be controlled between false positives and false negatives. To obtain the dice similarity coefficient, α and β must be set to 0.5. Setting β's > 0.5 more emphasis is given to false negatives in the slices with small target regions.

2.7 Training

In DL approaches, the available images are split into two data sets namely training and testing. The k-fold cross-validation strategy is used when few images are available. Consequently, CT studies are divided into k folds. In particular, the 111 patients were stratified in five-fold as follows: the dataset was divided into 5 subgroups of patients and each holdout method was repeated 5 times both for UNet and C-Net. At each round, each subgroup of the five was considered as a test set and the other 4 as training set. Cross-contamination was avoided between test and training sets.

Augmentation techniques were adopted through randomly rotations (20) and translation in both X (0.2) and Y (0.2) directions, shearing (10), horizontal flip and zooming (0.1) on the input training set. For the normalization of the data, for each CT study the subtraction of the mean and the division of the standard deviation were carried out in such a way that the numbers were more stable. The input parameters, for the learning process for both networks, were obtained using an initial set of 23 patients. Specifically, a learning rate of 0.0001 and 0.00001 for C-Net and UNet with Adam optimizer were adopted, respectively. A batch size of 8 slices for all experiments was used. The Tversky loss function was set with $\alpha = 0.3$ and $\beta = 0.7$ [25]. All models were trained with a maximum of 100 epochs. An automatic stopping criterion was adopted: the training phase stopped when the loss decreased after 10 epochs. A high-end HPC system equipped with a GPU (NVIDIA QUADRO P4000 with 8 GB of RAM, 1792 CUDA Cores) was used to train all networks and run inference.

2.8 Evaluation Metrics

The performance of the proposed approaches was based on the dice similarity coefficient (which measures the spatial overlap between the reference volume and the segmented volume), sensitivity, volume overlap error, volume difference and positive predictive value calculated as mean, standard variation and confidence interval [26]. In general, with a dice similarity coefficient equal to 0% no overlap means, and with a value of 100% the perfect overlap is achieved.

$$DSC = (2 \times TP)/(2 \times TP + FP + FN) \times 100\% \tag{2}$$

where TP, FP, and FN are the number of true positives, false positives, and false negatives respectively.

Sensitivity is the true positive rate and is defined as:

$$Sensitivity = (TP)/(TN + FN) \times 100\% \tag{3}$$

where TN is the number of true negative.

Finally, VOE, VD, and PPV are defined respectively as:

$$\text{VOE} = 1 - (TP)/(TP + FP + FN) \tag{4}$$

$$\text{VD} = (FN - FP)/(2TP + FP + FN) \tag{5}$$

$$\text{PPV} = (TP)/(TP + FN) \tag{6}$$

One-way ANOVA test was applied to test the significance of differences of performance between UNet and C-Net.

3 Results

Our study was based on the biomedical application of CNN methods, including UNet and C-ENet models. The latter is a CNN based on ENet model, both marked by high accuracy and fast inference. However, we obtained C-ENet by ENet with opportune improvements: for instance, $128 \times 64 \times 64$ output is replaced by a $256 \times 64 \times 64$ output in C-ENet, resulting in a higher DSC distribution and a decrease of variability. Then, we applied DL models in order to improve image segmentation approaches, starting from CT images of a cohort of pre-TIPS patients. Considering the retrospective features of the analyses, the data were obtained from our hospital and 111 patients were enrolled for the study. The images were split in two datasets: training and testing sets. The enrolled patients were divided into five subgroups, according to the k-fold cross-validation strategy, used in the presence of few samples. Each subgroup was investigated, using both C-ENet and UNet methods. Then, each subgroup was considered as test set and the other four as training set, avoiding any cross-contamination among test and training sets.

We applied the proposed segmentation approaches to identify and contour cirrhotic liver imaging, in pre-TIPS patients and we provided a comparison with the results of the C-ENet and UNet as showed in Fig. 1. Table 1 shows the performance evaluation using the k-fold strategy. C-ENet showed the highest DSC $87.70 \pm 4.84\%$, while UNet achieved a DSC of $85.33 \pm 3.62\%$. Figure2 reveals how C-ENet and UNet models achieved a training DSC greater than 80% in less than 5 epochs and in less than 25 respectively. At the analysis of variance, the p-value corresponding to the F-statistic of one-way ANOVA was less than 0.05, suggesting that C-ENet and UNet were significantly different (see Table 2).

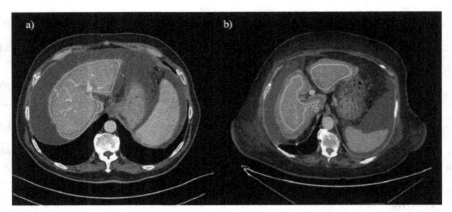

Fig. 1. Comparison of segmentation performance in two different slices for (**a**) patient #007, and (**b**) patient #019. Manual (yellow), C-ENet (red), and UNet (green) segmentations are superimposed. In the first study, C-ENET and UNet obtained the best DSCs (94.24% and 85.25%, respectively). In the second study, C-ENET and UNet showed the worst DSCs (77.50% and 76.13%, respectively) while ENET maintained similar performance compared to the first study (94.24%).

Table 1. Performance of DL networks.

	DSC	VOE	VD	PPV	Sensitivity
C-ENet					
Mean	87.70%	21.58%	19.37%	86.15%	91.23%
± std	4.84%	7.52%	14.11%	10.79%	8.33%
± CI (95%)	2.02%	3.14%	5.90%	4.51%	3.48%
UNet					
Mean	85.33%	25.42%	20.47%	88.31%	84.61%
± std	3.62%	5.39%	12.09%	10.53%	9.48%
± CI (95%)	1.51%	2.25%	5.05%	4.40%	3.96%

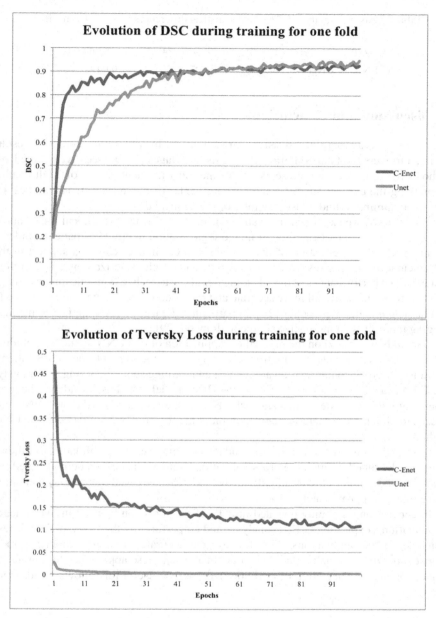

Fig. 2. Training DSC and Tversky loss plots for C-ENet and UNet.

Table 2. ANOVA on the DSC showed statistical differences between DL methods.

ANOVA	F Value	F critic value	p-Value
C-ENet vs. UNet	3.2365	4.0727	0.0492

4 Discussion and Conclusions

Liver cirrhosis is a progressive disease characterized by liver function alterations, resulting in an irreversible fatal condition, during its late stages [1]. In recent years, the liver cirrhosis rising incidence represents one of the most frequent causes of adult deaths, intensifying the clinical attention and concern [27]. For this reason, many studies are carried out aiming to find a fast diagnosis of this clinical disease.

In this study, we examined innovative DL methods to support clinical issues about a faster and more accurate method of image segmentation in pre-TIPS patients. Indeed, the automatic characterization of liver cirrhosis in CT images can be a support in the real calculation of features, in order to avoid manual characterizations and resulting mistakes. The performances of the DL strategies allow to realize synthetic images, image classifications and above all more accurate and reproducible segmentations compared to the classical manual approaches [28]. In particular, the use of CNN applied to medical imaging represents an innovative source to draw on [29].

Our study was based on the biomedical application of two CNN methods, including UNet and C-ENet models starting from CT images of a cohort of 111 pre-TIPS patients avoiding any cross-contamination among test and training sets. According to our analyses, C-ENet achieved a higher DSC than the UNet model, which is considered the most promising method in the biomedical field. Hence, these data showed that C-ENet can be used to obtain more accurate segmentation of the liver region, compared to the UNet method.

Despite the limited number of cases and the lack of the external validation to validate a final model tuned through the cross-validation strategy, our results demonstrated the feasibility and validity/efficacy of C-ENet method, which showed accurate segmentation with a DSC of approximately 87%.

In conclusion, our study revealed how DL algorithms can be used in liver images segmentations, exploiting C-ENet analyses and outperforming the UNet method. These user-independent applications allow for fast and accurate analyses without any radiologist supervision. Finally, the clinical application of these approaches for automatic delineation and segmentation of cirrhotic liver may be useful for following radiomics studies.

References

1. Roerecke, M., et al.: Alcohol consumption and risk of liver cirrhosis: a systematic review and meta-analysis. Am. J. Gastroenterol. **114**, 1574–1586 (2019). https://doi.org/10.14309/ajg.0000000000000340
2. Ginès, P., Krag, A., Abraldes, J.G., Solà, E., Fabrellas, N., Kamath, P.S.: Liver cirrhosis. Lancet **398**, 1359–1376 (2021). https://doi.org/10.1016/S0140-6736(21)01374-X

3. Smith, A.J., Baumgartner, K., Bositis, C.M.: Cirrhosis: diagnosis and management. Am. Fam. Physician **100**(12), 759–770 (2019)
4. Fan, Y., Li, Y., Chu, Y., Liu, J., Cui, L., Zhang, D.: Toll-like receptors recognize intestinal microbes in liver cirrhosis. Front. Immunol. **12**, 99 (2021). https://doi.org/10.3389/fimmu.2021.608498
5. Lai, M., Afdhal, N.H.: Liver fibrosis determination. Gastroenterol. Clin. North Am. **48**, 281–289 (2019). https://doi.org/10.1016/j.gtc.2019.02.002
6. De Wit, K., et al.: Prevention of hepatic encephalopathy by administration of rifaximin and lactulose in patients with liver cirrhosis undergoing placement of a transjugular intrahepatic portosystemic shunt (TIPS): a multicentre randomised, double blind, placebo controlled t. BMJ Open Gastroenterol. **7**, (2020). https://doi.org/10.1136/bmjgast-2020-000531
7. Rajesh, S., et al.: Transjugular intrahepatic portosystemic shunt in cirrhosis: an exhaustive critical update. World J. Gastroenterol. **26**, 5561–5596 (2020). https://doi.org/10.3748/wjg.v26.i37.5561
8. Sun, S.H., et al.: Predicting death or recurrence of portal hypertension symptoms after TIPS procedures. Eur. Radiol. 32, 3346–3357 (2022). https://doi.org/10.1007/s00330-021-08437-0
9. Salvaggio, G., et al.: Deep learning network for segmentation of the prostate gland with median lobe enlargement in T2-weighted MR images: comparison with manual segmentation method. Curr. Probl. Diagn. Radiol. (2021). https://doi.org/10.1067/j.cpradiol.2021.06.006
10. Agnello, L., Comelli, A., Ardizzone, E., Vitabile, S.: Unsupervised tissue classification of brain MR images for voxel-based morphometry analysis. Int. J. Imaging Syst. Technol. **26**, 136–150 (2016). https://doi.org/10.1002/ima.22168
11. Laudicella, R., et al.: Artificial neural networks in cardiovascular diseases and its potential for clinical application in molecular imaging. Curr. Radiopharm. **14**, 209–219 (2020). https://doi.org/10.2174/1874471013666200621191259
12. Cutaia, G., et al.: Radiomics and prostate MRI: current role and future applications. J. Imaging **7**, 34 (2021). https://doi.org/10.3390/jimaging7020034
13. Salvaggio, G., et al.: Deep learning networks for automatic retroperitoneal sarcoma segmentation in computerized tomography. Appl. Sci. **12**, 1665 (2022). https://doi.org/10.3390/app12031665
14. Cuocolo, R., et al.: Deep learning whole-gland and zonal prostate segmentation on a public MRI dataset. J. Magn. Reson. Imaging **54**, 452–459 (2021). https://doi.org/10.1002/jmri.27585
15. Chen, C., et al.: Deep learning for cardiac image segmentation: a review. Front. Cardiovasc. Med. (2020). https://doi.org/10.3389/fcvm.2020.00025
16. Choy, G., et al.: Current applications and future impact of machine learning in radiology. Radiology **288**, 318–328 (2018). https://doi.org/10.1148/radiol.2018171820
17. Mitrea, D., Badea, R., Mitrea, P., Brad, S., Nedevschi, S.: Hepatocellular carcinoma automatic diagnosis within ceus and b-mode ultrasound images using advanced machine learning methods. Sensors. **21**, 1–31 (2021). https://doi.org/10.3390/s21062202
18. Zheng, R., et al.: Feasibility of automatic detection of small hepatocellular carcinoma (≤ 2 cm) in cirrhotic liver based on pattern matching and deep learning. Phys. Med. Biol. **66**, 085014 (2021). https://doi.org/10.1088/1361-6560/abf2f8
19. Perez, A.A., et al.: Deep learning CT-based quantitative visualization tool for liver volume estimation: defining normal and hepatomegaly. Radiology **302**, 336–342 (2022). https://doi.org/10.1148/radiol.2021210531
20. Stefano, A., Comelli, A.: Customized efficient neural network for covid-19 infected region identification in CT images. J. Imaging. **7**, 131 (2021). https://doi.org/10.3390/jimaging7080131

21. Stefano, A., et al.: Performance of radiomics features in the quantification of idiopathic pulmonary fibrosis from HRCT. Diagnostics **10**, 306. 10, 306 (2020). https://doi.org/10.3390/DIAGNOSTICS10050306

22. Paszke, A., Chaurasia, A., Kim, S., Culurciello, E.: ENet: A Deep Neural Network Architecture for Real-Time Semantic Segmentation, pp. 1–10 (2016)

23. Ronneberger, O., Fischer, P., Brox, T.: U-Net: convolutional networks for biomedical image segmentation. In: Navab, N., Hornegger, J., Wells, W.M., Frangi, A.F. (eds.) MICCAI 2015. LNCS, vol. 9351, pp. 234–241. Springer, Cham (2015). https://doi.org/10.1007/978-3-319-24574-4_28

24. Salehi, S.S.M., Erdogmus, D., Gholipour, A.: Tversky loss function for image segmentation using 3D fully convolutional deep networks. In: Wang, Q., Shi, Y., Suk, H.-I., Suzuki, K. (eds.) MLMI 2017. LNCS, vol. 10541, pp. 379–387. Springer, Cham (2017). https://doi.org/10.1007/978-3-319-67389-9_44

25. Alongi, P., et al.: Radiomics analysis of 18F-Choline PET/CT in the prediction of disease outcome in high-risk prostate cancer: an explorative study on machine learning feature classification in 94 patients. Eur. Radiol. **31**(7), 4595–4605 (2021). https://doi.org/10.1007/s00330-020-07617-8

26. Comelli, A., Stefano, A., Benfante, V., Russo, G.: Normal and abnormal tissue classification in positron emission tomography oncological studies. Pattern Recogn. Image Anal. **28**, 106–113 (2018). https://doi.org/10.1134/S1054661818010054

27. Hu, Y., et al.: A prediction model for 30-day deaths of cirrhotic patients in intensive care unit hospitalization. Med. (United States). **101**, E28752 (2022). https://doi.org/10.1097/MD.0000000000028752

28. Groendahl, A.R., et al.: A comparison of methods for fully automatic segmentation of tumors and involved nodes in PET/CT of head and neck cancers. Phys. Med. Biol. **66** (2021). https://doi.org/10.1088/1361-6560/abe553

29. Comelli, A., et al.: Deep learning approach for the segmentation of aneurysmal ascending aorta. Biomed. Eng. Lett. **11**(1), 15–24 (2020). https://doi.org/10.1007/s13534-020-00179-0

Combining Convolutional Neural Networks and Anatomical Shape-Based Priors for Cardiac Segmentation

Samuel Bignardi[1]([✉]) [iD], Anthony Yezzi[1] [iD], Navdeep Dahiya[1] [iD],
Albert Comelli[2] [iD], Alessandro Stefano[3] [iD], Marina Piccinelli[4] [iD],
and Ernest Garcia[4] [iD]

[1] Department of Electrical and Computer Engineering,
Georgia Institute of Technology, Atlanta, GA, USA
sbignardi3@gatech.edu
[2] Ri.MED Foundation, Via Bandiera 11, 90133 Palermo, Italy
[3] Institute of Molecular Bioimaging and Physiology,
National Research Council (IBFM-CNR), 90015 Cefalù, Italy
[4] Department of Radiology and Imaging Sciences,
Emory University School of Medicine, Atlanta, GA, USA

Abstract. We investigate whether leveraging high-resolution semantic segmentation from convolutional neural networks on Cardiac Tomography Angiography imaging, coupled with a shape-prior-based segmentation capable of enforcing the anatomical correctness can provide improved segmentation capabilities. While fully integrated approaches may be devised in principle, we investigate a simpler three-step approach for ease of implementation where, after leveraging a convolutional network to produce initial labels, we re-segment the labels using a fully geometric shaped-based algorithm followed by a post-processing refinement via active surfaces. Following the semantic segmentation, our second step is capable of generating a topologically correct cardiac model, albeit with lower resolution compared to the input labels, and is therefore capable of repairing any non-anatomical mislabeling. The post-processing step then recaptures the lost small-scale structure making the combined strategy successful in recovering a topologically correct segmentation of the imaging data of quality comparable, if not superior, to the initial labels. Our results show dice scores comparable to those obtained by using deep learning alone but with much improved performance in terms of Hausdorff distance due to the removal of erroneous islands and holes which often evade notice using only dice scores. In addition, by design, our segmentation is topologically correct. This preliminary investigation fully demonstrates the advantages of a hybrid semantic-geometric approach and motivates us in pursuing the investigation of a more integrated strategy in which semantic labels and geometric priors will be integrated as competing penalty terms within the optimization algorithm.

This work was supported by the National Institutes of Health (NIH) grant number R01-HL-143350.

Keywords: Convolutional neural networks · Deep learning · Principal component analysis · Anatomical modeling · Heart segmentation

1   Introduction

Early diagnosis has become increasingly important in modern medicine. Computer assisted approaches have assumed a dominant role in medical diagnosis, as they enable processing imaging data from large groups of patients in a time-efficient and cost-effective way [5]. While medical imaging techniques offer a window on the inside of the patient body, it is up to healthcare clinicians to interpret such image products. However, when blending information from different imaging modalities or when targeting a specific body area for treatment it becomes necessary to first obtain a geometric representation of the investigated anatomical feature [6–8,11]. The main challenge behind creating such a three-dimensional representation and recognizing common volumes of interest within imaging data from different acquisition modalities (that may have different resolutions and/or be affected by image distortion) is segmentation, whose challenges vary depending both on the physical phenomena leveraged by the imaging system and the investigated body area. Generally speaking, medical imagery suffers from poor contrast, low signal to noise ratio, faint or even invisible edges, or blurring of features due to patient movement (see for e.g. [1,16,18]); all factors known to hinder automatic and semi-automatic segmentation and that historically have led many practitioners to prefer the ostensibly more time-consuming manual segmentation over automated methods.

In this paper we consider the semi-automatic segmentation of Cardiac Tomography Angiography (CTA) data with the goal of reconstructing the heart anatomy for the diagnosis of ventricular and atrial function. In particular, the present contribution leverages previous work from this group [10] in which segmentation of main heart structures such as epicardium (Epi), left ventricle (LV), and right ventricle (RV), were obtained by optimizing a shape prior model-based implicit parametric representation of each anatomical structure of interest. In [10], segmentation is achieved by searching the optimal values of the parameters controlling the shape of priors which minimizes the difference between data and statistics within the segmented volumes. As described in Sect. 2.3, we leveraged principal component analysis (PCA) applied to a set of 30 clinical cases to capture the global geometry of each cardiac boundary surface. The obtained "principal modes", which in our formulation consist of a set of three-dimensional signed distance functions (SDF), constitute an orthogonal base for the above-mentioned geometries. These bases are used to generate a generic cardiac shape which is further modified by a pose transformation. The goal of the resulting iterative segmentation method in [10] is to determine both the optimal weights for the linear combination of shape modes as well as optimal values for the pose parameters. The optimization is achieved by minimizing a cost functional which depends, through the pose and the PCA weights, on the surfaces representing Epi, LV, and RV. Furthermore, additional penalty terms are included within the cost functional as soft constraints with the purpose of preventing overlap of the three surfaces as well as ordering the contrast statistics within each resulting segmented sub-volume. The main advantage of such a segmentation approach is to fully leverage a-priori knowledge of the heart structure and enforce precise and well-defined anatomical hierarchical relations between the surfaces representing *Epi*, *LV*, and *RV*.

The powerful benefit of employing a learning component (i.e. the PCA) engineered to learn strictly geometrical aspects from the data and enforcing as much prior knowledge as possible within our algorithm [9,12], is that the final segmentation is always correct from the topological perspective, as clearly shown in our previous work. In addition, the approach is extremely robust with respect to imaging anomalies that may be present in the CTA data. In contrast, we pay for this robustness by a loss of sensitivity to subtle details, which are still difficult to capture with the present segmentation strategy. As such, improvement in this area would be desirable.

On the one hand, recent developments in artificial intelligence offer unprecedented segmentation capabilities [4,11]. Given the CTA data volume, deep learning methods using layered Convolutional Neural Networks (CNN) are capable of producing labeled volumes, identifying background, myocardium (the volume enclosed between epicardium and ventricles), left ventricle, right ventricle at the voxel level. Therefore, CNN can easily capture fine scale structures. In addition, CNN offer one of the simplest solutions in terms of design choices, as the only parameters that need to be selected are those defining the structure of the neural network being used. Nevertheless, CNN present several limitations as well, as they are sensitive to the gray level range of the training set. Furthermore, while to some extent the network learns of structures at different scales from the training set, it does not inherently ensure topological correctness and may label pixels in a way that is incompatible with the real anatomy. We refer to this phenomenon as "rogue pixel clusters".

In the present contribution we investigate whether labels from CNN (i.e. voxel-wise tissue information) can be leveraged within our shape-prior-based (i.e. fully geometric) approach, and whether including such information may actually lead to better segmentation. While the most flexible mathematical way to include tissue information would be to introduce a penalty term within the cost functional driving the segmentation, thereby incorporating both greyscale information as well as CNN classifier labels (indeed, we proposed a similar approach in the context of cancer segmentation [6–8]), we explore a less complicated three-step approach (Fig. 1c) which will be much simpler to implement in practice. First we obtain a voxel-based classification using deep learning which is able to respond to sophisticated gray-scale patterns but which does not incorporate a geometric anatomical model. Second, we use our shape-based algorithm [10] to resegment the labeled volumes produced by the CNN, rather than the gray-scale values directly. As such, we incorporate geometry on top of labels that already performed the work of complex greyscale pattern matching. Third, we leverage three independent active surfaces (AS) which, starting from this optimized geometry from step two, are evolved with a distance penalty against this reference starting point. This third step helps soften the low dimensional shape constraint imposed during step two, which limits its ability to respond locally to fine scale shape variations present in the classifier labels. We show that, even in this simple three forward-step approach, combining CNN tissue classification with shape-based segmentation strategies introduces a tangible advantage beyond the deep learning by itself, motivating further studies in this direction.

2   Method

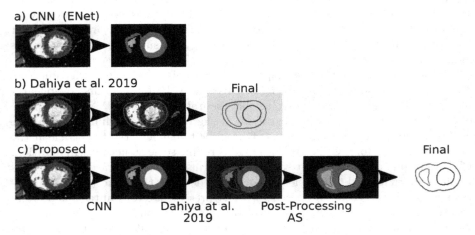

Fig. 1. Comparison of different approaches: a) Segmentation using CNN. Advantage: reaches voxel-wise resolution. b) direct segmentation using the prior-based approach from [10]. Advantage: completely geometric and topologically correct. c) Three-stages approach considered in this study. From left to right: i) Example CTA data. ii) Step 1; Labels produced by the CNN are shown as shades of gray. The example emphasizes a partially mislabeled case. iii) Step 2; re-segmentation using the algorithm [10]. Input labels are shown in the background onto which colored contours (red for *Epi*, blue for *LV*, and yellow for *RV*) showing the intersection of the output geometry with the considered slice are superimposed. iv) Step 3; Post-Processing. The input, i.e. the segmentation from step 2 is shown in the background. Contours from the final converged heart geometry are once again shown in color. v) Final contours, intersection between the 3D *Epi*, *LV*, and *RV* surfaces with this slice plane. (Color figure online)

2.1   Cardiac Tomography Angiography Data

In the following, we consider a dataset provided by the Nuclear Cardiology Laboratory at Emory University, comprising measurements acquired at different clinical and research centers, and using machines from different manufacturers (Siemens Somaton Definition, Siemens Sensation Cardiac 64, GE LightSpeed

46VCT and Philips Brilliance 64). The image acquisition was originally performed after review and approval by Emory University Institutional Review Board (USA), the Institutional Review Board of the University Hospital Val D'Hebron (Spain) and the Institutional Review Board of the Rambam Medical Hospital (Israel). Written informed consent was obtained from each patient in accordance with clinical guidelines on human research. Additional information on the dataset can be found in [14]. For all cases, a set of binary masks was manually segmented by our expert clinicians.

2.2 Deep Learning Segmentation (Step 1)

Based on previous results from [4], we adopted the *ENet* model. *ENet* is a neural network architecture optimized for high-precision and rapid inference semantic segmentation introduced in 2016 and later adapted for biomedical imaging applications (e.g. [4,17]). It is based i) on building blocks of residual networks, with each block consisting of 3 convolutional layers, and ii) on several types of convolutions to build an encoder/decoder style image segmentation network. The interested reader may refer to [13] for an in-depth description.

Training: We implemented *ENet* in python language, leveraging Keras and Tensorflow APIs and we run it on a high performance computing system equipped with GPU. The dataset used in this task consisted of 60 clinical cases on which we performed a stratified five-fold cross-validation. As such, patients were divided into 5 equal subsets, and the holdout method was repeated 5 times. We chose a learning rate of .0001 with the Adam optimizer, a batch size of 8 slices, and a maximum of 100 epochs. We leveraged the Tversky loss function [15] with parameters $\alpha = 0.3$ and $\beta = 0.7$ and the training was stopped once the loss did not decrease for 10 consecutive epochs. In order to avoid over-fitting and increase the training dataset, we applied data augmentation techniques such as image rotation, translation, and applying shearing, horizontal flip, and zoom. Finally, image standardization and normalization were also applied to obtain faster convergence and avoid numerical instability.

2.3 Anatomy-Based Segmentation (Step 2)

As second step of our simplified approach we use an improved version of the segmentation algorithm introduced in [10]. In the following we will summarize its main aspects while readers interested in the full development may refer to the aforementioned dedicated publication. The algorithm seeks to optimize shape and pose of three independent surfaces (*Epi*, *LV*, *RV*) so that the data volume is partitioned into four volumes corresponding to the background (outside *Epi*), the inside of the left and right ventricles (i.e. inside *LV* and inside *RV*) and the myocardium (i.e. the volume inside *Epi* but outside both ventricles). The optimal gray level within these volumes is also adaptively computed. Pose and shape parameters are evolved until the mismatch between the average gray level of the segmented volumes and those of the data being segmented are minimal. In practice, while optimizing such surfaces the algorithm seeks to minimize the following energy functional:

$$E_{\text{coupled}} = E_I + E_B + E_O \tag{1}$$

The first is a Chan-Vese like data fidelity term [2,3] for the interior of the heart volume and takes the form:

$$E_I = w_{RV} \int_{RV} (I - \mu_{RV})^2 \, d\mathbf{x} + w_{LV} \int_{LV} (I - \mu_{LV})^2 \, d\mathbf{x} + w_{Myo} \int_{Myo} (I - \mu_{Myo})^2 \, d\mathbf{x} \tag{2}$$

where I represent the data being segmented, and μ_{RV}, μ_{LV}, μ_{Myo} are average gray levels within the RV, LV, ad Myo volumes respectively. The second term models the background using a standard two level c-means clustering:

$$E_B = w_{BG} \int_{BG} \min \left((I - c_{lo})^2, (I - c_{hi})^2 \right) d\mathbf{x} \tag{3}$$

This approach accounts for bright features (e.g. ribs) that stand out over the mostly dark background and whose presence would otherwise produce an incorrect average value, affecting in turn the quality of the segmentation.

The term E_O is a penalty term designed to drastically increase whenever two surfaces overlap:

$$E_O = \beta_{LR} \int_{LV \cap RV} d\mathbf{x} + \beta_{LM} \int_{LV \cap Myo} d\mathbf{x} + \beta_{RM} \int_{RV \cap Myo} d\mathbf{x} \tag{4}$$

Finally, the combined energy (Eq. 1) is minimized imposing that a hierarchical relation exists between average statistics within each data sub-domain, namely:

$$c_{lo} <= \mu_{Myo} <= \mu_{RV} <= \mu_{LV} <= c_{hi} \tag{5}$$

which embodies the characteristic appearance of the corresponding anatomical structures within CTA images.

Shape Priors. Shape priors were built independently for each anatomical structure leveraging the PCA. To do so we employed a set of binary masks manually segmented by our expert clinicians from a set of 30 clinical cases, chosen as training set. We emphasize that the creation of shape priors is a stand-alone operation that is required to be performed only once. Furthermore, data set used for this task is independent from the one we used to train the CNN (Sect. 2.2). For each training case we converted the corresponding binary mask (i e. the stack of manually segmented slices), in a 3D signed distance function. The latter was then vectorized in lexicographical order and assembled as a column of the data matrix input to our PCA analysis. As output, the PCA returns a set of vectors comprising the mean and the principal components (or eigenvectors) of the matrix of residuals. These were re-assembled, by reversing the previous vectorization operation, back into 3D form. What we obtain is a set of 3D distance functions that constitute a base through which a wide variety of heart shapes can be represented. The task of our optimization/segmentation is to determine optimal weights for such a base and optimal values for the pose parameters.

Pose Parameters. The current implementation of the algorithm offers two pose modalities 1) the classic rigid-body approach, which comprises 3D rotation, translation and scale, and a "blended" approach. The latter, which we used in this study, requires the user to select a reference slice for the heart base and three points corresponding to the apexes (x, y and slice #) of *Epi*, *RV*, and *LV*. The pose optimization (for each of the three surfaces) consists of determining the necessary x and y translation as well as the $2D$ rotation at both the base and vertex slices. Rotation and translations at intermediate slices are then obtained by linear interpolation. Besides the obvious advantage of reducing the number of degrees of freedom to optimize, the main reason to prefer this modality is that it is capable of capturing the twist experienced by the cardiac muscle during its contraction. Capturing this aspect, which could not be reproduced by the rigid-body approach did indeed led to improved results when segmenting CTA data directly [10], and motivated our choice in this study as well.

2.4   Post-Processing Using Active Surfaces (step 3)

In the post-processing step, we use sign distance implicit representations ψ_{Epi}, ψ_{LV}, and ψ_{RV} for the *Epi*, *LV*, and *RV*, outputs from step 2 (Sect. 2.3), as a fixed reference geometry from which three independent active surfaces are evolved to fit the CNN labels. Leveraging active surfaces provides the necessary flexibility to capture subtle features observed by the CNN. However, without any constraint, the AS would just fit the labels exactly. Therefore we added to the cost function a penalty term designed to increase as the active surfaces depart from the reference geometry by using the same signed distance representations ψ_{Epi}, ψ_{LV}, and ψ_{RV} as distance weighted overlap priors. In this way, not only can we capture a level of detail comparable to that offered by the CNN, but the converged geometry respects anatomy.

$$E_{\text{surfaces}} = E_{\text{coupled}} + \omega_{\text{prior}} \underbrace{\left(\int_{RV} \psi_{RV}\, d\mathbf{x} + \int_{LV} \psi_{LV}\, d\mathbf{x} + \int_{Epi} \psi_{Epi}\, d\mathbf{x} \right)}_{\text{distance-weighted overlap to reference priors}}$$

3   Results

We tested the combined strategy described in Sects. 2.2–2.4 on 25 clinical cases. Concerning the algorithm [10] used in step 2, after providing the minimal input

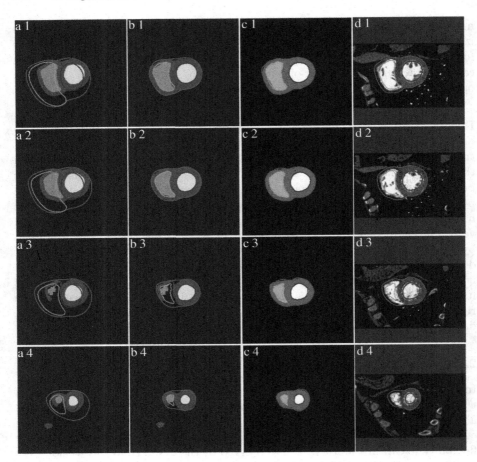

Fig. 2. Example of segmentation result for a selected case. Column *a* shows the output of step 1, the semantic segmentation from CNN (in shades of gray), while Red, blue and yellow lines represent the intersection of the shape of priors *Epi*, *LV*, and *RV* with the selected data slices before step 2 is started. Column *b* shows CNN labels, input to step 2, with superimposed the converged output of step 2. Column *c* shows segmentation results from step 2 as background (input to step 3), with superimposed the converged contours after post-processing (i.e. at the end of step 3). Finally, column *d* shows segmentation results superimposed to CTA images. (Color figure online)

required to start the segmentation process we let the optimization evolve automatically, without taking advantage of any of the several manual fine-tuning tools available. This operation alone was sufficient to eliminate all rogue pixel clusters. The average DICE score at the end of step 2 fell by almost 3 points but the Hausdorff distance errors were significantly reduced. The loss in DICE was fully recovered in the subsequent post-processing, even flipping into a slight average improvement overall. However, the quality of the results was greatly

Table 1. Segmentation performance in terms of DICE values. Columns labeled "CNN" show DICE scores obtained by employing deep learning alone while columns indicated as "Impr." show the change/improvement (with respect to the result from CNN) achieved by the proposed algorithm.

ID	Epi. CNN	Epi. Impr.	LV CNN	LV Impr.	RV CNN	RV Impr.
1	87.31	−0.95	94.94	0.00	96.32	−0.23
3	87.88	−0.09	95.25	0.01	95.66	−0.18
5	87.81	2.06	95.74	1.61	95.84	0.41
8	87.81	0.55	95.74	0.01	95.84	−0.01
9	87.27	−1.29	96.84	0.00	95.67	−1.05
10	88.82	−0.55	92.20	−0.01	94.34	−1.35
13	89.16	−0.38	96.37	−0.01	95.36	−0.11
14	83.44	0.41	96.09	0.00	94.88	−0.12
17	89.31	0.09	96.87	0.00	96.17	−0.29
19	86.19	−0.52	97.01	0.00	95.71	−0.54
24	87.48	0.79	92.46	0.00	90.56	−0.14
27	91.14	−0.07	96.94	0.00	96.50	−0.16
28	80.96	−1.14	92.26	0.00	92.55	−1.17
31	88.16	0.40	81.86	0.05	92.03	0.55
32	91.03	−2.15	96.88	0.00	96.14	−1.26
33	88.01	0.60	91.26	0.05	91.60	1.49
35	86.99	0.57	94.93	0.00	95.34	0.03
38	87.23	0.75	82.43	0.03	90.90	0.86
43	86.37	0.49	96.52	0.01	92.27	0.44
45	90.26	−0.21	96.87	0.00	95.32	−0.60
46	88.66	0.51	95.34	−0.01	93.82	0.34
47	84.18	0.80	96.49	0.00	91.31	0.61
57	87.39	0.39	96.70	0.01	92.98	0.28
59	87.95	0.07	91.93	0.00	93.70	−0.07
60	90.15	0.65	96.42	0.00	96.60	−0.46

improved in terms of the Hausdorff measure. Table 1 shows the DICE scores of the CNN semantic segmentation, while columns marked as "Impr." show the improvement over the CNN score achieved at the end of our workflow. As it can be observed, changes are marginal, mainly due to the fact that rogue pixel cluster, while obviously topologically wrong, do not contribute much to the DICE score. The achieved improvement is much more evident in terms of Hausdorff distance from the ground truth shown in Table 2. Finally, Fig. 2 shows intermediate and final results of the combined algorithm for a selected case in which the

Table 2. Segmentation performance of the proposed algorithm as compared to CNN. Values in the table are in terms of Hausdorff distance from the gold standard.

ID	CNN	Proposed method	ID	CNN	Proposed method	ID	CNN	Proposed method
1	15.1	17.0	19	83.4	7.4	38	13.8	13.8
3	49.7	5.8	24	47.5	6.7	43	25.7	7.0
5	5.9	5.3	27	36.4	6.0	45	7.6	5.9
8	80.8	4.5	28	9.3	9.3	46	28.2	11.0
9	68.3	7.0	31	33.4	12.3	47	37.0	10.6
10	14.5	12.6	32	40.0	9.8	57	8.8	7.4
13	7.3	7.2	33	130.0	13.8	59	22.1	7.0
14	44.0	7.5	35	42.7	13.0	60	33.9	5.2
17	61.9	7.0						

problem of rogue pixel clusters is particularly severe. In this case, CNN labels (Fig. 2, col. a) do provide pixel-wise detail that the algorithm [10] would not be able to capture alone. However, part of the labels is incorrect, as clearly seen in figures a3 and a4. While using CNN alone this error would be unrecoverable, the prior-based geometric algorithm (step 2) is able to correct the issue (Fig. 2, col. b). Finally, during post-processing (step 3), the augmented resolution from the CNN is fully exploited.

4   Conclusion

In the context of cardiac CTA segmentation, we investigated whether leveraging greyscale tissue information, in form of a highly detailed labeled data volume obtained from CNN processing in conjunction with our shape-based algorithm [10] may help obtaining improved segmentation performance when used in simple feed-forward combination. The algorithm in [10] consists of a prior-based shape optimization which, while sacrificing some of the pixel-wise detail offered by the CNN, fully enforces the anatomical correctness of the result. Notably, when CNN and [10] are applied to gray-scale CTA data independently, they both achieve very good performance (in terms of DICE score), with CNN being slightly better. Yet, the CNN result often shows mislabeled clusters of pixels that while not sufficient to impact the DICE score, are clearly topologically incorrect upon visual inspection, and which yield large errors when distance based metrics (such as Hausdorff) are utilized as an alternative metric. Therefore, the rationale to include label information is improve the segmentation of each anatomical part on the one hand, and remove non-anatomical features on the other. To explore this venue, we adopted a simplified approach in which we produce the labeled volume first, and then we segment the result using our prior-based algorithm followed by a last post-processing refinement based on active surfaces. We have shown that DICE score of the final segmented products is comparable to those obtained using CNN alone. However, the Hausdorff distance is drastically improved, demonstrating that the new result is much closer to the ground truth. Not only has tissue labeling improved our segmentation performance with respect to segmenting CTA directly, but the result from using CNN labels within our combined strategy has improved the result even beyond the original CNN performance. Most importantly, the segmented result is now guaranteed to be topologically correct and every "rogue pixel cluster" has been removed. These results clearly prove the potential value of a learning-geometric hybrid approach. As such, in future work we will explore a more integrated approach to combine semantic and geometric segmentation.

References

1. Boellaard, R., O'Doherty, M.J., Weber, W.A., et al.: FDG PET and PET/CT: EANM procedure guidelines for tumour PET imaging: version 1.0. Eur. J. Nucl. Med. Mol. Imaging **37**, 181–200 (2010). https://doi.org/10.1007/s00259-009-1297-4
2. Chan, T., Vese, L.: An active contour model without edges. In: Nielsen, M., Johansen, P., Olsen, O.F., Weickert, J. (eds.) Scale-Space 1999. LNCS, vol. 1682, pp. 141–151. Springer, Heidelberg (1999). https://doi.org/10.1007/3-540-48236-9_13
3. Chan, T., Vese, L.: A level set algorithm for minimizing the Mumford-Shah functional in image processing. In: IEEE Workshop on Variational and Level Set Methods in Computer Vision, pp. 161–168 (2001)
4. Comelli, A., et al.: Deep learning approach for the segmentation of aneurysmal ascending aorta. Biomed. Eng. Lett. **11**(1), 15–24 (2020). https://doi.org/10.1007/s13534-020-00179-0
5. Comelli, A., et al.: Development of a new fully three-dimensional methodology for tumours delineation in functional images. Comput. Biol. Med. **12** (2020). Article no. 103701, https://doi.org/10.1016/j.compbiomed.2020.10370
6. Comelli, A., et al.: K-nearest neighbor driving active contours to delineate biological tumor volumes. Eng. Appl. Artif. Intell. **81**, 133–144 (2019). https://doi.org/10.1016/j.engappai.2019.02.005
7. Comelli, A., et al.: Active contour algorithm with discriminant analysis for delineating tumors in positron emission tomography. Artif. Intell. Med. **94**, 67–78 (2019). https://doi.org/10.1016/j.artmed.2019.01.002
8. Comelli, A., et al.: A smart and operator independent system to delineate tumours in positron emission tomography scans. Comput. Biol. Med. **102**, 1–15 (2018). https://doi.org/10.1016/j.compbiomed.2018.09.002
9. Dahiya, N., Fan, Y., Bignardi, S., Sandhu, R., Yezzi, A.: Dependently coupled principal component analysis for bivariate inversion problems. In: Proceedings of the 25th International Conference on Pattern Recognition (ICPR), pp. 10592–10599 (2021). https://doi.org/10.1109/ICPR48806.2021.9413305
10. Dahiya, N., Yezzi, A., Piccinelli, M., Garcia, E.: Integrated 3D anatomical model for automatic myocardial segmentation in cardiac CT imagery. Comput. Methods Biomech. Biomed. Eng. Imaging Vis. **7**(5–6), 690–706 (2019)
11. D'Antoni, F., et al.: Artificial intelligence and computer vision in low back pain: a systematic review. Int. J. Environ. Res. Public Health **18** (2021). Art. no. 10909, https://doi.org/10.3390/ijerph182010909

12. Fan, Y., Dahiya, N., Bignardi, S., Sandhu, R., Yezzi, A.: Directionally paired principal component analysis for bivariate estimation problems. In: Proceedings of the 25th International Conference on Pattern Recognition (ICPR), pp. 10180–10187 (2021). https://doi.org/10.1109/ICPR48806.2021.9412245
13. Paszke, A., Chaurasia, A., Kim, S., Culurciello, E.: ENet: a deep neural network architecture for real-time semantic segmentation. ArXiv. 1606.02147 (2016)
14. Piccinelli, M., et al.: Diagnostic performance of the quantification of myocardium at risk from MPI SPECT/CTA 2G fusion for detecting obstructive coronary disease: a multicenter trial. J. Nucl. Cardiol. **25**(4), 1376–1386 (2017). https://doi.org/10.1007/s12350-017-0819-x
15. Salehi, S.S.M., Erdogmus, D., Gholipour, A.: Tversky loss function for image segmentation using 3D fully convolutional deep networks. In: Wang, Q., Shi, Y., Suk, H.-I., Suzuki, K. (eds.) MLMI 2017. LNCS, vol. 10541, pp. 379–387. Springer, Cham (2017). https://doi.org/10.1007/978-3-319-67389-9_44
16. Soret, M., Bacharach, S.L., Buvat, I.I.: Partial-volume effect in PET tumor imaging. J. Nucl. Med. **48**, 932–945 (2007). https://doi.org/10.2967/jnumed.106.035774
17. Stefano, A., Comelli, A.: Customized efficient neural network for COVID-19 infected region identification in CT images. J. Imaging **7**, 131 (2021). https://doi.org/10.3390/jimaging7080131
18. Verduna, F.R., et al.: Image quality in CT: from physical measurements to model observers. Phys. Med. **31**, 823–843 (2015)

A Predictive System to Classify Preoperative Grading of Rectal Cancer Using Radiomics Features

Ilaria Canfora[1], Giuseppe Cutaia[2,3] ⓘ, Marco Marcianò[4], Mauro Calamia[2],
Roberta Faraone[2], Roberto Cannella[2,3] ⓘ, Viviana Benfante[3,5] ⓘ,
Albert Comelli[5](✉) ⓘ, Giovanni Guercio[4], Lo Re Giuseppe[2],
and Giuseppe Salvaggio[2] ⓘ

[1] Oncological and Stomatological Sciences, University of Palermo, Via del Vespro 129, 90127 Palermo, Italy
[2] Section of Radiology - Department of Biomedicine, Neuroscience and Advanced Diagnostics (Bi.N.D.), University Hospital "Paolo Giaccone", Via del Vespro 129, 90127 Palermo, Italy
[3] Department of Health Promotion, Mother and Child Care, Internal Medicine and Medical Specialties, Molecular and Clinical Medicine, University of Palermo, 90127 Palermo, Italy
[4] Department of Surgical, Oncological and Stomatological Sciences, University of Palermo, Palermo, Via del Vespro 129, 90127 Palermo, Italy
[5] Ri.MED Foundation, Via Bandiera 11, 90133 Palermo, Italy
acomelli@fondazionerimed.com

Abstract. Although preoperative biopsy of rectal cancer (RC) is an essential step for confirmation of diagnosis, it currently fails to provide prognostic information to the clinician beyond a rough estimation of tumour grade. In this study we used a risk classification to stratified patient in low-risk and high-risk patients in relation to the disease free survival and the overall survival using histopathological post-operative features. The purpose of this study was to evaluate if low-risk and high-risk RC can be distinguished using a CT-based radiomics model. We retrospectively reviewed the preoperative abdominal contrast-enhanced CT of 40 patients with RC. CT portal-venous phase was used for manual RC segmentation by two radiologists. Radiomics parameters were extracted by using PyRadiomics (3.0) software, which automatically obtained a total of 120 radiomics features. An operator-independent statistical hybrid method was adopted for the selection and reduction of features, while discriminant analysis was used to construct the predictive model. Postoperative histopathological report was used as reference standard. Receiver operating characteristics (ROC) and areas under the ROC curve (AUROC) were calculated to evaluate the diagnostic performance of the most dis-criminating selected parameters. Sensitivity, specificity, and accuracy were calculated. In our study cohort, the original_shape_Maximum3DDiameter and origi-nal_shape_MajorAxisLength demonstrated a good performance in the differentiation between preoperative degree of RC, with an AUROC of 0.680%, sensitivity of 74.02%, specificity of 73.45%, positive predictive value of 81.47%, and accuracy of 73.71%. In conclusion, this preliminary analysis showed statistically significant differences in radiomics features between low-risk and high-risk RC.

P. L. Mazzeo et al. (Eds.): ICIAP 2022 Workshops, LNCS 13373, pp. 431–440, 2022.
https://doi.org/10.1007/978-3-031-13321-3_38

Keywords: Computed tomography · Rectal cancer · Texture analysis · Radiomics

1 Introduction

Rectal cancer (RC) is the third most common cancer in men and the second in women, as well as the fourth leading cause of death globally [1]. Over the past years there has been an improvement in RC management associated with a reduction of mortality and higher survival rates, mainly related to earlier diagnosis and more effective treatment [2]. Colorectal cancer's treatment may consist of one or a combination of the following: chemotherapy, biological or targeted therapy, radiation therapy or surgery. In locally advanced rectal cancer therapeutic strategy is strictly related to the stage and to the biological behavior of the neoplasia. Treatment is generally based on neoadjuvant radio-chemotherapy followed by anterior rectal recision or total mesorectal excision [3].

Surgical complications rates are high, with a mortality rate between 2% and 8%, up to 35% in elderly (>85 years old patients) [4].

It is, therefore, mandatory to select patients in subgroups with early stage disease, who can be submitted to surgical intervention, and "frail" patients in whom a high operative risk lays for a non-operative management, including chemo-radiotherapy, obtaining the same results in both populations in terms of survival and mortality. In this scenario, diagnostic imaging plays a crucial role for pre-treatment disease staging. Although high-resolution magnetic resonance imaging (MRI) is the standard staging modality for RC [5], contrast-enhanced computed tomography (CT) is frequently used for local and distant metastasis staging because it is more widely available [6], has faster acquisition time and is more practical than MRI [7]. Both CT and MRI have limited resolution in clinical applications so that researcher tried to find novel strategies to further increase the value of diagnostic imaging. Particularly, the main challenges of diagnostic imaging in preoperative RC staging are related to the differentiation of early RC (cT1–T2) from local advanced RC (cT3) [1]. Current Italian Association of Medical Oncology (AIOM) guidelines provide for compulsory pre-treatment histologic cancer diagnosis, to obtain a differential diagnosis with ulcers, lymphomas, pseudo polyposis and other lesions which do not require a surgical intervention. Information required in all biopsies histopathological reports: i) Histological type and ii) Tumor grading;

However, the limits of the method must be taken into account, as the lesion may not be representative of the behaviour of the lesion in its entirety, which may present a certain heterogeneity both from the point of view of the histotypes and the degree of differentiation. The most important independent prognostic factor in the CRC is the stage of the tumour. However, the fact that patients at the same pathological stage in the postoperative period present differences in terms of local recurrence and invasion suggests that pathological staging (TNM) is insufficient in these patients [8]. The situation requires the investigation of biological, molecular and morphological factors that may be related to the aggressive behaviour of the tumour in the cancer tissue. In the present study we used a classification method to stratified patient with RC in low-risk and high-risk patients. This classification takes into account some features obtained from post-operative histopathological result: cellular grading (High grade Who 2019), budding score ≥ 10, perineural invasion, perivascular invasion, tumor deposit and mucinous neoplasms. These features cannot be achieved from conventional diagnostic methods (CT or MRI) in pre-operative routine examination. In this setting, a post processing quantitative technique known as radiomics appears particularly promising, with encouraging evidence collected in recent years [9–12]. Specifically, radiomics is an emerging research area based on a extraction process of quantitative features from biomedical images in order to convert these images into high-dimensional and mineable data. These *radiomics features* can be extracted from MRI [13], CT [14], and Positron Emission Tomography (PET) [15] scans. The most important and commonly used features can be grouped into three large classes: i) Shape Features that describe geometric characteristics of the region of interest (ROI), ii) 1st Order Statistical Features, describing grey levels distribution within the ROI, iii) Texture Features, used to obtain information about grey levels patterns within the ROI.

These features may reveal predictive, or prognostic associations between biomedical images and medical outcomes since they capture cancer properties capable to support personalized support models for clinical decision, such as therapy response assessment or diagnosis [16, 17].

Some recent studies have supported the role of radiomics in RC staging with the goal of overcoming the limitations of conventional imaging and providing additional imaging biomarkers, allowing for the correct management of RC patients [18, 19].

Therefore, the aim of this study is to explore the role of radiomics features extracted from contrast-enhanced CT images to predict preoperative differentiation degree of rectal cancer.

2   Materials and Methods

The institutional review board approved this retrospective single-institution study. The requirement for written informed consent was waived.

2.1 Population

From January 2016 to August 2020, 59 consecutive patients were referred to our surgery department to perform intestinal resection for rectal adenocarcinoma.

The following exclusion criteria were considered for this study: (a) absence of CT examination before surgical treatment ($n = 12$); (b) pathological report of low-grade dysplasia, without diagnostic of invasive cancer ($n = 3$); (c) patient undergoing radiotherapy and/or surgical therapy for pathologies adjacent to the rectum (i.e., prostate or urinary bladder cancers) ($n = 4$).

2.2 CT Technique

All patients included in the study were studies with a standard preoperative CT protocol at the Radiology department of our Hospital.

Patients underwent an abdominal contrast-enhanced CT (CECT) scan on a 16-slice CT scanner (General Electric BrightSpeed, Milwaukee, WI, USA). Scanning parameters used were tube current with automatic mA modulation, peak tube voltage of 120 kV, rotation time 0.6 s, detector collimation 16 × 0.625 mm, field of view of 350 mm × 350 mm, matrix, 512 × 512.

CECT was performed by injecting about 1.5 mL/kg of iodinated contrast material (Xenetix, Guerbet, Roissy, France) at a flow of 3 mL/sec, followed by infusion of 20 mL of saline solution with a pump injector (Ulrich CT Plus 150, Ulrich Medical, Ulm, Germany).

Image acquisition was done using a baseline pre-contrast scan, an arterial and a portal-venous phase of the abdomen and pelvis. Arterial phase was obtained after 35–40 s of delay after intravenous injection of contrast material, and portal venous phase was performed after 70–80 s of delay.

All CTs were performed with the patient in supine position, during a single inspiratory breath-hold whenever possible.

2.3 Tumor Segmentation

Manual RC segmentation were performed by two radiologists with 15 and 5 years of experience in abdominal CT. The portal-venous phase CT images was used for manual segmentation. Each CT portal-venous exam was imported into an open-source DICOM viewer (Horos, LGPL license at Horosproject.org) in order to obtain RC volume by manual segmentation.

Lesion boundaries were manually traced with a contouring tool (pencil) slice by slice.

Lesion segmentation was performed by drawing ellipse-shaped regions of interest (ROI) including the whole RC visible on axial images. After that, the "compute volume"

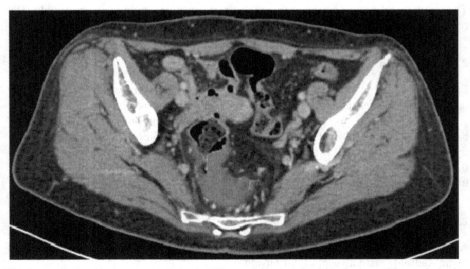

Fig. 1. Example of lesion segmentation on CT portal-venous phase in a patient with rectal cancer.

tool was used to obtain volume rendering of the entire tumor with the volume measurement. The entire process required 10–15 min per case. Example of lesion segmentation is provided in the Fig. 1.

2.4 Features Extraction

The radiomics parameters were extracted by using PyRadiomics (3.0) software [20], which automatically obtained a total of 120 radiomics features from each ROI, including first order texture features (which provide information related to the distribution of the gray level within the ROI, without considering the spatial relationships between the voxels), second order (which take into account the spatial relationships between the voxels), and third order features (evaluating the spatial relationship between three or more voxels). The texture parameters were obtained from the histogram analysis of the gray levels (e.g. mean, variance, asymmetry, kurtosis, and percentiles), the co-occurrence matrix was calculated in five measurements (e.g. contrast, correlation, sum of squares, inverse difference moment [IDM], sum average, sum variance, sum entropy, difference variance, difference entropy), while the run-length matrix was calculated in four directions (e.g run length nonuniformity [RLN], gray-level nonuniformity normalized [GLNN], long run emphasis [LRE], short run emphasis [SRE]). The detailed description of the radiomics parameters is available in the online manual of PyRadiomics [21].

2.5 Reference Standard

The reference standard was assessed by study coordinator, who had access to electronic patient medical records, including histopathological reports, but was not involved in lesions segmentations or features extraction.

The histopathological reports were obtained from the postoperative surgical specimens and they were used as a reference standard.

2.6 Computational and Statistical Analyses

Computational analysis of radiomics features was conducted by a senior scientist in biomedical imaging (with 9 years of experience on image and data processing and analysis). The analyzed lesions were grouped into preoperative degree differentiation of RC according to the reference standard.

An operator-independent statistical hybrid method was adopted for the selection and reduction of features, while discriminant analysis was used to construct the predictive model. To identify the most discriminant features and reduce redundancy of radiomics features with high correlation, a new descriptive-inferential mixed sequential approach was used [22]. Particularly, for each feature, the point-biserial correlation coefficient between features and dichotomous variable was calculated assuming a value of 1 or 0 for the reference standard. Subsequently, the features were sorted in descending order based on the absolute value of the point-biserial correlation coefficient. Then, a cycle began to add one column at a time performing a logistic regression analysis. Next, the p-value of the current iteration was compared to the p-value of the previous iteration.

The loop stopped when the p-value of the current iteration did not decrease from the previous iteration. In this way, the most discriminating features were identified.

The discriminant analysis was used to create a predictive model in this dataset such as in [23]. We trained the discriminant analysis with the most discriminant features to evaluated differences between preoperative degree of RC. The training activity had to be performed only one time and, once completed, the discriminant analysis was able to classify the newly encountered radiomics texture. To generate the formative input for the classifier, the results of the expert radiologist's assessment were used as gold standard. In our study, the k-fold strategy was used to split data into training and validation sets. In this way, the studies were divided into k-folds such as in [24]. One of the folds was used as the validation set and the remaining folds were combined in the training set. This process was repeated k-times using each fold as the validation set and the other remaining sets as the training set. In our study, $k = 5$ was empirically determined by trial-and-error strategy (k range: 5–15, step size of 5). To ensure disjointed validation sets, the leave-one-out approach was not adopted. In this way, more robust results can be obtained in implementing the classification model [25]. Receiver operating characteristics (ROC) with 95% confidence intervals (95% CI) and areas under the ROC curve (AUROC) were calculated to evaluate the diagnostic performance of the most discriminating selected parameters on CT portal-venous phase. Sensitivity, specificity, and accuracy were calculated.

The system used to provide the proposed computational statistical analysis was implemented in the Matlab R2019a simulation environment (MathWorks, Natick, MA, USA), running on an Intel Core i7 3.5 GHz, 16 GB iMac computer 1600 DDR3 MHz memory and OS X El Capitan.

3 Results

3.1 Population

The final study population consisted of 40 patients (18 males; 22 females; mean age 65.9 $\pm$ 0.44 years) with RC treated with surgical resection. Twenty-one patients (52.5%) had a high-grade RC, while the other 19 (47.5%) had a lower-grade RC.

Five patients (12.5%) had a rectosigmoid junction cancer, while in the other 35 (87.5%) patients (75%) the cancer was located in the rectum [10 (25%) in the low, 16 (40%) in the middle and 9 (22.5%) in the high rectum].

Characteristics of the patients, the degree of aggressiveness and the location of the tumor are reported in Table 1.

Table 1. Characteristics of the study population

Characteristics	Number (%)
Sex	18 (45.0%)
Males	22 (55.0%)
Females	

(*continued*)

Table 1. (*continued*)

Characteristics	Number (%)
Age (years)	65.9 ± 10.44
Histopathological grading High-grade Low-grade	21 (52.5%) 19 (47.5%)
Location Rectosigmoid junction Low rectum Middle rectum High rectum	5 (12.5%) 10 (25.0%) 16 (40.0%) 9 (22.5%)

3.2 Performance of Radiomics

The most discriminative radiomics features with their diagnostic performance are presented in the Table 2.

On CT portal-venous phase, the original_shape_Maximum3DDiameter and original_shape_MajorAxisLength were significantly different according to the histopathological grading. The model combining these two features demonstrated a fair performance in the differentiation between histopathological grading of RC, with an AUROC of 0.680 (95% C.I. 0.498–0.862; $p < 0.01$), sensitivity of 74.02%, specificity of 73.45%, positive predictive value of 81.47%, and accuracy of 73.71% (Fig. 2). According to the PyRadiomics documentation available on the following web site [21], the maximum 3D diameter is represented by the largest pairwise Euclidean distance existing between the vertices of the tumor surface mesh, and it is named Feret diameter; moreover Major Axis length identifies the length of the major axis of the ellipsoid in which the ROI is enclosed and the calculation of it results derived from the largest principal component. Voxels of ROI defined by centers of physical coordinates are on the base of principal component analysis and, for this reason, spacing, but not the shape mesh, is considered.

Table 2. Selected statistically significant radiomics features according to the histopathological degree of rectal cancer.

Feature	p value
Original shape maximum 3D diameter	$1.042010e{-}02$
Original shape MajorAxisLength	$2.487119e{-}03$

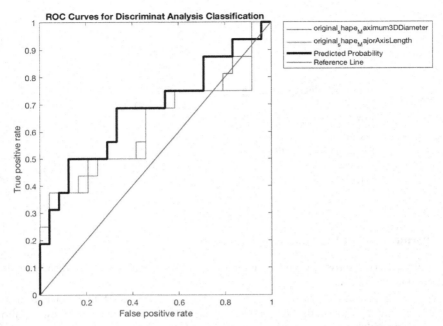

Fig. 2. Receiver operating characteristics curve of original_shape_Maximum3DDiameter and original_shape_MajorAxisLength on CT portal-venous phase.

4 Discussion

Rectal cancer is the third most common cancer in men, the second in women, and the fourth leading cause of death globally. Therefore, an accurate preoperative staging has a critical value in establishing the clinical and surgical treatment plans and predicting the prognosis. The main challenge of imaging for guiding treatment decisions, including surgery or neoadjuvant chemo-radiotherapy, in preoperative RC is the differentiation between low-grade and high-grade RC.

In this study cohort, the extraction and analysis of the quantitative information contained within the manually traced ROIs allowed to identify two independent features associated with the RC grading: the original_shape_Maximum3DDiameter and original_shape_MajorAxisLength. The combined radiomics model demonstrated a fair performance in the differentiation between histopathological grading of RC, with an AUROC of 0.680, sensitivity of 74.02%, specificity of 73.45%, positive predictive value of 81.47%, and accuracy of 73.71%, on CT portal-venous phase images. Therefore, under the assumption that imaging reflects not only the macroscopic features of tissues but also their cellular and molecular properties [26], the study allowed to evaluate tumor biological aggressiveness in accordance with the definitive postoperative histological examination and showed a good predictivity of tumor aggression.

Few studies are already exploring the predictive ability of CT-based radiomics signature for preoperative RC staging. Liang et al. proposed a 16-feature based radiomics signature to be a predictor in discriminating stage I–II from stage III–IV rectal cancer [27], which is in line with our results.

We acknowledge that the results of the current investigation are limited by several factors such as its retrospective nature and a relatively small sample size. Despite MRI is the gold standard imaging staging modality for patient with RC, CT exams is more widely available and easier to obtain in clinical setting and it is frequently required for distant metastases staging in patients with RC.

5 Conclusion

In conclusion, this study demonstrates that there is a statistically significant difference in radiomics features which can contribute to push the boundaries of conventional imaging, allowing differentiation between low- and high-grade RC.

References

1. Coppola, F., et al.: Radiomics and magnetic resonance imaging of rectal cancer: from engineering to clinical practice. Diagnostics (Basel, Switzerland) **11** (2021). https://doi.org/10.3390/DIAGNOSTICS11050756
2. Dekker, E., Tanis, P.J., Vleugels, J.L.A., Kasi, P.M., Wallace, M.B.: Colorectal cancer. Lancet **394**, 1467–1480 (2019). https://doi.org/10.1016/S0140-6736(19)32319-0
3. Sauer, R., et al.: Preoperative versus postoperative chemoradiotherapy for rectal cancer. N. Engl. J. Med. **351**, 1731–1740 (2004). https://doi.org/10.1056/NEJMoa040694
4. Paun, B.C., Cassie, S., MacLean, A.R., Dixon, E., Buie, W.D.: Postoperative complications following surgery for rectal cancer. Ann. Surg. **251**, 807–818 (2010). https://doi.org/10.1097/SLA.0b013e3181dae4ed
5. Glynne-Jones, R., et al.: Rectal cancer: ESMO clinical practice guidelines for diagnosis, treatment and follow-up. Ann. Oncol. **28**, iv22–iv40 (2017). https://doi.org/10.1093/annonc/mdx224
6. Balyasnikova, S., Brown, G.: Optimal imaging strategies for rectal cancer staging and ongoing management. Curr. Treat. Options Oncol. **17**(6), 1–11 (2016). https://doi.org/10.1007/s11864-016-0403-7
7. Hou, M., Sun, J.H.: Emerging applications of radiomics in rectal cancer: state of the art and future perspectives. World J. Gastroenterol. **27**, 3802–3814 (2021). https://doi.org/10.3748/wjg.v27.i25.3802
8. Park, K.-J., Choi, H.-J., Roh, M.-S., Kwon, H.-C., Kim, C.: Intensity of tumor budding and its prognostic implications in invasive colon carcinoma. Dis. Colon Rectum. **48**, 1597–1602 (2005). https://doi.org/10.1007/s10350-005-0060-6
9. Vernuccio, F., Cannella, R., Comelli, A., Salvaggio, G., Lagalla, R., Midiri, M.: Radiomics and artificial intelligence: new frontiers in medicine. Recent. Prog. Med. **111**(3), 130–135 (2020). Italian. https://doi.org/10.1701/3315.32853
10. Giambelluca, D., et al.: PI-RADS 3 lesions: role of prostate MRI texture analysis in the identification of prostate cancer. Curr. Probl. Diagn. Radiol. **50** (2019). https://doi.org/10.1067/J.CPRADIOL.2019.10.009
11. Cannella, R., la Grutta, L., Midiri, M., Bartolotta, T.V.: New advances in radiomics of gastrointestinal stromal tumors. World J. Gastroenterol. **26**, 4729–4738 (2020). https://doi.org/10.3748/WJG.V26.I32.4729

12. Caruana, G., et al.: Texture analysis in susceptibility-weighted imaging may be useful to differentiate acute from chronic multiple sclerosis lesions. Eur. Radiol. **30**(11), 6348–6356 (2020). https://doi.org/10.1007/s00330-020-06995-3
13. Cutaia, G., et al.: Radiomics and prostate MRI: current role and future applications. J. Imaging. **7**, 34 (2021). https://doi.org/10.3390/jimaging7020034
14. Stefano, A., et al.: Performance of radiomics features in the quantification of idiopathic pulmonary fibrosis from HRCT. Diagnostics. **10**, 306 (2020). https://doi.org/10.3390/diagnostics10050306
15. Stefano, A., et al.: Robustness of pet radiomics features: Impact of co-registration with MRI. Appl. Sci. **11**, 10170 (2021). https://doi.org/10.3390/app112110170
16. Banna, G.L., et al.: Predictive and prognostic value of early disease progression by PET evaluation in advanced non-small cell lung cancer. Oncology **92**, 39–47 (2016). https://doi.org/10.1159/000448005
17. Russo, G., et al.: Feasibility on the use of radiomics features of 11[C]-MET PET/CT in central nervous system tumours: preliminary results on potential grading discrimination using a machine learning model. Curr. Oncol. **28**, 5318–5331 (2021). https://doi.org/10.3390/curroncol28060444
18. Li, M., et al.: A clinical-radiomics nomogram for the preoperative prediction of lymph node metastasis in colorectal cancer. J. Transl. Med. **18**, 1 (2020). https://doi.org/10.1186/s12967-020-02215-0
19. Sun, Y., et al.: Radiomic features of pretreatment MRI could identify T stage in patients with rectal cancer: Preliminary findings. J. Magn. Reson. Imaging **48**, 615–621 (2018). https://doi.org/10.1002/jmri.25969
20. Van Griethuysen, J.J.M., et al.: Computational radiomics system to decode the radiographic phenotype. Cancer Res. **77**, e104–e107 (2017). https://doi.org/10.1158/0008-5472.CAN-17-0339
21. Pyradiomics, https://pyradiomics.readthedocs.io/en/latest/features.html. Accessed 11 Apr 2022
22. Barone, S., et al.: Hybrid descriptive-inferential method for key feature selection in prostate cancer radiomics. Appl. Stoch. Model. Bus. Ind. **37**, 961–972 (2021). https://doi.org/10.1002/asmb.2642
23. Alongi, P., et al.: Radiomics analysis of 18F-Choline PET/CT in the prediction of disease outcome in high-risk prostate cancer: an explorative study on machine learning feature classification in 94 patients. Eur. Radiol. **31**(7), 4595–4605 (2021). https://doi.org/10.1007/s00330-020-07617-8
24. Salvaggio, G., et al.: Deep learning networks for automatic retroperitoneal sarcoma segmentation in computerized tomography. Appl. Sci. **12**, 1665 (2022). https://doi.org/10.3390/app12031665
25. Stefano, A., Comelli, A.: Customized efficient neural network for covid-19 infected region identification in CT images. J. Imaging **7**, 131 (2021). https://doi.org/10.3390/jimaging7080131
26. De Cecco, C.N., et al.: Texture analysis as imaging biomarker of tumoral response to neoadjuvant chemoradiotherapy in rectal cancer patients studied with 3-T magnetic resonance. Invest. Radiol. **50**, 239–245 (2015). https://doi.org/10.1097/RLI.0000000000000116
27. Liang, C., et al.: The development and validation of a CT-based radiomics signature for the preoperative discrimination of stage I-II and stage III-IV colorectal cancer. Oncotarget **7**, 31401–31412 (2016). https://doi.org/10.18632/ONCOTARGET.8919

Unsupervised Brain Segmentation System Using K-Means and Neural Network

Riccardo Laudicella[1,2], Luca Agnello[3], and Albert Comelli[1](✉) ⓘ

[1] Ri.MED Foundation, Via Bandiera 11, 90133 Palermo, Italy
acomelli@fondazionerimed.com
[2] Nuclear Medicine Unit, University of Messina, Messina, Italy
[3] Palermo, Italy

Abstract. Voxel-based morphometry is an analysis technique used to quantify matter volume in the human brain from magnetic resonance imaging studies. Atrophies and morphologic changes can be signs of neuronal depletion that can lead to various degenerative diseases. Two of the most worldwide used tools for brain volume assessment and segmentation in white matter, grey matter, and cerebrospinal fluid are the Functional Magnetic Resonance Imaging of the Brain (FMRIB) Software Library (FSL) and Statistical Parameter Mapping (SPM). However, the main issue of these tools is related to the choice of the best parameter setting.

In this paper, a novel and unsupervised segmentation system, without any user parameter setting, that uses both the k-means clustering algorithm and artificial neural network is proposed. Performance of this system was evaluated on the Internet Brain Segmentation Repository (IBSR) dataset (v.2.0) and results were compared with FSL and SPM results.

The dice similarity score was calculated to compare the segmentations obtained with FSL, SPM, and the proposed system with the reference segmentations. The proposed system resulted fast and reliable, and reduced any error (the dice similarity score was greater than 83%, 86%, and 65% for white matter, grey matter, and cerebrospinal fluid, respectively) demonstrating an improvement in the discrimination among white matter, grey matter, and cerebrospinal fluid.

Keywords: Voxel-Based Morphometry · K-means · Artificial neural networks

1 Introduction

The evaluation of brain tissues in a quantitative manner is a predominant field in neuroscience [1, 2]. Since the first experimental studies, magnetic resonance imaging (MRI) has represented a valid non-invasive-modality for the study of the human brain in-vivo. Specifically, the brain can be divided into grey-matter (GM), white-matter (WM) and cerebrospinal fluid (CSF) [3]. In turn, the GM is identified in neuronal, glial and neuropil cells, namely dendrites and axons; the WM constitutes the axons that are myelinated cells acting as a connection between the cell bodies of the system central nervous system (CNS); CSF is instead a colourless liquid that permeates the CNS performing numerous trophic as well as protective functions. The efficiency of the conduction of electrical signals and brain stimuli is intrinsically linked to the structural integrity of the WM, which

P. L. Mazzeo et al. (Eds.): ICIAP 2022 Workshops, LNCS 13373, pp. 441–449, 2022.
https://doi.org/10.1007/978-3-031-13321-3_39

makes up 40–50% of the adult human brain. Macroscopically, the WM consists of a network of axons that connects the different brain regions thickly wrapped in myelin, a multi-lamellar sheath of protein matrix (30%) and lipid (70%), which envelops the axon to preserve the integrity of the neuronal signal determining its typical white colour. There are also small regions not enveloped by the myelin sheath, called "Ranvier nodes", which mediate the correct conduction of the electrical signal increasing its speed. Each myelin alteration results in one variation of the protein/lipid ratio with densitometry modification of the electrical signal, for which MRI appears to be a remarkably sensitive diagnostic technique. Namely, MRI allows a precise distinction of WM and GM, between normal and altered myelin: for a precise diagnosis, such radiological alterations must always be integrated with the careful evaluation of the lesion-morphological pattern, monitoring the temporal evolution of the lesions, always related to the clinic and characteristics of the patient. Therefore, MRI is nowadays the gold-standard technique for brain imaging, capable of evaluating neurological disorders associated with dementia, in which neuronal depletion determines atrophy usually accompanied by volumetric reduction of WM, and GM [3–5]. Atrophy can affect various brain areas: for the assessment of the temporal-mesial lobe and hippocampal atrophy, MRI images are mainly evaluated on coronal-oblique SE/TSE-T1 scans. Images should be acquired with thin sections (<5 mm), ideally obtained by reformatting a 3D T1-sagittal sequence weighted, acquired along with the entire brain with slightly higher layer thicknesses to the millimetre, with possibly isotropic resolution. Also, for this reason, the T1-weighted sequences are often referred to as "morphological", allowing for optimal differentiation of the WM from the GM, assessing the atrophy degree. Spin echo/Turbo spin-echo (SE/TSE)-T2 and Fluid attenuated inversion recovery (FLAIR)-T2 sequences are used, instead, in the evaluation of deep periventricular WM changes, detecting any areas of altered signal (hyper intensity), expression of perivascular gliosis from previous hypoxic-ischemic events, demyelination or subarachnoid perivascular spaces enlargement [6]. Further, the Gradient echo (GRE)-T2 sequences and the Susceptibility weighted imaging (SWI), on the other hand, allow localizing any micro bleeds, calcifications, metal ions ($Ca2+$, $Mn2+$, $Fe2+$).

Brain volumetric reductions are characteristic of almost all forms of primary and secondary dementia syndromes. Such reduction can be assessed through semi-automatic analysis software able to identify and quantify the different intracranial compartment tissues such as WM, GM, and CSF.

Voxel-Based Morphometry (VBM) is an analysis technique able to characterize the brain's anatomy [7]; medical image datasets are segmented and split into their constituent parts. This characterization is based on the MRI signal intensity, usually weighted in T1 or T2 sequences. VBM aims to determine if a specific voxel has a different intensity in one group instead of another, correlating morpho-volumetric variations and allowing to compare results between pathological subjects and healthy controls or longitudinal comparisons (i.e., follow-up studies).

Segmentation methods of CSF, GM and WM from MRI, based on statistics, geometrics, atlas and learning, are affected by several issues, i.e. noise, the intensity of non-uniform tissue (bias) and partial volume effect [8]. For this reason, a robust method of brain voxel classification is mandatory. Also, the radiomics feature extraction process from biomedical images depends on a reliable volume segmentation [9–13] which is, therefore, a necessary prerequisite for obtaining accurate and reproducible parameters associated with the target tissue. In the last years, many studies have investigated the accuracy of brain segmentation techniques (i.e. [14–22]); most of the used computer-aided design (CAD) tools for brain analysis are performed using the Functional Magnetic Resonance Imaging of the Brain (FMRIB) Software Library (FSL) [23] and the Statistical Parameter Mapping (SPM) [24]. Namely, FSL is composed of several tools for neuro-radiological images analysis; after a pre-processing phase where the "non-brain" tissues (i.e. bones) are removed from the MRI volume, the features from accelerated segment test (FAST) algorithm classifies the major cerebral tissues, i.e. WM, GM and CSF. It is based on the hidden Markov random field model and an associated algorithm of expectation-maximization. Differently, SPM is a MatLab plugin [25] for the segmentation of brain MRI volumes, which uses both functional and structural statistical methods of neuro-images analysis. It provides a probabilistic classification of the brain tissues increasing the precision of each tissue class. Both tools provide a satisfactory VBM analysis. However, the main issue of such techniques is related to the setup of a high number of parameters, that can lead to different and/or inaccurate segmentation results. The search for the most accurate parameters capable of obtain the quantitative results more similar to the "gold-standard" can be made through several manual attempts, representing a time-loss methodology with intra- and inter-operator result variability. Also, some of these parameters are difficult to interpret for medical operators and physicians that may need dedicated training. Therefore, potential errors caused by the operator variability have to be taken into account.

The aim of this study is to present a novel VBM analysis system capable of segment MRI 3D brain volume without user intervention and parameter setting. An Artificial Neural Network (ANN) has been trained using the voxels classified by an unsupervised k-means algorithm. Consequently, the proposed system avoids the above-mentioned issue using unsupervised clustering techniques that label voxels using the different intensity distribution of tissue signals. Next, the trained ANN is employed for segmentation purpose to discriminate among WM, GM and CSF. The obtained segmentations are compared with FSL and SPM results showing improvement.

2 Materials and Methods

A brief description of the algorithms used in the proposed system is reported in the following subsections.

2.1 K-Means Algorithm

The K-means algorithm is a clustering algorithm able to discriminate a set of objects into k groups depending on their characteristics. The goal of the algorithm is to minimize the total intra-cluster variance, and each cluster is identified by a centroid. The algorithm follows an iterative procedure: it initially creates k partitions assigning a random centroid for each partition; then, the centroid of each group is calculated, building a new partition by associating each entry point to the cluster whose centroid is closer to it. At that point, the centroids are recalculated for the new clusters until the algorithm minimize the objective function.

Briefly, the algorithm is composed of the following steps:

1. k points are placed into the space represented by the objects. These points represent the starting centroids.
2. Each object that has the closest centroid is assigned to cluster;
3. When all objects have been assigned, the positions of the k centroids are recalculated;
4. Steps 2 and 3 are repeated until the centroids no longer move. This produces a separation of the objects into k groups.

2.2 Feed-Forward Neural Network

An ANN is composed of "artificial neurons" that send activation signals to each other and can approximate a function with multiple inputs and outputs. For this reason, it can be used for a variety of tasks, like classification, descriptive modelling, clustering, function approximation, and time series prediction. In this context, a feed-forward neural network and the back-propagation learning algorithm that trains the ANN is considered. The feed-forward ANN is a graph of neurons, where each neuron computes an activation function of the inputs and sends output on its out-edges. Each input and output is weighted and shifted by a specific bias factor.

The network aims to learn a set of weights and biases that approximate an activation function. So the output of the activation function is the output of the neuron, according to the Eq. (1):

$$\text{Output} = \Sigma(w_k I_k) + \text{bias} \tag{1}$$

where w_k is the weight of the k-th in-edge, I_k is the input carried across the k-th in-edge, and bias is the bias of the neuron. The learning phase aims to find values that minimize the sum of squares error (SSE) of the training data. Given the topology of a neural network and the activation function of each neuron, the train is performed using pairs of sets of inputs and outputs (xi, yi). Xi denotes neuron input, while Yi is the desired output.

The SSE is computed as:

$$\text{SSE}(D) = \text{sum}((Yi - Zi)) \tag{2}$$

where D is the training set, and Zi is the set of outputs of the network given inputs Xi. In the back-propagation learning, weights and biases are assigned to a random continuous value between 1 and -1. Iteratively the algorithm trains the neural network, and updates weights and biases in each step, minimizing a gradient descent of the error respect weights and biases.

The learning algorithm can be divided into three phases:

1. Calculate the output of the network Zi, given the input set Xi;
2. Calculate Blame: if Yi is the desired value for Zi, and if they are different, the error is computed for each neuron. Blames are used to adjust weights and biases;

3. Adjust weights and biases, performing the gradient descent.

After the training session, the learning process is completed and the neural network can be used for classification purpose.

2.3 The Proposed System

The proposed method aims to segment a whole-brain T1-weighted MRI study automatically, classifying each voxel in CSF, GM and WM. The workflow of the proposed brain segmentation system is depicted in Fig. 1.

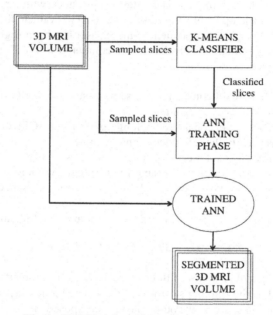

Fig. 1. The Workflow of the proposed method.

The system takes in input the MRI dataset. Each dataset is often composed of hundreds of slices (generally 50–300), in a Digital Imaging and COmmunications in Medicine (DICOM) format of 256×256 voxels. The dataset is then sampled taking a group of only 3 slices as training set: one slice is chosen near the neck zone, where the brain starts and the presence of the CSF matter is predominant with respect to GM and WM; one is chosen in the middle of the sequence, where WM and GM are little predominant with respect to CSF; the last slice is chosen in the upper section of the brain, where the WM is more present than the other two matters. At this point, these slices are the input of the k-means clustering algorithm. With k = 3 cluster, the k-means assigns each voxel to a cluster, labelling it with the cluster number (1 = CSF, 2 = GM, 3 = WM). Because of the nature of the k-means, labels are randomly assigned to the clusters: each group is then relabelled in according to the centroid value of each cluster. As a matter of fact, in the T1 sequence, the CSF has small intensity value, the WM has the highest intensity value, and the GM has a mean intensity included between the CSF and WM. The ANN training set is the combination of the input set (voxel intensity values) and the target set (voxel labels). When the training phase is completed, the trained ANN can segment and classify each voxel composing the whole brain volume.

3 Results

The public available Internet Brain Segmentation Repository (IBSR) dataset (v2.0) [26] is composed of 18 brain MRI T1-weighted acquisitions; brain volumes are skull stripped, so no-brain tissue has been removed. The dataset is provided with a reference segmentation of each brain made up by expert radiologists used to evaluate the goodness of the segmentation methodologies. Consequently, the dataset has been segmented using the proposed methodology and the results have been compared with FSL and SPM results.

Each segmented voxel can be a:

- True Positive (TP): a voxel considered the same tissue (CSF or GM or WM) both in reference and in calculated segmentation;
- False Positive (FP): a voxel considered belonging to a tissue (CSF or GM or WM) but not considered as such in the reference segmentation;
- False Negative (FN): a voxel that is excluded from a tissue (CSF or GM or WM) but considered to belong to that tissue in the reference segmentation;
- True Negative (TN): a voxel excluded both from the reference and calculated segmentation.
- The performance was evaluated using the dice similarity coefficient (DSC):

$$DSC = (2 * TP)/(2 * TP + FN + FP) \tag{3}$$

For each patient study, a series of three slices have been sampled with the k-means algorithm and used as the training set for the ANN. The hidden layer of the proposed ANN is composed of 30 neurons; the output layer is composed of 3 neurons, one for each output tissue [27]. The training of the ANN takes less than a minute, while the segmentation of the whole volume takes just a couple of seconds. Next, the segmentations have been compared with the reference segmentations, and DSCs have been calculated. The segmentation has been carried out also using FSL and SPM with defaults parameters. The obtained DSC results for all segmentation methodologies are shown in Table 1. The DSC takes into account both corrected and uncorrected labelled voxels, showing an improvement of the proposed system if compared to FSL and SPM. Also, the proposed unsupervised system results faster and without the need to set any parameter: segmentation of the whole dataset, composed of 18 × (256 * 256 * 128) voxels, has taken 504 s for FSL, 652 s for SPM, and 162 s for the proposed method.

Table 1. DSC for segmentations obtained using FSL, SPM, and the proposed system.

	CSF	GM	WM
FSL	53,3 ± 5,5	78,1 ± 2,5	87,1 ± 3,0
SPM	40,8 ± 4,3	79,8 ± 5,3	85,8 ± 2,3
Our system	65,4 ± 7,6	83,7 ± 4,1	86,2 ± 2,2

4 Conclusion

The ability to segment brain tissues accurately from MRI can substantially extend the utility of this important neuroimaging technique. Manual contouring is still a common choice in clinical practice. Unfortunately, it is very time-consuming and results tend to vary according to expertise and clinical specialization of the operator [28]. For this reason, many computer-aided segmentation systems supporting automatic or semi-automatic algorithms have been proposed so far [29]. In this study, a novel unsupervised system, that uses a k-means classifier and an artificial neural network, has been proposed. The proposed system results fast and reliable, reducing error introduced by other state-of-the-art segmentation systems [1, 23, 24]. Our system samples a small amount of data from the whole volume that is classified by using the k-means algorithm. Classified voxels are then used as the training set for the feed-forward ANN, which learns the segmentation phase. Each voxel of the whole volume is then segmented using the trained ANN, obtaining superior results if compared to FSL and SPM segmentation, as shown in Table 1. The developed system could be used as a Medical Decision Support System to help clinicians in treatment response evaluation of neurological diseases [4]. Despite the limitations pertaining to the proposed system, our results show reasonable segmentations of WM, GM and CSF based on standard MRI. The proposed study can also be used as a foundation for the development of additional, more complex segmentation procedures for tasks such as the automated labelling of brain areas. Consequently, further investigations are required with a larger number of patients in order to assess the prognostic usefulness and long-term clinical impact to correlate the obtained segmentation with clinical outcomes, progression-free survival and overall survival.

Finally, the inclusion of metabolic information from Positron Emission Tomography (PET) images will be reserved for future developments [30] also considering the unequivocal advancements reached by PET/MRI [31] and deep learning algorithms, e.g. [32, 33].

References

1. Dora, L., Agrawal, S., Panda, R., Abraham, A.: State-of-the-art methods for brain tissue segmentation: a review (2017)https://doi.org/10.1109/RBME.2017.2715350
2. Comelli, A., et al.: Tissue classification to support local active delineation of brain tumors. In: Zheng, Y., Williams, B.M., Chen, K.E. (eds.) MIUA 2019. CCIS, vol. 1065, pp. 3–14. Springer, Cham (2020). https://doi.org/10.1007/978-3-030-39343-4_1

3. Staffaroni, A.M., et al.: Neuroimaging in dementia. Semin. Neurol. **37**, 510–537 (2017). https://doi.org/10.1055/s-0037-1608808
4. Alongi, P., et al.: 18F-Florbetaben PET/CT to assess Alzheimer's disease: a new analysis method for regional amyloid quantification. J. Neuroimaging. **29**, 383–393 (2019). https://doi.org/10.1111/jon.12601
5. Alongi, P., et al.: Radiomics analysis of brain [18F]FDG PET/CT to predict Alzheimer's disease in patients with amyloid PET positivity: a preliminary report on the application of SPM cortical segmentation. Pyradiom. Mach. Learn. Anal. Diagn. **12**, 933 (2022). https://doi.org/10.3390/diagnostics12040933
6. Griffanti, L., et al.: Classification and characterization of periventricular and deep white matter hyperintensities on MRI: a study in older adults. Neuroimage **170**, 174–181 (2018). https://doi.org/10.1016/J.NEUROIMAGE.2017.03.024
7. Kennedy, D.N., Filipek, P.A., Caviness, V.S.: Anatomic segmentation and volumetric calculations in nuclear. Magn. Reson. Imaging (1989). https://doi.org/10.1109/42.20356
8. Stefano, A., Gallivanone, F., Messa, C.L., Gilardi, M.C.L., Castiglioni, I.: Metabolic impact of partial volume correction of [18F]FDG PET-CT oncological studies on the assessment of tumor response to treatment. Q. J. Nucl. Med. Mol. Imaging. **58**, 413–423 (2014)
9. Alongi, P., et al.: Radiomics analysis of 18F-Choline PET/CT in the prediction of disease outcome in high-risk prostate cancer: an explorative study on machine learning feature classification in 94 patients. Eur. Radiol. **31**(7), 4595–4605 (2021). https://doi.org/10.1007/s00330-020-07617-8
10. Vernuccio, F., Cannella, R., Comelli, A., Salvaggio, G., Lagalla, R., Midiri, M.: Radiomics and artificial intelligence: new frontiers in medicine. Recent. Prog. Med. **111**(3), 130–135 (2020). Italian. https://doi.org/10.1701/3315.32853
11. Comelli, A., et al.: A Kernel support vector machine based technique for Crohn's disease classification in human patients. In: Barolli, L., Terzo, O. (eds.) CISIS 2017. AISC, vol. 611, pp. 262–273. Springer, Cham (2018). https://doi.org/10.1007/978-3-319-61566-0_25
12. Licari, L., et al.: Use of the KSVM-based system for the definition, validation and identification of the incisional hernia recurrence risk factors. G. Chir. **40**, 32–38 (2019)
13. Cuocolo, R., et al.: Clinically significant prostate cancer detection on MRI: a radiomic shape features study. Eur. J. Radiol. **116**, 144–149 (2019). https://doi.org/10.1016/j.ejrad.2019.05.006
14. Tsang, O., Gholipour, A., Kehtarnavaz, N., Gopinath, K., Briggs, R., Panahi, I.: Comparison of tissue segmentation algorithms in neuroimage analysis software tools. In: Proceedings of the 30th Annual International Conference of the IEEE Engineering in Medicine and Biology Society, EMBS 2008 - "Personalized Healthcare through Technology.", pp. 3924–3928 (2008). https://doi.org/10.1109/iembs.2008.4650068
15. Klauschen, F., Goldman, A., Barra, V., Meyer-Lindenberg, A., Lundervold, A.: Evaluation of automated brain MR image segmentation and volumetry methods. Hum. Brain Mapp. **30**, 1310–1327 (2009). https://doi.org/10.1002/hbm.20599
16. Rajagopalan, V., Pioro, E.P.: Disparate voxel based morphometry (VBM) results between SPM and FSL softwares in ALS patients with frontotemporal dementia: Which VBM results to consider? BMC Neurol. 15, (2015). https://doi.org/10.1186/s12883-015-0274-8
17. Kazemi, K., Noorizadeh, N.: Quantitative comparison of SPM, FSL, and Brainsuite for Brain MR image segmentation. J. Biomed. Phys. Eng. **4**, 13–26 (2014)
18. Tudorascu, D.L., et al.: Reproducibility and bias in healthy brain segmentation: comparison of two popular neuroimaging platforms. Front. Neurosci. **10** (2016). https://doi.org/10.3389/fnins.2016.00503
19. Fellhauer, I., et al.: Comparison of automated brain segmentation using a brain phantom and patients with early Alzheimer's dementia or mild cognitive impairment (2015).https://doi.org/10.1016/j.pscychresns.2015.07.011

20. Stefano, A., et al.: A fully automatic method for biological target volume segmentation of brain metastases. Int. J. Imaging Syst. Technol. **26**, 29–37 (2016). https://doi.org/10.1002/ima.22154

21. Agnello, L., Comelli, A., Ardizzone, E., Vitabile, S.: Unsupervised tissue classification of brain MR images for voxel-based morphometry analysis. Int. J. Imaging Syst. Technol. **26**, 136–150 (2016). https://doi.org/10.1002/ima.22168

22. Comelli, A., Stefano, A.: A fully automated segmentation system of positron emission tomography studies. In: Zheng, Y., Williams, B.M., Ke., Chen (eds.) MIUA 2019. CCIS, vol. 1065, pp. 353–363. Springer, Cham (2020). https://doi.org/10.1007/978-3-030-39343-4_30

23. Woolrich, M.W., et al.: Bayesian analysis of neuroimaging data in FSL. Neuroimage **45**, S173–S186 (2009). https://doi.org/10.1016/j.neuroimage.2008.10.055

24. Friston, K.J.: Statistical Parametric Mapping: The Analysis of Functional Brain Images (2006)

25. Sharma, G., Martin, J.: MATLAB®: A language for parallel computing. Int. J. Parallel Program. **37**, 3–36 (2009). https://doi.org/10.1007/s10766-008-0082-5

26. Rohlfing, T.: Image similarity and tissue overlaps as surrogates for image registration accuracy: Widely used but unreliable. IEEE Trans. Med. Imaging. **31**, 153–163 (2012). https://doi.org/10.1109/TMI.2011.2163944

27. Hunter, D., Yu, H., Pukish, M.S., Kolbusz, J., Wilamowski, B.M.: Selection of proper neural network sizes and architectures-A comparative study. IEEE Trans. Ind. Informatics. (2012). https://doi.org/10.1109/TII.2012.2187914

28. Stefano, A., et al.: A graph-based method for PET image segmentation in radiotherapy planning: a pilot study. In: Petrosino, A. (ed.) ICIAP 2013. LNCS, vol. 8157, pp. 711–720. Springer, Heidelberg (2013). https://doi.org/10.1007/978-3-642-41184-7_72

29. Russo, G., et al.: Feasibility on the use of radiomics features of 11[C]-MET PET/CT in central nervous system tumours: Preliminary results on potential grading discrimination using a machine learning model. Curr. Oncol. **28**, 5318–5331 (2021). https://doi.org/10.3390/curroncol28060444

30. Comelli, A., Stefano, A., Benfante, V., Russo, G.: Normal and abnormal tissue classification in positron emission tomography oncological studies. Pattern Recognit. Image Anal. **28**, 106–113 (2018). https://doi.org/10.1134/S1054661818010054

31. Laudicella, R., Iagaru, A., Minutoli, F., Gaeta, M., Baldari, S., Bisdas, S.: PET/MR in neuro-oncology: is it ready for prime-time? Clin. Transl. Imaging **8**(4), 233–235 (2020). https://doi.org/10.1007/s40336-020-00377-x

32. Cuocolo, R., et al.: Deep learning whole-gland and zonal prostate segmentation on a public MRI dataset. J. Magn. Reson. Imaging. **54**, 452–459 (2021). https://doi.org/10.1002/jmri.27585

33. Stefano, A., Comelli, A.: Customized efficient neural network for covid-19 infected region identification in CT images. J. Imaging. **7**, 131 (2021). https://doi.org/10.3390/jimaging7080131

Combining Image and Geometry Processing Techniques for the Quantitative Analysis of Muscle-Skeletal Diseases

Martina Paccini[✉] 📵, Giuseppe Patané📵, and Michela Spagnuolo📵

Istituto di Matematica Applicata e Tecnologie Informatiche 'E. Magenes' - CNR,
Pavia, Italy
{martina.paccini,patane,michela.spagnuolo}@ge.imati.cnr.it

Abstract. For rheumatic diseases, it is fundamental to achieve an efficient medical evaluation of the patient's status and monitor the development of pathology. Acquiring and analyzing information on the pathology
progression are important steps to customize the therapy and slow the
disease's degeneration. This paper focuses on the localization of bone
erosion sites, which are a typical symptom of rheumatic disease progression, from both morphological and tissue perspectives. To this end, we
propose a *geometry-based approach*, which performs a *geometric analysis*
of 3D segmented surfaces, and a *texture-based approach*, which analyses
changes in the grey levels in a neighbour of the bone surface. These two
approaches are integrated to define a more complete tool for the analysis
and visualization of the input anatomical structures and the underlying
pathology. The performances of the different methods are evaluated on
the wrist district, acquired by a low-field magnetic resonance scanner.

Keywords: CADs · Biomedical image processing · Image-based 3D
reconstruction · 3D morphological analysis and visualization · Erosion
evaluation · Follow-up analysis · Image texture analysis

1 Introduction

Follow-up exams are commonly used to analyze degenerative diseases in most
medical branches. These exams consist of the analysis of the patient's status over
time. The importance of follow-up analysis resides in their support of the study
of the pathology development which, in turn, leads to personalized adjustments
to the therapy. In the rheumatological domain, a common sign of degeneration is the presence of bones' deformation, usually linked to an erosion process.
Affected patients suffer from severe pains and difficulties in the mobility of the
involved joints. The origin of erosive degeneration differs according to the particular undergoing pathology, but the result is an anomalous change in the tissues'

Supported by the Biannual Project "IMAGE-FUSION", FSE Regione Liguria.

composition, which leads to an alteration of the bone morphology. Indeed, it is important to consider the morphological changes in the segmented region (i.e., the segmented bones) as well as the tissue degeneration.

In recent years there has been an increasing interest in developing Computer-Aided Diagnosis (CAD) systems to improve disease diagnosis, treatment, and follow-up. CAD has become one of the major research subjects in medical imaging and diagnostic radiology and has been employed in the rheumatological domain for assisting physicians in the early detection of muscle-skeletal diseases, such as bone erosion in rheumatoid arthritis through the analysis of magnetic resonance images [3]. Even though advanced rendering techniques have been developed in recent years, the common practice still requires the study of individual 2D slices of the data. The first problem with a 2D visualization consists in the difficulty to determine the area and extent of the erosion, which is a 3D feature. Secondly, it is difficult to identify and compare the same bone erosion from 2D scans [23].

In this scenario, we focus on the enhancement of the patient's 3D data visualization through the combination of the geometrical analysis of 3D models and the evaluation of image intensities. In particular, this work proposes two approaches for the follow-up analysis of segmented anatomical structures. The *geometry-based approach* focuses on the identification of changes in the shape morphology; it is based on a geometrical analysis of 3D surface models of the bones and identifies geometric changes over time. The *texture-based approach* is based on an analysis of the image informative content (i.e., the tissue composition) in a neighbour of the bone surface and the alteration induced by the erosive process. We discuss the strengths and weaknesses of these two approaches and their integration into an accurate tool for the visualization and analysis of the evolution of muscle-skeletal pathology. After a review of related work (Sect. 2), we describe the evaluation of follow-up erosion based on geometry, segmented texture analysis, and an integrated approach (Sect. 3). Then, we discuss the evaluation and comparison of our approach to low-field MRI of the carpus (Sects. 4, 5).

2   Related Work

Medical images are at the core of rheumatic diseases analysis. Nowadays, two of the most frequently used imaging techniques for the study of rheumatic diseases are Computed Tomography (CT) and Magnetic Resonance (MR). Since MR acquires images non-invasively and without harmful radiations, it is commonly applied both in diagnosis and monitoring. For erosion detection, the MR exam provides a sensitivity higher than CT [7,21] and a better differentiation of small erosions when compared to US imaging [1]. Usually, the identification of critical sites, such as erosion or synovitis, has been performed by experts. This type of manual identification is error-prone [5], time-consuming, and can underestimate the extent of the damage [8], especially with 3D images. Indeed, the automatic identification of erosion sites and the analysis and quantification of image features through (automated) image processing are largely studied in the

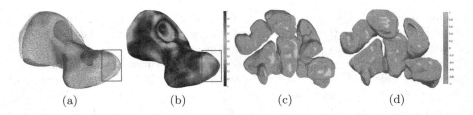

(a)   (b)   (c)   (d)

Fig. 1. (a, b) Inaccuracies of the registration method (a) with the relative influence on the identification of erosion regions (b). (c, d) Grey-level mapping and comparison of the surface texture derived from the MRI at baseline time (c) to the one derived from the MRI at follow-up time (d). Both mappings are performed on the 3D surface at follow-up. Changes in texture show the degeneration of the tissue composition induced by an erosion process.

field of rheumatic diseases [9,10,12,13]. With the diffusion of Artificial Intelligence, bone erosion has been identified in end-to-end systems [15,20]. However, largely reliable and clinically validated data sets for deep learning are not as fairly widespread in radiology as in other medical branches. Since bone erosion not only modifies the tissues' composition but also involves the bone morphology, the accurate analysis of the bone shape provides information on the location and extension of erosion sites (if any) on the bone surface.

Thanks to Computer Graphics algorithms (e.g., marching cubes [14]), 3D surface models are extracted from 3D images to accurately represent the anatomy of the patient and 3D morphological analysis provides results that are comparable to 2D image analysis. Follow-up studies evaluate the evolution of erosion sites on wrist bones exploiting 3D shape analysis on segmented images [3]. Analyzing parameters extracted from a 3D shape or a comparison of various shapes, it is possible to support general radiologic tasks with a particular focus also on follow-up exams [2,11]. A combination of image texture and shape analysis overcomes the limitations of the single approaches in the analysis of the erosion processes [18].

3   Proposed Approach

The proposed approach supports physicians in monitoring degenerative rheumatological diseases and can be included in CAD systems to improve image processing tools for the detection, visualization, and evaluation of abnormalities, and for the comparison of patient images and clinical data. We present the *geometry-based* (Sect. 3.1) and *texture-based* (Sect. 3.2) *analysis* of segmented MR images of the wrist, and their integration in a unified framework (Sect. 3.3). The geometry-based approach considers the geometric differences of 3D segmented surfaces, without examining tissue information. The texture-based approach identifies a degeneration in the tissue composition through an analysis of the changes in grey levels. Both approaches take advantage of the 3D segmentation of the anatomical structure, performed by experts and considered as ground truth without applying further processing (e.g., smoothing and re-meshing). From the geometric point of view, we visualize an explicit representation of the 3D segmented structures and perform a geometric evaluation of the surface shape. For the analysis of the tissues, the surface representation helps in the localization of the interesting regions inside the whole image volume avoiding the analysis of irrelevant areas of the image.

3.1 Geometry-Based Analysis

To evaluate the geometric differences that each bone presents over time, we compare the 3D surfaces of the carpus at baseline time with the one at follow-up time. The 3D surfaces are obtained by experts with the support of a dedicated system (Sect. 4), which includes the extraction of a 3D surface from the segmented image, post-processing, and smoothing. The analysis is carried out by co-registering the two wrists and evaluating local distances to identify shape changes and eroded regions. We consider two methods for the registration of the carpus at baseline and follow-up: the *Iterative Closest Point algorithm* (ICP) [4], and the *Coherent Point Drift algorithm* (CPD) [16]. Since we consider rigid registrations, there are no changes in the morphology of the bones and in the differences between baseline and follow-up, which identify the erosion sites.

After the registration, we compute the Hausdorff distance between the two co-registered districts to identify which bone presents an erosion. Calling $\mathbf{X}_1$ the 3D bone surface at t_1 and $\mathbf{X}_2$ the registered 3D surface at t_2, we identify eroded bones by their Hausdorff distance: $d(\mathbf{X}_1, \mathbf{X}_2) := \max\{d_{\mathbf{X}_1}(\mathbf{X}_2), d_{\mathbf{X}_2}(\mathbf{X}_1)\}$, where $d_{\mathbf{X}_1}(\mathbf{X}_2) := \max_{\mathbf{x} \in \mathbf{X}_1}\{\min_{\mathbf{y} \in \mathbf{X}_2}\{\|\mathbf{x} - \mathbf{y}\|_2\}\}$. Then, we evaluate the local distribution of the minimum distance of each vertex of the surface at t_2 from the vertices of the surface at t_1. Distances are then normalized to $[0, 1]$ to be comparable with the results obtained with the texture approach (Sect. 3.2). The regions of the bone, where the morphology has changed the most, present a higher value of distance distribution (close to 1), thus highlighting possible erosion processes. To help physicians in the visualization, we set a threshold for localizing the region of the bone that could present an erosion with a higher probability: $T = \overline{d_{\mathbf{X}_1}} + 3 * \sigma_{d_{\mathbf{X}_1}}$, were $\sigma_{d_{\mathbf{X}_1}}$ and $\overline{d_{\mathbf{X}_1}}$ represent the standard deviation and the mean of the distance distribution, respectively. Vertices that have a distance higher than T are visualized on the 3D surface with different colors (red), which allow a simple identification of the location of probable erosion.

3.2 Texture-Based Analysis

In our analysis, we consider a set of 3D T1-weighted MR images of the carpus (Sect. 4). Voxel intensities have been normalized between 0 and 1, being zero black and one white. The inner marrow bone, composed of fat tissue, results in high-intensity values. The outer layer of the bone, rich in minerals, is rendered black. Outside the bone, collagenous tissues (e.g., ligaments, tendons) and tissues with high water content (e.g., muscles, hyaline cartilage) are represented by low signals and, thus, by darker and intermediate grey levels. Once the degeneration

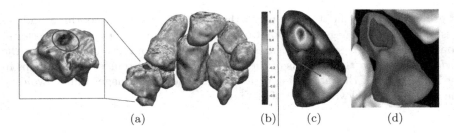

(a)   (b)| (c)   (d)

Fig. 2. (a, b) Texture difference close to −1 (red circle) can be associated with the healing process of the bone, thanks to the tailored therapy. (c-d) Scaphoid bone follow-up analysis of a patient with Rheumatoid Arthritis. Comparison of the erosion region identified by the experts (d) with the result of the geometrical analysis (c). The erosion is correctly identified (circle), but the distance distribution shows a false positive (arrow). (Color figure online)

affects the bone, the erosion deteriorates the cortical tissue at first and then proceeds to the internal layer. Indeed, erosion will be shown by a change in the voxel intensity levels.

Following [18], we generate a textured surface from an input MR image and its segmentation into bones. The segmented 3D surface is a triangle mesh, the volume image is composed of a sequence of 2D slices and is represented as a voxel grid. The image is loaded into a 3D grid, whose elements have the same dimension as the image voxels. In this way, every grid cell has its 3D coordinates to locate it in space and each grid cell is associated with a voxel and its grey level. Leveraging this data structure, three different criteria are defined to analyze the grey values in the proximity of the surface, depending on the method chosen to identify the correspondences between the surface vertices and the volume voxels. In the *Euclidean mapping*, the surface vertex **p** gets the grey-level of the voxel closest to **p** in terms of Euclidean distance. In the *internal mapping*, the closest voxels are searched only inside the surface, that is, inside the object's volume. In the *external mapping*, the closest voxels are searched only outside the surface, that is, outside the object's volume. Once every vertex of the surface has been associated with a voxel, the same grey level is associated with the correspondent voxel. The result of the grey-level mapping is a textured surface, where each vertex coordinate is associated with its specific colour, representative of the information contained in the image.

This approach focuses on the regions of the volume image that are near the bone surface by mapping the grey levels in the neighbour of the surface onto the 3D shape model. After co-registering the two surfaces, the follow-up 3D model is textured with the grey levels of both the MRI at baseline time (t_1) and at follow-up time (t_2), through the grey-levels mapping. Mapping the volume gray levels at time t_1 on the surface at time t_2, the follow-up 3D model shows either the volume situation at time t_1 and at time t_2. We focus on the correspondence criteria called *external mapping*, which explores the volume toward the external

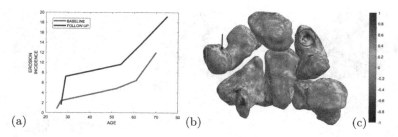

(a)   (b)   (c)

Fig. 3. (a) Incidence of bone erosion (percentage of bones that present erosion among all the bones in the data set) in relation to patient age at baseline (red) and follow-up (blue). (b, c) Erosion localization in the texture-based approach. The erosion is correctly identified (circle) but other healthy areas (arrow) false positives due to low image resolution. (Color figure online)

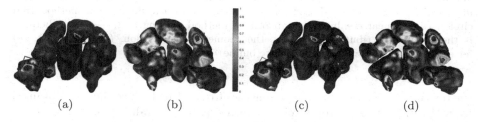

(a)   (b)   (c)   (d)

Fig. 4. Erosion localization on two different subjects, based on geometric analysis and threshold of the distance distribution. Red regions locate potential erosion, i.e., regions where the uncertainty of the erosion presence is minimal. Blue areas indicate regions associated with maximal uncertainty of erosion presence. The red rectangles indicate erosion identified by experts. (a, b) ICP registration algorithm and (c, d) CPD registration algorithm. The ICP algorithm suffers less from false positives. (Color figure online)

normal directions from the surface vertices since the erosion typically results from a degeneration of articular regions (Fig. 1(c, d)). The variations in texture are highlighted by computing the difference between the grey levels mapped from the baseline MRI onto the follow-up surface and the grey levels mapped from the follow-up MRI onto the follow-up surface. A higher value of difference indicates a region where the tissue has been substantially damaged, probably due to an erosion process. The colour map represents the tissue modification directly on the 3D surface.

3.3 Integrated Analysis

We present two approaches that integrate the information extracted by the geometry-based and texture-based approaches. Geometry-based and texture-based methods provide a follow-up district where each vertex is associated with a feature vector, composed of geometrical and texture information. In particular,

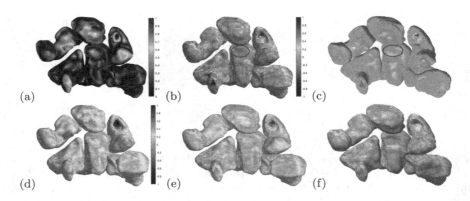

Fig. 5. (a, b, c) Comparison of the (a) geometry-based approach, (b) texture-based approach, and (c) their integration through multiplication approach. Small erosion identified by the geometry-based approach but not by the integration method (red circle). (d-f) Linear combination integration method varying ϵ: $d_1 + \epsilon * d_2$ where d_1 is the texture distribution and d_2 is the geometry distribution; (d) for $\epsilon = 1$, (e) for $\epsilon = 0.5$, (f) for $\epsilon = 0.2$. (Color figure online)

the texture information presents intensities from -1 to 1, since they are obtained from the difference of grey levels between 0 and 1. A value near 1 indicates a major change in the intensity of the image voxels, i.e., a radical change in tissue composition over time. A value of texture near -1 might indicate a healing process, where the extension of an existing erosion has been reduced due to a specific therapy [3]. Figure 2(a, b) shows the identification of an erosion where the texture provides negative values; the eroded volume is $171\,mm^3$ at baseline time and $57\,mm^3$ at follow-up time, thus indicating a reduction of the erosion.

The first option is to multiply the geometry and the texture values for each vertex. In this way, if a variation in geometry is associated with a high variation in texture (value near 1), then the result has a higher total value. The erosion site will be highlighted only if texture and geometry, show a major variation, confirming that the bone has developed both a change in morphology and tissue composition. The second option is a linear combination of geometric and texture information. Calling d_2 the distribution of the distances obtained by the geometry analysis and d_1 the distribution of the texture changes in the grey-levels analysis, the combined distribution is defined $d_1 + \epsilon * d_2$ with $\epsilon > 0$. Varying the value of ϵ, it is possible to emphasize geometric or texture information. If the clinician wants to surely identify all erosions, then ϵ will be increased. A low ϵ is more suitable for the identification of larger and persistent erosions. The manual setting of the parameter ϵ with the interactive visualization of the integrated results helps the physician in the analysis of the input data accordingly to their knowledge of the type of rheumatic disease, the mechanism of erosion development, and the evolution of the pathology.

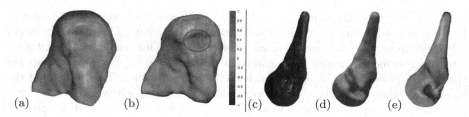

Fig. 6. Integrated approach ($\epsilon = 1$) result on the hamate bone before texture scaling (a) and after texture scaling, where the eroded region (red circle) results better highlighted (b). (c-e) identification of an erosion on a finger bone with geometrical approach (a), texture approach (b), and integrated approach with $\epsilon = 1$ (c). The results are coherent with the discussion presented for the wrist bones. (Color figure online)

4   Results and Discussions

The data set used for the analysis is composed of the 3D MRIs of the carpus associated with their segmentation performed by experts through a semi-automatic region-growing method [22]. The MRIs are obtained from a 0.2T extremity dedicated machine (Esaote-Artoscan) using 3D T1 weighted sequences with reconstruction on the axial and sagittal plane. The subjects suffer from degenerative rheumatoid illnesses at different stages. The carpus is one of the most indicated districts for the diagnosis and monitoring of rheumatic diseases since it is one of the first to show symptoms and damages linked to the pathology. For our analysis, we are interested in the 5 subjects that underwent follow-up exams. For each of those subjects, 2 exams are present: one at baseline time (t_1) and one at follow-up time (t_2). Every exam involves 25 bones, thus we analyzed 125 bones. Figure 3(a) shows the incidence of the erosions on the bones according to the patients' age. The highly complicated anatomical structure and the low-field images represent the core challenges that the approaches presented in this paper have to face.

In Fig. 2(c, d), we compare the identification of erosion sites performed by experts in the field with the result of the geometry-based analysis. The erosion site is correctly identified by the geometrical analysis, which presents a particularly high value of distance distribution in the exact location indicated by the experts. However, the results show the presence of *false positives*, i.e., areas of the bone that are classified as erosion but are healthy regions, for both the rigid registrations described in Sect. 3.1. This misclassification is related to the inaccuracies of the registration processes. Indeed, the rounded and symmetric shape of most of the bones affects the accuracy of the alignment of the district. According to Fig. 1(a, b), in the region where the two bones were not well aligned, the distance distribution presents higher intensity values than expected, even if no erosion process is involved. Nevertheless, the erosion sites highlighted by experts are correctly identified for both registration methods. Figure 4 shows the changes in the geometrical approach in relation to the registration method.

Regarding the image texture analysis, the difference between the texture at baseline and follow-up shows an inhomogeneous behaviour. The higher values of difference in texture are located in an erosion region. This result is coherent with what is expected as a major change in tissue composition implies a higher value of the difference between the texture at the two different times. The location of the erosion is correctly identified; however, a series of false-positive is present, even if characterized by differences lower than the real erosion locations (Fig. 3(b, c)). The inhomogeneities, as well as false positives, are due to the low resolution of the MRI images. This factor influences the results obtained using a texture-based approach; by increasing the resolution, we expect a more accurate result. The differences in texture related to a change in the registration are not significant, as the texture approach is robust to a rigid registration. Furthermore, the texture results provide the tissue density in the proximity of the surface, which helps the physician to focus on the relevant regions of the volume in a 3D environment and to evaluate the patient over time, even if the overall result presents some inhomogeneities.

The integrated method merges the information provided by the geometrical and texture analysis. In Fig. 5(c), the false positives are no longer present. The overall result is more homogeneous, thus indicating that geometry and texture information compensate for each other. Nevertheless, the integration result could miss some newly developed and small erosion. The red circles in Fig. 5 indicate the small erosion correctly localized by the geometrical approach, but missed by texture-based analysis. This result suggests that the erosion could be at its beginning, implying a minor change in geometry and a small change in the cortical bone tissue, which could be still partly intact. The integrated method is robust to the registration approach since the final result does not present significant changes related to the chosen algorithm. The second integration of texture and geometry is more flexible compared to the multiplication approach. Indeed, by varying the value of ϵ it is possible to tune the analysis to the type of search that the physician is carrying on.

Figure 5, shows three different integration results according to the variation of the ϵ value. Reducing the relevance of the geometric information ($\epsilon = 0.5$, $\epsilon = 0.2$), the resulting values lead to a more homogeneous result, i.e., the false positive areas decrease in number along with the reduction of the geometric information. However, an excessive reduction of the geometrical information brings also the presence of false negatives, that is the misclassification of erosion regions as healthy areas. Overall, the linear combination allows us to adjust the focus of the search and reach the desired trade-off between false negatives and false positives. The registration method used to align the baseline and follow-up exams does not influence the final results. Indeed, the presence of the texture information makes the final result robust to the rigid registration chosen, even if the geometrical analysis can be slightly influenced by the registration approach in terms of false positives.

To reduce the influence of the MRI's low resolution, without compromising the information brought by the texture, we performed a texture scaling on the final result. In this way, the most damaged regions of the bones are still highlighted, but the overall visualization results are clearer (Fig. 6(a, b)). Manually changing the parameter ϵ also provides the opportunity to support the quantitative evaluation metrics used for erosion in rheumatic diseases, such as the OMERACT rheumatoid arthritis MRI scoring system (RAMRIS) and the EULAR-OMERACT rheumatoid arthritis MRI reference image atlas. These scoring systems are established standards for synovitis, bone edema, and bone erosion scoring guided by standard reference images [17]. In particular, the bone erosion is evaluated separately for each bone with a score between 0–10, based on the proportion of eroded bone compared to the assessed bone volume, judged on all available images.

The manual setting of ϵ, could improve the precision of the scoring, showing interactively the result of the evaluation on the 3D model. Higher values of ϵ help localize early erosion. Lower values of the parameter ϵ are suited for existing localized erosion. The integrated approach combines different sources of information in an interactive visualization for the monitoring of the patient's status and his/her clinical history. Finally, these methods do not need previous knowledge of the analyzed structure, or the computation of mean shapes or atlases [6]. Moreover, the integrated method is general and can be applied to different anatomical structures (Fig. 6(c-e)).

5 Conclusions and Future Work

The paper presents a comparison of different approaches to support the medical follow-up analysis in radiology, with a special focus on erosion development in rheumatic diseases. The proposed geometry-based and texture-based approaches localize the initial appearance or evolution of erosion sites, thus providing physicians with a visual tool that could help and speed up erosion identification. Our approach can identify even the smallest erosion but classifies some regions of the bone that are still healthy as eroded areas. The texture-based analysis shows promising results, which can be improved with higher resolution images. The presence of false positives proposes or false negatives induce misinterpretations in the analysis of the therapy performance. The integration of texture-based and geometric information provides more homogeneous results.

The proposed approach is quite simple and can be easily integrated into current clinical workflows, such as systems assembled as packages, associated with specific imaging modalities (CT, MRI), and implemented as a part of PACS - Picture Archiving and Communication Systems [19]. The novelty of our approach resides in the possibility to integrate geometry- and texture-based representations of a morphological district and the underlying pathology in an interactive way to better support the analysis of the patient status by multidisciplinary experts. The method is general enough to be applied to different types of images and can adapt to different resolutions. Indeed, a higher quality image like a high-field MRI would bring more insights into the bone tissue condition than a low-field MRI. Leveraging other types of images, the texture content will be related to different tissue properties, opening the possibility to address other tasks, such as the evaluation of tumor extension after chemotherapy and the status of surrounding tissues, according to their encoding in the surface textures.

The main limitation of our work is the necessity of the district segmentation; however, different learning techniques could be leveraged to perform the required segmentation. Future work will be focused on the improvement of the integration method toward a fully automatic approach for a quantitative measure of erosion. This process would be easier in presence of more than one follow-up exam, especially for a comparison thought to be extremely patient-specific. A higher number of exams, other than helping the automatic adjustment of the ϵ parameter, could allow a more complete clinical validation.

References

1. Backhaus, M., et al.: Prospective two year follow up study comparing novel and conventional imaging procedures in patients with arthritic finger joints. Ann. Rheum. Dis. **61**(10), 895–904 (2002)
2. Banerjee, I., Catalano, C.E., Patané, G., Spagnuolo, M.: Semantic annotation of 3D anatomical models to support diagnosis and follow-up analysis of musculoskeletal pathologies. Int. J. Comput. Assist. Radiol. Surg. **11**(5), 707–720 (2015). https://doi.org/10.1007/s11548-015-1327-6
3. Barbieri, F., et al.: An MRI study of bone erosions healing in the wrist and metacarpophalangeal joints of patients with rheumatoid arthritis. In: Murino, V., Puppo, E., Sona, D., Cristani, M., Sansone, C. (eds.) ICIAP 2015. LNCS, vol. 9281, pp. 129–134. Springer, Cham (2015). https://doi.org/10.1007/978-3-319-23222-5_16
4. Besl, P.J., McKay, N.D.: Method for registration of 3D shapes. In: Sensor Fusion IV: Control Paradigms and Data Structures, vol. 1611, pp. 586–606. International Society for Optics and Photonics (1992)
5. Busby, L.P., Courtier, J.L., Glastonbury, C.M.: Bias in radiology: the how and why of misses and misinterpretations. Radiographics **38**(1), 236–247 (2018)
6. De Craene, M., du Bois d'Aische, A., Macq, B., Warfield, S.K.: Multi-subject registration for unbiased statistical atlas construction. In: Barillot, C., Haynor, D.R., Hellier, P. (eds.) MICCAI 2004. LNCS, vol. 3216, pp. 655–662. Springer, Heidelberg (2004). https://doi.org/10.1007/978-3-540-30135-6_80
7. Døhn, U.M., et al.: Detection of bone erosions in rheumatoid arthritis wrist joints with magnetic resonance imaging, computed tomography and radiography. Arthritis Res. Therapy **10**(1), R25 (2008)
8. Figueiredo, C.P., et al.: Methods for segmentation of rheumatoid arthritis bone erosions in high-resolution peripheral quantitative computed tomography (hr-pqct). In: Seminars in Arthritis and Rheumatism, vol. 47 (5), pp. 611–618. Elsevier (2018)
9. Gornale, S.S., Patravali, P.U., Manza, R.R.: A survey on exploration and classification of osteoarthritis using image processing techniques. Int. J. Sci. Eng. Res. **7**(6), 334–355 (2016)
10. Huo, Y., Vincken, K.L., van der Heijde, D., De Hair, M.J., Lafeber, F.P., Viergever, M.A.: Automatic quantification of radiographic finger joint space width of patients with early rheumatoid arthritis. IEEE Trans. Biomed. Eng. **63**(10), 2177–2186 (2015)

11. Joshi, A.A., Leahy, R.M., Badawi, R.D., Chaudhari, A.J.: Registration-based morphometry for shape analysis of the bones of the human wrist. IEEE Trans. Med. Imaging 35(2), 416–426 (2015)
12. Langs, G., Peloschek, P., Bischof, H., Kainberger, F.: Automatic quantification of joint space narrowing and erosions in rheumatoid arthritis. IEEE Trans. Med. Imaging 28(1), 151–164 (2008)
13. Leung, K.K., et al.: Automatic quantification of changes in bone in serial MR images of joints. IEEE Trans. Med. Imaging 25(12), 1617–1626 (2006)
14. Lorensen, W.E., Cline, H.E.: Marching cubes: a high resolution 3D surface construction algorithm. ACM SIGGRAPH Comput. Graph. 21(4), 163–169 (1987)
15. Murakami, S., Hatano, K., Tan, J.K., Kim, H., Aoki, T.: Automatic identification of bone erosions in rheumatoid arthritis from hand radiographs based on deep convolutional neural network. Multimedia Tools Appl. 77(9), 10921–10937 (2017). https://doi.org/10.1007/s11042-017-5449-4
16. Myronenko, A., Song, X.: Point set registration: coherent point drift. IEEE Trans. Pattern Anal. Mach. Intell. 32(12), 2262–2275 (2010)
17. Østergaard, M., et al.: An introduction to the eular-omeract rheumatoid arthritis MRI reference image atlas. Ann. Rheum. Dis. 64(suppl 1), i3–i7 (2005)
18. Paccini, M., Patané, G., Spagnuolo, M.: Analysis of 3D segmented anatomical districts through grey-levels mapping. Comput. Graphics 91, 179–188 (2020)
19. Parascandolo, P., Cesario, L., Vosilla, L., Viano, G.: Computer aided diagnosis: state-of-the-art and application to musculoskeletal diseases. In: Magnenat-Thalmann, N., Ratib, O., Choi, H.F. (eds.) 3D Multiscale Physiological Human, pp. 277–296. Springer, London (2014). https://doi.org/10.1007/978-1-4471-6275-9_12
20. Rohrbach, J., Reinhard, T., Sick, B., Dürr, O.: Bone erosion scoring for rheumatoid arthritis with deep convolutional neural networks. Comput. Electr. Eng. 78, 472–481 (2019)
21. Scheel, A., et al.: Prospective 7 year follow up imaging study comparing radiography, ultrasonography, and magnetic resonance imaging in rheumatoid arthritis finger joints. Ann. Rheum. Dis. 65(5), 595–600 (2006)
22. Tomatis, V., et al.: a database of segmented MRI images of the wrist and the hand in patients with rheumatic diseases. In: Murino, V., Puppo, E., Sona, D., Cristani, M., Sansone, C. (eds.) ICIAP 2015. LNCS, vol. 9281, pp. 143–150. Springer, Cham (2015). https://doi.org/10.1007/978-3-319-23222-5_18
23. Zheng, L., Chaudhari, A.J., Badawi, R.D., Ma, K.L.: Using global illumination in volume visualization of rheumatoid arthritis CT data. IEEE Comput. Graphics Appl. 34(6), 16–23 (2014)

Robustness of Radiomics Features to Varying Segmentation Algorithms in Magnetic Resonance Images

Luca Cairone[1] , Viviana Benfante[2,3,4] , Samuel Bignardi[5] ,
Franco Marinozzi[1] , Anthony Yezzi[5], Antonino Tuttolomondo[3] ,
Giuseppe Salvaggio[6] , Fabiano Bini[1] , and Albert Comelli[2(✉)]

[1] Department of Mechanical and Aerospace Engineering, Sapienza-University of Rome,
00184 Rome, Italy
[2] Ri.MED Foundation, Via Bandiera 11, 90133 Palermo, Italy
acomelli@fondazionerimed.com
[3] Department of Health Promotion, Mother and Child Care, Internal Medicine and Medical
Specialties, Molecular and Clinical Medicine, University of Palermo, 90127 Palermo, Italy
[4] Institute of Molecular Bioimaging and Physiology, National Research Council (IBFM-CNR),
90015 Cefalù, Italy
[5] Department of Electrical and Computer Engineering, Georgia Institute of Technology, Atlanta,
GA 30332, USA
[6] Section of Radiology, Department of Biomedicine, Neuroscience and Advanced Diagnostics
(Bi.N.D.), University of Palermo, 90100 Palermo, Italy

Abstract. Aim: To verify the accuracy of different segmentation algorithms applied on a dataset of 50 patients suffering from enlargement of the median lobe of the prostate district, to establish whether it is possible to support the work of medical physicians in radiomics analyses through semi-automatic segmentation approaches.

Materials and Methods: Seven algorithms were used for prostate segmentation in MR images and for the subsequent extraction of radiomics features. A statistical analysis was carried out considering the features extracted from semi-automatic and manual segmentations. The analysis was based on the ANOVA test, followed by the Tukey test to verify the repeatability of the algorithms, and on the calculation of the intraclass correlation coefficient to verify the reliability and robustness of the extracted features. Based on the correlation between the binary masks extracted for each algorithm and the corresponding binary mask of the medical physicians' segmentation, a volumetric analysis was conducted.

Results: The best semi-automatic algorithm to support the medical physician among those evaluated is the "Fill between slices" algorithm, which is also the fastest of all. The least reliable algorithms are those based on the similarity of grey levels.

Keywords: Deep learning · Segmentation · Prostate · MRI · ENet · UNet · ERFNet · Radiomics

© The Author(s), under exclusive license to Springer Nature Switzerland AG 2022
P. L. Mazzeo et al. (Eds.): ICIAP 2022 Workshops, LNCS 13373, pp. 462–472, 2022.
https://doi.org/10.1007/978-3-031-13321-3_41

1 Introduction

Prostate volume is a parameter widely used in the clinical environment by medical physicians, both for the diagnosis of benign or neoplastic pathologies (for example the prostate cancer or PCa) affecting this gland or in the presence of symptoms in the lower urinary tract, such as benign prostatic hyperplasia (BPH) [1, 2]. Furthermore, this parameter is considered an important prognostic value since the medical physician, by correctly estimating this volume, is able to prepare a specific therapeutic plan, such as radiotherapy and ablation [3]. Prostate volume is especially important when correlated with both PCa scores and BPH levels. Related to serum prostate specific antigen (PSA), and PCa, prostate volume may be essential for clinician's prognostic decisions [4]. Prostate volume is also used to calculate PSA density (PAS-D) that is the level of serum PSA divided by the prostate volume. The higher the PSA-D, the more likely it is that the PCa is clinically significant. EUA guideline [5] emphasized that the use of PSA-D remains currently limited due to the lack of standardization of prostate volume measurement (assessed by DRE or by imaging [TRUS or MRI using various techniques such as ellipsoid formula or planimetry]. The impact of this lack of standardization on the volume estimation remains under evaluated. The prostate district is very particular as it has variations (in some cases very clearly) from patient to patient; therefore, the presence of this physiological condition makes the segmentations and therefore the three-dimensional modeling of the prostate of the various patients even more different.

There are no articles in the scientific literature concerning the extraction of radiomics features [6] from this district with this specific physiological condition of prostate median lobe enlargement. In fact, there are only studies on radiomics regarding the presence of prostate cancer [7, 8]. The possibility of drawing on this information is given by the fact that the enlargement can lead to the development of a lesion; therefore, in a predictive key, the setting is made starting from study such as that of Schwier et al. [9].

Methods to visualize the volume of the prostate include various imaging techniques, such as computed tomography (CT) [10], PET [11], and magnetic resonance imaging (MRI) [12]. Specifically, MRI allows the detection of prostate volume in a more precise way as it approximates the prostate gland to an ellipsoid [13]. Indeed, an error in the calculations of the prostate volume is frequently linked to the presence of prostate median lobe enlargement [14] and this involves an overestimation of the prostatic volume as compared to the real volume of the sample [15], as shown in Fig. 1.

PI-RADS v2.1 [16] recommended to routinely report the prostate volume based on MRI, using manual or automated segmentation or calculations using ellipsoid formulation.

The formula for approximating the prostate volume (PV) [17] is

$$PV = \frac{\pi}{6} * anteroposteriorDiameter * longitudinalDiameter * transverseDiameter$$

(1)

MRI of the prostate region has two major problems that have been encountered: the prostate organ is made up of different heterogeneous tissues [12], therefore it is represented by different levels of gray, making segmentations more complicated with algorithms based on the principle of similarity of the levels themselves and the district is

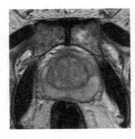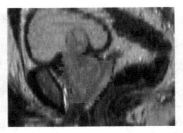

Fig. 1. 3D model prostate of patient 011 (medical physicians' manual segmentation): axial plane, sagittal plane, and 3D model.

made up of different pelvic organs, all characterized by being represented with similar gray levels to each other: this often involves some problems of over-segmentation.

The first step to perform biomedical imaging is to segment the target to extract many quantitative parameters from the biomedical images with the aim of doing radiomics studies [18, 19]. MRI radiomics studies are essential to stratify patients according to the degree of risk. Furthermore, the parameters extracted from the images, used as imaging biomarkers, associated with other clinical data will provide the patient with a more precise outcome. To make this happen and to avoid errors during the features extraction, radiomics requires a contouring of the target organ or tumor [20]. The target delineation must be repeatable and can be achieved semi-automatically or automatically. The purpose of this work is to verify the repeatability of seven different segmentation algorithms applied on a dataset of 50 patients suffering from enlargement of the median lobe of the prostate district, to establish whether it is possible to support the work of expert medical physicians (who provided the manual segmentations) with that of a biomedical engineer able to use software suitable for semi-automatic segmentation. Reference images were obtained by MRI and T2-weighted. The extraction of radiomics features was carried out. A statistical analysis was carried out with the aim to verify both the repeatability of the various algorithms by making a comparison with the medical physicians' manual segmentation and the robustness [21] of the features to demonstrate their reliability.

2   Materials and Methods

2.1   Material and Population

The population taken into consideration is made up of 50 patients aged between 53 and 83, with a mean of 66.08 and a standard deviation of 7.23, who underwent the magnetic resonance examination in a time range from 4 July 2016 (patients 058, 061 and 050) to 14 July 2017 (patient 009). This shows how this condition is present in a very wide range of the population.

MRI exams were performed using a 1.5 T magnet (Achieva, Philips Healthcare, Best, The Netherlands) with a phased-array pelvic coil (8-channel HD Torso XL). MRI scans were performed by means of a Turbo Spin-Echo (TSE) sequence. The most important metadata are shown in the Table 1.

Table 1. Most important metadata.

Parameters	T2wSENSE
Repetition time (ms)	3091
Echo time (ms)	100
Slice thickness (mm)	2.5
Flip angle (degrees)	90
Number of slices	40
Bits allocated	16
Bits stored	12
High bit	11
Pixel spacing	0.267
SAR	2

2.2 Segmentations

Once the various segmentations were completed, the binary masks for each of them were then extracted. For these masks there are only two possible levels of gray: the white gray level (value 1) is given to the voxels belonging to the segmentation while the black gray level (value 0) is given to the voxels belonging to the background. In addition to the various algorithms, these masks were also extracted from manual segmentations, in order to be able to carry out a statistical comparison between the semi-automatic and manual segmentations.

The semi-automatic algorithms used are the following:

– Grow from seeds (GFS), an algorithm based on Region Growing. It uses an iterative method based on the similarity between the voxels; to make the work carried out on each patient comparable, it was decided to select the seeds on 25% of the slices presenting the prostate organ.
– Watershed: it was chosen to select an object scale value equal to 2.00 mm for the segmentation; also in this case it was decided to select 25% of the slices containing the prostate organ.
– Fast Marching (FM), based on the similarity of the gray levels; due to the too many similarities of gray levels between the various organs of the district and to avoid overlapping problems in the slices where the portion of the prostate is not very large, it was necessary to reduce the volume of the segment to 50%.
– Fill between slices (FBS), an algorithm based on filling the slices starting from a sample of manually segmented slices (in this case too, the choice fell on 25% of the slices containing the prostate organ) and through the principle of similarity of gray levels.
– Clever Segmentation (CS), innovative technique based on Region Growing.
– Threshold. Due to the presence of too many similar gray levels throughout the district, we chose to fix the extreme values in 415 and 1439, by making several attempts on

all the datasets; as some voxels have not been segmented as they have gray levels excluded from the range, a manual post processing was necessary.

– Draw: an algorithm that allows the operator to manually outline the area of interest and to immediately segment the voxels present within this area.

2.3 Setup for Prostate District and Features Extraction

The software used for the extraction of radiomics features is Pyradiomics, an extension of the 3DSlicer. However, before proceeding with the extraction, an ad hoc study on the district was necessary to make the appropriate setting.

The process reported in [9] was replicated in this study and so two classes that by default are present on Pyradiomics were removed from the number of feature classes to be considered. They are: Neighbouring Gray Tone Difference Matrix or NGTDM features and Gray Level Dependence Matrix or GLDM features. Other features were eliminated because redundant or not useful for our purpose, thus making the procedure quicker. These features are Compactness1, Compactness2, SphericalDisproportion, SumAverage, Homogeneity1 and Homogeneity2 because directly correlated to other features and Flatness and LeastAxis because not useful for our purpose.

This leaves 5 classes (shape, statistical, Gray Level Co-occurrence Matrix or GLCM, Gray Level Run Length Matrix or GLRLM and Gray Level Size Zone Matrix or GLSZM) for 85 features. As regards the number of bins that determines the discretization of the voxel intensities, it was decided to leave the default value equal to 25. Wavelet filters haven't been used because their use does not significantly improve the repeatability of the algorithms compared to the non-use of filters.

2.4 Statistical Analysis

Once the features have been extracted, the study continues with the statistical analysis. The analysis starts with the construction of the ANOVA tables for each feature, from which it then continues with Tukey post-hoc test and the calculation of the intraclass correlation coefficient (ICC). All this was conducted using Matlab tools. For the ANOVA test, a table was created for each feature with 50 rows (patients) and 8 columns (algorithms + medical physician's segmentation). For each we have two null hypotheses. The most important one is about algorithms, and it is

$$H_0 : \mu_{:,1} = \mu_{:,2} = \cdots = \mu_{:,j} = \cdots = \mu_{:,8} \text{ with } j = 1, 2, 3 \ldots 8 \qquad (2)$$

with $\mu_{:,j}$ = average of the 50 observations of the column j.

For the ICC we have

$$ICC = \frac{\text{var}(\beta)}{(\text{var}(a) + \text{var}(\beta) + \text{var}(\varepsilon))} \qquad (3)$$

where var(β) is the variability of the interest group (that given by algorithms), var(α) is the variability given by patients and var (ε) is that given by error.

3   Results

The ANOVA test was used to check if there were algorithms that generate variant features with respect to the medical physicians' segmentation. However, since this test is only able to establish if there is at least one algorithm that differs, but not which one it is, we proceeded with Tukey's post-hoc test. Specifically, attention was paid to the number of features that for each algorithm differ in a statistically significant way from those of the medical physicians.

Specifically, we have that the features that differ in a statistically significant way are:

- 1 out of 85 (equal to 1.17%) for the Draw algorithm (the statistical feature Minimum)
- 24 features out of 85 (equal to 28.23%) for the Fill between slices algorithm
- 36 features out of 85 (equal to 42.35%) for the Threshold algorithm
- 59 features out of 85 (equal to 69.41%) for the Clever Segmentation algorithm
- 60 features out of 85 (equal to 70.58%) for the Grow from seeds algorithm
- 61 features out of 85 (equal to 71.76%) for the Watershed algorithm
- 62 features out of 85 (equal to 72.94%) for the Fast Marching algorithm

Statistical analysis approach was also used to demonstrate that the use of wavelet filters does not significantly improve the repeatability of the algorithms compared to the non-use of filters. In this case, the calculation was made only on the best result algorithm, therefore the Draw. In total there are 8 wavelet filters available. The extracted features are then grouped according to the reference filter. Except for the shape features which are 12 and are equally valid for all filters, 73 features are extracted for each filter, for a total of 596 features extracted for each segmentation. So, for each wavelet filter there are 85 features. The null hypothesis establishes that there is no statistical difference between the averages of the observations obtained by the two algorithms. If the p-value is less than 0.05, this null hypothesis is rejected, so the algorithm does not allow to obtain a feature like that obtained by the medical physicians. Conversely, if the p-value is greater than 0.05, the null hypothesis is not rejected, so for that observation the algorithm was able to simulate the manual segmentation obtained by the medical physicians.

Considering all filters, the features that differ in a statistically significant way are:

- 8 out of 85 (equal to 9.41%) using the LLH filter
- 2 out of 85 (equal to 2.35%) using the LHL filter
- 8 out of 85 (equal to 9.41%) using the LHH filter
- 5 out of 85 (equal to 5.88%) using the HLL filter
- 7 out of 85 (equal to 8.23%) using the HLH filter
- 8 out of 85 (equal to 9.41%) using the HHL filter
- 7 out of 85 (equal to 8.23%) using the HHH filter
- 9 out of 85 (equal to 10.58%) using the LLL filter

where L indicates a low-pass filter and H a high-pass filter, combined along the three possible directions.

Comparing the result obtained without the application of filters (1.17%) it is evident that the application of the filters does not vary excessively the repeatability of the algorithm, in fact the difference is always less than 10% and the Draw algorithm remains very reliable.

Considering the robustness of the features, the bar graph (Fig. 2) shows the average ICC value for each group of features. It is noted how the texture features have higher ICC, with the GLRLM group in the lead with an average ICC equal to 0.947, while the least reliable group (despite its reliability is still good) is the one of shape with an average ICC equal to 0.807.

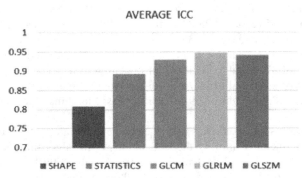

Fig. 2. Average ICC for each group of features

For the shape features, the highest value is assumed by the MajorAxisLength feature and is equal to 0.98. Following there are two features related to the volume, respectively MeshVolume with ICC equal to 0.968 and VoxelVolume with ICC equal to 0.968. The lower values, on the other hand, concern the shape and the surface. Absolutely, the Sphericity feature assumes the lowest value among all the groups, a value with a very low reliability equal to 0.159 Obviously, differences in shape generate differences in the surface, so much so that the SurfaceVolumeRatio feature with an ICC of 0.611 has a reliability that is considered moderate.

For the statistical features, the highest ICC value belongs to Median and is 0.99, followed by RootMeanSquared with 0.987, and Mean with 0.98558. The lowest ICC value, on the other hand, is 0.599 and belongs to Minimum. This is since while with the manual segmentation of the medical physicians no voxels belonging to the background are taken (hypointense with respect to the prostate), with the various semi-automatic segmentations the background is always partially included due to over-segmentations, and this significantly lowers the value of the voxel with the lowest intensity level. The average ICC of the group is 0.921.

For the GLCM features, the highest ICC values are 0.986, 0.985 and 0.985 respectively belonging to the features Inverse Difference Moment (Idm), InverseVariance and Autocorrelation. These three features are linked to the local homogeneity of the gray levels. The lowest ICC value is 0.755 of the Maximal Correlation Coefficient (MCC). The average ICC of the group is 0.93.

For the GLRLM features, the value of the ICC is very high for all features. The Run-Variance feature has the highest ICC of all 85 features and is equal to 0.993, followed by LongRunEmphasis with 0.991. The lowest values belong to the runs involving low gray levels: ShortRunLowGrayLevelEmphasis (0.801), LowGrayLevelRunEmphasis (0.814) and LongRunLowGrayLevelEmphasis (0.836).

Finally, for the GLSZM features too the ICC values are very high, with the maximum given by the LargeAreaHighGrayLevelEmphasis feature with 0.992, followed by ZoneVariance with 0.991. These results, extended to the zones, agree with the results obtained for the runs. Also with regard to the lower ICC values, attention is paid to the low gray levels with SmallAreaLowGrayLevelEmphasis, ZoneEntropy and LowGrayLevel-ZoneEmphasis with values of 0.786, 0.805 and 0.812 respectively. The average ICC of the group is 0.941.

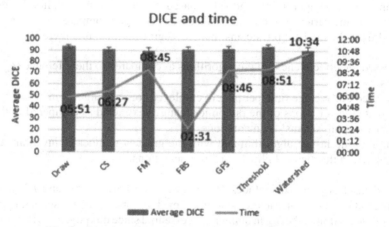

Fig. 3. Average value of the overlap index (DICE) and time.

From volumetric analyses, bar graphs were obtained to represent the average values, with the respective standard deviations (Fig. 3). All parameters, whose values vary between 0 and 1, are expressed as a percentage. A broken line is superimposed on these, representing the average segmentation times of each algorithm.

All segmentation algorithms have an average value of the overlap index (or DSC = DICE similarity coefficient) parameter greater than 90%, with the highest value obtained from the Threshold equal to 93.97% and the lowest obtained by Fast Marching equal to 90.08 (Fig. 3). Such high values indicate that in general the algorithms can faithfully reconstruct the prostate volume without moving away from the medical physicians' target.

In conclusion, the semi-automatic algorithm with the least number of features that differ from the gold standard is the Fill between slices (24 features out of 85), while the one with the highest number is the Fast Marching (62 features out of 85). The fastest algorithm is the Fill between slices with an average time equal to 02:31, the slowest is the

Watershed with a time of 10:34. The total mean value of the DICE is 91.85%, because all the algorithms are faithful in the morphological representation, with a standard deviation of ±1.56.

Therefore, considering overall the invariance of the features, the timing and the morpho-volumetric analysis, the best semi-automatic segmentation algorithm for this district is the Fill between slices.

4 Discussion and Conclusion

The ability to support the three-dimensional segmentation operation performed manually by a medical physician on DICOM nuclear MRI of a complex area such as that of the prostate is the basis of the studies carried out. We tried to evaluate which semiautomatic algorithms are more appropriate and valid, based on the quantity of radiomics features obtained from the various segmentations that are unchanged compared to the same ones extracted from the medical physicians' manual segmentations. It is therefore:

1. assessed the effectiveness of the algorithms as compared to the reference segmentations
2. measured the average time per patient employed for each algorithm
3. calculate the variations of the radiomics features extracted as compared to those of the medical physicians' segmentations
4. identified the fastest algorithm and with the greatest number of invariant features compared to the medical physicians' segmentations.

The dataset considered includes 50 patients aged between 53 and 83 years and physiological condition of enlargement of the median lobe of the prostate. Obtaining a correct segmentation of the organ of interest is essential since this physiological condition can cause the development of a lesion; therefore, the decision to support the medical physician's hand with semi-automatic algorithms affects the patient's health.

The various semi-automatic segmentation algorithms, used through the 3DSlicer software, which have been evaluated are: Grow from seeds, Watershed, Fast Marching, Fill between slices, Clever Segmentation and Threshold (applied as a mask). To these were added the segmentations obtained with a manual algorithm (the Draw), completely operator dependent, to verify how far a segmentation carried out by a biomedical engineer inexperienced in the sector can differ from that carried out by some medical physicians with years of experience.

While the segmentations were conducted, the times (total and average) were measured for each algorithm, since in the clinical setting the times are important; if there is therefore the possibility of obtaining a result compatible with that obtained by the medical physician in a shorter time, the advantage is obvious. Considering only the timing, the fastest algorithm turns out to be the Fill between slices with an average time per patient of 2 min 31 s, while the slowest is the Watershed with an average time per patient of 10 min 34 s due to an excessively slow initialization.

The absence of articles dealing with the radiomics features extraction of the district affected by this physiological condition has meant that the information has been drawn from articles that treat the prostate with the presence of cancer. This choice is made possible by the fact that the enlargement can lead to the tumor; therefore, in a predictive key, it is possible to use that same setting.

With the statistical analysis, it has been obtained that the Fill between slices algorithm has only 24 features out of 85 (equal to 28.23%) which vary significantly from a statistical point of view compared to the same ones extracted from the medical physicians' segmentation, followed by the Threshold with 36 (42.35%), to then arrive at four algorithms that are not at all reliable since they have a difference of around 70%: Clever Segmentation (69.41%), Grow from seeds (70.58%), Watershed (71.76%) and Fast Marching (72.94%). The manual algorithm we used showed only 1 feature different from that of the medical physicians (Minimum), demonstrating that the standard algorithm of the district remains the one based on a priori knowledge of the organ by the operator. Furthermore, it was decided to evaluate the reliability of the various extracted features by measuring the ratio between the variability of the interest group (that given by the algorithms) divided by the total one (given by algorithms, patients, and error). Only three features are unreliable and are the shape feature Sphericity with ICC = 0.159 (low reliability), the shape feature SurfaceVolumeRatio with ICC = 0.611 (moderate reliability) and the statistical feature Minimum with ICC = 0.599 (moderate reliability).

Finally, the morpho-volumetric analysis, carried out starting from obtaining the binary masks of each segmentation, demonstrated how from a purely volumetric point of view all the algorithms are very faithful to the reference segmentation.

Therefore, the best algorithm to support the medical physician's work, since it is faster and with the greatest number of invariant features, is the Fill between slices. On the other hand, algorithms based on the similarity of gray levels are not at all reliable in a district like that of the prostate that has too many gray levels.

This work will be the basis for the creation of a model that allows to predict the possible development of a tumor mass in the prostate organ of patients suffering from a physiological condition of the prostate median lobe enlargement. Deep learning methods will be also considered [22, 23].

References

1. Mobley, D., Feibus, A., Baum, N.: Benign prostatic hyperplasia and urinary symptoms: evaluation and treatment. Postgrad. Med. **127**, 301–307 (2015). https://doi.org/10.1080/00325481.2015.1018799
2. Mitterbergera, M., et al.: Ultrasound of the prostate. Cancer Imaging **10**, 40–48 (2010). https://doi.org/10.1102/1470-7330.2010.0004
3. Ghose, S., et al.: A survey of prostate segmentation methodologies in ultrasound, magnetic resonance and computed tomography images. Comput. Methods Programs Biomed. (2012). https://doi.org/10.1016/j.cmpb.2012.04.006
4. Jue, J.S., et al.: Re-examining prostate-specific antigen (PSA) density: defining the optimal PSA range and patients for using PSA density to predict prostate cancer using extended template biopsy. Urology **105**, 123–128 (2017). https://doi.org/10.1016/j.urology.2017.04.015
5. EAU Pocket Guidelines. Edn. Present. EAU Annu. Congr. Amsterdam (2022)
6. Cutaia, G., et al.: Radiomics and prostate MRI: current role and future applications. J. Imaging **7**, 34 (2021). https://doi.org/10.3390/jimaging7020034

7. Barone, S., et al.: Hybrid descriptive-inferential method for key feature selection in prostate cancer radiomics. Appl. Stoch. Model. Bus. Ind. **37**, 961–972 (2021). https://doi.org/10.1002/asmb.2642

8. Cuocolo, R., et al.: Machine learning applications in prostate cancer magnetic resonance imaging. Eur. Radiol. Exp. **3**, 35 (2019). https://doi.org/10.1186/s41747-019-0109-2

9. Schwier, M., et al.: Repeatability of multiparametric prostate MRI radiomics features. Sci. Rep. **9**, 1–16 (2019). https://doi.org/10.1038/s41598-019-45766-z

10. Alongi, P., et al.: Choline PET/CT features to predict survival outcome in high risk prostate cancer restaging: a preliminary machine-learning radiomics study. Q. J. Nucl. Med. Mol. Imaging (2020). https://doi.org/10.23736/s1824-4785.20.03227-6

11. Alongi, P., et al.: Radiomics analysis of 18F-Choline PET/CT in the prediction of disease outcome in high-risk prostate cancer: an explorative study on machine learning feature classification in 94 patients. Eur. Radiol. **31**(7), 4595–4605 (2021). https://doi.org/10.1007/s00330-020-07617-8

12. Cuocolo, R., et al.: Deep learning whole-gland and zonal prostate segmentation on a public MRI dataset. J. Magn. Reson. Imaging **54**, 452–459 (2021). https://doi.org/10.1002/jmri.27585

13. Comelli, A., et al.: Deep learning-based methods for prostate segmentation in magnetic resonance imaging. Appl. Sci. **11**, 1–13 (2021). https://doi.org/10.3390/app11020782

14. Salvaggio, G., et al.: Deep learning network for segmentation of the prostate gland with median lobe enlargement in T2-weighted MR images: comparison with manual segmentation method. Curr. Probl. Diagn. Radiol. (2021). https://doi.org/10.1067/j.cpradiol.2021.06.006

15. Chevrefils, C., Chériet, F., Grimard, G., Aubin, C.-E.: Watershed segmentation of intervertebral disk and spinal canal from MRI images. In: Kamel, M., Campilho, A. (eds.) ICIAR 2007. LNCS, vol. 4633, pp. 1017–1027. Springer, Heidelberg (2007). https://doi.org/10.1007/978-3-540-74260-9_90

16. Turkbey, B., et al.: Prostate imaging reporting and data system version 2.1: 2019 update of prostate imaging reporting and data system version 2. Eur. Urol. **76**, 340–351 (2019). https://doi.org/10.1016/J.EURURO.2019.02.033

17. Stanzione, A., et al.: Prostate volume estimation on MRI: accuracy and effects of ellipsoid and bullet-shaped measurements on PSA density. Acad. Radiol. (2020). https://doi.org/10.1016/j.acra.2020.05.014

18. Cuocolo, R., et al.: Clinically significant prostate cancer detection on MRI: a radiomic shape features study. Eur. J. Radiol. **116**, 144–149 (2019). https://doi.org/10.1016/j.ejrad.2019.05.006

19. Stefano, A., et al.: Performance of radiomics features in the quantification of idiopathic pulmonary fibrosis from HRCT. Diagnostics **10**, 306 (2020). https://doi.org/10.3390/diagnostics10050306

20. Russo, G., et al.: Feasibility on the use of radiomics features of 11[C]-MET PET/CT in central nervous system tumours: preliminary results on potential grading discrimination using a machine learning model. Curr. Oncol. **28**, 5318–5331 (2021). https://doi.org/10.3390/curroncol28060444

21. Stefano, A., et al.: Robustness of pet radiomics features: Impact of co-registration with mri. Appl. Sci. **11**, 10170 (2021). https://doi.org/10.3390/app112110170

22. Stefano, A., Comelli, A.: Customized efficient neural network for covid-19 infected region identification in ct images. J. Imaging **7**, 131 (2021). https://doi.org/10.3390/jimaging7080131

23. Salvaggio, G., et al.: deep learning networks for automatic retroperitoneal sarcoma segmentation in computerized tomography. Appl. Sci. **12**, 1665 (2022). https://doi.org/10.3390/app12031665

Deep-Learning and High Performance Computing to Boost Biomedical Applications - DeepHealth

Fast Learning Framework for Denoising of Ultrasound 2D Videos and 3D Images

Simone Cammarasana[1]([✉]) [ID], Paolo Nicolardi[2], and Giuseppe Patané[1] [ID]

[1] CNR-IMATI, Via De Marini 6, Genova 16149, Italy
simone.cammarasana@ge.imati.cnr.it
[2] Esaote S.p.A, Via E. Melen 77, Genova, Italy

Abstract. Ultrasound signals are widespread in medical diagnosis for muscle-skeletal, cardiac, and obstetrical diseases, due to the efficiency and non-invasiveness of the acquisition methodology. However, ultrasound acquisition introduces noise in the signal, which corrupts the reconstructed image and affects further processing steps, e.g., segmentation, quantitative analysis. We define a novel deep learning framework for the real-time denoising of ultrasound signals. Our framework replicates denoising algorithms that exploit spatiotemporal redundancy of the input signals (e.g., 2D videos, 3D images). The HPC implementation allows us to learn dedicated networks for different input signals and anatomical districts. Finally, our approach is general in terms of its building blocks and parameters of the deep learning and high-performance computing frameworks, i.e., we can select different denoising algorithms and deep learning architectures.

Keywords: US signals · Signals denoise · Real-time denoise · High-performance computing · Deep-learning framework

1 Introduction

Ultrasound (US, for short) *imaging* uses high-frequency sound waves to visualise soft tissues, such as internal organs, and to support the diagnosis of patients' diseases, due to the efficiency, cheapness, and non-invasiveness of the US acquisition. US images can be acquired at different planes, through the manual/automatic movement of the probe; furthermore, the physician can acquire both static and dynamic images. These acquisitions are associated with different input signals: 2D images, 2D videos, and 3D volumetric images. Each of these types of signals has its properties and advantages: dynamic 2D US images (i.e., videos) allow the physician to analyse the temporal variation of an anatomical feature (e.g., the movement of a muscle, the volume of the ventricle). This variation can be generated either by the shift of the probe or by the movement of the anatomical part. 3D volumetric images offer a full understanding of the spatial anatomy of the acquired region, against a more expensive tool for the acquisition

© The Author(s), under exclusive license to Springer Nature Switzerland AG 2022
P. L. Mazzeo et al. (Eds.): ICIAP 2022 Workshops, LNCS 13373, pp. 475–486, 2022.
https://doi.org/10.1007/978-3-031-13321-3_42

(e.g., automatic 3D probes). US 2D images are simple to acquire and process, but they offer a limited view of the anatomical part of interest.

In this context, our goal is the development of a fast learning framework for denoising of ultrasound 2D videos and 3D images (Sect. 2). The proposed framework is based on the training of a neural network to learn and replicate the behaviour of the denoising algorithms (e.g., BM4D, Vidosat). Then, an image-to-image architecture learns to predict images, which has been denoised through an algorithm that exploits the properties of the signal (e.g., temporal/spatial redundancy). With this approach, we use a standard learning architecture, still exploiting the characteristics of the denoising algorithm. We also avoid the use of more complex architectures (e.g., spatiotemporal networks), and we avoid managing videos with different lengths for the training of the network. We specialise the training phase to specific anatomical districts and input signals. The real-time computation depends only on the execution time of the network prediction. As the main contribution, the proposed framework is general in terms of the input data (e.g., 3D images, time-dependent US videos), type of noise (e.g., speckle, Gaussian noise), resolution (e.g., isotropic, anisotropic) of the input signals, acquisition methodology, and anatomical district (Sect. 3). Our focus is the description of the pipeline, learning-based and HPC tools, rather than the implementation/user interface. Nevertheless, the proposed pipeline is replicable, subject to the availability of US data and adequate computing resources. For further details on the tests, we refer the reader to the video available at the URL: https://www.dropbox.com/s/27rdwez8dibwdxa/ICIAP21-HPC-3D-2DT. mp4?dl=0

2   Learning and HPC Framework for Real-Time US Denoising

Biomedical data include 2D videos of different anatomical districts (e.g., abdominal, cardiac, and obstetrical) and volumetric 3D images. 2D videos are acquired through 2D probes, which capture sequences of images at a given frequency. The resolution of the images is affected by the acquisition frequency of the video since some anatomical districts (e.g., cardiac) require a high frequency to better analyse the behaviour of anatomical features that quickly change during time. Through the probe oscillation within a given range, equally spaced slices are acquired and stacked into the 3D volume; volumetric images are intrinsically anisotropic, due to the different resolution of each slice, with respect to the resolution of the probe in its movement direction. We encode *2D images* as $m \times n$ matrices, *2D videos* as $m \times n \times t$ tensors, where each frame has a $m \times n$ resolution, and t frames are acquired. We represent *3D (volumetric) images* as $m \times n \times p$ tensors, where p planes are acquired, and each plane has a $m \times n$ resolution. We review previous work on image denoising (Sect. 2.1), introduce the proposed learning and HPC framework for real-time denoising of US 2D videos and volumetric images (Sect. 2.2), and discuss the experimental results (Sect. 2.3).

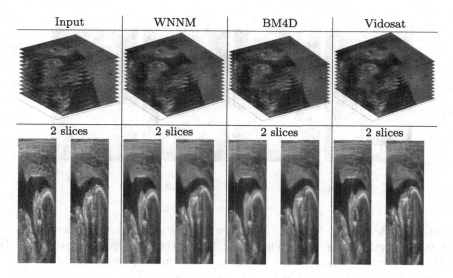

Fig. 1. Denoising of US volumetric image $408 \times 120 \times 36$ of the obstetric district.

2.1 Previous Work

2D denoising generally applies sparse transformations (e.g., *Block-Matching 3D - BM3D* [6]), low-rank approximations (e.g., *Low Rank Matrix Factorization - LRMF* [13]), deep-learning (*Block Matching-Convolutional Neural Network - BM-CNN* [3]). The extension *Block Matching 4D* (BM4D) [16] of the BM3D algorithm to volumetric images exploits grouping and collaborative filters, where similar voxels are stacked together into 4D groups. A variant of non-local means denoising to 3D biomedical images [17] takes into account the spatially varying noise levels across the volumetric data, and automatically adjusts the strength of the filter, through a noise estimation approach. The K-SVD algorithm [2] represents the signal as a sparse linear combination of atoms from an over-complete dictionary; the atoms are iteratively updated through an SVD of the representation error, to better fit the data. A 3D blockwise version of the non-local means filter with wavelet sub-bands [5] is applied to biomedical images. A learning-based method is applied to denoise 3D biomedical data [18], through a residual encoder-decoder Wasserstein generative adversarial network.

Vidosat [23] applies online transform learning to 2D video denoising; the patches are computed either from corresponding 2D patches in successive frames or using an online block matching technique, fully exploiting the spatio-temporal data correlation. In VBM3D [15], 3D spatio-temporal volumes are constructed by tracking blocks along trajectories, which are defined by the motion vectors. Then, the denoising of the blocks is achieved through collaborative filtering, by transforming each block through a decorrelating 4-D separable transform; finally, the shrinkage and inverse transformation generate the denoised output. The formulation of the denoising of mixed noise as a low-rank matrix completion

Raw   BM4D   Vidosat   WNNM

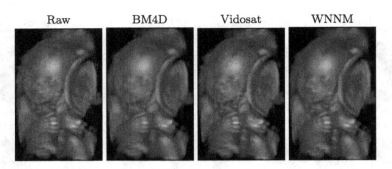

Fig. 2. Ray-casting [20] rendering of Fig. 1

problem [11] leads to a denoising scheme without strong assumptions on the statistical properties of the noise. The application of the non-separable oriented 3-D dual-tree wavelet transformation [21] gives a motion-based multi-scale decomposition for video and isolates in its sub-bands motion along with different directions. Among state-of-the-art methods, we select three denoising methods: 2D-based method (e.g., *Weighted Nuclear Norm Minimisation* - WNNM [7]), 3D-based method (BM4D), and Vidosat. In particular, 2D and volumetric methods (i.e., WNNM, BM4D) account for the spatial relationship among patches, to exploit data similarity and remove the noise component. In contrast, video denoising (e.g., Vidosat) exploits both the spatial and the temporal dimensions of the data. Our framework is general with respect to the denoising algorithm, which generates the target images, by exploiting spatio-temporal features of the signal. Each of the algorithms in the related work is applicable for the generation of the target images and the training of the corresponding learning model. The selection of the proper algorithm depends on the preferences of the user/the application.

2.2   Proposed Denoising Framework

The main requirements of a denoising algorithm for US signals are the magnitude of the removed noise, edge preservation, and real-time computation. The proposed framework satisfies these requirements, except for the execution time, which does not satisfy the real-time need of US applications. To achieve a real-time computation and maintain good results in terms of denoising and edges preservation, we design and implement a deep learning framework that exploits HPC and replicates the proposed denoising algorithms.

Proposed Framework. Our framework is based on the training of a neural network to learn and replicate the behaviour of the denoising algorithms. In the first phase, the denoising of different input signals is performed through dedicated algorithms (e.g., BM4D, Vidosat) which exploits the spatiotemporal reduncancy. Then, the network is trained on a collection of pairs of US images: the input (i.e., the raw image) and the target (i.e., the image denoised with the proper filter).

(a) Ground truth - frame 6 (b) Ground truth - frame 129

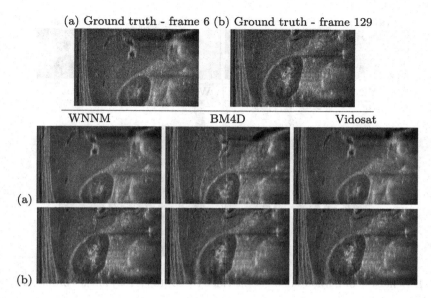

Fig. 3. Denoising of 2 frames of a 2D US video (560 × 359 × 256) of the abdomen.

We train a specific network for each district, thus obtaining a more precise result when predicting the denoised image, as each network is specialised to the input anatomical features. Furthermore, images from different input signals (e.g., 2D videos, 3D images) are used to train specific networks. The real-time denoising depends only on the execution time of the network prediction.

Our framework is general with respect to the learning architecture. We select *Pix2Pix* [10], an image-to-image *Generative Adversarial Network* (GAN), where the generator is a U-net [19], the discriminator is an encoding network [14], and the loss function is based on the binary cross-entropy. To implement a parallel and distributed framework in TensorFlow2, we define an HPC implementation of the selected learning network, taking advantage of a large US data set, and of the CINECA-Marconi100 cluster [1], exploiting both CPUs (IBM POWER9 AC922) and GPUs (NVIDIA Volta V100). Through the proposed HPC framework, we train multiple networks with large data sets in a reasonable time for the target medical application, thus increasing the specialisation to anatomical districts and input signals, and consequently the accuracy of the deep learning framework.

2.3 Experimental Results

2D Denoising Methods. WNNM is natively applicable to 2D images, and it is applied to 2D videos, through frame-by-frame denoising, and to 3D volumetric images, through slice-by-slice denoising. The application of WNNM to 2D videos/3D images does not exploit any knowledge of the temporal/spatial redundancy of the signal.

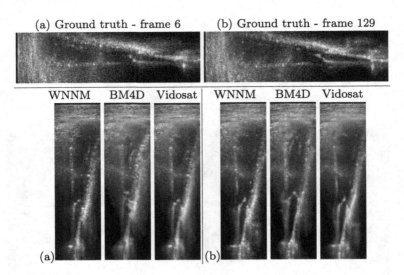

Fig. 4. Denoising of 2 frames of a 2D US video ($592 \times 168 \times 233$) of the cardiac district.

3D Volumetric Denoising Methods. BM4D is natively applicable to 3D volumetric images, which will be applied to 2D videos; in this case, the temporal dimension is assumed as the third dimension of the volumetric data. We follow two main approaches; given a 2D video $m \times n \times t$, where $m \times n$ is the resolution of a single frame, and t is the number of frames, BM4D can be applied to

- the full video: in this case, the $m \times n \times t$ tensor is the input video and the output is a tensor representing the smoothed video;
- consecutive portions of the video: in this case, the smoothing of each frame t_i is performed through the denoising of the tensor $m \times n \times 2k$, where 2k is the interval of frames centred in i, from $i - k$ to $i + k$. This procedure is repeated starting from the frame k, for each frame of the video, i.e., $t - k$ times.

2D Video Denoising Methods. Vidosat is natively applicable to 2D videos but can be applied to volumetric images, by considering the third spatial dimension as the temporal dimension of dynamic data. Both full video and consecutive portions (i.e., blocks of frames) can be considered as input of the denoising algorithm.

Denoising Results on US Signals. Figure 1 shows the denoising results of WNNM, BM4D, and Vidosat, with *US volumetric images*. Analysing the images sectioned in the slice direction, WNNM and BM4D have better results in terms of noise removal and anatomical features preservation, while Vidosat has a slight scattering effect. To integrate this evaluation, we apply a ray-casting algorithm [20] to visualise a 2D rendering of the volumetric data (Fig. 2). This visualisation allows us to better analyse the consistency among slices; in fact,

(a) Ground truth - frame 6 (b) Ground truth - frame 129

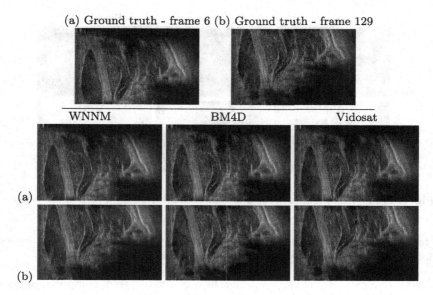

Fig. 5. Denoising of 2 frames of a US video (600 × 380 × 155) of the muscle-skeletal district.

BM4D has a smoother rendering than WNNM, which is affected by a scattering effect, due to the phase shift between adjacent slices. Finally, Vidosat rendering is affected by the lower noise removal and BM4D has the best results on denoising 3D volumetric images, in terms of noise removal, anatomical features preservation, and slices consistency. Figures 3, 4, and 5 show the denoising results on *2D videos*, on different anatomical districts: abdominal, cardiac, muscle-skeletal. We select the window-moving version of BM4D, WNNM is applied *frame by frame*, and Vidosat is applied on the whole 2D video. Vidosat shows the best results in terms of noise removal and anatomical features preservation; also, the blurring effect is barely present. WNNM is not affected by blurring effects, since it is applied frame by frame. However, the noise reduction of WNNM is lower than BM4D and Vidosat, since WNNM does not exploit any knowledge among consecutive frames. BM4D has a higher blurring effect and a lower noise reduction than Vidosat. Indeed, we select BM4D and Vidosat for generating the target images from 3D images and 2D videos, respectively.

Framework Prediction. Our learning-based framework allows us to predict the denoised output of a 2D video (Fig. 6), and a 3D image (Fig. 7). In both cases, the predicted image is very similar to the target image; the output appears smooth, still preserving anatomic features and edges. The predicted images do not present any artefacts or blurring effects. The smoothing intensity depends on the target images in the training data set; images with higher smoothing generate a network that learns higher denoising of the input image. Furthermore,

Input   Target   Prediction

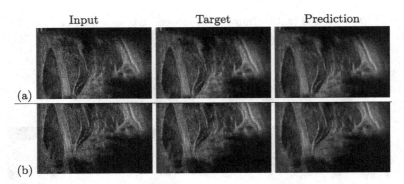

Fig. 6. Framework prediction for 2 muscle-skeletal frames (a, b) of a 2D video.

our framework allows the user to train several networks with a different level of smoothing and to select the preferred output among different choices.

Quantitative Error. Table 1 summarises the quantitative error computed between the target and the predicted images, for different signals (e.g., 2D videos, 3D images) and anatomical districts (e.g., obstetric, cardiac), and measured through the Peak Signal-to-Noise Ratio (PSNR) and Structural Similarity Index Measure (SSIM) metrics. The Peak Signal-to-Noise Ratio (PSNR) measures the Mean Squared Error (MSE) through a logarithmic scale; the Structural Similarity Index Measure (SSIM) measures the perceived similarity of two images, calculated on different windows. Given two identical images, the PSNR and SSIM values are equal to $+\infty$ and 1, respectively. Images extracted from volumetric data and 2D videos are used to train separated networks. Each network is specific for an anatomical district (e.g., obstetric, cardiac). The selection of the anatomical regions depends on different parameters: the type of probe, the acquisition modality, the quantitative/qualitative analysis (e.g., segmentation, morphological evaluation), the post-processing algorithms. Furthermore, different anatomical districts lead to different types of signals: for example, in the cardiac district, the movement of the cardiac valve is acquired by the probe, while in the abdominal district, the movement of the probe is performed by the physician. The experimental results show that our framework can correctly denoise the signal through an image-to-image prediction, for both 3D images and 2D videos. For example, the prediction of obstetric 3D images shows an average PSNR value of 33.15, while the prediction of cardiac videos shows an average PSNR value of 34.62. According to [4], the specialisation of the learning model for different anatomical districts allows us to improve the prediction results on 2D images.

Execution Time and Computational Cost. Table 2 shows the *execution time* of the denoising methods, with different data set (i.e., 2D video, volumetric image). BM4D is the fastest method, taking 75 s for processing a $408 \times 120 \times 36$ volumetric image, while Vidosat and WNNM take 161 and 1260 s, respectively. None of these methods reaches the real-time requirement for denoising.

Input		Target		Prediction	
(a)	(b)	(a)	(b)	(a)	(b)

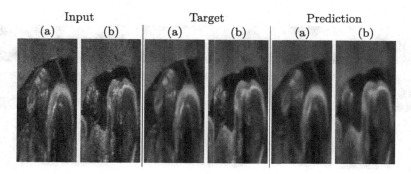

Fig. 7. Framework prediction for two slices (a, b) of a 3D image of the obstetric district.

Table 1. PSNR and SSIM metrics computed between the target and the prediction image, as average value among the 20 signals of each test data set: muscle-skeletal videos (Msk.), cardiac videos (Card.), obstetric 3D images (Ob.).

Signal	Msk.	Card.	Ob.
PSNR	28.12	34.62	33.15
SSIM	0.963	0.978	0.970

The analysis of the execution time of the framework is divided into an *offline training* and an *online prediction*. To test the training phase of the deep learning framework on the HPC implementation (Sect. 2.2), we exploit 8 nodes, each one composed of 32 cores and 4 accelerators, for a theoretical computational performance of 260 TFLOPS, and 220 GB of memory per node. The parallel implementation of the deep learning framework reduces the computation time of the training phase by at least 100 orders of magnitude compared to a serial implementation on a standard workstation, with an average execution time of less than 0.1 s per epoch on a single image, i.e., about 2 h on a data set of 500 images, with 150 epochs. For the volumetric data set, we use 15 3D images composed of 36 stacks, for a total amount of 540 2D images. For the video data set, we use several videos of different lengths for each anatomical district; we train each network with a minimum amount of 500 2D images. All the images/videos are part of the private Esaote S.p.A. data set.

The execution time of the prediction is crucial for the real-time implementation of our framework. We test the denoising prediction on GPU-based hardware, which replicates the hardware of a US scanner currently in use. Given a set of US images from different districts, the average execution time is 25 ms per image, thus confirming their real-time computation. The proposed method allows the user to denoise each image during the acquisition of the video/volumetric signal since the spatio-temporal information is not required. For this reason, the execution time is about 25 ms per frame/stack, but its computation is contemporary to the acquisition of the subsequent frames/stacks. We underline that the input

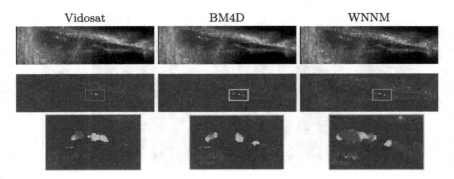

Fig. 8. Displacement analysis of the mitral valve in the cardiac district: optical flow (1st row), optical magnitude (2nd row), magnitude magnification (3rd row). The denoising through specific algorithms allows us different characterizations of the morphological features of the anatomical part.

Table 2. With reference to the tests in Figs. 1 and 5, we report the execution time of the denoising methods tested on 2D video and volumetric data.

Method	WNNM	BM4D	Vidosat
2D video [s]	26820	1506	3338
3D image [s]	1260	75	161

resolution of the network is 600×600, which is reached through the zero-padding of each input image. The computational cost of the prediction depends on the resolution of the input image and on the architecture of the network: in particular, the computational cost of a convolution operation is $\mathcal{O}(r/s_r \cdot c/s_c) \cdot (f_r \cdot f_c) \cdot f$; in our application, the input image has a resolution of $r = c = 600$, the kernel-filter size on rows and columns is $f_r = f_c = 4$, the stride on rows and columns is $s_r = s_c = 2$, we use 10 convolution and 10 deconvolution operators, and a number of kernel-filters from 32 to 512.

3   Discussion and Conclusions

Denoising of US images is relevant both for post-processing and visual evaluation by medical experts. Several works show the benefits of denoising for *segmentation* [24], *feature extraction* [9], *classification* [22], and *super-resolution* [12]. For example, we analyse the optical flow [8] of US videos, by evaluating the movement of relevant anatomical features. Figure 8 shows that the denoising through Vidosat and BM4D allows us to improve the characterisation of the movement of the mitral valve, and to better estimate its movement during the opening/closing phases. In US denoising, the main goal is to achieve the best compromise between noise removal, features preservation, and real-time execution. The use of deep learning allows us to reach real-time performance, which is required by the clinical practice while preserving the denoising results of state-of-the-art methods, which are time-consuming.

We analyse the results of different denoising methods, applied to US 2D videos and 3D volumetric data. The application of a 2D method (e.g., WNNM) does not allow us to reach good results in terms of denoising, and consistency among consecutive frames/slices. From our analysis, a volumetric-based denoising method (i.e., BM4D) has the best results when applied to volumetric data, and a video-based denoising method (i.e., Vidosat) has the best results when applied to 2D videos, as expected. This result confirms that these methods keep their performance/applicability when used with US data. Then, our framework allows us to tune the denoising algorithm to obtain the best denoising results, as this tuning only affects the training phase, while the real-time computation of the denoised image is performed through the prediction of the network. Our framework allows us to replicate in real-time the denoising results of the denoising algorithms, according to the property of the input signal and the anatomic district. The HPC allows us to train multiple networks for different districts and input signals, and to use large data set of images. As future work, we plan to evaluate specific learning-based networks for different types of signal (e.g., video-to-video network). Furthermore, we plan to further validate the denoising results through the perceptual evaluation of physicians.

Acknowledgements. We thank the Reviewers for their constructive comments, which helped us to improve the presentation of the paper. This research is partially carried out as part of an Industrial PhD project funded by CNR-IMATI and Esaote S.p.A. Tests on CINECA Cluster are supported by the ISCRA-C Project HP10CVHIXD.

References

1. Cineca marconi100. https://www.top500.org/system/179845/. Accessed 20 Apr 2022
2. Aharon, M., Elad, M., Bruckstein, A.: K-SVD: an algorithm for designing overcomplete dictionaries for sparse representation. IEEE Trans. Signal Process. **54**(11), 4311–4322 (2006)
3. Ahn, B., Cho, N.I.: Block-matching convolutional neural network for image denoising. arXiv:1704.00524 (2017)
4. Cammarasana, S., Nicolardi, P., Patanè, G.: A universal deep learning framework for real-time denoising of ultrasound images. arXiv preprint arXiv:2101.09122 (2021)
5. Coupé, P., Hellier, P., Prima, S., Kervrann, C., Barillot, C.: 3D wavelet subbands mixing for image denoising. Int. J. Biomed. Imaging 2008 (2008)
6. Dabov, K., Foi, A., Katkovnik, V., Egiazarian, K.: Image denoising with block-matching and 3D filtering. In: Image Processing: Algorithms and Systems, Neural Networks, and Machine Learning, vol. 6064, p. 606414 (2006)
7. Gu, S., Zhang, L., Zuo, W., Feng, X.: Weighted nuclear norm minimization with application to image denoising. In: Proceedings of the IEEE Conference on Computer Vision and Pattern Recognition, pp. 2862–2869 (2014)
8. Horn, B.K., Schunck, B.G.: Determining optical flow. Artif. Intell. **17**(1–3), 185–203 (1981)

9. Iakovidis, D.K., Keramidas, E.G., Maroulis, D.: Fuzzy local binary patterns for ultrasound texture characterization. In: Campilho, A., Kamel, M. (eds.) ICIAR 2008. LNCS, vol. 5112, pp. 750–759. Springer, Heidelberg (2008). https://doi.org/10.1007/978-3-540-69812-8_74

10. Isola, P., Zhu, J.Y., Zhou, T., Efros, A.A.: Image-to-image translation with conditional adversarial networks. In: Conference on Computer Vision and Pattern Recognition, pp. 1125–1134 (2017)

11. Ji, H., Liu, C., Shen, Z., Xu, Y.: Robust video denoising using low rank matrix completion. In: 2010 IEEE Computer Society Conference on Computer Vision and Pattern Recognition, pp. 1791–1798. IEEE (2010)

12. Khavari, P., Asif, A., Rivaz, H.: Non-local super resolution in ultrasound imaging. In: 20th International Workshop on Multimedia Signal Processing (MMSP), pp. 1–6. IEEE (2018)

13. Kishore Kumar, N., Schneider, J.: Literature survey on low rank approximation of matrices. Linear Multilinear Algebra 65(11), 2212–2244 (2017)

14. Krizhevsky, A., Sutskever, I., Hinton, G.E.: Imagenet classification with deep convolutional neural networks. In: Advances in Neural Information Processing Systems, pp. 1097–1105 (2012)

15. Maggioni, M., Boracchi, G., Foi, A., Egiazarian, K.: Video denoising, deblocking, and enhancement through separable 4-d nonlocal spatiotemporal transforms. IEEE Trans. Image Process. 21(9), 3952–3966 (2012)

16. Maggioni, M., Katkovnik, V., Egiazarian, K., Foi, A.: Nonlocal transform-domain filter for volumetric data denoising and reconstruction. IEEE Trans. Image Process. 22(1), 119–133 (2012)

17. Manjón, J.V., Coupé, P., Martí-Bonmatí, L., Collins, D.L., Robles, M.: Adaptive non-local means denoising of MR images with spatially varying noise levels. J. Magn. Reson. Imaging 31(1), 192–203 (2010)

18. Ran, M., et al.: Denoising of 3D magnetic resonance images using a residual encoder-decoder Wasserstein generative adversarial network. Med. Image Anal. 55, 165–180 (2019)

19. Ronneberger, O., Fischer, P., Brox, T.: U-Net: convolutional networks for biomedical image segmentation. In: Navab, N., Hornegger, J., Wells, W.M., Frangi, A.F. (eds.) MICCAI 2015. LNCS, vol. 9351, pp. 234–241. Springer, Cham (2015). https://doi.org/10.1007/978-3-319-24574-4_28

20. Roth, S.D.: Ray casting for modeling solids. Comput. Graphics Image Process. 18(2), 109–144 (1982)

21. Selesnick, I.W., Li, K.Y.: Video denoising using 2d and 3d dual-tree complex wavelet transforms. In: Wavelets: Applications in Signal and Image Processing X, vol. 5207, pp. 607–618. International Society for Optics and Photonics (2003)

22. Wei, M., et al.: A benign and malignant breast tumor classification method via efficiently combining texture and morphological features on ultrasound images. Comput. Math. Meth. Med. 2020 (2020)

23. Wen, B., Ravishankar, S., Bresler, Y.: VIDOSAT: High-dimensional sparsifying transform learning for online video denoising. IEEE Trans. Image Process. 28(4), 1691–1704 (2018)

24. Yang, F., Qin, W., Xie, Y., Wen, T., Gu, J.: A shape-optimized framework for kidney segmentation in ultrasound images using NLTV denoising and DRLSE. Biomed. Eng. Online 11(1), 1–13 (2012)

Lung Nodules Segmentation with DeepHealth Toolkit

Hafiza Ayesha Hoor Chaudhry[1]([✉]) , Riccardo Renzulli[1] , Daniele Perlo[2] ,
Francesca Santinelli[3], Stefano Tibaldi[3] , Carmen Cristiano[3], Marco Grosso[3] ,
Attilio Fiandrotti[1] , Maurizio Lucenteforte[1] , and Davide Cavagnino[1]

[1] University of Turin, Turin, Italy
hafizaayeshahoor.chaudhry@unito.it
[2] Fondazione Ricerca Molinette Onlus, Turin, Italy
[3] Città della Salute e della Scienza di Torino, Turin, Italy

Abstract. The accurate and consistent border segmentation plays an
important role in the tumor volume estimation and its treatment in the
field of Medical Image Segmentation. Globally, Lung cancer is one of
the leading causes of death and the early detection of lung nodules is
essential for the early cancer diagnosis and survival rate of patients. The
goal of this study was to demonstrate the feasibility of Deephealth toolkit
including PyECVL and PyEDDL libraries to precisely segment lung nodules. Experiments for lung nodules segmentation has been carried out on
UniToChest using PyECVL and PyEDDL, for data pre-processing as
well as neural network training. The results depict accurate segmentation of lung nodules across a wide diameter range and better accuracy
over a traditional detection approach. The datasets and the code used
in this paper are publicly available as a baseline reference.

Keywords: Medical image segmentation · Deep learning · U-Net ·
Dataset · Chest CT scan · Lung nodules · DeepHealth

1 Introduction and Background

Lung cancer has surpassed breast and prostate cancer, and has become the leading cause of death for men and women in 2021 [22]. Medical Imaging plays a
crucial part in the early detection and proper monitoring of cancer patients [11].
Traditionally, a thoracic *Computed Tomography* (CT) scan of the lungs is performed first, which produces high resolution images of the chest structures [18].
Due to the level of detail, great image quality and clear resolution CT scans have
become the most popular choice to visualize lung nodules [24]. National Lung
Screening Trial (NLST) has also conducted a study that shows the decrease
in mortality rate of the lung cancer patients by screening with low-dose CT
(LDCT), hence emphasising the role of medical imaging in the recovery process
[1,23].

P. L. Mazzeo et al. (Eds.): ICIAP 2022 Workshops, LNCS 13373, pp. 487–497, 2022.
https://doi.org/10.1007/978-3-031-13321-3_43

Automated Lung Nodule segmentation done using CT scans could pass essential information to the *Computer-Aided Diagnosis* (CAD) employed for lung cancer diagnosis. A robust lung segmentation method could save the time taken by manual nodule analysis and also remove the inter-observer variability found in many studies [15]. Several CAD systems based on traditional or deep learning image processing techniques have been proposed over the last decade for the detection and segmentation of lung nodules [12,13,25]. The variations in size and shape of the nodules, the patients' gender and age, the imaging device model and brand, and the resemblance between the nodules and their surroundings make this a challenging problem.

After the detection of lung nodules using medical imaging, the protocol is to have regular follow-up scans from 3 to 12 months, to monitor the growth rate of nodules [14]. To avoid the over diagnosing and to deal with slow growing cancer, the protocols have set the tumor doubling time as an indicator for malignant nodules [10,20]. To access the tumor response, Response Evaluation Criteria in Solid Tumors (RECIST) is used as a standard, that focuses on the diameter measurement of tumor in uni-direction and linearly [8]. There is a lot of work being done in developing accurate and consistent segmentations of lung tumors for the purpose of response assessment, tumor diagnosis, and staging, which can result in giving linear and volumetric assessments of the tumor size, shape and the tumor change rates.

The largest European lung cancer trail, Nederlands Leuvens Longkanker Screenings Onderzoek (NELSON) trial, focuses on predicting the risk of malignancy in lung nodules. Currently, there are various segmentation algorithms that are automated or semi-automated working on segmentation, detection and classification of lung nodules, but it's difficult to analyse and inter-compare the robustness of them all. A study was conducted using NELSON's data and three different software systems for the malignancy risk assessment task. These systems calculated different tumor doubling time and the results conclude that due to this variation the classification of lung nodules is affected [26].

New lung segmentation algorithms based on learning methods are introduced periodically. Hence there is a dire need of a platform where the user can access different deep learning and computer vision algorithms, analyse them and use them off-the-shelf. This is where our contribution comes in: here we introduce Deephealth toolkit, a complete deep learning and computer vision solution that can be easily used by all developers, includes most commonly available deep learning and computer vision algorithms and provides easy integration of data between them. It also has its own visualisation and image editing tools, therefore providing support from data pre-processing to network fine-tuning.

2   DeepHealth Toolkit (DHt)

Owing to the success of *Artificial Intelligence* (AI) and learning-based methods in the health sector, The European Union is funding AI based projects to cater to this challenging field. Deephealth [5,16] is a health-centered project, part of this effort, that aims to do large-scale experimental research using AI. For this purpose multiple large-scale open access datasets are gathered, UniToChest [17] is one them [2,9,17].

The DeepHealth toolkit (DHt) is the framework of Deephealth that is developed to provide one platform for easy deployment of Deep Learning and Computer Vision applications [3]. It uses High Performance Computing, Big Data and Cloud Computing for providing off the shelf services for all Image Processing related tasks. The Deephealth toolkit consists of European Computer Vision Library (ECVL), European Distributed Deep Learning Library (EDDL), and a front-end interface. In this paper we have used EDDL and ECVL to train deep learning network on UniToChest dataset.

2.1   ECVL

The European Computer Vision Library (ECVL) is a general purpose library that is Image centered. It supports basic functionalities like Image read/write, Image manipulation, integration, parallel image augmentation to advance features like dataset parsing and batch creation. The main objective of ECVL is to provide integration and data exchange between existing Computer Vision (CV), Image processing libraries, and EDDL. Different operating systems including Windows, Mac, and Linux are supported on ECVL. The ECVL contains generic algorithms employed with the Deep Learning library. The Image class in ECVL has a generic tensor model and provides an Hardware Abstraction Layer (HAL) allowing it to run on GPU and FGPU. It also has Memory Management flexibility support for different devices. Moreover, there is also a Visualiser for 3D volumes like CT scan slices in ECVL. The user can observe different slices from various views using this visualizer. A basic Image Editor also comes with ECVL, including functionalities like brightness and contrast adjustment, rotation, flipping, etc. The programming language of ECVL is C++ but a Python version is also developed using a wrapper class, called the PyECVL, to support Python Ecosystem. The latest versions of ECVL and PyECVL along with documentation are publicly available on GitHub [6,19].

2.2   EDDL

The European Distributed Deep Learning Library (EDDL) is a general purpose library that includes most of the commonly available Deep Learning functionalities. In addition, EDDL also contains the functionalities that are needed within the Deep Health project, which covers 15 DeepHealth use cases. The main objective of building EDDL is to provide a general-purpose library that covers most of the functionalities needed by Deep Learning in the Health sector, is easy to use and integrate by developers, and becomes the most widely used Deep Learning library for Health. EDDL uses High-Performance Computing (HPC) and a Cloud infrastructure transparently. It provides Neural Network topology components and hardware-independent tensor operations. Using the Neural Network library both the training and inference of a model can be performed, along with a finer control on deeper levels like gradient manipulation or individual batches. The development language of EDDL is also C++ and a Python wrapper class PyEDDL is provided. The latest versions of EDDL and PyEDDL along with documentation are published publicly on GitHub [7,19].

3   The UniToChest Dataset

The *UniToChest* dataset has been collected within the EU-H2020 *DeepHealth* [5, 16] project and consists of more than 300k lung CT scans of pulmonary lungs from 623 different patients. The scans are in DICOM format and each scan comes with a manually annotated segmentation mask in black and white PNG format, both being 512 × 512 in size.

A comparison with similar datasets in Table 1 shows that UniToChest has more nodules with a wider diameter range especially at the top end. The UniToChest contains data collected from a gender-balanced population and spanning across a wide range of ages. Moreover, it includes images acquired using 10 different devices. The demographic details of patients and insights of the data collection process can be found in the original dataset paper (accepted to ICIAP 2022) [4]. For all the CT scan slices in UniToChest, the radiologist has manually segmented the present lung nodules to provide a segmentation mask. To ensure UE regulation on privacy all the patient identifiers are removed from the CT scan slices and the segmented masks.

Table 1. Comparison with similar public dataset shows that our dataset has more clinical lung cancer CT scan slices and annotated lung nodule count with a diverse diameter range.

Dataset	Number of patients	Number of scans	Total nodules count	Nodule diameter range (mm)
LIDC – IDRI	1010	244527	7371	2–69
LUNA16	1010	888	1836	3–33
UniToChest	623	306440	10071	1–136

For the purpose of training a neural network, we split the dataset into training, validation and test set randomly as 80-10-10 of patients. We maintain data consistency across multiple splits by assigning a single split to each patient. The data population with respect to the splits is summarized in Table 2. All the three sets (training, validation and test) have a 60 to 40 ratio between the number of male and female patients. Furthermore, the Table 3 presents an in-depth distribution of different nodule diameters within the three splits done for training of the neural network.

Table 2. Dataset population for the three splits we provide.

Splits	Number of patients	Number of dicoms	Number of masks
Training	498	250893	18534
Validation	62	26996	1712
Test	63	28551	2467
Total	623	306440	22713

Table 3. Nodule diameter distribution across three splits.

	<3 mm	<10 mm	<30 mm	>30 mm	Total
Training	149	6527	1861	249	8786
Validation	7	315	116	23	461
Test	21	575	195	33	824
Total	177	7417	2172	305	10071

4 Methodology

This section describes the proposed method for pulmonary nodules segmentation, including the preprocessing stage, the architecture of the deep neural convolutional architecture we rely upon and the relative training procedures. The data preprocessing stage has been accomplished using PyECVL 1.2.0 and for network training PyEDDL 1.3.0 is used.

4.1 Data Preprocessing

DICOM files produced by CT machines typically contain pixel intensity values in Hounsfield Units (HU), i.e. they indicate radiometric density per pixel (low values indicating air, higher values indicating bones). Following a standard medical practice, a clipped windowing transformation function is applied to such density values. The window width and center indicate the range of the Hounsfield Units covered inside the converted pixel values, everything outside this range will be equivalent to either zero or one. According to standard practice, we have used a window width of 1600 and a window center of −500 to account for the radiometric density of body structures actually useful for nodule detection.

4.2 Network Architecture

Our approach relies on the U-Net implementation [21]. The U-Net consists of Encoder and Decoder part. The encoder consists of 5 convolutional layers with max-pooling for featuremap downsampling. As in other convolutional architectures, as the size of the featuremaps shrinks the number of featuremaps increases by a two factor. The decoder includes 5 convolutional layers followed by an upconvolutions, where the size of the featuremaps increases while their number decreases at each layer. A number of encoder and decoder layers are matched with skip connections, where the feature maps generated by the respective encoder layer is concatenated with the output of decoder layer, enabling the precise learning and localization of image object by allowing different tradeoffs between semantic level and spatial accuracy of the featuremaps. The full architecture of U-Net can be observed in Fig. 1.

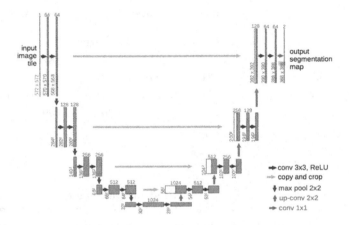

Fig. 1. U-Net architecture [21]

4.3   Training Procedure

The training method is fully supervised and consists in randomly initializing the network weights (*from scratch*) and then training the network for nodule segmentation minimizing the loss between the network output and the segmentation mask relative to the input image. As for similar segmentation tasks, we minimize the Dice loss since it has a derivative allowing for error gradient backpropagation and minimizing the Dice loss amounts to maximizing the IoU (Intersection over Union) between predicted and ground truth mask. Next, the network is trained over UniToChest training set for 200 epochs. For this training, only scans with one or more nodules have been considered, since we experimentally verified that other scans do not bring any useful information for segmentation. The CT slices are provided as input to the neural network in batches of 12, as that enabled a reasonable tradeoff between memory footprint and performance. We found beneficial resorting to on-the-fly data augmentation during the training to avoid overfitting to the training data. The augmentation technique we used consists in random flips and rotations (the very same transformations are also applied to the corresponding segmentation mask). The optimizer used in our experiment is Adam with a learning rate of 0.0001. The whole architecture has been implemented in PyEDDL and is available on github.[1]

5   Results and Discussion

In this section, we experiment over the UniToChest dataset with the neural network based method described in the previous section for nodule segmentation. All results are relative to UniToChest test set, i.e. images that have not been used at training time. For the experiments Docker image dhealth/pylibs-toolkit:1.2.0-1-cudnn with PyECVL 1.2.0 and PyEDDL 1.3.0 are used.

5.1   Experimental Setup

We used Weights & Biases for experiment tracking and visualizations to develop insights for this paper. To automate hyperparameter optimization of the number of workers and the queue ratio size of the ECVL dataloader, we run a sweep with 2 GPUs. In Fig. 2 we can see that with the aim of speed up the training process, assigning two workers (one per GPU) and a queue ratio size of eight (four per GPU) lead to better training times. Therefore, when using 4 GPUs we set the number of workers to 4 and the queue ratio size to 16.

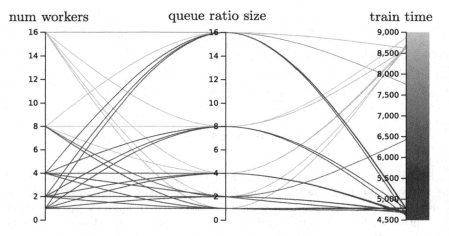

Fig. 2. Parallel hyperparameter sweep (grid search) for tuning the number of workers and the queue ratio size of the ECVL dataloader.

---

[1] https://github.com/deephealthproject/UC4_pipeline.

5.2   Nodules Segmentation

Firstly, for the lung nodule segmentation the neural network was trained using only the images from training split of UniToChest shown in Table 2 that had lung nodules in them i.e. having a respective nodule segmentation mask. The model that performed the best on validation set was picked. This model was then further trained and fine-tuned with 2% of images with black masks, i.e. 2% images that had no nodule segmentation mask, for a few epochs. Lastly, we compute the Dice and IoU scores on all the images of the test set (including images both with and without lung nodules). Figure 3 shows the Dice losses for training, validation and test set when training only on images with nodules. The Dice and IoU scores achieved on the full test set with a model finetuned using 2% of black masks are 0.75 and 0.73 respectively.

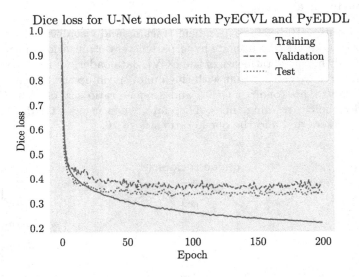

Fig. 3. Dice loss when training only on images with nodules.

Finally, Fig. 4 shows some samples of the segmentation mask predicted by the network (bottom row) for some sample test images (top row). Red pixels represent false negatives, green pixel false positives and yellow pixels correctly segmented pixels: most of the pixels are correctly segmented, a few errors remaining only at the borders of the nodule.

5.3   Computational Speed

DeepHealth libraries provide support for multiple GPUs. We performed experiments using 1, 2 and 4 GPUs with different batch sizes. We can see in Table 4 that running our experiments on bigger batch sizes and using more GPUs we can further speed up training and inference processes.

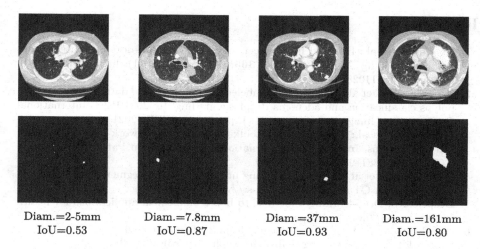

Diam.=2-5mm	Diam.=7.8mm	Diam.=37mm	Diam.=161mm
IoU=0.53	IoU=0.87	IoU=0.93	IoU=0.80

Fig. 4. Segmentation results on UnitoChest. Overlap (yellow) between predicted (red) and ground truth (green) masks is shown (top). Results over different nodule diameters and corresponding ground truth are also shown (bottom). (Color figure online)

Table 4. Average training time (seconds, per epoch) and inference time (seconds, per image) with different numbers of GPUs.

Number of GPUs	Batch size	Training time (s)	Inference time (s)
1	1	–	0.16
1	3	6723	0.14
2	6	4233	0.08
4	12	3303	0.04

6   Conclusion and Future Works

This paper proves the feasibility of the Deephealth toolkit and its libraries. In particular, PyECVL and PyEDDL in providing Deep Learning and Computer Vision off-the-shelf services. In this study we proposed a U-Net based architecture using PyEDDL that yields promising results at the segmentation of lung nodules from UniToChest. Future research directions of this work include exploiting similar datasets and perform an efficiency comparison with PyTorch.

Acknowledgement. This work has received funding from the European Union's Horizon 2020 research and innovation programme under grant agreement No 825111, *DeepHealth* Project.

References

1. Aberle, D., et al.: Reduced lung-cancer mortality with low-dose computed tomographic screening. N. Engl. J. Med. **365**(5), 395–409 (2011). https://doi.org/10.1056/NEJMoa1102873
2. Barbano, C.A., et al.: Unitopatho, a labeled histopathological dataset for colorectal polyps classification and adenoma dysplasia grading. In: 2021 IEEE International Conference on Image Processing (ICIP), pp. 76–80. IEEE (2021)
3. Cancilla, M., et al.: The deephealth toolkit: a unified framework to boost biomedical applications. In: 2020 25th International Conference on Pattern Recognition (ICPR), pp. 9881–9888. IEEE (2021)
4. Chaudhry, H., et al.: Unitochest: a lung image dataset for segmentation of cancerous nodules on CT scans (2022). https://www.iciap2021.org/
5. DeepHealth: Deep-learning and HPC to boost biomedical applications for health (2019). https://deephealth-project.eu/
6. ecvl: Ecvl (2022). https://github.com/deephealthproject/ecvl
7. eddl: Eddl (2022). https://github.com/deephealthproject/eddl
8. Eisenhauer, E.A., et al.: New response evaluation criteria in solid tumours: revised RECIST guideline (version 1.1). Eur. J. Cancer **45**(2), 228–247 (2009)
9. Gava, U., et al.: Unitobrain (2021). 10.21227/x8ea-vh16, https://dx.doi.org/10.21227/x8ea-vh16
10. Infante, M., Berghmans, T., Heuvelmans, M.A., Hillerdal, G., Oudkerk, M.: Slow-growing lung cancer as an emerging entity: from screening to clinical management. Eur. Respir. J. **42**(6), 1706–1722 (2013)
11. Knight, S.B., Crosbie, P.A., Balata, H., Chudziak, J., Hussell, T., Dive, C.: Progress and prospects of early detection in lung cancer. Open Biol. **7**(9) (2017). https://doi.org/10.1098/rsob.170070
12. LeCun, Y., Bengio, Y., Hinton, G.: Deep learning. Nature **521**(7553), 436–444 (2015)
13. Liu, H., et al.: A cascaded dual-pathway residual network for lung nodule segmentation in CT images. Physica Med. **63**, 112–121 (2019)
14. MacMahon, H., et al.: Guidelines for management of small pulmonary nodules detected on CT scans: a statement from the fleischner society. Radiology **237**(2), 395–400 (2005)
15. Marten, K., Auer, F., Schmidt, S., Kohl, G., Rummeny, E.J., Engelke, C.: Inadequacy of manual measurements compared to automated CT volumetry in assessment of treatment response of pulmonary metastases using RECIST criteria. Eur. Radiol. **16**(4), 781–790 (2006)
16. Oniga, D., et al.: Florea: applications of AI and HPC in the health domain. In: HPC, Big Data, and AI Convergence Towards Exascale: Challenge and Vision, p. 217 (2022)
17. Perlo, D., et al.: UniToChest (2022). https://doi.org/10.5281/zenodo.5797912
18. Puderbach, M., Kauczor, H.U.: Can lung MR replace lung CT? Pediatr. Radiol. **38**(S3), 439–451 (2008). https://doi.org/10.1007/s00247-008-0844-7
19. pyecvl: Pyecvl (2022). https://github.com/deephealthproject/pyecvl
20. Revel, M.P.: Avoiding overdiagnosis in lung cancer screening: the volume doubling time strategy. Eur. Respir. J. **42**, 1459–1463 (2013)
21. Ronneberger, O., Fischer, P., Brox, T.: U-Net: convolutional networks for biomedical image segmentation. In: Navab, N., Hornegger, J., Wells, W.M., Frangi, A.F. (eds.) MICCAI 2015. LNCS, vol. 9351, pp. 234–241. Springer, Cham (2015). https://doi.org/10.1007/978-3-319-24574-4_28

22. Siegel, R.L., Miller, K.D., Fuchs, H.E., Jemal, A.: Cancer statistics, 2021. CA: Can. J. Clin. **71**(1), 7–33 (2021). https://doi.org/10.3322/caac.21654
23. National Lung Screening Trial Research Team: Results of initial low-dose computed tomographic screening for lung cancer. New Engl. J. Med. **368**(21), 1980–1991 (2013)
24. Van Ginneken, B.: Computer-aided diagnosis in thoracic computed tomography. Imaging Dec. MRI **12**(3), 11–22 (2008)
25. Wu, J., Qian, T.: A survey of pulmonary nodule detection, segmentation and classification in computed tomography with deep learning techniques. J. Med. Artif. Intell. **2**(8), 1–12 (2019). https://doi.org/10.21037/jmai.2019.04.01
26. Zhao, Y.R., et al.: Comparison of three software systems for semi-automatic volumetry of pulmonary nodules on baseline and follow-up CT examinations. Acta Radiologica **55**(6), 691–698 (2014)

UniToBrain Dataset: A Brain Perfusion Dataset

Daniele Perlo[1] , Enzo Tartaglione[2(✉)] , Umberto Gava[3] ,
Federico D'Agata[3], Edwin Benninck[4], and Mauro Bergui[3]

[1] Fondazione Ricerca Molinette Onlus, Turin, Italy
[2] LTCI, Télécom Paris, Institut Polytechnique de Paris, Palaiseau, France
enzo.tartaglione@telecom-paris.fr
[3] Neuroscience Department, University of Turin, Turin, Italy
[4] University Medical Center Utrecht, Utrecht, The Netherlands

Abstract. The CT perfusion (CTP) is a medical exam for measuring
the passage of a bolus of contrast solution through the brain on a pixel-
by-pixel basis. The objective is to draw "perfusion maps" (namely cerebral blood volume, cerebral blood flow and time to peak) very rapidly for
ischemic lesions, and to be able to distinguish between core and penumbra regions. A precise and quick diagnosis, in a context of ischemic stroke,
can determine the fate of the brain tissues and guide the intervention and
treatment in emergency conditions.

In this work we present UniToBrain dataset, the very first open-
source dataset for CTP. It comprises a cohort of more than a hundred of
patients, and it is accompanied by patients metadata and ground truth
maps obtained with state-of-the-art algorithms. We also propose a novel
neural networks-based algorithm, using the European library *ECVL* and
EDDL for the image processing and developing deep learning models
respectively. The results obtained by the neural network models match
the ground truth and open the road towards potential sub-sampling of
the required number of CT maps, which impose heavy radiation doses
to the patients.

Keywords: Medical image synthesis · Deep learning · U-Net ·
Dataset · Perfusion map · Ischemic stroke · Brain CT scan ·
DeepHealth

1 Introduction and Clinical Background

The occlusion of a cerebral vessel causes a sudden decrease in blood flow in the
surrounding vascular territory, in comparison to its centre. The identification of
such an occlusion reliably, quickly and accurately is crucial in many emergency
scenarios like ischemic strokes [7]. The CT perfusion (CTP) is a medical exam
for measuring the passage of a bolus of contrast solution through the brain
on a pixel-by-pixel basis. CT perfusion is performed with a sampling time of
approximately 1 Hz. Based on these measurements, low-dose serial scans are

© The Author(s), under exclusive license to Springer Nature Switzerland AG 2022
P. L. Mazzeo et al. (Eds.): ICIAP 2022 Workshops, LNCS 13373, pp. 498–509, 2022.
https://doi.org/10.1007/978-3-031-13321-3_44

acquired from which blood time-density curves and several other parametric maps are calculated. The blood time-density curves correspond to the passage of the contrast agent into the brain tissue. The most relevant parameters used in clinical practice are maps representing Cerebral Blood Volume, Cerebral Blood Flow and Time To Peak (called CBF, CBV, TTP respectively) [1].

Ischemic lesions develop very rapidly, originating from the central area of the occluded vascular region and progressively expanding to increasingly peripheral regions. From the onset of symptoms, two different regions can be identified in the problematic ischemic area of the brain. The area of irreversible damage is the central region called *core*. The visible area of potential recovery and possible re-canalization, provided by the occluded vessel, is the peripheral *penumbra* region. Generally, CBV maps are used for core segmentation, while CBF and TTP for penumbra areas. Therefore, the identification of the core and of the penumbra can predict the fate of the brain tissue itself and guide physicians in re-perfusion treatments [7,17]. An example of colored perfusion maps and core-penumbra region is shown in Fig. 1. The extent of the core and its penumbra area can be estimated clinically based on symptoms and their time of onset, and using common perfusion techniques such as CTP.

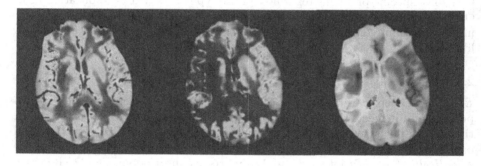

Fig. 1. Examples of perfusion maps, from left to right CBV, CBF and TTP. While core is the dark blue region in CBV, the penumbra is evident in CBF and TTP: in TTP it is particularly evident, in red. (Color figure online)

A time-intensity curve is the result of processing the signal intensity values over time. Several algorithms are used to perform deconvolution of time-intensity curves, but some of them are not public and may produce maps with divergences [12]. If we place ourselves in an ideal environment, where we find limited noise, limited variance and no artifacts created by patient motion during scanning, the optimal choice for obtaining realistic, accessible and reproducible maps is an analysis performed pixel by pixel, such as the one performed by deconvolution-based algorithms. Unfortunately, in the real clinical case, the information must be redundant in order to overcome the problems caused by the presence of noise, large variances and motion artifacts. In practice, this results in obtaining more brain slices, requiring more patient X-ray exposition, more

500 D. Perlo et al.

acquisitions, estimation of an Arterial Input Function (AIF), and a series of spatial pre-processing steps for noise and variance reduction.

2 DeepHealth Related Works

The European Union is spending significant amount of resources properly leading the AI development and research to maintain its proper position in this emergent and challenging context. EU funds projects to deploy pilots and large-scale experimental research solutions by combining the latest discovered technologies in artificial intelligence. The same effort is spent to support AI technologies like distributed high-performance computing, cloud computing and big data support. *DeepHealth* [6,13] is an example of this effort, that is thought (and developed) as a health-focused project. CTP data gathered for UniToBrain dataset are part of a larger collection of open-access datasets [3,14] developed for the DeepHealth project. The European framework of *DeepHealth*, called *DeepHealth Toolkit*, is a single entity that aims to use heterogeneous architectures, such as high-performance computing, big data and cloud computing, to provide deep learning capabilities and computer vision off-the-shelf services. *DeepHealth Toolkit*'s purpose is to make it easier to develop and deploy new applications that solve specific problems regardless of the type of context or application field. Our contribution is achieved with the support the *DeepHealth Toolkit*, by taking into account some of its main components, in particular *EDDL* and *ECVL* libraries.

2.1 EDDL

EDDL is a deep learning library that was originally developed to be general-purpose and it meets the AI development needs inside the DeepHealth context, therefore with the aim to be used in healthcare applications. *EDDL* is a free and open source software library, available on online repository as a core part of the *DeepHealth Toolkit*. It integrates and supports the most popular and well known Artificial Neural Network (ANN) topologies, by including both convolutional and recurrent models. *EDDL* aims to simplify the development of hardware-specific accelerated deep learning mechanisms by providing hardware-independent tensor operations and ANN topologies components like activation functions, regularization functions, optimization methods, and multiple types of different layers. The neural network library contains both high-level tools, such as training and evaluation of a model, and low-level tools that allow finer control of each step in the training or inference loop, like individual epochs, batches, or gradients manipulation.

2.2 ECVL

The *European Computer Vision Library (ECVL)* is the *DeepHealth* computer vision library, developed to be general-purpose, with a special focus on supporting healthcare applications. It provides high-level computer vision capabilities, by providing also specialized and hardware accelerated implementations of commonly used image processing algorithms in deep learning. *ECVL's* design revolves around the pivotal concept of `Image` as the centerpiece of the entire library. Special features are included in the library for medical image data manipulation. These images are often retrieved with proprietary or multi-scan formats, such as DICOM, NIfTI and others virtual slide formats. `Image` provides the arithmetic instruments in order to apply mathematical operations between images and scalars. More common affine image transformations, such as rotating, scaling, mirroring, and color space changes are available. *ECVL* is accompanied by a *Python API* called `pyecvl`, just like `pyeddl`, whose main advantage is that it not only speeds up application developments but also integrates with the rich *Python* ecosystem of scientific programming tools. Support for *NumPy* allows developers to process data with many other scientific tools. `pyecvl`, as well as other toolkits, is available as open-source software.

3   The *UniToBrain* Dataset

The University of Turin (UniTo) released the open-access dataset UniToBrain collected within DeepHealth project [6]. UniToBrain [9] is a dataset of Computed Tomography (CT) perfusion images (CTP). The dataset includes 258 patients from multiple health institutions. Perfusion data were obtained from hospital Picture archiving and communication system (PACS) of *Città della Salute e della Scienza di Torino* by Neuroradiology Division in Molinette Hospital, by doing a retrospective research.

All the data collected within this study are retrieved with procedures complying with institutional ethical standards, the 1964 Declaration of Helsinki and its subsequent amendments, or comparable ethical standards. In addition, the requirement for written informed consent was waived because this was a retrospective study.

Perfusion maps, including CBF, CBV, TTP, were calculated using a standard spatial pre-processing pipeline followed by a nonlinear regression (NLR) method based on a state-of-the-art fast model developed and described by Bennink *et al.* [4]. A motion correction is required and was performed using a rigid registration method. Next, all images were pre-processed by implementing a bilateral filter [11]. Estimates of the AIF and vein output function (VOF) were made automatically using a sample of 100 voxels. The impulse response function (IRF) of perfused tissue is described by the model developed by Bennink *et al.*, in terms of CBV and tracer delay, which is fundamental in the clinical context of ischemic stroke. The tissue temporal attenuation curve and associated maps (CBV, CBF, and TTP) are then estimated using the AIF and IRF calculated by that method [4]. Along with the dataset, we provide some utility files, by using the *DeepHealth Toolkit*, in order to pre-process the DICOM files, the ground-truth maps and to load the dataset for ANN training purposes.

3.1 *DeepHealth Toolkit* Integration

The *DeepHealth Toolkit* is a versatile deep learning system with fully integrated image processing and computer vision capabilities that uses HPC and cloud infrastructure to perform parallel and decentralized AI inference and learning processes. The toolkit is designed to handle large and growing datasets, by matching the nature of medical image datasets. To that end, the *DeepHealth Toolkit* solution aims to transparently integrate the latest parallel programming technologies to leverage the parallel performance capabilities of HPC and cloud infrastructures, by including symmetric multiprocessors (SMPs), graphics processing units (GPUs) and various other computing acceleration technologies. The toolkit also includes features that can be used for training and inference by abstracting the complexity of different computational resources and facilitating architecture developments adopted in the learning and inference phases. The following scripts for data management are then provided along with the dataset:

dicomtonpy.py: It converts the DICOM files in the dataset to *NumPy* arrays. These are 3D arrays, where CT slices at the same height are piled-up over the temporal acquisition. Here pyecvl is used in order to convert and resize the ground-truth images.

dataloader_pyeddl.py: Dataloader for the pyeddl deep learning framework. It converts the numpy arrays in normalized tensors, which can be provided as input to standard deep learning models using the European library *EDDL*. The reader can look at https://github.com/EIDOSlab/UC3-UNITOBrain to have a full companion code where a U-Net model is trained over the dataset.

dataloader_pytorch.py: Dataloader for the *PyTorch* deep learning framework. The behaviour is the same of dataloader_pyeddl.py.

4 Methodology

Employing Deep Learning approaches to the problem of deconvolving time-intensity curves, offers several potential advantages over canonical algorithms. Indeed, DL allows the extraction of information and features that are relatively insensitive to noise, misalignment and variance. Gava *et al.* [10] shows whether a properly trained Convolutional Neural Network (CNN), based on a U-Net-like structure, on a pre-processed dataset of CTP images, can generate clinically relevant parametric maps of CBV, CBF and time to peak TTP.

Since this specific model has been originally thought for medical images segmentation [15], and in this case the goal is to generate parametric images, some changes to the standard model are introduced. There is evidence that this CNN model is effective in other tasks, other than image segmentation, as well [8]. In contrast to similar state-of-the-art U-Net based methods, no extra information, like the above mentioned arterial input function AIF, has been provided to the U-Net model.

4.1 Data Preprocessing

The raw pre-processing inputs are a collection of multiple CT scans and multiple targets maps for each patient, in *DICOM* format. *DICOM* is an acronym for *Digital Imaging and Communications in Medicine* and it is the standard for the communication and management of medical imaging information and related metadata. Each target map corresponds to the output of the perfusion scan at a certain scan height of the patient's brain. In order to synthesize a representative map of the patient's blood flow over time, CT scans are performed at different time points. Thus, given a target perfusion, we have to search between the patient CT scans for all the images acquired at the same height. All the CT scans for the same patient are ordered following their acquisition time point. Therefore CT images can be viewed as 3D tensors, with the third dimension being the time axis. In practice, the input pre-processing consists in finding all grayscale images correlated by the scan height and grouping them in a single image tensor, whose depth has to be the number of available CT scan for a given target map. All pixel values in the image tensor drop in range $[0; 1]$. Figure 2 summarizes this input pre-processing step.

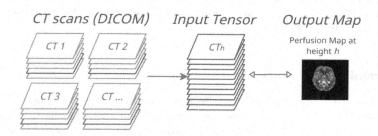

Fig. 2. A representation of the *UniToBrain* input pre-processing step. CT scans at the same scan height h are staked together in order to create U-Net input tensor.

4.2 Network Architecture

The pre-processed images are the only input for the trained U-Net network architecture [15]. Here, we consider using it for inference on perfusion maps. The overall model can be found in Fig. 3. This particular neural network architecture has been originally developed for image segmentation: however, it proved to be effective also to solve other image generation tasks. For our purpose, we reproduce the suggested modifications [10] at the architectural level to fit the problem. For segmentation tasks, a common state-of-the-art choice is to use max-pooling layers for sub-sampling. This operator, however, introduces a non-linear behavior which prevents the forward propagation of great part of the information content [16]. According to the paper, we have used average pooling layers in place of max pool since sparse features are not expected to be extracted. A sigmoid function is used to estimate each pixel intensity for the CNN output image. Hence, depending on the chosen time granularity, the number of input channels changes accordingly.

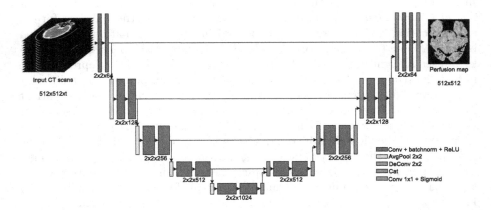

Fig. 3. A representation of the U-Net architecture used to generate perfusion maps. The model takes as input the scans acquired in different time instants. The images resolution is 512×512. After four encoding stages, the decoder stages produce a map with the same input resolution.

4.3   Training Procedure

The tensors, that are produced in the pre-processing step, are the only input provided to the trained U-Net architecture. In order to train our CNN, we use a widely used loss function definition for image generation tasks. We are using U-Net for perfusion map inference: instead of using standard cross entropy loss, or dice score/focal loss, which are typical for training segmentation tasks, we minimize the Mean Squared Error (MSE) loss between the required ground-truth and the CNN output. Additional information or data (e.g. AIF) are not provided to the CNN: all information is found in the pre-processed input CT images. The model is pre-trained to produce a 128×128 output map for 250 epochs, after that it is trained and tuned for 50 epochs to produce 512×512 maps, in which all pixel values fall into the range $[0; 1]$. The choice to pre-train the U-Net model with down-sampled images comes mainly from practical factors. Training on full resolution images requires a high consumption of GPU memory and the time needed to reach model convergence becomes very high. Training on down-sampled images allows to reach a solution in a much shorter time, since the task is simplified. The pre-training step produces a suitable set of starting parameters for the model: this type of approach is often used for training generative networks, and the results are comparable, and smoother, than those produced with very high dimensional image training. The training of the entire model for each target is done using the Adam optimization strategy, with a learning rate of 10^{-5} and batch size equals to 8.

5   Results and Discussion

The whole UniToBrain collection is composed from patients that differ not only in the number of exams or in the head positioning, but also their CT scans are acquired at different scan heights or scan angle. A sub-sample of 100 training subjects, and 15 for testing, was used in a submitted publication for the training and the testing of a Convolutional Neural Network [10]. This sub-sample is composed by patients from Molinette hospital only, each of them share the same features in terms of number of CT scans and acquisition parameters. The CTP acquisitions were performed using a GE 64 Scanner, and the parameters for the examination were defined as follows, the same for each case: 80 kV, 150 mAs, 44.5 s duration, 89 volumes (40 mm axial coverage), injection of iodinated contrast agent for 40 ml (300 mg/ml) at 4 ml/s speed. In this sub-sample, 8 perfusion maps are available for each target (CBV, CBF, and TTP) for each patient. Furthermore, each sample share the same number of CT scans: the same brain portion appears 89 times at different scan timing. Therefore, the number of scans that are stacked together to compose the U-Net input is the same. In our experimentation, we use the same data sub-sample.

We evaluate the concurrent `pyeddl` implementation on the UniTo HPC environment (HPC4AI [2]) with four 16 GB GPUs NVIDIA Tesla T4. All simulations with *EDDL* were performed using the "low memory" option available on the neural model building phase. Due to the size of the inputs, $512 \times 512 \times 89$ wide tensors, 2 samples are computed for each GPU for each training step.

Table 1. Correlation measures between full resolution U-Net outputs and related targets.

	Pearson index	DICE coefficient (binarized masks)
CBV	0.73	0.75
CBF	0.83	0.52
TTP	0.87	0.54

We propose the results for the three identified target perfusions. We report both MSE graphs from the pre-training phase at 128×128 resolution and from the fine-tuning step at 512×512 resolution, for 250 and 50 training epochs respectively. The evaluation of the resulting images is performed by the value of the loss Mean Square Error (MSE) function. MSE clearly indicates how much the predicted maps deviate from the target. Figure 4b reports that MSE reach promising values below 0.01. While CBF and CBV experiments show similarities in loss slopes in both phases, predicted TTP map has an higher mean MSE over

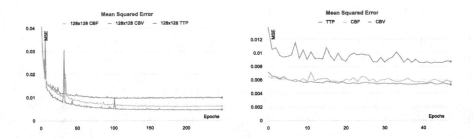

(a) Measurements at pre-training phase, (b) Measurements at fine-tuning phase,
for 128×128 pixels images.   for 512×512 pixels images.

Fig. 4. MSE loss metric during training: low is better, it indicates that the generated maps are numerically very close to the targets.

the training loop. MSE shows a slighter decrease for CBF and CBV curves, that suggests a lower gain for the pre-training at a lower resolution 128×128 pixels. The evaluation of each generated perfusion map, whose pixel values fall in the range $[0:1]$, is proposed by measuring the correlation between the CNN output and the ground-truth with the Pearson correlation index. We also evaluate the highlighted brain regions consistency for each map by calculating the Dice coefficient. In order to do that, we simply binarize the perfusion maps by threshold at half intensity range. We summarize the measurements in Table 1. Dice score suggests that CBF and TTP predictions tend to slightly over-estimate high-intensity regions. In particular, comparing the results with the Pearson index, we observe that an hard thresholding to half the intensity is not a good approach for the complex temporal and flow-related perfusion maps: for this reason, direct optimization of binarized images looks not to be a promising approach for this specific task. On the contrary, high Pearson indices suggest the success of the MSE optimization. Visual examples on the generated perfusion maps are reported in Fig. 5. In according to a team of 3 Molinette clinicians, the U-Net CNN approximates sufficient perfusion mismatch in brain tissues to create an information-rich perfusion map for patients with ischemic lesions. Clinicians analysis refer a good agreement between the CNN proposed method and the ground-truth in estimating hypo-perfused regions on CTP maps.

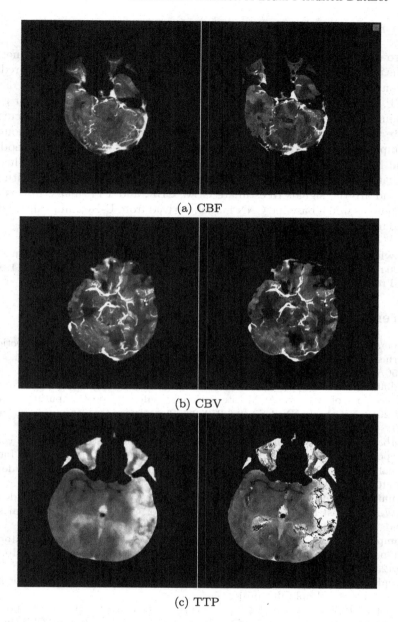

(a) CBF

(b) CBV

(c) TTP

Fig. 5. Examples of map predictions for each target type. The image on the left represents the U-Net output, while the ground-truth map is on the right.

6   Conclusion

The growing potential of machine learning-based perfusion analysis methods have the potentialities to lead to new improved acquisition protocols and reduced radiation doses. In this work we introduce UniToBrain, an open-source dataset for CTP, which allows us to evaluate a state-of-the-art DL approach for generate brain blood flow maps. We have observed that CNN models can accurately evaluate the perfusion parameters by using CT scans images only, without any other input information, while the standard decomposition-based methods for CT and MRI require AIF curves measured in the saphenous vein [5]. This suggests that CNNs are capable of combining the information associated with both tissue and arterial signals to estimate CBV, CBF, and TTP maps. In this work we propose as well a baseline CNN model, derived from U-Net, implemented and open-sourced using the new *DeepHealth Toolkit*.

Acknowledgement. This work has received funding from the European Union's Horizon 2020 research and innovation programme under grant agreement No. 825111, *DeepHealth* Project.

References

1. Albers, G.W., et al.: Thrombectomy for stroke at 6 to 16 hours with selection by perfusion imaging. New Engl. J. Med. **378**(8), 708–718 (2018). https://doi.org/10.1056/nejmoa1713973
2. Aldinucci, M., et al.: Hpc4ai: an AI-on-demand federated platform Endeavour. In: Proceedings of the 15th ACM International Conference on Computing Frontiers. CF 2018, New York, NY, USA, pp. 279–286. Association for Computing Machinery (2018). https://doi.org/10.1145/3203217.3205340
3. Barbano, C.A., et al.: Unitopatho, a labeled histopathological dataset for colorectal polyps classification and adenoma dysplasia grading. In: 2021 IEEE International Conference on Image Processing (ICIP). pp. 76–80 (2021). https://doi.org/10.1109/ICIP42928.2021.9506198
4. Bennink, E., Oosterbroek, J., Kudo, K., Viergever, M.A., Velthuis, B.K., de Jong, H.W.A.M.: Fast nonlinear regression method for CT brain perfusion analysis. J. Med. Imaging **3**(2) (2016). https://doi.org/10.1117/1.jmi.3.2.026003
5. Campbell, B.C., et al.: Imaging selection in ischemic stroke: feasibility of automated CT-perfusion analysis. Int. J. Stroke **10**(1), 51–54 (2014). https://doi.org/10.1111/ijs.12381
6. DeepHealth: Deep-learning and HPC to boost biomedical applications for health (2019). https://deephealth-project.eu/
7. Donahue, J., Wintermark, M.: Perfusion CT and acute stroke imaging: foundations, applications, and literature review. J. Neuroradiol. **42**(1), 21–29 (2015). https://doi.org/10.1016/j.neurad.2014.11.003
8. Falk, T., et al.: U-net: deep learning for cell counting, detection, and morphometry. Nat. Methods **16**(1), 67–70 (2018). https://doi.org/10.1038/s41592-018-0261-2
9. Gava, U., et al.: UniToBrain (2022). https://doi.org/10.21227/x8ea-vh16
10. Gava, U.A., et al.: Neural network-derived perfusion maps: a model-free approach to computed tomography perfusion in patients with acute ischemic stroke (2021). https://doi.org/10.1101/2021.01.13.21249757

11. Klein, S., Staring, M., Murphy, K., Viergever, M., Pluim, J.: elastix: a toolbox for intensity-based medical image registration. IEEE Trans. Med. Imaging **29**(1), 196–205 (2010). https://doi.org/10.1109/tmi.2009.2035616

12. Kudo, K., et al.: Differences in CT perfusion maps generated by different commercial software: Quantitative analysis by using identical source data of acute stroke patients. Radiology **254**(1), 200–209 (2010). https://doi.org/10.1148/radiol.254082000

13. Oniga, D., et al.: Applications of AI and HPC in health domain. In: HPC, Big Data, AI Convergence Toward Exascale: Challenge and Vision, chap. 11. CRC Press, Taylor & Francis Group (2021). ISBN: 9781032009841

14. Perlo, D., et al.: UniToChest (2022). https://doi.org/10.5281/zenodo.5797912

15. Ronneberger, O., Fischer, P., Brox, T.: U-Net: convolutional networks for biomedical image segmentation. In: Navab, N., Hornegger, J., Wells, W.M., Frangi, A.F. (eds.) MICCAI 2015. LNCS, vol. 9351, pp. 234–241. Springer, Cham (2015). https://doi.org/10.1007/978-3-319-24574-4_28

16. Sabour, S., Frosst, N., Hinton, G.E.: Dynamic routing between capsules. In: Proceedings of the 31st International Conference on Neural Information Processing Systems. NIPS 2017, Red Hook, NY, USA, pp. 3859–3869. Curran Associates Inc. (2017). https://doi.org/10.5555/3294996.3295142

17. Wannamaker, R., et al.: Computed tomographic perfusion predicts poor outcomes in a randomized trial of endovascular therapy. Stroke **49**(6), 1426–1433 (2018). https://doi.org/10.1161/strokeaha.117.019806

A Compact Deep Ensemble for High Quality Skin Lesion Classification

Anita Giovanetti$^{(\boxtimes)}$ [ID], Laura Canalini [ID], and Paolo Perliti Scorzoni [ID]

Università degli Studi di Modena e Reggio Emilia - Dipartimento di Ingegneria "Enzo Ferrari", Modena, Italy
{anita.giovanetti,laura.canalini,paolo.perlitiscorzoni}@unimore.it

Abstract. Convolutional Neural Networks (CNNs) are widely employed in the medical imaging field. In dermoscopic image analysis, the large amount of data provided by the International Skin Imaging Collaboration (ISIC) encouraged the development of several machine learning solutions to the skin lesion images classification problem. This paper introduces an ensemble of image-only based and image-and-metadata based CNN architectures to classify skin lesions as melanoma or non-melanoma. In order to achieve this goal, we analyzed how models performance are affected by the amount of available data, image resolution, data augmentation pipeline, metadata importance and target choice. The proposed solution achieved an AUC score of 0.9477 on the official ISIC2020 test set. All the experiments were performed employing the ECVL and EDDL libraries, developed within the european DeepHealth project.

Keywords: Convolutional Neural Networks (CNNs) · Skin lesion · Classification

1 Introduction

Melanoma is a malignant tumor of the skin which shows a constantly growing incidence all over the world. Numerous studies suggest it doubled in the last 10 years. According to epidemiological studies presented by the GLOBO-CAN (Global Cancer Observatory), melanoma has reached more than 320 000 new cases per year worldwide [32], with a slightly higher incidence among men (170 000 cases versus 150 000 cases among women). In particular, in Italy the estimate of melanomas is nearly 7 300 new cases per year among men and 6 700 among women, mainly affecting people aged between 30 and 60 years [21].

Although melanoma represents only a small percentage of tumors affecting the skin, it is responsible for most of skin cancer deaths. According to the statistics of 2020 [32], in Europe the mortality rate for melanoma cancer is 46.2%. Early diagnosis plays an essential role in treatment. Unfortunately, the recent COVID-19 pandemic and the consequent lockdown had an overall negative impact regarding timely diagnosis, leading to the increase of waiting time

P. L. Mazzeo et al. (Eds.): ICIAP 2022 Workshops, LNCS 13373, pp. 510–521, 2022.
https://doi.org/10.1007/978-3-031-13321-3_45

in the hospitals booking agendas as well as to medical examinations canceled by patients themselves due to their fear of COVID-19 infections.

The need for early and accurate diagnosis combined with the new possibilities offered by modern digital dermatoscopes, justifies the significant increase of publications regarding the use of machine learning algorithms in the field of skin imaging, a narrow branch of medical imaging focused on analysis and classification of images representing skin lesions. Although each lesion may differ from others in minimal details, deep convolutional neural networks have recently shown their great potential in melanoma recognition.

The aim of this article is to present an ensemble of Convolutional Neural Networks realized by means of the ECVL (European Computer Vision Library) and EDDL (European Distributed Deep Learning Library), developed within the H2020 DeepHealth project [9], that integrates five different models that vary in architecture, input data (i.e., image and metadata or only image), and data preprocessing to address the skin lesion classification problem. A brief analysis of the state-of-the-art solutions in the medical field is also included.

2 Related Work

Dermoscopic Images. Skin cancer is the most prevalent type of cancer and melanoma is its most deadly form [25,26]. When recognized and treated in its earliest stages, melanoma is readily curable with minor surgery. Skin cancer is mainly diagnosed visually with an initial clinical screening followed by dermoscopy, biopsy and histopathological examination.

As detailed in the next subsection, the extensive use of dermoscopic images combined with the recent advancements in deep learning based computer vision have resulted in a great effort to develop different approaches to solve the problem of automated skin lesion classification. In the last years, multiple organizations such as the International Skin Imaging Collaboration (ISIC) have released dermoscopic datasets labeled with their skin lesion categories and associated with image-level and clinical-level metadata. The main goal is to achieve standards for the use of digitized images of skin lesions to assist the recognition of skin cancer, with a particular focus on melanoma, through clinical decision support and automated diagnosis. Specifically, ISIC Archive contains over 150 000 total images, of which approximately 70 000 are public [3]: the 2019 and 2020 challenge training sets count respectively 25 331 and 33 126 images; 10 982 more images are from the 2020 test set.

The dataset used to perform the experiments described in this paper is explored in Sect. 3.

CNNs for Classification. Machine learning and deep learning are widely used in the medical imaging field. In particular, Convolutional Neural Networks are the most common deep learning approach for medical image analysis and retrieval [5], detection of cancer forms (such as those affecting breasts, lungs, prostate, colon, liver, and brain) [20], renal biopsy [29], maxillofacial imagery [10,11,22], and many other application fields [8,12,13,27,28,30,31]. CNNs implemented in the work described in this paper are ResNet [18], ResNeXt [35], ResNeSt [37] and EfficientNet [33].

Proposed in 2014 by He et al., ResNet is successful in introducing the Residual Block and its Skip Connection to solve the vanishing gradient problem [7], resulting in the improvement of scaling up techniques to achieve better accuracy.

In 2016, Xie et al. proposed ResNeXt, a ResNet variant in which the building blocks are split in parallel (introducing the cardinality dimension), and summed together for the output.

The following year, SE-Net (Squeeze-and-Excitation Net) [19] improved the representative power of the network thanks to its SE block, a mechanism that allows the network to perform the recalibration of the features, in order to be able to selectively emphasize the informative features and suppress the less useful ones.

ResNeSt inherits the SE-block from Se-Net and the cardinality from ResNeXt to introduce a model that integrates the channel-level attention strategy with the multi-path network structure.

Finally, in 2019 EfficientNet achieved state-of-the-art accuracy on ImageNet providing a new scaling up method that uniformly increases the dimensions of depth, width, and resolution. EfficientNet is still one of the best performing networks, challenged in the last period only by the boost of Vision Transformers [14] even in the image classification task.

An in-depth description of how some of these models have been implemented in an ensemble method is provided in Sect. 4.

Deep Learning in Skin Imaging. With the support of massive parallel architecture (Graphic Processing Unites, GPUs), deep learning techniques increased their popularity and recently have been proposed also for dermoscopic image analysis [6,36].

Esteva et al. studied pre-trained CNNs for skin cancer classification over a dataset of 129 450 clinical images and compared the performance of those neural networks to the accuracy of expert dermatologists. The results of this study demonstrated an artificial intelligence capable of classifying skin cancer with a level of competence comparable to dermatologists [15].

Mahbod et al. used a pre-trained AlexNet and VGG-16 architecture to extract deep features from dermoscopic images for skin lesion classification. The proposed architecture showed to achieve very good classification performance, yielding an area under the receiver operating characteristic curve (AUC) of 83.83% for melanoma classification and of 97.55% for seborrheic keratosis classification [24].

The winners of the ISIC 2019 Skin Lesion Classification Challenge [4] proposed an ensemble of multi-resolution models, in which EfficientNets prevail, in order to perform the tasks of skin lesion classification using only-image and image-and-metadata as input data, combined with extensive data augmentation and loss balancing [16]. On the ISIC official test set their method is ranked first for both tasks with an AUC score of 0.636 and 0.634 respectively.

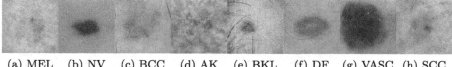

(a) MEL   (b) NV   (c) BCC   (d) AK   (e) BKL   (f) DF   (g) VASC   (h) SCC

Fig. 1. Samples of the 2019 ISIC dataset training set. (a) Melanoma, (b) Melanocytic Nevus, (c) Basal Cell Carcinoma, (d) Actinic Keratosis, (e) Benign Keratosis, (f) Dermatofibroma, (g) Vascular Lesion, (h) Squamous Cell Carcinoma.

Table 1. Datasets description

	ISIC2019	ISIC2020	ISIC2019 + ISIC2020
Training images	25 331	33 126	58 457
Melanoma images	4 509	581	5 090

Wei et al. suggested a lightweight skin cancer recognition model with feature discrimination based on fine-grained classification principle. Compared to the existing multi-CNN fusion method, the framework can achieve an approximate (or even higher) model performance with a lower number of model parameters end-to-end [34].

3   Dataset

Since 2016, ISIC hosts challenges to engage the computer science community to improve dermatologic diagnostic accuracy through machine learning solutions. In addition, ISIC periodically expands its ISIC Archive, an open source platform with publicly available images of skin lesions. The dermoscopic images contained in the archive are associated with clinical metadata, such as patient's *age* and *sex*, lesion's *anatomic site*, *diagnosis* and the relative *benign/malignant* target, and more. In the 2019 challenge the *diagnosis* feature corresponds to 9 ground-truth category of the skin lesion (Fig. 1): Melanoma (MEL), Melanocytic Nevus (NV), Benign Keratosis Lesion (BKL), Basal Cell Carcinoma (BCC), Actinic Keratosis (AK), Squamous Cell Carcinoma (SCC), Vascular Lesion (VASC), Dermatofibroma (DF) plus the *unknown* (UNK) class (without samples in the training set), to which the images that cannot be classified in the other categories belong.

The current most numerous datasets provided by ISIC are the ones associated to the 2019 and 2020 challenges. As detailed in Table 1, both datasets are heavily unbalanced with respect to the melanoma class, to which belong only the 8.78% of samples. For the sake of completeness, the distribution of each skin lesion category is reported in Table 2.

Since deep learning models perform better with large amount of data, the experiments described in Sect. 5 use the concatenation of both 2019 and 2020

Table 2. Classes distribution within the datasets

Label	ISIC2019	ISIC2020	ISIC2019 + ISIC2020
NV	50.8%	15.7%	31.12%
MEL	17.8%	1.8%	8.78%
BCC	13%	–	5.73%
BKL	10%	0.7%	4.89%
AK	3%	–	1.49%
SCC	2.4%	–	1.08%
VASC	1%	–	0.44%
DF	0.9%	–	0.41%
UNK	–	81.9%	46.06%

training images as a single dataset. Three new datasets are created from the original, each containing the images resized to 512×512, 768×768 and 1024×1024 respectively. In this way it is possible to compare the performance of models in classifying images starting from different resolutions. Moreover, during the training step, images are pre-processed with a pipeline of Data Augmentation techniques (it could be the *Full pipeline* or the *Reduced pipeline*), implemented to reduce overfitting. The transformations in the pipelines are applied to the image with a specific probability and they are chosen considering that dermoscopic images present very high resolution, but low colour variability. For this reason, the transforms mostly emphasize contrast and contours. All of these transformations have been performed through the augmentation functionalities of ECVL. They have to be wrapped into a container, that can be a *SequentialContainer* (i.e., all the augmentations in the container are performed sequentially) or a *OneOfContainer* (i.e., only one of the augmentations in the container is performed with a certain probability). Containers can be nested in order to apply the needed set of augmentations.

Full Pipeline. It consists of a sequence of: *Transpose*, *Vertical Flip*, *Mirroring*, *Scale*, *Rotate* and *Resize*, which are operators that do not alter the semantic content; changing the *Brightness* and *Contrast* of the image randomly; *Coarse Dropout*, which removes rectangular regions in the image; *Normalize* and finally a blurring and a distorting transformations (Fig. 2).

Reduced Pipeline. It is a reduced version of the *Full pipeline*, consisting only of *Transpose*, *Vertical Flip*, *Mirroring* and *Normalize* transformations.

3.1   Metadata

ISIC provides the metadata associated to each image. From those information, we obtained our own set of metadata, some of which are related to the image itself,

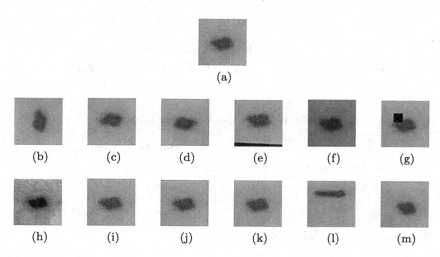

Fig. 2. Data Augmentations - Full pipeline. (a) Original, (b) Transpose, (c) Vertical Flip, (d) Mirror, (e) Scale and Rotate, (f) Brightness and Contrast, (g) Coarse Dropout, (h) Normalize, (i) Gaussian Blur, (j) Laplace Noise, (k) Optical distortion, (l) Grid distortion, (m) Elastic transform

such as *image_name* (i.e., the name of the image), *filepath* (i.e., path where the image is stored), *fold* (i.e., fold index to which the image is assigned by the Cross Validation Stratified 5-Fold strategy) and *is_ext* (which is 1 if the image belongs to the 2019 dataset, 0 otherwise). However, others are related to the patient and its skin lesion, such as *patient_id, sex, age_approx, anatom_site* (i.e., the location of the lesion on the patient's body), *diagnosis* (i.e., skin lesion category or *unknown*), *benign_malignant* (where benign stands for non-melanoma, while malignant stands for melanoma), *target* (i.e., the corresponding binary numeric value of the *bening_malignant* feature).

Since the images originally belong to two different datasets, it is necessary to map the values of the *diagnosis* feature from the 2020 to the 2019 diagnosis, to maintain consistency between the labels and the metadata.

Feature Importance. Feature importance is a class of techniques that score the features provided as input to a predictive model, based on how relevant they are in predicting the target. In particular, the Gradient Boosting algorithm shows that the *age_approx* feature is the most significant in target prediction [38]. Afterwards, the features *anatom_site* and *sex*.

For this reason, even models that classify images by integrating information extrapolated from metadata are included in the ensemble described in Sect. 5.1. For example, Table 3 shows that an image-and-metadata EfficientNet-b3 model performs better than the same model receiving only dermoscopic images as input data.

Table 3. Image-only model VS image-and-metadata model

Model	Target	Resize	Augm.	Metadata	AUC
EfficientNet-b3	9	512	Full	**False**	**0.9127**
EfficientNet-b3	9	512	Full	**True**	**0.9340**

Table 4. Multi-class VS binary target

Model	Target	Resize	Augm.	Metadata	Accuracy
ResNet-152	9	256	Full	True	**93,7%**
ResNet-152	2	256	Full	True	**92,9%**

4   Classification Models

During the experimental phase, different Convolutional Neural Network models proved to be effective solutions for the skin lesion images classification task: ResNet-152, ResNest-101, ResNeXt-50, EfficientNet-b3, EfficientNet-b4, EfficientNet-b5, EfficientNet-b6, EfficientNet-b7.

As in a typical image classification problem, each tested CNN model has been loaded in EDDL pretrained on ImageNet and its last layer is replaced so that the output dimension equals the target dimension. Experiments showed better results when using *diagnosis* as target instead of *benign_malignant*. Table 4 illustrates that ResNet-152 trained to predict 9 diagnoses achieved more effective results than the same model trained on binary target. In fact, a CNN trained on a binary target must become particularly efficient at distinguish melanoma from all the others lesions. On the other hand, a CNN with a 9-dimensional output layer is trained to learn all the skin lesion categories and their details, so that the model can gather more information. In this case, to validate the performance of the network trained with a 9-dimensional target we decided to measure its accuracy on the validation set (described in Sect. 5) and to compare it with the accuracy achieved with a binary target. In fact, the official ISIC2020 Challenge metric (AUC) provided to measure only the model's capability of classifying skin lesions as melanoma or non-melanoma, i.e. with binary target.

The architecture of the model that processes images and metadata is composed by a CNN that performs feature extraction from the dermoscopic images, a Fully Connected Neural Network (FCNN) for clinical metadata processing and a Fully Connected (Dense) layer followed by a Softmax layer, which takes both the outputs of the CNN and of the FCNN in input to return the class distribution (Fig. 3). Specifically, the metadata-FCNN is composed of two blocks, each containing a Dense layer followed by batch normalization and ReLU activation, interspersed with a Dropout. Its 128-dimensional output is concatenated with the CNN's feature vector (which size depends on the number of output features of the CNN's last layer, excluding the prediction head), followed by the final classification layer.

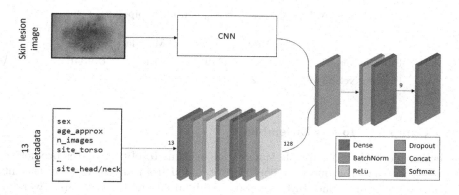

Fig. 3. Architecture for image and metadata processing

5   Experimental Results

The dataset used for training and evaluating the proposed models includes 58 457 dermoscopic images, as the concatenation of the ISIC2019 and ISIC2020 datasets. Images are resized to different resolutions, ranging from 256×256 to 768×768.

The Cross Validation Stratified 5-Folds technique splits the training set into 5 smaller sets (i.e., 5 folds) according to three criteria: folds are created such that they had the same class distribution as the entire dataset, images belonging to the same patient are put into the same fold and the patient's images count distribution is balanced within the folds, i.e. some patients have as many as 115 images and some patients have as few as 2 images, so each fold has an equal number of patients with 115 images, with 100, with 70, with 50, with 5, with 2, etc. This makes validation more reliable. Then, each model is trained using $k-1$ folds as training data, with the aim of minimizing the Cross-Entropy loss, and it is validated on the remaining part of the data computing the model's accuracy. The ADAM algorithm [23] is used to optimize the loss, and the learning rate is set to 3×10^{-5}.

As shown in Table 4, a model trained to predict a 9-dimensional target performs better than the same model trained to predict a binary target. For this reason, the *diagnosis* feature is used as label. All the models have been trained for 18 epochs, which was sufficient to achieve satisfactory results.

Table 5 reports the comparison between the AUC score achieved by an EfficientNet-b3 model which receives input data processed with the *Full pipeline* and then with the *Reduced Pipeline*. As expected, performance improves if images are transformed with the *Full pipeline*. Moreover, experiments have shown that good diversity can be achieved by inserting models that process metadata into the final ensemble.

Table 5. Full VS reduced augmentation pipeline

Model	Target	Resize	Augm.	Metadata	AUC
EfficientNet-b3	9	512	**Full**	True	**0.9340**
EfficientNet-b3	9	512	**Reduced**	True	**0.9104**

5.1 Compact Models Ensemble

Ensemble methods use multiple learning algorithms to obtain better predictive performance than the one that could be obtained from any of the constituent learning algorithms alone. In this paper, the final ensemble is a simple average of the five more reliable models' probability ranks. Specifically, for each model predictions on the official ISIC2020 test set, the rank function is used to compute numerical data ranks (1 through n, where n is equal to the test set size) based on target probability predicted for each image. Equal probabilities are assigned a rank that is the average of the ranks of those values and then the rank values are expressed as a percentage. Finally, ensemble method consists in computing the new target value for each test sample as the average of the models ranks associated to the sample.

Each of the five multi-class classifiers employed in the ensemble is evaluated considering the melanoma class vs. the rest. Since the ground truth of the ISIC2020 test set has not yet been released, the only metric available is the AUC, provided by the challenge once the predictions have been submitted. Table 6 shows the configuration of the models ensemble that achieved our best AUC score. On the ISIC 2020 Skin Lesion Classification Challenge Leaderboard [4], our ensemble ranked fourth with a more compact models ensemble compared to the top three and with a difference of only 0.0013 from the AUC score of the winning proposal (Table 7).

The winning strategy [17] differs in the choice of augmentations techniques and hyperparameters and it is important to underscore that it consists of an ensemble of 18 models unlike ours which has only 5.

Instead, the second-place-winner [1] built an ensemble of 15 image-only-models, in which EfficientNets prevail, trained with 3-dimensional target: *melanoma*, *nevus* and *other* classes.

Finally, the third-place-winner [2] built an ensemble of 8 image-and-metadata models, in which EfficientNets prevail.

Table 6. Compact models ensemble

Model	Resize	Augm. Pipeline	Metadata	AUC
Eff-b3	512	Full	True	0.9340
Eff-b4	448	Full	False	0.9333
Eff-b5	768	Full	True	0.9337
Eff-b5	384	Full	False	0.9317
ResNet-152	256	Reduced	False	0.9281
Ensemble				**0.9477**

Table 7. ISIC 2020 leaderboard

	Team	# Models in ensemble	AUC
1	All Data are Ext	18	0.9490
2	Aloe	15	0.948
3	Deloitte Analytics Spain	8	0.9484
4	**Ours**	**5**	**0.9477**

6 Conclusions

This paper introduces an effective method to solve the dermoscopic images classification task. The proposed solution takes advantages of the larger number of training images obtained from the union of the ISIC2019 and the ISIC2020 archives. In addition, replacing the last layer of the models with a 9-dimensional layer to use the *diagnosis* attribute as target has proven to be a successful approach. Finally, the ensemble of different Convolutional Neural Network models, with and without metadata, further increases the AUC of the classification. These experiments led to a final compact ensemble that achieved a very satisfactory AUC score on the test set with a relatively low computational effort, compared to the competitors.

Future research directions will hence include an investigation to find a reliable solution that can assist dermatologists in their diagnosis.

Acknowledgments. This project has received funding from the European Union's Horizon 2020 research and innovation programme under grant agreement No 825111, DeepHealth Project.

References

1. ISIC 2020–2nd place solution. https://github.com/i-pan/kaggle-melanoma/blob/master/documentation.pdf
2. ISIC 2020–3rd place solution. https://github.com/Masdevallia/3rd-place-kaggle-siim-isic-melanoma-classification
3. ISIC Archive. https://www.isic-archive.com
4. ISIC Leaderboards. https://challenge.isic-archive.com/leaderboards/live/
5. Allegretti, S., Bolelli, F., Pollastri, F., Longhitano, S., Pellacani, G., Grana, C.: Supporting skin lesion diagnosis with content-based image retrieval. In: 2020 25th International Conference on Pattern Recognition (ICPR), pp. 8053–8060 (2021)
6. Barata, C., Celebi, M.E., Marques, J.S.: Explainable skin lesion diagnosis using taxonomies. Pattern Recogn. **110**, 107413 (2021)
7. Bengio, Y., Simard, P., Frasconi, P., et al.: Learning long-term dependencies with gradient descent is difficult. IEEE Trans. Neural Networks **5**(2), 157–166 (1994)
8. Bigazzi, R., Landi, F., Cascianelli, S., Baraldi, L., Cornia, M., Cucchiara, R.: Focus on impact: indoor exploration with intrinsic motivation. IEEE Robot. Autom. Lett. **7**, 2985–2992 (2022)

9. Cancilla, M., et al.: The deephealth toolkit: a unified framework to boost biomedical applications. In: 2020 25th International Conference on Pattern Recognition (ICPR), pp. 9881–9888. IEEE (2021)
10. Cipriano, M., et al.: Deep Segmentation of the Mandibular Canal: a New 3D Annotated Dataset of CBCT Volumes, pp. 1–11. IEEE Access (2022)
11. Cipriano, M., Allegretti, S., Bolelli, F., Pollastri, F., Grana, C.: Improving segmentation of the inferior alveolar nerve through deep label propagation. In: Proceedings of the IEEE/CVF Conference on Computer Vision and Pattern Recognition (CVPR), pp. 1–10. IEEE (2022)
12. Cornia, M., Baraldi, L., Cucchiara, R.: Smart: training shallow memory-aware transformers for robotic explainability. In: Proceedings of the International Conference on Robotics and Automation (2020)
13. Cornia, M., Baraldi, L., Serra, G., Cucchiara, R.: Sam: pushing the limits of saliency prediction models. In: Proceedings of the IEEE Conference on Computer Vision and Pattern Recognition Workshops (2018)
14. Dosovitskiy, A., et al.: An image is worth 16x16 words: transformers for image recognition at scale. arXiv preprint arXiv:2010.11929 (2020)
15. Esteva, A., et al.: Dermatologist-level classification of skin cancer with deep neural networks. Nature **542**(7639), 115–118 (2017)
16. Gessert, N., Nielsen, M., Shaikh, M., Werner, R., Schlaefer, A.: Skin lesion classification using loss balancing and ensembles of multi-resolution EfficientNets. línea], ISIC Chellange (2019)
17. Ha, Q., Liu, B., Liu, F.: Identifying melanoma images using EfficientNet ensemble: winning solution to the SIIM-ISIC melanoma classification challenge. CoRR abs/2010.05351 (2020). https://arxiv.org/abs/2010.05351
18. He, K., Zhang, X., Ren, S., Sun, J.: Deep residual learning for image recognition. In: 2016 IEEE Conference on Computer Vision and Pattern Recognition (CVPR), pp. 770–778 (2016)
19. Hu, J., Shen, L., Sun, G.: Squeeze-and-excitation networks. In: Proceedings of the IEEE Conference on Computer Vision and Pattern Recognition, pp. 7132–7141 (2018)
20. Hu, Z., Tang, J., Wang, Z., Zhang, K., Zhang, L., Sun, Q.: Deep learning for image-based cancer detection and diagnosis - a survey. Pattern Recogn. **83**, 134–149 (2018)
21. Istituto Superiore di Sanità: L'epidemiologia per la sanità pubblica - melanoma. https://www.epicentro.iss.it/melanoma/
22. Jaskari, J., et al.: Deep learning method for mandibular canal segmentation in dental cone beam computed tomography volumes. Sci. Rep. **10**(1), 1–8 (2020)
23. Kingma, D.P., Ba, J.: Adam: A method for stochastic optimization. arXiv preprint arXiv:1412.6980 (2014)
24. Mahbod, A., Schaefer, G., Wang, C., Ecker, R., Ellinge, I.: Skin lesion classification using hybrid deep neural networks. In: ICASSP 2019–2019 IEEE International Conference on Acoustics, Speech and Signal Processing (ICASSP), pp. 1229–1233. IEEE (2019)
25. Melanoma Research Alliance: Melanoma Statistics. https://www.curemelanoma.org/about-melanoma/melanoma-101/melanoma-statistics-2/
26. Pellacani, G., Grana, C., Seidenari, S.: Algorithmic reproduction of asymmetry and border cut-off parameters according to the ABCD rule for dermoscopy. J. Eur. Acad. Dermatol. Venereol. **20**(10), 1214–1219 (2006)
27. Pollastri, F., Bolelli, F., Paredes, R., Grana, C.: Augmenting data with GANs to segment melanoma skin lesions. Multimedia Tools Appl. **79**, 15575–15592 (2019)

28. Pollastri, F., Cipriano, M., Bolelli, F., Grana, C.: Long-range 3D self-attention for MRI prostate segmentation. In: 2022 IEEE 18th International Symposium on Biomedical Imaging (ISBI), pp. 1–5. IEEE, March 2021
29. Pollastri, F., et al.: Confidence calibration for deep renal biopsy immunofluorescence image classification. In: 2020 25th International Conference on Pattern Recognition (ICPR), pp. 1–8. IEEE (2021)
30. Pollastri, F., et al.: A Deep Analysis on High ResolutionDermoscopic Images Classification. IET Comput. Vision 15(7), 514–526 (2021)
31. Ronneberger, O., Fischer, P., Brox, T.: U-Net: convolutional networks for biomedical image segmentation. In: Navab, N., Hornegger, J., Wells, W.M., Frangi, A.F. (eds.) MICCAI 2015. LNCS, vol. 9351, pp. 234–241. Springer, Cham (2015). https://doi.org/10.1007/978-3-319-24574-4_28
32. Sung, H., et al.: Global cancer statistics 2020: Globocan estimates of incidence and mortality worldwide for 36 cancers in 185 countries. CA Can. J. Clin. 71(3), 209–249 (2021)
33. Tan, M., Le, Q.: EfficientNet: rethinking model scaling for convolutional neural networks. In: International Conference on Machine Learning, pp. 6105–6114 (2019)
34. Wei, L., Ding, K., Hu, H.: Automatic skin cancer detection in dermoscopy images based on ensemble lightweight deep learning network. IEEE Access 8, 99633–99647 (2020)
35. Xie, S., Girshick, R., Dollár, P., Tu, Z., He, K.: Aggregated residual transformations for deep neural networks. In: 2017 IEEE Conference on Computer Vision and Pattern Recognition (CVPR), pp. 1492–1500 (2017)
36. Yuan, Y., Chao, M., Lo, Y.: Automatic skin lesion segmentation using deep fully convolutional networks with Jaccard distance. IEEE Trans. Med. Imaging 36(9), 1876–1886 (2017)
37. Zhang, H., et al.: Resnest: Split-attention networks. arXiv preprint arXiv:2004.08955 (2020)
38. Zhanshan, L., Zhaogeng, L.: Feature selection algorithm based on XGBoost. J. Commun. 40(10), 101 (2019)

Automatic Detection of Epileptic Seizures with Recurrent and Convolutional Neural Networks

Salvador Carrión, Álvaro López-Chilet, Javier Martínez-Bernia,
Joan Coll-Alonso, Daniel Chorro-Juan, and Jon Ander Gómez[✉]

Pattern Recognition and Human Language Technology Research Center, Universitat
Politècnica de València, Camí de Vera, 46022 València, Spain
{salcarpo,allochi,jamarbe2,jcolalo,dchojua,jon}@upv.es

Abstract. Computer-aided diagnosis based on intelligent systems is
an effective strategy to improve the efficiency of healthcare systems
while reducing their costs. In this work, the epilepsy detection task is
approached in two different ways, recurrent and convolutional neural
networks, within a patient-specific scheme. Additionally, a detector function and its effects on seizure detection performance are presented. Our
results suggest that it is possible to detect seizures from scalp EEGs with
acceptable results for some patients, and that the DeepHealth framework
is a proper deep learning software for medical research.

Keywords: Deep learning · Neural networks · Epilepsy ·
Electroencephalogram

1 Introduction

The progress in technology and medicine has been improving humanity's quality
of life over history. The 21st century is currently living a technological revolution,
where Artificial Intelligence seems to be one of the most critical technologies for
the future. This discipline is developing in giant steps, and the possibility of using
AI techniques to help individuals in healthcare has motivated many researchers
to develop systems that could improve the quality of life of many people. This
work is focused on the Automatic Detection of Epileptic Seizures from scalp
Electroencephalograms (EEG) and presents two deep learning based solutions
to approach the problem.

Epilepsy is a chronic non-communicable disease of the brain that affects
around 50 million people worldwide. According to the World Health Organization, this disease is characterised by recurrent seizures, which are episodes
of involuntary movement that involve parts of the body or even the entire

---

This project has received funding from the European Commission - Horizon 2020
(H2020) under the DeepHealth Project (grant agreement no 825111), and the SELENE
project (grant agreement no 871467).

P. L. Mazzeo et al. (Eds.): ICIAP 2022 Workshops, LNCS 13373, pp. 522–532, 2022.
https://doi.org/10.1007/978-3-031-13321-3_46

body. Early detection and immediate warning of these seizures could significantly improve the quality of life of these people. Additionally, detecting these seizures with high reliability could help better understand this disease as well as open the door to improve existing treatments or computer-aided diagnosis to help neurologists.

The most common way of detecting seizures is through the analysis of the scalp Electroencephalogram (EEG), which is a non-invasive recording of the electrical activity of the brain. The main difficulty in this use case lies in the significant variability between different patients and also among the brain states of the same patient. In the EEG signals, it is possible to find different patterns corresponding to seizure periods of the same patient. Additionally, since seizures are rare events, algorithm designers must create solutions that work with limited seizure data. Nonetheless, with more research and advanced neural models, we are convinced that seizures could be detected automatically by intelligent systems with the required quality.

The main contributions of this work are the following:

- A recurrent approach to solve the seizure detection problem with raw EEG signals.
- A convolutional approach to solve the seizure detection problem with raw EEG signals.

This paper is organized as follows: Sect. 2 analyses state of the art for Epileptic Seizure Detection from EEG signals. Section 3 gives an introduction to the DeepHealth framework and its features. Section 4 describes all the parts of our experimentation setup. Section 5 shows the experiments carried out and their results. Section 6 presents our conclusions. Finally, Sect. 7 concludes the paper by giving our future research lines.

2 Related Work

Epilepsy detection using EEG signals has been approached with many different solutions, which generally rely on a first process of feature extraction and selection, and a machine learning classifier afterwards. Most of the approaches achieve high scores on detecting seizures, in terms of sensitivity and specificity. One of the first solutions that were successful was a self-organized map (SOM) neural network to detect seizures in a 24 long-term EEG recordings. This was presented in [4] in 1996 by Gabor et al., and they demonstrated the possibility of automatic seizure detection. In [6], discrete wavelet transform (DWT) was used in order to extract features from the EEG signals, and the method achieved a 76.0% of sensitivity on detecting seizures.

In [8], a novel algorithm for feature extraction called MinMaxHist is presented, with the purpose of describing the waveform characteristics of the spikes and sharp waves of the EEG signals in order to classify the events by using these kinds of features. The solution achieved 86.27% of accuracy in a patient-independent classifier. In [7], there was designed a feature vector with spectral features using filter banks to measure the energy falling within the passband of each filter. They classified the feature vectors into ictal or interictal using a SVM and generated non-linear boundaries with a RBF kernel. Overall, 96% of the 173 test seizures were detected with an average detection latency of 4.6 s. Finally, in [3] they trained a CNN with raw signals in order to get the probability of each time window of being ictal. Afterwards, they proposed an onset-offset detector for determining the seizure onsets and offsets. The model correctly detected 90% of the seizures of the CHB-MIT Database. In [1], a deep convolutional autoencoder with a Bi-LSTM classifier achieved a 98.86% of accuracy in the CHB-MIT dataset, trained with raw signal. Additionally, an undersampling technique is applied to the Interictal class samples, in order to balance the data before feeding the network.

Regarding preprocessing techniques, in most of the works the signal is processed before using it. The common way is to extract spatial and spectral features in order to create a feature vector that is classified by a machine learning based system. In this work, the aim is to show different perspectives of approaching the task without applying any preprocessing to the data.

3   The DeepHealth Framework

The DeepHealth Framework is a flexible and scalable framework for running on HPC and Big Data environments based on two core technology libraries developed within the DeepHealth project: the European Distributed Deep Learning Library (EDDL) and the European Computer Vision Library (ECVL). These libraries will take full advantage of the current and coming development of HPC systems, and will provide a transparent use of heterogeneous hardware accelerators to optimise the training of predictive models, while considering performance and accuracy trade-offs.

Both libraries are being integrated into seven software platforms with the DeepHealth project. In a similar way, other commercial or research software platforms will have the possibility of integrating the two libraries, given that both are delivered as free and open-source software. Additionally, European large industry companies and SMEs will have the chance of using the DeepHealth Framework for training predictive models on Hybrid HPC + Big Data architectures and export the trained networks using the standard ONNX format [2], so, if their software applications already integrated another DL library able to read the ONNX format, all work is done.

The software used in this work involves the EDDL library, used to build and train the deep learning models, pyedflib to read EDF signals, and scikit-learn for some metrics calculation. The code is available in GitHub https://github.com/deephealthproject/UC13_pipeline.

4   Experimental Setup

4.1   Dataset

In the involved task of this work, the dataset used was the CHB-MIT Scalp EEG database, available on PhysioNet [5]. This dataset is composed of 24 sessions of scalp Electroencephalogram recordings from 23 pediatric subjects from the Children's Hospital of Boston. Each patient contains between 9 and 42 continuous signal files of one hour long in most of the cases. The recordings are in EDF (European Data Format), and the sampling rate 256 Hz. The signals are composed of many channels, each one related to a pair of electrodes located on the scalp, according to the international 10–20 system standard. For this task, a total of 23 channels were used, which are the ones that repeat the most in the dataset, ignoring some extra channels in some cases and files with fewer channels. Each patient has a summary file that contains some annotations, such as the starting and ending times of the seizures. These annotations were used to label the signals into interictal and ictal segments, preparing the data for a binary classification task. An example of an EEG from subject *chb01* can be seen in Fig. 1.

The recordings of each subject were divided in three subsets, using a 65% of the recordings for training, a 15% for validation and the 20% left for testing. As seizures usually last a few seconds, the class distribution is highly unbalanced, with more than 900 h of interictal periods and just 3 h of ictal periods in the whole dataset.

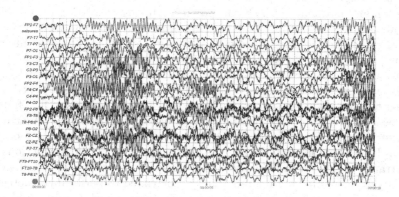

Fig. 1. This is a 10 s extract of an EEG recording from patient *chb01*. Snapshot taken from the LightWave visualizer of Physionet [5].

4.2   Training Details

Our solution for the epilepsy detection task involves a classifier based on neural networks and a post inference process that will act as a seizure detector. For each one of the patients, a classifier will be trained only with data from the same patient, following a patient-specific approach. The first classification part will be approached by two different architectures: recurrent neural networks and convolutional neural networks.

In the recurrent approach, the input of the network are sequences of one-second-long periods extracted from raw signal. To generate each sequence, a one-second-long sliding window is shifted through the signal every 500 ms. In such a way that every single sample corresponds to a period of one second of the signal, which is overlapped at 50% with its surrounding previous and next samples.

Each time step, the network looks at a sequence of the last 10 s of the signal in order to predict the current state. In this approach, the channels that compose the signal are passed one by one by the same network, and the results are combined to make the prediction at each step. The model architecture has a single recurrent layer, followed by a fully-connected part. For the recurrent layer type, a Long Short-Term Memory (LSTM) and a Gated Recurrent Unit (GRU) were tested.

Alternatively, the convolutional approach is focused on classifying periods of 10 s extracted from the signal, by applying a first convolution along the temporal axis, similar to a Time Delay Neural Network (TDNN), followed by more convolutions with 3×3 kernels to extract features and reduce the dimensionality. The input for this second approach are periods of 10 s shifted each 0.25 s, and the signal channels are all processed together at once, giving an input size of 2560×23, corresponding to the time dimension and the 23 channels that compose the signal. This approach applies Gaussian noise to the input, L2 regularization and Dropout, with the purpose of reducing overfitting caused by the class imbalance. In addition, in the training process of both approaches the generated mini-batches are class-balanced, applying undersampling to the interictal data and oversampling to the ictal data.

Both approaches perform a Z-score normalization to the data, but the input for the classifiers is raw signal, without any processing technique applied.

After the classification part, there is a post inference process with a function acting as a seizure detector. This function is based on a finite-state machine of two states: interictal and ictal. As the outputs of the network are ones or zeros (one for Ictal, zero for Interictal), the function analyses the predictions and makes transitions between the states, so it can raise alarms when a seizure onset is detected. It has some parameters that can be tuned to perform the detection: the size of the analysis window; α_{pos}, the minimum ratio of positive predictions needed inside the window to trigger a transition from Interictal to Ictal; α_{neg}, the maximum ratio of positive predictions needed inside the window to trigger a transition from Ictal to Interictal; and the detection threshold, which is the number of seconds that the model will be allowed to detect each seizure.

4.3   Evaluation Metrics

To evaluate our neural network models, the following metrics were monitored:

- **Accuracy**: Proportion of correct predictions among the total number of cases examined.
- **Balanced Accuracy**: Arithmetic mean of sensitivity and specificity.
- **F1-score (Macro)**: Harmonic mean of the precision and recall. Macro indicates the arithmetic mean of all the F1-scores per class.

For the detection of seizure events, the following metrics were evaluated:

- **Percentage of correctly detected seizures**: Recall associated to the detection of events.
- **Average latency**: Average time in seconds that the model needs to detect the seizures.
- **False Alarms per Hour**: Number of false alarms raised by a model per hour.

5   Experimentation

To begin with the experiments, a subset of eight patients was selected in order to find which one of the approaches performed better, as well as to find the best training configurations. This was done because of resources and time limits, as each configuration had to be trained and tested for each patient specifically. This subset was composed by patients *chb01*, *chb03*, *chb05*, *chb08*, *chb12*, *chb14*, *chb15* and *chb24*. After the best model and configuration were selected, it was tested with all of the subjects. At the end, different configurations for the post inference function parameters were analysed.

5.1   Results

First of all, both approaches (recurrent and convolutional) were trained and tested with the above mentioned subset of eight patients using SGD and Adam as optimizers and different initial learning rates, ranging from 1e−3 to 1e−6. The best results for these neural network classifiers are summarized in Table 1. As it can be seen, the accuracy of the models is quite high, but it is an overly optimistic metric because the dataset is unbalanced. Regarding the balanced accuracy, which is a good metric for unbalanced datasets, the best model is the recurrent one with the GRU layer trained with Adam, which achieved a 91.24%. Nevertheless, the convolutional model achieved the highest F1-Score, so it is also a possible candidate to be selected for testing with all of the patients.

In order to select between recurrent and convolutional models, the post-inference process was performed and the detection of seizures was evaluated with the best model of each approach. The results of the post-inference process for these models are summarized in Table 2. As it can be observed, the convolutional model detected 80% of the test seizures, with an average latency of 9.3 s and 2.76 false alarms per hour. The recurrent model performed worse, especially in the

Table 1. Summary of the results obtained by the four configurations that best performed with the subset of eight patients. These results are the averaged values for the eight subjects.

Model	Optimizer	Accuracy (%)	F1-score	Balanced accuracy (%)
GRU	Adam (1e−6)	96.06	0.7215	91.24
GRU	SGD (1e−5)	88.24	0.5457	88.70
LSTM	Adam (1e−5)	99.10	0.7806	76.26
CONV	Adam (1e−6)	98.77	0.8084	85.31

Table 2. Results after the post-inference process of the test samples with the subset of eight patients. These results are the averaged values for the eight subjects.

Model	Optimizer	Detected seizures (%)	Avg latency (s)	False alarms per hour
GRU	Adam (1e−6)	76.67%	6.96	14.32
CONV	Adam (1e−6)	80.00%	9.30	2.76

number of false alarms per hour, with an average of 14.32. The average latency for detection was lower on this model, but there were many more false alarms.

After these first experiments with a subset of patients, the convolutional model was selected to be tested on the whole dataset. Table 3 shows the results achieved by the convolutional model for all the patients of the dataset after the post-inference process. In general, the model detected 56.67% of the seizures, with an average latency of 9.51 s and 2.15 false alarms on average. As it can be seen in Table 3, most of the patients only have one or two seizures in many hours in the test subset, so the percentage of detected seizures is very sensitive, with extreme observable values of 0% and 100%, which makes the average not very meaningful, even though it is weighted to the number of seizures of each patient.

There are 9 patients for whom the model could not detect any seizure in the test subset and 10 patients with a 100% of detected seizures. If we look at the 15 patients for whom the model could detect at least one seizure, the average rate of detected seizures is 85.93%, the average latency is 9.51 s and the average rate of false alarms per hour 2.31. Moreover, there are remarkable results for patients *chb02*, *chb05*, *chb09* and *chb10*, with a 100% of detected seizures and no false alarms. Finally, the best results in terms of accurate and fast detection were obtained with patients *chb03* and *chb10*: with 3.12 s of latency and 0.22 false alarms per hour in the case of patient *chb03*, and with 4.88 s of latency and no false alarms in the case of patient *chb10*. All the seizures of these two patients in the test subset were detected (2 seizures each).

Table 3. Results after the post-inference process with the selected model for all the subjects of the dataset.

Patient id	No. seizures	Detected seizures	Average latency (s)	False alarms per hour	Tested hours
chb01	2	100.00%	8.38	0.62	9.62
chb02	1	100.00%	6.25	0.00	8.98
chb03	2	100.00%	3.12	0.22	8.98
chb04	2	0.00%		6.86	35.16
chb05	1	100.00%	7.00	0.00	7.98
chb06	2	0.00%		3.46	15.03
chb07	1	0.00%		0.05	19.34
chb08	1	100.00%	17.00	1.40	4.99
chb09	1	100.00%	9.50	0.00	13.62
chb10	2	100.00%	4.88	0.00	13.98
chb11	1	100.00%	5.00	0.91	8.77
chb12	11	81.82%	12.72	3.18	5.98
chb13	4	50.00%	11.75	1.00	2.99
chb14	2	50.00%	9.75	9.45	6.98
chb15	7	57.14%	7.06	2.78	8.98
chb16	4	0.00%		0.00	4.99
chb17	1	0.00%		1.80	4.99
chb18	2	100.00%	11.12	4.57	8.98
chb19	1	0.00%		0.25	7.90
chb20	2	50.00%	14.00	3.84	7.54
chb21	1	0.00%		6.77	7.98
chb22	1	0.00%		0.29	6.98
chb23	4	0.00%		0.00	12.88
chb24	4	100.00%	6.31	0.32	6.28
Average		**56.67%**	**9.51**	**2.15**	**10.00**

Finally, after selecting the best model and testing it with all of the patients, an extra experiment was done in order to analyse the performance of the post-inference process function, by varying some of its parameters.

First, the length of the analysis window used in the post-inference function was in the range of 10 to 80 predictions. This length indicates how many predictions from the past the function has to use for predicting the current state. As in the case of the convolutional approach, predictions are performed every 0.25 s, so a window length of 80 will analyze the last 20 s to decide on changing of state (from interictal to ictal or vice-versa). The hyper-parameters α_{pos} and α_{neg} were set to 0.4, the same values used in all of the previous experiments. The results of this experiment can be observed in Fig. 2. It can be noticed that as the analysis window gets longer, the latency increases and the number of false alarms is reduced. This is because the model can observe more predictions in order to predict if there is a seizure, so it is more confident on the predictions, but also slower because the latency is affected. The percentage of detected seizures is not much affected by these changes.

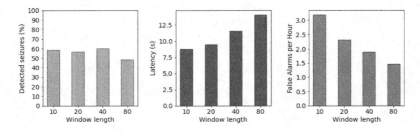

Fig. 2. Experimentation with different window lengths in the post-inference function.

The second experiment was devoted to see the effect of the hyper-parameters α_{pos} and α_{neg} on the performance. The following configurations were tested:

> **Configuration A**: $\alpha_{pos} = \alpha_{neg} = 0.2$
> **Configuration B**: $\alpha_{pos} = \alpha_{neg} = 0.4$
> **Configuration C**: $\alpha_{pos} = \alpha_{neg} = 0.8$
> **Configuration D**: $\alpha_{pos} = 0.8, \alpha_{neg} = 0.2$

Figure 3 shows the results for configurations A, B, C and D with a fixed window length of 20 predictions.

It can be observed that the configurations can vary the performance in terms of latency and false alarms. As higher are the values of α_{pos} and α_{neg}, the function needs more positive predictions inside the analysis window in order to raise an alarm, therefore the alarms are more delayed and the false alarms are

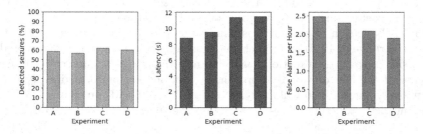

Fig. 3. Experimentation with configurations A, B, C, and D for the hyper-parameters α_{pos} and α_{neg} in the post-inference function.

reduced, because the model is more confident. Regarding the detection rate, it does not seem to be affected by these variations either.

6   Conclusions

This work was focused on Epileptic Seizure Detection and presented two approaches, one based on recurrent neural networks and the other based on convolutional neural networks. In both approaches raw data was used as input. Despite recurrent neural networks are designed to learn dependencies inherent to sequential data, the convolutional approach presented in this work achieved better results.

The task addressed in this work is challenging mainly for two reasons: (i) A strong imbalance of samples of each class in the dataset. The target class (ictal) has much fewer samples than the other class (inter-ictal). (ii) The high variability between patients. In fact, the results obtained and presented in previous sections are not consistent for all the patients; the models worked well for some patients but were not enough good for others.

A post-inference process was used in both approaches with a function acting as a seizure detector. The experimentation results show that it is possible to reach a trade-off between fast detection and a low number of false alarms by adjusting the parameters of the post-inference function.

Finally, the obtained results show that it is possible to achieve a good enough performance to detect seizures in the case of some patients, and suggest that, with more research and more data, the epilepsy detection task could be addressed with more reliable models; what could improve the quality of life of many people affected by Epilepsy. Additionally, the European Deep Learning Distributed Library (EDDL) showed to be a solid candidate to work with Deep Learning tasks.

7   Future Work

A patient-specific schema was used in this work. So that the model used for each patient was trained from scratch using only its data. This strategy led to run many experiments, and many more are still to be done, either following a patient-specific schema or a patient-independent schema. Nonetheless, our interests are in the following line of research:

- Test more models and configurations with all the subjects.
- Find a solvent feature extraction technique to improve results.
- Test our solution with other EEG datasets.
- Explore the seizure prediction task.

References

1. Ahmed, A., Magdy, B.: A deep learning approach for automatic seizure detection in children with epilepsy. Front. Comput. Neurosci. **15** (2021). https://doi.org/10.3389/fncom.2021.650050
2. Bai, J., Lu, F., Zhang, K., et al.: ONNX: Open Neural Network Exchange (2019). https://github.com/onnx/onnx
3. Boonyakitanont, P., Lek-uthai, A., Songsiri, J.: Automatic epileptic seizure onset-offset detection based on CNN in scalp EEG. In: ICASSP 2020–2020 IEEE International Conference on Acoustics, Speech and Signal Processing (ICASSP), pp. 1225–1229 (2020). https://doi.org/10.1109/ICASSP40776.2020.9053143
4. Gabor, A.J., Leach, R.R., Dowla, F.U.: Automated seizure detection using a self-organizing neural network. Electroencephalogr. Clin. Neurophysiol. **99**, 257–266 (1996). https://doi.org/10.1016/0013-4694(96)96001-0
5. Goldberger, A.L., et al.: PhysioBank, PhysioToolkit, and PhysioNet: components of a new research resource for complex physiologic signals. Circulation **101**(23), E215–E220 (2000). https://doi.org/10.1161/01.cir.101.23.e215
6. Saab, M.E., Gotman, J.: A system to detect the onset of epileptic seizures in scalp EEG. Clin. Neurophysiol. **116**, 427–442 (2005). https://doi.org/10.1016/J.CLINPH.2004.08.004
7. Shoeb, A., Guttag, J.: Application of machine learning to epileptic seizure detection. In: Proceedings of the 27th International Conference on International Conference on Machine Learning. ICML 2010, Omnipress, Madison, WI, USA, pp. 975–982 (2010)
8. Yang, S., et al.: Selection of features for patient-independent detection of seizure events using scalp EEG signals. Comput. Biol. Med. **119**, 103671 (2020). https://doi.org/10.1016/J.COMPBIOMED.2020.103671

Enabling Efficient Training of Convolutional Neural Networks for Histopathology Images

Mohammed H. Alali[1,2]([✉])[ID], Arman Roohi[1][ID], and Jitender S. Deogun[1]

[1] University of Nebraska-Lincoln, Lincoln, NE 68503, USA
alali@huskers.unl.edu
[2] Prince Sattam Bin Abdulaziz University, Al-Kharj, Saudi Arabia

Abstract. Convolutional Neural Networks (CNNs) have gained lots of attention in various digital imaging applications. They have proven to produce incredible results, especially on big data, that require high processing demands. With the increasing size of datasets, especially in computational pathology, CNN processing takes even longer and uses higher computational resources. Considerable research has been conducted to improve the efficiency of CNN, such as quantization. This paper aims to apply efficient training and inference of ResNet using quantization on histopathology images, the Patch Camelyon (PCam) dataset. An analysis for efficient approaches to classify histopathology images is presented. First, the original RGB-colored images are evaluated. Then, compression methods such as channel reduction and sparsity are applied. When comparing sparsity on grayscale with RGB modes, classification accuracy is relatively the same, but the total number of MACs is less in sparsity on grayscale by 77% than RGB. A higher classification result was achieved by grayscale mode, which requires much fewer MACs than the original RGB mode. Our method's low energy and processing make this project suitable for inference on wearable healthcare low powered devices and mobile hospitals in rural areas or developing countries. This also assists pathologists by presenting a preliminary diagnosis.

Keywords: Deep learning · Quantization · Computational Pathology

1 Introduction

Convolutional Neural Networks (CNNs) offer significant superiority for use on small and large -scale data-sets due to the exceptional performance on image classification and recognition tasks, achieving close to human-level perception rates. Nonetheless, to achieve the advantages, the processing demands of high-depth CNNs spanning hundreds of layers face serious computational and memory resources challenges. These bottlenecks have been motivating the development of promising approaches to improve CNN efficiency at both software and hardware levels [29,31]. From an algorithm point-of-view, the use of shallower but

P. L. Mazzeo et al. (Eds.): ICIAP 2022 Workshops, LNCS 13373, pp. 533–544, 2022.
https://doi.org/10.1007/978-3-031-13321-3_47

wider CNN models, quantization, pruning, model distillation, etc., have been explored extensively. Lately, leveraging weights and activations with low bit-width reduces computational complexity and model size (storage components). For instance, bit-wise convolution between the inputs and low bit-width weights has been demonstrated in [42] by converting conventional Multiplication-And-Accumulate (MAC) operations into their corresponding AND and/or XOR operations. However, such conversion cannot necessarily guarantee high efficiency in a hardware implementation that may engage various instruction encoding and operand access aspects. In an extreme quantization, Binary Convolutional Neural Network (BNN) has achieved acceptable accuracy by relaxing the demands for some high precision calculations, where it binarizes weight/input through the forward path [8]. From the hardware point of view, in order to improve the efficiency of CNNs, comprehensive studies for developing accelerators using GPUs, FPGAs, and ASICs have been researched. Due to the isolated computing units and memory elements utilized in conventional von-Neumann designs, severe challenges, such as high leakage power consumption, limited memory bandwidth channels, and long memory access latency. Consequently, different designs as a non-von Neumann architecture, including *near* and *in* -memory computing architectures, have been introduced and implemented to address the challenges mentioned above [30]. There are many promising applications of accelerating deep learning algorithms.

Deep learning (DL) has been successful and shows tremendous improvement in digital pathology [9,19,23,33,34]. Pathologists examine histopathology cancer images for diagnosis. These images show the underlying tissue architecture, such as cell nuclei, glands, and lymphocytes. Some diseases, such as lymphatic infiltration of cancer, can only be diagnosed using histopathology images [14]. However, these diagnoses may vary across pathologists and the same pathologist across time. This introduces variability in the diagnosis process alongside the inherent variability in the cancerous appearance [20,38,40]. The nuclei patterns in histopathology images are irregular and complex. This makes it hard to recognize the nuclei. [3] A pathologist's availability may be limited and expensive. This poses an urgent need for automatic processing of histopathology images in order to achieve a better and faster diagnosis. Applying deep learning (DL) in digital pathology provides a second opinion to pathologists that would allow them to produce a better diagnosis and reduce their workload. In addition, it serves as a quality measure for pathologists' recommendations and also can be used to train new pathologists [38]. Incorporating diagnostic decisions from DL with pathologists would produce more reliable results since errors in human diagnosis and machine diagnosis are not usually the same type [39].

Since almost all wearable healthcare devices are resource-constrained from both computational and storage perspectives, developing appropriate and promising techniques is vital but challenging. Therefore, we plan to evaluate the effectiveness of low bitwidth inference on CNN to produce a lower energy model with comparable results. This paper presents a comprehensive analysis for efficient approaches to classify histopathology images accurately. First, we aim to evaluate the processing of the original RGB (red, green, blue) colored images and then apply different compression methods, including channel reduction and sparsity. Finally, all possible combinations of these compression methods are considered, and their effectiveness is examined and compared.

2   Background

CNNs have shown great promise for a wide range of applications, including image classification [21], speech recognition [13], language processing [22], computer games [18], and autonomous car driving [26]. However, gaining high accuracy needs more complex computation; therefore, demand for accelerating of CNNs becomes more important day by day. Another essential key for CNNs is energy consumption. For instance. the energy cost per 32b operation in the 45nm technology is approximately equal to $3pj$ for arithmetic operation, whereas the energy consumption for off-chip memory accesses is approximately equal to $640pj$ [17]. To solve these issues, researchers proposed various hardware/software co-design approaches [5,6,10,11,27,28], including ASIC designs and quantization.

Quantization is defined as the process of approximating a continuous signal by a set of discrete symbols or integer values. The quantization technique is typically performed during inference. One simple way to compress neural networks is by reducing precision values. Although using this method was proposed as far back as the 1990s [2,12], attention to the quantization again began in the 2010s s when researchers [35] used 8-bit weight values rather than 32-bit floating-point (FP32) weight to accelerate inference without a significant accuracy loss. Using 8-bit weight values accelerates inference and reduces bandwidth, energy, and on-chip area. There are two essential methods to replace floating-point values with a single bit: 1) stochastic and 2) deterministic [7]. The stochastic methods consider the value of input or global statistics to determine the value of the weights. While, in deterministic methods, weight is determined directly based on their values. For example, using a sign function, the positive weights will be replaced with $+1$, and others with -1.

2.1   Dataset

The Camelyon16 dataset [4] contains hematoxylin and eosin (H&E) stained whole-slide images of lymph nodes from breast cancer patients. The data was collected in the Netherlands. The information was released in the Grand Challenge 2016, which detects breast cancer metastasis in lymph nodes. The PatchCamelyon (PCam) dataset [37] that is derived from Camelyon16 is used in this paper. The PCam consists of 327,680 histopathologic color images of 96×96 pixels. Each image represents the presence or absence of metastasic tissue, making it a binary classification task. Class 1 represent 50% of the dataset, and so class 0. The dataset is partitioned as follows: 262,144 for training, 32,768 for validation, and 32,768 for testing. Figure 1 shows examples of images with metastasis and non-metastasis cancer cases.

Metastasis (class 1)   Non-metastasis (class 0)

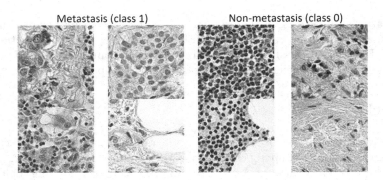

Fig. 1. Sample images from the metastasis and non-metastasis classes. (Color figure online)

We will review the most popular papers that analyze deep learning classification on PatchCamelyon (PCam) dataset [37], our target dataset. A unique model was developed based on DenseNet, called P4M-DenseNet. It was then concluded that rotation and reflection of the PCam dataset are helpful and cannot be learned through data augmentation. [37] An equivariant version of MobileNetV2 was designed and quantized on int8. The model was tested on PCam. [25] A modified scale-equivariant DenseNet model, called S-DensNet, was developed that utilizes the symmetry structure of convolutional tasks was evaluated on PCam by [41].

3   Methodology

In this section, the work pipeline is discussed in detail. First, we obtain the PCam dataset, and sample images are shown in Fig. 1. Second, a quantized ResNet56 model based on DoReFa-Net is created with different bitwidth lengths, specifically (1, 2, 4, 8, 32) for weights and activation parameters. According to DoReFa-Net implementation, the first and last layers of the model are not quantized, and the bias is added to weight parameters in these two layers. This mitigates the problem of losing information due to reducing bitwidth in calculations. We want to develop an algorithm to train histopathology images using low bit-width and then perform inference on low energy devices. W-bits represent the number of bits used for synapses weights between convolutional layers. A-bits represent the number of bits used for the activation matrix, which is the output of a convolution layer. No quantization is used when using full precision, bitwidth is 32, as it is not computationally efficient [42]. We propose using three combinations of color modes: grayscale, sparsity on grayscale, and sparsity on RGB. Our main idea is to convert original RGB images into different representations that use lower energy and result in comparable testing accuracy. Grayscale representation only uses one channel instead of three channels (RGB) in every image. This gives a representation with a two-third decrease in data size. Sparsity on RGB removes white pixels that might not be necessary for final diagnosis. These white

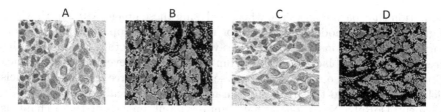

Fig. 2. An example image from the dataset with random rotation. A) shows the original RGB. B) shows the image after applying sparsity on RGB. C) shows the image after applying grayscale. D) shows the image after applying sparsity on grayscale. (Color figure online)

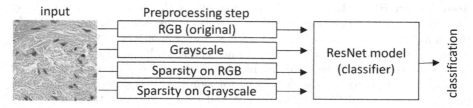

Fig. 3. After reading an image, four independent preprocessing steps are applied. 1) Keeping the original RGB image. 2) Converting it to grayscale. 3) Increasing sparsity of the original RGB image. 4) Increasing sparsity of the grayscale image. ResNet model is trained on the selected color mode from the previous step. The model then is evaluated on the testing dataset to get classification accuracy. (Color figure online)

pixels are replaced by black pixels, making convolutional operations run faster by skipping these black pixels. Sparsity on grayscale is used to merge both reduction methods and produce a more reduced representation that might be used for very low-energy devices.

3.1   Four Examined Modes

There are four modes of experiments based on the color status of the PCam dataset: RGB, grayscale, sparsity on RGB, and sparsity on grayscale. An example of each color mode is shown in Fig. 2. These modes are used to create a dataset for training and inference on the model. For data augmentation, random rotation is applied to the dataset, such as in Fig. 2C and Fig. 2D. The steps of our process are shown in Fig. 3.

RGB. In this mode, the original colored dataset is used as-is. Every pixel in an image is defined by three numbers corresponding to red, blue, and green. Every number is between 0 and 255, where 0 is black, and 255 is white.

Grayscale. In this mode, the original RGB-colored images are converted into grayscale images. Several studies show that converting histopathology images to grayscale results in lower accuracy because grayscale images may miss relevant information that pathologists use when analyzing these images [19,24]. However, the grayscale color mode can be used for normalizing histopathology images by ignoring stain variations [36]. Usually, grayscale images contain one channel that represents white to black variation, from 0 to 255. However, due to technical reasons, we had to use a grayscale representation with three identical channels, which doesn't change the image appearance. The technical reason is that we implement DoReFa-Net version that requires input images of three channels, not one channel. We did not change the number of channels in the model's input layer to be consistent with all color modes but used a grayscale of three identical channels. We do not make any changes the network architecture for any specific color mode.

Sparsity on RGB. In this mode, the sparsity of the dataset is increased. By sparsity, we mean the percentage of black pixels in every image in the dataset. As shown in Fig. 1, the dataset contains H&E stained histopathology images. These images contain purple color for the cell's nuclei and pink color for the cytoplasm [1]. The remaining color is white. We increase the sparsity of the dataset in order to evaluate the change in the model's performance. This is done by reading each pixel in each colored 96 × 96 px image and converting each whitish pixel to black (zero). There is no clear definition of a whitish color. However, we found that it is safe to consider whitish pixels greater or equal to 200 on the scale of 0 (black) to 255 (white). Converting whitish pixels to black increases sparsity in the image, making hardware implementation more accessible and faster. In hardware processing of convolutional operations, black pixels are skipped and not processed. Hence, the processing becomes more efficient. The PCam images contain 20% whitish pixels on average. Converting these pixels into black should, generally, reduce the processing time.

Sparsity on Grayscale. We integrated the two approaches to benefit from the previous two color modes. Specifically, we take grayscale images described above and apply the sparsity step described above. This results in a dataset of grayscale images with increased sparsity.

4   Experimental Results and Discussion

4.1   Model

Our model is a modified version of ResNet56 [15], which contains 56 convolutional layers. The model starts with the conv2d layer, followed by model layers, then a batch normalization layer, and finally a linear (dense) layer. The first conv2d applies 16 kernels of size 3 × 3. The model layers are organized into 26 blocks. Each block starts with activation quantization, then batch normalization, then conv2d with quantized weights, then a batch normalization. The block ends with a conv2d with quantized weights. Blocks number 9 and 18 are different from the others. They contain strided conv2d and skip connections.

Table 1. Classification inference/testing results for All color modes.

a-bits	w-bits	RGB	Sparsity on RGB	Grayscale	Sparsity on grayscale
1	1	0.72	0.77	0.81	0.80
1	2	0.80	0.78	0.81	0.80
1	4	0.77	0.79	0.81	0.81
1	8	0.74	0.77	0.81	0.80
2	1	0.78	0.81	0.85	0.83
2	2	0.81	0.82	**0.86**	**0.84**
2	4	0.81	0.82	0.85	0.83
2	8	0.81	0.81	**0.86**	0.81
4	1	0.78	0.82	0.85	0.80
4	2	0.83	0.79	0.85	0.83
4	4	0.79	0.81	**0.86**	0.81
4	8	0.78	0.83	0.84	0.81
8	1	**0.84**	0.79	0.85	0.82
8	2	0.78	**0.85**	0.85	0.82
8	4	0.80	0.83	0.85	0.81
8	8	0.80	0.81	**0.86**	0.82
32	32	0.83	0.77	0.85	0.83

4.2   Accuracy Analysis

In this section, we present classification results using the PCam dataset in the four-color modes described in the previous Sect. 3. The reported accuracy is calculated using *sklearn.metrics.accuracy_score*, which is the number of correctly classified images divided by the total number of images in the testing dataset.

Training Details. The model is optimized using a Stochastic Gradient Descent (SGD) with batch size 32 and cross entropy loss for 100 epochs. The learning rate starts at 1e−4 and is divided by ten gradually every 20 training epochs. The best parameters were selected based on validation loss. Training was performed using PyTorch on a single NVIDIA Tesla V100 GPU. The same training procedure and hyperparameters are used for all four color modes.

RGB. Results of RGB mode can be found in Table 1. The best accuracy of 84% from experiment setting of 8 bits for a-bits and 1-bit for w-bit, abbreviated as 8-1. Details of this accuracy result of 8-1 are shown in Table 2. The accuracy drops to 82% when training the same model with the full precision of 32 a-bits and 32 w-bits.

Grayscale. Table 1 shows classification results from the dataset in a grayscale mode. The best accuracy of 86% is achieved using these configurations for a-bits and w-bits: 2-2, 2-8, 4-4, and 8-8. Table 2 shows the detailed result for 2-2 configuration.

Sparsity on RGB. Results in Table 1 show sparsity on RGB mode prediction accuracies for all configurations. The model gives an accuracy of 77% with full

Table 2. Detailed results of the best configurations for each color mode: True positive (TP), true negative (TN), false positive (FP), false negative (FN), true positive rate (TPR), true negative rate (TNR), and accuracy. The Activation (A) and Weights (W) bitwidth are shown. To have fair comparison, the baseline method contains no quantization and no further optimization.

Color mode	TN	TP	FN	FP	TNR	TPR	Accuracy	A-W bits
RGB (original)	0.90	0.78	0.10	0.22	0.80	0.87	0.84	8-1
Grayscale	**0.91**	0.81	0.09	0.19	0.83	**0.90**	0.86	2-8
Sparsity on RGB	0.88	**0.93**	0.12	0.07	**0.93**	0.89	0.85	8-2
Sparsity on Grayscale	0.84	**0.84**	0.16	0.16	**0.84**	0.84	0.84	2-2
RGB (original) [baseline]	0.90	0.75	0.10	0.25	0.78	0.88	0.83	32-32

precision. However, it produces the best accuracy of 85% when using 8 a-bits and 2 w-bits, 8-2. The detailed result of this configuration is shown in Table 2.

Sparsity on Grayscale. Table 1 shows the classification results of the model when using the sparsity on the grayscale dataset. The model produces an accuracy of 83% when using full precision of weights and activation parameters. However, the accuracy jumps slightly to 84% when using 2 a-bits 2 w-bits, abbreviated as 2-2. Table 2 shows a detailed result for 2-2 configuration.

4.3   Comparing Results of the Four Modes

This section presents a comparison of processing the four-color models in training and inference. Table 2 shows the detailed classification results of all color modes. The true positive rate (TPR) is shown, which is the sensitivity rate. This rate means the number of sick people that are correctly identified as sick. Additionally, the true negative rate (TNR) is shown. This rate is the specificity rate, which means the number of healthy people that are correctly identified as not sick. We have added our baseline method, which is RGB (original) with 32-32 configuration that contains no optimization and no quantization. It is clearly demonstrated that grayscale mode gives the highest true positive rate. The highest true negative rate achieved by the sparsity on RGB mode. These results emphasize our hypothesis that compression methods, such as channel reduction or sparsity, may achieve better classification results than original RGB color mode.

4.4   Performance Analysis

With the same cache design, using the gray_sparse technique, we almost achieved one-sixth cache misses compared to the RGB inputs, which decreases data movement overhead and consequently reduces power consumption significantly. Although additional hardware components are required to handle the zero-skipping approach, the imposed overhead is negligible compared to the arithmetic logic unit and memory access instructions.

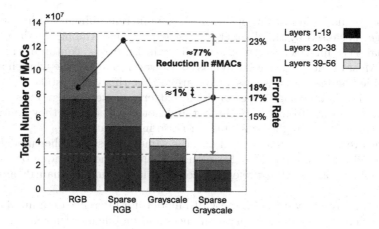

Fig. 4. Total number of MACs *vs.* error rate regarding different approaches.

Herein, because the main portions (>99%) of various deep and convolutional neural networks are occupied by MAC operations [32], we consider the total number of MACs as the main performance metrics for both power consumption and execution time. Moreover, the energy consumption of data-intensive (memory-enteric) applications such as CNN is usually dominated by data accesses to on-chip storage and off-chip memory. For example, in [16], authors showed that reading a 32-bit floating-point value from the main memory and moving it to the higher level of a memory hierarchy takes around two orders of magnitudes than performing a multiplication for the same data within a processor. The same analysis can be performed for the execution time; the lower the number of MACs, the lower the execution time. Figure 4 depicts the total number of MACs for four different implementations with respect to the error rate. Furthermore, the quantized results can be achieved by aggressively scaling the baseline model; for example, 8-bit integers approximately obtain ×4 speedup or/and energy efficiency compared to a 32-bit floating-point implementation.

5   Conclusion

In this project, we used low bitwidth ResNet56 based on DoReFa-Net quantization on histopathology images. We found that compression methods such as grayscale and sparsity could help in giving comparable or better prediction accuracy than original RGB images. This could help in deploying digital diagnostic systems on healthcare wearable devices or low power devices. We found that grayscale images gives a true positive rate of 3% more than the original RGB.

There are many limitations of this work. An inherent difficulty in histopathology images is caused by the diversity in tissue patterns. Among the dataset, we found that 4178 images contain at least 95% whitish pixels, containing no tissue pattern. Most of these images are in class 0. However, a few of the whitish images are classified as metastasis, class 1. We argue that this is a mistake in labeling because it labels an image with no tissue pattern as metastasis. These images should be discarded from the beginning and not used because they contain no tissue pattern. They might be a cause of noise in the dataset.

For future work, we plan to evaluate the same process on other models such as ResNet56 and AlexNet. We also plan to evaluate the technique on another histopathology dataset that preferably contains larger images than PCam, such as TCGA.

Our goal is to allow using low bitwidth models for inference on limited energy devices such as mobile devices on ambulances and mobile hospitals in rural areas or in developing countries. We aim to assist pathologists and facilitate their work in order for them to produce a final clear decision using different tools.

References

1. Araújo, T., et al.: Classification of breast cancer histology images using convolutional neural networks. PLoS ONE **12**(6), e0177544 (2017). https://doi.org/10.1371/journal.pone.0177544
2. Balzer, W., et al.: Weight quantization in Boltzmann machines. Neural Netw. **4**(3), 405–409 (1991). https://doi.org/10.1016/0893-6080(91)90077-I
3. Beevi, K.S., et al.: Automatic mitosis detection in breast histopathology images using convolutional neural network based deep transfer learning. Biocybern. Biomed. Eng. **39**(1), 214–223 (2019). https://doi.org/10.1016/j.bbe.2018.10.007
4. Bejnordi, B.E., et al.: Diagnostic assessment of deep learning algorithms for detection of lymph node metastases in women with breast cancer. JAMA **318**(22), 2199–2210 (2017). https://doi.org/10.1001/jama.2017.14585
5. Chakradhar, S., et al.: A dynamically configurable coprocessor for convolutional neural networks. In: Proceedings of the 37th Annual International Symposium on Computer Architecture, pp. 247–257 (2010). https://doi.org/10.1145/1815961.1815993
6. Chen, T., et al.: DianNao: a small-footprint high-throughput accelerator for ubiquitous machine-learning. ACM SIGARCH Comput. Archit. News **42**(1), 269–284 (2014). https://doi.org/10.1145/2654822.2541967
7. Courbariaux, M., et al.: BinaryConnect: training deep neural networks with binary weights during propagations. In: Advances in Neural Information Processing Systems, pp. 3123–3131 (2015). 10.48550/arXiv. 1511.00363
8. Courbariaux, M., et al.: Binarized neural networks: training deep neural networks with weights and activations constrained to +1 or −1. arXiv preprint arXiv:1602.02830 (2016). https://doi.org/10.48550/arXiv.1602.02830
9. Cruz-Roa, A., et al.: High-throughput adaptive sampling for whole-slide histopathology image analysis (HASHI) via convolutional neural networks: application to invasive breast cancer detection. PloS One **13**(5) (2018). https://doi.org/10.1371/journal.pone.0196828

10. Du, Z., et al.: ShiDianNao: shifting vision processing closer to the sensor. In: Proceedings of the 42nd Annual International Symposium on Computer Architecture, pp. 92–104 (2015). https://doi.org/10.1145/2749469.2750389

11. Farabet, C., et al.: CNP: an FPGA-based processor for convolutional networks. In: 2009 Intl Conference on Field Programmable Logic and Applications, pp. 32–37. IEEE (2009). https://doi.org/10.1109/FPL.2009.5272559

12. Fiesler, E., et al.: Weight discretization paradigm for optical neural networks. In: Optical Interconnections and Networks, vol. 1281, pp. 164–173. Intl Society for Optics and Photonics (1990). https://doi.org/10.1117/12.20700

13. Graves, A., et al.: Speech recognition with deep recurrent neural networks. In: 2013 IEEE International Conference on Acoustics, Speech and Signal Processing, pp. 6645–6649. IEEE (2013). https://doi.org/10.1109/ICASSP.2013.6638947

14. Gurcan, M.N., et al.: Histopathological image analysis: a review. IEEE Rev. Biomed. Eng. **2**, 147–171 (2009). https://doi.org/10.1109/RBME.2009.2034865

15. He, K., et al.: Deep residual learning for image recognition. In: Proceedings of the IEEE conference on Computer Vision and Pattern Recognition, pp. 770–778 (2016). https://doi.org/10.1109/CVPR.2016.90

16. Horowitz, M.: 1.1 computing's energy problem (and what we can do about it). In: 2014 IEEE International Solid-State Circuits Conference Digest of Technical Papers (ISSCC), pp. 10–14. IEEE (2014). https://doi.org/10.1109/ISSCC.2014.6757323

17. Horowitz, M.: Energy table for 45nm process. In: Stanford VLSI wiki (2014)

18. Kim, M., Kim, J., Lee, D., Son, J., Lee, W.: A study on autoplay model using DNN in turn-based RPG. In: Bhatia, S.K., Tiwari, S., Ruidan, S., Trivedi, M.C., Mishra, K.K. (eds.) Advances in Computer, Communication and Computational Sciences. AISC, vol. 1158, pp. 399–407. Springer, Singapore (2021). https://doi.org/10.1007/978-981-15-4409-5_36

19. Komura, D., Ishikawa, S.: Machine learning methods for histopathological image analysis. Comput. Struct. Biotechnol. J. **16**, 34–42 (2018). https://doi.org/10.1016/j.csbj.2018.01.001

20. Korbar, B., et al.: Deep learning for classification of colorectal polyps on whole-slide images. J. Pathol. Inform. **8** (2017). https://doi.org/10.4103/jpi.jpi_34_17

21. Krizhevsky, A., et al.: ImageNet classification with deep convolutional neural networks. In: Advances in Neural Information Processing Systems 25, pp. 1097–1105 (2012). https://doi.org/10.1145/3065386

22. Landolt, S., et al.: A taxonomy for deep learning in natural language processing. In: Hawaii International Conference on System Sciences (2021). https://doi.org/10.24251/HICSS.2021.129

23. Litjens, G., et al.: A survey on deep learning in medical image analysis. Med. Image Anal. **42**, 60–88 (2017). https://doi.org/10.1016/j.media.2017.07.005

24. Mejbri, S., et al.: Deep analysis of CNN settings for new cancer whole-slide histological images segmentation: the case of small training sets. In: 6th International Conference on BioImaging (BIOIMAGING 2019), pp. 120–128 (2019). https://doi.org/10.5220/0007406601200128

25. Mohamed, M., et al.: A data and compute efficient design for limited-resources deep learning. arXiv preprint arXiv:2004.09691 (2020)

26. Parashar, A., et al.: Automated guided autonomous car using deep learning and computer vision. In: Autonomous Driving and Advanced Driver-Assistance Systems (ADAS): Apps, Development, Legal Issues, and Testing, p. 219 (2021). https://doi.org/10.1201/9781003048381-10

27. Qadeer, W., et al.: Convolution engine: balancing efficiency & flexibility in specialized computing. In: Proceedings of the 40th Annual International Symposium on Computer Architecture, pp. 24–35 (2013). https://doi.org/10.1145/2485922.2485925

28. Qiu, J., et al.: Going deeper with embedded FPGA platform for convolutional neural network. In: Proceedings of the 2016 ACM/SIGDA International Symposium on Field-Programmable Gate Arrays, pp. 26–35 (2016). https://doi.org/10.1145/2847263.2847265

29. Roohi, A., et al.: ApGAN: approximate GAN for robust low energy learning from imprecise components. IEEE Trans. Comput. **69**(3), 349–360 (2019). https://doi.org/10.1109/TC.2019.2949042

30. Roohi, A., et al.: Processing-in-memory acceleration of convolutional neural networks for energy-efficiency, and power-intermittency resilience. In: 20th International Symposium on Quality Electronic Design (ISQED), pp. 8–13. IEEE (2019). https://doi.org/10.1109/ISQED.2019.8697572

31. Roohi, A., et al.: RNSim: efficient deep neural network accelerator using residue number systems. In: 2021 IEEE/ACM International Conference On Computer Aided Design (ICCAD), pp. 1–9. IEEE (2021). https://doi.org/10.1109/ICCAD51958.2021.9643531

32. Sharma, H., et al.: Bit fusion: bit-level dynamically composable architecture for accelerating deep neural network. In: 2018 ACM/IEEE 45th Annual International Symposium on Computer Architecture (ISCA), pp. 764–775. IEEE (2018). https://doi.org/10.1109/ISCA.2018.00069

33. Shen, D., et al.: Deep learning in medical image analysis. Annu. Rev. Biomed. Eng. **19**, 221–248 (2017). https://doi.org/10.1146/annurev-bioeng-071516-044442

34. Srinidhi, C.L., et al.: Deep neural network models for computational histopathology: a survey. Med. Image Anal. 101813 (2020). https://doi.org/10.1016/j.media.2020.101813

35. Vanhoucke, V., Senior, A., Mao, M.Z.: Improving the speed of neural networks on CPUs. In: Deep Learning and Unsupervised Feature Learning Workshop, NIPS 2011 (2011)

36. Vasiljević, J., et al.: Towards histopathological stain invariance by unsupervised domain augmentation using generative adversarial networks. Neurocomputing **460**, 277–291 (2021). https://doi.org/10.1016/j.neucom.2021.07.005

37. Veeling, B.S., Linmans, J., Winkens, J., Cohen, T., Welling, M.: Rotation equivariant CNNs for digital pathology. In: Frangi, A.F., Schnabel, J.A., Davatzikos, C., Alberola-López, C., Fichtinger, G. (eds.) MICCAI 2018. LNCS, vol. 11071, pp. 210–218. Springer, Cham (2018). https://doi.org/10.1007/978-3-030-00934-2_24

38. Veta, M., et al.: Breast cancer histopathology image analysis: a review. IEEE Trans. Biomed. Eng. **61**(5), 1400–1411 (2014). https://doi.org/10.1109/TBME.2014.2303852

39. Wang, D., et al.: Deep learning for identifying metastatic breast cancer. arXiv preprint arXiv:1606.05718 (2016)

40. Wei, J.W., et al.: Pathologist-level classification of histologic patterns on resected lung adenocarcinoma slides with deep neural networks. Sci. Rep. **9**(1) (2019). https://doi.org/10.1038/s41598-019-40041-7

41. Worrall, D., Welling, M.: Deep scale-spaces: equivariance over scale. In: Advances in Neural Information Processing Systems 32 (2019). https://doi.org/10.5555/3454287.3454949

42. Zhou, S., et al.: DoReFa-Net: training low bitwidth convolutional neural networks with low bitwidth gradients. arXiv preprint arXiv:1606.06160 (2016)

AI Support for Accelerating Histopathological Slide Examinations of Prostate Cancer in Clinical Studies

Mauro Del Rio[1], Luca Lianas[1], Oskar Aspegren[2,4],
Giovanni Busonera[1], Francesco Versaci[1], Renata Zelic[3,4],
Per H. Vincent[3,4], Simone Leo[1], Andreas Pettersson[3,4], Olof Akre[3,4],
and Luca Pireddu[1(✉)]

[1] Visual and Data-Intensive Computing, CRS4, 09050 Pula (CA), Italy
{mauro.delrio,luca.lianas,giovanni.busonera,francesco.versaci,
simone.leo,luca.pireddu}@crs4.it
[2] Department of Clinical Pathology and Cancer Diagnostics,
Karolinska University Hospital, 17176 Stockholm, Sweden
[3] Department of Pelvic Cancer, Karolinska University Hospital,
17176 Stockholm, Sweden
[4] Department of Molecular Medicine and Surgery, Karolinska Institutet,
17176 Stockholm, Sweden KI, Sweden

Abstract. While studies in pathology are essential for the progress in the diagnostic and prognostic techniques in the field, pathologist time is becoming an increasingly scarce resource, and can indeed become the limiting factor in the feasibility of studies to be performed. In this work, we demonstrate how the Digital Pathology platform by CRS4, for supporting research studies in digital pathology, has been augmented by the addition of AI-based features to accelerate image examination to reduce the pathologist time required for clinical studies. The platform has been extended to provide computationally generated annotations and visual cues to help the pathologist prioritize high-interest image areas. The system includes an image annotation pipeline with DeepHealth-based deep learning models for tissue identification and prostate cancer identification. Annotations are viewed through the platform's virtual microscope and can be controlled interactively (e.g., thresholding, coloring). Moreover, the platform captures inference provenance information and archives it as RO-Crate artifacts containing data and metadata required for reproducibility. We evaluate the models and the inference pipeline, achieving AUC of 0.986 and 0.969 for tissue and cancer identification, respectively, and verifying linear dependence of execution speed on image tissue content. Finally, we describe the ongoing clinical validation of the contribution, including preliminary results, and discuss feedback from clinical professionals regarding the overall approach.

Keywords: Digital pathology · Artificial intelligence · Workflows

M. Del Rio and L. Lianas—These authors contributed equally to this work.

© The Author(s) 2022
P. L. Mazzeo et al. (Eds.): ICIAP 2022 Workshops, LNCS 13373, pp. 545–556, 2022.
https://doi.org/10.1007/978-3-031-13321-3_48

1   Introduction

The examination and annotation of images of tissue samples is a critical part of clinical studies in the field of pathology – that is, the medical discipline that diagnoses disease from tissue and relevant clinical data. In such studies, tissue characteristics are identified and analyzed, along with other patient traits, in the search for information useful to improve clinical practice. The tissue samples are collected by either surgery or biopsy. Slices of these specimens are then mounted on glass slides, stained (coloured) and, finally, scanned by special-purpose digital optical microscopes. The resulting digital pathology images – often referred to as slides, like the glass slides from which they are scanned – are very high in resolution (typically 40× magnification, which results in images with a resolution in the order of tens of Gigapixels and a size 1–5 GB per compressed image). The examination and image annotation required of pathologists to conduct such clinical studies is defined in detail by the study protocol, and it is generally much more time-consuming than examining slides for regular clinical diagnostic practice. For instance, study protocols may require the annotation and measurement of additional exploratory features that are not currently part of any clinical diagnostic or prognostic protocol. Therefore, pathologist time tends to become the limiting factor in the feasibility of the studies – a situation worsened by the declining number of pathologists and the rise in biopsy volumes. Computer-aided pathology holds a lot of potential to ameliorate the situation by accelerating the slide examination and annotation process and reducing the required human effort through the use of AI methodologies [21].

In this setting, the support of bespoke software can be very valuable to facilitate the rigorous application of the study protocol and the correct management of such a study: the Digital Pathology (DP) Platform by CRS4 [27] is a system exactly for this purpose. It provides a platform for configuring vertical applications for managing, examining and annotating digital pathology images within the context of clinical research. It supports all major virtual slide formats and provides users with a web application that includes a virtual microscope, allowing the on-line interactive remote visualization and annotation of very large virtual slides, without loss of quality with respect to optical microscopes [33]. The platform also provides a palette of tools to accurately draw and measure regions of interest (ROIs) following irregular tissue contours. Using the platform, a vertical application has been created for studies on prostate cancer. In addition to general annotations, the application adds specifically detailed prostate cancer ROI annotation labels. A minimally customized variant of this configuration of the platform has been used to conduct the Prognostic Factors for Mortality in Prostate Cancer (ProMort) study [34], and another is currently being used in a study aiming to improve prostate cancer prognosis through the integration of advanced statistical modeling and the inclusion of new prognostic variables [28].

In this work, we describe how we extended the DP Platform with AI-based functionality to better support the examination and annotation of digital pathology slides in the context of clinical studies. The remainder of the manuscript is structured as follows: Sect. 2 provides relevant background; Sect. 3 describes the main contributions, including the inference pipeline, the deep learning models, the visualization strategy and the collection of provenance information; Sect. 4 describes the evaluation and discusses the results; finally, Sect. 5 concludes the work.

2   Background and Related Work

The DeepHealth Toolkit. The DeepHealth toolkit [8] is an open source deep learning framework. It is specifically tailored to be easily applied to biomedical data (for instance, it includes functionality to read digital pathology images) and to leverage heterogeneous computing resources (e.g., high-performance computing clusters, cloud computing platforms, GPU and FPGA accelerators). The toolkit's deep learning (EDDL) and computer vision (ECVL) libraries have been used (through their respective Python APIs) to implement the AI functionality described in this work.

Related Work. To the best of the authors' knowledge, no other software platform has been published that aims to support the execution of clinical studies in digital pathology in a way analogous to the DP Platform. However, much work has been published in related fields. For instance, OMERO provides whole-slide image (WSI) data management functionality, and it is also one of the key components of the DP Platform; it provides generic key-value image annotation that is not specialized on any particular domain. Other tools like QuPath [5], Orbit [25], FastPathology [20], ASAP [4], PathML [6] provide functionality to view and annotate slides; some even support machine/deep learning based segmentation and classification. However, these tools do not aim to support the execution of clinical study protocols, nor to provide domain-specific annotation tools. Recently, the PANDA challenge [7] has catalyzed efforts on the application of deep learning techniques to prostate cancer histopathology; however, PANDA focuses on prostate cancer prognosis, rather than identifying cancer tissue in prostate tissue images. Work has also been done on characterizing the aggressiveness of cancer tissue based on its appearance [26].

3   Slide Examination Support System

The DP Platform is a multi-component system consisting of an image repository/server, an annotation management service and a web application. The image repository is based on the OpenMicroscopy OMERO server [1] – the same system that is behind some large-scale public image repositories [13,30] – which has been extended with the purpose-built ome_seadragon software component [17] to add support for the Deep Zoom Image format [10] and web-based viewers for high-resolution zoomable images, such as the OpenSeadragon [18]. The user-facing web application interacts with the image and annotation services to provide functionality such as the virtual microscope, the annotation tools, etc.

In this work, the DP Platform has been augmented with new functionality to support the examination of histopathological slides by pathologists through computational annotation of the images. This functionality has been achieved by implementing a computational annotation pipeline that integrates multiple specialized deep learning models for image analysis, as well as custom visualization and examination tools that leverage the model predictions. In addition, to enhance the reproducibility of the computational results, the provenance information of the predictions is captured in RO-Crate artifacts [24] and stored with the annotations. The extended platform's architecture is illustrated in Fig. 1. The following subsections describe the components in more detail.

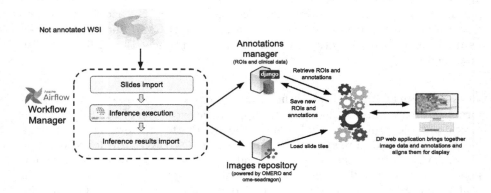

Fig. 1. The extended DP platform software architecture

3.1 Computational Annotation Pipeline

Computational annotation of digital pathology images has been integrated into the DP Platform through its slide import and pre-processing workflow. The workflow has been extended to apply AI-based analyses to digital pathology images at this stage. The added complexity of the process motivated the integration of the Apache Airflow workflow manager [3] into the platform as a process automation subsystem, providing sophisticated workflow execution and monitoring functionality (both programmatic and graphical).

As illustrated in Fig. 1, the image import pipeline is composed of three main stages: the first and third perform platform-specific data and metadata management; the "Inference execution" stage uses AI models to automatically analyze images. The computational pipeline of this stage is defined using the Common Workflow Language (CWL) [2] and executed using CWL-Airflow [16] – an implementation of CWL for Airflow. The choice of a standard workflow language improves workflow portability and facilitates the integration of novel data provenance approaches (see Sect. 3.4). The inference stage performs the following steps on the digital pathology image: a low-resolution mask of the tissue is inferenced (downsample factor of 2^9) and used to select the areas of the image that warrant further processing; the tissue mask is refined by repeating tissue inference at a higher magnification level (downsample factor of 2^4) on tissue areas recognized in step 1; cancer inference is performed at high magnification level (downsample factor of 2) on tissue areas recognized in step 1.

Each deep learning model is packaged as an executable Docker container image that provides inference functionality through a common interface – these images are based on pre-built DeepHealth toolkit images [11]. The abstract interface exposes the whole slide to the model, allowing it to support any kind of ensemble or complex model design. The generated annotations are stored using either Zarr [32] or TileDB [19]: both are modern formats for storing large N-dimensional arrays in a chunked, compressed and cloud-friendly data structure (at the moment the workflow implementation can be configured to use either solution). The import workflow invokes the inferencing containers, makes the data and previous predictions in the pipeline accessible to them (by mounting appropriate data volumes on the container), retrieves the resulting annotations and imports them into the annotations manager. The DP import workflow can be configured to run any number of annotating container images.

3.2   Deep Learning Image Annotation Models

Identification of Tissue. We have created a neural network model with the PyEDDL and PyECVL libraries for the identification of tissue areas on histological images. This model allows the platform to completely automate the tissue annotation phase in the clinical annotation process. To create the model, training, validation, and test sets were generated by manual annotation of background and tissue areas from a set of sample slides. Selected samples also contained different kinds of objects that can be found in the background – for example, markers and glue – which can easily generate errors in simple automated tissue recognition approaches, and which were also problematic for preliminary versions of the model. For this particular task, we defined a pixel-based model architecture made of dense layers which classifies input RGB pixels one-at-a-time, as opposed to patch-based architectures that are frequently used for image segmentation problems – such as U-Net [22] – which produce a single output for a given patch of pixels in input. This approach made it very simple to generate training data for the model by selecting blocks of pixels from tissue and background image areas, with no need to annotate samples of the tissue-background interface.

Identification of Prostate Cancer Areas. A second deep learning model has been developed to recognize adenocarcinoma of the prostate. Based on initial experiments, a patch classification approach was adopted: we decompose the histopathology slides into patches of size 256×256 pixels and classify each tissue patch as a whole as benign/malignant. Moreover, initial exploratory work brought us to select the VGG-16 network architecture [23]. The convolutional layers of the network are pre-trained with the ImageNet dataset [12] (without freezing any layer parameter), improving convergence speed and overall accuracy with respect to starting with models that were either completely untrained or using the Glorot [14] or He [15] initializations. To mitigate the effects of overfitting, dropout layers were added to the classification part of the network. Other solutions were also tested during model development, ranging from regularization techniques to data augmentation, as well as reducing the number of parameters of the fully connected classifier and using staining normalization – based on stain separation with preservation of the sample structure. These did not provide significant improvements in inference performance.

To create the model, a set of 417 slide images were scanned using a 3DHistech Pannoramic 250 Flash II at 40× magnification (pixel size of approximately 0.1945 µm/pixel). The slide images were examined and annotated by pathologists (using the DP Platform). From these, a training dataset of about 123K patches was generated (38K normal and 85K cancer patches) and saved to a scalable Cassandra-based patch repository [29]. Leveraging our custom Cassandra-based data loader, we created two kinds of balanced split configurations: the first, composed of two splits (80% training and 20% validation), was used for rapid evaluation of different training hyperparameter configurations; the second, composed of five equally sized splits, was used to more robustly evaluate promising models through cross-validation. Like the tissue identification model, this one was also developed with the PyEDDL and PyECVL libraries.

3.3   Visualization of Computational Annotations

The DP Platform has been extended with functionality to visualize the results of inference by deep learning models and use them to provide visual cues to assist the end user in the examination of the image. The outputs of the models developed for this use case are 2D arrays of "scores" at the pixel or patch level: in particular, the tissue detection model classifies single pixels, while cancer prediction works on whole patches. We have implemented two alternative visualization methods for these computational annotations: the heatmap and the vectorial ROI. These methods have both been integrated into the DP Platform's virtual microscope and produce visual artifacts that can be dynamically controlled by the user and overlaid onto the image (see Fig. 2).

The heatmap visualization (Fig. 2a), which is used for the cancer detection feature, is used to focus the attention of the pathologist on potentially relevant regions (like specific cancer patterns). To render the model outputs as heatmaps, the results produced by the models are registered into the DP Platform as new annotations of the slide and stored as arrays; they are then rendered at run time by a dedicated module by appropriately slicing the data and applying a color map. The web application includes controls to dynamically adjust the heatmap's opacity and to specify a threshold to cut off non-significant values.

On the other hand, the visualization of vectorial ROIs, which are used for the tissue detector output, requires additional post-processing on the model's 2D matrix output. Specifically, the continuous value matrix is transformed into a boolean mask by applying a configured threshold value. The mask is further processed to identify clusters of "true" values bigger than a set threshold (smaller clusters are not useful for the clinical review) and compute the enclosing geometry defining the ROI (Fig. 2b).

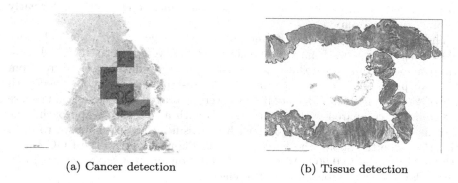

(a) Cancer detection   (b) Tissue detection

Fig. 2. Heatmap visualizations and tissue ROIs rendered in the Virtual Microscope, generated respectively from the outputs of the cancer and tissue identification models.

3.4   Prediction Provenance with RO-Crate

At the conclusion of the inference workflow execution for a given slide, the DP Platform generates an RO-Crate object (with the ro-crate-py library [9]) to capture the provenance data of the tissue and cancer predictions generated by the inference process. The RO-Crate references the slide, the predictions, the CWL inference workflow definition and its input parameters (including the model's specific Docker image tag). The RO-Crates thus created serve as archivable snapshots of prediction runs, and they are expected to greatly enhance the reproducibility of the predictions; they can even be a part of a more articulate graph that also documents the provenance of the slides by using the Common Provenance Model [31].

4   Evaluation and Discussion

Evaluation of the Tissue Predictive Model. The tissue predictive model was trained using a balanced dataset of about 30M pixels (i.e., 30M RGB triplets). The training took about 18.5 min (30 epochs, about 37 s for each epoch) running on a Nvidia RTX 2080Ti GPU with 12 GB RAM. We evaluated the model's accuracy with a balanced test set of 6M pixels. A maximum accuracy of 0.96 was achieved by setting the classification threshold (to assign the class of a pixel starting from its prediction score) to 0.65. The ROC curve (Fig. 3a) shows that the model can have its maximum sensitivity without increasing the false positive rate beyond 10%. The AUC is 0.986; the F1-score, which is 0.96 when using the threshold classification value of 0.65.

Evaluation of Cancer Predictive Model. The cancer prediction model was trained starting from a dataset composed of 384 annotated slides (taken from 200 different cases) resulting in 123,148 patches measuring 256×256 pixels each. The training was performed on a single GPU (Nvidia Titan RTX with 24 GB RAM) and the epoch time was on average 467 s (std 3.8 s). The minimum number of epochs needed to get the best validation accuracy, including 20 epochs for early stopping, ranged from 35 to 73.

The final evaluation was performed on a test set generated from 149 slides (taken from 109 cases), from which 66,698 patches were extracted. We characterized model performance through a five-fold cross validation procedure, from which we produced five different models. All test patches were classified with each of the five models. The predictions were averaged to have a single score that could be compared with the true labels with a soft voting approach. The resulting maximum accuracy is 0.91 with a classification threshold set to 0.58. With the same threshold, the F1-score is 0.9. Figure 3b shows the ROC curve, with an AUC equal to 0.969. All training, validation and test sets were generated to be balanced with respect to the two classes.

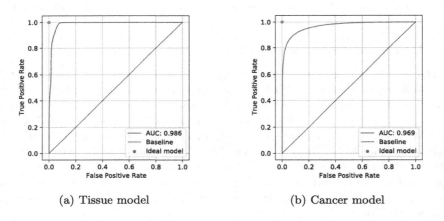

(a) Tissue model   (b) Cancer model

Fig. 3. ROC curves for the image analysis models

Computational Inference Pipeline Performance. We tested the inference pipeline described in Sect. 3.1 to characterize its overall speed and verify its linear progression with respect to the slide's tissue content. Experiments were conducted on node equipped with an Intel(R) Xeon(R) W-2145 CPU @ 3.70 GHz (8 cores, 16 threads), 128 GB RAM, a NVIDIA Quadro RTX 5000 (16 GB RAM), and a 3-HDD ZFS. The test set was composed of 203 WSI. Each slide was captured with a 3DHistech Pannoramic 250 Flash II scanner at a magnification of 40× (pixel size of approximately 0.1945 μm/pixel) and has a resolution of 112,908×265,513 pixels; the average tissue coverage per slide is 1.5%. Note that all prediction times are comprehensive of I/O operations for reading slides and writing results.

We report wall clock execution times of the inference pipeline in Fig. 4a. The various pipeline stages are executed serially and each occupies the single GPU on the test system. The difference between the execution time of the whole pipeline and the sum of the individual steps is used for the data management work performed by the pipeline, such as packaging the output of the models as Zarr arrays and registering them with the platform.

The execution time of the tissue mask refinement and cancer identification steps is dependent on the amount of tissue on the image, which explains the increased variability in the execution times for these steps. Our experiments show that the execution time of the pipeline's application of these models grows linearly with the image's tissue coverage (see Fig. 4b).

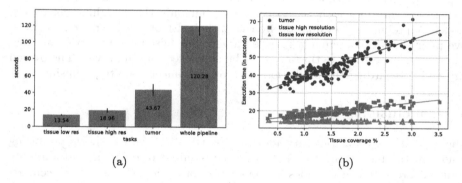

(a)   (b)

Fig. 4. (a) Average execution times of the prediction pipeline and its tasks. (b) Execution time of inference steps with respect to tissue coverage.

Clinical Evaluation. The AI-based slide examination functionality that has been added to the DP Platform is undergoing clinical evaluation based on measuring the time of annotation and assessment of the slides by the pathologist; this evaluation parameter is in line with the main goal of the platform's AI-based features to support the examination by an expert, rather than fully automate the process. While the full evaluation is not yet complete, in this work we report the preliminary results, as well as the feedback collected from the evaluating pathologist.

The review protocol followed for the clinical evaluation involves two steps: identification and measurement of the ROIs of relevance in the slide (in particular, identification of tissue cores and invasive cancerous areas within them); for each identified ROI, annotation of relevant clinical features (e.g., cancerous or inflammatory patterns, cancer staging scores, etc.). The evaluation is being conducted in three different stages: 1) Baseline, without any AI support tools; 2) Intermediate, with the examination supported by the tissue recognition model;

3) Final: with the examination supported by both the tissue and cancer identification models.

We present results for the Baseline and Intermediate evaluation stages. Annotation times were measured on 139 slides for the Baseline stage and 131 slides for the Intermediate stage. The clinical examination focused on the single cancerous tissue core per slide considered most relevant and sufficient for diagnostic purposes. For the Baseline stage, we measured an average annotation time of 11 min. For the Intermediate stage, the average annotation time per slide was 9 min. At the time of writing, the Final evaluation phase is in progress and no data on annotation time is available yet.

These preliminary evaluations suggest that the AI-based support tools presented here successfully reduce the time required for cancer slide examination and annotation by a pathologist. We expect the addition of sufficiently accurate cancer-identification functionality to further accelerate annotation in the Final stage, as the pathologist will no longer need to examine the full area of each tissue core in search for cancer areas, but only those highlighted by the model. A preliminary evaluation by the pathologist of the predictions of invasive prostate adenocarcinoma revealed a very low false-negative error rate and a false-positive error rate that needs to be addressed and improved. The overall impression regarding the predictions of prostate cancer is quite promising.

5   Conclusion

The new AI-based functionality added to the DP Platform has shown promising results in the reduction of pathologist time required to examine and annotate digitized prostate cancer slides in the context of clinical studies. The accuracy and computational performance of these new tools has been experimentally evaluated and their clinical evaluation is in progress. The software used for this work has been released under the MIT open source license and the code is available on GitHub (https://github.com/deephealthproject/promort_pipeline, https://github.com/crs4/slaid, https://github.com/crs4/deephealth-pipelines).

Acknowledgements. This work has been supported by the DeepHealth and EOSC-Life projects, both funded by the European Union's Horizon 2020 research and innovation programme (respectively under grant agreement numbers 825111 and 824087), and by the SVDC project funded by the Sardinian Regional Authority.

References

1. Allan, C., et al.: OMERO: flexible, model-driven data management for experimental biology. Nat. Methods **9**(3), 245–253 (2012)
2. Amstutz, P., et al.: Common workflow language, v1. 0 (2016)
3. Apache Airflow (2022). https://airflow.apache.org
4. ASAP. https://github.com/computationalpathologygroup/ASAP
5. Bankhead, P., et al.: QuPath: open source software for digital pathology image analysis. Sci. Rep. **7**(1) (2017)

6. Berman, A.G., Orchard, W.R., Gehrung, M., Markowetz, F.: PathML: a unified framework for whole-slide image analysis with deep learning. medRxiv (2021)
7. Bulten, W., et al.: Artificial intelligence for diagnosis and Gleason grading of prostate cancer: the PANDA challenge. Nat. Med. **28**, 154–163 (2022)
8. Cancilla, M., et al.: The DeepHealth toolkit: a unified framework to boost biomedical applications. In: 2020 25th International Conference on Pattern Recognition (ICPR), pp. 9881–9888 (2021)
9. De Geest, P., et al.: ro-crate-py (2022). https://zenodo.org/record/6594974#.YuOBJEzhXGg
10. Deep Zoom Image format. https://docs.microsoft.com/en-us/previous-versions/windows/dotnet-windows-silverlight/cc645050(v=vs.95)?redirectedfrom=MSDN
11. Deephealth dockerhub organization. https://hub.docker.com/u/dhealth
12. Deng, J., Dong, W., Socher, R., Li, L.J., Li, K., Fei-Fei, L.: ImageNet: a large-scale hierarchical image database. In: 2009 IEEE Conference on Computer Vision and Pattern Recognition, pp. 248–255. IEEE (2009)
13. Ellenberg, J., et al.: A call for public archives for biological image data. Nat. Methods **15**(11), 849–854 (2018)
14. Glorot, X., Bengio, Y.: Understanding the difficulty of training deep feedforward neural networks. In: Teh, Y.W., Titterington, M. (eds.) Proceedings of the Thirteenth International Conference on Artificial Intelligence and Statistics. Proceedings of Machine Learning Research, vol. 9, pp. 249–256. PMLR, 13–15 May 2010
15. He, K., Zhang, X., Ren, S., Sun, J.: Delving deep into rectifiers: surpassing human-level performance on ImageNet classification. In: 2015 IEEE International Conference on Computer Vision (ICCV), pp. 1026–1034 (2015). https://doi.org/10.1109/ICCV.2015.123
16. Kotliar, M., Kartashov, A.V., Barski, A.: CWL-airflow: a lightweight pipeline manager supporting common workflow language. Gigascience **8**(7), giz084 (2019)
17. ome-seadragon (2022). https://github.com/crs4/ome_seadragon
18. OpenSeadragon (2022). https://openseadragon.github.io
19. Papadopoulos, S., Datta, K., Madden, S., Mattson, T.: The TileDB array data storage manager. Proc. VLDB Endowment **10**(4), 349–360 (2016)
20. Pedersen, A., Valla, M., Bofin, A.M., De Frutos, J.P., Reinertsen, I., Smistad, E.: FastPathology: an open-source platform for deep learning-based research and decision support in digital pathology. IEEE Access **9**, 58216–58229 (2021)
21. Regitnig, P., Müller, H., Holzinger, A.: Expectations of artificial intelligence for pathology. In: Holzinger, A., Goebel, R., Mengel, M., Müller, H. (eds.) Artificial Intelligence and Machine Learning for Digital Pathology. LNCS (LNAI), vol. 12090, pp. 1–15. Springer, Cham (2020). https://doi.org/10.1007/978-3-030-50402-1_1
22. Ronneberger, O., Fischer, P., Brox, T.: U-Net: convolutional networks for biomedical image segmentation. In: Navab, N., Hornegger, J., Wells, W.M., Frangi, A.F. (eds.) MICCAI 2015. LNCS, vol. 9351, pp. 234–241. Springer, Cham (2015). https://doi.org/10.1007/978-3-319-24574-4_28
23. Simonyan, K., Zisserman, A.: Very deep convolutional networks for large-scale image recognition. In: Bengio, Y., LeCun, Y. (eds.) 3rd International Conference on Learning Representations, ICLR 2015, San Diego, CA, USA, 7–9 May 2015, Conference Track Proceedings (2015). http://arxiv.org/abs/1409.1556
24. Soiland-Reyes, S., et al.: Packaging research artefacts with RO-Crate. Data Sci. **5**(2), 97–138 (2022). https://zenodo.org/record/6594974#.YuOBJEzhXGg
25. Stritt, M., Stalder, A.K., Vezzali, E.: Orbit image analysis: an open-source whole slide image analysis tool. PLoS Comput. Biol. **16**(2), e1007313 (2020)

26. Ström, P., Kartasalo, K., Olsson, H., Solorzano, L., Delahunt, B., Berney, D.M., Bostwick, D.G., Evans, A.J., Grignon, D.J., Humphrey, P.A., et al.: Artificial intelligence for diagnosis and grading of prostate cancer in biopsies: a population-based, diagnostic study. Lancet Oncol. **21**(2), 222–232 (2020)
27. The Digital Pathology platform. https://github.com/crs4/ProMort
28. Turin prostate cancer prognostication study. https://sites.google.com/view/studio-tpcp/
29. Versaci, F., Busonera, G.: Scaling deep learning data management with Cassandra DB. In: 2021 IEEE International Conference on Big Data (Big Data), December 2021. https://doi.org/10.1109/BigData52589.2021.9672005
30. Williams, E., et al.: Image data resource: a bioimage data integration and publication platform. Nat. Methods **15**(11), 984–984 (2018). (vol 14, pg 775, 2017)
31. Wittner, R., et al.: ISO 23494: biotechnology – provenance information model for biological specimen and data. In: Glavic, B., Braganholo, V., Koop, D. (eds.) IPAW 2020-2021. LNCS, vol. 12839, pp. 222–225. Springer, Cham (2021). https://doi.org/10.1007/978-3-030-80960-7_16
32. Zarr. https://zarr.readthedocs.io/en/stable/
33. Zelic, R., et al.: Interchangeability of light and virtual microscopy for histopathological evaluation of prostate cancer. Sci. Rep. **11**(1), 1–11 (2021)
34. Zelic, R., et al.: Estimation of relative and absolute risks in a competing-risks setting using a nested case-control study design: example from the promort study. Am. J. Epidemiol. **188**(6), 1165–1173 (2019)

Detection of Pulmonary Conditions Using the DeepHealth Framework

Salvador Carrión, Álvaro López-Chilet, Javier Martínez-Bernia,
Joan Coll-Alonso, Daniel Chorro-Juan, and Jon Ander Gómez[✉]

Pattern Recognition and Human Language Technology Research Center,
Universitat Politècnica de València, Camí de Vera, 46022 València, Spain
{salcarpo,allochi,jamarbe2,jcolalo,dchojua,jon}@upv.es

Abstract. Medical diagnosis assisted by intelligent systems is an effective strategy to increase the efficiency of healthcare systems while reducing their costs. This work is focused on detecting pulmonary conditions from X-ray images using the DeepHealth framework. Our results suggest that it is possible to discriminate pulmonary conditions compatible with the COVID-19 disease from other conditions and healthy individuals. Hence, it could be stated that the DeepHealth framework is a suitable deep-learning software with which to perform reliable medical research. However, more medical data and research are still necessary to train deep learning models that could be trusted by medical personnel.

Keywords: Deep learning · Computer vision · Neural networks · Medical imaging · Covid19

1 Introduction

Medical diagnosis is a highly complex process involving a large number of factors. Due to this complexity, the scientific community working in the health sector focuses its efforts on developing systems to assist medical personnel in order to increase its efficiency. With this goal in mind, this work was focused on detecting pulmonary conditions compatible with the COVID-19 disease using chest X-ray images. It might seem that with the success of PCR tests specifically designed for its detection, there would be no reason to perform an X-ray scan on a potential COVID-19 patient. However, in medical practice, it is common to perform chest X-ray scans on patients presenting respiratory problems, so having an automated system for COVID-19 detection using X-ray images can save healthcare systems a lot of time and money.

The significant variability between patients makes the detection of pulmonary conditions from X-ray images a non-trivial problem. In addition to this, COVID-19 can produce symptoms compatible with other diseases, making their diagnosis even more complex. Nonetheless, with more data and more advanced deep

This project has received funding from the European Commission - Horizon 2020 (H2020) under the DeepHealth Project (grant agreement no 825111) and the SELENE project (grant agreement no 871467).

P. L. Mazzeo et al. (Eds.): ICIAP 2022 Workshops, LNCS 13373, pp. 557–566, 2022.
https://doi.org/10.1007/978-3-031-13321-3_49

learning models, we are confident that these pathologies can be discriminated with the required robustness so that the models can be deployed in production environments.

The main contributions of this work are the following:

- Ready-to-use pre-trained models to detect COVID-19 related pulmonary conditions in chest X-Ray images with a balanced accuracy of 83.5%, a precision of 0.90, and a recall of 0.95 in the dataset used in this work.
- A deep learning approach to address the problem of multi-labeling X-ray images giving a score for each target pulmonary condition.
- Lungs alignment from the extraction of the region of interest where lungs appear in the X-ray image, i.e., semantic segmentation to delimit the silhouette of the lungs.

This paper is organized as follows: Sect. 2 analyses state of the art for COVID-19 and other pulmonary conditions detection using X-ray images. Section 3 gives an introduction to the DeepHealth framework and its features. Section 4 describes all the parts of our experimentation setup. Section 5 shows the experiments carried out and their results. Section 6 presents our conclusions. Finally, Sect. 7 concludes the paper by giving our future research lines.

2   Related Work

Due to the immense impact of COVID-19 and the necessity of quick and reliable screening methods, many studies have arisen to use X-ray images for providing a fast way to detect infected patients. A lot of deep learning approaches have been developed thanks to the power of CNNs to recognize patterns from the images and use such patterns to make predictions.

In the literature, many works can be found achieving high accuracy in classifying chest X-ray images, usually in two (healthy vs. COVID-19) or three (healthy vs. pneumonia vs. COVID-19) classes classification tasks. In Khan et al. [6], they used a novel architecture called STM-RENet combined with Channel Boosting, using two pre-trained models, to perform the two-class classification task achieving an accuracy of 96.53%. In de Moura et al. [4], some architectures well-known in Computer Vision and pre-trained with Imagenet (DenseNet-121 and DenseNet161; ResNet-18 and ResNet-34; VGG-16 and VGG-19) were used to build classification models for the three-class classification task achieving an accuracy of 97.44%. In Kumar et al. [7], a CNN with inception blocks was applied to solve the three-class classification task achieving an accuracy of 97.6%. The model predictions were analyzed using GRAD-CAM (Selvaraju et al. [13]) to see heat maps on the input images with the most relevant pixels for the model in order to make the prediction. In Bhattacharyya et al. [2], they used first a Conditional GAN to segment the lungs; with the extracted lungs, they applied different feature extractors, a Pre-trained VGG19, and the CV algorithm BRISK. The extracted features were combined and fed to a final Random Forest classifier that makes the final prediction, achieving an accuracy of 96.6% in the three-class classification task. In Nayak et al. [8], they tested different popular CNN architectures (AlexNet, VGG-16, GoogleNet, MobileNet-V2, SqueezeNet, ResNet-34, ResNet-50, and Inception-V) pre-trained with the ImageNet dataset, and concluded that the ResNet-34 was the one achieving the best results with an accuracy of 98.33% in the two-class classification task. In Qi et al. [10], they followed a semi-supervised approach using a Teacher-Student architecture to perform the three-class classification task achieving an accuracy of 93%. The model used had two inputs, where one of them was the original image, and the other was a three-channel image where each channel was a filtered version of the original image with three different filters.

One of the problems of working with medical data is the lack of images. The available datasets are usually small, and it is challenging to train robust models with a good generalization ability. A crucial technique to deal with the lack of data is applying Data Augmentation during the training phase. In the works analyzed here, the common practice is to apply affine transformations like Rotation, Flip, Scaling, and Shear. Furthermore, in some cases, other transformations are also applied: Gaussian Noise in Nayak et al. [8]; Elastic Transform, CutBlur, MotionBlur, Intensity Shift, and CutNoise in Kumar et al. [7].

From the analyzed works, it can be seen that researchers usually take more than one dataset to create a more extensive dataset for training; for example, in Nayak et al. [8], they picked the COVID-19 images from one dataset and the healthy samples from another one. This kind of combination can introduce a bias that the model can use just for classifying the samples depending on specific characteristics of each dataset and not original medical-related patterns of COVID-19. In Cruz et al. [3], the authors analyze various COVID-19 datasets and discuss the kinds of biases that can be present when using these datasets. We think this practice is hazardous in these kinds of use cases and even more when the samples of each class come from different datasets.

3   The DeepHealth Framework

The DeepHealth Framework is a flexible and scalable framework for running on HPC and Big Data environments based on two core technology libraries developed within the DeepHealth project: the European Distributed Deep Learning Library (EDDL) and the European Computer Vision Library (ECVL). These libraries will take full advantage of the current and coming development of HPC systems. They will provide a transparent use of heterogeneous hardware accelerators to optimize the training of predictive models while considering performance and accuracy trade-offs.

Both libraries are being integrated into seven software platforms with the DeepHealth project. Similarly, other commercial or research software platforms will have the possibility of integrating the two libraries, given that both are delivered as free and open-source software. Additionally, European large industry companies and SMEs will have the chance of using the DeepHealth Framework for training predictive models on Hybrid HPC + Big Data architectures and export the trained networks using the standard ONNX format [1], so, if their software applications already integrated another DL library able to read the ONNX format, all work is done. The integration of ECVL and EDDL makes it a robust framework with the ability to deal with real-world medical problems by building state-of-the-art models. While ECVL provides support for medical image formats such as DICOM or NIfTI, the EDDL gives the possibility to conduct experiments with modern neural networks on different hardware devices and in a single machine or a distributed environment.

The training pipeline developed in this work uses ECVL to load the images, apply some data augmentation techniques and create the training batches. The EDDL is used to build and train the deep learning models, using the cuDNN implementation as the backend. In addition, two external libraries were used: scikit-image [14] was used to apply the image normalization in the preprocessing step, and scikit-learn [9] to compute some evaluation metrics. The code is available on GitHub (https://github.com/deephealthproject/UC15_pipeline).

4   Experimental Setup

4.1   Datasets

For the COVID-19 classification task, we used the BIMCV-COVID19 dataset [5]. The dataset is divided into two splits, the BIMCV-COVID19+, which contains the data of COVID-19 patients, and the BIMCV-COVID19−, which contains the data of non-COVID-19 patients. For each patient in the dataset, we have one or more sessions available, and each can have one or more X-ray images. Each patient has a list of pathologies that can be used as labels. There are 190 different labels, but the distribution is very unbalanced. We considered just four labels because of their popularity and relation with COVID-19: "covid19", "normal", "pneumonia" and "infiltrates". We prepared two classification tasks, one for binary classification between "normal" and "covid19", and another for multi-label classification with the four labels (each patient has more than one label, e.g., it can have "infiltrates" and "pneumonia"). From all the available images, we selected just the ones with Anterior-Posterior or Posterior-Anterior views, leaving the ones from the side. We collected 2,083 samples and divided them into three partitions: 1,667 for training, 208 for validation, and 208 for testing. The partition was made at a patient level to avoid having images from the same patient in different splits. The distribution of labels inside each split is shown in Table 1.

4.2   Training Details

The training images were padded and resized to 512 × 512 and 256 × 256, as the original size was too large to manage (ranging from 2500 to 4000px, height and width). Then their contrast was improved by applying the Contrast Limited Adaptive Histogram Equalization (CLAHE) algorithm (See Fig. 1).

Table 1. Dataset partitions: The dataset is not balanced and the classes are not mutually exclusive.

Label	Train		Validation		Test	
Covid	592	(33.95%)	77	(32.69%)	76	(35.10%)
Normal	219	(43.79%)	29	(43.27%)	29	(38.46%)
Pneumonia	730	(35.51%)	90	(37.02%)	80	(36.54%)
Infiltrates	566	(13.14%)	68	(13.94%)	73	(13.94%)
Total images	1667	(100%)	208	(100%)	208	(100%)

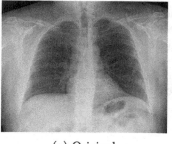 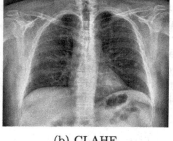

(a) Original   (b) CLAHE

Fig. 1. Image preprocessing: All images were padded, resized (lanczos) and normalized using the Contrast Limited Adaptive Histogram Equalization (CLAHE).

To parallelize the loading of the training images and perform the data augmentation on the fly, the ECVL library was used. The augmentations applied were: Horizontal mirroring, Rotation (from -15 to $15\,°C$), Brightness (beta from 0 to 70), and GammaContrast (gamma from 0.6 to 1.4).

Multiple neural network topologies were tested for this task. Specifically, we made use of Imagenet pre-trained models such as VGG-{16, 19}, VGG-{16, 19} with Batch Normalization and ResNet-{18, 50, 101, 152}. These models were downloaded from the ONNX hub and loaded into the EDDL library for training and inference. From each neural model, we added on its top a new classifier with a dense layer with half the number of input features as units, followed by a ReLu activation, a DropOut with a drop rate of 0.4, and finally, a dense layer with Softmax activation to perform the classification. Experiments have shown that pre-trained weights improve training performance and stability.

Next, the weights of the base model (pre-trained feature extractor) were frozen so that the new extension on top of it could be trained for 50 epochs. These were the necessary number of iterations to determine where the loss function became flat. Then, we fine-tuned the entire model with a very small learning rate ($1e-5$) using SGD for another 50 epochs. To avoid overfitting during training, we applied weight decay (L2) with a penalty of $1e-5$, besides the data augmentation and the dropout layers.

All models were trained using a machine with one NVIDIA RTX 3090 GPU (24 GB VRAM), an AMD Ryzen 9 5950X CPU, and 32 GB of RAM. By using this configuration and taking as reference the training time of the experiment with 256×256 size shown in Table 2. The average training time per batch is 0.055 and 0.016 s for inference. As a result, each training epoch, including training and validation, lasts 15 s on average.

4.3 Evaluation Metrics

To evaluate our models, we used the following metrics:

- **Accuracy**: Proportion of correct predictions among the total number of cases examined.
- **Precision (P)**: Fraction of relevant instances among the retrieved instances.
- **Recall (R)**: Fraction of relevant instances that were retrieved.
- **F1-score (f1)**: Harmonic mean of the precision and recall.
- **Intersection Over Union (IoU)**: Estimates how well a predicted mask matches the ground truth.

5 Experimentation

5.1 Lung Alignment

Given the limited memory in our GPUs and the need for using the maximum resolution possible in our images, we decided to crop the lungs regions, excluding all information outside the region of interest (See Fig. 2). To do so, we first segmented the lungs of 250 X-ray images manually, using the tool CVAT [12]. Next, a U-net architecture was used to semi-automatically label the remaining lungs following a *human-in-the-loop* strategy to reduce human effort, and with which we could efficiently segment the lungs of 2,083 X-ray images, obtaining an IoU of 0.95. That is, we trained a *weak* segmentation model to segment the non-annotated images (no mask) automatically. By making use of these automatically segmented images, we extended the training set, including the automatic segmentations qualified as *correct* and discarding those qualified as *incorrect*. In addition to this, we manually segmented the hard negatives to boost the performance of our model. For the neural architecture, we used the U-Net described in [11] since it is a well-known and widely used neural architecture for image segmentation tasks. As feature extractor we experimented with different models pre-trained on ImageNet such as VGG16, ResNet34, ResNet50, ResNet101, InceptionV3. However, since most of them offered similar results, we finally chose the ResNet34 architecture as it required fewer parameters.

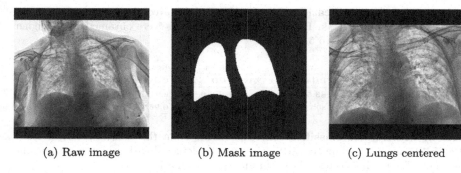

| (a) Raw image | (b) Mask image | (c) Lungs centered |

Fig. 2. Lungs alignment: To align the lung images (cropping and centering), we first trained a U-net model to segment the lungs regions. Then, we combined the bounding boxes of the segmented regions to extract the region of interest.

5.2   Detecting Pulmonary Conditions

We experimented with two classification tasks given the selected samples from the BIMCV-COVID19 dataset:

– **Task 1**: A binary classification task of "normal" vs "covid19".
– **Task 2**: A multi-label classification task with the four selected labels: "normal", "covid19", "pneumonia" and "infiltrates".

The preprocessing steps, data augmentation, and models used are the same for tasks 1 and 2. The difference appears in the loss functions used and the output layers of the models.

For task 1, the loss functions used are Binary Cross-Entropy (BCE) and regular Cross-Entropy (CE). We used BCE when the label is represented as 0 or 1, and we only used one output neuron in the last layer of the model. The CE was applied when we encoded the labels as one-hot vectors of length two. Regarding task 2, as we are doing a multi-label classification, we used one-hot vectors of length four to encode the labels. In this case, we tried two loss functions: BCE, applying it to each output unit; and Mean Squared Error (MSE).

The best results for the two-class classification task are shown in Table 2. The ResNet101 (pre-trained with Imagenet) was the best model architecture for 256×256 and 512×512 images. We also observed that increasing the image size does not improve the results; in fact, the best results were obtained with 256×256 images.

Table 2. Binary classification: The ResNet-101 achieved the best results for the "covid19" vs. "normal" task. However, no improvements were obtained when higher resolutions were used (256 to 512).

Model	Size	Acc (%)	Balanced Acc (%)	Precision		Recall		F1-score	
				COVID	Normal	COVID	Normal	COVID	Normal
ResNet101	256 × 256	**88.57**	**83.57**	**0.9**	0.84	0.95	**0.72**	**0.92**	**0.78**
ResNet101	512 × 512	87.62	80.78	0.88	**0.86**	**0.96**	0.66	**0.92**	0.75

Table 3. Multi-label classification: The results from the multi-label ResNet101 (512 × 512) show that while "covid19" class can be detected with a high precision, the "pneumonia" and "infiltrates" classes are more problematic.

Metric	Normal	COVID	Pneumonia	Infiltrates
Accuracy	**0.84**	0.72	**0.6**	0.63
Precision	0.42	**0.80**	0.46	0.47
Recall	0.38	0.32	0.3	**0.49**
F1-score	0.4	0.45	0.36	**0.48**

The best model configuration found in the multi-label task is the 512 × 512 model shown in Table 2. The difference is that the output layer has four neurons and a Sigmoid activation function for the multi-label classification. The loss function used was BCE applied to each output unit independently. The results of this experiment for each class are shown in Table 3. The results obtained indicate that these models are not good enough to be deployed in a production environment. However, the limited amount of training data has to be taken into account since it is to be expected that the accuracy of these models can be significantly improved with more data.

Finally, tabular data (age and sex) was also used to improve the performance of the model. This tabular data was incorporated as a second input connected to a non-linear MLP and concatenated to the final layer of the model. However, no significant results were obtained.

6   Conclusions

This work was focused on detecting pulmonary conditions from X-ray images using the DeepHealth framework.

First, a dataset for lung segmentation was created to extract the regions of interest (lungs) using a U-net model, with the goal of increasing the lungs' resolution but without increasing their input image size.

Next, we trained several ResNet models (pre-trained with Imagenet) to classify pulmonary conditions, framed as binary or multi-label classification problems, obtaining slightly better results for the binary classification models. Similarly, tabular data (age and sex) was also used to improve the performance of the model, although no significant results were obtained. However, as there are no published results on the BIMCV-COVID19 dataset yet, it is not easy to establish quantitative comparisons with other works. Nonetheless, we would like to highlight the ease of use of the framework for developing advanced deep learning models for medical use cases.

Finally, our work suggests that the DeepHealth Framework is a robust framework to perform reliable medical research. However, given the limited amount of medical data available and the high variability between patients, more research and larger medical datasets are needed before these models can be safely deployed in production environments.

7 Future Work

Many experiments have been left for the future due to time constraints. Nonetheless, we are interested in exploring the following ideas:

- Can we improve the COVID-19 detection by running a sliding window on a very large image?
- Can we improve the results by using more X-ray images (from other datasets) to pre-train an autoencoder and then use the encoder part as the backbone for the final classifier model?

References

1. Bai, J., Lu, F., Zhang, K., et al.: ONNX: Open Neural Network Exchange (2019). https://github.com/onnx/onnx
2. Bhattacharyya, A., Bhaik, D., Kumar, S., Thakur, P., Sharma, R., Pachori, R.B.: A deep learning based approach for automatic detection of Covid-19 cases using chest X-ray images. Biomed. Signal Process. Control **71**, 103182 (2022). https://doi.org/10.1016/j.bspc.2021.103182. https://www.sciencedirect.com/science/article/pii/S1746809421007795
3. Cruz, B.G.S., Sölter, J., Bossa, M.N., Husch, A.D.: On the composition and limitations of publicly available Covid-19 X-ray imaging datasets. arXiv preprint arXiv:2008.11572 (2020)
4. de Moura, J., Novo, J., Ortega, M.: Fully automatic deep convolutional approaches for the analysis of Covid-19 using chest X-ray images. Appl. Soft Comput. **115**, 108190 (2022). https://doi.org/10.1016/j.asoc.2021.108190. https://www.sciencedirect.com/science/article/pii/S156849462101036X
5. de la Iglesia Vayá, M., et al.: BIMCV COVID-19+: a large annotated dataset of RX and CT images from COVID-19 patients (2021). https://doi.org/10.21227/w3aw-rv39. https://dx.doi.org/10.21227/w3aw-rv39
6. Khan, S.H., Sohail, A., Khan, A., Lee, Y.S.: COVID-19 detection in chest X-ray images using a new channel boosted CNN. Diagnostics **12**(2) (2022). https://doi.org/10.3390/diagnostics12020267. https://www.mdpi.com/2075-4418/12/2/267
7. Kumar, A., Tripathi, A.R., Satapathy, S.C., Zhang, Y.D.: SARS-Net: COVID-19 detection from chest X-rays by combining graph convolutional network and convolutional neural network. Pattern Recogn. **122**, 108255 (2022). https://doi.org/10.1016/j.patcog.2021.108255. https://www.sciencedirect.com/science/article/pii/S0031320321004350

8. Nayak, S.R., Nayak, D.R., Sinha, U., Arora, V., Pachori, R.B.: Application of deep learning techniques for detection of COVID-19 cases using chest x-ray images: a comprehensive study. Biomed. Signal Process. Control **64**, 102365 (2021). https://doi.org/10.1016/j.bspc.2020.102365. https://www.sciencedirect.com/science/article/pii/S1746809420304717

9. Pedregosa, F., et al.: Scikit-learn: machine learning in Python. J. Mach. Learn. Res. **12**, 2825–2830 (2011)

10. Qi, X., Foran, D.J., Nosher, J.L., Hacihaliloglu, I.: Multi-feature semi-supervised learning for COVID-19 diagnosis from chest X-ray images. In: Lian, C., Cao, X., Rekik, I., Xu, X., Yan, P. (eds.) MLMI 2021. LNCS, vol. 12966, pp. 151–160. Springer, Cham (2021). https://doi.org/10.1007/978-3-030-87589-3_16

11. Ronneberger, O., Fischer, P., Brox, T.: U-Net: convolutional networks for biomedical image segmentation. CoRR abs/1505.04597 (2015). http://arxiv.org/abs/1505.04597

12. Sekachev, B., et al.: opencv/cvat: v1.1.0, August 2020. https://doi.org/10.5281/zenodo.4009388

13. Selvaraju, R.R., Das, A., Vedantam, R., Cogswell, M., Parikh, D., Batra, D.: Grad-CAM: why did you say that? Visual explanations from deep networks via gradient-based localization. CoRR abs/1610.02391 (2016). http://arxiv.org/abs/1610.02391

14. Van der Walt, S., et al.: scikit-image: image processing in Python. PeerJ **2**, e453 (2014)

Author Index

Printed in the United States
by Baker & Taylor Publisher Services